The Global Encyclopaedia of Informality

FRINGE

Series Editors
Alena Ledeneva and Peter Zusi, School of Slavonic and
East European Studies, UCL

The FRINGE series explores the roles that complexity, ambivalence and immeasurability play in social and cultural phenomena. A cross-disciplinary initiative bringing together researchers from the humanities, social sciences and area studies, the series examines how seemingly opposed notions such as centrality and marginality, clarity and ambiguity, can shift and converge when embedded in everyday practices.

Alena Ledeneva is Professor of Politics and Society at the School of Slavonic and East European Studies of UCL.

Pert Zusi is Associate Professor of Czech and Comparative Literature at the School of Slavonic and East European Studies of UCL.

First published in 2024 by
UCL Press
University College London
Gower Street
London WC1E 6BT

Available to download free: www.uclpress.co.uk

Collection © Editor, 2024
Text © Contributors, 2024
Images © Contributors and copyright holders named in the captions, 2024

The authors have asserted their rights under the Copyright, Designs and Patents Act 1988 to be identified as the authors of this work.

A CIP catalogue record for this book is available from The British Library.

Any third-party material in this book is not covered by the book's Creative Commons licence. Details of the copyright ownership and permitted use of third-party material is given in the image (or extract) credit lines. If you would like to reuse any third-party material not covered by the book's Creative Commons licence, you will need to obtain permission directly from the copyright owner.

This book is published under a Creative Commons Attribution-Non-Commercial 4.0 International licence (CC BY-NC 4.0), https://creativecommons.org/licenses/by-nc/4.0/. This licence allows you to share and adapt the work for non-commercial use providing attribution is made to the author and publisher (but not in any way that suggests that they endorse you or your use of the work) and any changes are indicated.

Attribution should include the following information:

Ledeneva, A. (ed). 2024. *The Global Encyclopaedia of Informality: A hitchhiker's guide to informal problem-solving in human life, Volume 3*. London: UCL Press. DOI: https://doi.org/10.14324/111.9781800086142

Further details about Creative Commons licences are available at https://creativecommons.org/licenses/

ISBN: 978-1-80008-616-6 (Hbk.)
ISBN: 978-1-80008-615-9 (Pbk.)
ISBN: 978-1-80008-614-2 (PDF)
ISBN: 978-1-80008-617-3 (epub)
DOI: https://doi.org/10.14324/111.9781800086142

The Global Encyclopaedia of Informality

A hitchhiker's guide to informal problem-solving in human life

Volume 3

Edited by Alena Ledeneva

with

Elizabeth Teague, Petra Matijevic, Gian Marco Moisé, Piotr Majda and Malika Toqmadi

Series editors' preface

The UCL Press FRINGE series presents work related to the themes of the UCL FRINGE Centre for the Study of Social and Cultural Complexity.

The FRINGE series is a platform for cross-disciplinary analysis and the development of 'area studies without borders'. 'FRINGE' is an acronym standing for Fluidity, Resistance, Invisibility, Neutrality, Grey zones, and Elusiveness – categories fundamental to the themes that the Centre supports. The oxymoron in the notion of a 'FRINGE CENTRE' expresses our interest in (1) the tensions between 'area studies' and more traditional academic disciplines; and (2) social, political, and cultural trajectories from 'centres to fringes' and inversely from 'fringes to centres'.

A Hitchhiker's Guide to Informal Problem-Solving in Human Life is the third volume of *The Global Encyclopaedia of Informality*. It continues to advance the central themes of the series – informality, human cooperation, local knowledge and global conjunctions, context-sensitive comparisons and context-free patterns for area studies without borders. This time, the journey into societies' open secrets, unwritten rules and hidden practices is, quite literally, life-long: it starts with an 'anchor baby' born in the United States and ends with the practices of digitalising death rituals in China. If a planetary hitchhiker visited Earth, this volume would be a perfect guide to informal problem-solving, or know-how, which all insiders tend to use without sharing it with outsiders.

The volume resonates with the core objectives of the FRINGE series both theoretically and empirically. Theoretically, the volume points to the centrality of the informal, which remains a key feature of human experience, even if fluid, invisible and resistant to articulation. It focuses on the potential of informality studies and argues that network-based expertise, such as that of the researchers represented in this volume, is itself a solution to the problem of compartmentalisation of knowledge and the extinction of polymaths. International experts in economics, social psychology, anthropology, urban planning, architecture, sociology, political science and young scholars alike join forces in addressing global challenges and capturing key changes in contemporary societies around the world.

The limitations of state-centric approaches to tackling global crises transfer the pressure onto individual migrants and entrepreneurs; families of those in need of care, job or dwelling; and communities and networks capable of self-governing. The main argument of the proposed volume is the need to re-evaluate the potential of informal cooperation in human life, which reduces social and cultural complexity, uncertainty, divisiveness of societies, as well as to integrate such informal cooperation into policies for digital, demographic and ecological challenges.

Alena Ledeneva and Peter Zusi
School of Slavonic and East European Studies, UCL

To Nina Sofia Woodgates

Contents

List of figures	xv
List of tables	xix
Informal shortcuts at complex crossings: a preface	xxi
Acknowledgements	xxix

The raison d'etre of informality studies: an introduction Alena Ledeneva	1

1 Being born 27
   Introduction: reproduction and emotional ambivalence by
   Michele Rivkin-Fish 27
   1.1 *Mei bao ma* (China) by Hui Guo 31
   1.2 *Khamstvo* (USSR, Russia) by Anastasia Novkunskaya,
        Daria Litvina and Anna Temkina 33
   1.3 *Selektivni abortus/tuđa večera* (Montenegro)
        by Diāna Kiščenko 36
   1.4 *Xiaoerni* (China) by Ling Meng 38
   1.5 *Parovoziki* (Russia) by Ekaterina Pereprosova 41
   1.6 *Cumătrism* (Moldova) by Andrei Iovu 44
   1.7 *Obnalichivanie* (Russia) by James McMeehan Roberts 46
   1.8 *Rabenmutter* (Germany, Austria, German-speaking
        Switzerland) by Elena Denisova-Schmidt and Lena
        Nicolas-Kryzhko 50
   1.9 *Uklonenie ot alimentov* (Russia) by Ekaterina Ivanova 53
   1.10 *Babushki* (Russia) by Anna Shadrina 56
   Bibliography to Chapter 1 59

2 Growing up 67
   Introduction: a psychological perspective on socialisation by
   Thomas Tsichtis 67
   2.1 *Les rallyes mondains* (France) by Alexandre Lieure 69
   2.2 *Mianzi* (China) by Long Zhang 73
   2.3 *Runs* (Nigeria) by Olumuyiwa K. Ojo and Olusola Ayandele 76
   2.4 *Neijuan* (China) by Haoxuan Mao 79

		2.5	*Słoiki* (Poland) by Mathilde Ollivo	81
		2.6	*Pokhorony okurka* (Russia and USSR) by Kirill Melnikov	83
		2.7	*Hikikomori* (Japan) by Taiga Kambara	86
		2.8	*Gaser* (Serbia and the Western Balkans) by Barbara Frey and Dragana Mrvoš	88
		2.9	*Lesboseksprosvet* (Russia) by Polina Kislitsyna	89
		2.10	*New normal* (Global) by Dmitry Kurnosov and Anna Varfolomeeva	93
		Bibliography to Chapter 2		96
	3	Adjusting to the digital age		105
		Introduction: digitally mediated (mis)trust by James Maguire and Kristoffer Albris		105
		3.1	*Shuahaoping* (China) by Xiangyi Liao	108
		3.2	*Travel influencers* (Global) by Eugénie Pereira Couttolenc	112
		3.3	*Follower buying* (Global) by Christina Zimmermann	114
		3.4	*Ticket touting* (Global) by Patricia Donovan	117
		3.5	*Doxing* (Global) by James Morgan	121
		3.6	*Catfishing* (Global) by Jade Jacobs	123
		3.7	*Revenge porn* (Global) by Julia Schur	126
		3.8	*Telefon gap zadan* (Tajikistan) by Swetlana Torno	129
		Bibliography to Chapter 3		131
	4	Getting married		139
		Introduction: marriage and informality by Péter Berta		139
		4.1	*Caili* (China) by Ling Zhang	142
		4.2	*Ala kachuu* (Kyrgyzstan) by Alberica Camerani	144
		4.3	*Mendanghudui* (China) by Shiqi Yin	148
		4.4	*Nikoh* (Tajikistan) by Madina Gazieva	150
		4.5	*Sdelat' ZAGS* (Tajik diaspora in Russia) by Elena Borisova	153
		4.6	*Bridezilla* (UK, North America, Australia) by Julia Carter	156
		4.7	*Karmir khndzor* (Armenia) by Anna Temkina and Lilit Zakaryan	160
		4.8	*Kelin* (Central Asia) by Tommaso Aguzzi	164
		4.9	*Ernai* (China) by Ouxiang Ji	166
		4.10	*Toqal/Tokal* (Kazakhstan) by Nursultan Suleimenov	169
		4.11	*Burrnesha* (Albania) by Ellen Robertson	172
		Bibliography to Chapter 4		175
	5	Belonging and social exclusion		183
		Introduction: gender, social exclusion and the dark side of informal networks by Sven Horak and Fadi Alsarhan		183
		5.1	*KhTsB* (Armenia) by Armine Petrosyan	188
		5.2	*Pečenje rakije* (Serbia) by Maria Vivod	191
		5.3	*Hemşehricilik* (Turkey) by Eda Pamuksuzer	195
		5.4	*Ahbap-çavuş ilişkisi* (Turkey) by Semih Ergelen	197

	5.5	*Grypsowanie* (Poland) by Piotr Majda	200
	5.6	*Meso* (Cyprus and Greece) by George Hajipavli	203
	5.7	*Palanca* (Mexico) by David Arellano-Gault and Luis Jair Trejo-Alonso	206
	5.8	*Kabel* (Malaysia) by Christian Giordano	210
	5.9	*Fanju* (China) by Lang Liu	214
	5.10	*Enchufismo* (Spain) by Ignacio Fradejas-García	217
	5.11	*A molestar a otro lado* (Guatemala) by Jose Godinez and Denise Dunlap	220
	Bibliography to Chapter 5		223
6	**Alternative currencies of support**		**231**
	Introduction: sharing norms by Elodie Douarin		231
	6.1	*Znaki vnimaniya* (Russia and FSU) by Conor Murray	234
	6.2	*Sinnamjai* (Thailand) by Wasin Punthong and Attasit Pankaew	236
	6.3	*Joro* (Kyrgyzstan) by Arzuu Sheranova	241
	6.4	*Sadaqa* (Kazakhstan and Kyrgyzstan) by Aisalkyn Botoeva	244
	6.5	*Ashar* (Kyrgyzstan) by Arzuu Sheranova	247
	6.6	*Nisia* (Georgia) by Megi Kartsivadze	249
	6.7	*Cassa peota* (Italy) by Giulio Benedetti	251
	6.8	*Chernaya kassa* (Kyrgyzstan) by Arzuu Sheranova	254
	6.9	*Moai* (Japan) by Abel Polese	257
	6.10	*Koshumcha* (Kyrgyzstan) by Eugenia Pesci	260
	6.11	*Pujogŭm* (South Korea) by You Kyung Byun	263
	6.12	*Poclon* (Wallachia, Romania) by Vasile Mihai Olaru	265
	Bibliography to Chapter 6		268
7	**Gaining an advantage**		**275**
	Introduction: trickster by Mark Lipovetsky		275
	7.1	*Chanchullo* (Central America) by Denise Dunlap and Jose Godinez	279
	7.2	*Gorroneo* (Spain and Hispanic America) by Ignacio Fradejas-García	281
	7.3	*(Za)chachmęcenie* (Poland) by Alisa Musanovic	284
	7.4	*Nokofio* (Ghana) by Dagna Rams	287
	7.5	*Chaa pani* (India) by Ajeet Kaur	289
	7.6	*Duit kopi* (Malaysia) by Christian Giordano	292
	7.7	*Aumento* (Lowland South America) by Daniela Peluso	294
	7.8	*Pari pod masata* (Bulgaria) by Kristina Tsabala	297
	7.9	*Otkat vizy* (Russia) by Olga Tkach	300
	Bibliography to Chapter 7		304
8	**Informal income**		**311**
	Introduction: informal economy by Colin C. Williams		311
	8.1	*Svart arbete* (Sweden) by Lotta Björklund Larsen	314
	8.2	*Travail au noir* (France) by Carla Montigny	317

	8.3	*Caporalato* (Italy) by Francesco Bagnardi	320
	8.4	*Paga globale* (Italy) by Giulio Benedetti	322
	8.5	*Shabashniki* (USSR, Russia) by Nikolay Erofeev	325
	8.6	*Khaltura* (USSR) by Taisiia Nahorna	329
	8.7	*Stacze kolejkowi* (Poland) by Nikolaos Olma	332
	8.8	*Taksovanie* (Uzbekistan) by Nikolaos Olma	335
	8.9	*Trotro* (Ghana) by Jennifer Hart	338
	8.10	*Pfandsammeln* (Germany) by Annika Kurze	342
	8.11	*Andare in giro* (Italy) by Isabella Clough Marinaro	345
	Bibliography to Chapter 8		348

9	Becoming an entrepreneur		355
	Introduction: entrepreneurship by Abel Polese		355
	9.1	*Combina* (Israel) by Ina Kubbe	358
	9.2	*Manteros* (Spain) by Horacio Espinosa	362
	9.3	*Tenderpreneur* (South Africa) by Laurence Piper and Andrew Charman	365
	9.4	*Mzungu price* (Kenya) by Yunqiao Xu	369
	9.5	*Churning* (Canada) by Katie Kilroy-Marac	371
	9.6	*Double Irish* (Ireland) by Julia Schmalz	374
	9.7	*Palyonka* (Russia) by Zoya Kotelnikova	377
	9.8	*Mertvye dushi* (Russian Federation, from 1991) by Ekaterina Vorobeva	379
	9.9	*Bin diwar/fazaee* (Iraq and the Kurdistan Region of Iraq) by Hemn Namiq Jameel	383
	Bibliography to Chapter 9		385

10	Living on the edge		393
	Introduction: triangulating ethnicity, networks and migration by Endre Sik		393
	10.1	*Vorovskie pasporta* (Russia) by Andrey V. Gornostaev	396
	10.2	*Saksy* (Poland) by Krzysztof Kruk	400
	10.3	*Ściągnąć* (Poland) by Anne White	403
	10.4	*Trailing spouses* (India) by Shalini Grover and Sanna Schliewe	406
	10.5	*Mulas* (Cuba) by Concetta Russo	409
	10.6	*Simsar, samsara* (Middle East and North Africa) by Alberica Camerani	412
	10.7	*Jak igrač* (North Macedonia) by Borjan Gjuzelov	414
	10.8	*Nojukusha* (Japan) by Hideo Aoki	417
	10.9	*La débrouille* (Former French and Belgian colonies in sub-Saharan Africa) by Cécile B. Vigouroux	420
	10.10	*No. 8 wire* (New Zealand) by Grace Reynolds	423
	Bibliography to Chapter 10		426

11	Settling in		433
	Introduction: informal housing and beyond by Anthony Boanada-Fuchs and Vanessa Boanada Fuchs		433
	11.1	*Colonias* (USA) by Michael J. Pisani	439
	11.2	*Chabolismo* (Spain) by Noel A. Manzano Gómez	443
	11.3	*Samozakhvat* (Kyrgyzstan) by Eliza Isabaeva	447
	11.4	*Zaniato* (Abkhazia and Nagorno-Karabakh, Caucasus) by Andrea Peinhopf	450
	11.5	*Xiaochanquan* (China) by Cinzia Losavio	454
	11.6	*Chuồng cọp* (Vietnam) by Francisco García Moro	458
	11.7	*Divlja gradnja* (Countries of Former Yugoslavia) by Fynn-Morten Heckert	462
	11.8	*Vrtičkarstvo* (Slovenia) by Petra Matijevic	465
	11.9	*Informal housing of the rich* (Global) by Udo Grashoff	469
	Bibliography to Chapter 11		470
12	Engaging politically		477
	Introduction: political participation by Uta Staiger		477
	12.1	*Voto di scambio* (Italy) by Alberica Camerani	482
	12.2	*Vote buying/vote selling* (Western Balkans) by Jovan Bliznakovski	486
	12.3	*Party soldiers* (Western Balkans) by Jovan Bliznakovski	488
	12.4	*Maliks* (Afghanistan) by Jennifer Brick Murtazashvili	492
	12.5	*Titushky* (Ukraine) by Michal Pszyk	494
	12.6	*Krumpliosztás* (Hungary) by Zsofia Stavri	498
	12.7	*Mungu idekh* (Mongolia) by Marissa Smith	500
	12.8	*Parillada* (Spanish-speaking Amazonia) by Daniela Peluso	503
	12.9	*Ne talasaj* (Bosnia and Herzegovina, Croatia, Serbia and Montenegro) by Emina Ribo	505
	Bibliography to Chapter 12		508
13	Ageing power		517
	Introduction: demystifying ageing and power by Gemma Carney and Mia Gray		517
	13.1	*OBON* (Kyrgyzstan) by Elmira Satybaldieva	520
	13.2	*Jirga/shura* (Afghanistan) by Madeleine O. Nosworthy	523
	13.3	*Aqsaqal* (Kazakhstan) by Talshyn Tokyzhanova	527
	13.4	*Mullahs* (Afghanistan) by Jennifer Brick Murtazashvili	529
	13.5	*Amakudari* (Japan) by Hayato Moriyama	531
	13.6	*Jajmani* (South Asia) by Soumya Mishra	535
	13.7	*Partiti* (Corsica) by Paul Thomé	538
	13.8	*Caciquismo* (Mexico) by Fausto Carbajal Glass	541
	13.9	*Maan tapa* (Finland) by Simo Mannila	543

13.10	*Duang muang* (Thailand) by Akkharaphong Khamkhun, Pridi Banomyong and Wasin Punthong	545
13.11	*Okkul't* (Russia) by Valeriy Solovey	549
Bibliography to Chapter 13		552

14 Informal care and the end — 559

Introduction: elderly care and ambivalence by Elena Zdravomyslova — 559

14.1	*Baksy* (Kazakhstan) by Lyazzat Utesheva	564
14.2	*Bajanje and vilarkas* (Serbia and the Western Balkans) by Maria Vivod	568
14.3	*Tchop* (Caucasus) by Maria Vyatchina	571
14.4	*Kako mati* (Greece) by Eugenia Roussou	574
14.5	*Marmotagem* (Brazil) by Giovanna Capponi	577
14.6	*ThetaHealing* (USA, Russia) by Tatiana Loboda	579
14.7	*Indulgence* (Global) by Elena Denisova-Schmidt and Sibylle Krause	583
14.8	*Ehsan* (Azerbaijan) by Turkhan Sadigov	585
14.9	*Pomeni* (Moldova) by Gian Marco Moisé	588
14.10	*Mingbi* (China) by Yizhou Xu	591

Bibliography to Chapter 14 — 594

Concluding remarks: the Big Three and informality — 601
Jan Nederveen Pieterse

Glossary — 607
Index — 615

List of figures

0.0.1	Complexity at the crossing Korte Prinsengracht and Haarlemmerstraat, Amsterdam, Netherlands	xxi
0.1.1	Transformation map of informality: from informality through migration to gender inequality	6
0.1.2	Transformation map of informality: informal economies	9
0.1.3	Transformation map of informality: urban informality	10
0.1.4	Transformation map of informality: informal networks	11
1.4.1	Diagram of a *xiaoerni*'s life	39
1.7.1	'Attention, owners of maternity capital certificates, I help in receiving funds.'	48
2.2.1	The logogram for *mianzi* interpreted by the author	74
2.3.1	One of many cheating techniques	77
3.4.1	Ticket resale	119
3.4.2	Ticket touting typologies	120
4.2.1	Once they kidnapped me. Elzada's story	145
4.2.2	Once they kidnapped me. Nargiza's story	146
4.6.1	Sample wedding cakes at a national wedding show, UK	157
4.7.1	An invitation to a feminist NGO performance	161
4.11.1	Sworn virgin. 2016	173
5.1.1	Survey results on *KhTsB* contacts used to access services	189
5.1.2	*KhTsB*, illustration	190
5.2.1	Home *rakija* distillation equipment, August 2019, Novi Sad, Serbia	193
5.5.1	A diagram showing newcomers' possible paths upon arrival in the cell	202
5.7.1	*Palanca* (lever) in Mexico	207
5.9.1	A wedding *fanju* in Nantong, Jiangsu, China	214
6.3.1	A *chaikhana* in Osh, a typical public tea-serving space where *joro* gatherings take place	242
6.7.1	*Peota* boats were used for leisure trips funded by the *casse*	253

6.8.1	A laid *dastorkon* for *chernaya kassa* in Osh, Kyrgyzstan	255
6.11.1	The front of a *pujogŭm* envelope, with the writing 祝結婚 (*ch'ukkyŏrhon*), meaning 'wedding celebration'	264
7.7.1	The transportation of illegal wood	295
7.9.1	The practice of *visa running*	302
7.9.2	Example of a bus fare list doing daily trips to Finland	303
8.7.1	People lining up to buy paczki (filled doughnuts) in Warsaw, Poland	333
8.9.1	*Trotro* on the road in Accra, Ghana	339
9.2.1	*Manteros* carrying their packages on their backs, Barcelona, Spain	363
9.2.2	Street art depicting a *mantero*, Barrio del Raval, Barcelona, Spain	364
9.4.1	Masai Market, Nairobi, Kenya	369
10.1.1	A counterfeit printed passport, 1752	397
11.1.1	*Colonia* home in Hidalgo County, Texas, USA	441
11.2.1	*Chabolas*, around 1960	444
11.2.2	*Chabolas* in 1981	445
11.3.1	Ak Zhar squatter settlement to the north of Bishkek	447
11.4.1	Photo of *zaniato* in Shusha, Nagorno-Karabakh, where Armenians occupied houses of displaced Azeris after the war in the early 1990s	451
11.4.2	Terrace of the abandoned restaurant Amra	453
11.5.1	Small property rights housing on village residential plot in Zhuhai, Guangdong province	455
11.5.2	An urban village in Guangzhou city core being swallowed up by urban encroachment, December 2016	456
11.6.1	Khu thập thể Trung Tự. Hanoi, 2019	460
11.7.1	Informal settlement Malo Brdo in the heart of Podgorica, Montenegro	463
11.8.1	View of a housing estate in Ljubljana from *vrtički*	466
12.3.1	Influence of political party membership on employment (opinion poll)	490
12.5.1	Vadym Titushko charging at a photographer, Kyiv, 18 May 2013	495
13.2.1	A Grand *Jirga* in Moqur, Afghanistan	524
13.7.1	The isolated location of Corsican villages contributes greatly to a Corsican sense of identity and to the formation of *partiti*	538
13.10.1	A *duang* tablet forecasts and enhances one's *duang*	546

14.2.1	*Salivanje strave* ('melting the fear')	569
14.2.2	The fairy-seer Ivanka, in Kulma Topolnica, Eastern Serbia, April 2015	570
14.3.1	The advertisement for *tchop* treatment on public transportation. Makhachkala, 2019	572
14.4.1	A lay healer performing *ksematiasma* in northern Greece	575
14.9.1	Built-in table and chairs in tombs	589

List of tables

4.1.1	The changing pattern of the three main gifts	143
4.1.2	Data on 'bride price' in rural areas	143
6.2.1	Respondents' rankings of the importance of *sinnamjai*	239
8.6.1	*Khaltura* or *shabashka*? A comparison	329
11.0	Informality ideas in various disciplines and discourses	434
13.5.1	First *amakudari* posts in selected ministries and government agencies	533

Informal shortcuts at complex crossings: a preface

Alena Ledeneva
Founder of the Global Informality Project

In the post-apocalyptic scenario of Douglas Adams' 1979 novel *The Hitchhiker's Guide to the Galaxy*, one person escapes the destruction of Earth and struggles to explain to aliens what humanity was like. Other sci-fi civilisations may be more advanced, but they fail to understand us. It may be that they are missing the informal dimension that escapes official records and data monitoring but remains central for problem-solving in human life. This volume aims to fill that void.

Our journey to the world's open secrets, unwritten rules and hidden practices starts at a crossroads in Amsterdam, a YouTube video of which has attracted millions of viewers (2018). The video captures the intricate way in which pedestrians, cyclists and car and truck drivers negotiate the right of way at a complex crossroads, which is a perfect metaphor for the invisibility, omnipresence and importance of unwritten rules on the one hand, and human cooperation on the other.

Figure 0.0.1 depicts both the complexity of the constraints that shape daily routines and the role of human contact in overcoming them,

Figure 0.0.1 Complexity at the crossing Korte Prinsengracht and Haarlemmerstraat, Amsterdam, Netherlands. © Thomas Schlijper.

xxi

often without much awareness on the part of the participants. The metaphor of driving is a perfect example of interaction between culture-specific behaviours and universally accepted rules.

Humans are social animals. Yuval Harari emphasises the crucial role of cooperation in the rise of humans over other species (2011). Social cooperation has made us what we are. We are born connected to other people, and as we grow up we cooperate initially with family and friends, before gradually expanding our connections to our neighbourhood, school, town, country and the world. Just as cooperation is a profound part of our life story, it runs deep through our economies and societies. Routes of migration, maps of networks, directions of trade, mutual help and sharing access to resources, and economic and political activities presented in this volume are all aspects of human cooperation. Human cooperation is also a major source of meaning and happiness for human beings. The COVID-19 pandemic, as a natural experiment, showed that while digital technology allows people to cooperate productively from remote locations, it falls short of providing the experience that makes them mentally healthy and happy. Human beings need to be close to each other, to smile, to rub shoulders, to share a joke and to laugh at it together. The pandemic has proved that informality is essential for mental health, well-being, and happiness at individual and societal levels all over the world. Not surprisingly, during lockdown many companies and individuals tried, with limited success, to recreate informal gatherings online.

This volume continues the FRINGE series, which develops an innovative understanding of the significance of fringes and explores patterns of social and cultural complexity. The focus on elusive, taken-for-granted and banal practices of problem-solving or 'ways of getting things done' in this volume resumes the bottom-up approach undertaken in the first two volumes of *The Global Encyclopaedia of Informality* that started the series. The previous volumes identified such practices across the globe, charted the grey zones and blurred boundaries in the key domains of human cooperation – re-distribution, solidarity, market, domination – and distinguished four types of ambivalence essential for capturing practices resistant to articulation, visualisation and measurement.

The third volume adds a human touch, emotional ambivalence and the positionality angle to the story of social and cultural complexity. It explores how contexts create identities in terms of age, gender, sexuality, ethnicity, class and status and how the identities influence, and bias, one's outlook on the world. In post-socialist Uzbekistan, for example, veiled tensions around car ownership, which is seen as an essential part of manhood, a token of coming-of-age for young men or even a prerequisite for marriage, result in women being excluded from the informal provision of taxi service (*taksovanie*). Adding such nuances highlights the implications of informality: the extensive time that men in Tashkent, and more widely in Central Asia, spend in garages leads to the emergence of a subculture that only serves to reinforce male sociability, male bonding and narratives of masculinity. *Taksovanie* gives men not only a certain amount of informal income, but also a degree of autonomy and freedom (see *taksovanie*, 8.8 in this volume; Sopranzetti 2017). Such informal practices emerge as a corollary of retreat of the state and austerity, when the state blanket has shrunk, even in the most developed economies.

The cluster of practices, within which *taksovanie* falls, offers a comparative look at underreported income in developing economies and the most developed European democracies (see *svart arbete* in Sweden, 8.1 and *travail au noir* in France, 8.2 in this volume). While identifying the underresearched practices in remote corners of the world, this collection of informal practices, clustered and viewed from a variety of perspectives in social sciences and area studies, reveals novel connecting points and patterns of human cooperation.

For a hitchhiker, the practices included in this volume unfold in the so-called 'biographical approach' that corresponds to the stages of experience in individual lives (Berger and Berger 1976). To this end, the journey begins with a chapter on birth, and proceeds with experiences of growing up, youth socialisation, marriage and mutual help, the world of work and migration, political participation, exercising rights and, finally, ageing, illness and dying. Each chapter opens with a conceptual introduction written from a particular disciplinary perspective that informs but also benefits from informality studies. The ambition overall is to frame informal problem-solving from the multidisciplinary perspective and highlight the nuances of coping strategies from the participants' point of view. So the story of informal problem-solving practices over the span of human life as narrated in this volume is also the story of human cooperation told from multiple angles and perspectives.

Such informal yet powerful problem-solving practices tend to escape articulation in official discourse but are often captured in the vernacular. The uniting principle of this collection of entries from over 70 countries and world regions is that they refer to practices circumventing formal constraints, captured in slang. Euphemisms for instrumental exchanges, and other informal shortcuts – that can be interpreted in terms of Wittgenstein's language games and participants' ability 'to go on' in a situation – are of particular interest since they not only serve the purpose of polite conversation but also highlight the necessity to embed, socialise and normalise instrumentality (Wittgenstein in Hamilton 2014). Vernaculars of informality, as Henig and Makovicky have argued, are essential for deception and self-deception, for adhering to the norms while playing them to one's own advantage and for talking about morally reprehensible exchanges in terms of morally acceptable patterns of cover-up, such as sharing, tipping or charity (Henig and Makovicky 2017; Makovicky and Henig in Ledeneva et al. 2018; see also Chapter 5, Belonging and social exclusion and Chapter 6, Alternative currencies of support in this volume).

This volume allows one to travel across time and space, so any 'hitchhiking' reader can choose their own route to trace people's challenges geographically and historically. The reader might like to take up the 'budget' option – practices used by the poor and underprivileged – the 'weapons of the weak' or strategies of survival, which are more commonly associated with informality studies. One can also travel in business class, as it were, and study informal ways to solve the problems of the wealthy and the powerful, such as strategies of tax optimisation, strategic migration or resort to traditional medicine and occult practices. For example, a well-to-do Chinese mother can give birth to an *anchor baby* in the United States with a long-term plan to educate her child there and obtain a US passport that would, prospectively, allow for family unification in the United States. In another example of problem-solving, Canadian middle-class women resort to the help of professional organisers to deal with the pressure of overwhelming possessions and *churning*. Each chapter closes with a detailed bibliography which frames the case studies, so that the reader may continue to study the informal practices, networks or institutions that sparked their interest, and place them in a global, and comparative, context.

If one pursues biographical logic, the next stop after birth is growing up, which is complicated in many corners of the world. You may be faced with the pressure of being a student in Nigeria, the stress of competition in Asia, the absurdity behind subordination in the Russian army, labelling and the general psychological trauma of being a teenager, all discussed in Chapter 2, where the pressure of, and resistance to, formal constraints go hand in hand with peer pressure.

Chapter 3 focuses on the digital age, whereby through experiencing bullying, catfishing or tinder swindling one learns not to trust the digital media world. To avoid the perils associated with being inexperienced, lonely, vulnerable or depressed, or unable to fall in love, one may find refuge in an arranged marriage. Following the West Balkans tradition of inheritance, there is an option for a woman to live her life as a man, thus remaining single and waiting for a male heir in the extended family to take over and ensure the continuation of the male inheritance line. This book's journey through the world's diversity of practices, customary in one place and travelling to other locations through diasporas, labour or forced migration, reveals the uniqueness of one's own life, but also points out the patterns of cooperation characteristic of humanity overall, as illustrated in the chapters on informal networks, informal income and alternative currencies of support.

For a post-human hitchhiker, human life with its ageing, illnesses, anxiety and continuous problem-solving may look like a struggle, yet a struggle softened by a human touch, human emotion, human cooperation. This volume addresses the issues of emotional ambivalence, whereby the family, the people you love, intended to nurture and support you, are also the ones who can inflict the most pain. It emphasises the pressures of the digital age, intended to unite and integrate yet results in division and polarisation. The informal practices assembled here can teach the designers of the digital age how people really work and what they want in the aftermath of the pandemic-driven reflection period. The underlying patterns of informal practices in this volume demonstrate the urgency of alleviating tensions between continuity and all-too-rapid change and/or create shortcuts to tackle the central problem of modern societies: uncertainty (Bauman 2000; Rabinow and Samimian-Darash 2015).

Migration crises, the COVID-19 pandemic, climate change, political divides, democracy backsliding and trends to improve life/work balance have created 'a new normal' associated with both a new high in uncertainty and misinformation and a new low in levels of fairness and inequality. People's experiences of lockdown and related pandemic management measures varied enormously depending on their health, age and socioeconomic status. People suffering from a chronic disease faced reduced access to health care for non-COVID-19 conditions. The switch to online education put underprivileged students at a disadvantage. Children and adolescents with lower economic status or with a migration background and limited living space experienced significant challenges to their mental health. In addition, lockdown restrictions increased the risk of gender-based violence due to the mental effects of isolation and barriers to victim support (Kurnosov and Varfolomeeva 2020).

Maintaining mental health became a major challenge for human beings living in such contexts, as previously prevalent life strategies became redundant. The natural experiment caused by the pandemic lockdowns highlights the importance of informality in human life. The chapters on gaining advantage, informal income and entrepreneurship demonstrate how the paradox of uncertain, under-determined futures and standardised, over-determined regulatory frameworks is resolved through individually enacted and context-bound informal shortcuts, yet collectively recognised and documented in a context-free slang.

This volume opens a discussion on cyber informality and digital mistrust. Technologies based on blockchain algorithms, big data, internet platforms and cryptocurrencies have been imagined, designed and used as explicitly open-access spaces that obliterate the distinction between formal and informal to facilitate horizontal relations and to flatten formal hierarchies. The informality perspective on the study of boundary-crossing and boundary-creation, freedom and restraint, and crime and regulation in cyberspace offers interesting parallels with the dynamics of the formal and informal in human societies, and is yet to be researched. To this end, we could argue that any new technology will be associated with the emergence of new informal practices. One should also ask if artificial intelligence (AI) can generate informal shortcuts, or hacks, and whether and how it can be trained to recognise them (Schneier 2023). Finally, there is a need to develop theoretical frameworks that allow conceptualisation of the association between digital innovation and informal practices.

In its cross-disciplinary embrace, the perspective of informality studies in this volume overcomes fragmentation of local knowledge and invites verification and comparison without losing the context within which informal practices are embedded. This volume is a collective effort of open-minded researchers, which resulted in 'network expertise', an approach that merits a longer explanation and historical grounding. For the hitchhiker who is itching to start their journey, this is the time to check out the glossary in the end or go straight to Chapter 1. For the patient reader, I would like to explain the relevance of informality studies for the challenges of the twenty-first century in more detail and reflect on the ways in which network-based expertise relates to past methods of coping with the fragmentation of knowledge, the nineteenth-century encyclopaedists such as Diderot and Voltaire, and the idea of polymaths, as well as offer a summary of skills to equip an avid informality scholar.

Bibliography

Adams, D. N. 1979. *The Hitchhiker's Guide to the Galaxy*. New York: Harmony Books.
Bauman, Z. 2000. *Liquid Modernity*. Cambridge: Polity Press.
Berger, P. L. and Berger, B. 1976. *Sociology: A Biographical Approach*. New York: Penguin Books.
Hale, H. E. 2019. 'The Continuing Evolution of Russia's Political System'. *Developments in Russian Politics* 9: 261–76.
Harari, Y. N. 2011. *Sapiens: A Brief History of Humankind*. New York: Random House.
Hamilton, A. 2014. *Routledge Philosophy Guidebook to Wittgenstein and On Certainty*. London: Routledge.
Henig, D. and Makovicky, N. 2017. *Economies of Favour after Socialism*. Oxford: Oxford University Press.
Kurnosov, D. and Varfolomeeva, A. 2020. 'Constructing the Not-So-New Normal'. *Anthropology in Action* 27(2): 28–32.
Makovicky, N. and Henig, D. 2018. 'Introduction: Vernaculars of Informality'. In *The Global Encyclopaedia of Informality: Towards Understanding of Social and Cultural Complexity, Volumes 1–2*, edited by A. Ledeneva et al., 125–8. London: UCL Press.
Marková, I. 2003. *Dialogicality and Social Representations: The Dynamics of Mind*. Cambridge: Cambridge University Press.
Rabinow, P. and Samimian-Darash, L. 2015. *Modes of Uncertainty: Anthropological Cases*. Chicago: The University of Chicago Press.
Sopranzetti, C. (ed.) 2018. *Owners of the Map: Motorcycle Taxi Drivers, Mobility, and Politics in Bangkok*. Oakland: University of California Press.
Schneier, B. 2023. *A Hacker's Mind: How the Powerful Bend Society's Rules, and How to Bend Them Back*. New York: W. W. Norton & Company.
YouTube. 2018. 'Unbelievably busy bicycle crossing in Amsterdam'. www.youtube.com/watch?v=pqQSwQLDIK8

Acknowledgements

We cannot express enough gratitude to our authors who have been patient and cooperative in the process of putting together this complex volume. Without them, the third volume or, indeed, the Global Informality Project overall, would not be possible. We have been honoured to benefit from the conceptual contributions to this volume by Péter Berta, Anthony and Vanessa Boanada Fuchs, Gemma Carney and Mia Gray, Elodie Douarin, Sven Horak and Fadi Alsarhan, Mark Lipovetsky, James Maguire and Kristoffer Albris, Jan Nederveen Pieterse, Abel Polese, Michele Rivkin-Fish, Endre Sik, Uta Staiger, Thomas Tsichtis, Colin C. Williams and Elena Zdravomyslova who have helped us to frame the empirical data on informal problem-solving around the globe from multiple disciplinary perspectives. My students on the *Informal Practices in Post-communist Societies* course at UCL School of Slavonic and Est European Studies (SSEES) over the years deserve our special gratitude for being such enthusiastic researchers. Their entries represent a significant share of this volume. Their expertise and insights into youth issues in the digitalised era have been invaluable for this collection. We are particularly indebted to the late Christian Giordano, Natsuko Oka, Phil Hanson and Elizabeth Teague who had been part of the success of this project and donated their time, expertise and editing skills to the encyclopaedia.

We are grateful to Abhinav Chugh of the World Economic Forum Strategic Insights and Contextual Intelligence team, who initiated the mapping of informality from the transformative perspective. Our authors Tommaso Aguzzi, Giulio Benedetti, Alberica Camerani, Alexandra Fernandes, Piotr Majda and Eugenia Pesci, fellows of the EC-funded MSCA-ITN project MARKETS, led by Abel Polese, have taken part in this initiative and explored other avenues of visualisation of informality. Talshyn Tokyzhanova has created the ChatGPT definition of informality as part of the 2023 MARKETS Global Informality Project workshop in Leuven. Madeline Nosworthy has helped improve the project website design (www.in-formality.com). Matthew Cooper at Simple by Design has kept the website hosted and upgraded.

We have mostly relied on the kindness of strangers who volunteered their expertise and time to contribute to the Global Informality Project Online Encyclopaedia, but this published volume has also benefited from synergy with the Horizon 2020 projects: 'Closing the gap between formal and informal institutions in the Balkans' (INFORM, Grant agreement No. 693537) and 'Mapping uncertainties, challenges and future opportunities of emerging markets: informal barriers, business environments and future trends in Eastern Europe, The Caucasus and Central Asia' (MARKETS, Grant agreement 861034). This explains the prevalence of entries from the Western Balkans and Central Asian countries of the former Soviet Union. Most PhD candidates in the MARKETS project attended the UCL research-led course on *Informal Practices in Post-communist Societies* and prepared entries for this volume. MSCA-ITN fellows Piotr Majda and Malika Toqmadi were involved in the editing process, together with Gian Marco Moisé and Petra Matijevic who managed and directed the Global Informality Project online. Piotr Majda led on the illustrations and designed the AI-generated cover for this volume.

The Paris Institute for Advanced Studies has been both a spiritual and spacial starting point of *The Global Encyclopaedia of Informality*. We are grateful for the Institute's continued support of the project in various forms and the 2018 book launch at Quay d'Anjou, once a residence of Charles Baudelaire, himself a *flaneur*, the lonely wanderer of Parisian streets, almost a hitchhiker. We thank all our global ambassadors who helped with the global book launches of the first two volumes and created momentum for the third. We are grateful to hosting institutions in Basel, Belgrade, Berlin, Boston, Dar Salaam, Kyoto, Lund, Malatya, New York, Riga, San Diego, Santa Barbara, Stanford, Tokyo, Washington and many others for their hospitality and effort in promoting our work (www.in-formality.com/wiki/index.php?title=Project_events). Professors Anna Temkina and Elena Zdravomyslova at the Gender Studies Institute, European University at St. Petersburg, together with their students, helped generate the vision for this volume. The case on Network Leadership: Global Informality Project, prepared for INSEAD business school by Stanislav Shekshnia and Alexandra Matveeva, has been instructive for the development of the project, as it articulated the method, documented the progress and offered scenarios for the future.

Annie Jael Kwan, Denis Maksimov, Michal Murawski and Kasia Sobucka, the curators of the Palace of Ritual exhibition in Venice, integrated the theme of informality into their programme and added a performative dimension to the dissemination of the Global Informality Project findings. Brainstorming with Lucy Ash, Steve Titherington and

Simon Pitts at BBC World Service, who became interested in how one accesses things money cannot buy, resulted in the idea of including 'hitchhiker's guide' in the title of this volume.

We wish to thank all our colleagues at UCL SSEES who helped in their various ways. The late Philippa Hetherington (1981–2022) promoted a biopolitics angle and had planned to write a conceptual introduction for this volume. Peter Zusi and Michal Murawski at the FRINGE Centre supported students' placement schemes for the project; Mukesh Hindocha, Lisa Walters and Shevanese Anderson facilitated FRINGE Centre activities and students' volunteer activities. The UCL SSEES-Digital Humanities internship scheme that has been in operation since 2017 has helped us to keep the online database of new entries updated and improved. We thank Orla Delaney, Binxia Xu, Xi Cao and Oksana Walsh who supported the Online Encyclopaedia. The FRINGE Centre student volunteers Yvonne Preda and Charlotte Solomou helped with editing, Ouxiang Ji and Benny Mao were super-efficient in putting together the mammoth file for this third volume of the encyclopaedia, which incidentally has hit the Google Docs word ceiling. All visuals, copyright and access to online sources have been checked and double-checked by Piotr Majda and Malika Toqmadi; all links were valid as of 2 April 2023.

Last, but not least, we extend our deepest thanks to our UCL Press editor, Chris Penfold, who has been supportive of the project from the start. It was a pleasure to work with the UCL Press production team led by Jaimee Biggins, the copy editor Anna Paterson, the indexer Kim Stringer, the Newgen production team Helen Nicholson and Dawn Preston, and the designers who continue to make the FRINGE series look so smart.

The critical importance of the anonymous reviews commissioned by UCL Press and the peer reviewers within our own network of authors goes without saying. Without a critical eye, a cross-check of entries arriving at different times and from various locations, we would not have been able to put such a varied collection together.

On behalf of the editorial team, and also the authors, I would like to thank our respective families, who supported us but also suffered through this encyclopaedic endeavour during COVID-19. Special thanks go to baby Nina Sofia Woodgates, whose birth in 2020 inspired the structuring of this volume.

The raison d'etre of informality studies: an introduction

Alena Ledeneva
UCL, UK

The first reader of *A Hitchhiker's Guide to Informal Problem-Solving in Human Life*, its anonymous reviewer, summed up the volume as follows:

> Along with the first two volumes of *The Global Encyclopaedia of Informality*, it sets the boundaries, rules and standards of what is shaping up to be the field of informality studies. These standards include a *cross-disciplinary approach* (which combines approaches and insights into political sciences, sociology, social anthropology, social psychology, organisational theory, behavioural economics, and other disciplines); *the network expertise* (which is a response to the problem produced by the contradictory tendencies of the growing volume and complexity of knowledge on the one hand, and scholars' hyper-specialisation and the fragmentation of academic knowledge, on the other); *a bottom-up perspective* (that gives voice to the witnesses of informal practices in local contexts); *the means of identification of informal practices* (which often escape articulation in official discourse, but must have a name in the local jargon); *focusing on 'what works'* (rather than 'what should work' or the reasons why public policies 'do not work'); *context-sensitive comparisons* (comparisons of similar informal practices from various parts of the world, which provide a generalization of knowledge without losing sight of the local context); and *keeping in mind the ambivalence of informal practices* (their substantive, functional, normative, and motivational ambivalence).

I will explain why these principles are central to informality studies and why informality plays such an important role in finding solutions to twenty-first-century problems.

1. The problem-oriented approach

The rapid deployment of the Internet and other digital technologies in the last two decades has amplified two conflicting trends which have been developing since the second half of the nineteenth century – knowledge fragmentation and the need for integration. As the depth and complexity of knowledge has been increasing exponentially, the specialisation of scholars has been increasing at a similar rate. Because of the fragmentation of academic knowledge, individual scholars are unable to tackle complex problems which require urgent solutions (Harari 2018; Keller 2022). One clear example of this is climate change, itself only a part of the sustainability problem, which requires a multitude of scientific perspectives as well as an understanding of societies and their foundational principle – human cooperation. In his 1948 article 'Science and Complexity', Warren Weaver stated:

> These new problems [of complexity] … require science to make a third great advance, an advance that must be even greater than the nineteenth-century conquest of problems of simplicity or the twentieth-century victory over problems of disorganized complexity. Science must, over the next 50 years, learn to deal with these problems of organized complexity.
> (1948: 540 quoted in Castellani 2014)

In order to achieve this:

> an open learning environment would need to be created, where students could be introduced to new and innovative notions of complexity, critical thinking, data visualisation and modelling, as well as the challenges of mixed-methods, interdisciplinary teamwork, global complexity, and big data! In short, the social sciences would need to be 'opened-up,' as Weaver called for in 1948 …!
> (Castellani 2014; see also Byrne and Callaghan 2014)

Three-quarters of a century later, we continue to call for social sciences to develop methodologies that capture contexts in order to resolve the ambivalence of informal practices and map their complexity. Using mixed methods, cross-disciplinary teamwork and institutional architecture as a means of bridging intellectual boundaries remains a challenge, even if one accepts the limitations of individual expertise.

According to the cultural historian Peter Burke, historically, the challenges scattered across different fields had been addressed by individuals with encyclopaedic knowledge, or polymaths, such as Da Vinci, Erasmus, Pascal, Newton, von Humboldt, Pareto and Keynes (Burke 2020: 2), but deepening specialisation and increasing complexity of knowledge have made them virtually impossible to overcome. Today's scholars need to collaborate and overcome the limits of specialisation to reproduce a similar effect.

As early as the 1920s, top-down, institutional initiatives to facilitate collaboration between different fields of study led to the creation of the Institute for Social Research in Frankfurt and the Rockefeller Foundation programme for the social sciences (Jay 1973; Ruml 1930). In the 1920s and 1930s, leading US universities – Yale, Harvard, Chicago – attempted to unite professors from different fields. In the social sciences, extended departments, joint seminars and discussion groups were organised to enable collaboration and integration. In 1940, Chicago University set up a multidisciplinary Committee on Human Development that linked natural and social sciences (Burke 2020: 224). A new format for interdisciplinary research under which scholars from different fields worked, conversed and collaborated under one roof – the Institute of Advanced Studies – emerged in 1931 at Princeton University. It was adopted throughout the Western world in the 1960s, mostly due to support of interdisciplinary research by Western governments in the aftermath of the Second World War. In Burke's view, 'in the case of humanities and social sciences ... the results of these initiatives were disappointing' and many interdisciplinary research centres, interdisciplinary committees and educational programmes ceased to exist (Burke 2020: 228).

The so-called area studies, government-sponsored research collaboration initiatives, continue to this day. The School of Slavonic and East European Studies (SSEES) in London was founded in 1915. In the aftermath of World War II, the US administration, eager to learn about its rival the USSR, joined forces with private foundations in order to establish cross-disciplinary research centres dedicated to Soviet or Russian studies. Later on, similar institutions were created to study the Middle East, South-East Asia, China and Latin America, now focused on decolonising efforts to interrogate and transform the institutional, structural and epistemological legacies of colonialism (see for example, https://blogs.soas.ac.uk/decolonisingsoas/).

Area studies-based collaborations have also produced a new generation of problem-centred fields and programmes: development studies, studies of women and minorities, cultural studies, global studies, media studies, religious studies, post-colonial studies, cognitive studies, liminality studies and so on. These have evolved bottom-up in response to social issues, as opposed to the top-down efforts to promote cross-disciplinarity. According to Burke, the problem-solving focus has been much more productive. Development studies grounded in neo-institutional theory have led the way. One example of success is Elinor Ostrom's project on governing the commons, which was awarded the Nobel Memorial Prize in Economic Sciences. The evidence compiled by Ostrom supported the theory that local communities are best at managing their own natural resources as they are the ones who use them, and she argued that the resources should be regulated at a local level, rather than a higher, centralised authority without a direct access to the resources. However, when bureaucracies adopt these results for their own use, the outcomes may differ significantly (Hart 2009). Urban studies 'hold the record for the number of disciplines involved in its programs in different universities – anthropology, archaeology, architecture, economics, geography, history, literature, politics and sociology – held together by a concern with major urban problems such as poverty and violence' (Burke 2020: 233). Due to the visibility of issues of informal settlements, urban studies takes the lead in research on informality and sets the policy agenda on urban development around the globe.

Similar to how formal institutions command more attention than informal ones on the subject of solving complex research problems, top-down institutional approaches to interdisciplinarity receive the most coverage. However, it has always been complemented and even preceded by bottom-up, informal ways to overcome the fragmentation of knowledge and enable collaborations between scholars from different fields. Burke describes 'The Club' established in London by Samuel Johnson and Joshua Reynolds in 1764 as an early example of such cross-fertilisation. Members of The Club who represented different professions met at a London tavern and discussed matters of shared interest. Similar informal groupings proliferated in London, Boston and many European cities towards the end of the nineteenth century and into the twentieth century, the most famous being the Vienna Circle; History of Ideas Club, Baltimore; Ratio Club, London; Parisian salons and the like (Burke 2020: 233).

Most informal groups had a limited life (from 5 to 15 years), included a small number of participants with different backgrounds and managed to make significant advances in understanding specific problems as opposed to producing breakthrough scientific discoveries. Their strengths lay in the strong motivation and cognitive diversity of the participants, as well as flexibility of interaction free from any formal constraints or obligations. Their weaknesses were limited resources, including time and lack of a specific research agenda or a need to deliver (the case of the off-the-record Bilderberg club, established in 1954, might be an exception here).

Both top-down and bottom-up efforts to facilitate some interdisciplinary collaboration demonstrate the potential of these groups as well as their limitations. Both require a unifying force that holds the participants together. The format of a high table at Oxbridge colleges generates cross-discipline discussions and exchange of perspectives. However, it is only when the researchers cooperate to address a specific problem that their collaboration becomes sustainable and produces remarkable outcomes (Burke 2020: 228). Harvard Business School professor Amy Edmondson argues that effective collaboration between professionals with diverse backgrounds takes place when they face a challenge that is equally important to all of them but cannot be resolved without others who have complementary skills and knowledge (Edmondson 2012). The 'network expertise' assembled within the Global Informality Project (GIP) somewhat matches Edmondson's idea of 'teaming'.

First, it would not be possible to assemble this global collection of informal practices without the collaboration of researchers across cultures, disciplines and methods. Hundreds of scholars from all over the globe, willing to capture, map and describe informal practices, were united by the challenge of shedding light on informality and its role in the world. Second, most informal practices of problem-solving described in this encyclopaedia are themselves based on the teaming principle – people face challenges which they are unable to overcome simply by relying on existing, top-down, formal mechanisms, so they turn to other people with whom they have no formal bonds but whose help is indispensable. By combining resources, they overcome the challenge and find a solution. Third, the 'network expertise' approach relies on the classics: the strength of the weak ties (Granovetter 1973), activated by the 'network leadership' (Shekshnia and Matveeva 2019a, 2019b). Finally, there are wider forces at play that sparked interest in informality studies in the search for alternative solutions to societal problems and sustainability. One example is the 'Strategic interactive map of informality', set in motion by the World Economic Forum (WEF) strategic intelligence team (WEF 2022).

2. From capturing to mapping informality

Visualisation of informal practices and their impact helps to accomplish what *The Global Encyclopaedia of Informality* attempts to achieve: to capture specific informal practices in a context-sensitive way, to map the patterns of informality around the world and to document the ambivalent impact of informal practices on people engaged in them, societies in which they take place, and global public goods (www.in-formality.com).

The critical role of informal practices as a means of solving problems that people face at various stages in their lives has been neglected for centuries. Most commonly, informality has been associated with its visible and measurable types: informal settlements and informal economy. However, the last two decades witnessed a successful effort to capture and map less visible practices. Social network analysis (SNA) has produced major breakthroughs (Butts 2008). This shift was also due to the qualitative research produced by a new generation of scholars who use mixed methods and innovative approaches to record less observable aspects of informality such as informal networks, informal governance, informal exchanges and informal currencies (Giordano and Hayoz 2013; Morris and Polese 2013; Henig and Makovicky 2017; Polese et al. 2022a).

A WEF strategic intelligence team working on strategic insights and contextual intelligence monitors forces that drive transformational change across economies, industries and systems. When approached to create an informal economy map, the GIP team sought to integrate

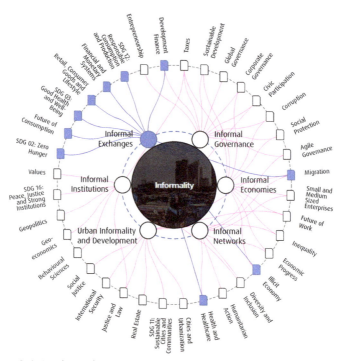

Figure 0.1.1 (Cont.)

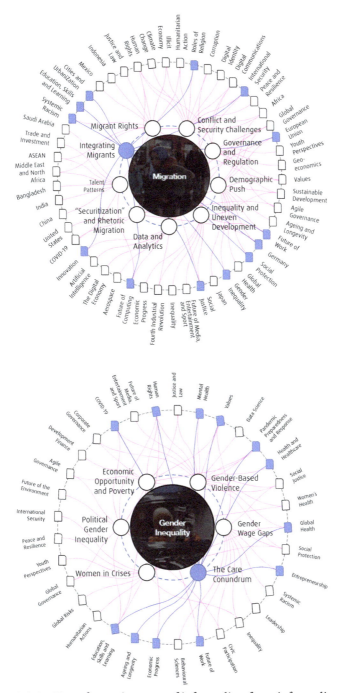

Figure 0.1.1 Transformation map of informality: from informality through migration to gender inequality CC BY-NC-ND 4.0. © World Economic Forum Strategic Intelligence.

social and cultural complexity into strategic thinking, with a particular emphasis on those invisible and less measurable aspects of informality that make the latter so pervasive and omnipresent. In cooperation with doctoral students funded by the EC Marie-Curie innovative training network, and WEF tech specialists, six key constituents of informality were established (WEF 2022). Each one is associated with global issues and contexts, links to other interactive strategic maps and gets updated by new resources pulled by the AI algorithm. The interactive map comes to life when you select one of the six nodes. The blue lines in Figure 0.1.1 illustrate just one of the multiple tracks linking informality to the world's strategic policy agenda.

Let us examine the key issues traditionally associated with informality, starting with the informal economy, the area that perhaps has attracted the most attention (Morris 2019; Polese et al. 2019). Forming part of the national economy, the informal economy, however, escapes direct regulation and is not registered for tax purposes. According to Eurostat, the size of the informal economy ranges from 1 per cent of the whole economy in Norway to 28 per cent in Romania. Survey-based indices of the informal economy in emerging markets report much higher estimates of the share of shadow economies in the gross domestic product (GDP) (Putniņš and Sauka 2015; Polese et al. 2022b; see also Colin Williams' conceptual introduction to Chapter 8 in this volume).

Like most informal practices, informal economic activities are ambivalent. On the one hand, they create value for entrepreneurs and additional goods and services for consumers, and they create jobs for employees and put otherwise idle resources to productive use. On the other hand, they lead to the loss of public revenue, which undermines the financing of social security systems and the sustainability of public finances and erodes public trust in formal institutions.

The strategic map links informal economies to economic progress, corruption, inequality, employment, sustainability and public finances, as depicted in Figure 0.1.2, while urban informality, perhaps counterintuitively, is related to real estate development business and civic participation, urbanisation and international security, migration and corporate governance (see Figure 0.1.3).

Urban informality embraces everyday tactics that people use to appropriate and claim space, cope with scarce resources and strategically bypass or bend official regulations. It can be readily observed in the form of unregulated occupation of public or private buildings (squatting), land grabbing, construction of buildings for residential and commercial purposes without permits, establishing of slums and shantytowns and the

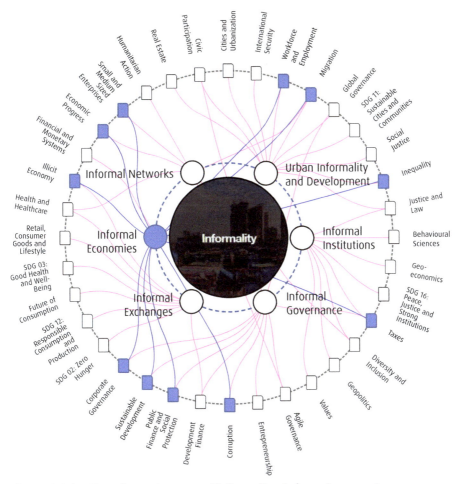

Figure 0.1.2 Transformation map of informality: informal economies. CC BY-NC-ND 4.0. © World Economic Forum Strategic Intelligence.

emergence of temporary, unregulated settlements as a result of the mass displacement of populations due to war or natural disasters (see typology in the introduction to Chapter 11). Informal settlements are not only a result of housing shortages; their formation can be a strategic choice made in response to the lack of affordable housing and access to employment opportunities in urban areas where employment opportunities tend to be concentrated. *Colonias* in the USA (see 11.1 in this volume), *favelas* in Brazil, slum cities in India and *campamentos* in Chile accommodate millions of people. Less visible, perhaps, is the informal housing of the rich (Pow 2017; Martínez and Chiodelli 2021).

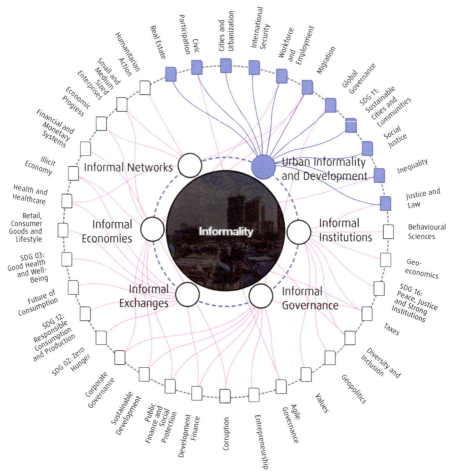

Figure 0.1.3 Transformation map of informality: urban informality. CC BY-NC-ND 4.0. © World Economic Forum Strategic Intelligence.

The focus on informal networks in Figure 0.1.4 reveals the less obvious side of informality – the impact of personal connections on various aspects of human and social life. Whether it is about knowing the right person to find accommodation, arrange transport, release a package held at customs, or find a tutor, in many parts of the world connections are indispensable for getting things done. Connections are part and parcel of cooperation and solidarity, and their strength and quantity directly affect one's quality of life. Strong connections guarantee better support and informal care as people are more likely to help those with whom they share a bond. Informal networks offer a sense of belonging and bonding ties that correlate with well-being and happiness, and even

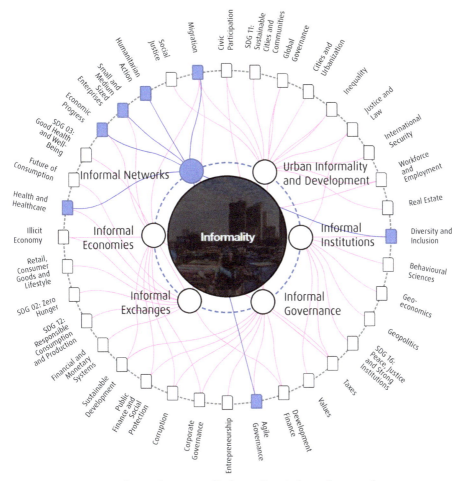

Figure 0.1.4 Transformation map of informality: informal networks. CC BY-NC-ND 4.0. © World Economic Forum Strategic Intelligence.

weaker connections serve as bridging ties. The networks channel social capital that serves to improve life chances and provide practical benefits to everyone involved, as captured in the entry about the reproduction of aristocrats in France (see *les rallyes mondains*, 2.1 in this volume), alongside the emotional benefits associated with friendship, security and happiness.

However, a wealth of social capital can also have a negative effect by encouraging dependence on informal contacts and generating corrupt behaviour. Informal networks can restrict personal choice and have a 'lock-in' effect. Ultimately, individuals might feel trapped by the expectations of their connections. While insiders experience the burden of inclusion, outsiders feel deprived and excluded from access to resources and opportunities. As Chapter 5 on belonging and Chapter 7 on gaining advantage show, this duality also applies to informal social networks, which foster sociability and cohesion for insiders while excluding outsiders.

Interpreting the invisible part of the informal iceberg is not a straightforward undertaking. The focus on the invisible, unarticulated and immeasurable in informality studies concurs with the school of suspicion, associated with Paul Ricoeur's famous analysis of the great 'masters of suspicion', each of whom came up with an idea of falseness of consciousness – Karl Marx (class interest), Sigmund Freud (sex) and Friedrich Nietzsche (will power) (Ricoeur 2008 [1970]; Coyne 2020). Informality studies seeks to relativise the intellectual rigidity and intrinsic biases of approaches based on formalisation, visibility, articulation and measurability. The strategic interactive maps of informality have made a step in this direction by complicating the picture of the world with evidence of informal shortcuts that pervade contemporary societies.

3. The drivers of informality studies

In embracing both the developing and developed world, informal studies complements the global studies agenda with a bottom-up perspective that gives a voice to participants in liminal spaces and grey zones – often an undervalued source of policy solutions (Marinaro 2022). Informality studies enables the bridging and bonding of scholars with area studies expertise from all over the globe, thus creating a platform to explore deep structures of collective existence and critical analysis of contextuality (Geertz 1990).

In the last two decades, scholars of post-communist societies have made a remarkable contribution to the field of informality (see Polese 2023 for a review). The relationship between informality and the state has been scrutinised: from the connivance of the state and exploitation of informal refuse collectors, carers of the elderly and other service providers, to turning a blind eye to activities parallel to the state or not worth regulating (see *Pfandsammeln*, 8.10 in this volume; *Andare in giro*, 8.11 in this volume; *Babushki*, 1.10 in this volume; Rivkin-Fish and Zdravomyslova introductions to Chapters 1 and 14 in this volume). Once a peripheral theme of informality, associated with area studies, post-communist regimes and underdeveloped economies, has become mainstream, as formalised policies aimed at better governance continued to fail. The black box of informal institutions has been unpacked, and informal networks, channelling social values and peer pressure to conform with them became part of the transformative policy agenda (North 1990; Ostrom 1998; Minbaeva et al. 2022). The disciplinary divide in studying informal institutions, networks and practices has been partially overcome by intense cross-discipline collaboration within large-scale projects, application of network expertise, surveys and comparative research (Ledeneva 2010; Morris and Polese 2013; Ledeneva et al. 2018).

Several factors have created a demand for deeper understanding of informality as part of the global intellectual agenda (Harari 2018). The failure of global governance vis-à-vis nation states led to countless crises – geopolitical, environmental, the COVID-19 pandemic, migration – and pushed for novel, non-bureaucratic ways to solve global problems. Critical reviews of hegemonic discourses – via decolonisation and woke culture – questioned the assumptions of the historical and social roles of formal institutions. The transformations of the twenty-first century – the crisis of liberal ideology, the omnipresence of the Internet, the emergence of a gig economy and AI-based services, the rise of social media and political polarisation – undermined the normative analyses that had previously sidelined informality as marginal and detrimental to the effectiveness of formal institutions and created a need to assess the role of the informal in the new context. A focus on resilience and the ability to deal with uncertainty changed the angle on informality from traditionally suspect or borderline corrupt, to the problem-solving potential in the context of the 'new normal' (Stuart et al. 2018). Here I elaborate on the three main factors driving researchers' and practitioners' interest in informality studies and the impact thereof.

Facing uncertainty

Unregulated migration, the COVID-19 pandemic, extreme weather, political polarisation, the wars in Ukraine and the Middle East, energy shortages and wild fluctuations of major currencies are only the most recent crises that have put severe pressure on governments and created an unprecedented level of uncertainty that has become the salient characteristic of the contemporary world. Solutions grounded in economics, theory of probability and game theory, with their emphasis on human rationality, strong institutions (including international bodies like the United Nations [UN], North Atlantic Treaty Organization [NATO], World Trade Organization [WTO] and International Monetary Fund [IMF]), bilateral and multilateral treaties and negotiations, preventive risk identification and mitigation strategies have mostly failed to address the new challenges.

In order to make sense of realities that bypass traditional theoretical frames and resist institutions of global governance and integrate them into policy, scholars in economics, management and political science turned to behavioural economics, experimental methods and nudge policy approaches (Ahn and Ostrom 2002; Thaler and Sunstein 2008; Sunstein and Reisch 2017; Hodgeson 2021). In times of crisis, informal practices, associated with flexibility and intuition grounded in social norms and cultural values, affect the default mode of rules and procedures. It is essential to provide insights for studying alternative ways of dealing with uncertainty individually, collectively and at policy level.

Transcending West-centric transitional paradigms

Of the hundred countries that could be identified as transitional by the twenty-first century, no more than twenty are on a path to a well-functioning democracy. Most of the countries do not appear to be consolidating democratic institutions, while others have regressed into authoritarianism (Carothers 2002: 9–10). The sheer number of adjectives to describe these democracies as formal, façade, pseudo, weak, illiberal, sovereign, managed or virtual points to the problem with the key assumption of the transition paradigm: transition can be prompted at will by political elites, top-down, regardless of the country's predisposition for democracy and should be based on the creation of strong institutions, which will lead to flourishing economies, prosperous societies and effective states. The establishment and strengthening of such institutions became the core of the liberal reforms and democratisation efforts that swept the world from the 1980s to the 2000s, despite warnings of the effects of cultural and social norms on governance structures and emphasis on the habitual behaviour and irrational decision-making in the context of peer pressure and community-driven interests. Organisational theory posits that agents' actions and rationality reflect the norms pervading their workplace, so the principal–agent models of the public sector must integrate the collective action theory (Ahn and Ostrom 2002; Marquette and Peiffer 2015). The backsliding of democracies in many countries, including the new members of the EU from Central and Eastern Europe adopting the so-called 'no-predisposition' approach, gave way to comparative analyses that identified patterns of governance, fundamental for understanding the grey zones of political regimes, exiting from, or returning to, authoritarianism. These patterns are referred to as patronal politics in Eurasia (Hale 2014, 2019), subversive institutions, stubborn structures or informal institutions (Bunce 1999; Lauth 2000; Helmke and Levitsky 2004, 2006; Gel'man 2017; Magyar and Madlovich 2020), or informal governance (Christiansen and Piattoni 2003, Christiansen and Neuhold 2012, Ledeneva 2013; Baez-Camargo and Ledeneva 2017).

Thirty years after the fall of communism in Europe, scholars from different disciplines have joined forces to develop more balanced perspectives and reflect upon the pathways of post-communist transitions (Douarin and Havrylyshyn 2021) and subsequent 'democratic backsliding' (Cianetti et al. 2020). New conceptual frameworks for dealing with the path dependence of post-communist regimes (Magyar and Madlovich 2020) and critical review of their legacies and lessons have benefited wider intellectual frameworks (Kubik and Linch 2013; Duncan and Schimpfössl 2019), and facilitated new fields of study such as informal politics (Gill 2023: 410).

Balancing out ahistoric, state-centric thinking

In most sources, the prerequisites for governance include the power to act and the authority to do so. Governing is usually associated with the formal institutions of a modern state. However, historically, the modern state and its institutions are relatively recent phenomena, bound to specific factors facilitating their emergence and global dominance. The relevance of the West-centric concept of the state for countries run by Sharia law is questionable (Acemoglu et al. 2002) as it plays down the role of religion. The practical and ideological hegemony of state-led governance resulted in a loaded, if not stigmatised, understanding of non-Western, non-formalised processes of government, culminating in a rather naïve belief in the linear triumph of modernity over tradition. In this vein, the top-down perspective on informality, especially when associated with poverty, underdevelopment and the informal sector, has colonial roots (Hart 1973; Gerxhani 2004; Acemoglu et al. 2001, 2002).

Normative and classic institutionalist perspectives view informality as subversive, bad and obsolete, if not outright corrupt and illegal, and thus something to cast aside or erase from modern societies dominated by strong institutions, representative democracy and top-down governance. However, in recent decades the impact of informality has increased not only in emerging countries but also in liberal democracies. Dichotomic, normative thinking fails to explain the persistence of informality, because it cannot capture the ambivalent nature of informality: it creates issues while resolving problems. In later academic literature, informality is predominantly viewed in association with corruption, poor governance and the draining of resources from the formal sector.

4. Skills to study informality

Scholars of informality face an intrinsic challenge. The unarticulated, or hidden, nature of informal practices makes their measurement problematic and their research dependent predominantly on qualitative methods. Data collection relies on the participants' willingness and ability to articulate practices for observers. Insiders' biases may distort the outsiders' interpretations, and vice versa. Controlling for positionality is essential. In addition, a researcher of informality, and an eager informality critic alike, may want to exercise caution in capturing, mapping or targeting informality, given the warning against 'allowing the informal economic practices to be portrayed as a kind of democratic resistance' (Misztal 2002; Hart 2009: 1). The following must-have research skills can enable one to see and assess the world through the lens of informality.

Operationalising informality

Is informality indeed a *lens* through which we observe human cooperation in particular times and spaces? Is it an *umbrella* concept embracing the variety of forms of human cooperation? Is it a *pattern* of cooperation that re-emerges in different contexts and is fundamentally repetitive? Do we even need a definition for it? To paraphrase Nietzsche, informality is a term that has history, rather than a definition. Without attempting to achieve consensus, and in the spirit of the social and cultural complexity in informality studies, it might still be useful to question the widespread assumptions about informality. Let us take issue with the ChatGPT-generated definition that does not distinguish between the concept and the practices it refers to:

> Informality refers to behavior, relationships, or structures that operate outside of formal rules, norms, or procedures. In social or economic contexts, informality can refer to practices that are not regulated or recognized by the state or other formal institutions, such as informal labor markets or unregistered businesses. Informality can also refer to social behavior that is relaxed, casual, or unstructured, as opposed to formal, rigid, or traditional. The term can be used in a variety of contexts, including politics, economics, sociology, and culture, to describe phenomena that are not fully regulated or institutionalized.
>
> (Generated 28 March 2023)

Three assumptions come to the fore: (1) informal behaviour takes place *outside* formal rules, norms and procedures, rather than penetrating, exploiting and diverting them, (2) the definition relies on the formal–informal *dichotomy* rather than shades of grey in the interrelation of its poles and (3) it promotes the residual principle, what is not formal is informal, whereby the state is perceived to be the centre (independent variable) that shapes and regulates informal behaviour (dependent variable). On these three counts, the ChatGPT definition lacks sophistication and does not go beyond a dichotomic, black-and-white, top-down account of informality.

In response to the question on the spread of informality, the ChatGPT fared much better by emphasising the global and universal nature of informality:

> Informality is a global phenomenon that is present in both developed and developing countries. It is estimated that more than half of the world's workforce is employed in informal jobs, with the highest rates of informality in developing countries. In many developing countries, informal employment can account for as much as 80–90% of the workforce, particularly in rural areas and in the service sector. However, informality is not limited to developing countries and can also be found in developed countries, particularly in the form of undeclared work, self-employment, and irregular employment arrangements.
>
> (Generated 28 March 2023)

The operationalisation of informality as informal employment is somewhat limited, especially from the perspective of urban studies and other angles as represented in this volume. Disaggregating informality into informal ways of problem-solving is the means by which it is operationalised in the GIP. In other words, researchers have operationalised the concept of informality in a context-sensitive way that suited their research needs best.

Exercising cross-disciplinarity

Tackling informality requires a cross-disciplinary perspective. The following discipline-based concepts are essential for understanding informality: informal institutions in political sciences, informal networks in sociology, informal practices in social anthropology, governmentality in social theory and informal governance in management studies, informal power in organisational theory, informal influence in social psychology and trust in behavioural economics. The cross-disciplinary perspective allows us to reflect on the choice of conceptual tools used to understand and describe a range of informal problem-solving practices presented in this volume.

Most of these concepts are needed to explore a commonplace practice of *kabel*, the use of connections in Malaysia, 5.8 in this volume. To understand *kabel* one has to grasp its history, its political significance and ideological nature of bargaining powers, economic functions and the social skills and divisions that *kabel* produces. A cross-disciplinary analysis of *kabel* networks, practices, exchanges and relationships was necessary to conceptualise this everywhere-and-nowhere phenomenon. In turn, research on *kabel* is relevant for the study of social capital, consumption, labour markets, entrepreneurship, trust, mobility, migration, remittance economies and gender in Malaysia.

Bringing entries from different area studies and disciplines under one roof does not necessarily create cross-discipline or cross-area studies knowledge. What it does do, however, is create an informational platform for further collaboration between scholars with different backgrounds around specific research questions or problems, which produces a collective polymath effect.

The first two volumes of the encyclopaedia enabled such cross-discipline and cross-area studies endeavours, published in the UCL Press FRINGE series and as special issues of peer-reviewed journals (www.in-formality.com/wiki/index.php?title=Related_Publications). We anticipate that this collection will also inspire new projects and cooperation for the future volumes of this Encyclopaedia. The teaming method, a collaboration of people with different backgrounds and specialisations in order to solve a specific problem, applied to informality studies can become a powerful tool for developing novel approaches to policy making.

Globalising knowledge: area studies without borders

An informality scholar contributes to the globalising of knowledge about informal problem-solving and creates datasets for context-sensitive comparisons, as well as feeds from wider frameworks of thought (see introductions to chapters in this volume; Kennedy 2014). The local wisdom and know-how embedded in informality are maintained and transmitted through informal practices. By criss-crossing evidence emanating from different corners of the world, this volume seeks to overcome the limitations of understanding local knowledge, unwritten rules and hidden practices in societies other than one's own. We aim to reach out to other disciplines and area studies in order to generate networks for problem-solving. We facilitate public engagement with issues around informality. Specific ways in which knowledge, images, symbols and practices are shared locally or globally reveal some universal patterns, the fractals of informality. Looking at the case studies in the encyclopaedia, we can attempt so-called 'context-sensitive comparisons', thus facilitating the globalising of knowledge, yet without losing local context. Our organisation of material transcends the geographical principle and area studies divide to highlight the universal patterns of problem-solving in societies.

Superseding dichotomies

In the Western sociological literature, informality is conceptualised as the opposite of formality, following Erving Goffman's conception of 'role distance' and frontstage–backstage dichotomy (Goffman 2002 [1959]). On stage, actors ought to perform according to their scripts; backstage, they can relax and use backstage language. Do these opposites help or impede our grasp of grey areas and blurred boundaries?

This encyclopaedia highlights how the space between the two 'opposites' is filled with tension, which makes them mutually inclusive. Many informal practices have ambivalent names and meanings, and/or are left deliberately unclear, or have multiple, context-bound meanings. In Chinese mandarin, for example, there is no word for dichotomy, and the words for East and West are not opposites. The language implies what the Chinese philosophical tradition has long argued: opposites always coexist (Marková 2002). The tension between the formal and informal constitutes the very terrain upon which the forces of interaction unfold. Although this statement may appear trivial, it has important, symmetrical, implications.

If studying the informal is not possible without the formal, the reverse should also be true. When researching formal institutions, networks or practices, one should not lose sight of their informal underpinnings, if only for their potential in problem-solving. For example, the role of informal networks in governance has become a prominent concern in the field of organisational behaviour in response to the ineffectiveness of international organisations in local settings, as well as a partial solution to the problem (Horak et al. 2020; Marková 2003; Minbaeva et al. 2023).

Context-sensitive comparisons

What is context in the analysis of formal–informal interaction is a question that calls for the *gestalt* principles of figure-ground and symmetry. If one focuses on formal institutions, informal institutions, networks and practices constitute the background, or context, within which the workings of formal institutions unfold against the interplay of historical, cultural, social and interpersonal factors. However, when the focus shifts to hidden, under-researched or unarticulated informal practices, that is, informality, formal frameworks (legal, bureaucratic, official) themselves can be perceived as contextual. Mastering the contexts and acquiring skills of context sensitivity can be achieved by comparative analysis of the complex interplay of the formal and informal in each of the compared cases and an assessment of the similarity/difference of all constituents in the formal–informal interaction.

For example, a comparative study of *blat* in Russia and *guanxi* in China not only highlighted similarities and differences in the functionality of seemingly parallel practices, in their formal frameworks and their transformations, but also pointed to the complex interplay between formal and informal (Ledeneva 2008). A comparative study of informal institutions, networks and practices in Russia and China led to the conclusion that even when focusing on the informal its formal counterpart is part and parcel of the comparative analysis. The symmetry principle means that the reverse is also true.

Switching between figure and background allows us to navigate the grey zones between sociability and instrumentality in relationships, between need and greed in corrupt exchanges, between us and them in applying double standards and between private and public in double motives.

Informal practices are ambivalent by nature; they provide solutions but also create problems, they produce competitive advantage for an individual at the expense of a larger group and they privilege members of a closed circle over strangers.

To identify universal patterns but preserve the context that helps differentiate the modes of human interaction and modalities of our perception of it has been a paradoxical yet effective tool in tackling ambivalence. In addition to the emotional ambivalence coined by Swiss psychiatrist Eugen Bleuler in the early twentieth century (Bleuler 1914), Robert K. Merton identified and developed the concept of sociological ambivalence, associated with clashing demands on professionals such as doctors and teachers, resulting in their oscillating behaviour. A doctor, for example, should be both compassionate and impartial in treating patients. The poles themselves are not the problem; it is the uncertainty of which one transpires in which context that creates the dilemma. The tension of ambivalence is resolved temporarily and situationally, thus producing a context-bound oscillation that differentiates ambivalence from ambiguity. Cases of non-resolution of the clashing constraints are those where the notions of ambivalence and ambiguity overlap. The challenge for informality scholars is to examine an informal practice through the lens of ambivalence and acquire the critical skills of a master of suspicion.

Looking for paradoxes that are resolved by informal practices in particular contexts and clustering similar contexts has become a major conceptual tool to capture, map and measure informal practices that escape articulation in official discourse but represent the know-how of what works in the vernacular (Ledeneva 2018: 1).

Mastering ambivalence

The previous two volumes of *The Global Encyclopaedia of Informality* revealed the significance of the ambivalence of informal practices, networks and institutions (Ledeneva et al. 2018). Four types of ambivalence relevant to informality studies were distinguished: substantive, functional, normative and motivational. These four types, associated with doublethink, double standards, double deed and double incentives, can also be traced in this volume.

The blurred boundaries between sociable and instrumental in relationships means that it is not possible to disentangle a relationship from the (ab)use of that relationship. Being neither or both is possible. The *substantive ambivalence* of informal exchanges rules out any single categorisation of the way in which gifts, favours, transfers and transactions are given, taken or exchanged. The ambivalent nature of relationships – seen as social by participants, but as instrumental by observers – points to the fact that a clear-cut categorisation is not possible. Relationships are both social and instrumental. Positionality is crucial in defining the interested or disinterested nature of informal exchanges and draws attention to timing, obligation of the recipient, domination of the donor, logic of antagonism or alliance, personalisation or anonymity, as well as the interconnectedness of public and private contexts in navigating the complexity of social exchanges.

The same pattern can be seen in double standards at play, whereby the comfort of belonging, inclusion and sharing an identity seamlessly leads to the exclusion of others – the *normative ambivalence*. Kinship and local communities reward members with a safety net and support, but also restrict individual rights. Social networks in so-called open access societies are declared open yet are filled with hidden social filters. The double standards applied to 'us' and 'them', to insiders and outsiders, differ considerably depending on the context, but a common pattern is the ambivalent nature of belonging; enabling but also constraining (Barsukova and Denisova-Schmidt 2022; Staiger's introduction, Bliznakovski's entry 12.3 and others in Chapter 12 in this volume).

Informality tends to be stigmatised as dysfunctional, yet it is a powerful resource, if one focuses on 'what works', rather than on what should work. A master of *functional ambivalence* explores the enabling power of constraints. Paradoxically, practices subversive of formal constraints, such as geographical borders, regulations circumstances (such as food shortages), are also supportive of them and help them reproduce. Bending the rules also implies complying with and reinforcing them. The coping strategies described in the entries are often conceptualised as a 'weapons of the weak', channelling resistance to existing constraints, thereby subverting but also supporting them (Scott 1985). Participants commonly justify their strategies of gaining advantage or gaming the system as a forced choice, a necessity, a need, rather than as seeking an unfair advantage (see Lipovetsky's introduction and other entries in Chapter 7, for example Peluso 7.7). Outsiders, however, are likely to interpret this as bending the rules.

Finally, *motivational ambivalence* resides in the grey zones of informal power connecting the public and the private domains. Blurring of the boundaries between the public and the private calls into question the adequacy of the public–private dichotomy for grasping symbiotic patterns and complex constellations in present-day societies, which is not exercised exclusively top-down or bottom-up. Practices of informal power such as co-optation, co-dependence and informal control, as depicted in the 3C model of informal governance, are often diffuse (Baez-Camargo and Ledeneva 2017). These may be exercised through collective action, provision of access to material resources (privileges, allowances or loans) or symbolic resources (such as access to decision makers). In most cases, informal power is exercised in non-violent and more nuanced forms of indirect pressure, resulting in compliance and even self-censorship (Gerlach et al. 2019).

The third volume goes beyond these four types of ambivalence and highlights emotional ambivalence and points to the centrality of gender, age, sexuality, ethnicity, class and status. In line with the previous volumes, this collection challenges the widespread assumption that informality is driven by a purely pragmatic approach to solving problems and is associated with poverty, underdevelopment, the Global South, oppressive regimes or the former socialist countries of Eastern Europe and Central Asia. By embracing informal practices that support people throughout their entire lives, the third volume offers nuances of gender and age, ethnicity and migration, beliefs and spirituality, care and emotions, and everything that makes us human. Equipped with the skills of operationalising informality, exercising cross-disciplinarity, globalising knowledge, superseding dichotomies, implementing context-sensitive comparisons and mastering ambivalence, the patient and informed hitchhiker is now ready to face the uncertainty of the journey through this book.

Bibliography

Acemoglu, D., Johnson, S. and Robinson, J. A. 2001. 'The Colonial Origins of Comparative Development: An Empirical Investigation'. *The American Economic Review* 91(5): 1369–401.

Acemoglu, D., Johnson, S. and Robinson, J. A. 2002. 'Reversal of Fortune: Geography and Institutions in the Making of the Modern World Income Distribution'. *The Quarterly Journal of Economics* 117(4): 1231–94.

Ahn, T. K. and Ostrom, E. 2002. 'Social Capital and The Second-Generation Theories of Collective Action: An Analytical Approach to the Forms of Social Capital'. *Annual Meeting of the American Political Science Association*. Available online. www.researchgate.net/profile/T-Ahn/publication/239561534_SOCIAL_CAPITAL_AND_THE_SECOND-GENERATION_THEORIES_OF_COLLECTIVE_ACTION_AN_ANALYTICAL_APPROACH_TO_THE_FORMS_OF_SOCIAL_CAPITAL/links/00b495314b340c8bfa000000/SOCIAL-CAPITAL-AND-THE-SECOND-GEN

Baez-Camargo, C. and Ledeneva, A. 2017. 'Where Does Informality Stop and Corruption Begin? Informal Governance and The Public/Private Crossover in Mexico, Russia and Tanzania'. *Slavonic & East European Review* 95(1): 49–75.

Barsukova, S. and Denisova-Schmidt, E. 2022. 'Double Standards as Modus Operandi: Mixing Business and Politics in Russia'. *Europe-Asia Studies* 74(6): 990–1005.

Bleuler, E. 1914. *The Ambivalence*. Dedication for the inauguration of the new buildings of the University of Zurich 18 April 1914 (the medical faculty). Zurich: Schulthess & Co.: 95–106.

Bunce, V. 1999. *Subversive Institutions: The Design and the Destruction of Socialism and the State*. New York: Cambridge University Press.

Burke, P. 2020. *The Polymath*. New Haven and London: Yale University Press.

Butts, C. T. 2008. 'Social Network Analysis with SNA'. *Journal of Statistical Software* 24: 1–51.

Byrne, D. and Callaghan, G. 2014. *Complexity and the Social Sciences: The State of the Art*. Abingdon: Routledge.

Carothers, T. 2002. 'The End of the Transition Paradigm'. *Journal of Democracy* 13(1): 5–21.

Castellani, B. 2014. 'Complexity and the Failure of Quantitative Social Science'. *Focus* 14.

Christiansen, T. and Piattoni, S. (eds) 2003. *Informal Governance in the European Union*. Northampton: Edward Elgar Publishing.

Christiansen, T. and Neuhold, C. (eds) 2012. *International Handbook on Informal Governance*. Northampton: Edward Elgar Publishing.

Cianetti, L., Dawson, J. and Hanley, S. (eds) 2020. *Rethinking 'Democratic Backsliding' in Central and Eastern Europe*. Abingdon: Routledge.

Coyne, R. 2020. *Reframing the Masters of Suspicion: Marx, Nietzsche, and Freud*. London: Bloomsbury.

Douarin, E. and Havrylyshyn, O. (eds) 2021. *The Palgrave Handbook of Comparative Economics.* London: Palgrave Macmillan.

Duncan, P. J. and Schimpfössl, E. 2019. *Socialism, Capitalism and Alternatives: Area Studies and Global Theories.* London: UCL Press.

Edmondson, A. C. 2012. *Teaming: How Organisations Learn, Innovate and Compete in the Knowledge Economy.* San Francisco: John Wiley & Sons.

Geertz, C. 1990. 'History and Anthropology'. *New Literary History* 21(2): 321–35.

Gel'man, V. 2017. 'Political Foundations of Bad Governance in Post-Soviet Eurasia: Towards a Research Agenda'. *East European Politics* 33(4): 496–516.

Gerlach, P., Teodorescu, K. and Hertwig, R. 2019. 'The Truth about Lies: A Meta-Analysis on Dishonest Behavior'. *Psychological Bulletin* 145(1): 1.

Gerxhani, K. 2004. 'The Informal Sector in Developed and Less Developed Countries: A Literature Survey'. *Public Choice* 120(3): 267–300.

Gill, G. 2023. *Routledge Handbook of Russian Politics and Society.* 2nd ed. 410–23.

Giordano, C. and Hayoz, N. (eds) 2013. *Informality in Eastern Europe: Structures, Political Cultures and Social Practices.* New York: Peter Lang.

Goffman, E. 2002 [1959]. *The Presentation of Self in Everyday Life.* New York: Garden City.

Granovetter, M. S. 1973. 'The Strength of Weak Ties'. *American Journal of Sociology* 78(6): 1360–80.

Hale, H. E. 2014. *Patronal Politics: Eurasian Regime Dynamics in Comparative Perspective.* New York: Cambridge University Press.

Hale, H. E. 2019. 'The Continuing Evolution of Russia's Political System'. *Developments in Russian Politics* 9: 261–76.

Harari, Y. N. 2018. *21 Lessons for the 21st Century.* Random House.

Hart, K. 1973. 'Informal Income Opportunities and Urban Employment in Ghana'. *The Journal of Modern African Studies* 11(1): 61–89.

Hart, K. 2009. 'On the Informal Economy: The Political History of an Ethnographic Concept'. CEB Working Paper 09/042.

Helmke, G. and Levitsky, S. 2004. 'Informal Institutions and Comparative Politics: A Research Agenda'. *Perspectives on Politics* 2(4): 725–40.

Helmke, G. and Levitsky, S. (eds) 2006. *Informal Institutions and Democracy: Lessons from Latin America.* Baltimore: John Hopkins University Press.

Henig, D. and Makovicky, N. 2017. *Economies of Favour after Socialism.* Oxford: Oxford University Press.

Hodgson, G. M. 2021. 'Culture and Institutions: A Review of Joel Mokyr's *A Culture of Growth*'. *Journal of Institutional Economics*: 1–10.

Horak, S., Afiouni, F., Bian, Y., Ledeneva, A., Muratbekova-Touron, M. and Fey, C. F. 2020. 'Informal Networks: Dark Sides, Bright Sides, and Unexplored Dimensions'. *Management and Organization Review* 16(3): 511–42.

Jay, M. 1973. *The Dialectical Imagination: A History of Frankfurt School and the Institute for Social Research 1923–1950.* Berkeley: University of California Press.

Keller, A. 2022. Les grands enjeux de notre temps: des défis systémiques [The Great Issues of Our Times]. IPSA, 10 November, www.youtube.com/watch?v=CtOQGDWF9vY.

Kennedy, M. D. 2014. *Globalising Knowledge: Intellectuals, Universities, and Publics in Transformation.* Redwood: Stanford University Press.

Kubik, J. and Linch, A. (eds) 2013. *Postcommunism from Within: Social Justice, Mobilization, and Hegemony.* Vol. 8. New York: NYU Press.

Lauth, H. J. 2000. 'Informal Institutions and Democracy'. *Democratization* 7(4): 21–50.

Ledeneva, A. 2008. '*Blat* and *Guanxi*: Informal Practices in Russia and China'. *Comparative Studies in Society and History* 50(1): 118–44.

Ledeneva, A. 2010. 'Créer des ponts entre les disciplines. Institutions, réseaux, pratiques' [Bridging Disciplines: Institutions, Networks and Practices]. In *Les Paradoxes de l'Économie Informelle. A Qui Profitent les Règles?*, edited by L. Fontaine and F. Weber. Paris: Editions Karthala.

Ledeneva, A. 2013. Russia's Practical Norms and Informal Governance: The Origins of Endemic Corruption. *Social Research: An International Quarterly* 80(4): 1135–62.

Ledeneva, A., Bailey, A., Barron, S., Curro, C. and Teague, E. (eds) 2018. *The Global Encyclopaedia of Informality: Towards Understanding of Social and Cultural Complexity, Volumes 1–2.* London: UCL Press.

Magyar, B. and Madlovics, B. 2020. *The Anatomy of Post-Communist Regimes: A Conceptual Framework.* Budapest: Central European University Press.

Marinaro, I. C. 2022. *Inhabiting Liminal Spaces: Informalities in Governance, Housing, and Economic Activity in Contemporary Italy*. Abingdon: Routledge.
Marková, I. 2002. 'Thinking and Antinomies'. In *Dialogicality and Thinking, the Dynamics of Mind*. Chapter 2. Cambridge: Cambridge University Press.
Marková, I. 2003. *Dialogicality and Social Representations: The Dynamics of Mind*. Cambridge: Cambridge University Press.
Marquette, H. and Peiffer, C. 2015. *Corruption and Collective Action*. London: DLP Research Paper.
Martínez, S. A. V. and Chiodelli, F. 2021. 'Informal Housing of the Rich: Clustering, Isolating, and Concealing in Bogotá, Colombia'. *Habitat International*: 112.
Minbaeva, D. B., Ledeneva, A., Muratbekova-Touron, M. and Horak, S. 2023. 'Explaining the Persistence of Informal Institutions: The Role of Informal Networks'. *Academy of Management Review* 48(3): 556–74.
Misztal, B. 2002. *Informality: Social Theory and Contemporary Practice*. Abingdon: Routledge.
Morris, J. 2019. 'The Informal Economy and Post-Socialism: Imbricated Perspectives on Labor, the State, and Social Embeddedness'. *Demokratizatsiya: The Journal of Post-Soviet Democratization* 27(1): 9–30.
Morris, J. and Polese, A. (eds) 2013. *The Informal Post-socialist Economy: Embedded Practices and Livelihoods*. Abingdon: Routledge.
North, D. C. 1990. *Institutions, Institutional Change and Economic Performance*. Cambridge: Cambridge University Press.
Ostrom, E. (1998). 'A Behavioral Approach to the Rational Choice Theory of Collective Action: Presidential Address, American Political Science Association, 1997'. *American Political Science Review* 92(1): 1–22.
Polese, A. 2023 'What is Informality? The Art of Bypassing the State in Eurasian Spaces – and Beyond'. *Eurasian Geography and Economics* 64(3): 322–64.
Polese, A., Russo, A. and Strazzari, F. (eds) 2019. *Governance Beyond the Law: The Immoral, the Illegal, the Criminal*. London: Palgrave Macmillan.
Polese, A., Urinboyev, R., Svensson, M., Adams, L. and Kerikmäe, T. 2022a. 'Political vs. Everyday Forms of Governance in Uzbekistan: The Illegal, Immoral, and Illegitimate'. In *Informality, Labour Mobility and Precariousness* edited by A. Polese, 223–47. Cham: Palgrave Macmillan.
Polese, A., Moisé, G. M., Tokyzhanova, T., Aguzzi, T., Kerikmäe, T., Sagynbaeva, A., Sauka, A. and Seliverstova, O. 2022b. 'Informality versus Shadow Economy: Reflecting on the First Results of a Manager's Survey in Kyrgyzstan'. *Central Asian Survey*: 1–22.
Pow, C. P. 2017. 'Elite Informality, Spaces of Exception and the Super-Rich in Singapore'. In *Cities and the Super-Rich*, edited by R. Forrest, S. Y. Koh and B. Wissink, 223–47. Cham: Palgrave Macmillan.
Putniņš, T. J. and Sauka, A. 2015. 'Measuring the Shadow Economy using Company Managers'. *Journal of Comparative Economics* 43(2): 471–90.
Ricoeur, P. 2008 [1970]. *Freud and Philosophy: An Essay on Interpretation*. Translated by Denis Savage. New Haven: Yale University Press.
Ruml, B. 1930. 'Recent Trends in Social Science'. In *The New Social Science*, edited by L. R. White, 99–111. Chicago: University of Chicago.
Scott, J. C. 1985. *Weapons of the Weak: Everyday Forms of Peasant Resistance*. New Haven: Yale University Press.
Shekshnia, S. and Matveeva, A. 2019a. 'The Network Leadership (A): Global Informality Project'. Fontainebleau: INSEAD.
Shekshnia, S. and Matveeva, A. 2019b. 'The Network Leadership (B): Global Encyclopaedia of Informality'. Fontainebleau: INSEAD.
Stuart, E., Samman, E. and Hunt, A. 2018. *Informal Is the New Normal: Improving the Lives of Workers at Risk of being Left Behind*. Vol. 530. London: Overseas Development Institute.
Sunstein, C. R. and Reisch, L. A. 2017. *The Economics of Nudge*. London: Routledge.
Thaler, R. H. and Sunstein, C. R. 2008. *Nudge: Improving Decisions about Health, Wealth, and Happiness*. New Haven: Yale University Press.
WEF. 2022. 'Strategic Interactive Maps of Informality', https://intelligence.weforum.org/topics/a1G68000000KzI5EAC

1
Being born

Introduction: reproduction and emotional ambivalence

Michele Rivkin-Fish
University of North Carolina, USA

Ethnographies related to procreation reveal the complex ways informal activities and relationships emerge in reproduction, kinship and family life. Bringing children into the world and raising them are simultaneously personal journeys for parents and major concerns of states; the latter pursues their own agendas related to population dynamics and the need for productive citizens. Birth, and the prevention of birth, are potentially costly (or lucrative) endeavours, depending on your social position. Informal practices surrounding reproduction are thus motivated by both economic and emotional goals.

For people unable to conceive or bear children, surrogacy in the twenty-first century is increasingly common. Its profitability and ambivalent moral status generate numerous informal practices. During the industry's early years, US surrogacy agencies encouraged commissioning mothers to treat their surrogates as part of the family. These informal tactics aimed to distract surrogates from bonding with the growing foetus. Yet the agencies instruct families to distance themselves from the surrogate and preserve the nuclear family façade (Ragone 1994). Emotions can thus be cynically manipulated for economic gain. With the globalisation of surrogate labour, debates over its exploitative nature have multiplied. Siegl's ethnography reveals how commissioning couples justify their actions by emphasising their surrogates' 'happiness' at helping others, or by contending that surrogates exert 'free choice' (Siegl 2023). Although surrogates are motivated by the need for money, the ethical quandaries at stake are gradually being erased by informal rationalisations, including an insistence on positive emotions.

Abortion offers significant examples of informal relations arising for personal and political autonomy. In many US states, laws require abortion providers to communicate certain non-medical, and often scientifically untrue, information in order to try to change their patients' minds. Ethnographic research found that clinics fulfil the letter of the law while upholding the commitment to reproductive choice: staff preface their script by explaining what it is state mandated to say, but not state mandated to hear (Buchbinder 2016). In contexts where abortion is criminalised, women are vulnerable to greed and/or moral judgement as they seek informal arrangements (Kligman 1998). For example, in Brazil, women who cannot afford to pay for illegal abortions initiate terminations and arrive at the hospital to have the procedure completed, claiming miscarriage. Despite Brazilian health care services' rhetoric promising 'humanised' medicine, discrimination against women experiencing miscarriages (who are suspected of having induced abortions) is pervasive (McCallum et al. 2016). With increasing abortion restrictions across the United States, scholars would do well to follow the informal strategies that surround this politicised procedure; they are bound to be motivated by economic interests, moral rationales and emotionally managed justifications (Keys 2010).

The study of reproduction reveals how economic motivations for informal practice are rarely the single factor; emotional goals are often intertwined with the pursuit of social advantage and economic gain. For example, providing a child with US citizenship through childbirth tourism is reminiscent of 'intensive mothering' – practices cultivating a child's well-being in emotional and economic terms (Shpakovskaya 2015). Mothers give their children skills and advantages while gaining a sense of personal accomplishment and social respect for themselves. Such informal efforts should be seen not only as individual choices, but as personal journeys shaped by macro-level forces. The societal expectation that women have ambitious careers sits alongside continuing norms of maternal responsibility for child rearing and neoliberal competition in the workforce. Intensive mothering is an informal response to the persistence of gendered inequalities in a competitive world. These dynamics reveal that multiple incentives, desires and deterrents mediate informal relationships.

Contrary to anti-corruption campaigns, which focus on economically motivated illegality, many informal practices are justified by moral and emotional obligations. The Moldovan system of *cumătrism* networks, a version of the godparent-godchild relationship, is exemplary. *Cumătru* relationships provide a child with economic support and spiritual guidance from a trusted elder. The fact that the godchild demonstrates respect and deference, not economic return, is significant. The emotional components of these relationships shape their perceived morality and help explain why efforts to exclude *cumătrism* influence from public institutions often fail.

Economic and emotional motivations are also intertwined in *uklonenie ot alimentov* or Russian men's practice of evading child support payments by hiding their income. At first glance, this seems entirely motivated by economic interests. Yet pride is also at stake. Culturally, in Russia masculinity is tied to being a breadwinner and maintaining control over one's expenditures. Men thus perceive state mandates for child support to be a direct attack on their personal dignity. Russian women, consequently, mostly arrange informal support with their ex-husbands. Knowing that men have multiple strategies for evading state mandates, women place their hopes in a man's moral sense of obligation to be a 'good father' rather than aligning their claims with state power.

The combination of economic and emotional advantage, and the related sense of moral virtue attached to many informal relationships, are explored in a rich ethnography of single mothers in Russia (Utrata 2015). The common assumption that older women have no need for a personal life, and a cultural norm that *babushki* universally provide care, allow both the economic and emotional value of *babushkas*' labour to be ignored (Utrata 2015). Yet when adult daughters take their mothers' help as *babushki* for granted, *babushki* respond with a variety of emotions. The obligations tacitly assumed in informal relations and linked to feelings of connection, virtue and love may also produce ambivalence and even resentment. And as public policies and economic incentives change, the meanings and expectations of kinship roles also shift. Emotions are a central feature to informal strategies in both institutional and domestic spheres; and ambivalent, contradictory emotions abound.

The emotional and moral components of informal practices challenge the distinction between public and private spheres. Staff in Russian public institutions are known to use *khamstvo*, rudeness and aggression, against those with less power (Temkina et al. 2021). Yet when workers encounter clients through their friendship networks, kin-based feelings of obligation are aroused. Inside the public space of the medical facility, informal relations carve out privileged spheres of kindness and solicitude. For this reason, many pregnant women sought to give birth with a clinician known through their informal networks rather than through official, bureaucratic channels. Physicians also prefer caring for people with whom they had personal network connections, because such patients were likely to recognise the doctors' expertise, rather than suspecting the doctors were indifferent or incompetent (Rivkin-Fish 2005). Indeed, in the 1990s, Russian maternity care patients who offered their doctors bribes were met with resentment for implying the doctor's competence must be bought; by contrast, patients who presented economically meaningless but sincere gifts of thanks cultivated relationships with doctors that often continued outside the medical context. These relationships involved informal favours across institutional and domestic boundaries, revealing that the distinction between public and private spheres should not be reified.

Temkina (2020) and Temkina and Rivkin-Fish (2020) show how neoliberal health care reforms have transformed Russian doctor-patient dynamics. In the 2000s, the Russian state introduced competition to improve maternity care; all birthing women were now free to choose their doctor. Simultaneously, women began discussing their childbirth experiences on new internet forums and doctors began acquiring public reputations. With consumer recognition, physicians gained moral recognition and salary increases. These official incentive systems reduced the use of informal acquaintance relations and made bribes virtually unnecessary. Interestingly, however, women whose friendship networks included doctors still preferred to access care informally, expecting these channels to ensure the strongest moral and emotional commitments.

In examining informal practices related to birth, abortion, maternity care and kinship, anthropologists reveal the limitations of economists' assumption that human rationality always prioritises maximising individual utility. Economic goals are tied to and often subordinated to emotional aspirations; mothers prioritise their children's long-term well-being over their own financial comfort, and physicians long for professional respect over economically valuable bribes. Godparents enjoy social prestige and respect in return for providing economic and social guidance. Emotions can also be objects of manipulation to secure social goals, such as securing a newborn from its surrogate mother or stigmatising abortion. Divorced fathers crave the pride of being breadwinners and turn their caregiving into a moral statement of personal virtue while resisting state control and even abandoning their children if mandated to pay by law. Women seeking child support payments hedge their bets by catering to men's emotions. Public policies that seek to reduce informal economic activities and the social protections of nepotism must consider the emotional dimensions of care, obligation and inequality that are central to informality.

1.1 *Mei bao ma* (China)
Hui Guo
Alumna, School of Slavonic and East European Studies, UCL, UK

Mei bao ma (美宝妈) – literally 'mother of an American baby' – refers to the practice of 'birthright tourism', whereby Chinese mothers-to-be travel to the USA with a purpose of acquiring US citizenship for their child and, in the long term, for themselves and their family. This practice is based on the legal principle *jus soli*, the 'right of soil' in Latin, that grants citizenship to those born on a particular territory (Wydra 2010: 2; Scott 1930: 58). *Jus soli* is exercised in 33 countries, among which the USA and Canada are the only developed countries (World Atlas 2018). Chinese birthright tourism practice is aimed at increasing social capital, enhancing one's social standing and creating opportunities to develop new connections, perceived as important in Chinese society (also see *guanxi*, 1.12 Volume 1).

While birthright citizenship is legal, birthright tourism is informal. While not illegal, it exploits the *jus soli* doctrine for personal advantage. Donald Trump has voiced his concern over the so-called 'anchor babies' in the USA (Flanagin 2015). Acquiring birthright citizenship is seen by some as an exploitative strategy and a 'sinister kind of way of achieving U.S. citizenship' (KCET 2018). For a family, an 'anchor baby' is a long-term strategy for entitlement to permanent US residency, and for enhancing family's life chances and education possibilities. The parents may join the child once they reach 21 years of age, although there is no guarantee that such an application will be successful (Semotiuk 2014).

Concerns over this 'abusive and exploitative' practice are related to fears that the increasing number of birth tourists would drain the health care and public welfare systems (Woord 2018). In 2018 it was reported that every year around 40,000 babies are born in the US to Chinese mothers on travel visas (Fonrouge 2018). However, birthright tourists are not eligible for health care or travel insurance. The parents must bear the cost themselves: 32,093 USD for a vaginal birth and 51,125 USD for C-section, inclusive of newborn care (Glenza 2018). When the parents declare giving birth as the reason for their visit to the USA at the visa application stage, they must provide evidence that they are able to cover all medical costs, thereby adding no financial pressure on the health care system (Oni 2016).

It is estimated that *mei bao ma* tourists accounted for about 1 per cent of the 2.2 million Chinese tourists visiting the US in 2014 (Ramakrishnan 2015). This new trend, associated with luxury and affluence in China, stems from the increasing wealth of the middle class. As China opens up to the world, better-off people contemplate possibilities for solving their problems and plan for the future. Initially, birthright tourism was used to circumvent China's one-child policy, rigidly enforced between 1979 and 2015. Birthright tourism began to increase when China became 'plagued by health scandals that have instilled fear into expectant mothers', such as adulterated infant milk powder and the lack of epidural anaesthesia during labour (Sheehan 2015).

Pull factors associated with benefits of an American citizenship also played a role. Holding a US passport allows a visa-free or visa-on-arrival travel to 174 countries, thus increasing children's opportunities, but the most cited reason for birthright tourism is 'education of the next generation'. A child with an American passport will be able to apply to study at Chinese international schools, which are more affordable than private schools and hold higher standards of education (Bourgon 2017). Pursuing higher education in China as an international student is a less competitive option compared to the annual battle of 10 million students applying for 6.6 million spots at Chinese universities (Richburg 2010). Children born in the USA can stay in the US and enrol in free public education. They are entitled to numerous benefits such as access to better educational resources and more diverse campuses, bypassing high overseas tuition fees and qualifying for government aid, scholarships and government jobs (Jacob 2017: 156). Yet to study in the US, the child must have legal guardianship or custody from a US citizen. Children of parents unable to obtain a visa or custody often return to China.

Taking part in the *mei bao ma* idea can be expensive. Giving birth in American hospitals is considered the costliest in the world. Further costs come from stays at '*mei bao ma* hotels' after giving birth: between 29,048 USD and 43,573 USD for the duration of their stay (Lin 2017). Maternity hotels host women during the period of 'postnatal confinement' before and after birth, a norm for Chinese mothers (Haque 2017). The multi-billion-dollar maternity hotel industry is a significant driver of the increase of birthright tourism and provides support at every stage, from consultation and visa application to hospital care and entertainment. The hotels offer a wide range of services for the wealthier Chinese clients, such as curated meals, valet service, organised tours, hospital care, recreation classes, on-site nurses, translation services and assistance with visa applications. This lucrative tourist industry is often cash-based, and profits fall outside of the US formal economy (KCET 2018). According to indirect estimates, companies that 'skirted tax law, flouted immigration laws and helped their clients to defraud US hospitals of tens of thousands of dollars for each baby born' failed to report over 1 million USD profit per maternity hotel (Phillip 2015).

Cheaper and simpler birthright 'loopholes' also exist for less wealthy families (Grant 2015: 165). Saipan in the Mariana Islands in the Pacific Ocean falls within the US *jus soli* jurisdiction. Chinese citizens can visit the island visa-free for up to 45 days, with a simple procedure to extend their stay. The number of *mei bao ma* who entered as tourists increased from 8 in 2009 to 472 in 2017. The growth is not overwhelming, considering the size of the Chinese population; nevertheless it is significant and expected to increase further.

1.2 *Khamstvo* (USSR, Russia)
Anastasia Novkunskaya, Daria Litvina and Anna Temkina
European University at St. Petersburg, Russia

Khamstvo – a communicative code of rudeness – signifies emotional and verbal abuse, which had been widespread in public sector services in the Soviet Union. Some examples of *khamstvo* can also be found in contemporary encounters. *Khamstvo* normally characterises communicative situations when members of social groups assert their situational authority in a rude manner. *Khamstvo* was typical for the *proletariat* and professional groups that had exclusive access to scarce resources, such as sales clerks, medical personnel, accountants, and staff for communal and housing services (Koenker 2019).

Khamstvo was embedded in the fabric of Soviet everyday life. Multiple examples of *khamstvo* can be found in literary epics of early Soviet times – in Tolstoy's *The Road to Calvary* that covers the period 1914–9 and Bulgakov's *Heart of a Dog* that depicts the aftermath of the early twenty-century revolutions in Russia. The snap redistribution of power in that period and further economic, political and social changes provided institutionally favourable conditions for the spread of *khamstvo*. *Khamstvo* can either be employed occasionally or become a habitual mode of behaviour, routinely performed in public: on transport, in queues, on the streets. It is more likely to be widespread in authoritarian and top-down regulated regimes where the rigidity of rules is combined with poor services.

The Soviet planned economy resulted in a constant deficit of goods and services (even essential ones), unavailable even for a higher price (see *blat*, 1.1 Volume 1). This made service workers the de facto gatekeepers of centrally distributed scarce resources. Their situational authority, giving them power to make decisions about the welfare of others, made them eligible to perform *khamstvo* – to assert this authority in a rude manner. These gatekeepers could facilitate or limit access to goods or services, and such examples were widespread in late socialist fiction, such as Dovlatov's essay on *This untranslatable word – khamstvo* (Dovlatov 2005).

Soviet maternity wards were physically closed to visitors and could be characterised as quasi total institutions, harbouring opaque rules and practices and resistant to challenges from the outside (Goffman 1961; Davies 1989). Consequently, they were secure spaces for health care practitioners to exercise direct power and control over women and subordinate them to uniform medical procedures, without regard for their feelings (Rivkin-Fish 2005). Maternity wards have since changed, yet *khamstvo* (even though reduced and lost status of normality in interactions) remains an important tool to control women and place them under clinicians' authority.

The rigidity of the centralised socialist health care system was somewhat alleviated by a system of informal and paid care (Stepurko et al. 2013; Cook 2015). In order to avoid the uniform over-medicalisation of mothers during pregnancy and the emotionally traumatic experience of giving birth in Soviet hospitals (including *khamstvo* of personnel), women mobilised their families and networks and resorted to informal practices. These included personal introductions and referrals (*blat*, see 1.1 Volume 1) and informal agreements arranged through social networks and informal payments. The contacts were used to find a doctor that could offer personal care, thus reducing negative experience and stress during childbirth, in exchange for an out-of-pocket payment. While *blat* (see 1.1 Volume 1) could not change the emotional pressure put on patients by the doctors, or reduce manifestations of *khamstvo* overall, personal referrals could boost the competitive advantage of patients and ensure doctors' attention, sincere concern, thereby forgoing *khamstvo*. The system of out-of-pocket payments helped further improve the provider-patient relationship, by making emotional support part of the deal. Thus, *khamstvo* captured a complex emotional regime. On the one hand, it was on display in both bureaucratic and non-bureaucratic medical settings, but never openly admitted by the Soviet doctors, who positioned themselves as experts 'teaching' women proper behaviour. On the other hand, the trade of emotional support through informal channels was also widely known, albeit as an 'open secret'.

Dominant in Soviet paternalistic maternity care, *khamstvo* remains present despite the significant changes in maternity care after the collapse of the Soviet Union. In in-depth interviews conducted by the authors

(Temkina et al. 2022) for the research project 'Choice, control and trust in childbirth' in 2017, women shared examples of *khamstvo* communication they had experienced on maternity wards: 'The midwives were so angry, so conniving and insolent … I asked her, "Well, what about the test results?". She snapped at me: "How would I know, it's none of my business", and so on' (mother, 25 years old). 'Yes, they are boorish. They yell, damn it, but they don't just yell, they discipline' (mother, 30 years old).

Khamstvo manifested as emotional abuse in health care could be considered an emotional regime or an institutionalised behaviour. The vulnerability and dependence of patients together with the isolation of medical institutions reinforce the staff's sense of superiority. The institutionalisation of *khamstvo* is indicative of the prevalence of the collective over the individual in Russia. This regime enables health care providers to neglect women's emotional needs for care and subordinate these needs to the clinical, organisational and bureaucratic demands. *Khamstvo* in maternity wards used to be perceived as legitimate by both the health care providers and, to some extent, by the childbearing women.

Khamstvo shapes the attitudes of all participants, including the clinicians themselves, who often claim to feel helpless within the paternalistic hierarchies of the state. Doctors and midwives often perceive themselves to be in a subordinate, and vulnerable, position, which makes them exercise familiarity and aggression as effective instruments to make women obey (Litvina et al. 2019). Protagonists of this view appeal to the necessity of controlling, manipulating and, in some cases, exercising power. Unlike in other medical settings, such as *psikhushka* (see 8.7, 8.8 Volume 1), they exercise power verbally and emotionally, rather than physically. Women are labelled as 'ignorant' and 'infantile' and forced to cooperate and behave properly during childbirth, purportedly for their own and their baby's sake. Paternalistic aggression is used to generate shame to affect patient behaviour and to subordinate an individual to the 'correct' way of behaving. Clinicians justify their way of communication as a preventive measure against 'wrong or shameful' behaviour from pregnant women and do not identify it as *khamstvo*. At the same time, they perceive the women's tactics against *khamstvo*, such as lodging a complaint or taking a video of such behaviour, as aggressive, so they respond to such action with *khamstvo*.

Late Soviet-era state medical services were characterised by over-regulation, rigidity of medical hierarchies and shortages of resources. *Khamstvo* in maternity wards generated a power style and a code of rudeness that sought to discipline women and subject them to both the impersonal rules and the clinicians' discretion in interpreting them.

Because women were completely dependent on the medical staff, they had to accept these rules and codes as inevitable, beyond women's control and impossible to challenge (Temkina 2016). To feel bound by fate is considered a constitutive element of the emotional regime of *khamstvo* and can be considered its intrinsic vehicle, reproduced in institutions at the organisational level. Patients who had no choice but to use state medical facilities employed bottom-up strategies of personalisation to counter *khamstvo*, a top-down strategy of the staff. Some structural prerequisites and communication characteristics of *khamstvo* were transferred onto Russian contemporary medical institutions and are still typical for certain medical specialists and settings (Temkina et al. 2021).

1.3 *Selektivni abortus/tuđa večera* (Montenegro)
Diāna Kiščenko
Faculty of Communication, Rīga Stradiņš University, Latvia

In Montenegro, *selektivni abortus* (literally 'selective abortion') denotes a deliberate termination of pregnancy based on the predicted sex of the child. Worldwide, this practice is understood as an abortion of the female foetus. One of the main causes leading to sex-selective abortion in Montenegro, as elsewhere, is the preference for a son facilitated by access to medical technologies. Historically, women in Montenegro were expected to give birth to a son in order to ensure continuation of the husband's family lineage. To ensure a male heir, women used to give birth as many times as necessary until a son was produced (Milich 1995). Prenatal medical technologies such as ultrasound, amniocentesis, chorionic villus sampling and cell-free foetal DNA testing allow parents to determine the sex of the foetus in early pregnancy and make decisions regarding termination based on this information.

In Montenegro law, sex-selective abortion is prohibited, while abortion is legal, with no restrictions regarding termination during the first ten weeks of pregnancy (Ministarstvo Zdravlja 2009). No official records of sex-selective abortion exist, so the scale of sex-selective abortions performed in the country is speculative. A method of monitoring such practices accepted worldwide is to compare statistical data on newborns to the standard biological ratio of 104–106 newborn boys to 100 newborn girls (UNFPA 2012: 9). When the number of male newborns exceeds 106, there is reason to suspect human intervention, that is, female foetuses were aborted. It is statistically challenging to assess the situation in Montenegro due to its low number of annual births. Based on the 2000–8 cumulative data, the sex ratio at birth was estimated at 109.7 newborn boys to 100 girls, while in 2017, the ratio was 107.2. Thus, Montenegro has been slightly affected by the practice of sex-selection abortion, with the ratio fluctuating below 110 (Chao et al. 2019, note the correction). Sex-selective abortions have been driven by three factors: society's continuing preference for sons, access to technologies such as ultrasound and amniocentesis and decreasing fertility levels (Guilmoto 2010).

The preference for a son tends to be linked to the general attitude towards women and girls that is formed by patriarchal, patrilineal and patrilocal characteristics of society (Patel 2007: 293). Montenegro's traditional social and kinship systems were male-centred: men had a central power and resources in society, family name and assets were inherited by male lineage, sons were expected to live close to their father and take care of ageing parents. Being a woman in Montenegro meant getting married, moving away from your family, moving with and taking care of your husband's household, serving your new family and bearing children (Denich 1974). Historically, women's position in Montenegro was characterised with a pejorative expression *ćerka je tuđa večera* (the daughter serves someone else's dinner) to suggest that having a daughter is a worthless investment as she will sooner or later leave her natal family and serve her husband's family. Once they are married, the woman will no longer be her father's concern; her husband's family's will take on this responsibility. A son, on the other hand, is seen as a valuable asset as he will provide care and help, continue the family's lineage and maintain the family's property. Even though attempts were made to reduce these patriarchal patterns during the socialist period, they were not overcome, only suppressed (Petrović 2014). Today, these customary norms and perceptions merge with modern technology to result in the practice of sex-selective abortions.

The preference for boys had numerous implications. There is a shortage of women in Montenegrin rural areas as rural women migrate to cities and abroad for education and work, and men stay to manage the property. Relationships and marriages with women from neighbouring countries is becoming increasingly common, especially between Montenegrins and Albanians. In 2017 the Montenegrin news portal *Vijesti* broke the story about men in the northern part of the country who paid a broker for brides from neighbouring Albania. The transactions failed to take place when the men were swindled out of their money

(2,500–10,000 Euros each), but of course they could not report the case to the police (Skorupan 2017).

While the current shortage of marriageable women in rural areas relates largely to rural-urban migration, in the future it will likely be exacerbated by biomedical technologies. Condemning the preference for a son, prenatal testing and sex-selective abortion, a non-governmental women's rights organisation, Centar za ženska prava, together with McCann (marketing company), in 2017 launched a social campaign Neželjena ('unwanted'), driven by the idea of unwanted daughters in Montenegro. The campaign petitioned for a change in the law that would prevent the abuse of prenatal testing for selective abortion (Centar za ženska prava 2017).

According to UNFPA, practices of the termination of female foetuses are also widespread in East and South Asia (China, India, the Republic of Korea and Vietnam) and Caucasus (Azerbaijan, Armenia and Georgia). India has one of the most skewed birth sex ratios (110.5 newborn boys to 100 newborn girls) (UNFPA 2012: 20). In the Indian practice of *kanya bhroon hatya* (killing of the female foetus, Sanskrit term used in formal contexts, Patel 2007), sons are preferred because of dowry customs, kinship patterns and the subordinate position of women in society (Patel 2007: 293, 343). The shortage of Asian women eligible for marriage has profound socio-economic effects. In India and China women risk being kidnapped or trafficked for the purpose of marriage or sexual exploitation (UNFPA 2012: 2).

Several approaches are adopted in the study of sex-selective abortion and son preference (Eklund 2011: 19). The outcome approach quantifies human behaviour and is conducted by demographers, economists and public health researchers. The causal approach tends to embrace the cultural embeddedness of the practice, its social contexts and economic and legal constraints and is carried out by social anthropologists and sociologists. Studies combining such approaches and mixed-method research also exist.

1.4 *Xiaoerni* (China)
Ling Meng
Department of Applied Social Sciences, The Hong Kong Polytechnic University, Hong Kong

Xiaoerni (小二妮) refers to a family's second-born daughter; it is a regional dialect term to describe a special group, mainly in rural northern China, such as in the provinces of Shandong, Henan, Shanxi, Hebei

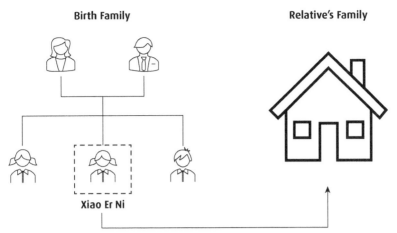

Figure 1.4.1 Diagram of a *xiaoerni*'s life. © Ling Meng 2021.

(Li 1993; Chen 2004; Johnson 2016). *Xiaoerni* usually has a unique life experience. The girl has an elder sister but grows up in a relative's family (see Figure 1.4.1).

This adulteration of the family highlights the conflict between birth control policy and traditional fertility culture that has been prevalent since the 1980s. This phenomenon originates from informal strategies practised by Chinese families whose traditional fertility culture allows them to resist family planning policies. Because they cannot change the gender of newborn children, families conceal their children's birth.

With no social security support, traditionally, rural families raised sons in order to support or take care of the parents in their old age (*yang er fang lao*). Furthermore, this preference for male children is a way for families to preserve their reputation, or *mianzi*, in the local community so as not to be ridiculed for having no male offspring. However, confronted with enforced population control, the goal of having a son may not be achieved. According to the 1.5-child policy, before 2016, in rural China, a couple was allowed to have at most two children if the first child was a girl (Scharping 2003; Greenhalgh and Winckler 2005). A family is lucky if their firstborn is a boy, but if they are less fortunate and their firstborn is a girl, the couple are then allowed to produce a son. However, complications arise when the second child is also a girl. In accordance with the regulations of the 1.5-child policy, a family with two daughters is no longer permitted to have more children. Nevertheless, it is impossible for families with deep-rooted traditional fertility values to accept not having sons. Despite being aware that they are directly contradicting state policy, these families are unwilling to give up the ideal fertility goal.

When the second girl is born, families are faced with a choice: they can either 'resign themselves to their fate' (*ren ming*), accepting the situation of having two daughters, or they can arrange backroom dealings with local cadres to 'spend money to buy birth' (*hua qian mai sheng yu*). Nevertheless, although many families are not willing to 'accept fate', they also do not have the ability or the money to receive protection from a local cadre. Under these circumstances, hiding the second daughter becomes an option. Placing the second daughter within extended family is a relatively conservative strategy; neither passive resignation nor aggressive resistance, instead representing a reasonable solution between a rigid policy regulation and a flexible blood bond. On one hand, this practice is cruel in that it prevents the second daughter from living with her biological parents, but on the other hand, the practice is moderate because it does not deprive the second daughter of her life and does not abandon her completely (Chu 2001; Huang 2012; Johnson 2016; Shi and Kennedy 2016). In some families, the second daughter is adopted out on a temporary basis and eventually returned. However, many urban families are pressured by the one-child policy to hide and adopt out their firstborn daughter to relatives in rural areas.

In local practice, *xiaoerni* is often described as 'wounded' or 'dead' when she is born. In fact, the girl is brought up by the extended family, such as maternal grandparents, paternal aunts and maternal aunts. In general, in-laws do not live near the birth family, which makes it easier to avoid family planning inspection until a son is born. After that, the adopted daughter can return to her birth family. In most cases, the birth family provides economic support for their 'adopted-out' daughter, whereas the foster family is responsible for the girl's care.

Legally speaking, the birth of *xiaoerni* does not violate the 1.5-child policy. However, the children are not legally registered and are excluded from official population statistics. Hence, regardless of whether she stays with her biological or relative's family, fleeing from sudden unannounced inspection is normal for *xiaoerni*. If discovered, the second daughter's biological parents would be subject to strict birth control punishment, such as contraception, sterilisation or forced abortion, which would deprive them of the chance to produce another child.

For the *xiaoerni* and her two families, obtaining legal status and leading a normal life are key issues. In general, there are two strategies for families to obtain household registration (*hukou*). The first strategy is for biological parents to directly assign the second daughter's *hukou* to their own family, mainly through a population census or by seeking *guanxi* (see 1.12 Volume 1). Using this method, the birth family is usually required to pay a fine. The other strategy is for relatives, particularly unmarried or childless male relatives, register the second daughter's *hukou* in the name of their adopted daughter, thus evading fines for disregarding family planning policy. Regardless of how the household is settled, it is essential to invite local cadres to meals, spend money on them, give them gifts (*songli*, see 2.2 Volume 1) and exploit *guanxi* to solicit help.

Since 2016, the one-child policy in mainland China and its 1.5-child version in rural areas are no longer enforced, but the residual effects of this policy are still evident. *Xiaoernis* represent one of the unintended consequences of a series of complicated mechanisms, and their lives are deeply shaped by these events before their birth. These children have become the 'hidden group', whose lives are determined by national policy and their families. Illegal labels and perplexing identities accompany them throughout their life, contributing to long-lasting, complex psychological and practical consequences. Furthermore, individual strategies have been adopted by this group (sometimes together with their families) to redefine their fate. For example, these children always conceal their identities as *xiaoerni* during their education and some may also discard the same in marriage.

1.5 **Parovoziki** (Russia)
Ekaterina Pereprosova
Centre de recherche sur les liens sociaux, Université Paris Descartes, France

The term *parovoziki*, literally 'little trains' in Russian, refers to the practices emerging around the custom of not separating siblings when they are fostered. The term was coined in 2008 when fostering began to be promoted as a form of orphan care, facilitated by articles 145, 152, 153 of the Federal Decree No 49 and integrated into the Family Code of Russian Federation. The size of the sibling group to be placed with foster parents depends on the parents' fostering experience, their living conditions and economic resources. Up to two children may be placed with a first-time foster family; while the more experienced, 'professional' candidates can foster three or more children. Thus, the term refers primarily to the application stage, when a willing foster family contacts the local childcare authorities or meets the child selected from the local or federal database of orphans. Should this child have a sibling, the placement becomes contingent on their inseparability. The term is also used to denote a situation whereby the family that fosters a child has priority in fostering the child's siblings should they become orphans at a later stage. This is normally a result of the decision by social services to remove the siblings, for example children born to mothers with limited parental rights, from their biological family. In this case, the family fostering the newborn's siblings is solicited by social services for placement before other candidates. Despite their right to decline, this kind of additional placement is common.

The norm of placing siblings within the same family is not, however, set in stone. Social workers and childcare authorities retain some room for manoeuvre and ultimately have the power to revoke a *parovoziki* placement should they assess this to be in 'the best interest of the child', as stipulated by article 145 of the decree. If they regard the placement of the newly fostered sibling to the foster family as unsatisfactory, or detrimental to other siblings, they can either separate them and move the foster candidate to another foster family or they can separate siblings into different groups within the public residential institution. The policy of the inseparability of siblings, however flexible, is nevertheless an important departure from practices predominant in the state residential institutions that place children in groups according to their age, regardless of their family ties.

Fostering *parovoziki* groups is a beneficial outcome of the deinstitutionalisation of public policies, informed by observing the detrimental effects on child socialisation in Soviet orphanages, or 'total institutions' (Goffman 1961; Becker 1985). The *parovoziki* placements are part of a wider effort to create a family-like environment by reorganising residential institutions into smaller-group homes with in-house educators and by promoting family-based forms of care. In 2010, following President Dmitry Medvedev's call for a society with 'no un-adopted children' in Russia (Kulmala et al. 2017), fostering and adoption became social policy priorities, and their rise became the principal measure of the effectiveness of deinstitutionalisation (Kulmala 2017). By law, foster and adoptive families are entitled to social guarantees as well as various financial and property benefits, such as property grants for fostering several children and maternity capital grants (*masterinsky kapital*) for adopting a child as a second child of the family. Therefore, the increasing rates of family-based forms of care over the past decade has changed the profile of children in institutional care. According to an analysis of the official statistics for 2015, 42 per cent of children in institutional care have a physical disability and 67 per cent a psychological disability

(Biryukova and Sinyavskaya 2017). Ninety-one per cent of children in institutional care are more than six years old, of which 69 per cent are between 7 and 15 years old and 21 per cent are older than 16 (Biryukova and Sinyavskaya 2017). Siblings constitute 53 per cent of all children in institutional care, according to a report published by the Russian charity fund 'Nuzhna Pomosch' (Tinchurin et al. 2018). As such, this number suggests that *parovoziki* siblings may be at a disadvantage in terms of being adopted (Rudov 2015; Semya et al. 2016; Biryukova and Sinyavskaya 2017). The very existence of the *parovoziki* slang indicates the pervasiveness of the problem associated with siblings in need of a foster home.

To improve the experience of children for whom entering family-based care has been difficult, various charity funds and non-profit organisations initiate foster parents training that focuses on specific issues encountered in fostering teenagers, siblings and children with disabilities: behavioural problems, communication with the biological family and health issues. Some organisations offer psychological support and monitor processes of attachment and kinship construction. The organisations may also offer intervention in critical situations, for example to prevent a child being removed from the foster home and being returned to the residential institution.

Several regional development programmes also address this problem and encourage placements of several children at a time, most commonly siblings, children with disabilities and children over ten years old. Such programmes are aimed at improving the living conditions of foster families. A pilot project in the Moscow region, funded by the state, for example, grants a flat to the family willing to foster five children at once, three of whom must be over ten years old or have a disability. However, this programme has been criticised by several non-profit organisations that raised concerns about the lack of adequate qualifications of foster parents applying to participate. Other projects include building a village for foster families as part of the Smart Schooling project (*Umnaja Shkola*) in the Irkutsk region, an educational complex, intended to house 30 foster families and 150 foster children, the latter of whom would represent approximately 15 per cent of the Smart School's students. Due to the context-bound nature of the problem, child placement projects remain rather local, with *parovoziki*, children with disabilities and teenagers presenting a major challenge. Faced with this challenge, the childcare authorities and expert community called for an amendment to decree No 423 to allow siblings who did not grow up together to be separated. By prioritising the well-being of an individual over the imperative to maintain family ties of the sibling group, this proposal highlights the importance of each child's social ties constructed in institutional and foster family placements, as well as the importance of socialisation contexts themselves.

1.6 **Cumătrism** (Moldova)
Andrei Iovu
Alumnus, School of Slavonic and East European Studies, UCL, UK

The term *cumătrism* stands for the use of informal networks in the Republic of Moldova. While not in the official dictionary of Romanian language, in mass media and the vernacular the word is widely used and has two meanings. First, *cumătrism* refers to the system of kinship relations created in the event called *cumătria*, associated with the religious ritual of christening a child. The second meaning has a pejorative connotation and describes the unmerited promotion of a candidate to a certain position, based on being a *cumătru* to someone with status. These two meanings are close to those of *kumstvo* in Montenegro (see 3.6 Volume 1), where the term stands for both the relationship with a godfather and the use of this relationship as competitive advantage. *Cumătrism* also occurs in Romania, where similar relations are associated with local customs. In both of these countries, the practice has connotations of political patronage, similar to the *padrino system* in the Philippines (see 7.10 Volume 1), *uruuchuluk* in Kyrgyzstan (see 3.3 Volume 1) and *yongo* in South Korea (see 3.5 Volume 1).

Cumătrism can be understood as a type of patron-client network but using a less direct form of 'political patronage' based on traditions and customs (Weingrod 1968: 379). The 'clients' are the child's parents, and the patron is the *cumătru*. A *cumătru* can help the child to find employment, facilitate bureaucratic procedures or offer political protection or legal immunity. The extent of such services vary according to the power and outreach of the *cumătru*. Like in a patron-client relationship, the 'patron' provides services and the 'client' reciprocates with respect and submissiveness.

In preparation for a child's christening, parents provide the priest with the names of people who will take part and become the child's second parents, *cumătri*. At the party to celebrate the event, the *cumătri* play a central role and perform a prescribed set of rituals. The child's parents offer gifts to the *cumătri* in recognition of their acceptance to become kin, and in return the *cumătri* offer them money and gifts. The christening and the associated rituals transform the relationship between families, and from that moment on, they become kin. There are no limits to the number of *cumătri* that a christened child can have, but there are guidelines for their selection that suggest that parents should consider *cumătri* who can serve as lifelong support and spiritual guides for their child, such as family friends or people they admire and respect.

In other words, parents are encouraged to think about establishing 'strategic' informal networks using the occasion of christening. Without explicitly stating it, parents select *cumătri* by carefully considering which friendships to 'institutionalise' and which liaisons with business partners, artists, politicians or other 'people with influence' – not all of whom parents have close relationships with – to solidify. For each child, parents tend to choose different *cumătri*, so the birth of each baby presents another opportunity to expand the overall size of the network by adding new kinship ties. The responsibilities and commitments of a *cumătru* are first, to the christened child and second, but more importantly, to the child's parents. The obligations entail mutual respect and care, the exchange of gifts and participation in family events. Once created, this bond is for life and cannot be revoked.

The *cumătrism* parties operate according to the 'norms of reciprocity' (Gouldner 1977). The services and benefits they exchange might be difficult to obtain outside of these relations but are not necessarily equivalent or reciprocated immediately. In the long run, the *cumătrism* network balances out the exchange. The logic of a 'good turn deserves another' is enforced by peer pressure, and failing to provide help is considered to be an offence and a violation of the vows. *Cumătrism* is a 'cultural ghost' – it is well known and commonly practised, yet only a few academic sources refer to or study it. It is Moldova's 'open secret' (Ledeneva 2011) that embodies its ambivalence: on the one hand, *cumătrism* is understood as a 'home-grown custom', on the other, it is often associated with corruption: 'Cumatrism (networks of those helping each other) ... proposes that patterns of patron-client relationships and kinship exist beneath the official structures of state, turning politics into a process of non-transparent decisions and allocations' (Johannsen 2004: 37, 40).

Most Moldovans become *cumătri* several times during their lifetime. The practice is hard to avoid. Since it is not limited to particular regions or social groups and is equally present in urban and rural areas, Moldovans tend to see it as universal. Yet, since *cumătrism* is taken to belong to the private domain, people will not speak of it openly. *Cumătrism* prioritises personal relations over professionalism, competence or merit. A *cumătru* that hires relatives in a private company might justify this by claiming to support the idea of family business. *Cumătrism* becomes more problematic in the public sphere, where it violates the principles of fairness and equality of access and leads to 'conflicts of interests'.

Tackling *cumătrism* in the Moldovan public domain began in 2008 with attempts to harmonise national legislation on the conflict of interest with international benchmarks. Two laws were passed as a result but with limited effect. The 'Law regarding the code of conduct for public servants' stipulated that officials should avoid any conflict of interest, but did not define which relations and actions constitute conflict (*Lege privind Codul de conduită a funcționarului public, nr. 25-XVI din 22.02.2008, Monitorul Oficial nr. 74–75/243 din 11.04.2008, art. 12*). The law regarding conflict of interest defines the categories of kinship as follows: 'husband (wife), persons related by blood or those that become kin by adoption (parents, children, brothers, sisters, grandmothers, grandsons, uncles, aunt) and persons who are kin by affinity (sister-in-law, brother-in-law, father-in-law, and mother-in-law)' (*Lege cu privire la Conflictul de Interese, nr. 16 din 15.02.2008, Monitorul Oficial Nr. 94–96 din 30.05.2008, art. 2*) – but did not include *cumătri* as kin 'by affinity' as proposed by Transparency International in their reports (Transparency International Moldova 2008). Ratifying international agreements and adopting legislation on conflict of interest without including kinship relations established by local customs failed to provide effective measures against informal practices that were found to undercut the quality of public service and governance.

Since the 2010s *cumătria* selection has undergone considerable changes, with the choice of *cumătri* driven by their professional skills rather than status. But *cumătrism* remains a widely accessed practice of strengthening kin-like ties that help people to find employment, avoid red tape and gain a competitive advantage. As it is common to solicit favours not only from one's *cumătru*, but also from the *cumătri* of the *cumătru*, the Moldovan *cumătrism* operates as a network-based economy of favours, as well as a cultural practice.

1.7 *Obnalichivanie* (Russia)
James McMeehan Roberts
Alumnus, School of Slavonic and East European Studies, UCL, UK

Obnalichivanie materinskogo kapitala, or the encashment of maternity capital, is a spin-off from the maternity benefit programme in Russia, introduced in January 2007 to boost Russia's declining birth rate. It provides mothers with access to funds when they give birth to, or adopt, a second or subsequent child. The capital is not provided in cash; rather, a certificate is issued, to be exchanged for one of several specific services. The claimant's use of the certificate can only be implemented once the child is three years old and includes the following options:

- To improve the family's living conditions by the acquisition, construction or refurbishment of an individual home, or to pay an initial payment on a credit or mortgage loan used for the acquisition or improvement of a property;
- To use towards the cost of the child's education, including pre-school;
- To support children with disabilities; or
- To pay into an individual pension account for the mother.

Initially the sum provided to a mother by the state was 250,000 roubles (equivalent to about 11,000 USD at that time). The value of certificates has increased steadily to take account of inflation, reaching 466,617 roubles from 1 January 2020 (approximately 7,600 USD). In January 2020, President Putin announced an extension of the programme to include the first child and the increase of support for the second child to 616,617 roubles (10,000 USD).

The share of federal funds attributed to this benefit has been substantial, even before the 2020 increases. The scheme is administered by the Pension Fund of Russia (PFR), which stated in its 2018 annual report that 8.3 million certificates were issued and over 2 trillion roubles dispersed between 2007 and 2017 (Pension Fund of the Russian Federation Annual Report 2018). Nearly four million of those certificates are still unused, most likely due to the impractical terms of use. In 2017 the amount paid out was 311.8 billion roubles, amounting to 1.9 per cent of total federal expenditure.

To date, 98.6 per cent of this budget has been used for the first option: 'improvement of the family's living conditions'. Among the poorer social classes in Russia, the most pressing needs of most new parents are not property-related, but food, clothing, warmth – the basics of everyday life. Cash therefore has infinitely higher utility than the certificate. The face value of Maternity Capital Certificates is substantially higher than the annual disposable income of the majority of Russian families: the Russian Statistical Service states that the average monthly wage was 46,674 roubles as of January 2020 – 650 USD per month or 7,800 USD per year. It is not surprising that from the time of its introduction, there has been a high demand for the conversion of certificates into cash.

As early as 2010, a large contingent of agents, or brokers, arose promptly to offer a service of *obnalichivanie*, or cashing out. They seek out clients openly on the Internet, in newspapers and on social media – but also through posters on bus shelters, lamp-posts, apartment blocks and any other available public spaces (see Figure 1.7.1). They promise fast cash, often within one day, and minimum administrative hassle. *Obnalichivanie* is an offence under the Criminal Code as an embezzlement of public funds and is punishable by a fine and imprisonment. Sanctions depend on whether the scam is organised by an individual or a group. Individuals can face fines of up to 120,000 roubles or one year's salary plus the return of all money obtained fraudulently, and up to two years in prison. Organised groups can face fines of up to 1 million roubles or three years' salary and five to ten years in prison. Certificate holders making use of these services are either unaware of the legalities, or are willing to take the risk, potentially jeopardising a significant amount of the cash.

These schemes operate in a variety of ways. For example, a near-worthless property in a remote location is priced at the level of a Maternity Capital Certificate's value. A credit cooperative or microfinance company, often set up for the purpose, advances a loan to the certificate owner, who is able to purchase the property. On completion of the purchase, the relevant documentation and certificate are sent to the PFR, which sends the money directly to the providers of the credit, who then pass on part of the money to the claimant. In some cases, even the property itself is fictitious.

Figure 1.7.1 'Attention, owners of maternity capital certificates, I help in receiving funds.' © Info Orel/infoorel.ru.

These schemes are particularly accessible to realtors, who can easily find suitably dilapidated properties, or to employees of credit cooperatives who can provide documentation for fictitious loans. Civil servants working for the PFR have also been seen to have a hand in these schemes. Brokers usually charge a fee of perhaps a third of the certificate value. In some cases, however, the brokers keep the total sum and disappear. This has prompted some victims to report their loss to the authorities, resulting in their own prosecution.

In the traditional spirit of *blat* (see 1.1 Volume 1), some certificate holders find a solution within their own circle, for example buying a property from their parents or other relatives or friends, but not occupying the house. The vendors give part or all of the money to the notional purchasers.

This criminal activity began in 2010, as soon as the first certificates issued became eligible for use (BFM.ru 2012). The delay until the first children born under the scheme reached their third birthday provided ample time for criminal networks to develop, and to design adequate methodologies. In January 2012, the Ministry of Internal Affairs, responsible for the investigation of the crimes, announced it had uncovered a nationwide criminal ring operating in 246 different cities, which had successfully set up approximately 300 different 'front' companies to undertake the loan and property purchase transactions. The crimes had been carried out over the previous two years (Demoscope Weekly 2012).

A second type of crime associated with maternity capital is obtaining certificates for which there is no entitlement. One large scheme in the North Caucasus in 2012 involved gynaecologists registering non-existent births and passing the documents to accomplices at local PFR branches. The fraudulent organisation created in excess of 160 fictitious births and gained 65 million roubles. Interestingly, the following year, the Presidential Envoy to the North Caucasus reported that 110,000 births had been registered in the previous years, yet school registration numbers did not match this figure (*Forbes* Russia 2013). It has been suggested that this could be the result of fraud related to Maternity Capital. Such a level of misrepresentation would not only bring into question the effectiveness of the Maternity Capital programme, but also the State Statistical Service's published fertility rates.

The scale of maternity capital fraud is difficult to quantify precisely. No official figures are published and the matter has not been publicly discussed. The PFR declines to answer questions on the subject, claiming that identifying fraudulent schemes is the responsibility of law enforcement agencies. The Ministry of Internal Affairs does not provide statistics, and has recently stopped posting details of related prosecutions on its website and removed all relevant previous posts. Of the 70 cases they reported between 2015 and 2019, 84 per cent involved property transactions, representing 95 per cent of individual criminal events and 97 per cent of the cash value attributed to the benefit (670 million roubles out of 690 million) (author's analysis based on data available at the Ministry of Internal Affairs in September 2019).

The design of the benefit is the main driver of fraud. Families in serious financial need are accredited with a certificate that entitles them to receive a large sum of money. Yet when they try to access the money, they find that the restrictive conditions hinder them from profiting from the benefit.

The changes to Russia's maternity capital benefits announced by Vladimir Putin in January 2020 will significantly increase the cost of the maternity capital scheme. About 40 per cent of Russian women have only one child in their lifetime. They will constitute a whole new class of claimants. Additionally, they will be the first children of those who go on to have more. The certificate value for second children is increased by a third. Over time, the cost of the programme will more than treble, to a level twice the current federal spending on health care. At the same time, it will double the number of potential targets for the fraudsters (McMeehan Roberts 2020).

1.8 **Rabenmutter** (Germany, Austria, German-speaking Switzerland)
Elena Denisova-Schmidt
School of Humanities and Social Sciences, University of St.Gallen, Switzerland
and
Lena Nicolas-Kryzhko
Independent researcher

Rabenmutter (literally 'raven mother') is a German expression used to denote a bad mother, who does not take sufficient care of her children, often because she is combining family with work. This derogatory term is used for a 'loveless, hard-hearted mother who neglects her children' or for an egoistic woman who refuses to have children due to economic or emotional circumstances (Duden 2020). According to an old German belief, the raven cares little for its offspring and pushes them out of the nest when it no longer wants to feed them. The term reinforces the traditional division of roles where women are supposed to dedicate themselves to the family while men are the breadwinners. Even in present-day German-speaking Europe, highly educated women stop working or work part-time once they have children in order to provide 'sufficient' care to their families. The reasons underlying the perception that combining work and motherhood is bad are deeply rooted in the historical, social and economic context.

The traditional model has been dominant in German-speaking Europe and many other countries for centuries and is grounded in the household hierarchy, the distribution of functions and the allocation of resources. Consider the rules of behaviour in the family suggested by Adolph Freiherr Knigge (1752–96) in his famous *Über den Umgang mit Menschen* (1788), which is today simply known as *Knigge*, or the Russian *Domostroi* (literally, *Domestic Order*) from the sixteenth century. Whereas boys went to school and were educated and trained to earn a living for the family, girls stayed at home to help with the household chores and take care of their younger brothers and sisters. The twentieth century has brought important changes in perceptions of gender equality, access to higher education and voting rights, but not as evenly across Europe as expected. The 1971 reform of voting rights for women in Switzerland, a country where cantons determine their own legislation, reached its smallest canton, Appenzell Innerrhoden, only in 1990 by a decision of the Swiss Supreme Court (116 Ia 359, 27 November 1990). Until 1984, married women in Switzerland were supposed to provide a written statement from their husbands allowing them to work. The progressive reforms aimed at ensuring equality between men and women were not implemented at the same pace across Europe. Whereas the representation of men and women in higher education is almost equal (women slightly outnumber men in German-speaking countries), in professional life, especially in top management positions and academia, men significantly outnumber women.

While the majority of countries, including German-speaking Europe, managed to reach a high level of equality in higher education, the inequality in professional life persists. The main reason for such a reversal in numbers reflects the inability of modern societies to reconcile women's professional ambitions with their family duties. Women focus (or are expected to by different stakeholders) on their families more than on their careers. Often, women do not receive enough support from their families, the state, their employers and society to be able to continue with their careers and their professional growth (Mühling and Schwarze 2011; Giudici and Schumacher 2017; Bund et al. 2019). According to a recent study, the gender gap in lifetime earnings for people currently in their mid-30s will reach 45 per cent in western Germany and 40 per cent in eastern Germany. Experts argue that part-time employment and childcare are the main reasons for this difference (Bönke et al. 2020).

Former German chancellor Angela Merkel, a strong role model who has been called the most powerful woman in the world (cf. Forbes Ranking 2019), but who is also often called *Mutti* (a diminutive form of mother), has a reputation in Germany for being a *Rabenmutter* despite the fact that she has no children. In Merkel's first electoral campaign, her rival Gerhard Schröder (b. 1944) and his spouse, Doris Schröder-Köpf, claimed that she could not support or even understand the problems of working mothers because she is not one herself. Merkel is neither a 'Mutter' nor a 'Rabenmutter', but 'only' a politician (Poelchau 2010). Another senior German female politician, Ursula von der Leyen, President of the European Commission, has also been called a *Rabenmutter*. In contrast to Merkel, von der Leyen has seven children. She started her political career in her mid-40s and was attacked by the media and society as a *Rabenmutter*. The *Rabenmutter* rhetoric appears across the political spectrum. When Andrea Nahles gave birth while serving as the first chairwoman of the Social Democratic Party (2018–19), she went back to work after eight weeks of maternity leave and as a result was publicly scolded as a *Rabenmutter*. Nahles issued a public statement explaining that her child was well taken care of and that she was able to combine both maternity and a political career (Jakat 2010). It has been noted that Nahles must have felt under pressure to return to work, as positions such as Minister of Labour and Social Affairs demand presence (Brigitte 2010). Leading female politicians who gave birth during their terms have often been smeared as *Rabenmutter* by their male colleagues (Schmidt 2014).

Businesswomen also endure the double pressure of public disapproval on the one hand and demands of the job on the other. A 2019 survey found that 'only 8.7 per cent of senior managers in Germany's 160 listed companies were women' and only five of the biggest companies in Germany had a female chief executive (EY survey quoted in Boulton and Chazan 2019). The slow change in female representation means that it 'would take until 2048 for a third of management roles to be occupied by women' (Boulton and Chazan 2019). The same is true in academia: a 2015 study by the European Commission concluded that women remain underrepresented in university faculties in Germany (17.3 per cent), Austria (20.3 per cent), as well as Switzerland (19.3 per cent) (Campbell et al. 2015).

Experts argue that, in addition to the organisational structures that neglect the needs of female employees, many working mothers still suffer from 'the double whammy of unhelpful taxation and educational systems' (Boulton and Chazan 2019). The German tax system that used to disadvantage married women with children now has provisions for daycare opportunities for pre-school children and after-school options for schoolchildren and youth. The media highlight successful role models for women in the workplace, which should significantly reduce the stigma of a *Rabenmutter*.

The stigmatisation of the reversal of traditional gender roles is a global problem. There are similar terms that refer to absent mothers in other languages. In Russian-speaking communities, these women are called 'cuckoos' (*kukushki*), the birds that allegedly leave their eggs in other birds' nests to hatch. In the United States, the term 'deadbeat mother' refers to mothers refusing to provide financial support and fulfil other obligations for their children. The problems of working mothers – childcare and equal pay – as well as other women's rights issues were addressed by every Democratic candidate for the 2020 US presidential election (Connley 2019). In Japan, female students face discrimination when they are denied entrance to medical schools because 'many female students who graduate end up leaving the actual medical practice to give birth and raise children' (BBC 2018).

1.9 *Uklonenie ot alimentov* (Russia)
Ekaterina Ivanova
School of Social and Political Sciences, Faculty of Arts,
The University of Melbourne, Australia

Uklonenie ot alimentov, literally 'evading alimony', includes a range of practices aimed at reducing the amount of formal child support payments while remaining within the bounds of the law and divorce settlement. The most common method of alimony evasion in Russia is through lowering one's official salary, which constitutes the base for automatic deductions of alimony. The difference between the official salary and earned income is pocketed, free from deductions by the state, corporate tax and social dues.

According to the Russian Family Code, alimony is paid as part of a divorce settlement by the non-resident parent to the one who is awarded custody and takes care of the children. Child support legislation maintains two options of alimony arrangements: either the resident parent brings the process of alimony collection to the state, or parents make a private informal agreement regarding the amount and the preferable method of payment. In a formal settlement, the court imposes a receiving order and forwards it to the bailiff service, which ensures that deductions are enacted. Based on the court order, the accounting department of the employer withholds part of the employee's salary and transfers it to the resident parent.

In an informal settlement, parents exercise discretion in making their own arrangements regarding alimony. However, their informal transfers are invisible to the state, and the resident parent is unable to bring the case to court should non-payments occur. The majority of divorcing parents – around 60 per cent – chose informal arrangements (or did not have any agreements at all) and only 38 per cent stated their payments were being imposed by court. The Family Code has a provision for parents to notarise their private agreement, thus making it official and enforceable, but in practice less than 1 per cent of couples use this option (Rzhanitsyna 2012: 17).

The advantage of court-imposed alimony is state control. Thus, in cases of non-compliance the bailiff service is responsible for tracing the liable party and collecting arrears. As a result, a common strategy to evade court-imposed alimony is to understate the official salary base from which it is deducted. Liable parents opt for grey, or shadow, payments (*seraya zarplata, tenevaya zarplata*), whereby part of their income, usually not exceeding the official wage minimum, is paid officially, and the most substantial part is paid in cash, off the books. Employers tend to be complicit in such schemes as they benefit from the reduction of corporate and social taxes also payable from the official salary base.

The unofficial part of the salary is paid in envelopes, or simple envelope-like folded paper, and referred to as salary in an envelope (*zarplata v konverte*). Such practices are not exclusive to Russia, but their scale differs from country to country. In Russia, grey salaries are common and widespread (at least 25 per cent of salaries is not reported, according to a business daily RBK.ru [2019]), and seem not to be perceived as morally reprehensible. Informal wages are present across sector, economic class and type of employer. They are seen as an illicit strategy of tax evasion, which benefits the parties, both companies and workers, at least in the short term (see also *alga aploksnē*, 6.27 Volume 2, *rad na crno*, 5.24 Volume 2, *cash in hand*, 6.1 Volume 2). In the case of child support minimisation, however, the scheme can benefit non-resident parents. If liable parents want to pay less, they can ask their employers to pay salaries in an envelope. The legitimising narratives for minimising child support are similar to those of tax evasion, inclusive of freedom in choosing a way to support the child and creating some leverage to see the child, thus preserving some power of discretion for those who want it.

There are further strategies to hide income and wealth that empower fathers in divorce settlement. Registering property on a third party, placing business revenues offshore, and other ways of hiding benefits can deepen the gender inequality associated with childbearing and care. Liable parents can also manipulate Russian child support legislation. If a divorced father has another child, the mother of the new child can also claim child support from him (even if they are unmarried and even if he lives with them) in order to reduce the child support payments deducted on behalf of his previous family (since child support is divided equally between all man's children). Nevertheless, these strategies remain under the radar of public outcry, while alimony evasion via grey salary is the most common practice reflected in the public discourse on evading fathers as well as in research.

Despite the gender-neutral language of the Russian family and child support legislation, evasion of alimony is a gendered social problem. The vast majority – over 93 per cent – of children stay with their mothers after separation, and fathers become the non-resident parents liable to pay alimony (Rzhanitsyna 2012: 14). Subsequently, a typical alimony non-payer (*neplatel'shchik*) is male, and many Russians are familiar with 'deadbeat fathers' through public discourse and personal experience. It is widely acknowledged that men often take advantage of informal employment practices to minimise the payments imposed by court (Rzhanitsyna 2015: 65). This is an 'open secret' that many fathers are not embarrassed about and confessed with little hesitation that they personally used such a strategy to reduce their alimony payments (Ivanova 2018). There are exceptions, of course, but they do not affect the public image of the gender gap, deepened by divorce parenting and alimony issues.

Child support evasion is an acknowledged problem, albeit the scope of it is difficult to estimate directly, precisely because many evaders manage to retain the façade of formal compliance with the law. Research and indirect assessments provide some insights. For example, less than 50 per cent of resident parents in Russia claimed they ever received alimony (Rzhanitsyna 2012: 17). Half of those who received alimony said that it was 50 per cent or less of the monthly child subsistence minimum (Ovcharova 2010: 24). That is, the received sums tend to balance on the edge of minimal support.

Alimony evasion cannot simply be accounted for by fathers' reluctance to provide for their children after divorce. Qualitative research has shown that it is court-imposed payments that many fathers oppose (Ivanova 2018). Alimony after divorce is a sore subject for men as it touches on crucial features of masculinity. One of the keystones of masculine identity in many cultures is the breadwinner status, which provides men with financial power and control over financial decision-making within the household. In Russia, despite a historically high level of female employment, men are still expected to be the primary, if not the sole, breadwinner (Kiblitskaya 2000; Ashwin and Isupova 2014; Lipasova 2016; Yusupova 2017). Marital separation alters monetary relations in families, from voluntary bestowal to compulsory entitlements (Zelizer 1996; for the adaptation of Zelizer's classification of monetary transfers to child support, see Bradshaw et al. 1999; Natalier and Hewitt 2010; Ivanova 2018). Such transformation is sensitive to fathers, as they continue to define alimony as 'their' money and claim accountability on its expenditure (Ivanova 2018). Consequently, many Russian fathers perceive court-imposed alimony as unfair as it unconditionally entitles their ex-partners to a part of his income and creates legal constraints for their movement (non-payers, for example, can be held when crossing the border of the Russian Federation). Thus, many opt to pay informally.

Such gendered attitudes are not unique to Russia; similar narratives can be found elsewhere (Natalier and Hewitt 2010, 2014), but in Russia, court-imposed alimony carries an additional stigma. Many mothers share negative attitudes towards an official alimony and prefer to agree on informal transfers for the sake of peace-keeping and a 'good divorce', even at the risk of not being able to enforce their informal agreements. However, in cases of confrontation, where mothers wish to formalise alimony, fathers then resort to the grey salary strategy, or at least threaten to do so. The awareness of the widespread practices of alimony evasion undermines the effectiveness of this legal provision. Mothers refuse to apply for official child support because they believe that their time, energy and effort will result in less than they would have gotten informally. Thus, Russian fathers generally have more bargaining power and discretion in decision-making regarding alimony payments.

1.10 *Babushki* (Russia)
Anna Shadrina
School of Slavonic and East European Studies, UCL, UK

In Russia and many other former Soviet republics, the term *babushki* denotes a family support-system that relies on the intense involvement of grandparents (mostly grandmothers) in childcare and housework. *Babushki* is the plural form of *babushka* (Russian for grandmother). Scholars of the post-Soviet family such as Tiaynen (2013), Utrata (2015),

Shadrina (2018) and Solari (2018) do not translate *babushki* into English in order to emphasise that, in the Russian-speaking world, the concept transcends the literal family definition of grandmother. In Russian-speaking countries, all middle-aged and older women are, regardless of their family situation, commonly called *babushki*. This concept reflects a distinct mode of the social reproduction of motherhood. Until the end of the twentieth century, the expectation that women would have children earlier in life and be able to become young *babushki* energetic enough to assist their daughters with childcare was widely accepted (Perelli-Harris and Isupova 2013: 143–6).

On an individual level, the word *babushka* signifies a socially approved identity for women of pensionable age based on practices related to family care. This reflects the expectation that, once they have passed their reproductive period, women will end their professional careers and individual activity. Despite the cultural predominance of the ideal of the nuclear family, child rearing in Russia often involves two parenting adults: a mother and a grandmother, with men on the margins of family life (Utrata 2015: 123–50, 185). Although the role of the father and grandfather is important in Russian society (Ashwin and Lytkina 2004), the family remains women-centred (Ashwin and Lytkina 2004: 58, 215, 221). Even with co-residential fathers, everyday life for many families is supported by 'extended mothering' (Rotkirch 2000: 121). While involved fatherhood has just started to become the norm among educated men, women still tend to spend two or three times more of their time on children's upbringing than do men (Rimashevskaya et al. 2016: 28).

Families with breadwinning mothers and grandmothers engaged in housework and childcare are also found among African American communities in the US (Utrata 2015: 126) and Southern Europe (Herlofson and Hagestad 2012: 26). It is traditionally assumed in many post-Soviet countries that *babushki* make a conscious and willing choice to disengage from active social life in order to take on unpaid childcare simply because they love their children and grandchildren. At the same time, it should be acknowledged that this building block of informal welfare emerged as an outcome of ideological pressure on young families to have children sooner rather than later, of women's early pensionable age and of the lack of fathers' involvement in childcare. The contribution made by *babushki* in terms of love and individual choice is not, however, recognised as an investment worthy of formal compensation (Utrata 2015: 124, 127).

Multigenerational households with women's hierarchical networks typified pre-revolutionary Russian families (Olson and Adonyeva 2013: 44–91). Russia's rapid industrialisation at the beginning of the twentieth century and the reconstruction of the Soviet economy after the Second World War required the widespread mobilisation of human resources, including women (Teplova 2007: 287). The importance of the role of women was further increased as a result of the reduction of the male population caused by the First World War, the Civil War that followed the 1917 Bolshevik Revolution, Stalin's purges and, last but not least, the Second World War. As a result, several generations of Soviet citizens were raised without fathers.

The deficit of men amplified women's familial ties and the dominant ideology of the division of gender roles in the family. *Babushki* served as a vital substitute for the lack of paternal involvement, insufficient state support and the high male mortality rate. The fact that women could retire from work and receive a pension at the age of 55 enabled many women to care for their children and grandchildren. While Soviet women were expected to implement the ideal of 'mother-worker', men were seen as the main component of the labour force. Women, by contrast, were seen as dependent on the state, which provided maternal benefits and services.

Because of the shortage of single-family housing in the USSR in the 1950s and 1960s, extended-family living arrangements remained the norm (Semenova and Thompson 2004). Moreover, by the end of the Soviet era, the number of families being cared for by single mothers was rising in Russia: the number of marriages declined, divorce rates rose and the number of births to unmarried mothers increased. With no guarantee of employment after the collapse of the USSR, no state-funded accommodation and significant cutbacks of state subsidies for childcare and after-school activities, the contribution of *babushki* to the family's well-being became even more crucial (Utrata 2015: 6, 128).

At the end of the twentieth century, the leading socially approved model of childcare in Western countries was the expert-guided ideology of 'intensive mothering' (Hays 1996). This denotes a child-centred approach that requires an unprecedented amount of emotional involvement, financial resources and various professional competences to ensure the best social start for children. This trend became noticeable in Russia at the beginning of the twenty-first century. As a result, middle-class Russian mothers aspiring to live up to the standards of 'intensive mothering' started to limit grandmothers' involvement and rely on commercial childcare (Sivak 2018). At the same time, many women of pensionable age were forced to stay in employment in order to supplement their meagre pensions, so the retirement threshold de facto began to rise. In 2018, the Russian government announced that, over a 15-year period, it would increase the retirement age from 60 to 65 for men and from 55 to 60 for women (State Duma of the Russian Federation 2018).

Since the opportunities for post-pension employment are extremely limited in Russia, the role of an involved *babushka* is motivation for many women of pensionable age to leave an unsatisfactory job. Due to insufficient institutional elderly care in Russia, playing the role of *babushki* in their daughters' families represents an investment for old age for members of poorer social groups, as grandmothers expect their work and care to be reciprocated later on in life. According to empirical studies, parents are more likely to provide support to children from whom they expect to receive help in their old age (Grundy 2005).

Following a Western trend, too, Russian fathers may have to increase the amount of childcare and housework that they undertake. Weakening kin networks, minimal state support for families and the fact that *babushki* will have to stay in work longer may force fathers and grandfathers to step in to compensate (Utrata 2015: 148).

Bibliography to Chapter 1

Introduction: reproduction and emotional ambivalence
Michele Rivkin-Fish

Buchbinder, M. 2016. 'Scripting Dissent: US Abortion Laws, State Power, and the Politics of Scripted Speech'. *American Anthropologist* 118(4): 772–83.
Keys, J. 2010. 'Running the Gauntlet: Women's Use of Emotion Management Techniques in the Abortion Experience'. *Symbolic Interaction* 33(1): 41–70.
Kligman, G. 1998. *The Politics of Duplicity: Controlling Reproduction in Ceausescu's Romania*. Berkeley: University of California Press.
McCallum, C., Menezes, G. and Reis, A. P. 2016. 'The Dilemma of a Practice: Experiences of Abortion in a Public Maternity Hospital in the City of Salvador, Bahia'. *História, Ciências, Saúde – Manguinhos* 23(1): 37–56.
Ragone, H. 1994. *Surrogate Motherhood: Conception in the Heart*. Boulder: Westview Press.
Rivkin-Fish, M. 2005. *Women's Health in Post-Soviet Russia: The Politics of Intervention*. Bloomington: Indiana University Press.
Shpakovskaya, L. 2015. 'How to be a Good Mother: The Case of Middle-Class Mothering in Russia'. *Europe-Asia Studies* 67(10): 1571–86.
Siegl, V. 2023. *Intimate Strangers: Commercial Surrogacy in Russia and Ukraine and the Making of Truth*. Ithaca: Cornell University Press.
Temkina, A. 2020. '"Childbirth is not a Car Rental": Mothers and Obstetricians Negotiating Customer Service in Russian Commercial Maternity Care'. *Critical Public Health* 30(5): 521–32.
Temkina, A. and Rivkin-Fish, M. 2020. 'Creating Health Care Consumers: The Negotiation of Un/official Payments, Power and Trust in Russian Maternity Care'. *Social Theory & Health* 18(1): 340–57.
Temkina, A., Litvina, D. and Novkunskaya, A. 2021. 'Emotional Styles in Russian Maternity Hospitals: Juggling Between *Khamstvo* and Smiling'. *Emotions and Society* 3(1): 95–113.
Utrata, J. 2015. *Women Without Men: Single Mothers and Family Change in the New Russia*. Ithaca: Cornell University Press.

1.1 *Mei bao ma* (China)
Hui Guo

Bourgon, L. 2017. 'Why Women Are Coming to Canada Just to Give Birth'. *Maclean's*. 8 August. www.macleans.ca/society/health/why-women-are-coming-to-canada-just-to-give-birth/
Flanagin, J. 2015. 'Birthright Citizenship is a Hallmark of New World Democracies'. *Quartz*. 25 August. https://qz.com/487492/birthright-citizenship-is-a-hallmark-of-new-world-democracies/
Fonrouge, G. 2018. 'Feds Crack Down on Birth Tourism at "Maternity Hotels"'. *New York Post*, 10 January.
Glenza, J. 2018. 'Why Does It Cost $32,093 Just to Give Birth in America?'. *Guardian*, 16 January. www.theguardian.com/us-news/2018/jan/16/why-does-it-cost-32093-just-to-give-birth-in-america
Grant, T. 2015. 'Made in America: Medical Tourism and Birth Tourism Leading to a Larger Base of Transient Citizenship'. *Virginia Journal of Social Policy & the Law* 22(1): 160–78.
Haque, A. 2017. 'Why British Chinese Mothers Won't Go Out after Giving Birth'. *BBC News*, 13 November. www.bbc.co.uk/news/health-41930497
Jacob, F. 2017. 'Birth Tourism'. In *The SAGE International Encyclopaedia of Travel and Tourism*, edited by L. L. Lowry, 1–6. SAGE Publications.
KCET. 2018. '"Birth Tourism", Fair Path to Citizenship or Legal Loophole?'. 30 March. https://web.archive.org/web/20190414060221/https://www.kcet.org/shows/socal-connected/birth-tourism-fair-path-to-citizenship-or-legal-loophole-0
Lin, W. 2017. 'Why Wealthy Chinese Women Are Flocking to LA to Give Birth'. *Jing Daily*. 8 July. https://jingdaily.com/los-angeles-chinese-birth-tourism/
Oni, J. 2016. 'Foreigners Seeking US Citizenship for Children Flout Law, Can Endanger Babies'. *VOA News*. 6 December. www.voanews.com/a/foreigners-seeking-american-citizenship-children-flout-law-endanger-babies/3626080.html
Phillip, A. 2015. 'Inside the Shadowy World of Birth Tourism at "Maternity Hotels"'. *The Washington Post*, 5 March. www.washingtonpost.com/news/post-nation/wp/2015/03/05/the-shadowy-world-of-birth-tourism-at-californias-luxury-maternity-hotels/?noredirect=on&utm_term=.c7430387a4f3
Ramakrishnan, K. 2015. 'Asian Birth Tourism, Numbers in Perspective'. *Data Bits*. 27 August. http://aapidata.com/blog/birth-tourism/
Richburg, K. B. 2010. 'For Many Pregnant Chinese, a U.S. Passport for Baby Remains a Powerful Lure'. *The Washington Post*. 18 July. www.washingtonpost.com/wp-dyn/content/article/2010/07/17/AR2010071701402.html
Scott, J. B. 1930. 'Nationality: *Jus Soli* or *Jus Sanguinis*'. *The American Journal of International Law* 24(1): 58–64.
Semotiuk, A. J. 2014. 'Immigration: The Myth of the "Anchor Baby"'. *Forbes*, 22 September. www.forbes.com/sites/andyjsemotiuk/2014/09/22/immigration-the-myth-of-the-anchor-baby/#7b7e512fe801
Sheehan, M. 2015. 'Born in the USA: Why Chinese "Birth Tourism" Is Booming in California'. *Huffington Post*, 6 December. www.huffingtonpost.co.uk/entry/china-us-birth-tourism_n_7187180
Woord, G. 2018. 'Petition Targets "Abusive and Exploitative" Birth Tourism'. *Vancouver Courier*, 27 March. www.vancourier.com/news/petition-targets-abusive-and-exploitative-birth-tourism-1.23214628
World Atlas. 2018. 'Countries Who Offer Birthright Citizenship'. www.worldatlas.com/articles/countries-who-offer-birthright-citizenship.html
Wydra, E. 2010. 'Birthright Citizenship: A Constitutional Guarantee'. *Advance* 4: 111.

1.2 *Khamstvo* (USSR, Russia)
Anastasia Novkunskaya

Cook, L. 2015. 'Constraints on Universal Health Care in the Russian Federation: Inequality, Informality, and the Failures of Mandatory Medical Insurance Reforms'. *Journal of Self-Governance and Management Economics* 3(4): 37–60.
Davies, C. 1989. 'Goffman's Concept of the Total Institution: Criticisms and Revisions'. *Human Studies* 12(1/2): 77–95.

Dovlatov, S. 2005. 'Eto neperevodimoe slovo – "khamstvo"'. In *Sobranie Sochineniy v 4-h Tomah*, 323–7. St. Petersburg: Azbuka-klassika.

Goffman, E. 1961. *Asylums: Essays on the Social Situation of Mental Patients and Other Inmates*. New York: Anchor.

Koenker, D. 2019. 'The Smile Behind the Sales Counter: Soviet Shop Assistants on the Road to Full Communism'. *Journal of Social History* 54 (3): 872–96.

Litvina, D., Temkina, A. and Novkunskaya, A. 2019. 'Multiple Vulnerabilities in Medical Settings: Invisible Suffering of Doctors'. *Societies* 10(1): 5.

Rivkin-Fish, M. 2005. *Women's Health in Post-Soviet Russia: The Politics of Intervention*. Bloomington: Indiana University Press.

Stepurko, T., Pavlova, M., Levenets, O., Gryga, I. and Groot, W. 2013. 'Informal Patient Payments in Maternity Hospitals in Kiev, Ukraine'. *International Journal of Health Planning Management* 28(2): 169–87.

Temkina, A. 2016. 'Russian Middle Class Intimacy and Family Life: The Life Project and Its Constraints'. In *Cultural Patterns and Life Stories*, edited by K. Joesalu and A. Kannike. Tallinn: Tallinn University Press.

Temkina A., Novkunskaya A. and Litvina D. 2021. 'Emotional Regimes in Russian Maternity Hospitals: Juggling between Khamstvo and Smiling'. *Emotions and Society* 3(1): 95–113.

Temkina A., Novkunskaya A. and Litvina D. 2022. *Pregnancy and Birth in Russia: The Struggle for 'Good Care'*. London: Taylor & Francis.

1.3 *Selektivni abortus/tuđa večera* (Montenegro)
Diāna Kiščenko

Centar za ženska prava. 2017. 'Neželjena – Kampanja Protiv Prenatalnog Odabira Pola'. 17 November. https://womensrightscenter.org/kampanja-protiv-prenatalnog-odabira-pola/

Chao, F., Gerland, P., Cook, A. R. and Alkema, L. 2019. 'Systematic Assessment of the Sex Ratio at Birth for All Countries and Estimation of National Imbalances and Regional Reference Levels'. *Proceedings of the National Academy of Sciences* 116(19): 9303–11.

Denich, B. 1974. 'Sex and Power in the Balkans'. In *Women, Culture, and Society*, edited by L. Lamphere and M. Zimbalist Rosaldo, 243–62. Stanford: Stanford University Press.

Eklund, L. 2011. *Rethinking Son Preference: Gender, Population Dynamics and Social Change in the People's Republic of China*. PhD dissertation, Lund University.

Guilmoto, C. Z. 2010. 'Longer-Term Disruptions to Demographic Structures in China and India Resulting from Skewed Sex Ratios at Birth'. *Asian Population Studies* 6(1): 3–24.

Milich, Z. 1995. *A Stranger's Supper: An Oral History of Centenarian Women in Montenegro*. New York: Twayne Publishers.

Ministarstvo Zdravlja. 2009. 'Zakon o Uslovima i Postupku za Prekid Trudnoće'. www.gov.me/clanak/zakon-o-uslovima-i-postupku-za-prekid-trudnoce

Patel, T. (ed.) 2007. *Sex-Selective Abortion in India: Gender, Society and New Reproductive Technologies*. New Delhi: Sage Publications.

Petrović, I. 2014. 'Promena Vrednosnih Orijentacija Ekonomske Elite – Patrijarhalnost, Autoritarnost, Nacionalizam'. In *Ekonomska Elita u Srbiji u Periodu Konsolidacije Kapitalističkog Poretka*, edited by M. Lazić, 215–46. Beograd: ISIFF, Čigoja štampa.

Skorupan, A. 2017. 'Bez Novca I Obećane Nevjeste Iz Albanije Ostalo Nekoliko Muškaraca Sa Sjevera'. *Vijesti*. 12 April. www.vijesti.me/vijesti/drustvo/bez-novca-i-obecane-nevjeste-iz-albanije-ostalo-nekoliko-muskaraca-sa-sjevera

UNFPA. 2012. Sex Imbalances at Birth: Current Trends, Consequences and Policy Implications. www.unfpa.org/sites/default/files/pub-pdf/Sex%20Imbalances%20at%20Birth.%20PDF%20UNFPA%20APRO%20publication%202012.pdf

1.4 *Xiaoerni* (China)
Ling Meng

Chen, X. X. 2004. 'The Local Society Process: Based on Games in the Family Planning Policy of Chen Village'. *Sociological Studies* (3): 93–102.

Chu, J. 2001. 'Prenatal Sex Determination and Sex-Selective Abortion in Rural Central China'. *Population and Development Review* 27(2): 259–81.

Greenhalgh, S. and Winckler, E. A. 2005. *Governing China's Population: From Leninist to Neoliberal Biopolitics*. Stanford, CA: Stanford University Press.

Huang, H. L. 2012. *The Missing Girls and Women of China, Hong Kong, and Taiwan: A Sociological Study of Infanticide, Forced Prostitution, Political Imprisonment, 'Ghost Brides', Runaways, and Thrownaways, 1900–2000s*. Jefferson, NC: McFarland & Company.

Johnson, K. A. 2016. *China's Hidden Children: Abandonment, Adoption, and the Human Costs of the One-Child Policy*. Chicago: University of Chicago Press.

Li, Y. H. 1993. *Procreation and Chinese Village Culture*. Hong Kong: Oxford University Press.

Scharping, T. 2003. *Birth Control in China 1949–2000: Population Policy and Demographic Development*. New York: Routledge.

Shi, Y. and Kennedy, J. J. 2016. 'Delayed Registration and Identifying the Missing Girls in China'. *The China Quarterly* 228: 1018–38.

1.5 *Parovoziki* (Russia)
Ekaterina Pereprosova

Becker, H. 1985. *Outsiders: Etudes de Sociologie de la Déviance*. Paris: Editions Métailié.

Biryukova, S. and Sinyavskaya, O. 2017. 'Children out of Parental Care in Russia: What We Can Learn from the Statistics'. *The Journal of Social Policy Studies* 15(3): 367–82.

Goffman, E. 1961. *Asylums: Essays on the Social Situation of Mental Patients and Other Inmates*. NY: Garden City, Anchor Books, Doubleday & Co.

Kulmala, M. 2017. 'Paradigm Shift in Russian Child Welfare Policy'. *Russian Analytical Digest* 200(28): 5–11.

Kulmala, M., Rasell, M. and Chernova, Zh. 2017. 'Overhauling Russia's Child Welfare System: Institutional and Ideational Factors Behind the Paradigm Shift'. *The Journal of Social Policy Studies* 15(3): 353–66.

Rudov, A. G. 2015. 'Analysis of Statistic Data and Evaluation of the State of Orphanhood in Russia. Family Based Forms of Care'. *Charity Fund Semya*.

Semya, G. V., Zaitsev G. O. and Zaitseva N. G. 2016. 'Preventing Social Orphanhood: The Russian Model'. *Psychological Science and Education* 21(1): 67–82.

Tinchurin A., Yaznevitch E., Ivanova N., Freik N. and Silaev, P. 2018. 'Sirotstvo v regionakh RF'. *Nuzhna pomosh*, 2 November. https://nuzhnapomosh.ru/research/2018/sirotstvo-v-regionakh-rf/

1.6 *Cumătrism* (Moldova)
Andrei Iovu

Gouldner, A. 1977. 'The Norm of Reciprocity', in Schmidt, S. (ed.). *Friends, Followers and Factions: A Reader in Political Clientelism*. Berkeley: University of California Press.

Johannsen, L. 2004. 'State of the State in Moldova'. *Demstar Research Report* 24.

Ledeneva, A. 2011. 'Open Secrets and Knowing Smiles'. *East European Politics and Society* 25(4): 720–36.

Transparency International Moldova. 2008. *Transparency International Cercetează Fenomenul Conflictului de Interese în Moldova*, www.civic.md/stagii/7-stiri/3675-transparency-international-cerceteazae-fenomenul-conflictului-de-interese-arn-moldova.html

Weingrod, A. 1968. 'Patrons, Patronage, and Political Parties'. *Comparative Studies in Society and History* 10(4): 377–400.

1.7 *Obnalichivanie* (Russia)
James McMeehan Roberts

BFM.ru. 2012. 'MVD Vskrylo Aferu s Materinskim Kapitalom v 246 Gorodah'. 12 January. www.bfm.ru/news/166963

Demoscope Weekly. 2012. www.demoscope.ru/weekly/arc/s_map_529.php

Forbes Russia. 2013. 'Na Severnom Kavkaze ne Mogut Nayti 110 Tysyach Detey'. 14 March. www.forbes.ru/news/235650-na-severnom-kavkaze-ne-mogut-naiti-110-tysyach-detei

McMeehan Roberts, J. 2020. 'Putin's Pursuit of the Baby Boom – The Next Chapter'. UCL SSEES Post-Soviet Brief. https://sway.office.com/APVaVyizgmjd0QFG

Pension Fund of the Russian Federation. 2018. '*Annual Report 2017*'. www.pfrf.ru/en/about/annual_report/

1.8 *Rabenmutter* (Germany, Austria, German-Speaking Switzerland)
Elena Denisova-Schmidt and Lena Nicolas-Kryzhko

BBC. 2018. 'Japan Medical Schools "Rigged Women's Results"'. 14 December. www.bbc.com/news/world-asia-46568975

Boulton. L. and Chazan, G. 2019. '"Rabenmutter!" How German Business Culture Still Sidelines Women'. *Financial Times*. 17 October. www.ft.com/content/1ea8686e-d551-11e9-8d46-8def889b4137

Bönke, T., Glaubitz, R., Göbler, K., Harnack, A., Pape, A. and Wetter, M. 2020. 'Wer gewinnt? Wer verliert? Die Entwicklung und Prognose von Lebenserwerbseinkommen in Deutschland'. Berlin: Bertelsmann Stiftung.

Brigitte. 2010. 'Andrea Nahles: Für Abgeordnete gibt's keine Elternzeit'. 18 November. www.brigitte.de/aktuell/gesellschaft/interview--andrea-nahles---fuer-abgeordnete-gibt-s-keine-elternzeit--10223986.html

Bund, K., Geisler, A., Kunze, A. and S. Venohr. 2019. 'Was Frauen im Job erleben'. 14 August. www.zeit.de/2019/34/diskriminierung-arbeitsplatz-frauen-job-sexismus-gleichberechtigung

Campbell, D., Archambault, E., Tippett, C., et al. 2016. *She Figures Handbook 2015*. European Commission Directorate-General for Research and Innovation. https://data.europa.eu/doi/10.2777/402057

Connley, C. 2019. 'Abortion, Equal Pay, Family Leave: Here are All the Women's Rights Policies Proposed by 2020 Candidates So Far'. CNBC. 24 June. www.cnbc.com/2019/06/24/all-the-womens-rights-policies-proposed-by-2020-candidates-so-far.html

Duden. 2020. Rabenmutter. www.duden.de/rechtschreibung/Rabenmutter

Forbes Ranking. 2019. 'The World's 100 Most Powerful Women'. www.forbes.com/power-women/list/

Giudici, F. and R. Schumacher. 2017. 'Erwerbstätigkeit von Müttern in der Schweiz: Entwicklung und Individuelle Faktoren'. Social Change in Switzerland, 10.

Jakat, L. 2010. 'SPD: Karrierekämpfe: Andrea Nahles – Schwanger und Furcht um den Job'. Süddeutsche Zeitung. 17 November. www.sueddeutsche.de/politik/spd-karrierekaempfe-andrea-nahles-schwanger-und-angst-um-den-job-1.1024626

Mühling, T. and Schwarze, J. (eds). 2011. *Lebensbedingungen von Familien in Deutschland, Schweden und Frankreich. Ein familienpolitischer Vergleich*. Leverkusen: Barbara Budrich.

Poelchau, N. 2010. 'Die "Rabenmutter"'. Süddeutsche Zeitung. 17 May. www.sueddeutsche.de/kultur/aus-dem-sz-magazin-die-rabenmutter-1.254876

Schmidt, S. 2014. *Vereinbarkeit von politischer Karriere und Familie untersucht anhand einer Umfrage von Mitgliedern des Deutschen Bundestages der 16. Legislaturperiode*. Berlin: FU Berlin.

1.9 *Uklonenie ot alimentov* (Russia)
Ekaterina Ivanova

Bradshaw J., Stimson, C., Skinner, C. and Williams, J. 1999. *Absent Fathers?* London: Psychology Press.

Ivanova. E. A. 2018. 'Alimenty Kak Mnozhestvennye Den'gi: Kontributsiya, Obyazatel'stvo ili Zabota? Issledovanie Praktik Soderzhaniya Rebenka Ottsami Posle Razvoda'. *Journal of Economics* 19(4): 101–33.

Kiblitskaya, M. 2000. 'Once We Were Kings: Male Experiences of Loss of Status at Work in Postcommunist Russia'. In *Gender, State and Society in Soviet and Post-Soviet Russia*, edited by S. Ashwin, 90–104. Abingdon: Routledge.

Lipasova, A. 2016. 'Fatherhood Models in the Middle Class of Contemporary Russia'. *Russian Sociological Review* 15(4): 202–14.

Natalier, K. and Hewitt, B. 2010. '"It's Not Just About the Money": Non-resident Fathers' Perspectives on Paying Child Support'. *Sociology* 44(3): 489–505.

Natalier, K. and Hewitt, B. 2014. 'Separated Parents Reproducing and Undoing Gender Through Defining Legitimate Uses of Child Support'. *Gender & Society* 28(6): 904–25.

Ovcharova, L. (ed.) 2010. *Determinanty Reproduktivnogo Povedeniya Naseleniya I Faktory Semejnogo Neblagopoluchiya: Rezul'taty Panel'nyh Issledovanij*. Moscow: HSE Independent Institute for Social Policy.

RBK.ru. 2019. Ekonomisty *Otsenili Chislo Rossiyan s Tenevymi Zarplatami*. 10 December. www.rbc.ru/economics/10/12/2019/5dee50109a79474ae5293e3d

Rzhanitsyna, L. 2012. '*Alimenty v Rossii: Analiz Problem i Strategiya v Interesakh Dete'j'*. Moscow: IE RAS.

Rzhanitsyna, L. 2015. 'Ulutsheniye Poloscheniya Detey v Razvedennyih Semyah'. *Sociological Research* 3: 65–9.

Yusupova, M. 2017. *Shifting Masculine Terrains: Russian Men in Russia and the UK*. PhD dissertation, University of Manchester.

Zelizer, V. 1996. 'Payments and Social Ties'. *Sociological Forum* 11(3): 481–95.

1.10 *Babushki* (Russia)
Anna Shadrina

Ashwin, S. and Lytkina, T. 2004. 'Men in Crisis in Russia: The Role of Domestic Marginalization'. *Gender & Society* 18(2): 189–206.

Ashwin, S. and Isupova, O. 2014. '"Behind Every Great Man …": The Male Marriage Wage Premium Examined Qualitatively'. *Journal of Marriage and Family* 76(1): 37–55.

Grundy, E. 2005. 'Reciprocity in Relationships: Socio-Economic and Health Influences on Intergenerational Exchanges between Third Age Parents and their Adult Children in Great Britain'. *British Journal of Sociology* 56(2): 233–55.

Hays, S. 1996. *The Cultural Contradictions of Motherhood*. New Haven and London: Yale University Press.

Herlofson, K. and Hagestad, G. O. 2012. 'Transformations in the Role of Grandparents Across Welfare States'. In *Contemporary Grandparenting: Changing Family Relationships in Global Contexts*, edited by S. Arber and V. Timonen, 25–51. Chicago: University of Chicago Press.

Olson, L. J. and Adonyeva, S. 2013. *The Worlds of Russian Village Women: Tradition, Transgression, Compromise*. Madison: University of Wisconsin Press.

Perelli-Harris, B. and Isupova, O. 2013. 'Crisis and Control: Russia's Dramatic Fertility Decline and Efforts to Increase It'. In *Fertility Rates and Population Decline. No Time for Children?* edited by A. Buchanan and A. Rotkirch, 141–56. Basingstoke: Palgrave Macmillan.

Rimashevskaya, N. M., Malysheva, M. M., Pislkakova-Parker, M. P., Morozova, T. V. and Limanskaya, V. O. 2016. *State of Russia's Fathers*. Moscow: The Institute of Socio-Economic Studies of Population of the Russian Academy of Sciences, Laboratory for Gender Studies.

Rotkirch, A. 2000. *The Men's Question: Loves and Lives in Late 20th Century Russia*. University of Helsinki, Department of Social Policy. Research Report 1/2000.

Semenova, V. and Thompson, P. 2004. 'Family Model and Transgenerational Influences: Grandparents, Parents and Children in Moscow and Leningrad from the Soviet to the Market Era'. In *On Living through Soviet Russia*, edited by D. Bertaux, P. Thompson and A. Rotkirch, 120–45. London: Routledge.

Shadrina, A. 2018. 'Narrating the Gender Order: Why Do Older Single Women in Russia Say That They Do Not Want to Be in Relationships with Men?'. In *Gender and Choice After Socialism*, edited by L. Attwood, E. Schimpfossl and M. Yusupova, 81–109. London: Palgrave Macmillan.

Sivak, E. 2018. 'Managing Grandparental Involvement in Child-Rearing in the Context of Intensive Parenting'. *Sociological Research Online* July: 1–17.

Solari, C. D. 2018. *On the Shoulders of Grandmothers: Gender, Migration, and Post-Soviet Nation-State Building*. New York: Routledge.

State Duma of the Russian Federation. 2018. *O Vnesenii Izmeneniy v Otdel'nyye Zakonodatel'nyye Akty Rossiyskoy Federatsii po Voprosam Naznacheniya i Vyplaty Pensiy (V Chasti Povysheniya*

Normativnogo Pensionnogo Vozrasta). https://web.archive.org/web/20191004081439/ https://sozd.duma.gov.ru/bill/489161-7

Teplova, T. 2007. 'Welfare State Transformation, Childcare, and Women's Work in Russia'. *Social Politics* 14(3): 284–322.

Tiaynen, T. 2013. *Babushka in Flux: Grandmothers and Family-Making Between Russian Karelia and Finland*. Tampere: Tampere University Press.

Utrata, J. 2015. *Women without Men: Single Mothers and Family Change in the New Russia*. Ithaca and London: Cornell University Press.

2
Growing up

Introduction: a psychological perspective on socialisation

Thomas Tsichtis
Alumnus, London School of Economics, UK

Human beings are complex, and this complexity is apparent not only in the unique developmental trajectories of each person but also in the interconnected and permeable sociocultural worlds they inhabit (Rosa and Valsiner 2018). Growing individuals, group formations and culturally shared, collective settings, in various geographical localities, illustrated in this chapter, are not simply descriptive addenda to different understandings of human development. Rather, they are at the core of how persons develop and come to actively participate in their day-to-day lives from their early years (Cole 1998; Jovchelovitch 2008).

Practices of everyday life rely on multiple norms, rules and procedures tied with the perspectives of those involved. Though possibly entrenched, these norms, rules and procedures are not static and mechanistically repeatable, but open to negotiation and creative change (Zittoun and Gillespie 2016; Jovchelovitch 2019). To navigate this complex sociocultural landscape, a few key conceptual points are required to help articulate patterns of practices and render them visible. Two such concepts are socialisation and social contexts.

The processes of socialisation generate shared norms and values which help individuals orient themselves in the societal sphere. The internalisation of such norms can be described as a process of interplay between personal experience and the sociocultural arrangements that orchestrate it (Zittoun and Gillespie 2015a). Other persons are heavily involved in the process: they psychologically accompany an individual in their experiential environment by providing support, care, expertise and social knowledge (Cole 1998; Gillespie and Cornish 2010). With their engagement, a person gradually becomes an active social agent that receives the know-how, and world view, internalised or employed in transactions with the social world (Vygotsky 1978; Zittoun et al. 2013). This internalisation is not instantaneous as its development takes time and requires various 'back and forth' and 'in and out' of the social world that enable a person to occupy and experience different social positions – from being a child to becoming a parent, from a beneficiary to a benefactor, from a reader to a writer – each with its own psychological perspective. Through this movement, one develops an internal landscape of perspectives that to some extent mirrors one's social position in society (Gillespie and Martin 2014).

Internalisation is mediated by a multitude of tools, signs and artefacts (Gillespie and Zittoun 2010; Zittoun and Gillespie 2015a). Narratives, depictions, sounds, organised activities, all standing between the material realm and historically precipitated or new meanings, function as collective sociocultural resources which persons may draw upon and actively use in order to make sense of who they are, how they are recognised and how 'to go on' in their social milieu (Cole 1998; Howarth et al. 2015). That is not to say, however, that these resources deny individuals a role; they may limit but they also enable. Just as in the dynamic theoretical constructs of Bourdieu's *habitus* and Giddens' *structuration*, sociocultural milieus exceed persons and groups, being shaped by wider economic, historical and political circumstances, but they also contribute to their reproduction and change (Bourdieu 2008 [1977]; Howarth et al. 2013; Giddens 2020).

The concept of social context is another useful heuristic in tracing societal processes which continuously permeate personal and collective day-to-day life (Jovchelovitch 2019). Social contexts can be understood as (un)official, (un)explicated backgrounds (Zerubavel 1985, 2015), or as microworlds actively filtered through available systems of knowledge and enacted through practices (Jovchelovitch 2019). In other words, a context can be simplified as 'what is going on, what is the case and what someone may or may not, has or has not, can or cannot do'. In both senses, they specify the interrelation between persons, groups and structures of the sociocultural worlds that these persons inhabit, yet also allowing the possibility of being challenged and creatively rearranged (Howarth 2006; Zittoun and Gillespie 2016).

Given their dynamic character, social contexts are not easy to categorise. Complexity aside, in their various formations, social contexts impact personal and collective developmental trajectories, thus shaping the human's iterative and dialogical making of reality, both on the intrapersonal, interpersonal and group level (Marková 2016). The 'dialogical spirit' that characterises social contexts is also the connecting point with processes of public deliberation and change (Linell 2009). Both in the form of dynamic backgrounds and interconnected microworlds, social contexts become articulated, negotiated and challenged and changed in a constant process of world making (Howarth et al. 2013; Power et al. 2023). The particulars are not always officially mapped and institutionally charted, and often require a cross-disciplinary approach.

Some cross-disciplinary analyses are provided in the following entries. Sociocultural resources, exchange of social positions, circulating social knowledge and social contexts are discussed through the themes of gender identification, family involvement and social recognition. In parallel, their ripple effects related to honourable positions, life and academic prospects, issues of political prioritisation, official and unofficial welfare support as well as recognition in terms of who is active and productive in the community are brought to the fore.

To conclude, human development can be captured through the concepts of socialisation and social context. These concepts help in mapping development as it is being lived in '(un)official' social worlds that are populated by other persons, groups, communities, networks, practices and institutions (Jovchelovitch 2019). Through processes of movement from 'the inside' to 'outside', across time and space, in combination with the 'know-hows' and 'whats' as well as in the 'mundane' unfolding of personal and collective trajectories, threads of sociocultural activity and practices are weaved together in the tapestry of everyday, human affairs which is constantly *in the making* (Zittoun and Gillespie 2015b; Power et al. 2023). Tracing various permutations of sociocultural activities – from teenage socialisation and rebellion to the emerging practices and actionable solutions to problems – is a way of understanding human development and the directions it can take into a collective future (Jovchelovitch 2008; Power et al. 2023).

2.1 **Les rallyes mondains** (France)
Alexandre Lieure
Alumnus, School of Slavonic and East European Studies, UCL, UK

Les rallyes mondains in France are informal groups that bring together young aristocrats for cultural and networking events on a regular basis and over several years. Children take part in *rallyes* from the age of

11 until they reach young adulthood, usually around 19 years old. During the first years of the *rallyes*, children participate in cultural activities such as historical visits and dancing lessons, intended to prepare them for their future life as fully fledged members of the aristocracy. During the final years of a *rallyes*, cultural activities turn into fancy balls – *les soirées dansantes* – during which teenagers are expected to put into practice the rules of good conduct they were taught in the previous stage, while hopefully making lasting connections. According to French sociologists Michel Pinçon and Monique Pinçon-Charlot (PPM hereafter), the *rallyes mondains* are a key element in the overall structure of French aristocracy (PPM 2007, 2009). They enable young aristocrats to meet their peers and develop a sense of community, which reinforces the cohesiveness of the group (PPM 2007: 41).

Research suggests that the *rallyes mondains* as known today find their roots in 1950s France. During the post-war period, aristocratic families found it progressively difficult to arrange marriages for their children. *Rallyes* seem to have emerged from this increasing need to prevent misalliances and preserve the social homogeneity of the group. The organisation of fancy receptions and balls where young aristocrats could meet one another was not a novel practice as such. *L'art de recevoir* – the art of hospitality – is a well-documented practice among the French high society of the nineteenth and early twentieth centuries. Nevertheless, it is only through the *rallyes* that it became institutionalised.

The initial function of the *rallyes* as a matrimonial enterprise is reflected in their structure. Female participants host the *soirées dansantes* in order to show their mastery of the different social skills expected from them as future wives, that is, hosting sumptuous receptions, establishing and maintaining beneficial and lasting relations. Girls usually team up in order to reduce costs. Furthermore, *rallyes* are organised and supervised by a few mothers from renowned aristocratic families. As PPM note, women have always played a crucial role in the management of social capital in aristocratic circles (PPM 2009: 28). Male participants, on the other hand, are only invited to the *rallyes* and are therefore free to participate in several. In addition, their mothers are expected to organise cultural activities in the first years of the *rallyes*.

Each individual *rallye* attracts around 200 individuals. Selection of participants is operated through a system of informal cooptation, which ensures the social and religious homogeneity of the group. Indeed, *rallyes* tend to recruit children who share the same religious beliefs, but as a practice, the *rallyes mondains* are found mainly in Catholic circles but also

Protestant and Jewish communities (PPM 2009: 17–24). Belonging to the same families, schools and neighbourhoods, as well as being of a similar age, are the main criteria for joining the same *rallye*. For their *soirée dansante*, however, each hostess is allowed to invite up to 50 extra persons external to the *rallyes*. This practice enables different communities within the aristocracy to connect, creating a closed and well-connected microcosm. For instance, teenagers attending Paris' most prestigious schools tend to all know one another on a level that goes beyond that of mere acquaintance, having a good sense of everyone's familial ties and social status.

There are several active *rallyes* running at the same time, and new *rallyes* are being created as a new generation of children comes of age. Although it is hard to quantify precisely, there are probably around 20 *rallyes* running simultaneously for each generation in Paris. While Parisian *rallyes* are the most prestigious – often attracting people from French provinces and expats from neighbouring countries – they can also be found in other French cities.

Interpreting the *rallyes* simply as a veiled matrimonial agency for young bourgeois or aristocratic families taking control of their children's social circle would, however, be misleading. As several testimonies reveal, the *rallyes* take place far too early for participants to find their future spouse or make useful lasting relations (Gallien 2005b: part 2, 13–15min). The crucial period occurs later, in *grandes écoles*, at prestigious universities, where young aristocrats will form a strong professional network and find a respectable spouse. The real value of *rallyes* lies therefore elsewhere. They constitute a complementary level of education to those provided by families and private schools; the *rallyes* experience perfects an already perfect education (PPM 2007: 41). This view is actually shared by participants themselves, parents and children alike (Gallien 2005a: part 1, 11min).

The types of learning dispensed within these informal groups are several. First, during the initial stage of the *rallyes*, which consists of cultural activities, teenagers experience their cultural heritage as members of the aristocracy. This cultural capital is, and always will be, an integral part of their life, whether personal or social (PPM 2009: 17–24). Culture is what defines them as individuals and as a group, therefore serves as a basis for social relations. In the participants' view, culture is what makes someone respectable and becomes a pretext to build ties within the *rallyes*. The second type of learning follows on from the first and relates to who/what a young aristocrat ought to be. Indeed, a very recurrent theme raised by *rallyes* participants is the importance of respecting the rules of good conduct, that is, learning the practice of how to behave in society (Gallien 2005a: part 1, 7–11min). They are aristocrats and therefore should behave accordingly.

Having internalised who they are and who they ought to be, young aristocrats learn to recognise one another. This group awareness enables young aristocrats to identify with ease which connections should be pursued, and which should not, thus enhancing inward dynamics and undermining those outside the group. This is quite evident with female participants when asked about future husband expectations (Gallien 2005a: part 1, 13–15min). They automatically assign higher moral values to male participants as opposed to males outside the *rallyes* networks, often portrayed as having bad looks, being foolish, unstable and taking drugs (Gallien 2005a: part 1, 13–15min). Thus, the boundaries of the social group are effectively reaffirmed, which in turn contributes to the further enforcement of norms, sanctions and trust within it.

In more general terms, the *rallyes* act as what Bourdieu denotes a *rite of institution* (1982). Indeed, not only do they prepare participants to become the new generation of the aristocracy, but they also serve to differentiate the aristocracy from lower classes further. The ritual assigns specific social properties – such as behaviours and codes specific to the aristocracy – to those who undergo it (Bourdieu 1982). Aristocrats recognise non-aristocrats and vice versa. Thus, together with education, family name, wealth and other rites of institution, the *rallyes* further shapes the external perception of the group as naturally and legitimately superior.

Finally, the *rallyes* can also be understood in terms of competence and disposition towards social capital. Indeed, as Bourdieu states, social capital 'is not profitable or even conceivable unless one invests in it a specific competence (knowledge of genealogical relationships and of real connections and skill at using them, etc.) and an acquired disposition to acquire and maintain this competence' (Bourdieu 1986: 252–3). From the youngest age, *rallyes* participants are made aware of the invaluable importance of social capital for their future life. They learn how to transform contingent, ordinary social relations into usable and lasting obligations, how to navigate their way through social networks and identify their key features and nodes. Therefore, the social competences and dispositions acquired during the *rallyes mondains* prevent social capital from ever becoming a public good, ensuring the overall cohesion of the aristocracy and the reproduction of power structures.

2.2 *Mianzi* (China)
Long Zhang
Department of Sociology, Nankai University, Tianjin City, China

Mianzi (面子) in Chinese, literally 'face', refers to the recognition of an individual's social status and prestige in the eyes of others. *Mianzi* can be earned, saved, borrowed and manoeuvred (Hu 1944; Hwang 1987; Kinnison 2017). As demonstrated by Goffman's research on face-work, concern for self-image (that is, how one is perceived by others) is commonplace worldwide (1972). However, in the social-cultural context of China, there are especially prominent concerns related to the practice of *mianzi*. These concerns highlight aspects of personal relations and interactions largely ignored in non-Chinese societies (Qi 2011).

For Chinese people, *mianzi* is perceived not to be particularly relevant in both close relations and among complete strangers (Hwang 1987). In close relations, such as with family members, an individual tends to be more relaxed and display a more 'authentic' version of him or herself. Among complete strangers, interactions are often superficial and short-lived, and an individual is rarely worried about strangers' perceptions of them. Rather, *mianzi* is most prominent in intermediary or mixed relations, or within the *guanxi* (关系) (see 1.12 Volume 1) network. This network includes friends, colleagues, classmates, fellow villagers, neighbours, and so on.

In a *guanxi* network, the amount of *mianzi* reflects the individual's social status and, to a certain extent, the person's position in the network. Those who have more *mianzi* usually find it easier to utilise their *guanxi* to gain resources (Hwang 1987). If A makes a request to B, and B accepts, then we can say that B gives *mianzi* to A. Meanwhile, the fact that B has helped A means that a social debt is owed to B, so A should provide *mianzi* to B in return. If A does not have enough *mianzi* to gain help from B, then A may need to 'borrow' *mianzi* from C, asking B to help A for the sake of C's *mianzi*. In general, C should be a person who has close *guanxi* with A and has *mianzi* for B.

In order to increase one's *mianzi*, some people may deliberately highlight their special *guanxi* with powerful figures, by inviting an influential figure to give a speech at a wedding, hanging a celebrity's calligraphy or painting in a prominent place at home, and so on. In addition, daily interactions between an individual and other people in the network also affect one's *mianzi*. Such interactions may include whether gifts are exchanged in accordance with commonly recognised rules, whether one gives *mianzi* to another in certain situations, and so on.

Because *mianzi* can be manoeuvred to a certain degree, variations exist to the extent to which a person's *mianzi* is 'valid' (实) or 'hollow' (虚). If a person is wealthy or possesses a certain ability commensurate with one's reputation, we can consider the person's *mianzi* to be 'valid'. In contrast, if a person produces an image of him or herself through subterfuge or posturing, then that person's *mianzi* is hollow (see Figure 2.2.1 as a metaphor). According to this understanding, exaggerating a particular *guanxi* with a powerful figure is a specific strategy for establishing 'hollow *mianzi*'. However, the distinction between 'valid *mianzi*' and 'hollow *mianzi*' is not absolute; for example, a businessman gaining hollow *mianzi* mainly through exaggerating his *guanxi* with a powerful official may still have more advantage in a competitive bidding, thus turning the hollow *mianzi* into a valid one.

Many Chinese people are concerned with protecting the *mianzi* of others, especially those of higher social status. Hurting someone's *mianzi* may cause embarrassment to that person, or even anger them, and could damage their interpersonal *guanxi* (Kipnis 1995). Common strategies to save the *mianzi* of others include avoiding public criticism preferring more euphemistic, general and vague comments; avoiding outright refusal of requests and, instead, making a perfunctory effort even when the request cannot be really fulfilled; avoiding public confrontation with elders and superiors and, instead, behaving as submissively as possible (Hu 1944; Hwang 1987).

According to Zhai's (2013) research, defence of leaders' *mianzi* constitutes a distinctive feature of the relationship between superiors

Figure 2.2.1   The logogram for *mianzi* interpreted by the author.
© Long Zhang.

and subordinates in the Chinese bureaucracy. For example, if a superior makes a mistake, they rarely admit it voluntarily in order to save *mianzi*; moreover, even if the subordinates are aware that their superior has made a mistake, they often choose to cover up the mistake or justify the misconduct to assist their leader save *mianzi*. This phenomenon exists both in traditional Chinese bureaucracy and among communist cadres, which shows considerable historical continuity.

This is also true the other way around. In Chinese bureaucracy, wise leaders also know the importance of maintaining the *mianzi* of their subordinates and avoid embarrassing their subordinates in public. The business magazine *Forbes* once reported how, in a large multinational company located in Shanghai, a US superior severely criticised his Chinese subordinate in a meeting, causing him to fall silent and then leave the meeting. Based on this story, the *Forbes* reporter advised foreign managers to be fully aware of Chinese people's sensitivity to public criticism: 'when your Chinese employees lose face, you lose them' (Vorhauser-Smith 2012).

In traditional Chinese culture, maintaining *mianzi* perpetuates unequal gender relations. According to the traditional principles of Confucianism, the expected image of a couple in public is 'husband sings and wife echoes' (夫唱妇随), which means that a wife should show deference to her husband and offer him as much *mianzi* as possible in front of other people. According to Chan's (2006) research, the perception that their *mianzi* has not been preserved constitutes an important reason why some Chinese husbands feel dissatisfied with their wives and in some cases even commit domestic violence.

The *mianzi* practice also perpetuates gender inequality in that having a son is traditionally viewed as generating *mianzi* for all family members, while having a daughter does not add anything to their *mianzi*. Given this perception, giving birth to a boy represents more than mere security; it is linked to the status and prestige of the family members in the community and network (Li and Shang 2012). Some young mothers may even feel that giving birth to a son affects their *mianzi* in the entire kinship network and community. This linking of a child's gender with the parents' *mianzi* has led to intentional gender selection and lower survival rates for girls.

However, the *mianzi* earned by raising a son is a double-edged sword. When a young man prepares for marriage, his parents are often obliged to prepare a substantial *caili* (see 4.1 in this volume) and even to buy an apartment for the newlyweds, for which the parents may accumulate a huge debt. The amount of *caili* and the quality of the apartment has an impact on the *mianzi* of the bridegroom's family in the previous community and in the newly established network with the bride's family (Wang et al. 2020). If, despite the heavy financial burden this presents, the bridegroom's parents fail to gain enough return from their son, their life actually becomes much harder due to their excessive investment in gaining a hollow *mianzi*. As a Chinese proverb says, people may 'suffer in life through dying to gain *mianzi*' (死要面子活受罪).

2.3 **Runs** (Nigeria)
Olumuyiwa K. Ojo and Olusola Ayandele
Department of General Studies, The Polytechnic, Ibadan, Nigeria

The term *runs* in Nigerian English and pidgin English refers to diverse acts of cheating in the Nigerian educational system. The euphemism derived from the English verb for moving fast by using one's feet is used to downplay the gravity of the offence or to cover up the act of gaining an advantage by illegitimate means.

Runs (used in the plural form) is used for a plethora of borderline illegal or immoral activities among students of higher institutions (Ojo et al. 2020). It describes various subversions of established rules and regulations during the students' stay on campus, from admission to graduation. The practices are common and take place in collusion with faculty, non-academic staff, business centre operators and others. A number of typologies of runs in higher institutions can be found in academic literature (see also Ojebode et al. 2010; Ekundayo 2013). The four basic forms of *runs* exchanges include: (1) sex for higher marks, or 'sex for grade', (2) 'money for grade', (3) examination malpractice and (4) the use of fake documents.

According to most Nigerian traditional ethos on morals and values known as *omoluabi* (Yoruba), a person should strive to promote integrity, service, hard work, humility and concern for others. According to some, these principles have been eroded in contemporary Nigeria (Adegoju 2007). Several indigenous languages spoken by Nigerians euphemise illicit exchanges and petty bribery to cover up corrupt practices (Auwal 1987: 293; Yagboyaju 2018): *egunje* in Yoruba, *Chuachua* or *Toshiyar baki* in Hausa, and *Igbuozu* in Igbo. These cleverly crafted words have helped petty corruption thrive among Nigerians, but the public remains critical of elite corruption. Acknowledging this gap, Goodluck Jonathan, the former president of Nigeria, said in a televised statement that 'stealing is not the same thing as corruption' (Aribisala 2014). Nigerian youth,

Figure 2.3.1 One of many cheating techniques. Pexels.

socialised in the context of systemic corruption, does not consider it morally wrong to engage in runs and refuses to accept normative views (Okoli 1997).

Research has established the use of language from other spheres of life to refer to specific *runs*: words and phrases from business, religion, technology, gambling, transportation and sports, as well as slang from popular culture. Terms that refer to the first type of *runs* exchanges are, for example, a *runs* girl, denoting someone who is willing to trade sex or money for a higher mark (Okorie and Bamidele 2016: 10), and a *runs* guy, referring to someone carrying out illicit transactions or brokering between sides. The *runs* of 'sex for grade' are referred to as 'trade by barter' (business), 'praise and worship' (religion), 'swap' (technology) and 'farase' or 'using body to get it' (local slang).

The pervasiveness of inappropriate sexual transactions between students and staff in higher education has been reported in the news in Nigeria and beyond: *runs* include girls engaging in strategic sexual relationships with school officials to enhance their academic performance, and boys paying for the services of female prostitutes to have sex with school officials on their behalf in exchange for higher marks (Alagbe 2016). A BBC *Africa Eye* undercover documentary on 'sex for grades' captured four male lecturers blackmailing female students and soliciting sex in exchange for marks required for admission to universities in Nigeria and Ghana (Mordi 2019). A Nigerian professor was sentenced to two years in prison for forcing a female student to have sex with him by threatening to award a fail mark otherwise (Adebayo and Busari 2018).

The second category of *runs* exchanges involves bribing academic and non-academic staff with cash to pass exams or improve marks. The euphemisms for this type of *runs* include: 'sorting, following-up, or subscribing' (from business), 'making a shortcut or an upgrade' (from transportation or technology), 'betting on the lucky number four' (*aja 4 gbera*, from virtual dog race gambling), considered to be the luckiest number, and 'peace offering' (from religious contexts). An interested student, known as a 'subscriber', finds a *runs guy* to act as an intermediary. Money is paid as a 'peace offering' to 'sort out' academic matters or to establish a 'shortcut' for a member of staff in charge of processing examination results to 'upgrade' the student's mark. Reports have been made about the role of poverty in forcing students to engage in robbery or prostitution to make enough money to pay for an improvement of their marks (Oko and Adie 2016).

The euphemistic language devised by students successfully shifts attention away from the negative connotations of fraud and cheating during examinations to the more linguistically neutral or positive implications associated with problem-solving. The *runs* euphemism for practices perpetrated by students to deceive invigilators, escape scrutiny or avoid detection during examinations is not the only one. Answers to examination questions inscribed on laps, arms and palms like body art are known as 'tattoos', while unauthorised materials smuggled into examination halls by students are known as *microchips* or *panpa*. These materials are similarly euphemised as *crib sheets* or *ponies* in English, *spickzettel* in German and *shpargalka* or *shpora* in Russian (Denisova-Schmidt 2017). Formation denotes a strategic seating plan or arrangement that would allow weak students to copy from stronger ones with or without the invigilator's connivance.

The fourth category of *runs* refers to the use of fake certificates, clearance slips, fees receipts and other documents forged by students to gain admission to institutions of their choice or sustain their studentship there. Popular terms in this category include *scam*, a direct word for fraudulent acts, an *FK*, a phonemic abbreviation of the word fake, *ike*, a *yoruba lingo* for plastic, with its connotation of an inferior material and *ro'dan*, a local word meaning performing deceptive magic. Prospective students often engage a broker, a *runs guy*, who owns a business centre as a cover for forging documents, admission fraud and certificate racketeering. Such brokers may also liaise with the higher education staff. Students who commenced their adult lives by cheating with *ike* or *FK* or getting involved in *ro'dan* and *scam*, might express regret about having built their careers on a false foundation which led to unfulfilled dreams. In the short-term, students who get caught can be dismissed from the school or have their certificates revoked (Kigotho 2004).

2.4 **Neijuan** (China)
Haoxuan Mao
Alumnus, School of Slavonic and East European Studies, UCL, UK

Neijuan is a Chinese expression for internal depletion and stifling due to intensified competition (*nei* stands for 'inner' and *juan* for 'circle'). Group anxiety generated by *neijuan* is particularly evident among younger generations as a result of increasing economic competition.

Seen as the origin of contemporary *neijuan*, agricultural involution was first proposed to describe the long-term stagnation of living standards due to the massive employment in Java's agriculture without a subsequent increase in per capita output (Geertz 1963). The understanding of the term then evolved to explain people's tendency to waste time and resources on meaningless things, leading to underdeveloped growth and internal depletion (Huang 1990). In the fierce competitive context of contemporary Chinese economy, *neijuan* has hence been adapted to describe all sectors of society.

Neijuan is evident in many workplaces where employees, fearing their superiors will consider leaving work on time a symptom of the fact that they do not work enough, will wait until everyone else has left the office before they leave, even if they have completed their tasks. On occasion, entire offices have stayed at work overnight.

Another driver of *neijuan* is the points system adopted by technology companies. For example, Alibaba's performance ranking system was identified by the *Financial Times* (2021) as the cause of the brutal working conditions of employees of the Chinese giant. In Chinese tech companies, such as TikTok, the so-called *996 system* is common. It decodes as 9am, the start of the working day, 9pm, the end of the working day, and a 6-day working week, a form of 'slavery in the modern workplace' (Wang 2020). Employees exposed to unhealthy corporate cultures rooted in productivity at the expense of their well-being easily fall into *neijuan*.

Heavy competition puts small-business owners under stress. *Neijuan* pushes them to lower their prices to keep up with the competition, resulting in a subsequent decrease in the quality of goods. This idea was explained by Sun, a young start-up owner in the catering industry, who argued that to compete with giants in the industry and takeaway platforms, he had to keep the prices of products as low as possible and hold frequent promotions. Faced with huge losses, he eventually went out of business (BBC 2021).

Top-down formal policies, such as the process to obtain a registered residence (*hukou*), can indirectly contribute to *neijuan*. Having a local *hukou* is a prerequisite for buying a house in the big cities of China, and the scale of salaries determines the outcome of a *hukou* application. Although *hukou* does not have a market price, candidates who receive a wage higher than the social security payment and meet other informal conditions are more likely to acquire a Shanghai *hukou*. Various sources suggest that from 2013 to 2023, the annual social security payments in Shanghai have almost double. As such, with a fixed number of *hukou* to assign, if everyone starts to raise the base and personal tax, the competition increases.

Considering 'diligence' is the word that is most often taught by Chinese parents to their young children (Wang et al. 2012), family face (*mianzi*) is a bottom-up drive for *neijuan*. Career success and a decent social status are the main sources for *mianzi*, and parents encourage their children to work hard to gain a competitive edge over their peers and to establish a strong family reputation, '*wang zi cheng long*' (literally 'hope that children achieve success'). This pressure already starts in pre-school, where children aged 3–6 are encouraged to engage in extra-curricular tutorial training (Li 2021).

Scarce educational opportunities and employment pressures can lead to an excessive focus on academic achievement (Luo et al. 2013). A senior student at Renmin University of China (Xinhua Net 2020) disclosed that when a word requirement for an essay is around 3,000 words, many students choose to write over 10,000 words to achieve a higher grade. Unlike in the West, Chinese teachers tend to acquiesce to this behaviour, resulting in almost everyone's assignments going well over the requirement, even if there is a fixed percentage of students who can get a full grade. This intensified competition prevents young people from understanding when the effort they make is enough, even if they are forced to stop.

In China, where young people's parents have moved from poverty to affluence, and where millennials have risen rapidly through the opportunities of the Internet, Generation Z is faced with high house prices and limited opportunities (*China Daily* 2018). As such, *neijuan* translates into the frustration of middle-class young people facing a window of missed opportunity. Although having grown up witnessing their elders' rapid development with the dividends of China's rapid economic growth, the reality is not what they expected. On the other hand, a person who does not strive for success or actively withdraws from intensified competition diminishes the pressure that comes with *neijuan* only to fall into *tangping*, pursuing a life without desire (Bai 2019). This value is dismissed by authorities and mainstream media that refer to *tangping* as 'shameful behaviour' (Xinhua Net 2021). While *tangping* and *moyu* (slacking off at work) are defence mechanisms, for young people it remains difficult to escape the social pressure of *neijuan*.

Despite its one-child policy, China's population grew by 400 million from 1980 to 2020 (World Bank 2021), clashing with the current trend of slowing economic development in East Asia (World Bank 2021). The economic slowdown will make employment difficult, intensifying the pursuit for higher academic qualifications (Sun 2008). Phenomena like *neijuan* can be found in Korea and Japan, known as *inner circle* (BBC Korean 2021) and *unanimous internal competition* (Nicovideo News 2020), respectively. Given that Confucianism is the foundation of East Asian cultural context, diligence (*qin*) and courtesy (*li*) are considered significant reasons for the birth of *neijuan* in East Asian countries (China Global Television Network 2020, 2020b).

2.5 **Słoiki** (Poland)
Mathilde Ollivo
Alumna, School of Slavonic and East European Studies, UCL, UK

Słoiki means 'jars' in Polish, but the term is also used to describe people who migrate from the countryside to big cities in Poland. These internal migrants are known for bringing conserved food (products, meals and so on) from the countryside to, for example, Warsaw, in jars. Stereotypical *słoik* (singular form of *słoiki*) is a young person, between 20 and 35 years old, who leaves their hometown for work or study. Once they arrive in a city, they typically share a flat with other migrants. In 2014, more than half of all *słoiki* were under 30, and 9 out of 10 were under 45 and were mainly coming from regions surrounding Warsaw and eastern cities like Lublin or Zamość (Pifczyk 2015). Commuting between their places of work/study and their hometown allows *słoiki* to limit their everyday expenses for food, as they tend to travel back home every weekend to restock, while also maintaining strong familial ties.

The *słoiki* practice is linked to solidarity within the family, focused on supporting the migrant. It is a substitutive survival strategy aiming at limiting the costs of living in the city and occurring as a response to the inability of the post-socialist state to respond to the urbanisation process. During the communist period (1944–89), goods shortages failed to generate a political response (Stenning et al. 2010: 144–74) which led to the growth of an underground economy and the increasing unease between the 'haves' and the 'have-nots' following Poland's admission to the European Union in 2004 (Podkalicka and Potkanska 2015: 95–119). Joining the EU amplified inequalities between the rural and urban areas. Therefore, bringing food with them during their pendulum migration 'helps migrants to survive in the cities' (Mroczkowska 2019: 228). From a microeconomic perspective, the living costs for *słoiki* are lower since they buy less food. However, the money saved by food mobility is at least partially used to travel back to the countryside.

Another explanation for the existence of *słoiki* is the intergenerational asymmetrical help, a practice that maintains ties within the family. Mauss (1924) suggests that gifts are never truly free and implicate a reciprocity, sometimes hints at hierarchy and antagonism. Providing their children with food in a jar is a way of ensuring they will come back to the house as they need to return or refill the empty jars. The jar becomes the 'representation of permanence and continuity of the family relationship' (Bachórz 2018: 139), a material embodiment of the relationship. This pendulum migration ensures the continuity of family roles, which are an important source of identity in Poland (Dunn 2004). This link between the *słoiki* and their families is, however, also ambivalent as the received food provides economic security but entails compliance and dependence.

Being a *słoik* is also a way of building an identity, with ambivalent results. There is the normative ambivalence, grounded on the divide between 'us' and 'them', based on identities, inclusion and exclusion, locals and migrants. Upon arriving in a new city, one needs to boost social capital. According to Bourdieu, social capital is one's capacity to mobilise relations to achieve goals. Yet, *słoiki* tend to remain attached to their home community to the detriment of forming networks in a new city. In this context, 'foodways are the key means of defining group identities, bonds and community building, both at the local level of the family and neighbourhood and at the regional and state level' (Mroczkowska 2019: 223).

However, this identity may have ambivalent consequences. A *słoik* willing to gain access to the middle class in order to integrate into the urban way of life will cut their ties to the homestead as it constrains their integration since bringing food from the home is perceived as a 'downshifting strategy seen as a symbol of lifestyle inadequacy and conservatism' (Bachórz 2018: 134). The term *słoiki* then becomes a label that reinforces the boundaries between 'us' and 'them', defined along the centre/periphery axis. In such a setting, being a *słoik* is to belong to a certain group with a real lock-in effect. By socialising within their safety net, they remain 'outsiders' and do not socialise with insiders, which may result in future difficulties in finding a job through informal networks and contacts.

2.6 *Pokhorony okurka* (Russia and USSR)
Kirill Melnikov
Institute of Philosophy and Law, Ural Division of the Russian Academy of Sciences, Russia

Pokhorony okurka refers to informal punishment in the Russian (and previously the Soviet) army, translated as 'a cigarette butt funeral'. The term refers to 'educating' soldiers caught smoking in prohibited areas. If such a violation is identified, the guilty soldier and his unit are ordered to carry out a march and dig a metaphorical grave for the cigarette. The commander gives a sarcastic funeral speech about the cigarette butt, soldiers shovel soil onto it and march back to their base. Depending on the gravity of the misconduct, its frequency and the discretion and creativity of the commander, particular scenarios may vary. The punishment can be intensified by its suddenness; for instance, the unit can be woken up in the middle of the night by an alert. A forced march can be complicated by the request to undertake it in full uniform (including helmet and bulletproof vest). The length of the march and the size of the pit can also vary. The ritual can be accompanied by the appointment of guards of honour, the three-volley salute and other ceremonial procedures inherent in military funerals. The diversity of these scenarios highlights the traditional, informal and entrenched nature of this practice.

Tracing the origins of *pokhorony okurka* is complicated. The analysis of blogs and memoirs confirms that it has been taking place since at least the 1980s, and practices of informal punishment were the exception rather than the rule in the 1950s (Manoilin 2004: 46–87; Zirtran 2014). Most likely, the penetration of informal punishment into the Soviet army is associated with the general spread of the non-statutory relations (*neustavnye otnosheniia*). While some practices of non-statutory relations can be traced back to the army of the Russian Empire (Tutolmin 2007), the proliferation of informal relations as a general trend began in the 1960s and is often seen as a result of several overlapping trends.

In the 1960s, veterans of the Second World War began retiring from commanding positions. While no systematic scholarly accounts exist, it is commonly believed that veterans, due to their unconditional authority and prestige as battlefront participants, did not need additional sources of legitimacy and, therefore, avoided hazing. Additionally, the shared combat experience often requires trusting in-group relations – the life lesson veterans might have brought to the post-war army.

The veteran retirement coincided with a shortage of recruits caused by the losses of the USSR in the war. In order to compensate for demographic losses, the Politburo resorted to conscripting men with criminal backgrounds (Tutolmin 2007). This measure was introduced as a form of rehabilitation of former prisoners, but in reality, prison subculture saturated the army. The proliferation of informal disciplinary techniques was enhanced by the degradation of the system of sergeant education. After reducing conscription from three to two years in 1968, regimental schools for sergeants were abolished. As a result, any qualitative distinction between soldiers and sergeants was erased, and posts for junior commanders began to be allotted to conscripts. The lack of competence of the new generation of sergeants and the continuous necessity to manage the army collective introduced informal ways of getting things done.

Different forms of informal punishments have a long history in the Soviet and Russian army. What makes them so durable, and why, despite the vast variety of formal penalty options (*Konsul'tant Plus* 2007: 55), do informal punishments still thrive?

The first reason is that applying informal punishment allows commanders to avoid responsibility. The formal penalty requires proof that a soldier had committed misconduct, as stated in the Disciplinary Bylaw (81). If misconduct lacks proof, the commander himself can be subject to investigation. Informal punishment allows superior officers to circumvent this hazardous procedure and to disguise punishment as a physical exercise.

Second, informal punishment allows commanders to apply it collectively. Sticking to the formal order of disciplinary action assumes compliance with the principle of personalisation of punishment, whereas collective punishment shapes the mechanism of *krugovaya poruka* (joint responsibility) (also see Ledeneva 2006: 91–114), where everyone looks after everyone else in the unit. *Pokhorony okurka*, in which the guilty soldier's entire unit must collectively undertake the forced march, induces guilt in the culprit towards the team. Informal punishment employs one of the most potent fears – the fear of social isolation. Given that the harsh conditions in the army require friendship and support, potential deprivation of such support leads to strong self-censorship. Collective punishment is not unique to the Russian army. The same mechanisms are present in the US, for instance. A US infantry officer reported that 'mass punishment has been a part of the military for many years' (Soler 2015). Scholars analysing the mechanisms of collective sanctions in the US military point out that manifestations of joint responsibility are often quite cruel. Recruits whose violations have frequently led to group punishment are sometimes beaten up in line with the custom known as the 'blanket party' (Heckathorn 1988: 538). These practices are reflected in iconic films such as *Full Metal Jacket* and *Hacksaw Ridge*.

The third reason is that there is an element of laughter culture or the culture of 'army absurdity' (Bannikov 2002: 191–204) in informal punishment. The practice of *pokhorony okurka* is ostentatiously absurd and grotesque. Besides the fact that it is disproportionately severe in relation to the misconduct committed, it also represents a parody and a social oxymoron, which combine the incompatible – a funeral (something meaningful and even sacred for an army) and a cigarette butt (something minor and mundane). Humour and absurdity fulfil several essential functions in the army. First, absurdity is the vehicle of initial army socialisation. In his book *Asylums*, Erving Goffman states that total institutions, and the army in particular, mortifies itself by, among other things, destroying the perception of causality and logic upon entering it (Goffman 1961: 14). At the same time, humour and irony are ingredients in socio-psychological relaxation. 'Humour saves a person from the oppressive awareness of his subordinate position and is given to man as a moment of inner freedom' (Bannikov 2002: 203). While in the first months, absurd humour can play a 'socialising' role, it can be a tool of relaxation later on.

The fourth reason is that the role of informal punishment is not only to punish but rather to normalise the subject in a 'disciplinary institution' (Foucault 1979) or to disrupt self-perception in a 'total institution' (Goffman 1961). Besides breaking the link between cause and effect, informal punishment also uses more subtle ways of disruption of the self. As Goffman states, 'one of the most telling ways in which one's economy of action can be disrupted is the obligation to request permission or supplies for minor activities that one can execute on one's own on the outside, such as smoking, shaving, going to the toilet, telephoning, spending money, or mailing letters' (Goffman 1961: 41). Having been subjected to the practice of *pokhorony okurka*, the soldier will tread more carefully next time – he will ask his commander for permission to smoke.

Informal punishment is a natural way to maintain discipline within total institutions. As long as the army retains the basic features of total institutions, practices of informal punishment will continue. An all-volunteer military can significantly limit the scope of such practices since it disrupts the central feature of total institutions – the inability to choose where, when and how to work, sleep and relax.

2.7 *Hikikomori* (Japan)
Taiga Kambara
Alumna, School of Slavonic and East European Studies, UCL, UK

Hikikomori is a Japanese word that translates as to 'shut oneself in'. It is the repurposing of a term that refers to people who refuse to have contact with the outside world. According to the official categorisation of the Ministry of Health, Labor and Welfare of Japan, a *hikikomori* is someone who has refused to have any contact with people for more than six months (Kawakami 2010).

Similar to *hikikomori*, there are NEET people, an acronym identifying those who are Not in Employment, Education, nor Training. Although NEET strictly speaking only refers to people who are unemployed and unwilling to work, these two terms are frequently used interchangeably, as they are often used for people with similar characteristics. Even the Japanese Ministry of Health, Labor and Welfare grouped these two bodies when conducting a survey regarding the reality of *hikikomori* (Iriya 2010).

Although the term is specific to Japan, the phenomenon is spread around the globe. The third edition of the handbook published by the American Psychological Association, or DSM-III, referred to patients with similar traits as displaying 'social withdrawal' (Iriya 2010). The first case of the term being used outside Japan is in Italy in the late 2000s (Katsura and Sugiyama 2019).

Despite being a practice that can be observed around the globe, there are several key factors that distinguish the Japanese case. First, the country saw a massive spike in young unemployed people following the burst of the economic bubble in the late 1990s (Futagami 2013). This, in tandem with a culture of shame, led to an increase of *hikikomori*. While highly capable, many young people were circumstantially unfortunate and found their unemployment shameful. To avoid having the finger pointed at them and being gossiped about behind their backs, they avoided human contact entirely. Parents of these young people were typically baby boomers raised during the height of economic growth. Often referred to as 'economic animals', these people were taught to work hard and consume even harder for the sake of the economy (Futagami 2013). The contrast between the parents' mindset and the economic reality that these young people were experiencing led to rising pressures within the household, where parents would be the first to shun their children for being unemployed.

In recent years, *hikikomori* has taken on a new problematic dimension. Known as the 8050 problem, the ageing population of Japan is becoming increasingly incapable of supporting *hikikomori* children (Kawakami 2010). The problem is referred to as 8050 because the first group of *hikikomori* people who were hit during the 'ice age of employment', in the late 1990s, are now turning 50 years old and their parents nearing 80. Although these ageing *hikikomori* may currently be able to live off their parents' income or social security, if they were to pass away, the 50-year-olds who have never worked would remain without any means to support themselves. Until now, the long lifespan of Japanese citizens has delayed this threat, but at the same time, in return it has prevented this terrible problem from being brought to light until it was exacerbated to the point of no return.

The greater implication of the existence of *hikikomori* links back to the question of what type of informal category the practice falls into. Essentially, in present-day Japan, the practice was caused by the incompetence of formal institutions to provide stable unemployment relief and employment opportunities following the burst of the economic bubble. To those who were unemployed, or never employed to begin with, the close personal space and parental support functioned as a financial, social and mental safety net.

That is not to say, however, that formal institutions are the only ones to blame. For instance, *amakudari*, the preferential treatment of retired civil servants when hiring for managerial positions, has produced an overwhelmingly favourable set of benefits to more senior citizens and employees, but doomed the economic and social prospects of younger citizens in Japan. In times of hardship, Japanese culture tends to undermine the importance of its youngest members to prioritise older citizens (Futagami 2013).

The covert nature of this practice makes it difficult to study and measure, but in the past decade the topic has become less of a taboo, leading to more research being conducted. However, since no one, including the Japanese Ministry of Health, Labor and Welfare, has been able to accurately document the *hikikomori*, it is difficult to have an overall picture of the phenomenon (Iriya 2010).

2.8 **Gaser** (Serbia and the Western Balkans)
Barbara Frey
Faculty of Business, Economics and Management Information Systems, University of Regensburg, Germany
and
Dragana Mrvoš
School of Interdisciplinary Global Studies, University of South Florida, USA

Gaser is an expression used in reference to a teenager or a young adult, a member of the street subculture that emerged in Serbia, and later in the other countries of former Yugoslavia, in the early 2010s. The root of the word *gaser* is the noun *gas* (gas), and its use stems from the expression *ide gas*, which has a dual meaning: to start a party, as well as to flex (to brag). In the wider context, *ide gas* is the youth's motto that denotes an overall display of luxurious, pretentious and self-centred lifestyle (Rosić 2020).

The possession of expensive attires has become a critical element of social demarcation for Serbian youth. As an illustration, peers often rely on a smartphone application to examine each other's attires to determine whether it is the original brand or a fake (Jovanović 2019). Only branded gifts are desirable and sought after by students as they are perceived to convey social prestige (Jovanović 2019). Consequently, a divide between those who cannot afford expensive wardrobes (*fušeri*) and those who can afford extravagant items (*gaseri*) creates the risk of social exclusion, peer violence, psychological, and sometimes physical, abuse of the materially vulnerable (Jovanović 2019).

Through exclusion and abuse of and violence towards low-income and socially vulnerable families, *gaseri* influence social structures but also reflect the existing levels of social inequality in Serbia (Jorgensen and Phillips 2002: 61). For example, the richest 20 per cent have 'a nearly 10 times higher equivalent income than the poorest 20 per cent' (The Social Inclusion and Poverty Reduction Unit of the Government of the Republic of Serbia [SIPRU] 2018). Along with a high degree of inequality, the share of people whose disposable income is below the relative poverty line is 21.7 per cent (Statistical Office of the Republic of Serbia 2020). Alongside social inequality and subjugation of the materially deprived, *gaser*'s subculture focuses on nihilism and hedonism, as exemplified in the *trep folk*, or *Balkan trep* music that they listen to. As a novel music genre, *trep folk* blends trap hop with folk music melodies and instruments, characteristic of Balkan folk music. More importantly, themes explored in this music describe the Balkan youth's everyday struggle to get rich while aspiring to party, have fun and enjoy drugs (Kaluža 2018: 23).

In this regard, *gaseri* identify with the lyrics of Bondisimo's (2020) song 'GASnaMAX': *'Ništa me ne zanima flexujem danima'* ('I am flexing for days not interested in doing anything'). Similarly, they relate to the lyrics of another popular *trap* performer Mimi Mercedez singing *'I da nisam čula reč / ako ne donosi keš'* ('I do not want to hear a word if you do not bring cash') with over 20 million views on YouTube (Mimi Mercedez 2017). The most popular Balkan trap performers, Jala Brat, Buba Corelli and Rasta boast more than 100 million views on YouTube, while singing almost exclusively about promiscuous women, golden watches, jewellery and macho men. The lyrics of the most popular *trep folk* performers do not appeal to national sentiment, but to a communal Balkan feeling consisting of longing for better living conditions (Dumnić Vilotijević 2020: 7, 10). *Trep folk* artists are popular among young people in the entire ex-Yugoslav area, including Slovenia and North Macedonia, and their artistic themes are based on 'values' of global materialism and consumerism, rather than on national or ethnic sentiments (Dragojlo 2019).

Although the lack of nationalist rhetoric in the *trep folk* music is a glimmer of hope in the otherwise economically wrecked region, burdened with divided history of national identities (Kaluža 2021: 163–4), *gaseri* promote an identity centred around wealth, rebelling against school, knowledge, empathy, hard work and commitment (Bugarin 2021). Because 'nothing is safe, or permanent', *gaseri* are prone to emotional distress leading to depression, anxiety, alcoholism or drug addiction (Bugarin 2021). Subcultures comparable to *gaser* exist beyond the ex-Yugoslav cultural space, albeit with comparable differences: *gazari* in Bulgaria (BGJargon 2022), *cocalar* in Romania (Costescu 2013: 262), *eshay* in Australia (Lill 2014; de Lacey 2020), *gopnik* in Russia (Gracheva et al. 2018) and chav in the UK (Martin 2009).

2.9 **Lesboseksprosvet** (Russia)
Polina Kislitsyna
Independent researcher, St. Petersburg, Russia

Lesboseksprosvet, an abbreviation for lesbian sex education, refers to grassroots initiatives aimed at disseminating information about safer sex among queer women in Russia. The term was coined in 2017 by one of the key figures in these activities, Sasha Kazantseva. The abbreviation includes three parts: *lesbiyskiy* (lesbian), *seks* (sex) and *prosvet* (enlightenment). *Seksprosvet*, or 'sex enlightenment' (*seksual'noe prosveshchenie*) has an idiomatic sounding of the twentieth-century revolutionary 'newspeak' that emerged in the aftermath of the 1917 Bolshevik revolution and included multiple variations on the theme of political and cultural education of the illiterate masses: *politpros*, *kul'tprosvet* and many others. *Lesboseksprosvet* of the twenty-first century is not associated with any organisation, movement or community. 'Enlightening' takes place at the grassroots level, through practices of sharing texts, videos, lectures, workshops and other forms of information production, devoted to sexual relationships between women. The thematic range of these activities includes lesbian health care, protection against sexually transmitted infections (STIs), psychological safety in sexual relations, diversity of sexual practices and preferences, and sexual consent.

There is no formal sex education in contemporary Russia. The Soviet youth learned about sex informally: from their peers, through courtyard games and childish folklore, as well as classical art representation of nude bodies and sexual scenes (Rotkirch 2000). In tune with Soviet morals, the theme of sexuality remains tabooed, and politicised. Late Soviet publications on sexual relationships linked sexuality solely with marriage and reproduction (Temkina 2009). In the post-Soviet period, the discourse on sexuality became somewhat liberalised and less censored. Some gynaecologists engaged in the preventive dissemination of information about STIs, mainly in response to a sharp peak in STIs since the collapse of the USSR. At the same time, most of them called for sexual abstinence before marriage as a way of protection against STIs and unwanted pregnancy. Medical discourse about sexuality still included the concept of moral purity inherited from the Soviet past (Rivkin-Fish 1999; Rivkin-Fish and Samokhvalov 2009).

In the 1990–2000s, there were ongoing debates on school sex education. The opponents stated that sex education implies the seduction of children and promotion of Western values. Sexual counselling at the time contained gender stereotyping and avoided any discussion of complicated topics including homosexuality (Snarskaya 2009). Although the subject of homosexuality began to emerge in public discourse in the 1990s, those mentions had little to do with educational information. Established in 1989, *SPEED-Info* (AIDS-Info), a monthly newspaper aimed at disseminating information about AIDS and safer sex, focused mainly on heterosexual relations, despite homosexuals being the predominant risk group.

In the small number of publications on homosexuality, the phenomenon was referred to as something forbidden, shameful, disgusting or, at least, obscene (Attwood 1996). Therefore, sex education in Russia was exclusively heteronormative.

The 2013 ban of the propaganda of non-traditional relations among minors, adopted as federal law, prevents the dissemination of any information about homosexuality in Russia. Besides, doctors and psychologists do not pursue the specific expertise of working with LGBTQ (lesbian, gay, bisexual, transgender and queer) people. In some cases, these specialists themselves appear to be a source of the spread of homophobia. They do not follow international standards and do not disseminate relevant information on sexuality. In such conditions, it is hard to obtain knowledge about sex or sexual health for queers.

Nonetheless, as in many countries, there are non-governmental organisations and communities that support people in Russia and work to prevent the spread of HIV. Some of these organisations work with men who have sex with men, so information about safer sex between men and their health care does circulate in some ways in Russia. Yet, even organisations working with marginalised groups seem to reproduce gender inequality by not channelling similar information for women who have sex with women. This issue is not exclusively typical for Russia: in the US, the UK and Australia the same problems exist (Richardson 2000; Power et al. 2009). Lesbians and bisexual women tend to be excluded from dominant discourses on sexual health risk. Furthermore, sex between women is often believed to be safe, as it does not involve potentially dangerous penetration and does not require contraception. Research on this problematic in Russia is limited, but some reports by the media and safe sex activists suggest that even doctors are often ignorant of the need to protect against STIs for lesbians.

Lesboseksprosvet practices of sex education for queer women have emerged online. One of the first in this respect was the blog 'Washed hands' (*Pomyla ruki*) on Telegram, a messenger and blogging platform, that was created by Sasha Kazantseva in 2017. The title of the blog reflects the irony in associating the safety of lesbian sex with the simple rules of hand hygiene. The blog has a limited number of followers: just over 44,000 as of 2023. In interviews, Kazantseva points to the lack of information on lesbian sex and health care in Russia as the major drive for her activities. As a social media influencer, she started running workshops and lectures in St. Petersburg and Moscow and pursued the offline format in other big cities in Russia. Due to Kazantseva's efforts, but not exclusively, lesbian sex education has developed in both virtual and real

Russian queer communities. In 2020, there were more than 30 blogs on different platforms (Instagram, Telegram, YouTube and so on) and about 20 YouTube videos that discuss lesbian sexuality and health in Russian. Although this may seem like a small number, this kind of information was largely inaccessible a few years ago. As the idea of women's sexual health become more accepted, more bloggers, who write about sex in general, bring up specific *lesbosexprosvet* issues. Notably, the number of people who blog about the subject is increasing. In the continuing absence of formal sex education and increasing censorship, independent bloggers and media assume the role of information providers and disseminators of good practices.

Kazantseva and other protagonists of *lesboseksprosvet* raise awareness of health care among queer women. On all platforms and in all formats, they channel advice on the means of barrier contraception that can be used for sexual contact between women and where they can be found. For example, since dental dams used as protection in oral sex are hard to find in Russian shops, they provide instructions of how to make them from a common latex condom and using sheets of latex instead. Health advice, such as regular visits to a gynaecologist and regular testing for STIs, is provided, together with details of lesbian-friendly gynaecologists. Yet physical safety in sex is not the only concern of *lesboseksprosvet*. It also promotes psychological safety and mental health agenda, which include the necessity of sexual consent, discussion of one's sexual preferences with partners and possible risks. Thus, creating a language to describe various sexual techniques and methods of masturbation used by queer women is an essential part of this novel discourse.

In addition to immediate sex education, the goals of *lesboseksprosvet* are to enhance visibility of queer women, legitimise lesbian sexuality and gradually expand the discursive space allotted to them, even if these goals are not expressed in those very words by the protagonists. This is achieved through the conceptualisation of lesbian sex as part of the medical discourse. The case of *lesboseksprosvet* may be considered as self-medicalisation by subjects excluded from medical control, a bottom-up initiative for those who seek to become objects of health care (Conrad 2007). Therefore, the medicalisation of sexual relations between women appears to be a way of normalising them.

Importantly, the grassroots initiatives of *lesboseksprosvet* create multiple platforms and network-based alternatives to official medicine where queer women can solve their health problems and get information about lesbian sexuality without feeling excluded. Some LGBT and feminist organisations, independent media and even private medical clinics support initiatives related to *lesboseksprosvet*, but it falls short of institutional support and largely confined to a grassroots solidarity in resisting the predominant climate of ignorance and homophobia.

2.10 **New normal** (Global)

Dmitry Kurnosov
Faculty of Law, University of Helsinki, Finland
and
Anna Varfolomeeva
Helsinki Institute of Sustainability Science, University of Helsinki, Finland

The *new normal* is an umbrella term that signifies a profound shift in familiar routines. It is widespread in journalism and the academic world and denotes a variety of societal changes. During the COVID-19 pandemic, the term acquired new popularity and a degree of formal recognition. Authorities, businesses and the media frequently used the term *the new normal* to contextualise the impact of the mitigation measures (such as, for example, mask mandates or social distancing) on the usual routines and practices. The term gained popularity after the 2007–9 global financial crisis, to describe the challenges of the post-crisis landscape, including structural unemployment, growing public debt and a much greater influence of politics on economics (El-Erian 2010) or, in a more upbeat way, to describe the wake of the financial crisis as an environment rich in possibilities for company executives (Davis 2009).

The term *the new normal* has been widely used in academic publications. For example, in political science it is relied upon to reflect shifts in consumption (Etzioni 2014). In environmental studies, the term is applied to describe the higher average summer temperatures due to climate change (Camargo and Seth 2016). Journalists use *the new normal* to describe events ranging from a terrorist attack to a sports team starting a season without a long-term coach (Dufresne 2012; *The Economist* 2016). The term has also been used in popular culture. The Australian rock band Cog named its 2005 album *The New Normal*, reflecting on the changed social environment in the wake of the 9/11 attacks in the United States in 2001. The American sitcom *The New Normal* that aired between 2012 and 2013 followed a fictional gay couple and the surrogate mother of their child in Los Angeles and alluded that the alternatives to the conventional nuclear family were becoming more mainstream.

Some argued that *the new normal* could integrate the quintessential human experiences such as pain and struggle into dominating perceptions of 'normality' (Maisel 2013). Yet the versatility of the notion led others to dismiss it as useless, a 'linguistic equivalent of a shrug, merely another way of saying, "Whaddaya gonna do?"' (Pepper Trail 2018), or as able to 'reduce a couple of words to a vacuous cliché' (Cox 2020).

During the COVID-19 pandemic, the term *the new normal* took hold almost instantly. Its ambiguity seemed to perfectly fit the cataclysmic event of yet unknown duration. However, the primary use of the term during the pandemic shifted. It was mainly used to describe the realities shaped by a new multitude of rules and policies adopted by public authorities and businesses. The contexts of the pandemic use of *the new normal* vary between countries. In Spain, it is deeply integrated into the official discourse. In April 2020, the Spanish Government adopted 'The Plan of Transition to the New Normal' (Plan Para La Transicion Hasta La Nueva Normalidad). Its eventual goal was to establish 'the main parameters and instruments for the adaptation of society as a whole to the new normality'. Specifically, the plan envisaged capacity restrictions in all types of public establishments (La Moncloa 2020). A year later, the Spanish Parliament adopted a permanent law for managing the pandemic and referred to it as 'The Law of New Normal' (Ley de Nueva Normalidad). In contrast, in Russia under almost no circumstances was the term (*novaia normal'nost'*), or an analogous expression, used in official contexts. A possible explanation is the difference in legal frameworks for pandemic management used in Spain and Russia. While the former moved from the formal state of emergency to ordinary legislation, the latter maintained an ambiguous semi-emergency regime – the state of 'high alert' (Karaseva 2020).

Escalating change can lead to 'more of the same' by reinforcing the existing configurations (Højer et al. 2018). For instance, a conflict over religious symbols can entrench the prevailing sentiments, be it towards secularism or immigrants (Højer et al. 2018). Similarly, *the new normal* may help strengthen existing inequalities and therefore become the *not-so-new normal.* For instance, the 'normalisation' of LGBTQ characters in *The New Normal* sitcom may have reinforced the stereotyping of sexual minorities (Byrd Jr. 2014). Responses to school shootings in the United States often establish the *not-so-new normal* – new routines provide psychological comfort but do not help to resolve the problem (Fogel 2018).

The COVID-19 pandemic might follow a similar trajectory and strengthen existing societal divides (Kurnosov and Varfolomeeva 2020). Many early indicators suggest that the COVID-19 crisis has reinforced hierarchies and inequalities. Some of the indicators correspond to the consequences of the public health responses to earlier epidemic outbreaks. In 2003, the Canadian city of Toronto quarantined more than fifteen thousand people to prevent the spread of the SARS virus. Subsequent surveys indicated that many quarantined residents believed they did not receive sufficient information about their health condition and the possible dangers of the virus. Some of those quarantined displayed symptoms of depression and post-traumatic stress disorder (Hawryluck et al. 2004). The early stages of the COVID-19 pandemic saw a similarly forceful use of quarantines that resulted in feelings of extreme isolation and in blurring the lines between care and control (Varfolomeeva 2020). In some jurisdictions (such as Mainland China, Singapore and Russia before April 2020) all people testing positive for COVID-19 were hospitalised, while in others (including Australia, New Zealand and Mongolia) all foreign arrivals were placed in mandatory institutional isolation. For COVID-19 patients, the sense of isolation was exacerbated by the lack of information about the disease and its treatment (Kurnosov and Varfolomeeva 2020). Information shortages in health institutions resembled a conscious tactic to obscure the limited knowledge of the virus and maintain a doctor-patient hierarchy.

Some official responses to the COVID-19 pandemic were termed 'hygiene theatre' (Thompson 2020) and also bear the hallmarks of the *not-so-new normal*. 'Hygiene theatre' denotes actions that are visible to the public but have little to do with actual disease control, such as spraying subway stations and streets with disinfectants, conducting temperature checks and introducing glove mandates. These measures may establish psychological comfort as they are easily noticeable. However, they waste scarce resources and obscure vital public health messages by distracting citizens from more efficient ways to combat the virus (Thompson 2020, 2021). Such measures are deemed ineffective by public health experts, yet continue to be maintained. Even more problematic are situations when the authorities target minority groups to promote public health measures, such as by restricting immigration (Davies 2020). For example, the United States government (under both Trump and Biden administrations) has relied on epidemic control as the basis for denying asylum-seekers entry into the country. At the same time, the United States did not restrict any other type of immigration (American Immigration Council 2021). Enforcing measures that are driven by public opinion strengthens existing societal inequalities.

The experiences of lockdowns and related pandemic management measures depend on one's health, age and socioeconomic status. People with chronic disease encountered a reduced access to health care for non-COVID-19 conditions during the pandemic (Bambra et al. 2020; Mansfield et al. 2021). The switch to online education was found to more likely put at a disadvantage underprivileged students who experienced a larger decline in learning in comparison to their peers (Di Pietro et al. 2020). Children and adolescents with lower economic status or with a migration background and limited living space have experienced significant challenges to their mental health during lockdowns (Ravens-Sieberer et al. 2021). In addition, lockdown restrictions increased the risk of gender-based violence due to the mental effects of isolation and barriers to victim support (Acosta 2020, Bambra et al. 2020).

Inequalities intensified during the rollout of COVID-19 vaccines. At the beginning of November 2021, over half of the world population had received at least one vaccination dose (Mathieu et al. 2021). However, 82 per cent of vaccines were distributed to high- and upper-middle-income countries (Furlong and Deutsch 2021). Only 4 per cent of the population in low-income countries received a vaccination by that time (Mathieu et al. 2021). Vaccines themselves are valued unequally, in a way that reflects the disparities between countries. Richer countries donated vaccines they deemed as less safe to poorer countries (Zinets 2021). The same vaccine, like the Oxford-AstraZeneca, was officially recognised in some European Union countries only if it was produced in Europe rather than in the AstraZeneca factory in India (Euractiv 2021).

Finally, the COVID-19 pandemic had uneven effects that depended on ethnicity, wealth and gender, for example, the stigmatisation of ethnic minorities (Li and Nicholson 2021), the growth in income disparities (Palomino et al. 2020) and an exacerbation of gender inequality (Fisher and Ryan 2021). These, too, produced a state of *not-so-new normal*.

Bibliography to Chapter 2

Introduction: a psychological perspective on socialisation
Thomas Tsichtis

Bourdieu, P. 2008 [1977]. *Outline of a Theory of Practice*. Cambridge: Cambridge University Press.
Cole, M. 1998. *Cultural Psychology: A Once and Future Discipline*. Cambridge, MA: Harvard University Press.
Giddens, A. 2020. 'Modernity and Self-identity: Self and Society in the Late Modern Age'. In *The New Social Theory Reader*, edited by S. Seldman and C. A. Alexander, 354–61. London: Routledge.
Gillespie, A. and Cornish, F. 2010. 'Intersubjectivity: Towards a Dialogical Analysis'. *Journal for the Theory of Social Behaviour* 40(1): 19–46.

Gillespie, A. and Zittoun, T. 2010. 'Using Resources: Conceptualizing the Mediation and Reflective Use of Tools and Signs'. *Culture & Psychology* 16(1): 37–62.

Gillespie, A. and Martin, J. 2014. 'Position Exchange Theory: A Socio-material Basis for Discursive and Psychological Positioning'. *New Ideas in Psychology* 32: 73–9.

Howarth, C. 2006. 'A Social Representation Is Not a Quiet Thing: Exploring the Critical Potential of Social Representations Theory'. *British Journal of Social Psychology* 45(1): 65–86.

Howarth, C., Campbell, C., Cornish, F., Franks, B., Garcia-Lorenzo, L., Gillespie, A., Gleibs, I., Gonvales-Portelinha, I., Jovchelovitch, S., Lahlou, S., Mannell, J., Reader, T. and Tennant, C. 2013. 'Insights from Societal Psychology: The Contextual Politics of Change'. *Journal of Social and Political Psychology* 1(1): 364–84.

Howarth, C., Cornish, F. and Gillespie, A. 2015. 'Making Community: Diversity, Movement and Interdependence'. In *The Cambridge Handbook of Social Representations*, edited by G. E. Sammut, E. Andreouli, G. Gaskell and J. Valsiner, 179–90. Cambridge: Cambridge University Press.

Jovchelovitch, S. 2008. 'The Rehabilitation of Common Sense: Social Representations, Science and Cognitive Polyphasia'. *Journal for the Theory of Social Behaviour* 38(4): 431–48.

Jovchelovitch, S. 2019. *Knowledge in Context: Representations, Community and Culture*. 2nd ed. London: Routledge.

Linell, P. 2009. *Rethinking Language, Mind, and World Dialogically*. Charlotte, NC: Information Age Publishing.

Marková, I. 2016. *The Dialogical Mind: Common Sense and Ethics*. Cambridge: Cambridge University Press.

Power, S. A., Zittoun, T., Akkerman, S., Wagoner, B., Cabra, M., Cornish, F., Hawlina, H., Heasman, B., Mahendran, K., Psaltis, C. and Rajala, A. 2023. 'Social Psychology of and for World-making'. *Personality and Social Psychology Review*, 1–15.

Rosa, A. and Valsiner, J. 2018. 'The Human Psyche Lives in Semiospheres'. In *The Cambridge Handbook of Sociocultural Psychology*, 2nd ed., edited by A. Rosa and J. Valsiner, 1–22. Cambridge: Cambridge University Press.

Vygotsky, L. S. 1978. *Mind in Society: The Development of Higher Psychological Processes*. Cambridge, Massachusetts, London: Harvard University Press.

Zerubavel, E. 1985. *Hidden Rhythms: Schedules and Calendars in Social Life*. Berkley, CA: University of California Press.

Zerubavel, E. 2015. *Hidden in Plain Sight: The Social Structure of Irrelevance*. New York: Oxford University Press.

Zittoun, T. and Gillespie, A. 2015a. 'Internalization: How Culture Becomes Mind'. *Culture & Psychology* 21(4): 477–91.

Zittoun, T. and Gillespie, A. 2015b. 'Body and Mind Moving between Contexts'. In *Integrating Experiences: Body and Mind Moving Between Contexts*, edited by B. Wagoner, N. Chaudhary and P. Hviid, 3–49. Charlotte, NC: Information Age Publishing.

Zittoun, T. and Gillespie, A. 2016. 'Imagination: Creating Alternatives in Everyday Life'. In *The Palgrave Handbook of Creativity and Culture Research*, edited by V. P. Glăveanu, 225–42. London: Palgrave Macmillan.

Zittoun, T., Vedeler, D., Salgago, J. and Valsiner, J. 2013. *Human Development in the Life Course: Melodies of Living*. Cambridge: Cambridge University Press.

2.1 *Les rallyes mondains* (France)
Alexandre Lieure

Bourdieu P. 1982. Les Rites Comme Actes D'institution. In: *Actes De La Recherche En Sciences Sociales* 43(1): 58–63. Rites et fétiches.

Bourdieu, P. 1986. 'The Forms of Capital'. In *Handbook of Theory and Research for the Sociology of Education*, edited by J. Richardson, 241–58. New York: Greenwood.

Gallien, A. 2005a. *Baisemains et Mocassins*. Arte Documentary. Part 1. www.dailymotion.com/video/xblugg_baisemains-et-mocassins-montage-1_school

Gallien, A. 2005b. *Baisemains et Mocassins*. Arte Documentary. Part 2. www.dailymotion.com/video/xblupy_baisemains-et-mocassins-montage-2_school

Pinçon, M. and Pinçon-Charlot, M. 2007. *Les Ghettos du Gotta: Comment la Bourgeoisie Defend ses Espaces*, Paris: Editions du Seuil.
Pinçon, M. and Pinçon-Charlot, M. 2009. *Sociologie de la Bourgeoisie*. Paris: La Découverte.

2.2 *Mianzi* (China)
Long Zhang

Chan, K. L. 2006. 'The Chinese Concept of Face and Violence against Women'. *International Social Work* 49(1): 65–73.
Goffman, E. 1972. 'On Face-Work: An Analysis of Ritual Elements in Social Interaction'. In *Interaction Ritual: Essays on Face-to-face Behaviour*, edited by E. Goffman, 5–46. London: The Penguin Press.
Hu, H. C. 1944. 'The Chinese Concepts of "Face"'. *American Anthropologist* 46(1): 45–64.
Hwang, K. 1987. 'Face and Favor: The Chinese Power Game'. *American Journal of Sociology* 92(4): 944–74.
Kinnison, L. Q. 2017. 'Power, Integrity, and Mask – An Attempt to Disentangle the Chinese Face Concept'. *Journal of Pragmatics* 114: 32–48.
Kipnis, A. B. 1995. 'Face: An Adaptable Discourse of Social Surfaces'. *Positions* 3(1): 119–48.
Li, W. D. and Shang, W. J. 2012. 'Nanhai Pianhao Zuowei Yizhong Shengyu Wenhua de Shengchan yu Zaishengchan'. *Funv Yanjiu Luncong* 110(2): 36–43.
Qi, X. 2011. 'Face: A Chinese Concept in a Global Sociology'. *Journal of Sociology* 47(3): 279–96.
Vorhauser-Smith, Sylvia. 2012. 'When Your Chinese Employees Lose Face, You Lose Them'. *Forbes*. 29 May. www.forbes.com/sites/sylviavorhausersmith/2012/05/29/when-your-chinese-employees-lose-face-you-lose-them-2/?sh=2e26f92964ba
Wang, S. N., Jia, Y. J. and Tian, C. 2020. 'Yi Caili: Lun Nongcun Caili Xingcheng Jizhi Zhong de Daode Qianruxing–Jiyu Gansu L Xian de Anli Fenxi'. *Shehui* 40(1): 1–24.
Zhai, X. W. 2013. *Renqing, Mianzi yu Quanli de Zaishengchan*. Beijing: Beijing Daxue Chubanshe.

2.3 *Runs* (Nigeria)
Olumuyiwa K. Ojo and Olusola Ayandele

Adebayo, B. and Busari, S. 2018. 'Lecturer Demanded Sex in Return for Better Grades, Nigerian Student Says'. CNN International+. 23 May. http://edition.cnn.com/2018/05/23/africa/sex-for-grades-university-nigeria-intl
Adegoju, A. 2007. 'Corruption of Language and Nigeria's Debased Value System'. *Nebula* 4(3): 339–56.
Alagbe, J. 2016. 'School Where Prostitutes Assist Male Students to Get Marks'. *Punch*. 9 April. www.punchng.com/school-where-prostitutes-assist-male-students-to-get-marks/
Aribisala, F. 2014. 'Nigerian Politicians Are Thieves, But They Are Not Corrupt'. *Vanguard*. 22 July. www.vanguardngr.com/2014/07/nigerian-politicians-thieves-corrupt/
Auwal, N. 1987. 'A Hausa Vocabulary on Corruption and Political Oppression'. *Corruption and Reform* 2(3): 293–6.
Denisova-Schmidt, E. 2017. 'The Challenges of Academic Integrity in Higher Education: Current Trends and Outlook'. In *CIHE Perspectives*, Vol. 5. Boston: Boston College.
Ekundayo, S. B. 2013. 'Lexico-Semantic "Intraference" in Educated Nigerian English (ENE)'. *International Journal of English Linguistics* 3(6): 17–30.
Kigotho, W. 2004. *Nigerian University Revokes Thousands of Diplomas in Crackdown on Academic Fraud*. The Chronicle of Higher Education, 1 November. www.utexas.edu/conferences/africa/ads/19.html
Mordi, K. 2019. '"Sex for Grades": Undercover in West African Universities'. BBC. 7 October. www.bbc.com/news/av/world-africa-49907376/sex-for-grades-undercovers-in-west-african-universities
Ojebode, A., Togunde, D. and Adelakun, A. 2010. 'Beyond Money and Gifts: Social Capital as Motivation for Cross Generational Dating among Tertiary School Female Students in South West Nigeria'. *The International Journal of Interdisciplinary Social Sciences* 4: 169–82.

Ojo, O. K., Ayandele, O. and Egbeleye, S. A. 2020. 'Euphemisms of Corruption among Students of Higher Institutions in South West Nigeria'. *Journal of Language and Education* 6(1): 72–82.

Oko, S. U. and Adie, R. I. 2016. 'Examination Malpractice: Causes, Effects and Possible Ways of Curbing the Menace. A Study of Cross River University of Technology'. *International Journal of Managerial Studies and Research* 4(1): 59–65.

Okoli, C. E. 1997. 'Examination Malpractice, the Bone of Our Society'. In *Emergent Issues in Nigeria Education*, edited by A. Ejiogu and K. Alani, 343–8. Lagos: Unilag Consult Publication.

Okorie, M. M. and Bamidele, O. 2016. 'Language and Class Resistance in Nigeria: A Foucauldian Perspective'. *Africology: The Journal of Pan African Studies* 9(6): 4–15.

Yagboyaju, D. A. 2018. 'Egunje (Nigeria)'. In *The Global Encyclopaedia of Informality, Volume 2: Understanding Social and Cultural Complexity*, Vol. 2, edited by A. Ledeneva et al., 147–51. London: UCL Press.

2.4 *Neijuan* (China)
Haoxuan Mao

Bai, M. 2019. 'Jiwa for All, No Escape from the "High Screening" Game'. *Contemporary Workers* 11.

BBC. 2021. 'Young Chinese People Struggling Between "Neijuan" and "Tangping"'. 2 June. www.bbc.com/zhongwen/simp/chinese-news-57304453

BBC Korean. 2021. 'Inner circle: "Even if You Work Hard, You Can't Succeed"' Chinese Youth Burnout'. 15 June. www.bbc.com/korean/international-57451262

China Daily. 2018. 'The Young People Who Are Struggling Today, How Many Opportunities Are There for Them in the Future?' 8 August. http://china.chinadaily.com.cn/2018-08/08/content_36730490.htm

China Global Television Network. 2020a. 'Behind "996" Schedule: Work to a Better Life, Not ICU'. 16 April. https://news.cgtn.com/news/3d3d774d336b544f33457a6333566d54/index.html

China Global Television Network. 2020b. '"Involution": The Anxieties of Our Time Summed Up in One Word'. 4 December. https://reurl.cc/yrkGY2

Financial Times. 2021. '"Obedience and Fear": The Brutal Working Conditions Behind China's Tech Boom'. 9 June. www.ft.com/content/37e9e0c6-952e-4fcf-9318-786ebd5e3a3d

Geertz, C. 1963. *Agricultural Involution: The Processes of Ecological Change in Indonesia*. Berkeley: University of California Press.

Huang, P. 1990. *The Peasant Family and Rural Development in the Yangzi Delta, 1350–1988*. Stanford: Stanford University Press.

Li, Y. 2021. 'A Study on the Choice of Early Childhood Training Institutions by Parents of Pre-school Children in the Context of the *Jiwa*'. *Journal of Heilongjiang Institute of Teacher Development* 40(11).

Luo, R., Tamis-LeMonda, C. S. and Song, L. 2013. 'Chinese Parents' Goals and Practices in Early Childhood'. *Early Childhood Research Quarterly* 28(4), 843–57.

Nicovideo News. 2020. 'Korean Society Seen from China "There is Absurd Competition and Exhaustion Inside"'. 29 December. https://news.nicovideo.jp/watch/nw8718877

Sun, C. 2008. 'Analyzing the Phenomenon of Difficult Employment of High Education and the Formation of the Trend of Pursuing High Education'. *Consumerist* (8): 236–7.

Wang, J. J. 2020. 'How Managers Use Culture and Controls to Impose a "996" Work Regime in China That Constitutes Modern Slavery'. *Accounting & Finance* 60(4): 4331–59.

Wang, X. L., Bernas, R. and Eberhard, P. 2012. 'When a Lie is Not a Lie: Understanding Chinese Working-class Mothers' Moral Teaching and Moral Conduct'. *Social Development* 21(1): 68–87.

World Bank. 2021. GDP Growth (China, Japan, Korea); Population, Total (China, Japan, Korea). https://data.worldbank.org/indicator/

Xinhua Net. 2020. 'University Students' "Neijuan": Competition or Internal Conflict?'. 9 November. www.xinhuanet.com/2020-11/09/c_1126713666.htm

Xinhua Net. 2021. 'Where Is the Sense of Justice When It Is Shameful to "Tangping"?' 20 May. www.xinhuanet.com/comments/2021-05/20/c_1127467232.htm

2.5 *Słoiki* (Poland)
Mathilde Ollivo

Bachórz, A. 2018. '"It's Just a Constant Exchange of Containers": Distribution of Home-made Food as an Element of Polish Family Lifestyles'. Working Paper. *Instytut Archeologii i Etnologii Polskiej Akademii Nauk*.
Dunn, E. 2004. *Privatizing Poland: Baby Food, Big Business, and the Remaking of Labor*. New York: Cornell University Press.
Mauss, M. 1924. 'Essai sur le Don. Forme Et Raison De L'échange Dans Les Sociétés Archaïques'. *L'Année Sociologique* 2: 1.
Mroczkowska, J. 2019. 'Pork Politics: The Scales of Home-made Food in Eastern Poland'. *Appetite* 140: 223–30.
Pifczyk, S. 2015. 'Sprawdziliśmy, Skąd Pochodzą Warszawskie 'Słoik'. 29 June. https://biqdata.wyborcza.pl/biqdata/7,159116,22152976,sprawdzilismy-skad-pochodza-warszawskie-sloiki.html
Podkalicka, A. M. and Potkanska, D. 2015. 'On the Meaning of Popular Representations of Low-Budget Urban Practices in Poland: The Case of Cultural Translation', *Ephemera* 15(1): 95–119.
Stenning, A., Rochovska, A., Smith, A. and Świątek, S. 2010. *Domesticating Neoliberalism: Spaces of Economic Practice and Social Reproduction in Post-socialist Cities*. Hoboken: Blackwell Publishing.

2.6 *Pokhorony okurka* (Russia and USSR)
Kirill Melnikov

Bannikov, K. 2002. *The Anthropology of Regimented Societies. Relations of Dominance in Social Interactions among Russian Soldiers*. Moscow: Izdatel'stvo Nauka.
Foucault, M. 1979. *Discipline and Punish: The Birth of the Prison*. New York: Vintage Books.
Goffman, E. 1961. *Asylums: Essays on the Social Situation of Mental Patients and Other Inmates*. New York: Anchor Books.
Heckathorn, D. 1988. 'Collective Sanctions and the Creation of Prisoner's Dilemma Norms'. *American Journal of Sociology* 94: 535–62.
Konsul'tant Plus. 2007. 'Distsiplinarnyi Ustav Vooruzhennykh Sil Rossiiskoi Federatsii'. 10 November. www.consultant.ru/document/cons_doc_LAW_72806/c401b0ba6064c7e607a9ea1b9aeb05e4d7e20fdf/
Ledeneva, A. 2006. *How Russia Really Works: The Informal Practices That Shaped Post-Soviet Politics and Business*. Cornell University Press.
Manoilin, V. 2004. *Bazirovanie VMF SSSR*. St. Petersburg: Neva.
Soler, K. 2015. 'The Failures of Mass Punishment'. U.S. Patriot Tactical. 17 June. https://blog.uspatriottactical.com/the-failures-of-mass-punishment/
Tutolmin, S. 2007. 'Dedovshchina: Retrospektiva', Fond Imperskogo Vozrozhdeniia. 22 October. https://web.archive.org/web/20190603034650/www.fondiv.ru/articles/3/189/
Zirtran. 2014. 'Pokhorony Bychka v Armii'. Pikabu.ru. 26 March. https://pikabu.ru/story/pokhoronyi_byichka_v_armii_2111061

2.7 *Hikikomori* (Japan)
Taiga Kambara

Borocz, J. 2000. 'Informality Rules'. *East European Politics and Societies* 14(2): 348–80.
Coser, R. L. 1966. 'Role Distance, Sociological Ambivalence, and Transitional Status Systems'. *American Journal of Sociology* 72: 173–87.
Dannefer, D. 1984. 'Adult Development and Social Theory: A Paradigmatic Reappraisal', *American Sociological Review* 49, 100–11.
Futagami, N. 2013. *Family Construction of NEET and Hikikomori*. Ichikawa: NPO New Start.

Habermas, J. 1987. *The Theory of Communicative Action, Lifeworld and System: A Functionalist Critique*, Vol. 2. Cambridge: Polity Press.
Helmke, G. and Levitsky, S. 2004. 'Informal Institutions and Comparative Politics: A Research Agenda', *Perspectives on Politics* 2(4): 725–40.
Iriya, H. 2010. 'Research on Hikikomori Youth: A Case Study'. *University of Tokyo Graduate School of Medicine* (1): 23–4.
Katsura, R. and Sugiyama, A. 2019. 'The Relationship between Psychological Withdrawal and Social Activity (1): Generation Comparison of Psychological Withdrawal and Interpersonal Communication'. *Kawaura Gakuen Women's University* 258.
Kawakami, N. 2010. 'The Reality and Related Factors of the "Hikikomori"'. *World Mental Health Japan Survey*. University of Tokyo, Graduate School of Medicine.
Marshall, V. W. 1995. 'The Micro-Macro Link in the Sociology of Aging'. In *Images of Aging in Western Societies: Proceedings of the 2nd Images of Aging Conference*, edited by C. Hummel and C. Lalive D'Epinay, 337–71.

2.8 *Gaser* (Serbia and the Western Balkans)
Barbara Frey and Dragana Mrvoš

BGJargon. 2022. 'гъзар'. www.bgjargon.com/word/meaning/%D0%B3%D1%8A%D0%B7%D0%B0%D1%80
Bondisimo. 2020. 'GASnaMAX'. YouTube. www.youtube.com/watch?v=8H2ODxMMTlo
Bugarin, A. 2021. 'Gaseri – Neautentična Omladinska Potkultura'. *Voice*. 23 June. https://voice.org.rs/gaseri-neautenticna-omladinska-potkultura/
Costescu, E. 2013. 'Brave New Virtual Worlds – A Socio-Historical Approach'. *Research and Science Today* 5(1): 256–66.
de Lacey, A. 2020. '"Wot do u call it? Doofdoof": Articulations of Glocality in Australian Grime Music'. *Global Hip Hop Studies* 1(1): 115–41.
Dragojlo, S. 2019. 'Trep Cajke: Kapitalistički Realizam'. *Bilten: Regionalni Portal*. 6 January. www.bilten.org/?p=28232#
Dumnić Vilotijević, M. 2020. 'The Balkans of the Balkans: The Meaning of Autobalkanism in Regional Popular Music'. *Arts* 9(2): 70. https://doi.org/10.3390/arts9020070
Gracheva, A. S., Ivanina, E. O., Markov, Y. and Gorbunova, E. 2018. 'Search for Familiar and Dangerous: Not Seeing Gopnik in the Crowd'. Higher School of Economics Research Paper No. WP BRP 96/PSY/2018. https://papers.ssrn.com/sol3/papers.cfm?abstract_id=3269227
Jørgensen, M. and Phillips, L. 2002. *Discourse Analysis as Theory and Method*. London: SAGE.
Jovanović, B. 2019. 'Diskriminacija Među Mladima: Ili Si Fušer Ili Si Gaser'. *Novosti*. 17 October. www.novosti.rs/vesti/lifestyle.303.html:824154-Diskriminacija-medju-mladima-Ili-si-fuser-ili-si-gaser
Kaluža, J. 2018. 'Reality of Trap: Trap Music and Its Emancipatory Potential'. *IAFOR Journal of Media, Communication & Film* 5(1): 23–42.
Kaluža, J. 2021. 'Importer, Authentifier, Revendre. La Trap Music Dans Les Balkans'. In: *Trap: Rap, Drogue, Argent, Survie*, edited by G. Heuguet and E. Menu, 157–75. Paris: Audimat Éditions.
Lill, A. 2014. 'From Local to Global: The Evolution of Musical Play in Secondary Schools'. *International Journal of Play* 3(3): 251–66.
Martin, G. 2009. 'Subculture, Style, Chavs and Consumer Capitalism: Towards A Critical Cultural Criminology of Youth'. *Crime, Media, Culture* 5(2): 123–45.
Mimi Mercedez (Feat. Rimski). 2017. 'Samo Keš'. YouTube. www.youtube.com/watch?v=ZI2Mo26kw4U
Rosić, B. 2020. 'Ko Su "Gaseri": Simboli Uličnih Demonstracija Od Džoa Bageriste Do Neke Nove Dece'. *Nedeljnik*. 28 December. www.nedeljnik.rs/ko-su-gaseri-simboli-ulicnih-demonstracija-od-dzoa-bageriste-do-neke-nove-dece/
Statistical Office of the Republic of Serbia. 2020. *Poverty and Social Inequality*. www.stat.gov.rs/en-us/vesti/20211015-siromastvo-i-socijalna-nejednakost-2020/?s=0102
The Social Inclusion and Poverty Reduction Unit of the Government of the Republic of Serbia (SIPRU). 2018. *Inequality*. http://socijalnoukljucivanje.gov.rs/en/social-inclusion-in-rs/poverty-statistics/inequality/

2.9 *Lesboseksprosvet* (Russia)
Polina Kislitsyna

Attwood, L. 1996. 'Young People, Sex and Sexual Identity'. In *Gender, Generation and Identity in Contemporary Russia*, edited by H. Pilkington, 103–28. London: Routledge.

Conrad, P. 2007. *The Medicalization of Society*. Baltimore: Johns Hopkins University Press.

Power, J., McNair, R. and Carr, S. 2009. 'Absent Sexual Scripts: Lesbian and Bisexual Women's Knowledge, Attitudes and Action Regarding Safer Sex and Sexual Health Information'. *Culture, Health & Sexuality* 11(1): 67–81.

Richardson, D. 2000. 'The Social Construction of Immunity: HIV Risk Perception and Prevention among Lesbians and Bisexual Women'. *Culture, Health & Sexuality* 2(1): 33–49.

Rivkin-Fish, M. 1999. 'Sexuality Education in Russia: Defining Pleasure and Danger for a Fledgling Democratic Society'. *Social Science & Medicine* 49(6): 801–14.

Rivkin-Fish M. and Samokhvalov V. 2009. 'Seksual'noe Obrazovanie ш Razvitie Lichnosti: Pereosmyslenie Professional'noy Vlasti' [Sexual Education and Personal Development: Rethinking of Professional Power]. In *Zdorov'e i Doverie: Gendernyi Podkhod k Reproduktivnoy Meditsine* [Health and Trust: Gender Approach to Reproductive Medicine], edited by E. Zdravomyslova and A. Temkina, 21–50. St. Petersburg: EU SP Press.

Rotkirch, A. 2000. *The Man Question: Loves and Lives in Late 20th Century Russia*. Helsinki: University of Helsinki, Department of Social Policy.

Snarskaya, O. 2009. 'Seksual'noe Obrazovanie Kak Sfera Proizvodstva Gendernykh Razlichiy I Kostruirovaniya Predstavleniy O "Natsii"' [Sexual Education as Reproduction of Gender Differences and Construction of Conceptions of 'Nation']. In *Zdorov'e i Doverie: Gendernyi Podkhod k Reproduktivnoy Meditsine* [Health and Trust: Gender Approach to Reproductive Medicine], edited by E. Zdravomyslova and A. Temkina, 51–89. St. Petersburg: EU SP Press.

Temkina, A. 2009. 'Polovoe Prosveshchenie Kak Moral'noe Vospitanie (Pozdnesovetskie diskursy o seksualnosti)' [Sexual Education as Moral Upbringing (Late Soviet Discourses of Sexuality)]. In *Zdorov'e i Doverie: Gendernyi Podkhod k Reproduktivnoy Meditsine* [Health and Trust: Gender Approach to Reproductive Medicine], edited by E. Zdravomyslova and A. Temkina, 90–107. St. Petersburg: EU SP Press.

2.10 *New normal* (Global)
Dmitry Kurnosov and Anna Varfolomeeva

Acosta, M. 2020. 'Gender-based Violence during the Pandemic and Lockdown'. *Spanish Journal of Legal Medicine* 46(3): 139–45.

American Immigration Council. 2021. 'A Guide to Title 42 Expulsions at the Border'. American Immigration Council. 15 October. www.americanimmigrationcouncil.org/research/guide-title-42-expulsions-border

Bambra, C., Riordan, R., Ford, J. and Matthews, F. 2020. 'The COVID-19 Pandemic and Health Inequalities'. *Journal of Epidemiology Community Health* 74(11): 964–8.

Byrd Jr., R. 2014. *The (Not so) New Normal: A Queer Critique of LGBT Characters and Themes in Primetime Network Television Situational Comedies*. PhD Thesis, University of Southern Mississippi. https://aquila.usm.edu/dissertations/757/

Camargo, S. and Seth, A. 2016. 'Hottest Summers the New Normal'. *Environmental Research Letters* 11(8).

Cox, J. 2020. 'COVID-19 and the Corporate Cliché: Why We Need to Stop Talking about "The New Normal"'. *Forbes*, 22 April. www.forbes.com/sites/josiecox/2020/04/22/covid-19-corporate-cliche-why-we-need-to-stop-talking-about-the-new-normal/

Davies, G. 2020. 'Does Evidence-Based EU Law Survive the COVID-19 Pandemic? Considering the Status in EU Law of Lockdown Measures Which Affect Free Movement'. *Frontiers in Human Dynamics* 2.

Davis, I. 2009. 'The New Normal'. McKinsey & Company. 1 March. www.mckinsey.com/business-functions/strategy-and-corporate-finance/our-insights/the-new-normal

Di Pietro, G., Biagi, F., Costa, P., Karpiński, Z. and Mazza, J. 2020. 'The Likely Impact of COVID-19 on Education: Reflections based on the Existing Literature and Recent International Datasets'.

Publications Office of the European Union. https://publications.jrc.ec.europa.eu/repository/handle/JRC121071

Dufresne, C. 2012. 'Penn State Football: Without Joe Paterno, a "New Normal"'. *The Boston Herald*. 31 August. www.bostonherald.com/2012/08/31/penn-state-football-without-joe-paterno-a-new-normal/

El-Erian M. 2010. 'Navigating the New Normal in Industrial Countries'. IMF, 10 October. www.imf.org/en/News/Articles/2015/09/28/04/53/sp101010

Etzioni, A. 2014. 'Politics and Culture in an Age of Austerity'. *International Journal of Politics, Culture and Society* 27(4): 389–407.

Euractiv. 2021. 'Indian-made Astrazeneca Vaccine Not Recognised in EU'. *Euractiv*, 26 July. www.euractiv.com/section/politics/short_news/indian-made-astrazeneca-vaccine-not-recognised-in-eu/

Fisher, A. and Ryan, M. 2021. 'Gender Inequalities during COVID-19'. *Group Processes and Intergroup Relations* 24(2): 237–45.

Fogel, S. 2018. 'The Not-So-New Normal'. *Families in Society: The Journal of Contemporary Social Services* 99(2): 91–2.

Furlong, A. and Deutsch, J. 2021. 'Rich Countries Look to Third Shots, Poor Countries to Half-doses in "Two-track" Pandemic'. *Politico*, 24 August. www.politico.eu/article/coronavirus-vaccine-booster-shots-two-track-pandemic/

Hawryluck, L., Gold, W., Robinson, S., Pogorski, S., Galea, S. and Styra, R. 2004. 'SARS Control and Psychological Effects of Quarantine, Toronto, Canada'. *Emerging Infectious Diseases* 10(7): 1206–12.

Højer, L., Kublitz, A., Puri, S. and Bandak, A. 2018. 'Escalations: Theorizing Sudden Accelerating Change'. *Anthropological Theory* 18(1): 36–58.

Karaseva, A. 2020. 'The Legal Void and COVID-19 Governance'. *Social Anthropology* 28(2): 294–5.

Kurnosov, D. and Varfolomeeva, A. 2020. 'Constructing the Not-So-New Normal'. *Anthropology in Action* 27(2): 28–32.

La Moncloa. 2020. 'Lockdown Easing Measures for Phase 3 of the Plan for a Transition to the New Normal published in Spanish OSG'. *La Moncloa*, 30 April. www.lamoncloa.gob.es/lang/en/gobierno/news/Paginas/2020/20200530measures-phase3.aspx

Li, Y. and Nicholson, H. 2021. 'When "Model Minorities" Become "Yellow Peril" – Othering and the Racialization of Asian Americans in the COVID-19 Pandemic'. *Sociology Compass* 15(2).

Maisel, R. E. 2013. 'The New Normal: Mental Health in the Context of Inevitable Struggle'. *Psychology Today* 13, www.psychologytoday.com/us/blog/rethinking-mental-health/201302/the-new-normal

Mansfield, K., Mathur, R., Tazare, J., Henderson, A., Mulick, A., Carreira, H., et al., 2021. 'Indirect Acute Effects of the COVID-19 Pandemic on Physical and Mental Health in the UK: A Population-based Study'. *Lancet Digital Health* 3(4): E217–30.

Mathieu, E., Ritchie, H., Ortiz-Ospina, E., et al. 2021. *A Global Database of COVID-19 Vaccinations*. Nat Hum Behav. https://ourworldindata.org/covid-vaccinations

Palomino, J., Rodríguez, J. and Sebastian, R. 2020. 'Wage Inequality and Poverty Effects of Lockdown and Social Distancing in Europe'. *European Economic Review* 129.

Pepper Trail. 2018. 'There's Nothing Normal about "the New Normal"'. *High Country News*, 12 June. www.hcn.org/articles/opinion-theres-nothing-normal-about-the-new-normal

Ravens-Sieberer, U., Kaman, A., Erhart, M., Devine, J., Schlack, R. and Otto, C. 2021. 'Impact of the COVID-19 Pandemic on Quality of Life and Mental Health in Children and Adolescents in Germany'. *European Child and Adolescent Psychiatry* 31(6): 879–89.

The Economist. 2016. 'The New Normal'. 26 March. www.economist.com/leaders/2016/03/26/the-new-normal

Thompson, D. 2020. 'Hygiene Theater Is a Huge Waste of Time'. *The Atlantic*, 27 July. www.theatlantic.com/ideas/archive/2020/07/scourge-hygiene-theater/614599/

Thompson, D. 2021. 'Deep Cleaning Isn't a Victimless Crime'. *The Atlantic*, 13 April. www.theatlantic.com/ideas/archive/2021/04/end-hygiene-theater/618576/

Varfolomeeva, A. 2020. 'Care/Punishment Dilemma in COVID-19 Hospital Treatment'. *Social Anthropology* 28(2): 375–6.

Zinets, N. 2021. 'Ukraine Receives 500,000 Doses of COVID-19 Vaccines from Denmark'. *Reuters*, 4 August.

3
Adjusting to the digital age

Introduction: digitally mediated (mis)trust

James Maguire
IT University of Copenhagen, Denmark
and
Kristoffer Albris
Center for Social Data Science, University of Copenhagen, Denmark

While there is little agreement within academia, and beyond, as to the precise meaning of the term 'trust', there is broad consensus as to its importance across various societal scales; whether it be relations between states, within communities, institutions and organisations, or the plethora of interpersonal relationships that are formative of everyday practice. Trust is said to enhance our ability to make agreements with one another, to uphold contractual arrangements, to promote self-expression, to reduce crime and even to generate more happiness. In welfare societies, in particular, trust is seen as a key societal resource that must be nurtured and protected in order to maintain standards of welfare in challenging times. In recent decades, trust has also become an object of rigorous measurement and an important rhetorical asset in political discourse. As a result, measuring the general level of trust between groups and institutions in society is increasingly seen as a primary health indicator of the body politic.

Within academia, research conceptualising trust has primarily developed within the confines of social sciences. In economics, trust is broadly seen as a way of reducing complexity and facilitating smoother exchanges of information within economic systems (Lorenz 1988; Williamson 1993; Moore 1994). Political scientists talk of trust in various modes: institutional, social and political. In particular, they focus on the role of trust in legitimising political and electoral systems, or on how trust in government institutions varies across different socio-political groups (Hardin 2004; Rose et al. 2013; Sønderskov and Dinesen 2016). In sociology, trust has long been an integral component in ongoing discussions about social cohesion and social capital (Simmel 1950; Putnam 2000; Hooghe 2007), and the distribution of power between and within groups in society (Seligman 2000; Luhmann 2017). In anthropology, trust and its shadow, mistrust (Carey 2017), are emphasised as having culturally specific, social and economic forms (Carey 2017; Mühlfried 2018, 2019). Anthropologists, therefore, often analyse trust as embedded within ethical regimes and institutional economies of information, audit accountability and transparency (Strathern 2000; Jiménez 2011).

In the digital era, scholars have begun to question whether an explosion in digitally mediated relations is not only conditional upon long-standing relations of trust, but also potentially disruptive of those very relations. While trust in technology, knowledge and expertise has been a long-standing area of social scientific enquiry – especially within Science and Technology Studies (STS) (MacKenzie 1998; Jasanoff 2009) and the history of technology (Porter 1996) – rapid digitalisation, we claim, inflects questions of trust in ways that are both historically congruent and disjunctive. One of the consequences of the encroachment of digitalisation into multiple veins of social life, be they formal or informal, is that it is oftentimes conceived as the ground upon which our grand challenges are deemed solvable (think climate, health and migration). Simultaneously the litany of controversies over disinformation, data ethics and predictive technologies grows daily, as does the appearance of large technology companies performing *mea culpa* before democratically elected legislatures around the world – asking the public to, once again, trust them.

So, there is a clear sense of unease around who, what, if and how we can trust in an ever-increasingly digitally mediated world. Examples are rife, whether it be doxing, revenge porn, trolling or deep fakes. And while we are routinely exposed to, and have become habituated by, the seduction of digitalisation's promises, such unease with its effects and consequences continues apace. Trust, it strikes us, has become the rhetorical ground upon which these debates and conflicts play out. As the overly inflated liberatory democratic claims of internet 2.0 now creak and moan under the weight of serial misuse, the clarion call to reclaim trust in technology has never been more resounding.

A number of scholars have pointed towards questions of trust as residing at the heart of 'surveillance capitalism' (Morozov 2013; Cheney-Lippold 2017; Zuboff 2019; Amoore 2020; Doctorow 2020). The effort to create fully datafied societies, they argue, is shrouded in under-articulated risks where questions of monitoring and compliance have already begun to supersede those of governance. For Amoore (2020) and Zuboff (2019) in particular, this represents a form of 'machinic' sociality and politics that displaces responsibility, mutual obligation and reciprocity – the very forms that social scientists argue trust takes – and, in the process, erases the need for trust.

While this critique is squarely aimed at the need to rethink the role of computational practices in contemporary societies – along with their assorted suite of connective platforms and industries – it seems to have fallen upon deaf ears as technology actors embrace 'machinic' modalities even more enthusiastically by designing for trust within digital infrastructures and software architectures. We see this through the growth of distributed ledger technologies (DLTs), particularly blockchain, where exchanges between actors are putatively subject to full transparency in order not to have to rely on trust as a social form, but rather to embed it, as a technical form, within architectural and infrastructural arrangements. This form of trust, known variously as trustless trust or methodological mistrust (Bruun et al. 2020; Gad 2023), indexes a clear move towards more machinic enactments of social relations. Take, for example, platform services such as eBay or Trustpilot, who, in their desire to document the entire history of transactions between market actors, rather than reconfiguring trust to a level that is needed in order to reduce complexity and enhance information flow (Luhmann 2017), turn it into something that inhibits market relations.

In our view, such a focus on designing for trust is too narrowly conceived given its implicit understanding of trust as something that can be designed for. We believe that trust is far too dynamic and relational to be contained within the strictures of such mechanical forms of design. In our own field, anthropology, there is a growing move towards ethnographically grounded work on the social forms that trust – along with its shadow concepts (Jiménez and Willerslev 2007; Strathern 2011) mistrust, and distrust – takes: the practices through which these forms are generated, the infrastructures and architectures that encode and envelop them as well as the conflicts that engender them. And, significantly, how digital technologies and platforms generate new conditions for what constitutes trust and what trust symbolises in public debate.

It is here that a more critical voice is necessary. Asking engineers, designers or coders to lay the grounds for what trust is, or is not, does not seem sufficient. Neither is staying within the logics of the machine whose grounds we want to critique – its computational frames, forms, ideologies and premises. The contemporary desire to develop digital infrastructures as purely computational artefacts misses some of the central socio-technical messages that have emerged from various streams of social science over the last few decades, namely that the development and use of technologies are always embedded in various social and political relations. Additionally, engineering citizens through enhanced digital competencies – improving the tech literacy, coding skills and data analytics of students – while having some merit, represents a somewhat myopic remedy to the increasing hegemony of computational logics. The problem, it strikes us, is of a larger order than merely tinkering with skill sets.

As such, we celebrate scholarly engagements that unearth the multiplicity of trust as a conglomerate term, particularly as it travels and translates through various places, practices, systems of thought and domains. If, as we claim, digitalisation is a historically contingent, culturally specific set of processes and practices that operate through an assemblage of actors across national and regional boundaries, then attending to its diversity across these categories is a must. While Silicon Valley has become an almost mythical 'ground zero' for the ideas, platforms and techniques that undergird the unfolding of 'global' digitalisation, the ways in which such ideas travel and translate into other contexts is less than clear. Examining these ethnographic contexts – formal and informal – is one way to develop a conceptually rich understanding of digitally mediated trust, its relations, mutations and shadows.

3.1 *Shuahaoping* (China)
Xiangyi Liao
Alumnus, School of Slavonic and East European Studies, UCL, UK

The Chinese term *shuahaoping* (刷好评) means 'brushing' (*shua*) good reviews (*haoping*) and refers to the practice of publishing false user reviews for products or services to improve one's business reputation, usually by using low-skilled hired labour. The buzzword *shua* (刷) means to access resources necessary for improving an individual's current situation through informal, unfair, repeated but effective action. Many things can be 'brushed': ranks (*shuadengji*, 刷等级), experience (*shuajingyan*,

刷经验), or purchase orders (*shuadan*, 刷单). *Shuahaoping* is often used interchangeably with the expressions *shuaxinyu* (刷信誉, to brush reputation) and *shuaxinyong* (刷信用, to brush credit).

Glowing reviews of a purchased commodity conventionally represent consumer approval. However, in China, positive reviews on certain online selling platforms are associated with *shuahaoping*. This practice is so prevalent that it has become the new *qianguize* (潜规则, an underlying, unspoken rule) in the online retailing industry. Research of eight shopping platforms suggested that the average rate of fake reviews is as high as 45 per cent, with the highest rate in one sample reaching 83 per cent (Shangshanruoshui 2017). Despite their frequency, fake reviews are rarely sanctioned. One study found that out of 4,109 sellers who posted *shuahaoping* jobs online within two months, only 89 (2.2 per cent) were detected and penalised by the Alibaba Group's Taobao website, the leading e-commerce platform in China (Xu et al. 2015: 1297).

This low detection rate can be partly attributed to the careful process with which *shuahaoping* is conducted. According to an insider report, *shuahaoping* does not entail only leaving a positive review for a product. *Shuashou* (刷手), the low-skilled workers hired to perform *shuahaoping*, go through the entire shopping process of actual consumers, apart from receiving the goods: they search for products, browse through product pages, bargain with online sellers, make purchases and receive parcels, which are usually empty (Xiao 2015). As each purchasing step adeptly follows that of an authentic order, there is no evidence to prove that these orders and reviews are fake. In fact, professional *shuashou* who form an underground market of elevating seller reputation guarantee that they are able to prevent *shuahaoping* from being detected by the e-commerce platform (Xu et al 2015: 1296).

Shuahaoping bears resemblance to click-farming, defined in dictionaries as 'employing low-paid workers to click on particular parts of web pages, especially approval buttons in social media as a way of making businesses seem popular'. In both practices, third parties are involved in misleading expressions in order to promote their employers or the designated commodities. However, while click-farmers can fulfil the task by simply clicking their mouse, for the *shuashou* the task entails a more complicated process and rigid requirements. Common requirements in the *shuashou* job description include: (1) to own a verified account with the person's real name, more than one month of user history and a credit rating higher than two stars (stars are given by the e-commerce platform according to the number of successful purchasing orders and reviewed products), (2) to order less than four times per week and less than eight times per month and (3) to never have more than seven paid-for products at one time, either ordered or received. These requirements are put in place to avoid arousing the suspicion of the platform's detection algorithm (Xiao 2015).

More experienced sellers opt for a variant of *shuahaoping* called *haopingfanxian* (好评返现) or 'cashback on good reviews', in which authentic customers are offered financial incentives to carry out *shuahaoping*. The seller encloses a card in the goods package with a message encouraging consumers to write enthusiastic reviews and with detailed instructions on how they can receive a small cash reward. Consumers who want the cashback are normally required to write at least 15 Chinese characters and must occasionally provide a picture of themselves using the product to enhance the veracity of their faked review. As everything falsified resembles the authentic practice down to the last detail, proving that users are not expressing their genuine fondness of the commodities remains a challenge.

Although this practice is widespread in online shopping websites, similar practices were in existence before the emergence of e-commerce. Traditionally, when a merchant entered a new market where they had no *guanxi* (see 1.12 Volume 1) connections, they would enlist the help of *meizi* (媒子) intermediaries to facilitate trade. Some *meizi* were instructed to act as potential buyers, approaching and pottering about the market stall, creating an illusion that the merchant's goods were in high demand and attracting real consumers. Others pretended to be regular, loyal customers recommending a seller's product to help convince potential buyers into making purchases. *Shuahaoping* is the evolutionary product of an old practice that has withstood the test of time and that the anonymous digital environment only helped grow further.

Many scholars believe *shuahaoping* to be a severe violation of business ethics, a challenge to the established rules and a deceptive act to the detriment of consumers, and should therefore be prevented (Malbon 2013; Li and Lou 2015; Peng et al. 2016). Their studies suggest that the subversive side of *shuahaoping* might lead to an increase in the seller-buyer information asymmetry and disrupt the order of e-commerce. The information asymmetry refers to the ability of sellers to conceal product information from buyers in the online shopping environment. Incorporating customer feedback on which future buyers can make their decisions intends to combat this asymmetry. However, *shuahaoping* manufactures good reviews and manipulates online shopping platforms. This induced information asymmetry impedes the communication between actual product users and potential buyers. When online retailing websites are plagued with falsified reviews, their businesses become untrustworthy. Moreover, where glowing reviews are easily available, authentic feedback no longer encourages sellers to improve their products. Sellers' survival becomes dependent upon more positive reviews, which defeats the original purpose of the review system.

Yet paradoxically, *shuahaoping* also supports the e-commerce industry. By inviting consumers to make purchases, this fake-it-till-you-make-it strategy saves new products from the curse of novelty. On average, 3,000 new products are launched every day on Tmall, another Alibaba retail website (Andrews 2018). New products without reviews are difficult to sell. Newcomers in e-commerce do not yet have a presentable reputation score since they lack good reviews. In an economy of low trust like China (Zhang and Ke 2002: 2), overly suspicious consumers will not consider buying from such sellers. For the startups, a motive for using *shuahaoping* is simply to obtain positive 'reference letters' to help their first customers make a purchase decision. After their first sale, the quality of their products alone invites genuine favourable reviews from actual buyers. For new online businesses, fake reviews are better than no reviews, since they boost sales and reputation by creating some degree of 'trust' in a distrusting market.

Shuahaoping does not necessarily lead to fraud. Instead, it keeps the market active. In most cases, sellers do not choose to use *shuahaoping* with the intention of misleading real customers, since misleading them will generate negative reviews. As the fake positive reviews reflect the real features of their products, their purpose is to retain new customers and establish a core of regular buyers. Their rationale for displaying more favourable reviews comes from the fact that the number of positive reviews plays a decisive role in consumers' final choice if the same product is sold by several sellers. Without *shuahaoping* to provide competitive advantage, some sellers would be squeezed out of the market not because they sell shoddy commodities, but because they do not have enough fake reviews to win consumers' trust. Thus, *shuahaoping* has been helping online shopping platforms to build a vibrant community of sellers and consumers, which in turn has supported e-commerce. Sellers who commit fraud do exist, but they are low in numbers and aim to make a quick profit. The difference of intention separates fraud from informality.

Shuahaoping is difficult to eradicate because of the dual role it plays in the development of e-commerce. Analogous to *guanxi*, the more effort that is made to eradicate it, the more covert it will become. For *shuahaoping*, this would mean that online sellers would spend even more resources on *shuahaoping* in order to avoid detection. This would increase transaction costs, which would translate into more expensive products – which would ultimately punish consumers as well as sellers.

3.2 **Travel influencers** (Global)
Eugénie Pereira Couttolenc
Faculté des Sciences humaines et sociales, Université Paris Cité, France

Travel influencers shape opinions and inspire travellers by sharing their experiences on social media. They provide online advice on where to find the best places to rest, where to have fun and how to avoid typical tourist traps (Fabry 2008: 13). Named *influenceur voyage* in French, *influencer viajeros* in Spanish or *wang hong* in Chinese, these individuals represent a 'new type of independent third-party' (Freberg et al. 2011: 90) who claims to embody an authentic voice in a profit-oriented leisure market while having a significant impact on it (Xu and Pratt 2018: 958).

It is generally admitted that influencers create their original content out of passion. Nevertheless, sponsorship affiliations are widespread among social media influencers. Classical actors of the tourist sector seek to partner with the most followed opinion leaders in order to reach a broader audience (Bayle 2019). Indeed, new communicative behaviours on the Internet have completely changed the way destinations are sold. Web 2.0 has been transforming tourism globally by both empowering people 'to identify, customise and purchase tourism products' and to undertake 'reservations in a fraction of time' (Buhalis and Law 2008: 609–10). Data shows that, even before 2007, user-generated content has been creating more than 10 billion USD in online travel purchases per year (Xu and Pratt 2018: 958). Unlike cases of follower buying, *travel influencers* have a real content-engaged audience. Ratings, comments, regular assessments from travellers are game-changers. Touristic promotion is no longer centred on the benefits of a location, but on understanding consumers' demands (Fabry 2008: 13).

To measure influencers' weight, companies rely on the number of daily hits on a blog, the number of times a post is shared, or the number of followers it attracts (Freberg et al. 2011: 90). Micro-influencers normally broadcast their activities to anything from 1,000 to 100,000 individuals, whereas expert influencers draw millions (Bayle 2019). Travel influencers navigate and publish their narratives on different web platforms, adapting and catering the content to their respective audience.

For instance, a blog enables tourists with practical information to organise their stay abroad. Instagram allows exploring visual and esthetical aspects of the leisure trip. YouTube is a dynamic and vivid invitation to reproduce the examples proposed in the videos. As new generations turn to online social media for travel information, the tourism industry is facing increasing economic challenges.

Influence is a very popular concept in management disciplines (de Vaublanc 2019: 237–9). The notion is nonetheless not recent in social sciences. In the thirteenth century, the word was known to be used in astrology and meant to define the *fluxus* which supposedly flowed from the stars to change the fate of men (Huyghe 2009: 139). Today, the meaning of this term remains linked to persuasion. While advertising strategies operate through many iterations of the product's benefits, influence is more easily related to reasoning and seduction. The goal is to modify people's mental paradigms so they can 'choose' to act according to expected behaviours (Huyghe 2009: 141). To make this kind of exhortation effective, web community managers have to prove they are entitled to make recommendations (Charaudeau 2009: 6–7). Their voice must be perceived as a truthful, informed and inspiring source (Xu and Pratt 2018: 959). Producing texts, images and videos based on the real experience of travel allows internet users to provide advice. The perception of the authenticity of content creators' statements is based both on the process of publishing these testimonials and the tone intended to be familiar and enthusiastic (Rosier 2006: 117). Addressing travel topics in an informal way differentiates these spokespersons from the formal discourse of touristic industry communication, and gives them more credibility.

Despite the playful tone, social media influencers are highly skilled. Their capacity to create and animate multiple social web communities requires technical and publishing aptitude. Indeed, in order to improve their visibility on the Internet they must know how to optimise their ranking in search engines by using html language or by sharing hyperlinks with other web players (Cardon 2013: 33). To maintain their audience's interest, they need to write and publish new content regularly. In addition, they have to show and demonstrate knowledge of their field to make their voice as credible as that of an expert (Juillet and Racouchot 2012: 162–3). To do so, they structure their posts with the same textual organisation and headings that characterise guidebooks and travel magazines ('the top ten best places to visit', 'the 10 best cheap eats in …', 'where to stay', 'things to do'). They take similar pictures to those of the adverts established in the tourism industry featuring beautiful views and people enjoying them.

Verbally, they use discursive routines that mainly appear in promotion leaflets. Descriptions of destinations are full of exclusively positive reviews with no or a small number of negative comments that are immediately neutralised. Indeed, to counterbalance any possible negative impressions of tourists, travel influencers systematically underline, after a negative comment, a positive aspect or some advantage (Kerbrat-Orecchioni 2004: 137). They use adjectives specific to the semantic fields of magic and authenticity to characterise the uniqueness of the place in the same way tourist brochures do (Dann 1996: 55–62). Through these semiotic and discursive strategies, *travel influencers* nourish people's desire to travel (MacCannell 2013: xvi). Those abilities are all directed at one objective: to build in discourse the image of a credible recommendation.

The activity of *travel influencers* consists of transforming a web community into potential consumers through equally seductive and authentic testimonials seasoned with apparent amateurism. As travellers are overwhelmed by touristic offers, digital nomads emerge as truthful voices. They create, for their followers, discursive, visual and graphic injunctions to desire the world through travel.

3.3 **Follower buying** (Global)
Christina Zimmermann
Alumna, School of Slavonic and East European Studies, UCL, UK

Follower buying denotes the acquisition of online followers by purchasing them from an intermediary supplier. Followers are online supporters, admirers or disciples and a feature of user accounts on social media platforms or blogs. They indicate the user's degree of popularity, since information about the number of followers is usually public. Buying followers bypasses the investment into slow and arduous gaining of followers by purchasing an agreed-upon number of follower accounts, thus faking the follower interest. *Follower buying* attracted attention following *The New York Times*' exposure of high-profile public figures' accounts that were linked to fake followers (Confessore et al. 2018). It is possible to buy fake followers for the majority of online social media, video and music platforms, for instance Instagram, Facebook, X (formerly Twitter) or the Chinese Sina Weibo.

Follower buying is closely related to *shuahaoping*, the purchase of positive comments and user reviews about goods or services, but differs in that it does not necessarily include online interaction. Ordinarily, a 'real' follower who subscribes or follows a user account out of interest engages with the content by commenting or liking. A 'fake follower' or 'zombie fan' (*jiang shi hao*) is either a computer-algorithm (i.e. bot) or a human operator who is not genuinely interested in the content (i.e. troll).

Follower buying differs from façade-creating strategies, like the Potemkin villages or window-dressing, in that the spectators of the façade are drawn to becoming part of the façade itself. The aim of buying fake followers is often to use them as bait to catch real followers. An increase in real followers is a multi-factor process that nearly automatically ensures an increase of the user's 'credibility' and functions as 'social proof' (Cialdini 1987). This can incite a positive bandwagon effect (Colman 2003), further ignited by the platforms' recommendation algorithms that tend to suggest users to follow accounts with a high number of followers (Confessore et al. 2018).

The reasons for buying followers are monetary, non-monetary or hybrid. Most commonly, *follower buying* is pursued to increase revenue of businesses and entrepreneurs by attracting new customers via positive signalling. A high number of followers is especially attractive to novel market entrants who have yet to prove their credibility and the quality of their products. *Follower buying* in this case is a form of deceitful marketing, legally grey and offering an unfair competitive advantage to those accumulating followers through the development of unique selling points, special knowledge and competence.

The non-monetary motivation is to improve one's social standing increase one's influence. It is typical for private persons, athletes and politicians to conceal a lack of public interest in order to prevent 'losing face' (Lim and Bowers 1991) or undermining personal self-esteem, national pride or authority (also vertical crowdsourcing).

The hybrid motivation combines monetary and non-monetary interests. Actors, musicians, pundits and influencers may buy followers to boost their personal self-esteem, but the resulting success of self-branding and increased popularity boosts their market value and their income. An influencer with a sufficiently large group of followers is more likely to get sponsorship deals from companies or other engagement opportunities. In influencer marketing, accounts with 1,000 to 10,000 followers are known as 'nano' influencers, while those with more than 1,000,000 followers are 'mega' influencers (Mediakix 2019).

Although paying internet users directly for following is possible, the more efficient method entails paying specialised online services since it minimises organisational and monetary costs. Suppliers specialise in particular social media websites and countries and offer diverse follower-bundles. Common online follower suppliers for Instagram include Buzzoid, Stormlikes and MrInsta. In 2020, 100 followers could be purchased for about 3 USD; for 300 USD one could receive 100,000 followers within 48 hours.

Follower buying involves informal or illegal cyber practices that make use of identity fraud, spoofing or theft, such as catfishing or sock puppetry (Stone and Ritchel 2007). Despite promises that the suppliers deliver 'real' followers, purchased followers are usually trolls or computer-generated bots using fake, hacked or inactive user accounts (Biaheza 2019; Groeper 2019). Depending on the sophistication of the algorithm used by suppliers, bot follower accounts can host posts containing images and profile descriptions, and they can engage with the client's content via likes and standardised comments.

Follower buying is not geographically bound; however, it is more common in countries where online reputation and social media marketing gained importance and was in greater demand among the upper and middle class. The fake followers' accounts, on the other hand, tend to be supplied by labour from emerging economies (Biaheza 2019). Countries such as China (where the practice is known as *mai fen si*) and India have large socio-economic disparities that produce both demand and supply for *follower buying* (Instant Help 2022). It is often unclear how the fake accounts were created and whether they are operated by computer bots or human trolls. Trolls are often underaged workers using personal accounts or working with multiple accounts on *click farms* (Associated Press 2017). Known underground groups creating bot-accounts and using trolling are the (supposedly shutdown) Chinese Internet Water Army (*wǎngluò shuǐjūn*) and the Russian Troll Army (*Armia trollej Russii*) (Lawrence 2015; Low 2018). Large follower-supplying businesses, such as Rantic (formerly SocialVEVO and Swenzy) and Devumi, were registered in the US but provided a global service that connected the 'first world problems' of striving for more followers and attention with earning an informal income in emerging economies to fulfil one's basic needs.

Since *follower buying* is a strategy of gaming the system, its extent depends on local legal frameworks. Chinese fake profile-creators were affected by the cybersecurity laws introduced in 2011 and 2017 (Shanghai Daily 2011; Zheng 2013). American follower suppliers, such as Devumi, were shut down in 2019 because they sold 'fake indicators of social media influence' (Federal Trade Commission 2019).

Strategies to increase the number of followers changed from 2008, when online self-promotion and influencer marketing first emerged

(Brown and Hayes 2008). Large-scale *follower buying* began in 2012 with the founding of *SocialVEVO*, the first big intermediary company specialising in *follower buying* (Alfonso et al. 2014). From 2019 to 2020, follower accumulation strategies substantially changed once Instagram influencers started promoting 'organic follower growth' and followers genuinely interested in the produced content (Groeper 2019; Ward 2019). New trends include purchasing trending hashtags to increase one's exposure and online visibility among real potential followers (Ocie 2019). Followers are attracted by utilising social media platform recommendation algorithms instead of faking the followers' existence.

The practice of *follower buying* creates mistrust and confusion about the validity of 'informational and normative influences' of social media (Burnkrant and Cousineau 1975). Companies that hire an influencer to promote their goods online rely on the influencer's network of followers as potential customers. If this network is a simulacrum of genuine interest, the company's consumer estimations are flawed, causing financial damage. An estimated 1.3 billion USD was lost in influencer marketing in 2019 (Graham 2019). In response, social media platforms modified their terms of service and their algorithms to detect fake followers and bots and to ban participation of fraudulent third parties. In turn, follower suppliers quickly adapted their algorithms so that lawmakers lagged behind. As not every social media platform could cope with the emerging formal constraints in this technological race, a market emerged for third-party auditing and vetting tools, such as IGaudit or Hypeauditor.

Most sources suggest that businesses and consumers are becoming increasingly aware of *follower buying* and drive demand to examine the authenticity of user accounts statistics. Influencers themselves have communicated how the practice of *follower buying* may ruin reputation and trust in the long run and began to promote 'organic growth' and 'honest work' instead.

3.4 **Ticket touting** (Global)
Patricia Donovan
Alumna, School of Slavonic and East European Studies, UCL, UK

Ticket touting, also known as ticket scalping, ticket resale or secondary ticketing, is a global practice that consists of purchasing tickets from legitimate outlets – particularly where demand is foreseen to outstrip supply – and then re-selling them at inflated prices. While ticket touting is often associated with the events industry – arts and entertainment – it may occur in any context involving ticketing, such as medical appointments and travel (Zhang 2016). The practice is long-standing, with historical records showing evidence of *ticket touting* for ship journeys in thirteenth-century France and for concert tickets in eighteenth-century London (Bird et al. 2013: 429–30).

Ticket touting relates to an economy of shortage – often of a luxury good – and is a market practice. Generally, *ticket touting* operates as a form of brokerage executed by either an entrepreneur broker or a gatekeeper broker, which occurs when an insider – commonly a promoter, venue, artist or primary ticket agent – intentionally participates in the touting process (Jancsics 2018: 207). *Ticket touting* may serve as an access practice when tickets are especially scarce due to desirability (in the events industry) or necessity; for example, in China, besides prevalent touting of arts and entertainment tickets, the touting of tickets for medical appointments is widespread and is facilitated via the provision of tickets by hospital staff to touts (Zhang 2016).

The practice of *ticket touting* includes a variety of methods of procurement and resale affecting the perceived legitimacy of the practice and its il/legality and un/ethicality (Drayer and Martin 2010: 47; Ledeneva 2018). On the procurement side, the most unethical and widely illegal forms of acquiring tickets for touting – the use of automated bots and selling fraudulent tickets – constitute cybercrime, while the least controversial transactions are simple resales at face value, which do not tend to be framed as touting and are not illegal. There is a wide range of potential grey areas within *ticket touting*, and this ambiguity is further exacerbated by the different laws and regulations that exist worldwide. France and Japan have each enacted wide-ranging anti-touting laws while, in the United Kingdom, unauthorised resale of tickets to football matches is illegal and yet no such provision exists for other types of events (Behr and Cloonan 2020: 98–9).

On the resale side, ticket touts have traditionally operated by physically standing outside venues to engage in spontaneous transactions of exchanging tickets for cash (Atkinson 2000: 157). While this form of exchange is still common, many touts now operate online. Another prominent form of resale is through licensed brokerage, typically with storefronts or kiosks in metropolitan areas alongside privately run websites, which provide a veneer of formality (Courty 2003: 88).

Technology plays a considerable role in twenty-first-century *ticket touting*: the existence of secondary ticketing websites and other online marketplaces facilitate transactions between consumers and touts, while digitalisation enables questionable ticket harvesting methods like bots

Figure 3.4.1 Ticket resale. Source: Unsplash.

and the use of multiple identities to circumvent ticket limits (Behr and Cloonan 2020: 100). Despite measures in place to prevent this, research suggests that ticketing websites experience almost twice the rate of malicious bot traffic that otherwise occurs across all industries with an online presence (Imperva 2019: 2). Significantly, bots artificially inflate ticket demand by rapidly completing a high volume of transactions and purchasing tickets from primary sources before human consumers can do so, forcing them to engage with touts to acquire tickets (Imperva 2019: 7, 9). Bots may also analyse market conditions by acquiring, or 'scraping', information such as current availability and demand to then inform touting strategies (Imperva 2019: 6). Legislation prohibiting the use of bots has been introduced even in places that have not otherwise implemented large-scale anti-touting measures, such as the UK and at the supranational level of the European Union (Lunny 2019; Behr and Cloonan 2020: 102).

Increasingly, primary ticket agents and suppliers appropriate some touting methods into their ostensibly legitimate business models to improve profits. Some primary ticket agents, including Ticketmaster, have integrated ticket resale directly into their primary platforms, even when such resale contravenes their own terms and conditions (Zou and Jiang 2020: 659). The tactic of integration appears to benefit both suppliers and consumers, with touts being the only ones at a disadvantage (Zou and Jiang 2020: 673). In other cases, artists and promoters circumvent

	Ticket source	Notes	
Authorised (Re)sale	Resale by consumer at face value	Agents may impose additional fees on buyers and sellers	↓ Decreasing perceived legitimacy
	Supplier officially sells selected tickets at an inflated price	May involve dynamic pricing, VIP or hospitality tickets	
Ticket touting	Tout obtains tickets directly from supplier	Wholly bypasses the primary consumer market	
	Supplier touts own tickets on secondary market	Wholly bypasses the primary consumer market	
	Purchasing tickets from primary sources for resale at profit	Classic form of ticket touting	
Cyber crime	Use of bots	Obtains large numbers of tickets rapidly	
	Fraud	Tickets being sold do not exist	

Figure 3.4.2 Ticket touting typologies. © Patricia Donovan.

the primary consumer market to instead tout their own tickets on the secondary market (Bennett et al. 2015: 1604). This method of surreptitiously gaining additional profit has been used by promoters since the 1950s and has been revealed more recently to occur at the express behest of performers themselves (Behr and Cloonan 2020: 96). Research indicates that various acts are impacted differently by touting, with secondary ticketing websites contributing to significant decreases in face value pricing of less popular acts and significant increases for the most popular acts (Bennett et al. 2015: 1611).

Ticket touting is also employed as a livelihood strategy by some individuals and small networks (Atkinson 2000: 166; Rosbrook-Thompson and Armstrong 2021: 200). Such touts may engage in related practices of small-scale entrepreneurship and petty capitalism, like the production and sale of counterfeit or unlicensed merchandise (Sugden 2007: 250–1). The existence of small *ticket touting* operations hinders accurate measurement of *ticket touting*'s full global and financial scale, though data from select industries and regions indicates that the practice is lucrative and widespread. For example, the size of the online secondary ticketing market for arts and entertainment alone is estimated to be worth approximately 15.19 billion USD (Lunny 2019).

Local names for *ticket touting* include *bagarinaggio* in Italy and *la revente de billets* in Francophone countries. In India, *dalali* – referring to fee-motivated brokerage practices – includes *ticket touting*. In Poland, ticket touts are named *koniki*, and *huangniu* (黄牛) in China. In English, *ticket touting* is a prominent type of scalping practice and is referred to as ticket scalping in non-British English – with the term scalping itself initially used in the nineteenth century to refer to the resale of 'unused portions of long-distance railway tickets' (Courty 2003: 88). Other goods that are frequently subject to scalping include electronics such as video game consoles (Courty and Nasiry 2016: 143). Additionally, queue-standing practices, like *stacze kolejkowi* in Poland (see 8.7 this volume), may include paying someone to queue at the box office.

3.5 **Doxing** (Global)
James Morgan
Alumnus, School of Slavonic and East European Studies, UCL, UK

Doxing, or *doxxing*, is most often understood as the act of releasing into the public domain an individual's private and personal information, such as their address, email or telephone number. An abbreviation of the phrase 'dropping documents', the term was coined around the turn of the twenty-first century to denote the practice employed by so-called internet hackers of publishing other hackers' personal information. *Doxing* has sometimes been used to describe the uncovering of a person's identity. For example, when Newsweek revealed the supposed identity of the founder of Bitcoin, the digital currency, the event was largely reported as a doxx[ing] (*The Economist* 2014).

In any case, the practice almost always compromises the individual's – the target – safety and is often used as a tool to attack the target. Anonymity is perceived to be an important factor in online interactions, and thus the threat of revealing someone's identity has taken on a greater significance. At the same time, the Internet aids doxers, whose 'research' often consists of following the data trail left by the target through their numerous online accounts.

Doxing only works in a world where people's personal information is not directly available to the public. The practice can be divided into the publication of legally and illegally obtained material. In the case of legally obtained material or information that is on the public record, its publication only has an impact if a small group is targeted. If everyone's address were to be posted online at once, it would be far less effective.

In the US, high-profile cases of *doxing* include hacking collective Anonymous' release in 2015 of the identities of alleged Ku Klux Klan members, the aforementioned identification of Satoshi Nakamoto, the founder of Bitcoin, in 2014, and the failed identification of one of the perpetrators of the Boston Marathon bombing the year before. In Belarus, doxing has been employed to expose riot police officers who have clashed with protestors (Tass 2020). In recent demonstrations in Hong Kong, the practice has been utilised by both sides of the conflict (*Guardian* 2019).

Doxing involves the unmasking of an individual, although the existence of the mask in question is not necessarily a consequence of anonymity provided by the Internet. Physical masks, such as those donned by riot police or KKK members, can be removed through this largely online practice. Part of the process of *doxing* also happens offline, as is shown by research into the 'Human Flesh Search', a crowdsourcing community serving as the main platform for the practice in China (Wang et al. 2010).

The website Doxbin.org provides a platform on which to anonymously post, or 'dump', other people's personal information. On any given day there can be more than 50 new posts to the website; on 18 January 2021 there were 63 new posts. The average age of targets was 21 years old, and the ratio of male to female 16:3. Eighty-nine per cent of posts revealed the target's address, and 71 per cent revealed the target's phone number. In this sense, *doxing* is understood by users of the website as the release of information that provides access, whether virtual or physical, to the target.

Fifty-seven per cent of posts included information about the target's relatives. The involvement of family members increases the severity of the act. However, the seriousness of such actions does not correlate to the seriousness of the allegations: only 42 per cent of posts attempted to justify the doxing, a reason which was not always clear, and a negligible amount attempted to provide evidence.

Even those acts of the practice purportedly carried out by recognised groups are shrouded in uncertainty because of the anonymous nature of their activity. For example, the aptly named collective Anonymous, which on the surface presents itself as a distinct group with recognised rules, is ridden with internal strife surrounding the true nature of its mission and common enemy. It simultaneously embodies socialist values, in that its targets often include corporations, government agencies and other centralised institutions, and at the same time engages in *doxing for the lulz* (a corruption of LOL, the phrase somewhat synonymous with 'for the fun of it').

Groups like Anonymous serve to direct the public's attention towards the most deserving targets. In turn, people look to such groups for direction and purpose, and as a way of getting actively involved in contemporary 'problems'. *Doxing* attempts to harness the power of the people; it attempts to make it easier for people to be activists by presenting them with a clear action plan.

Analogous forms of extra-judicial justice, or punishment, can be found in the practices of 'lynching' and *samosud*, in the United States and Russia respectively. Like *doxing*, the term 'lynching' is semantically charged, but whereas the former connotes criminal, malicious activity, the latter explicitly evokes violence: it always refers to extra-judicial execution. The two practices differ greatly in their breadth of engagement: while 'lynching', a historical practice rooted in nineteenth- and twentieth-century United States, is limited to the local, *doxing* is theoretically open to any user of the Internet.

The revelatory aspect of *doxing* links it to the practice of whistle-blowing: *doxing* can carry the same vigilante connotation of serving the public interest. But while the whistle-blower is usually identified (for example Edward Snowden), *doxing* is carried out by an unknown number of unidentified people. The *doxer* can also be doxed but is perceived to be anonymous. *Doxing* does not seek an attributed credibility or heroism. *Doxing* is permeated by the symbol of the mask: the mask worn by the perpetrator and the mask removed from the target. The mission of *doxing* is entirely reliant upon the target's desire for anonymity or privacy. And the mask of the perpetrators not only serves to obscure their identity, but also play out the ambiguity inherent in their act. As much as *doxers* try to hide their identity, they will equally try to mask their intention and motivation.

3.6 *Catfishing* (Global)
Jade Jacobs
Alumna, School of Slavonic and East European Studies, UCL, UK

Catfishing is an online practice whereby one creates a fake profile on a social networking site by using another person's name and/or pictures in order to form an intimate online relationship with a stranger.

Practices of *catfishing* have been investigated and popularised in a series of programmes called *Catfish: The TV Show* (MTV 2012). In one episode, a boy is desperate to meet a girl whom he has fallen in love with on Facebook (Jarrod & Abby, Season 1, Episode 5). However, when they meet the girl turns out to be a *catfish*: her real name is Melissa and she had used another woman's photos (Shana's) for her online profile. Melissa states the reason she used a fake identity was to help her overcome depression and her insecurities about her appearance. She maintains that 'I was completely myself' and all her feelings towards Jarrod were real although her physical attributes were not (MTV 2012). There are at least two victims in this case of *catfishing*: the boy who is *catfished* by the girl, and the person, like Shana, whose images, or parts of their identity are stolen to create fake profiles.

The example of Melissa reveals a core feature of *catfishing*: the construction of identity with ambivalent implications. While sharing an identity with others may bring 'the comfort of belonging' it can also lead 'to the exclusion of others' (Ledeneva 2018b: 213). Identity construction online involves creating 'a new text with borrowed properties to meet other users' expectations' to feel like they belong in society (Kottemann 2015: 89). The moral ambiguity of *catfishing* is only one side of the story. The other is the normative ambivalence, whereby the catfish relies on external expectations when creating a fake online identity but seeks recognition of the 'real me' and satisfaction of internal expectations in a personal meeting. Partiality of self, online and offline, accounts for the 'divisive identities' it creates. Understanding *catfishing* in this context helps to explain how 'multiple identities emerg[e] in complex societies' (Ledeneva 2018a: 10). The Internet becomes an 'identity lab' that enables users to create and 'experiment with new selves'. People believe that 'attractive people are considered more desirable dating partners' and therefore, to find love online they may present a false, or creative, accounting of themselves to feel more attractive (Toma and Hancock 2010: 335–7). This is evident in the first three seasons of *Catfish: The TV Show*. Out of 37 episodes analysed by the author, the most cited reason for *catfishing* was 'personal insecurities' (42 per cent). The Scandinavian informal practice *janteloven* sits in direct contrast to *catfishing* as it embodies the levelling principle, 'one should never try to be more, try to be different', thus rejecting the constructivist message of *catfishing* (Jakobsen 2018: 254).

The term *catfishing* was first coined in the documentary film *Catfish* in 2010 (Joost and Schulman 2010), which also explains the origins of the term. In order to keep codfish fresh when it was being transported from Alaska to China, fisherman would add catfish to the vat to 'keep the cod agile' (Joost and Schulman 2010). The documentary directors suggest that society needs catfish as 'they keep you guessing, they keep you thinking, they keep you fresh' (Joost and Schulman 2010). However, while the term may have been documented in 2010, practices of *catfishing* were already in existence prior to this, at least since 2007 when filming started. In a different context, the American reality television series *To Catch a Predator* (Hansen 2004), broadcast between 2004 and 2007, pointed to the practices of *catfishing* on the Internet. The show created fake online profiles of minors in order to catch the adults who preyed on them.

Due to the rise of capitalism in the 1980s, technology in the 1990s and the recession after the millennium, 'youth [has] stopped growing up' and what was once 'traditional markers of adulthood' have become 'delayed [and] disorderly' causing adulthood to be 'dramatically reimagined' (Silva 2013: 6–8). Scholars have emphasised the significance of *catfishing* as a practice emerging around the mid-2000s, 'a particular temporal moment in the life-cycle of neoliberal capitalism, the post-2008 financial crisis' (Lovelock 2016: 214). The 'good life' has 'become increasingly out of reach for the millennial generation who are represented within and addressed by *Catfish: The TV Show*' (Lovelock 2016: 214). People feel excluded because they are not meeting the markers of the 'good life', so they resort to *catfishing* as it allows them to alter their identities to make it appear as if they were succeeding and thus develop a sense of belonging.

In the age of 'fake news', *Catfishing* became increasingly universal and visible in societies through means of popular culture such as TV shows (Transparency International 2019). Multiple TV shows and media reports replicate *Catfish: The TV Show* (USA) in numerous spin-offs, including *Catfish Colombia 2014* (Facebook 2015), *Catfish Brasil 2016* (Facebook 2017) and *Catfish Mexico: The TV Show 2018* (Facebook 2018). Moreover, evidence suggests that *catfishing* occurs in many African countries, such as Nigeria and Ghana (Whitty and Buchanan 2016: 179; Ahmad 2018). As a practice, *catfishing* spreads through social networking sites, so it can be replicated in any country with sufficiently free access to the Internet. An increase in scale of the practice has been facilitated by the 'anonymity provided by most online spaces', as well as the need for the younger generation to feel as if they belong (Toma and Hancock 2010: 335).

It is difficult to measure the exact number of *catfishing* incidences across the globe, and, given the fact that *catfishing* occurs within the private sphere, it is likely to be underreported. Moreover, the number of fake accounts that exist on social networking sites do not necessarily equate to the number of instances of *catfishing*. Fake accounts can be used to commit fraud, impersonation, online romance scams or provide people with fake likes and followers, as well as serve state political agendas. An indirect way in which the scale of *catfishing* could be assessed quantitatively is by measuring the related practices, such as the online romance scam (which originates from *catfishing*). Qualitatively, it is essential, and may be more insightful, to use data on *catfishing* in order to indicate trends in the online practice. A Federal Bureau of Investigation (FBI) report of internet crime states that between 2014 and 2018, the number of instances of online romance scams rose from 5,833 to 18,493 (Internet Crime Complaint Centre 2014, 2018). This increase indicates, therefore, that despite increased visibility of the practice, *catfishing* is on the rise.

As *catfishing* has flourished, concerns about the practice have also grown. Thus, the 2016 survey on the psychological impact of *catfishing* reveals that most participants were 'affected negatively' by the practice (Whitty and Buchanan 2016: 180). Social networking sites have begun to implement preventative measures in an attempt to stop *catfishing*. In 2020, the messaging platform WhatsApp introduced a 'catfish-busting photo tool' which allows users to verify the legitimacy of a person's photo (Keach 2019). X, formerly Twitter, has addressed *catfishing* in its user policy. Impersonation is a 'violation of the Twitter Rules' and anyone who poses as another person in a 'confusing or deceptive manner' may be permanently suspended (Twitter Inc. 2019). However, despite these measures, the future of *catfishing* appears bright. This is indicative of the growing world of cyberinformality and identity in cyberspace where online practices associated with Bitcoin, hacktivism, follower buying are becoming increasingly prominent.

3.7 **Revenge porn** (Global)
Julia Schur
Legal Fellow at the Cyber Civil Rights Initiative and
Attorney at Law, Massachusetts; IP Litigation Associate,
New York, USA

Revenge porn comprises the non-consensual disclosure of private, sexually graphic, images of an individual. *Revenge porn* is a recent term, added to the Merriam Webster and Oxford English Dictionaries in 2016 (Maddocks 2018). It is commonly used to describe a vengeful ex-partner leaking private images of a sexual nature without the consent of the person depicted in the images. It is part of a wider set of harmful acts such as the habitual abuse of images by intimate partners, rapists and sex traffickers across mediums, including photographs, videos or synthetically made images (Franks and Citron 2014). *Revenge porn* can also colloquially refer to the actions of hackers who break into personal or corporate accounts, scammers who extort victims for money threatening the disclosure of actual, manufactured or even non-existent intimate images, as well as voyeurs who covertly capture images in private or public (such as 'upskirts' or 'down-blouses' images). In French the term is called *vengeance pornographique*, in Spanish *pornovenganza*, in Chinese *seqing fuchou* (色情复仇) and in Japanese *ribenjiporuno* (リベンジポルノ).

Revenge pornography is the popular term used for all forms of non-consensual pornography (Franks and Citron 2014: 346). It implies the purposeful dissemination of private, sexually explicit images to humiliate or harm the victim, often as revenge. In 2013, Dr Mary Anne Franks coined the term *non-consensual pornography*, an alternative term to *revenge porn* (Maddocks 2018: 348). Non-consensual pornography includes private, sexually graphic images and videos of an individual disclosed without consent and for no legitimate purpose (Franks 2017: 1251–8). It includes both images that were obtained without the person's consent, as well as images that were obtained with consent but within a private or confidential relationship. This term puts consent at the centre stage and focuses on intimate image abuse as a harm (Franks and Citron 2014: 345). The term refers to the exposure of the victim's 'sexual parts' but can also include images depicting a victim performing sexual acts or having been ejaculated on, even without their sexual parts being visible (Gonzalez 2015).

Revenge pornography is a global issue affecting victims worldwide. It is rooted in sexism and racism and is a form of bigotry and sexual harassment (Citron 2014). While non-consensual pornography is not a new phenomenon, its explosive growth is rooted in the technological innovations of digital photography, as well as the Internet, networked tools and mobile devices which have made it easier to share images (*People v. Austin* 2019). Networked tools have been diverted from their useful role in social communication and instead used to multiply and amplify their harmful effects. Exposing intimate images subjects the survivors of such acts to hatred, contempt and ridicule, impacting their health, safety, livelihoods, personal relationships and reputations. Occurrences of *revenge pornography* can be traced to 1980 when *Hustler*, a porn magazine, published stolen nude images of women (Maddocks 2018: 347). By 2012, victims' rights support groups had launched in Pakistan, India, the United States and the United Kingdom.

Studies have shown that 50 per cent of American adults share sexual texts and 70 per cent admitted to having received a nude photo (C. A. Goldberg n.d.). As many as 3,000 websites feature *revenge pornography* (C. A. Goldberg n.d.), many of which are entirely dedicated to exposing the victim's sexuality in an effort to humiliate, slut-shame, threaten and harass them, prompting hundreds of threatening messages in the comments section. 'Nonconsensual pornography does violence to essential social norms of trust at the core of social interaction' (Waldman

2017). Victims of the non-consensual disclosure of private images suffer significant emotional distress from the offenders' threats and actions. Perpetrators exploit intimacy and trust (Waldman 2017: 715).

To date, in the United States, there is no federal law that addresses non-consensual pornography. Forty-eight states, the District of Columbia and one US territory have some form of revenge pornography law in place (Cyber Civil Rights Initiative 2023). These laws are generally of limited effect, as they fail to categorise non-consensual pornography as a felony, reflecting social attitudes that have yet to appreciate the significance of the harms caused by non-consensual pornography and its often-irreversible nature. The US House of Representative passed the SHIELD Act (Stopping Harmful Image Exploitation and Limiting Distribution) which was approved by the House as part of the Violence Against Women Reauthorization Act (VAWA) of 2021 but was stripped out of the Senate version and did not become law when President Biden signed the VAWA. The SHIELD Act has, however, been reintroduced as a standalone bill. The bipartisan measure would criminalise the unauthorised disclosure of private, sexually explicit visual imagery and offenders could be imprisoned for up to two years, including for threatening to distribute such images (Cyber Civil Rights n.d.).

Frequently, victims have had to resort to other laws to protect themselves, including laws which address domestic violence, stalking and cyber-stalking, doxing, unlawful surveillance, sexual assault, harassment, hacking, tort of breach of confidentiality, and copyright law (Cyber Civil Rights Initiative n.d.). Non-consensual pornography is often a gendered crime which targets women, girls and sexual minorities more frequently than men and boys (Citron 2019). Individuals who identify as sexual minorities are more likely than heterosexual individuals to experience threats of, or actual, non-consensual pornography (Citron 2019). 'Research indicates that three per cent of Americans who use the internet have had someone threaten to post their nude photos, while two per cent have had someone do it. Those numbers jump considerably (to 15 per cent and seven per cent, respectively) among lesbian, gay, and bisexual individuals' (Citron 2019). Black non-Hispanic individuals, indigenous and disabled respondents and those who fall in the mid-to-low household income category are particularly vulnerable (Maddocks 2018: 37).

More recently, synthetic media has been used for *revenge pornography*. Synthetic media includes low- and high-quality Photoshop edits turning images, a majority of which are of women, into sexual nude images depicting identifiable persons (Chesney and Citron 2019: 1788). It also includes the machine-learning technologies used to create 'deep fake' sex videos – where people's faces and voices are inserted into pornography. The end results are increasingly difficult to debunk (Chesney and Citron 2019: 1788). Even though synthetic sex videos do not depict the featured individuals' actual genitals, breasts, buttocks and anuses, these images seize people's sexual and intimate identities. Much like non-consensual pornography, deep fake sex videos exercise dominion over people's sexuality, presenting it to others without their consent (Chesney and Citron 2019: 1772). They try to reduce individuals to sexual objects by creating a sexual identity not of the individual's own making and pushing it into the public domain without their consent.

3.8 *Telefon gap zadan* (Tajikistan)
Swetlana Torno
Heidelberg Centre for Transcultural Studies,
Heidelberg University, Germany

Telefon gap zadan or *ishk gap zadan*, literally 'to talk on the phone' or 'to [do] love talk', refers to courtship practices of young people in Tajikistan. The length and emotional intensity of the relationship varies considerably between cases, and at times individuals can have several online dating partners simultaneously. Young men and women that engage in 'love talk' defy established societal norms of gender segregation and Islamic morality, and hence, in public discourses mobile phones are often blamed for 'seducing young people' and held responsible for their 'moral decay'. Meanwhile, *telefon gap zadan* may – but most often does not – culminate in sexual involvement or marriage.

The spread of mobile technologies has reshaped courtship practices of the youth in Tajikistan and in Central Asian neighbouring countries (Kikuta 2019; Dall'Agnola and Thibault 2021). Similar to other Muslim contexts, it has opened up new spaces for intimate dynamics between the sexes and introduced novel challenges such as extended possibilities of surveillance as well as differing conditions to affirm one's morality (Costa 2016; Menin 2018; Walter 2021).

The number of mobile phone subscriptions in Tajikistan has been rising considerably since 2005 (3.9 per 100 people) and by 2015 surpassed the 100 per cent penetration rate (100.4 per 100 people) (World Bank 2022). In January 2022, there were 10.43 million mobile phone subscriptions, whereas the number of internet users amounted to 3.36 million or 34.9 per cent of the total population (Kemp 2022). There is little statistical data on the distribution of mobile phones among youth in Tajikistan. In my ethnographic research, I observed that only a small number of pupils possessed a mobile phone in 2014, whereas most university students had owned one since the onset of their studies (Torno 2020: 112). A survey conducted among young respondents aged 15 to 32 in 2015 found that they used their devices mainly for communication with family and friends (over 36 per cent), followed by accessing the Internet (26 per cent), and acquiring new information (11 per cent) (Safar 2015; Aliyev 2020).

Many phone liaisons in Tajikistan start from public spaces somewhere between one's place of residence and their place of work, study or leisure. Navigating these spaces provides an opportunity for young people to see or to be seen by the opposite sex and receive invitations for online dating. Young men might obtain a woman's phone number by asking her directly or via one of her friends or acquaintances. At times young men dictate their phone numbers to women they feel attracted to on the street while walking by, which is one reason why easy-to-remember numeric combinations are so popular in Tajikistan. Moreover, the phone numbers of young women are shared among male acquaintances or friends who are searching for a dating partner.

There is a high degree of variability and openness regarding the emotional intensity of online relationships. Some lovers exchange text messages daily and spend hours talking on the phone at night. Eventually, the relationship might break down due to a disagreement or an arranged marriage, at times leaving one of the partners heartbroken (*dil shikastan*). Romantic calls might spark women's interest initially but can become a nuisance when dating partners start becoming overly controlling, for example by calling too often or demanding their whereabouts and justifications for not answering their calls. In other cases, after getting to know each other and establishing trust, young women might agree to meet their beloved in a public space, often accompanied by a friend to uphold social and religious standards of modesty and to showcase their respectability. Young men are expected to pay the bill at restaurants and offer gifts such as headscarves, fabric for dresses and jewellery as a sign of their sincere intentions and manliness. If the lovers' parents agree to their children's choice, some romantic relationships culminate in marriage.

It is difficult to estimate how many young people in Tajikistan engage in online dating due to the clandestine nature of the practice and its potential to destroy a woman's reputation (*obru, sharmu hayo*). In contrast to men, who do not have to fear serious consequences for their misbehaviour, women are held responsible for maintaining their family's honour (*nomus*) and face higher policing of their daily mobility and sexuality (Harris 2004). While dating online, they often try to project themselves as modest, pious and respectable and carefully select the information they share. Especially at the outset of a phone liaison, many women are wary of sharing pictures of themselves with their lovers to prevent various forms of abuse, from the distribution of synthetically manipulated images to revenge porn. They often stress that young men are not interested in serious relationships and merely exploit (*istifoda burdan*) naïve women to satisfy their sexual desires. Such strategies help them set boundaries in flirtatious relations.

Over the twentieth and early twenty-first centuries, schools, universities, markets, shopping malls, cafés and parks have created possibilities for young people in Tajikistan to meet and engage in flirtatious romances while respecting established religious and social norms (Harris 2006). Mobile phones and social media platforms extend the previously existing spaces into the virtual domain and add the possibility to communicate instantaneously with the opposite sex without sharing physical space. Whereas public discourses commonly blame new communication technologies for leading young people towards immoral behaviour, most Tajik youth engage in 'love talk' without necessarily transgressing social norms and boundaries imposed by Islam.

Bibliography to Chapter 3

Introduction: digitally mediated (mis)trust
James Maguire and Kristoffer Albris

Amoore, L. 2020. *Cloud Ethics: Algorithms and the Attributes of Ourselves and Others*. Durham: Duke University Press.
Bruun, M. H., Andersen, A. O. and Mannov, A. 2020. 'Infrastructures of Trust and Distrust: The Politics and Ethics of Emerging Cryptographic Technologies'. *Anthropology Today* 36(2): 13–17.
Carey, M. 2017. *Mistrust*. Chicago: HAU Books.
Cheney-Lippold, J. 2017. *We Are Data: Algorithms and the Making of Our Digital Selves*. New York: NYU Press.
Doctorow, C. 2020. *How to Destroy Surveillance Capitalism*. New York: Stonesong Digital.
Gad, C. 2023. 'Trust and Mistrust in Computer Science and Social Inquiry: Making Sense of Complexities Provoked by the Prospect of Digitalizing Voting in Denmark'. *Journal of Cultural Economy*. Online first. DOI ttps://doi.org/10.1080/17530350.2023.2246991
Hardin, R. 2004. *Distrust*. New York: Sage.
Hooghe, M. 2007. 'Social Capital and Diversity Generalized Trust, Social Cohesion and Regimes of Diversity'. *Canadian Journal of Political Science/Revue Canadienne de Science Politique* 40(3): 709–32.
Jasanoff, S. 2009. *The Fifth Branch: Science Advisers as Policymakers*. Cambridge, MA: Harvard University Press.

Jiménez, A. C. 2011. 'Trust in Anthropology'. *Anthropological Theory* 11(2): 177–96.
Jiménez, A. C. and Willerslev, R. 2007. 'An Anthropological Concept of the Concept: Reversibility among the Siberian Yukaghirs'. *Journal of the Royal Anthropological Institute* 13(3): 527–44.
Lorenz, E. H. 1988. 'Neither Friends nor Strangers: Informal Networks of Subcontracting in French Industry'. In *Trust: Making and Breaking Cooperative Relations*, edited by D. Gambetta, 194–210. Oxford: Basil Blackwell.
Luhmann, N. 2017. *Trust and Power* (English edition). Cambridge: Polity Press.
MacKenzie, D. 1998. 'The Certainty Trough'. In *Exploring Expertise*, edited by R. Williams, W. Faulkner and J. Fleck, 325–9. London: Palgrave Macmillan.
Moore, M. 1994. 'How Difficult Is It to Construct Market Relations? A Commentary on Platteau'. *Journal of Development Studies* 30(4): 818–30.
Morozov, E. 2013. *To Save Everything, Click Here. The Folly of Technological Solutionism*. New York: PublicAffairs.
Mühlfried, F. 2018. *Mistrust: Ethnographic Approximations*. Bielefeld : Transcript Verlag.
Mühlfried, F. 2019. *Mistrust: A Global Perspective*. New York: Springer International Publishing.
Porter, T. M. 1996. *Trust in Numbers: The Pursuit of Objectivity in Science and Public Life*. Princeton: Princeton University Press.
Putnam, R. D. 2000. *Bowling Alone: The Collapse and Revival of American Community*. New York: Simon & Schuster.
Rose, R., Newton, K., Marien, S., Bollow, U., Bovens, M., Dekker, P. and van der Meer, T. 2013. *Political Trust: Why Context Matters*. Colchester: ECPR Press.
Seligman, A. B. 2000. *The Problem of Trust*. Princeton: Princeton University Press.
Simmel, G. 1950. *The Sociology of Georg Simmel*. New York: Simon & Schuster.
Sønderskov, K. M. and Dinesen, P. T. 2016. 'Trusting the State, Trusting Each Other? The Effect of Institutional Trust on Social Trust'. *Political Behavior* 38(1): 179–202.
Strathern, M. 2000. *Audit Cultures: Anthropological Studies in Accountability, Ethics, and the Academy*. London: Routledge.
Strathern. M. 2011. 'Sharing, Stealing and Borrowing Simultaneously'. In *Ownership and Appropriation*, edited by V. Strang and M. Busse. London: Berg Publishers.
Williamson, O. 1993. 'Calculativeness, Trust, and Economic Organization'. *Journal of Law and Economics* 36(2): 453–86.
Zuboff, S. 2019. *The Age of Surveillance Capitalism: The Fight for a Human Future at the New Frontier of Power: Barack Obama's Books of 2019*. London: Profile Books.

3.1 *Shuahaoping* (China)
Xiangyi Liao

Andrews, R. 2018. 'Tmall to Debut 20 Million Products This Year'. *Insideretail.hk*, 12 October. https://insideretail.asia/2018/10/12/tmall-to-debut-20-million-products-this-year/
Li, J. and Lou, C. 2015. 'Zaixian Shangpin Xujia Pinglun Xingcheng yu Yinxiang Zongshu', *Keji Chuangye Yuekan* 28: 38–9.
Malbon, J. 2013. 'Taking Fake Online Consumer Reviews Seriously'. *Journal of Consumer Policy* 36: 139–57.
Peng, L., Cui, G., Zhuang, M. and Chunyu, L. 2016. 'Consumer Perceptions of Online Review Deceptions: An Empirical Study in China'. *Journal of Consumer Marketing* 33: 269–80.
Shangshanruoshui. 2017. 'Yong Shuju Shuohua: Daodi Youduoshao Shangpin de Haoping Shi Shuaochulaide?'. *Douban*, 8 September. www.douban.com/group/topic/110457440/
Xiao, M. 2015. 'Wuhan Daxuesheng Wodi lianggeduoyue Jiekai Taobaomaijia Huaqian shuadan Neimu'. *Chutian Metropolis Daily*. 15 April.
Xu, H., Liu, D., Wang, H. and Stavrou, A. 2015. 'E-commerce Reputation Manipulation: The Emergence of Reputation-Escalation-as-a-Service'. *Proceedings of the 24th International Conference on World Wide Web*, 1296–306.
Zhang, W. and Ke, R. 2002. 'Trust in China: A Cross-Regional Analysis'. *Economic Research Journal* 10: 59–65.

3.2 *Travel influencers* (Global)
Eugénie Pereira Couttolenc

Bayle, N. 2019. 'Les Influenceurs Changent la Face du Marketing', *lemonde.fr*., 6 October. www.lemonde.fr/economie/article/2019/10/06/les-influenceurs-changent-la-face-du-marketing_6014435_3234.html

Buhalis, D. and Law, R. 2008. 'Progress in Information Technology and Tourism Management: 20 Years on and 10 Years after the Internet – The State of e-Tourism Research'. *Tourism Management* 29: 609–23.

Cardon, D. 2013. 'Dans l'esprit du PageRank – une enquête sur l'algorithme de Google'. *Réseaux* 177: 63–95.

Charaudeau, P. 2009. 'Le discours de manipulation entre persuasion et influence sociale'. *Patrick-Charaudeau*, 6 April. https://web.archive.org/web/20190819081628/http://www.patrick-charaudeau.com/IMG/pdf/Discours_Manipulation-_Texte_Lyon_.pdf

Dann, G. M. S. 1996. *The Language of Tourism, A Sociolinguistic Perspective*. Wallingford: Cab International.

de Vaublanc, G. 2019. *Image, réputation, influence – comment construire une stratégie pour vos marques*. Malakoff: Dunod.

Fabry, P. 2008. 'Le web 2.0 s'installe au cœur des stratégies touristiques'. *Espaces* 265: 12–18.

Freberg, K., Graham, K., McGaughey, K. and Freberg, L. A. 2011. 'Who Are the Social Media Influencers? A Study of Public Perceptions of Personality'. *Public Relations Review* 37: 90–2.

Huyghe, F. B. 2009. 'Influence'. *Medium* 18: 138–49.

Juillet, A. and Racouchot, B. 2012. 'L'influence, le noble art de l'intelligence économique'. *Communication et Organisation* 42: 161–74.

Kerbrat-Orecchioni, C. 2004. 'Suivez le guide! Les modalités de l'invitation au voyage dans les guides touristiques: l'exemple de l'"Île d'Aphrodite'. In *La communication touristique - Approches discursives de l'identité et de l'altérité,* edited by F. Baider M. Burger and D. Goutsos, 134–50. Paris: L'Harmattan.

MacCannell, D. 2013. *The Tourist: A New Theory of the Leisure Class*. Berkeley: University of California Press.

Rosier, L. 2006. 'De la vive voix à l'écriture vive. L'interjection et les nouveaux modes d'organisation textuels'. *Langages* 161: 112–27.

Xu, X. and Pratt, S. 2018. 'Social Media Influencers as Endorsers to Promote Travel Destinations: An Application of Self-congruence Theory to The Chinese Generation Y'. *Journal of Travel and Tourism Marketing* 7: 958–72.

3.3 *Follower buying* (Global)
Christina Zimmermann

Alfonso, F., Covucci, D. and Sadeque, S. 2014. 'Hoaxsters Bought us 75,000 Fake Followers in a New Kind of Twitter Attack'. The Daily Dot, 4 January. www.dailydot.com/debug/socialvevo-swenzy-fake-twitter-followers-spam-attack

Associated Press. 2017. 'Inside a Click Farm that Helps Fake Online Popularity'. *The New York Post*, 8 January. https://nypost.com/2017/06/13/inside-a-click-farm-that-helps-fake-online-popularity/

Biaheza. 2019. 'Buying Instagram Followers Experiment?'. 8 January. www.youtube.com/watch?v=ri1OhWTBYYQ

Brown, D. and Hayes, N. 2008. *Influencer Marketing*. Amsterdam: Elsevier/Butterworth-Heinemann.

Burnkrant, R. E. and Cousineau, A. 1975. 'Informational and Normative Social Influence in Buyer Behavior'. *Journal of Consumer Research* 2(3): 206–15.

Cialdini, R.B. 1987. *Influence*. Port Harcourt: A. Michel.

Colman, A. 2003. *Oxford Dictionary of Psychology*. New York: Oxford University Press.

Confessore, N., Dance, G., Harris, R. and Hansen, M. 2018. 'The Follower Factory'. *The New York Times*, 8 November. www.nytimes.com/interactive/2018/01/27/technology/social-media-bots.html

Federal Trade Commission. 2019. 'Devumi, Owner and CEO Settle FTC Charges They Sold Fake Indicators of Social Media Influence; Cosmetics Firm Sunday Riley, CEO Settle FTC Charges That Employees Posted Fake Online Reviews at CEO's Direction'. FTC. 21 October. www.ftc.gov/news-events/news/press-releases/2019/10/devumi-owner-ceo-settle-ftc-charges-they-sold-fake-indicators-social-media-influence-cosmetics-firm

Graham, M. 2019. 'Fake Followers in Influencer Marketing Will Cost Brands $1.3 Billion This Year, Report Says'. CNBC, 5 January. www.cnbc.com/2019/07/24/fake-followers-in-influencer-marketing-will-cost-1point3-billion-in-2019.html

Groeper, A. 2019 'Buying Followers on Instagram. What happens? Should you? (Buying Instagram Followers)'. www.youtube.com/watch?v=ml33s3x-63o

Instant Help. 2022. 'Rs 100 में 10K Followers Paid Followers for Instagram | How to Buy Instagram Likes,Followers,views'. 10 November. www.youtube.com/watch?v=X5OC3ItEOAY

Lawrence, A. 2015. 'Social Network Analysis Reveals Full Scale of Kremlin's Twitter Bot Campaign Global Voices'. *GlobalVoices*. 4 January. https://globalvoices.org/2015/04/02/analyzing-kremlin-twitter-bots/

Lim, T. S. and Bowers, J. W. 1991. 'Facework Solidarity, Approbation, and Tact'. *Human Communication Research* 17(3): 415–50.

Low, Z. 2018. 'Chinese Police Shut Down Trolls Paid US$4.3 Million to Blitz Websites'. *South China Morning Post*, 8 January. www.scmp.com/news/china/society/article/2177800/chinese-police-shut-down-water-army-internet-trolls-paid-43

Mediakix. 2019. 'What are "Micro-Influencers?" Definitions & Examples'. *Mediakix*, 7 October. https://web.archive.org/web/20190808030220/https://mediakix.com/blog/what-are-micro-influencers/

Ocie, S. 2019. 'How to Buy Active Instagram Followers in 2020'. *Influencive*, 1 January. www.influencive.com/how-to-buy-active-instagram-followers-in-2020/

Shanghai Daily. 2011. 'Taobao Takes Aim at "Internet Army"'. 8 January. www.china.org.cn/business/2011-01/07/content_21690990.htm

Stone, B. and Ritchel, M. 2007. 'The Hand That Controls the Sock Puppet Could Get Slapped'. *The New York Times*, 2 January. www.nytimes.com/2007/07/16/technology/16blog.html

Ward, A. 2019. 'How to Gain Instagram Followers Fast in 2020 (Grow From 0 to 5,000 Followers EASILY!)'. 7 January. www.youtube.com/watch?v=hnJ_xFPoFR0

Zheng, L. 2013. 'Social Media in Chinese Government: Drivers, Challenges and Capabilities'. *Government Information Quarterly* 30(4): 369–76.

3.4 Ticket touting (Global)
Patricia Donovan

Atkinson, M. 2000. 'Brother, Can You Spare a Seat? Developing Recipes of Knowledge in the Ticket Scalping Subculture'. *Sociology of Sport Journal* 17(2): 151–70.

Behr, A. and Cloonan, M. 2020. 'Going Spare? Concert Tickets, Touting and Cultural Value'. *International Journal of Cultural Policy* 26(1): 95–108.

Bennett, V. M., Seamans, R. and Zhu, F. 2015. 'Cannibalization and Option Value Effects of Secondary Markets: Evidence from the US Concert Industry'. *Strategic Management Journal* 36: 1599–614.

Bird, J., Peters, E. and Powell, J. (eds) 2013. 'Ticket-Scalping on a Crusade Ship, 1248'. In *Crusade and Christendom: Annotated Documents in Translation from Innocent III to the Fall of Acre, 1187–1291*, 429–430. Philadelphia: University of Pennsylvania Press.

Courty, P. 2003. 'Some Economics of Ticket Resale'. *The Journal of Economic Perspectives* 17(2): 85–97.

Courty, P. and Nasiry, J. 2016. 'Product Launches and Buying Frenzies: A Dynamic Perspective'. *Production and Operations Management* 25(1): 143–52.

Drayer, J. and Martin, N. T. 2010. 'Establishing Legitimacy in the Secondary Market: A Case Study of an NFL Market'. *Sport Management Review* 13(1): 39–49.

Imperva. 2019. *How Bots Affect Ticketing*. www.imperva.com/resources/resource-library/reports/how-bots-affect-ticketing/

Jancsics, D. 2018. 'Brokerage (general)'. In *The Global Encyclopaedia of Informality: Understanding Social and Cultural Complexity, Volume 2*, edited by Ledeneva, A. et al., 205–8. London: UCL Press.

Ledeneva, A. 2018. 'What is Informality'. *The Global Encyclopaedia of Informality Online*. www.informality.com/wiki/index.php?title=What_is_informality%3F

Lunny, O. 2019. 'Battle for $15.19 Billion Secondary Ticket Market Heats Up with First Europewide Anti Touting Law'. *Forbes*, 24 June. www.forbes.com/sites/oisinlunny/2019/06/24/the-battle-for-15-19b-secondary-ticket-market-heats-up-with-first-europe-wide-anti-touting-law/

Rosbrook-Thompson, J. and Armstrong, G. 2021. 'Mixed Occupancy: Mixed Occupations? Inequality and Employment on an Inner-city Housing Estate'. In *Urban Inequalities*, edited by I. Pardo and G. Prato, 193–214. Cham: Palgrave Macmillan.

Sugden, J. 2007. 'Inside the Grafters' Game: An Ethnographic Examination of Football's Underground Economy'. *Journal of Sport and Social Issues* 31(3): 242–58.

Zhang, W. 2016. '"Where Did the Tickets Go?" Ticket Touting in China'. *Live Music Exchange Blog*, 30 June. livemusicexchange.org/blog/where-did-the-tickets-go-ticket-touting-in-china-zhang-wenzhao/

Zou, T. and Jiang, B. 2020. 'Integration of Primary and Resale Platforms'. *Journal of Marketing Research* 57(4): 659–76.

3.5 *Doxing* (Global)
James Morgan

Guardian. 2019. 'Hong Kong Protests: Tech War Opens Up with Doxxing of Protesters and Police'. 20 September. www.theguardian.com/world/2019/sep/20/hong-kong-protests-tech-war-opens-up-with-doxxing-of-protesters-and-police

Tass. 2020. 'Personal Data of about 300 Belarusian Police Officers Doxed on Internet'. 16 September. https://tass.com/world/1201397

The Economist. 2014. 'What Doxxing Is, and Why It Matters: *The Economist* Explains'. 10 March. www.economist.com/the-economist-explains/2014/03/10/what-doxxing-is-and-why-it-matters

Wang, F. et al. 2010. 'A Study of the Human Flesh Search Engine: Crowd-Powered Expansion of Online Knowledge'. *Computer* 43(8): 45–53.

3.6 *Catfishing* (Global)
Jade Jacobs

Ahmad, A. 2018. 'How I Set Out to Catch a Romance Scammer'. BBC, 19 November. www.bbc.co.uk/news/uk-46260729

Facebook. 2015. Catfish Colombia. www.facebook.com/pg/catfishcolombia/

Facebook. 2017. Catfish Brasil. www.facebook.com/pg/catfishbrasilmtv/

Facebook. 2018. Catfish Mexico. www.facebook.com/pg/CatfishMexOficial/

Hansen, C. 2004. *To Catch a Predator* (TV series). USA: MSMBC.

Internet Crime Complaint Centre. 2014. *2014 Internet Crime Report*. www.ic3.gov/media/annualreport/2014_IC3Report.pdf

Internet Crime Complaint Centre. 2018. *2018 Internet Crime Report*. www.ic3.gov/media/annualreport/2018_IC3Report.pdf

Jakobsen, M. 2018. 'Janteloven/Jantelagen'. In *The Global Encyclopaedia of Informality: Understanding Social and Cultural Complexity, Volume 1*, edited by A. Ledeneva et al., 254–9. London: UCL Press.

Joost, H. and Schulman, A. 2010. *Catfish*. USA: Relatively Media.

Keach, S. 2019. 'Chat's Great: New WhatsApp Features for 2020 – Dark Mode, Self-deleting Texts and Catfish-busting Photo Tool'. *The Sun*. 27 December. www.thesun.co.uk/tech/10625579/

Kottemann, K. 2015. *The Rhetoric of Deliberate Deception: What Catfishing Can Teach Us*. PhD thesis. University of Louisiana at Lafayette.

Ledeneva, A. 2018a. 'Introduction: The Informal View of the World – Key Changes and Main Findings of the Global Informality Project'. In *The Global Encyclopaedia of Informality: Understanding Social and Cultural Complexity, Volume 1*, edited by A. Ledeneva et al., 1–27. London: UCL Press.

Ledeneva, A. 2018b. 'Solidarity: The Normative Ambivalence of Double Standards: "Us" vs "Them"'. In *The Global Encyclopaedia of Informality: Understanding Social and Cultural Complexity, Volume 1*, edited by A. Ledeneva et al., 213–15. London: UCL Press.

Lovelock, L. 2016. 'Catching a Catfish: Constructing the "Good" Social Media User in Reality Television'. *Television & New Media* 18: 203–17.

MTV. 2012. 'Catfish: The TV Show. Episode 5. Jarrod & Abby'. USA: Catfish Picture Company.

Silva, J. 2013. *Coming Up Short: Working-class Adulthood in an Age of Uncertainty*. New York: Oxford University Press.

Toma, C. and Hancock, J. 2010. 'Looks and Lies: The Role of Physical Attractiveness in Online Dating Self-presentation and Deception'. *Communication Research* 37: 335–51.

Transparency International. 2019. 'Fighting Corruption in the Age of "Fake News"'. www.transparency.org/en/news/fighting-corruption-in-the-age-of-fake-news

Twitter Inc. 2019. '15th Transparency Report: Increase in Proactive Enforcement on Accounts'. https://blog.twitter.com/en_us/topics/company/2019/twitter-transparency-report-2019.html

Whitty, M. and Buchanan, T. 2016. 'The Online Dating Romance Scam: The Psychological Impact on Victims – Both Financial and Non-Financial'. *Criminology & Criminal Justice* 16: 176–94.

3.7 *Revenge porn* (Global)
Julia Schur

C.A. Goldberg. 'Victims' Rights Law Firm. Revenge Porn and Internet Privacy'. www.cagoldberglaw.com/revenge-porn-and-internet-privacy/#1558405409607-ae142862-279d

Chesney, R. and Citron, D. K. 2019. 'Deep Fakes: A Looming Challenge for Privacy, Democracy and National Security'. *California Law Review* 107: 1753–820.

Citron, D. K. 2014. '"Revenge Porn" Should be a Crime in U.S'. CNN, 16 January. https://edition.cnn.com/2013/08/29/opinion/citron-revenge-porn/index.html

Citron, D. K. 2019. 'Sexual Privacy'. *Yale Law Journal* 128: 1870–960.

Cyber Civil Rights Initiative. n.d. Related Laws. www.cybercivilrights.org/related-laws/

Cyber Civil Rights Initiative. 2023. '48 States + DC + One Territory Now Have Revenge Porn Laws'. *Ballotpedia*, 13 March. https://ballotpedia.org/Nonconsensual_pornography_(revenge_porn)_laws_in_the_United_States

Franks, M. A. 2017. '"Revenge Porn" Reform: A View from the Front Lines'. *Florida Law Review* 69: 1251–337.

Franks, M. A. and Citron, D. K. 2014. 'Criminalizing Revenge Porn'. *Wake Forest Law Review* 49: 345–83.

Gonzalez, M. 2015. 'Infographic: The Anatomy of an Effective Revenge Porn Law'. *Cyber Civil Rights Initiative*. 23 January, www.cybercivilrights.org/anatomy-effective-revenge-porn-law

Gonzalez, M. 2021. 'Welcomes Passage of SHIELD Act as Amendment to Violence Against Women Reauthorization Act of 2021'. *Cyber Civil Rights Initiative*. 16 March, www.cybercivilrights.org/5014-2/

Maddocks, S. 2018. 'From Non-consensual Pornography to Image-based Sexual Abuse: Charting the Course of a Problem with Many Names'. *Australian Feminist Studies* 33(97): 345–61.

People v. Austin. 2019. IL 123910, at para 19. (asserting that nonconsensual pornography offenses are 'a unique crime fueled by technology'). www.illinoiscourts.gov/Resources/a9fc53e6-f934-48cb-86ac-54ff2eb8dde2/123910.pdf

Waldman, E. 2017. 'A Breach of Trust: Fighting "Revenge Porn"'. *Iowa Law Review* 102: 709–33.

3.8 *Telefon gap zadan* (Tajikistan)
Swetlana Torno

Aliyev, I. 2020. 'The Digital Generation and Startups in Tajikistan'. CAP Paper 229.
Costa, E. 2016. 'The Morality of Premarital Romances: Social Media, Flirting and Love in Southeast Turkey'. *Middle East Journal of Culture and Communication* 9(2): 199–215.
Dall'Agnola, J. and Thibault, H. 2021. 'Online Temptations: Divorce and Extramarital Affairs in Kazakhstan'. *Religions* 12: 654.
Harris, C. 2004. *Control and Subversion: Gender Relations in Tajikistan*. London: Pluto.
Harris, C. 2006. *Muslim Youth: Tensions and Transitions in Tajikistan*. Oxford: Westview Press.
Kemp, S. 2022. 'Digital 2022: Tajikistan'. Datareportal. 16 February, https://datareportal.com/reports/digital-2022-tajikistan
Kikuta, H. 2019. 'Mobile Phones and Self-Determination among Muslim Youth in Uzbekistan'. *Central Asian Survey* 38(2): 181–96.
Menin, L. 2018. 'Texting Romance: Mobile Phones, Intimacy and Gendered Moralities in Central Morocco'. *Contemporary Levant* 3(1): 66–78.
Safar, T. 2015. 'Smartfoni Tadzhikskoy Molodezhi: Pomoshnik, Istochnik Znaniy, ili Razvrat?'. *Radio Ozodi*. 6 May, https://rus.ozodi.org/a/26997924.html
Torno, S. 2020. '*Lebensläufe und Care/Sorge: Kontingenzen zwischen Aufwachsen und Altwerden in Tadschikistan*' [Life-courses and Care: Contingencies between Growing Up and Getting Old in Tajikistan]. PhD thesis, Heidelberg University.
Walter, A.-M. 2021. 'The Self in a Time of Constant Connectivity: Romantic Intimacy and the Ambiguous Promise of Mobile Phones for Young Women in Gilgit, Northern Pakistan'. *American Ethnologist* 48: 446–61.
World Bank. 2022. *Mobile Cellular Subscriptions (per 100 people) - Tajikistan*. https://data.worldbank.org/indicator/IT.CEL.SETS.P2?locations=TJ

4
Getting married

Introduction: marriage and informality

Péter Berta
Honorary Research Associate, School of Slavonic and East European Studies, UCL

The choice of partner in marriage drives many social practices regarded as particularly important sources of individual emotional, identity and biographical values. According to the dominant Western popular depiction of an ideal marriage, a strong contextual feature of the wedding is its openness to a small or wider public – as seen in the photos recording the most memorable moments of weddings that the creators post in large numbers on various social media sites, in the emergence of wedding organisation and wedding photography as separate professions, and in public forums of the wedding industry shaping fashion and consumer taste regarding marriage, such as various wedding magazines. However, it would be wrong to conclude from all this that in many social contexts the practices of choice of partner and marriage ceremony are not closely linked (at least in part) to the desire to achieve informality – quite the contrary.

In the case of many marriage subcultures (organised, for example, on ethnic or religious bases), some of the sociocultural expectations regarding choice of partner and the wedding differ from those accepted, expected and regarded as essential by the majority society. This is why the members of such marriage subcultures are inevitably forced to make their marriages more or less informal, that is, they adopt a strategy of relative marital secrecy to avoid possible legal and moral sanctions, or to avoid attracting negative media interest. Prime examples of this group of marriages are those made between minors in a legal environment that sets the attainment of legal maturity as a minimum condition for marriage – see for example the cases of the Gabor Roma in Romania (Berta 2019, 2023) or those of Fundamentalist Mormon polygamy (Bennion 2012; Quek 2018; Petrella 2023). Relative marital secrecy can also be applied where the choice of partner and the marriage have been made without the free, full and informed consent of one or both spouses, that is, in cases that can be regarded as forced marriage. Marital secrecy is relative in the aforementioned cases because naturally it does *not* extend to members of the given marriage subcultures.

In their 2020 path-breaking study on *Violence Against Women*, Chantler and McCarry draw attention to the significance of the informal practices and ideologies supporting premarital socialisation into/normalisation of forced marriage, and they also present a striking example of the close connection between informality and marriage (Chantler et al. 2017). The warning is that the concept of forced marriage should not be restricted to the events of partner selection and the wedding, otherwise, the multi-level and long-term process of informal parental and family preparation for such marriage as well as its complex effects remain invisible. The authors – and their interlocutors – recommended that forced marriage should be regarded not as a singular event, but as a 'process' or 'pattern of behaviour', that is, as a complex issue that covers 'a long period of time with the marriage itself just one element in this process' (Chantler and McCarry 2020: 106). This processual perspective on marriage allows not only a more thorough understanding of the consequences of the contextual dependency of individual agency and choice related to partner selection, but also makes it possible to map more precisely and comprehensively the subtle role and significance of the *informal* practices, strategies and techniques that play an active part in the premarital process of socialisation into/normalisation of forced marriage.

It has been argued that informality is a significant contextual factor not only in the processes of partner selection and marriage, but also the role it plays in divorces (Berta 2023). Among others, this is true of the arranged marriage culture of the Gabor Roma in Romania, where most divorces and remarriages occur in a couple's teenage years or early 20s – when the subjective constraint to meet parental expectations and the dependence on parents remains so strong that the young couples have not yet fully developed the ability to adopt a critical stance or effectively resist parental influence and manipulation. Among the Gabor Roma, almost all marriages, divorces and remarriages are arranged; in other words, these practices are primarily directed, supervised and authenticated by the parents and grandparents. Viewed from the perspective of the Romanian authorities, Gabor Roma marriages and divorces are informal and 'invisible' practices: they are not recorded in writing by the Roma, nor are they reported to or recorded by any Romanian authority.

The practice of arranged divorce is made possible within the Gabor Roma ethnic population primarily by the fact that many informal premarital conducive contexts and the coercive control exercised by parents, which are supported by structural and systemic (gendered, intergenerational and so on) inequalities and sociocultural expectations and ideals, continue to exist long after the wedding and have a big impact on the exercise of individual agency, autonomy and choice by both members of the couple regarding continuation or termination of their own marriage. The fact that among the Gabor Roma divorce is informal, that is, it is not supervised and controlled by the state and its authorities, results in the young couple being able to count *only* on the support and intervention of their extended families in the case of disputed questions (spousal conflicts or incompatibility, intention to divorce and so on) regarding their marriage. The high degree of ethnicised informality characteristic of Gabor Roma family life (including marriages and divorces) facilitates the long-term post-wedding survival of the aforementioned premarital informal conducive contexts and coercive control, and in this way significantly contributes to the restriction of the young couples' agency regarding the fate of their own marriage.

Many fascinating entries dealing with marriage in this section of the encyclopaedia offer an insight into the varied reasons and consequences of tensions that informality produces and explain why social judgements of informality are often ambivalent. In the context of preparation or performance of marriage, the entries refute the widespread assumption that informality is associated exclusively with poverty or underdevelopment. For example, Ling Zhang examines the concept of 'bride price' and the circumstances of its calculation in contemporary China, Alberica Camerani analyses the reasons and consequences of kidnapping as an informal pre-marriage practice in Kyrgyzstan and Julia Carter presents the emergence and complex meaning of an informal linguistic practice, coined as 'bridezillas' in Western media discourse in the Anglophone countries, to denote 'out of control' brides striving to control every aspect of their weddings. Madina Gazieva and Elena Borisova show the complex informality hidden in certain marriage rites through Tajik and Russian case studies. Anna Temkina and Lilit Zakaryan focus on gender imbalance in weddings in Armenia as the practice consists in verifying the bride's virginity. Similarly, Tommaso Aguzzi analyses the emergence and operation of informal family hierarchies and their effects on family members in Central Asia. Nursultan Suleimenov and Ouxiang Ji discuss the significance of informal polygyny, focusing in particular on the role and social judgement of second or unofficial wives in Kazakhstan and China. Finally, Ellen Robertson explores the non-marriage options for women in many Balkan countries, which means that they change their gender and live the rest of their lives as men.

4.1 *Caili* (China)
Ling Zhang
Alumna, School of Slavonic and East European Studies, UCL, UK

Caili is a Mandarin Chinese term meaning 'bride price', a betrothal gift given in money and assets by the groom and relatives to the bride and her family prior to the marriage. In rural areas, it is acceptable and associated with customary ways.

In the patrilocal context, marriage usually means marrying a bride into the groom's family while marrying her out of her own. The bride is normally given a dowry, money or property, by her parents for the marriage. However, a dowry is not compulsory, or considered less important. *Caili* has a long history in China (Jiang and Sánchez-Barricarte 2012), but with the growing Chinese economy it is becoming an excessive burden for many families. Economic growth itself cannot fully explain the scale and dramatic increase of the 'bride price', resulting also from the gender imbalance in China (Caldwell et al. 1983). Demand for women surpasses supply in the marital market, which gives females higher bargaining power (Lv 2006). In Chinese culture, parents usually regard finding a spouse for their child as their duty. The enthusiasm of parents fuels the request for a higher bride price, and surveys have indicated that the bride price is highly related to this type of competition. Bride prices symbolise compensation to the woman's family for the loss of a potential source of income (this duty to sustain parents is seen also in the Solomon Islands and Melanesia in the practice of *wantoks* and *kastom*) (see 3.8 Volume 1).

The history of betrothal gifts dates to the Western Zhou Dynasty (1045–771 BC), where betrothal gifts were regarded as a blessing and a symbol of the bond uniting the families of the couple. Since the Han dynasty (206 BC–AD 220) the extravagant spending in ceremonial events, as weddings and funerals, incentivised the practice of pricing wives. During the Tang dynasty (AD 618–907), betrothal gifts were

Table 4.1.1 The changing pattern of the three main gifts

Year	Betrothal gifts
1960s	Furniture including a bed, a cupboard, a chest of drawers, a chamber pot (nightstand), a table and four chairs.
1970s	A bike, a wristwatch and a sewing machine.
Late 1980s	A refrigerator, a television and a washing machine.
1990s	A computer, an air conditioner and a motorcycle.
2000s	A house, a car and cash.

considered an indispensable dimension of marriages. Once betrothal gifts were accepted by the family of the bride, the union became legally binding (Si and Wang 2018). The quantity and value of betrothal gifts reflected the families' wealth and social position.

Since the 1980s, the value of bride prices started to soar in both urban and rural regions. Traditionally, the number of betrothal gifts was three, and over the decades the identification of these gifts changed to include goods that were socially perceived as the most precious. In a competition to prove their higher social status families began to include more expensive gifts.

The increasing bride price can be attributed to two main reasons. First, the one-child policy has affected the sex-ratio balance, resulting

Table 4.1.2 Data on 'bride price' in rural areas

Time	Average 'bride price' RMB (USD)	Average annual household income RMB (USD)	Region	Source
2018	180,000 (26,865)	55,000 (8,208)	Heze city, Shandong province	Gong et al. (2018)
2016	108,764 (16,233)	12,138 (1,811)	Ganzhou city, Jiangzi province	Statistical data on bride price lawsuits https://wenshu.court.gov.cn/
2019	135,100 (20,164)	20,175 (3,011)	Shangqiu city, Henan province	Statistical data on bride price lawsuits https://wenshu.court.gov.cn/

in more men being born than women (this practice can also be seen in Montenegro as a result of *Selektivni abortus/tuđa večera*, see 1.3 in this volume). Jiang et al. (2015: 218) argued that being less in number, females have more options to choose from, while men have to compete, also economically, for their spouse. This demographic pressure is further reinforced by a social one. If they are not married by a certain age, Chinese men are referred to by their communities as 'bare branches'. In rural areas, a family with a 'bare branch' may be rejected by the community. To protect the reputation of the family and continue the paternal line, one of the main aims of parents is to find a spouse for their son. Second, the bride price reflects the prestige and social standing of both families. Higher bride prices might be set simply to show off, leading to competition between families. Parents will deliberately incur more costs in order to prove their superiority.

4.2 *Ala kachuu* (Kyrgyzstan)
Alberica Camerani
School of Law and Government, Dublin City University, Ireland

Ala kachuu is the act of abducting a woman for the purpose of marriage. Also known as (*kyz*) *ala kachuu*, it means 'take (the girl) and run' in Kyrgyz language. Kidnappings as a pre-marriage practice have been reported across several regions of the world. In the Soviet comedy *Kavkaskaya pleniza, ili Novye priklyucheniya Shurika* (Kidnapping, Caucasian Style), Shurik, the main character, is fooled into kidnapping a young woman as appropriate to local custom in a mountainous area of the Caucasus, where the practice is still carried out today. In Kyrgyzstan and in the South of Kazakhstan, there has been a steep surge in forced bride kidnappings since the end of the Soviet Union.

The *ala kachuu* vary in the degree of violence and consent: from an elopement of the bride that is consensual to the violent and non-consensual. Boundaries between the two are often blurred and difficult to discern. In the Kazakh language, the expression *qyz alyp qashu* (take the girl and run) can be specified further by adding adjectives *kelisimsiz* to denote a non-consensual abduction, or *kelisimmen* for consensual abduction (Werner 2009). In Kyrgyz tradition, even in the case of elopement, the bride has to display reluctance to marry as a way of asserting her innocence and purity.

According to the custom, the kidnapping is planned in advance and involves the future groom's friends and family. In the most common

Figure 4.2.1 Once they kidnapped me. Elzada's story. At the beginning they were trying to persuade me amicably: 'I also got married like this.' 'This has been the custom since the beginning of time.' 'Elders should be respected.' 'Woman's happiness.' Etc. © Tatiana Zelenskaya.

scenario, the groom, aided by young men, abducts the girl from the streets, forces her into a car and transports her to his house. There, everything has already been set up for the event. In a space delimited by a thin curtain in the living room, female family members are charged with persuading the future bride to wear a white scarf, which symbolises her consent, and to write a letter of marriage acceptance to her parents (Borbieva 2012). This process can last days. However, the more time goes by, the less likely the girl will be able to escape, because if she spends the night in the abductor's house, people will start to question her virginity (Werner et al. 2018). In the meantime, a delegation formed by the groom's family members (*achuu basar*, literally 'pain/anger relief') visits the bride's parents, informs them of the situation and by way of apology offers gifts, and a sheep as the bride price (*kalym*) (Becker et al. 2017).

Coercive methods to compel the girl to agree to the marriage include rape (Kim 2020), as well as a range of threatening techniques: curses, arranging for older women to lie on the doorstep, or placing bread in the doorway, so that if the girl tries to escape she will have to step over them, which is believed to bring bad luck. The abducted woman can potentially still refuse the marriage, but this rarely happens due to fear of repercussions (Amsler and Kleinbach 1999). A woman who succeeds in walking away from the kidnapper becomes less appealing for future marriages because she is considered impure and disrespectful to the Kyrgyz culture (Handrahan 2004). Usually, the bride's relatives do not oppose or rescue their daughter as the potential alternative of her not getting married at all is a highly undesirable outcome in Kyrgyzstan (Borbieva 2012).

Bride kidnapping is illegal and kidnappers may face up to ten years in prison according to articles 154 and 155, adopted in 2013. Nonetheless, these crimes are rarely reported and punishment is rarely enforced. In fact, *ala kachuu* practices generally enjoy social acceptance because it is believed to be a national tradition, suppressed during the Soviet Union. Yet, scholars suggest that in the pre-Soviet period bride kidnappings were rare (Werner et al. 2018). When they occurred, the punishment was severe because they violated both the *Adat*, the Kyrgyz customary law that requires the agreement between families for their children to enter marriage, and Islamic law, which requires consent from both the groom and bride (Kleinbach and Salimjanova 2007). Occasionally, consensual bride kidnappings in the form of elopement were orchestrated to counter parents' opposition to the marriage and/or to avoid wedding-related expenses. In the Soviet period, non-consensual marriage was officially banned in all its forms, but forced bride kidnapping started to be practised more frequently, especially towards the end of the Soviet Union (Werner 2009).

Figure 4.2.2 Once they kidnapped me. Nargiza's story. A girl should respect national traditions, and if she leaves now, then she will bring a curse upon herself and she will not be able to get married anymore. And also, a normal Kyrgyz girl can be happy only by being a wife and mother. No career nor education could bring the real 'woman's happiness'. And generally speaking, marry first and love will follow. © Tatiana Zelenskaya.

Given the reluctance to denounce these crimes, there is a lack of comprehensive data on the phenomenon. In 2018, The Ombudsman of Kyrgyzstan, declared that every year around five to seven thousand families, out of fifty thousand, are formed through bride kidnapping (Akyykatchy Kyrgyzskoy Respubliki 2018). A report provided by UNFPA (2016), which differentiates between consensual and non-consensual bride kidnapping, confirms that 22 per cent of Kyrgyz women were abducted, 16 per cent of them in a consensual manner and 6 per cent without consent. Earlier findings suggest that every year there are from 11,800 (Radio Free Europe/Radio Liberty 2014) to 16,000 (Luzyuk 2011) victims of *ala kachyy*. There was an upward trend in the years following independence, as the percentage of bride kidnapping rose from 33 per cent in 1999 to 45 per cent in 2004 (Ibraeva et al. 2011).

Scholars often link bride kidnapping to the ethnic nationalism that gained momentum after independence and considered it as an expression of the revival of patriarchy, with the aim of (re)gaining control of female bodies (Werner et al. 2018). In addition, unstable economic conditions may encourage this practice by financially limiting the possibility of meeting the traditionally high wedding expenses, such as in-law parties and celebrations and the dowry.

Bride kidnapping not only violates human rights and Kyrgyz legislation, but it also has long-lasting effects on families leading to domestic violence and higher rates of divorce. Among victims of *ala kachuu*, there have been frequent cases of suicide. In 2018 and 2021, two deadly cases of bride kidnapping sparked large protests in the country, where grassroot and civil society actors are raising awareness and demanding law enforcement and more severe punishments. In 2020, Open Line, a Bishek-based NGO, released a mobile phone game designed for young people to learn how to ask for help if they are victim of *ala kachuu* or if they witness a case. It is not only the media and the government that increasingly label bride kidnapping as a crime not a tradition (Kalikov 2021), but the Deputy Mufti has also stressed its incompatibility with Islam (Ulanova 2021). Despite these efforts, the practice is still widespread, and law enforcement officers tend to downplay the offence and attempt to reconcile the parties. In 2018, Burulai Turdaaly Kyzy was stabbed to death by her kidnapper in a room at the police station where they had been left unattended by police officials.

4.3 **Mendanghudui** (China)
Shiqi Yin
Alumnus, School of Slavonic and East European Studies, UCL, UK

Mén dāng hù duì (门当户对) is a Chinese idiom which means that families of the bride and groom share similar social and economic status. The English translation of the phrase is a 'marriage of the matching doors' (Hu 2016), or a 'good match'. It expresses a traditional Chinese perception of what comprises a good marriage and is viewed as a rule for choosing a marital partner. Although many young people in China, especially those with higher education living in large cities, regard it as a feudal idea, many still get married on the basis of *mendanghudui* (Tian 2017).

The term has a long history in China: *mendang* and *hudui* are integral parts of the ancient Chinese courtyard's gate architecture. The '*mendang*' is a pair of stone drums in front of the main gate which are said to ward off evil spirits (Wang 2020); the '*hudui*' are carved decorations on both sides of the door. This style of gate can still be seen in many parts of rural China today. Decorations on such gates symbolise the owner's status, economic power and identity.

The reasons for the longevity of *mendanghudui* in Chinese society are complex. One is related to the central role of family in the accumulation of wealth and influence. Marriage in China is not simply the union of two people but also the integration of two families. As a result, marriage is used as a method of combining two large families, expanding each other's power and sharing social resources, blessings and hardships (Gao 2017). The *mendanghudui* marriage can also be seen as a way of extending and securing *guanxi* (literally 'relationship' or 'connection') which is a prominent feature of Chinese society. Within *guanxi* people help their family members or even cover up for them. Furthermore, relatives of one's wife or husband or even relatives of one's children's wives or husbands are regarded as close and would be looked after in the same way.

In ancient China, the political status of the father determined the place of the entire family in the social hierarchy, which was more important than economic power (Tian 2017). However, as society changed, the importance of economic power increased significantly. Additionally, since the transition began in the 1980s, the requirements of *mendanghudui* have taken on new dimensions, with education becoming an important factor. Since the 1980s, China has been experiencing an increase in social and geographical mobility, in individualistic attitudes and a decline in the importance of the social economy based on family (Li 2008).

However, another reason for following the rule of *mendanghudui* is that it can reduce the amount of time people spend looking for a partner. In the past, young people had to listen to their parents when choosing whom to marry. Parents' pool of potential matches was mostly people around them or that of the *hongniang* (professional matchmakers, traditionally women). Nowadays, there are many dating websites or special apps available, but the information one receives in the search for a mate is limited and getting to know someone well requires a lot of time and effort. The *mendanghudui* criterion reduces this time. Most people believe that a similar family background and education level determines whether the basic profiles of two parties are similar, and from that compatibility of interests and personality traits can be inferred.

Indeed, wealth is not the only factor in *mendanghudui* considerations, because it implies that both parties have grown up in a similar environment and share a similar view of the world. There is a close relation between the worldview and the family background (Kang and Li 2016). As Fei (1999), a Chinese sociologist, puts it: 'a high degree of agreement is not easy to obtain, and can only be obtained through similar education and life experiences'. It is common sense in Chinese society that people with similar family backgrounds share similar experiences and understanding of the world. For example, they tend to agree on consumer choices and lifestyle, they are similar in their appreciation of culture and they can better understand each other in family life, which ensures enjoyment of marriage and contributes to its stability (Tian 2017).

Yet, *mendanghudui* can increase materialistic attitudes and deepen class divisions in society. In choosing a spouse for oneself or for one's children, a person might become mostly concerned with the potential spouse's family background and financial situation. In the long run, this may have a negative impact on society as people would start to measure their happiness in terms of money. The poorer partner may be criticised as vain for marrying for money rather than love. Another relevant phenomenon in China is *erdai*, the second generation, where *fuerdai*, the rich second generation refers to the younger generation who inherit their parents' wealth, whereas *guanerdai* means that both the younger generation and their elders are involved in politics. *Erdai* is often evidence of the tendency of social interests to consolidate (Yang 2014). Marriages based on *mendanghudui* also imply that these *erdai* combine, monopolise resources and form social barriers.

The study of this informal practice is not unique to China, but in academic circles is more commonly referred to as assortative mating. Gale and Shapley (1962) were the first to identify a stable marriage-matching mechanism in the marriage market from a mathematical and game theory perspective and proposed their Gale-Shapley algorithm as a model. After that, Becker (1973, 1974) introduced an economic model of marriage-matching. There is a large body of empirical research that analyses the marriage market in terms of age, social status, occupation, education and economic status. (Burgess and Wallin 1943; Becker 1974). Academics in this field divide marriage-matching into homogamy-matching (a concept close to *mendanghudui*) and gradient matching, that suggests that people are more likely to choose a partner with a better career and education than theirs.

Marriage may appear as a choice based solely on one's own will, but it is often tied to many factors including relations and resources. To a certain extent, *mendanghudui* is useful because it can act as guidance and set the standard for finding a partner, but for some, it serves the purpose of consolidating business and social position. Even those who do not worry about money may choose a *mendanghudui* marriage because they believe that people with similar backgrounds share similar experiences, interests and lifestyle. Yet, the practice easily reinforces money worship, resource monopolisation and class divisions.

4.4 *Nikoh* (Tajikistan)
Madina Gazieva
School of Law and Government, Dublin City University, Ireland

Nikah or *nikoh*, or marriage ceremony, is a mandatory practice in Islam, performed across the Muslim world and in countries with Muslim minorities, and does not involve an official, civic registration. Its popular social acceptability as evidence of a legitimate union between a man and woman can pose challenges to the regulatory attempts of the state, particular in relation to polygyny.

Aqd al-nikah in Arabic, or more common in Central Asia *nikah* or *nikoh*, is a religious marriage ceremony of the Muslim legal tradition recommended to live an exemplar life (Borisova 2021; Helie and Hoodfar 2021; Petersen 2021). *Nikah*, literally translated as 'contract of coitus', is a civil contract between a man and a woman legitimising their union, outside of which their relations would be considered as sin. The practice is performed across Muslim populations (from North Africa to Southeast Asia), including in Muslim-minority countries, within both Shi'a and Sunni Islam (Bredal 2018; Helie and Hoodfar 2021). Although not a strict requirement, the *nikah* is usually facilitated by an *imam* or *mullah*, and in Sunni Islam is performed in the presence of two male witnesses (Helie and Hoodfar 2021; Petersen 2021). The Twelver Shi'a branch additionally permits *nikah mut'ah* or *sigheh*, a temporary 'marriage of pleasure', commonly practised in Iran. The ceremony is performed without witnesses, creating a union where the woman receives a sum of money from the groom (Tremayne 2006).

Nikah's relation to the state is less straightforward than in historically Christian communities. In the West, certain religious institutions were integrated into secular practices, where the state regulates such passages of life. Marriage was institutionalised and now serves as a lever for social and economic organisation. In several European countries, failing to register a *nikah* marriage is considered illegal (Moors et al. 2018; Probert and Saleem 2018).

In Muslim-majority countries, widespread regulation of *nikah* took place over the course of the twentieth century with the adoption of European legal codes. Prior to this, registration was not enforced, such as in the Ottoman Empire or the former European colonies, where the handling of religious affairs was characterised by non-interference (Edgar 2006; Martykánová 2009). Unregistered marriages were labelled as *urfi* or customary, and only socially recognised. Despite the overall success of regulation, *urfi* marriage was sidelined, perceived as a way of hiding from society (Moors et al. 2018).

During the Soviet Union and following the Great Terror, the central government made concerted efforts to institutionalise religion and synchronise it with Soviet ideology (Edgar 2006). For Islam, this entailed the establishment of the SADUM (*Sovet po delam religioznykh kul'tov pri Sovete Ministrov SSSR*). The SADUM, was the official Soviet *muftiate*, a group of Islamic legal authorities who were led by a family of Muslim scholars based in Uzbekistan and whose activities were focused on Uzbekistan, Tajikistan and Kyrgyzstan. To foster a modern image, the SADUM developed a progressive and heavily bureaucratised 'Soviet Islam'. It criticised Central Asian wedding customs, taxed *sadaqqa* and required the registration of mosques, *imams* and *nikoh* ceremonies with the ZAGS (Tasar 2017). Despite these attempts, several rural families continued to perform unregistered *nikoh* marriages for polygyny or to marry their children before the legal age, registering them only once the wife was old enough (Harris 2000).

Presently, an official Central Asian marriage typically involves a *nikoh*, the state registration (ZAGS) and a *tui*, a traditional celebration organised for the community. In Tajikistan, marriage practices are heavily regulated, requiring medical checks for the bride and groom, evidence of the marriage registration from ZAGS and official approval to perform a *nikoh* (Borisova 2021). Since the fall of the Soviet Union, *nikoh* has been tied to several legal initiatives. First, in 2007 the Tajik government introduced a new law on *tanzim*, rites regulation which set limitations on expenditures and the number of celebrations for the wedding. Despite this regulation and many Tajiks agreeing to limit wedding-related overspending, families continue to break *tanzim* laws. Marriage in traditional Tajik communities is a key element of social life, the successful execution of which is a way of securing bonds between two families and asserting one's standing in the community (Borisova 2021).

Furthermore, during the Tajik civil war in the early 1990s, security concerns for young girls led families to give away their daughters to ensure their protection. For men, in turn, the war offered the opportunity to access women without societal control, leading to increased coercion and performance of *nikoh* without *tui* (Roche and Hohmann 2011). Despite being outlawed in Tajikistan, during the civil war polygyny increased due to the imbalance in the sex-ratio. With over fifty thousand deaths, poor economic conditions and social and psychological vulnerability, there was a shortage of husbands. Getting a second wife by means of *nikoh* was one way of mitigating these devastating effects (Cleuziou 2016), leading to its normalisation. After the war, the practice exploded because of the number of Tajik males migrating to Russia, which contributed to high divorce rates as men found new wives abroad (Cleuziou 2016; Thibault 2018).

Traditionally, divorce is executed by simply saying *talaq* ('repudiation') three times. Among migrants to Russia, *talaq* is often stated through text messages, a practice outlawed in Tajikistan since 2011, as well as Iran, Tunisia and Indonesia among others (Brenhouse 2011; Cabar.asia 2020). The high rates of migration and divorce had tragic repercussions for rural Tajik women, who traditionally live with their in-laws while their husbands are away. This makes the women vulnerable to domestic abuse and can result in them committing suicide, often with their children (Eurasianet 2018). At the same time, polygyny can offer women an alternative to widowhood by becoming second or third wives, or *toqal* as they are called in Kazakhstan. A second marriage can mitigate a woman's economic hardships, improve her social status and provide a form of companionship (Thibault 2018). In her analysis of polygamous relationships in Tajikistan, Juliette Cleuziou argued that instead of condemning it, the practice should be analysed through the 'prism of "sexual–economic exchange" … [which] better highlights the complexity of the "patriarchal bargain"' (Cleuziou 2016: 77). However, the illegality of polygyny does not allow women to access financial support for themselves and their children, leaving them subject to *talaq* without the protection of the law (Cleuziou 2016).

Given the secrecy of *nikoh* without ZAGS, there is an absence of official statistics on the practice or on the prevalence of polygyny (Najibullah 2016). One of the few official statistics is the divorce rate of one in every eight couples in a population of over eight million, indicative of an approximate ratio of potentially problematic outcomes (Cabar.asia 2020). Most scholars research the practice through interviews and ethnographies, and the extent of *nikoh* without ZAGS can be gauged through exposure to locals (Roche and Hohmann 2011; Thibault 2018; Cabar.asia 2020; Borisova 2021). Still, the tensions posed by *nikoh* are felt across European countries with Muslim minorities and beyond, where people engage in non-registration for a variety of reasons, only some of which are related to polygyny. This led to calls by scholars for more flexibility within European legal approaches to adapt to societal practices that continue to persist (Probert and Saleem 2018). Social acceptability of *nikoh* can thus be seen as a form of resistance to secular, 'external' mores, acting both as a source of salvation and oppression for women.

4.5 **Sdelat' ZAGS** (Tajik diaspora in Russia)
Elena Borisova
Department of Social Anthropology, School of Global Studies, University of Sussex, UK

Sdelat' ZAGS (ZAGS *kardan*) literally means 'to do the marriage registration'. ZAGS is an abbreviation for the Russian *Zapis' Aktov Grazhdanskogo Sostoianiia* – an office where people register their marital status, newborn children, paternity, change of names, and death. *Sdelat' ZAGS* stands for the practice widely used by migrants from Tajikistan: by officially registering a marriage with a Russian citizen they are eligible for the 'fast track' citizenship procedure. Once eligibility has been achieved and a migrant spouse secures a residence permit or citizenship, such marriages are usually discharged. In legal terms, it is a 'fictive marriage' (*fiktivnyi brak*), which, according to Russia's Family Code, occurs when one or both spouses register their marriage without the intention of starting a family. Such marriages are considered legally invalid, and citizenship acquired this way may be revoked. However, there are no legal mechanisms to ensure that marriages between Russian and foreign citizens are not fictive. The definition of intention is left to the discretion of the courts dealing with concrete cases, and the legal procedure must be initiated either by one of the spouses or a public prosecutor. This means that for migrants *sdelat' ZAGS* effectively remains a pathway to 'fast track' Russian citizenship vis-à-vis the Russian draconian migration regime.

From as early as the mid-1990s, migration from Tajikistan was to a large extent prompted by the ruination of the local economy, a sharp drop in the standard of living and the civil war (1992–97). Over the past three decades, labour migration to Russia has become the main livelihood strategy for many families, with the economy of Tajikistan becoming heavily reliant on migrant remittances as a source of poverty reduction and development. In 2020, Tajikistan featured on the list of the top five most remittance-dependent countries in relation to GDP (31 per cent) in the world (International Organization for Migration [IOM] 2020). Migrant remittances have inflated mobility expectations and made migration a highly desired option for younger generations. Migration has become a normalised dimension of male social becoming, opening a path to marriage and family life, and reshaping domestic moral economies, gender roles, ideas about social propriety and respectability, and people's experiences of time and place (Reeves 2012; Cleuziou 2017; Ibañez-Tirado 2019).

The question of how many migrants from Tajikistan are on the territory of Russia is far from having a straightforward answer. Different sources of data are based on various answers to the crucial question of who counts as a migrant. However, estimates provided by different scholars show that, of a population of 9.5 million people, there are around 700–800,000 Tajikistani nationals residing and working on the territory of Russia (Zotova and Cohen 2020). Migration in Tajikistan is highly gendered, with men constituting almost 90 per cent of the migration flow (Chudinovskikh and Denisenko 2020). The move to Russia is usually accompanied by downward social mobility. Most migrants are forced to engage in unqualified cheap labour, satisfying the Russian labour market's needs. Most of them are employed, often informally, in prestige state construction projects and in small businesses (Urinboyev 2020).

The contemporary Russian migration regime is rooted in the distinction between the resettlement of 'compatriots' (*sootechestvenniki*) and the temporary mobility of 'labour migrants' (*trudovye migranty*) (Abashin 2016). While the former is encouraged, the latter is subject to strict regulation that differentiates between 'legal' and 'illegal' migrants. One's migration status is closely tied to residency registration (*propiska*) and work documents as a labour licence (*trudovoi patent*). The condition of illegality emerges from the inconsistencies in Russian migration regulations, the tension between the law and its enforcement, the distinctive political economy of housing and the mediated production of documents vis-à-vis widespread police harassment and the historically informed dynamics of racialisation (Reeves 2013; Kubal 2016; Schenk 2018). This means that in struggling to reconcile the realities of exploitative work schedules, the pressing need to send money home and the necessity to document themselves, migrants often find themselves sliding into illegality and becoming deportable.

In Tajikistan, fears of collective entrapment and loss of opportunity to maintain transnational livelihoods coupled with an awareness of their asymmetrical relationship with the Russian migration regime have translated into the recent trend towards the mass search for a Russian passport (Borisova 2020). It came to be considered the best strategy to secure much-desired 'legality', reduce the risks of deportation and get access to better paid jobs and welfare services. Consequently, in 2018, 35,732 Tajikistani nationals secured Russian citizenship, while in 2020 the figure rose to 63,380 (Voices on Central Asia 2021). The majority of migrant workers from Tajikistan obtain Russian passports via a 'fast track' procedure (*uproshchennyi poriadok*), which allows one to reduce the time required from at least six years to a year (for the residence permit). However, many are ineligible, which is when registering a marriage in the state registration office (ZAGS) with a Russian citizen 'just for papers' (*radi dokumentov*) comes into play.

Although it is difficult to estimate the scope of this practice, fictive marriage is a well-trodden path to obtaining a Russian passport among Tajikistani migrant workers, while being a source of extra income for unmarried Russian women. Some migrant workers find a potential 'spouse' willing to help them as a favour among their Russian co-workers and acquaintances, while others turn to the services of intermediaries and meet their 'brides' only briefly on the day of the registration in ZAGS. Offers may vary from $150 in small towns and villages up to $3,000 in big cities, yet the payment does not guarantee that the marriage will take place.

Polygamy is outlawed in Russia, as well as in Tajikistan, which means that if a migrant worker is already officially married in Tajikistan, he must first divorce his wife and produce written evidence thereof. Thus, the practice of fictive marriages has caused a significant increase in divorce rates in Tajikistan, which became a matter of concern for the Tajik state and society. Tajik men registering marriages with Russian women sometimes raises anxiety about transnational polygyny among their Tajik families and contribute to the alarmist discourses about 'abandoned wives' (Bahovadinova 2018; Cieślewska 2021). However, the historical flexibility of forms of marriage in Tajikistan means that ordinary people do not attach value to the official state registration of marriage in ZAGS, and it is the Islamic ritual (*nikoh*) and the large-scale extravagant celebration (*tui*) that validate a union between a man and a woman for God and the community. Following the practices of the Soviet state, the Tajik government itself has struggled to make these practices more legally legible. It is precisely this flexibility that allows a certain degree of public consensus around fictive marriages. Although a match between a Tajik man and a Russian woman made for documents creates ambiguity, often migrant wives told me that they did not care whom their husbands are married to 'officially' as long as they continue to take care of their families.

4.6 **Bridezilla** (UK, North America, Australia)
Julia Carter
Department of Health and Social Sciences, University of the West of England, UK

The term *bridezilla* was coined by Diane White in a 1995 *Boston Globe* newspaper article to refer to 'out of control' brides (Moorhead 2018). The term caught on and has become part of a common wedding language used throughout Anglophone countries. *Bridezilla* is a portmanteau of 'bride' and 'Godzilla', the latter being a Japanese fictional monster originating in a series of Ishirô Honda films starting in 1954 (Engstrom 2012: 122). In Western media discourse in the UK, North America and Australia, *bridezilla* came to signify a monstrous version of a demure, virginal and hyper-feminised bride. She is 'out-of-control' as well as 'controlling' in the entitlement and demand for perfection on '"*her*" day': vulnerable and over-emotional, while being fierce, stubborn and military-like (Engstrom 2012: 171, emphasis in original). Interpreted at face value, this role could be seen as the epitome of feminist independence, autonomy and power. However, the connotation is not one of empowerment but rather of derision, emerging from hetero-patriarchal anxiety (Samek 2012: 11).

In Britain, wedding work – the planning, organisation and management of usually large wedding events – tends to be essentially the domain of women. This work is traditionally treated by heterosexual couples as an extension of domestic labour, and one in which women have far more invested than men (Carter and Duncan 2016). The work required to organise a traditional white wedding can be substantial, involving complex budgeting, hiring and liaising with multiple

Figure 4.6.1 Sample wedding cakes at a national wedding show, UK. © Julia Carter.

suppliers, managing guest lists, mediating between family members, negotiating with venues and much more. In interviews about weddings, grooms tend to report taking a background role in the wedding preparation, often stating that the wedding was for or about their bride-to-be (Carter and Duncan 2016, 2018). Similar views are expressed by the majority of women, some of whom would like more input from their male partners, but also accept the burden, even if reluctantly. These women commonly convey a fear of being seen as *bridezillas*. Like other forms of domestic labour in Britain and elsewhere, wedding work is overlooked as a form of feminised labour (Akorsu 2016), despite the fact that it is well remunerated when outsourced and certainly meets the national average wage in England (Indeed.co.uk 2019). As such, 'wedding work serves as a voluntary means by which women "*themselves*" continue to do domestic, unpaid work that prevents their own progress in the wider world, ... outside the realm of the feminine' (Engstrom 2012: 186–7, emphasis in original).

Heavy responsibility for the wedding work, alongside the demand for perfection in weddings (driven by the wedding industry and the media), have created a 'superbride' phenomenon in Britain (Boden 2003). The 'superbride' is a singular bridal consumer identity created (and targeted) by the wedding media, in particular bridal magazines. It combines two contrasting types of a 'childish fantasizer' and a 'project manager'. Under this consumer identity, brides are expected to have developed fantasies about their weddings (often harboured since childhood) and to fulfil their expectations through 'managing' the event, with the help of bridal consumer goods and services (for example, wedding cake suppliers as featured in Figure 4.6.1). Thus, the bridal identity – whether the 'superbride' or *bridezilla* – is enabled, or disabled, by acts of consumption (Illouz 1997). In other words, the *bridezilla* identity emerges from the 'wedding ideological complex' – a cultural obsession with white weddings which uphold some particular class-based, gendered and racial hierarchies and inequalities – which in turn supports the 'wedding-industrial complex' – a transnational wedding industry intent on maintaining and growing this cultural obsession with white weddings. For example, there are four National Wedding Shows in England every year and countless local exhibitions; since 2017 *Lux Life* (2019) magazine have hosted global wedding awards for those working in the wedding industry, and there are almost infinite resources for wedding couples online from Instagram and Pinterest (156,643,683 posts for #wedding on Instagram) to online magazines such as Brides.com, and local, national and international wedding planners, venues, honeymoon destinations and so on.

Through consumption practices becoming an essential part of most big white weddings from the 1980s onwards, women are able to construct a bridal identity that encompasses core features of white femininity: demure, soft, feminine and disciplined in bodily appearance and behaviour (Boden 2003). That is, she must be disciplined in her self-care – dieting, taking care of her skin and hair, beauty regimes – and she must comply with the discipline imposed by outside sources, such as bridal magazines, wedding-dress fitters, wedding shows, bridesmaids and so on. Thus, the bride becomes weighed down by expectations of behaviour: to be ultra-feminine, but also super-organised (women often organise wedding events alongside full-time work), and excited, but also in control of her emotions and body. The clash of such expectations inevitably creates an additional source of stress. Moreover, when a woman fails to meet such expectations or otherwise deviates from appropriate female-gendered bride-to-be behaviour, she is met with the disciplinary labels of a *bridezilla*. The narrative of *bridezilla*, perpetuated by wedding media, becomes internalised for women who subject themselves to self-surveillance in the attempt to avoid becoming monstrous.

While the 'monstrous' behaviour of the *bridezilla* could be interpreted as a rational response to taking on a project management job on top of existing responsibilities and inequalities in work and gender, the label *bridezilla* gains traction in a society which is considered 'postfeminist' (McRobbie 2009). Postfeminist societies exist where sexism and gendered inequalities are allowed to continue and even flourish because gender equality has supposedly been achieved and feminism is no longer needed or relevant: one can practice so-called 'enlightened sexism' (Douglas 2010). In such societies, the double standards towards women's allegedly voluntary labour in wedding work seem non-problematic. On the one hand, it is normal for women to undertake unequal (unpaid) labour in wedding work (as with other forms of domestic labour). On the other hand, it is acceptable for them to be morally judged when exhibiting supposedly inappropriately gendered behaviour in carrying out this work. Without a feminist ideology, women are not only loaded with resolving these conflicting constraints while lacking a language of inequality, but they are also led to believe that this is what they 'want'.

The *bridezilla*, therefore, operates to uphold 'binary gender constructs to discipline women while thinly disguising the hegemonic hetero-patriarchal structures undergirding … wedding culture' (Samek 2012: 11). It is the wedding culture, through the wedding media, that produces the ideal bridal identity coupled with its monstrous double – the *bridezilla*. This identity is recreated and reproduced by US films and TV shows such as: *Bridezillas* (2004–present), *The Wedding Planner* (2001) or *Bride Wars* (2009) to name a few. The *bridezilla* is the monstrous feminine, or uncontrollable femininity, that poses a threat to male power through her strength and deviance. An autonomous and powerful bride 'crystallizes the fears associated with feminine sexual, economic, and political power'; she both 'defies and reinforces sexist notions of femininity' (Samek 2012: 15). In a hetero-patriarchal society, brides and *bridezillas* are allowed to reign over their weddings because it is a temporary position, which is 'resolved and domesticated through the wedding ritual' (Samek 2012: 19). After her wedding day, a woman 'must rejoin the still-patriarchal world where she returns to the secondary status her gender still holds' (Engstrom 2012: 180). The *bridezilla* identity is both disciplinary (warning women against behaviour inappropriate to their normative gender identity) and temporary – it liberates women for a time, allowing them power, control and decision-making, the outcome of which – the wedding – returns them to the feminine realm where their short-lived power is relinquished. *Bridezilla* women are thus 'tamed' through both imposed norms of the temporary, wedding-related, consumption and their subsequent domestication.

While the ideal bride is an object of domination, the *bridezilla* is overly autonomous, breaking the codes of femininity twice, in her role as a 'woman' and as a 'bride'. For bridal women are expected to become event organisers, planners, managers, but they are warned not to go too far – not to step outside the bounds of acceptable femininity. Once they start to exhibit 'unacceptable' behaviour (such as demanding excessive perfection), they are labelled as monsters. As Samek notes, 'the *"bridezilla"* becomes monstrous by crossing or threatening to cross boundaries between human and nonhuman, normal and supernatural, properly gendered and gender-deviant' (2012: 15). In being unable to fulfil both roles of autonomous subject, project manager and working woman on the one hand, and feminine subordination, demureness and passivity on the other, the female subject is caught in a vortex of desire and repulsion, conscience and narcissism: she is 'beside herself' (Kristeva 1982: 1). The paradox of *bridezilla* is the abject horror mirror image of the blushing bride.

4.7 *Karmir khndzor* (Armenia)
Anna Temkina and Lilit Zakaryan
Department of the Sociology of Public Health and Gender, European University at St. Petersburg, Russia and National Academy of Sciences, Armenia

Karmir khndzor (Կարմիր խնձոր, literally 'red apple', Russian *krasnoe yabloko*) is a ritual practice in Armenia involving verifying the bride's virginity on the wedding night and rewarding her parents with a gift. The practice involves an inspection of bed sheets by the bride's or groom's parents for signs of blood. This is believed to confirm that the bride has not had sexual contact before the wedding. Upon thus proven virginity the bride's mother is gifted apples or cakes. According to tradition, when no blood is found, the bride is stigmatised, publicly shamed and banished from the household. The practice is meant to affirm the dignity of the bride and her parents for bringing up their daughter in an honourable way. This traditional gift-giving complements other practices of Armenian parental control over marriage, subordination and rigid division of labour ascribed to age and gender, and control over young women and their sexuality.

Testing the woman's purity – by way of testing her virginity – to affirm the honour and status of her family is present in a range of 'sheet ceremonies' in patriarchal societies from the Mediterranean cultures to Latin American peasantry and Indian castes, since the Middle Ages (Ortner 1978: 19; Kandiyoti 1988; Carpenter 2005). Parallels exist with the practice of *blaga rakija* in Macedonia. Female virginity is associated with social prestige since a woman's position in the social structure is defined by how 'pure' or 'polluting' she is (Ortner 1978: 24–6). This belief has been 'enforced by systematic and often quite severe control of women's social and especially sexual behaviour' (Ortner 1978: 19). Feminist

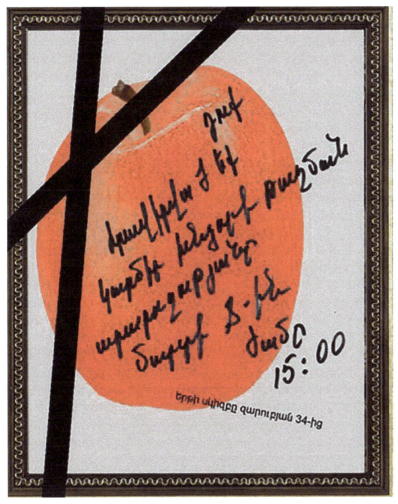

Figure 4.7.1 'We invite you to the funeral of the Red Apple on 8 of March at 3 pm.' An invitation to a feminist NGO performance. © Anna Temkina.

critics interpret the proof of virginity rituals as evidence of the patriarchy's double standards and control over female sexuality. According to Simone de Beauvoir, virginity is a patriarchal construct which objectifies women as the Other (1949).

Karmir khndzor is rarely mentioned in Armenian ethnography in the late nineteenth and early twentieth centuries because Armenian culture was mostly silent on the issues of sexuality. Predominantly male ethnographers did not investigate the wedding night ceremonies in sufficient detail with their female informants. If the bride was very young, the ritual was not performed on the wedding night at all and was postponed for several years (Shagoyan 2011: 497). Red apples used to play a different role in the local rituals accompanying the loss of the bride's virginity (Shagoyan 2011). As a symbol of fertility and with an erotic connotation, the apple was used as a gift box for silver jewellery, gifted to the bride. The spherical shape of the fruit symbolised integrity and perfection and the virginity of the bride was likewise interpreted as her 'integrity' (*tselostnost*, compare with *tselka*, 'virgin').

The current version of *karmir khndzor* that is practised throughout Armenia and in several diasporic communities became popular during the Soviet period with the increase of urban migration in the 1970s. The ritual has the following rules: on the morning after the wedding, a small group of women (the couple's godmother or groom's mother, maternal aunt or married sister), usually numbering two or three, bring the mother of the bride a tray of apples, sweets and cognac. The groom's mother invites her neighbours or close relatives, again usually two or three women, for coffee, tea, sweets and fruits. The godmother cuts the apples into four parts and shares them with the guests. Cakes in the shape of an apple are also an appropriate gift. The practice includes three steps: examination, sanctioning and validation. After the groom's mother or the other women check for traces of blood on the bedsheet of the bridal couple (examination), the bride receives a gift as reward for her confirmed virginity or a conviction and censure in case of failure (sanctioning). In the third step, a red apple or a tray with apples is sent as validation to the bride's mother, who awaits this sign accompanied by relatives or neighbours at her home (Poghosyan 2010; Shagoyan 2011).

Field research conducted in the mid-2000s revealed that *karmir khndzor* was performed most rigorously and diligently in rural areas where gender norms were more traditional and hierarchical. In the cities, the practice took a more moderate form – the ritual was performed but the virginity testing was more lenient (Temkina 2008, 2010). Several changes have helped redefine the practice since the 2000s (Temkina

2008, 2010; Poghosyan 2011). First, the ritual has been articulated in the public discourse by the media, NGOs and women's movements, and in academic discourse, educational programmes and university courses on gender, sociology, psychology and similar disciplines. Virginity has become politicised after several NGOs (Women's Resource Center of Armenia, UTOPIANA, WOW) organised actions and performances aimed at deconstructing the ritual with titles such as 'Red Apple is only for eating' and 'We invite you to the funeral of the Red Apple on 8 of March at 15 pm'. This has influenced younger generations' perception of *karmir khndzor* as they were more likely to see it as an old-fashioned practice of intimacy control. Second, it became possible to fabricate virginity. Women who had had premarital relationships could imitate their virginity for their husbands and/or mothers-in-law by undergoing a medical hymenoplasty procedure to reconstruct the hymen and demonstrate their cultural purity and honourable femininity. By medicalising the *karmir khndzor* practice, gynaecologists are in a position to help women construct a normal biography and improve their life chances for a normal marriage (Shahnazaryan 2015). Third, it became much more common for couples to refuse to take part in the ritual or to 'save' the woman's virginity. As sexual relationships became more liberal and regarded as belonging to an autonomous sphere of private life, *karmir khndzor* was relegated to a ceremonial and cultural symbol of a wedding and has lost the connection to virginity, as for example is the case of the wedding veil in Russia.

Karmir khndzor is caught up in the tensions between national identity and modernity. Since the ritual represents Armenian culture and traditional gender roles, those who refute the ritual risk being regarded as less than proper Armenian citizens and women. Yet those who rigidly follow the ritual will be seen as backward and conservative by its opponents. However, pro and con attitudes to *karmir khndzor* are better thought of as being located on a spectrum. Both young men and women may object to the virginity test acting as a mechanism of control over their intimacy and private life. In other cases, women may prefer to keep their virginity until marriage and to consider it an important cultural tradition that fosters kinship solidarity. Some may agree to preserve their virginity but dislike its public confirmation after the wedding. Many young people view non-marital sex as acceptable for both men and women and consider *karmir khndzor* completely archaic. As the patriarchal gender system lost its rigidness, the range of views on the practice indicate a lack of any societal consensus about the practice (see detailed scenarios for performing the ritual in Poghosyan 2010).

4.8 **Kelin** (Central Asia)
Tommaso Aguzzi
Tallinn University of Technology, Estonia

Ethnographers ascribe the origin of the informal tradition of becoming a *kelin* to the ancient nomadic family life where many social rituals and traditions were observed. It was customary for the newlyweds' parents and relatives to arrange marriages for the younger generations following the reception of a dowry by the bride's family, and for the bride to join the groom's family (Golden 2011). At the end of the nineteenth century, this custom became popular among Muslim populations, and at the beginning of the twentieth, in the Tsarist empire, where the so-called *kalym* was paid as a bride price to her parents (Brusina 2008).

Today, *kelins* are present in all Central Asian countries, some parts of the Caucasus region and Turkey. Studies found that the percentage of women living with their mother-in-law in Central Asia is statistically among the highest worldwide, with Tajikistan reporting 48.5 per cent of married women living with their in-law family (Bietsch et al. 2021). Unlike the Western nuclear family, the Central Asian family comprehends different generations. Marriage, for its part, represents an important institution that has implications for several aspects of family life, such as status, financial resources, social security, inheritance and descent. Family is hence a site where gender, social relationships and kin membership are negotiated and contested (Reynolds 2012).

In Central Asia, *kelins* occupy the lowest position in the family hierarchy and respond directly to the authority of their mother-in-law (*ene or kainene*). In this informal hierarchical spectrum, one can consider being *kelin* as a transitional phase, or rite of passage, between girlhood and motherhood, but also from stranger to full member of the family. The *kelin* follows the steps and guidance of the *baibishe*, the eldest woman in the family and the highest position that a woman can attain in traditional Central Asian communities. This status is achieved according to a seniority system after the woman has had grandchildren. In their first year after marriage, *kelins* are undertaking an 'apprenticeship' where they are closely followed and instructed by their mothers-in-law. In some cases, *kelins* are also subject to judgement regarding what they do, how they do it and how they look (for example, what they wear) by the in-law family members, and occasionally by the neighbours (Zhussipbek and Nagayeva 2021).

Within a family, several *kelins* married to the sons of the in-law family may live under the same roof. *Kelins* are usually responsible for the household (housekeeper or *khozyayka*), childcare and upbringing (her children and those of her husband's brothers if they live in the same house), buying groceries, running errands, cooking, cleaning, and serving meals and tea. *Kelins* are expected to honour the authority of their husbands and especially the senior members of the family, such as the *aqsaqal* and the *ene* (see 13.3 in this volume). In return they receive hospitality and, in some cases, honour and social status within the kinship circle. Women in this role are constantly mediating between the fulfilment of their own desires and the expectations of their husbands and in-law families (Reynolds 2012). For many women, the decision of becoming a *kelin* is imposed by peer pressure and results from the fear of accusation, smear or violence.

In most cases, this family position limits women's social and economic freedoms. In Central Asian patriarchal societies, women are relegated to housework and family care, without decision-making powers over assets or production activities (Lerman 2021). They are often forced to renounce their studies or professional careers, and this condition may be further exacerbated by labour migration, where a woman's husband leaves the home for extended periods and sends remittances to his family, thereby requiring the woman to stay with her in-laws to support them during his absence (Bietsch et al. 2021).

Nationalist propaganda goes hand in hand with what numerous scholars have called 're-traditionalisation' of Central Asian societies (Kudaibergenova 2018; Beyer and Finke 2019). This process is characterised by three elements. First, the division between the private (domestic) sphere, usually ascribed to women, and the public one, often consisting in male overrepresentation and female social exclusion. Second, the state's control over the female body proposing maternity as a moral female duty, made evident by the lack of fertility control campaigns and maternity support from the government. Third, the limited participation of women in the political sphere through the articulation of discourses on traditions and authenticity (Cleuziou and Direnberger 2016). This patriarchal rhetoric succeeds in creating a positive depiction of the obedient *kelin*, conveying this role an economic and social status to which young Central Asian women aspire by marrying at a young age (Ismailbekova 2016; Turaeva 2020).

Over the last decade, this tradition has attracted public attention due to the increase in episodes of domestic violence against women. In 2011, a TV series called *Kelinka Sabina* became very popular among Central Asian audiences. The series portrays the life of a young Kazakh woman who was kidnapped and forced into marriage in a remote Kazakh village. The attention towards this practice also triggered online debates and discussions on the *kelin*'s family role, with an increasing amount of online material on the topic, such as a *vade mecum* on how to be a good daughter-in-law or quizzes to test their abilities as daughters-in-law (Kudaibergenova 2018). As noted by experts in the field, media representation of patriarchy (for example, bride kidnapping, *ala kachuu*, or domestic abuses) 'normalizes it through the humor lens' (Dildabayeva 2021). On the other hand, this popularisation sparked the reaction of feminist activists, who expressed their dissent towards these practices. Another major problem is that *kelin* often get married at a very young age. According to national laws of Central Asian states, child marriage is formally forbidden, but in rural and deprived areas it is not uncommon for minors to get married (UNFPA EECARO 2014).

Phenomena that result from the re-traditionalisation of Central Asian societies require further research. In particular, ethnographic studies exploring the first-hand experience of Central Asian women are critical to gaining invaluable insights into their daily lives (Turaeva 2020). The COVID-19 pandemic and the imposed restrictions heavily affected women's domestic conditions and treatment by their family members, and episodes of domestic violence, abuse and femicide have been on the rise in Kazakhstan (UNFPA 2020; Kabylova 2021).

4.9 **Ernai** (China)
Ouxiang Ji
Alumnus, School of Slavonic and East European Studies, UCL, UK

Ernai is a term that denotes 'second wives' in China. Nowadays it refers to economically dependent mistresses who keep long-term stable extramarital relations with married men in exchange for material support. This practice is rooted in historical traditions of concubinage in imperial China. Decriminalisation of non-marital sex and of extramarital relationships in 1997, coupled with the economic boom, led to the proliferation of *ernai* – a de facto revival of polygamy in modern China.

Ernai is not simply a revival of an old practice but reflects the socialeconomic patterns in modern China. During the post-Maoist transition, China shifted its national focus from class struggle to economic development. As a result, consumerism has replaced the communist ideology (Onnis 2012). For the Party cadres and businessmen alike, 'men's behaviour is determined and measured by the accumulation of wealth and the status that affluence generates' (Zurndorfer 2016). Married rich men thus enjoy the privilege of having *ernai*, which is often connived by their first wives as a reward for economic success.

This informal polygamy also stems from the widening gap between the wealthy and the poor. China's Gini coefficient rapidly rose from 0.343 in 1978 to 0.491 in 2008, identifying it as one of the most unequal major economies in the world. The rich may keep many *ernai* while poor men might be reduced to a nearly celibate life due to financial difficulties. Likewise, since the post-Maoist transition, women from humble backgrounds move to large cities to seek opportunities. When they find themselves irrelevant and excluded from the city's prosperity, these females tend to trade their beauty and youth for luxuries, cars and real estate that they could never have afforded if they relied only on their economic success.

In addition to satisfying their lovers' desires, *ernai* bolstered men's fragile masculinity (Xiao 2011). Nowadays, by acquiring a mistress or *ernai* a Chinese man demonstrates his wealth and manliness. Masculinity is a cultural construct that requires constant maintenance through communication and social displays (Osburg 2016; Zurndorfer 2016). In social networks, *ernai* help harmonise her man's relationships with others by flattering his companions and catering to men's psychological needs by mirroring their social status (Zurndorfer 2016). The relationship of mutual trust is established among those with 'sufficient masculinity' via this male psychological bonding.

Apart from the social role, *ernai* boosts her man's masculinity in the private aspects of life. As described by Xiao in his article (2011), *ernai* Run's story is a case in point: she is continuously engaged in domestic activities like a de facto wife, providing emotional comfort and support for her partner Cai (Xiao 2011) who craves recognition by others of his value and self-dignity, as many middle-class men do. While Cai must do housework at home with his first wife, Run enables him, when they are together, to play the traditional family role of a husband taken care of by his devoted woman.

More than just bolstering her man's masculinity, *ernai* may also provide mental health support for her partner. In an interview, a Chinese journalist emphasised that *ernai* are spiritual confidants of stressed-out entrepreneurs. He explained that while foreigners may go to church, irreligious Chinese rich men only open their hearts to *ernai* (Osburg 2016). While legally recognised first wives understand only domestic issues and know little about the brutal competition in the market economy, *ernai*, as a part of the outside world, can easily comprehend their distress. Businessmen confide in *ernai* and communicate the stress of networking and trade deals with them as they view them as their soulmates, capable of consoling them.

The prevalence of *ernai* in modern China is incredibly high. Renmin University's study in 2013 estimates that 60 per cent of corrupt officials keep *ernai* or mistresses (Song 2013). Another report estimates that 300,000 babies were born to *ernai* by the end of the twentieth century, in Shenzhen alone (Shih 2007), and specific areas in the city are known as '*ernai* villages'. Hong Kongese *ernais*' children in Shenzhen accounted for five per cent of Hong Kong's population then.

Ernai is similar to but distinctive from other terms such as mistresses, concubines or prostitutes. Men having affairs with mistresses seek sex or love, and wives disdain their unfaithful husbands for cheating. In extramarital relationships, men and mistresses find each other desirable based on mutual attraction. However, first wives generally do not object to *ernai*, because their wealthy husbands have given them and their children financial dominance in return for permission to enjoy themselves in the outside world. Consequently, affairs with mistresses usually result in divorces while those with *ernai* do not. Furthermore, *ernai* are happy to have children with their 'husbands' if the payoff is sufficient, but mistresses will hardly ever do the same.

Ernai seem to be modern concubines in China, though their legitimacy remains questionable: it is an informal but not illegal practice in present-day China. They differ from prostitutes who only 'solve the problem', that is, satisfy men's basic physical needs (Osburg 2016). Social elites despise overt commercial sex with prostitutes, which is the solution for charmless men who are unable to attract mistresses or *ernai* with their appearances, fortunes or power. When the relationship ends, *ernai* would typically receive a 'buyout' compensation from her man. This compensation include stipends and properties that could support the *ernai* for the rest of her life and her children.

In the global context, informal polygamy or other similar extramarital relations are rather common. *Toqal*, a second or 'unofficial' wife in post-communist Kazakhstan, is very similar to the *ernai* in its neighbour country, China. *Toqal* derives from Islamic traditions, and other religions also endorse polygamous doctrines and practices. For instance, Fundamentalist Mormonism in Utah State in the USA practices polygamy, which was decriminalised in 2020.

Aside from polygamy based on centuries-old customs or religions, a variety of extramarital relationships similar to *ernai* exist worldwide. In Russian, *soderzhanka* stands for a kept woman, one who is living on the money of her partner. She plays the role between mistress and wife, as an *ernai* does in Chinese society. In the West, a similar phenomenon of *ernai* is the 'sugar baby' – typically a young person kept by a wealthier senior (Pardiwalla 2017).

As for the first wives, not all of them would tolerate *ernai*, and consequently this has become a major cause of family breakdowns (Onnis 2012). Wives' disgust regarding polygamy leads to divorce that hurts their children and destabilises society. Most surveyed Chinese interviewees considered the *ernai* phenomenon disdainful (Osburg 2016). In their opinion, keeping *ernai* is a 'feudal' lifestyle of the nouveau riche peasants, which should not have a place in modern society. As for impoverished men, they are stuck in chronic celibacy because financially successful men take a second or a third wife. For the government, the *ernai* problem is usually associated with corruption due to its extreme prevalence among public servants. The most extravagant statistic is that more than 90 per cent of party cadres convicted of corruption have an *ernai* (Watts 2007). As a result, excessive expenses on *ernai* are viewed as a drain on national wealth.

At present, utilitarianism dominates Chinese society as shown by the saying, 'people mock poverty more than prostitution' (*xiao pin bu xiao chang*). Like the ironic opening sentence in the nineteenth-century novel *Pride and Prejudice*: 'It is a truth universally acknowledged, that a single man in possession of a good fortune must be in want of a wife' (Austen 2003 [1813]), in China nowadays it is an unspoken understanding that 'a man of promise will contract a second wife' (Onnis 2012). Whether the *ernai* phenomenon will continue to prevail depends on social values. When material conditions are no longer considered significant factors in a marriage, people might choose their authentic love based on mutual affection and build more equal relationships that afford dignity.

4.10 *Toqal/Tokal* (Kazakhstan)
Nursultan Suleimenov
Alumnus, Law School, Warwick University, UK

Toqal is a Kazakh term that denotes a second or unofficial wife of a married man. This term has both the negative connotation of a morally reprehensible practice and a common association with wealth, such as in the Kazakh proverb: 'if a Kazakh gets rich, he takes a second wife'. The term derives from the Kazakh words, an adjective *toq*, meaning well-fed, and a verb *al* which means taking. The combined meaning communicates a simple message: if one can take care and afford it, why not get another wife (Khegay 2018). The roots of the phenomenon are linked to the tradition of polygamy, practised in other parts of the world for religious or demographic reasons (Vallely 2010).

Before Kazakhstan became a Soviet republic in 1936, Kazakh men had an official right to marry more than one wife, but no more than four women in total. However, only wealthy people from noble families could afford several wives (Najibullah 2011). A large family with several wives was a sign of a man's high status. The main function of the Kazakh polygamy was to solve the demographic crisis. A man could marry the *toqal* if she was a widow of a deceased relative (usually a brother), if there were no children in the first family, or with his first wife's consent.

Becoming part of the Soviet Union has resulted in the delegalisation of this tradition in Kazakhstan, as the Bolsheviks abolished polygamy in Russia and adjourning territories in 1917 (Yarmoshchuk and Zhetigenova 2019). This created a discrepancy between the law and practice in Kazakhstan during the Soviet period. Since the dissolution of the Soviet Union in 1991, polygamy in Kazakhstan remains officially prohibited, but it is decriminalised. In law, there is no provision for a 'second marriage' but there is a concept of 'cohabitation', which does not entail the same rights as official marriage (The Code of the Republic of Kazakhstan 'On Marriage (Matrimony) and Family 2019). In practice, male polygamy exists in Kazakhstan, as indicated in the open admission of Gabidulla Abdrakhimov, the former head of Shymkent, the third-largest city in Kazakhstan, and advisor to Prime Minister Mamin: 'I love both of my wives.' To the question, was polygamy permitted by law he replied: 'Allah allowed me to do this' (Yensebayeva 2019).

Kazakhstani parliament discussed the possibility of legalising male polygamy twice, in 2001 and 2008 (Shaykov 2008). Their main arguments were pragmatic (the need to improve the demographic situation), religious (polygamy is in men's nature and part of Muslim culture) and social (to accommodate for the needs of single women with the current imbalance between the number of women and men and to give them legal protection as a formal spouse). Some deputies pointed out that current practices of marrying a *toqal* have broken with Muslim and ancient Kazakh traditions. In Islam, the second wife could only be married with the official consent of the first wife – *baibishe*. There is also a provision that a man is obliged to ensure an equally worthy existence for all his wives. However, the canons of Islamic marriage law are based on the assumption that monogamous marriage is the most reasonable and relevant religious concept of godly fear and piety. The second, third or fourth wife is a canonical exception, which is condescendingly allowed by Islamic marriage law, but is determined by a number of possible circumstances. Sharia law does not contain calls for polygamy and does not consider it mandatory (Hussain 1965).

In Turkmenistan, where the Muslim population amounts to nearly 90 per cent, polygamy has been delegalised since September 2018, as spelt out in the Family Code and the Criminal Code. Moreover, the Turkmen legislation includes the definition of polygamy as cohabitation with two or more women at the same time when jointly managing a common household. The Turkmen Criminal Code states: 'A man who has several wives may face up to 2 years of corrective labour or a large fine' (Katsiev 2018).

As testified by a *baibishe*, polygamy is not an issue if it takes place openly (Najibullah 2011). Yet the contemporary practice of starting second families in Kazakhstan often resembles the covert extramarital relationships in non-Muslim societies. This makes the status of *toqal* closer to an 'official lover' than a 'second wife'. Since 2000, the use of the word *toqal* has become more prominent in Kazakhstani society. The economic growth in Kazakhstan due to the extraction and export of natural resources allowed a significant increase in income for the male population. The phenomenon of *toqal* became associated with businessmen and officials with higher salaries. Women from the second, unofficial family, began to be called *toqal* in reference to the long-standing Muslim tradition of polygamy in Kazakhstan.

In 1998, the capital of Kazakhstan was moved from Almaty to Astana (renamed as Nur-Sultan in 2019). An unintended consequence of the change was the need for officials to relocate, often without their wives and children, who were left behind in the old capital. This gave them the opportunity to start a second family. Due to officials living parallel lives in the two cities, the new capital Nur-Sultan is called the 'Toqal city' in the vernacular, while the old capital Almaty is called the 'city of baibishe' (Yarmoshchuk and Zhetigenova 2019).

The pragmatics of becoming the *toqal* are commonly associated with access to financial wealth. Indicative of the heavily masculine culture, every appointment of a young woman to a high position in Kazakhstan is accompanied by rumours about whose daughter or *toqal* this woman might be. Other stereotypes include a *toqal* either being a 'kept woman', ordinarily by a much older man, or someone who hopes to become the only wife one day. Some research draws a distinction between *toqal-wives* and *toqal-lovers* (Kaziyev 2017). *Toqal-wives* are usually ambitious women, unaffordable for the average Kazakhstani man. They have an excellent education, often under the patronage of their *agashka* (see 1.15 Volume 1) (Oka 2018: 86–8). They engage in business or charity affairs and earn a considerable income. They often have children with their protegé. *Toqal-lovers* are often financially independent and have professional skills and knowledge. They are described as looking for romance in relationships and the opportunity to lean on a strong male shoulder. Their 'husbands' may be middle-income Kazakhstani who can be responsible for protecting and caring for them and their children.

However, the *toqal* status has legal and social drawbacks for women. It does not carry legal protection and does not offer the right to property as a spouse. *Toqal* may not have the paternity of the child registered, because marriage is registered only in the mosque, and she is thus not entitled to child support if the relationship breaks down (Nur. kz 2015). Social condemnation of society is aimed mainly at *toqal* rather than the man who starts the 'second family'. Becoming a *toqal* is seen as a woman's voluntary choice. Kazakh TV presenter Laila Sultankyzyl, a *toqal* of a well-known businessman, Kairat Berkinbaev, according to media reports, expressed her position on being a *toqal* as follows:

> We live in a period of transformation, adaptation to changing living conditions as part of the global community. We are no longer the Kazakh steppes we were before the USSR. The influence of world cultures, both positive and negative, forms a new nation. So far, we are not doing very well. We are losing traditions that are important to us, and not everything that we are adopting we truly need. Our family institution is in serious crisis. One of us will have a family or two – it is not so important if our families are happy. Who needs our achievements and economic recovery if we are unhappy in the simplest and most necessary thing – in the family? Meanwhile, I, Laila Sultankyzy, having seen myself in the list of the seven most famous *toqal* of Kazakhstan in the press, declare that I am a WIFE. (Sultankyzyl 2013)

While some Kazakhstanis believe that it is normal to have a wife on the side, many *toqal* are offended by the term 'lover' since they consider themselves wives. However, being a *toqal* means having no guarantees that the practice will not be outlawed at some point in the future.

4.11 **Burrnesha** (Albania)
Ellen Robertson
Department of Psychology, University of Cambridge, UK

Burrnesha, Albanian sworn virgins, are physiological women, primarily from rural regions of northern Albania, who live as men and refrain from marriage or sexual activity. They adopt masculine dress, hairstyle, work roles, mannerisms and speech. They may even adopt behaviours that are typically only acceptable for men to practice in their communities, such as smoking, cursing, carrying arms and drinking liquor. They are sometimes visually indistinguishable from men. However, it is not socially acceptable for them to get married or to have sexual relations of any kind. There are some reports of sworn virgins having taken a formal oath of virginity; however, this seems more common in theory than in practice (Young 2001).

It is difficult to pinpoint with certainty the origin of this practice due to the lack of records. However, it was described in the *kanun*, an informal compilation of social rules passed down orally for centuries in these communities. This dates the custom from at least as early as the fifteenth century (Ilia 1993; Gjecovi 2010).

The *kanun* states that it is acceptable for women to live as men if there are no or few males in their family, if they wish to honourably reject an arranged marriage or if they simply desire to live as men (Ilia 1993; Gjecovi 2010). In practice women may choose to live as men for many other reasons, including to inherit their family's property or to fight in war. Overall, becoming a *burrneshe* is particularly instrumental

Figure 4.11.1 Sworn virgin. 2016. © Ellen Robertson.

in allowing women to live with their birth families; under typical circumstances they would move in with their husbands as soon as they were married. By living with their birth families sworn virgins are able to offer them various types of support. First, they provide practical support such as labour. Second, a family's status increases with the number of its male members. In this way sworn virgins contribute to the symbolic well-being of the family, which can have material consequences such as greater leverage in inheritance disputes (Durham 1910; Young 2001).

Sworn virgins not only live as men, but are also treated and respected as men. They are included in spaces typically reserved only for men, such as village meetings and the home's sitting/dining room. Under typical circumstances women have a much lower status than men and are excluded from many spaces and activities, so this shift is significant (Durham 1910; Young 2001). It is also considered safe for sworn virgins to walk alone far from home, for example to travel between villages or to herd goats. This increase in status is often justified as having been earned by the 'sacrifice' that they made in order to support their family as men.

There are several different terms used for these women in Albanian. The original term used in the *kanun* is *virgjineshe*, meaning virgin (see also *virdžina* or *tobelija* in the online encyclopaedia). However, today the word *burrneshe* (plural: *burrnesha*) is more commonly used. *Burrneshe* literally means man (*burre*) followed by a feminine ending (*-eshe*). Other terms are used less frequently, such as *sokoleshe*. *Sokol* literally means falcon but is used to denote a man of especially admirable and stereotypically masculine traits. As with the word *burrneshe*, the ending *-eshe* makes this semantically hyper-masculine word grammatically feminine. As such, these terms are simultaneously masculine and feminine, as opposed to representing a third gender category.

In Serbo-Croatian-speaking Balkan countries where this custom exists, these women are often referred to as *tobelija* (Horváth 2011). Meanwhile, in other languages the term for these women is usually a local equivalent of 'sworn virgin' (for example, *vergine giurata* in Italian) due to the understanding that they sometimes take an oath of virginity.

The words *burrneshe* and *sokoleshe* are titles that convey great respect and admiration. They signify bravery, wisdom and strength of character. Excluding sworn virgins' northern Albanian communities, the rest of the Albanian-speaking world usually uses these titles for women living as ordinary women who have earned the respect. For example, a woman who has confronted considerable hardship in responsible and honourable ways may be called a *burrneshe*.

The practice of sworn virgins has been reported in several Balkan nations. The highest number of them has been reported among ethnic Albanian communities of northern Albania and Kosovo. However, there have also been reports of ethnic Slavic sworn virgins in Montenegro, Bosnia, Croatia and Serbia (Young and Twigg 2009). The actual number of sworn virgins in existence is difficult to measure; however, an Albanologist and the sworn virgin expert Antonia Young estimates the number to be around 100 at the turn of the twenty-first century. Her *Women Who Become Men: Albanian Sworn Virgins* (2001) is the most thorough modern account of Albanian sworn virgins, highlighting the ambivalence of tradition that in this case makes a complete turnaround of customary gender divisions. Horváth's anthropological works interrogated the Western gaze in its portrayals of sworn virgins and the Balkans (Horváth 2011).

There are other cultures of the world where it is socially acceptable for people to assume the lifestyle of another gender for reasons other than gender identity. There is an Afghan practice called *bacha posh* whereby young girls may dress as boys. This satisfies the family's preference for a son while affording the girls more freedom and safety. However, unlike Albanian sworn virgins this practice ends at puberty, after which point it is considered socially unacceptable (Strochlic 2018).

Bibliography to Chapter 4

Introduction: marriage and informality
Péter Berta

Bennion, J. (2012) *Polygamy in Primetime: Media, Gender, and Politics in Mormon Fundamentalism*. Waltham: Brandeis University Press.

Berta, P. 2019. *Materializing Difference: Consumer Culture, Politics, and Ethnicity among Romanian Roma*. Toronto, Buffalo, London: University of Toronto Press.

Berta, P. 2023. 'Arranged Marriage as a Process: From Premarital Normalization of Arranged Marriage to Arranged Divorce and Arranged Remarriage'. In *Arranged Marriage: The Politics of Tradition, Resistance, and Change*, edited by P. Berta, 67–90. New Brunswick: Rutgers University Press.

Chantler, K. and McCarry, M. 2020. 'Forced Marriage, Coercive Control, and Conducive Contexts: The Experiences of Women in Scotland'. *Violence Against Women* 26(1): 89–109.

Chantler, K., Baker, V., MacKenzie, M., McCarry, M. and Mirza, N. 2017. 'Understanding Forced Marriage in Scotland: Equality, Poverty and Social Security'. *Scottish Government*. www.gov.scot/binaries/content/documents/govscot/publications/research-and-analysis/2017/01/understanding-forced-marriage-scotland/documents/00513514-pdf/00513514-pdf/govscot%3Adocument/00513514.pdf

Petrella, S. 2023. 'Nothing "Celestial" About It: Trafficking Underage Brides between Canada and the United States for the Purposes of Arranged Marriage'. In *Arranged Marriage: The Politics of Tradition, Resistance, and Change*, edited by P. Berta, 33–47. New Brunswick: Rutgers University Press.

Quek, K. 2018. *Marriage Trafficking: Women in Forced Wedlock*. London: Routledge.

4.1 *Caili* (China)
Ling Zhang

Caldwell, J. C., Reddy, P. H. and Caldwell, P. 1983. 'The Causes of Marriage Change in South India'. *Population Studies* 37(3): 343–61.
Gong, X., Qiao, X. and Cong, J. 2018. 'Social Lopsided Exchange: On High Bride Price in Rural Areas – Taking Village X, Town Q in Heze County as an Example'. In 2018 4th International Conference on Social Science and Higher Education (ICSSHE 2018). Atlantis Press.
Jiang, Q. and Sánchez-Barricarte, J. J. 2012. 'Bride Price in China: The Obstacle to "Bare Branches" Seeking Marriage'. *The History of the Family* 17(1): 2–15.
Jiang, Q., Zhang, Y. and Sánchez-Barricarte, J. J. 2015. 'Marriage Expenses in Rural China'. *The China Review* 15(1): 207–36.
Lv, J. (2006). 'An Investigation on Poverty in the Northern Rural Area in China'. *Chinese Writers* 22(19): 118–37.
Si, M. and Wang, J. 2018. 'Analysis of High Bride Price from a Cultural Perspective'. In 2nd International Conference on Art Studies: Science, Experience, Education (ICASSEE 2018). Amsterdam: Atlantis Press.

4.2 *Ala kachuu* (Kyrgyzstan)
Alberica Camerani

Akyykatchy Kyrgyzskoy Respubliki. 2018. 'Ala Kachuu – Pozornoye Yavleniye dlya Kyrgyzstana, – Ombudsmen', 6 June. https://ombudsman.kg/index.php?option=com_content&view=article&id=538:ала-качуу---позорное-явление-для-кыргызстана,---омбудсмен&catid=18&lang=ru&Itemid=330
Amsler, S. and Kleinbach, R. 1999. 'Bride Kidnapping in the Kyrgyz Republic'. *International Journal of Central Asian Studies* 4: 185–216.
Becker, C. M., Mirkasimov, B. and Steiner, S. 2017. 'Forced Marriage and Birth Outcomes'. *Demography* 54(4): 1401–23.
Borbieva, N. O. 2012. 'Kidnapping Women: Discourses of Emotion and Social Change in the Kyrgyz Republic'. *Anthropological Quarterly* 85(1): 141–69.
Handrahan, L. 2004. 'Hunting for Women: Bride-Kidnapping in Kyrgyzstan'. *International Feminist Journal of Politics* 6(2): 207–33.
Ibraeva, G., Moldosheva, A. and Niyazova, A. 2011. *World Development Report 2012: Gender Equality and Development: Kyrgyz Country Case Study*. World Bank. https://openknowledge.worldbank.org/server/api/core/bitstreams/3cbf4776-2807-58b1-a41e-a850a9d732be/content
Kalikov, M. 2021. '"Ala kachuu – eto ne traditsiya, eto ugolovno nakazuyemoye prestupleniye". Prem'yer Maripov otreagiroval na ubiystvo Ayzady Kanatbekovoy'. Kloop.kg, 8 April. https://kloop.kg/blog/2021/04/08/ala-kachuu-eto-ne-traditsiya-eto-ugolovno-nakazuemoe-prestuplenie-premer-maripov-otreagiroval-na-ubijstvo-ajzady-kanatbekovoj/
Kim, E. 2020. 'Re-Feminizing the Post-Soviet Women: Identity, Politics and Virginity Ceremonies in Contemporary Kyrgyzstan'. *Journal of Gender Studies* 29(6): 706–16.
Kleinbach, R. and Salimjanova, L. 2007. 'Kyz Ala Kachuu and Adat: Non-Consensual Bride Kidnapping and Tradition in Kyrgyzstan'. *Central Asian Survey* 26(2): 217–33.
Luzyuk, K. 2011. 'Yezhegodno v Kyrgyzstane pokhishchayetsya 16 tysyach chelovek'. Vesti.kg, 25 November. https://vesti.kg/obshchestvo/item/8879-ezhegodno-v-kyirgyizstane-pohischaetsya-16-tyisyach-chelovek.html
Radio Free Europe/Radio Liberty. 2014. 'Bride kidnapping in Kyrgyzstan', 29 May. www.rferl.org/a/bride-kidnapping-in-kyrgyzstan/25403604.html
Ulanova, B. 2021. 'Kadyr Malikov: Soglasno islamu, ala kachuu – bol'shoy grekh i tyazhkoye prestupleniye', *Kaktus Media*, 8 April. https://kaktus.media/doc/435370_kadyr_malikov:_soglasno_islamy_ala_kachyy_bolshoy_greh_i_tiajkoe_prestyplenie.html
UNFPA. 2016. 'Gender in Perception of Society. National Survey Results'. https://kyrgyzstan.unfpa.org/sites/default/files/pub-pdf/GSPS_english.pdf

Werner, C. 2009. 'Bride Abduction in Post-Soviet Central Asia: Marking a Shift towards Patriarchy through Local Discourses of Shame and Tradition'. *Journal of the Royal Anthropological Institute* 15(2): 314–31.
Werner, C. et al. 2018. 'Bride Kidnapping in Post-Soviet Eurasia: A Roundtable Discussion'. *Central Asian Survey* 37(4): 582–601.

4.3 *Mendanghudui* (China)
Shiqi Yin

Becker, G. S. 1973. 'A Theory of Marriage: Part I'. *The Journal of Political Economy* 82(2): 11–26.
Becker, G. S. 1974. 'A Theory of Marriage: Part II'. *The Journal of Political Economy* 82(2): 11–26.
Burgess, E. W. and Wallin, P. 1943. 'Homogamy in Social Characteristics'. *The American Journal of Sociology* 49(2): 109–24.
Fei, X. 1999. *From the Soil: The Foundations of Chinese Society*. Beijing: Peking University Press.
Gale, D. and Shapley, L. S. 1962. 'College Admissions and the Stability of Marriage'. *The American Mathematical Monthly* 69(1): 9–15.
Gao, X. 2017. 'The Traditional Chinese Concept of Marriage: "Mendanghudui"'. *Culture Journal* (07): 39–41.
Hu, Y. 2016. 'Marriage of Matching Doors'. *Demographic Research* 35: 557–80.
Kang, Y. and Li, Y. 2016. 'Exploring the Relationship between Inheriting Good Family Traditions and Establishing Correct "Three Views"'. *Innovation and Entrepreneurship Education* 7(02): 151–4.
Li, Y. 2008. 'Educational Matching in Marriage: Changes over 50 Years'. *Chinese Population Science* (3): 73–9.
Tian, Y. 2017. 'A Study on the Sociological Basis of "Door-to-Door Matching"'. *Talent* (33): 234–6.
Wang, F. 2020. 'The Origins of the Phrase "Mendanghudui"'. *The World of Literature and History* 2(06): 92.
Yang, W. 2014. 'Exploring the Consolidation of Social Classes in China during the Transition Period'. *Party School of the Central Committee of the Communist Party of China*.

4.4 *Nikoh* (Tajikistan)
Madina Gazieva

Borisova, E. 2021. '"Our Traditions Will Kill Us!": Negotiating Marriage Celebrations in the Face of Legal Regulation of Tradition in Tajikistan'. *Oriente Moderno* 100(2): 147–71.
Bredal, A. 2018. 'Contesting the Boundaries between Civil and Religious Marriage'. *Sociology of Islam* 6(3): 297–315.
Brenhouse, H. 2011. '"We R Over": Tajikistan's Religious Officials Ban Divorce by Text Message'. *Time*, 12 April. https://newsfeed.time.com/2011/04/12/we-r-over-tajikistans-religious-officials-ban-divorce-by-text-message/
Cabar.asia. 2020. 'Number of Divorces Grows in Tajikistan', 11 November. https://cabar.asia/en/number-of-divorces-grows-in-tajikistan
Cleuziou, J. 2016. '"A Second Wife is Not Really a Wife": Polygyny, Gender Relations and Economic Realities in Tajikistan'. *Central Asian Survey* 35(1): 76–90.
Edgar, A. 2006. 'Bolshevism, Patriarchy, and the Nation: The Soviet "Emancipation" of Muslim Women in Pan-Islamic Perspective'. *Slavic Review* 65(2): 252–72.
Eurasianet. 2018. 'The Conundrum of Tajikistan's Female Suicides', 1 November. https://eurasianet.org/the-conundrum-of-tajikistans-female-suicides
Harris, C. 2000. *Control and Subversion: Gender, Islam, and Socialism in Tajikistan*. PhD thesis, University of Amsterdam.
Helie, A. and Hoodfar, H. 2021. *Sexuality in Muslim Contexts: Restrictions and Resistance*. London: Zed Books.
Martykánová, D. 2009. 'Matching Sharia and "Governmentality": Muslim Marriage Legislation in the Late Ottoman Empire'. In *Institutional Change and Stability: Conflicts, Transitions and Social Values*, edited by A. Gémes, F. Peyrou and I. Xydopoulos, 168–70. Pisa: Pisa University Press.

Moors, A., Akhtar, R. C. and Probert, R. 2018. 'Contextualizing Muslim Religious-Only Marriages'. *Sociology of Islam* 6(3): 263–73.
Najibullah, F. 2016. 'Tajik Polygamy: "Secret" Second Wives Confront Risk, But Often It's Too Late'. *Radio Free Europe/Radio Liberty*, 26 October. www.refworld.org/docid/5a9fc630a.html
Petersen, J. 2021. 'The Islamic Juridical Vacuum and Islamic Authorities' Role in Divorce Cases'. *Naveiñ Reet: Nordic Journal of Law and Social Research* 10: 67–84.
Probert, R. and Saleem, S. 2018. 'The Legal Treatment of Islamic Marriage Ceremonies'. *Oxford Journal of Law and Religion* 7(3): 376–400.
Roche, S. and Hohmann, S. 2011. 'Wedding Rituals and the Struggle Over National Identities'. *Central Asian Survey* 30(1): 113–28.
Tasar, E. 2017. *Soviet and Muslim: The Institutionalization of Islam in Central Asia. 1943–1991*. Oxford: Oxford University Press.
Thibault, H. 2018. 'Labour Migration, Sex, and Polygyny: Negotiating Patriarchy in Tajikistan'. *Ethnic and Racial Studies* 41(15): 2809–26.
Tremayne, S. 2006. 'Modernity and Early Marriage in Iran: A View from Within'. *Journal of Middle East Women's Studies* 2(1): 65–94.

4.5 *Sdelat' ZAGS* (Tajik diaspora in Russia)
Elena Borisova

Abashin, S. 2016. 'Migration Policies in Russia: Laws and Debates'. In *Migrant Workers in Russia*, edited by K. Aitamurto and A.-L. Heusala, 16–34. Milton Park: Taylor & Francis.
Bahovadinova, M. 2018. 'Representing the Social Costs of Migration: Abandoned Wives or Nonchalant Women'. www.academia.edu/37760944/Representing_the_Social_Costs_of_Migration_Abandoned_Wives_or_Nonchalant_Women
Borisova, E. 2020. 'The Limits of Strategic Citizenship: Affective Engagements with Russian Passports in the Context of Migration from Tajikistan'. *Social Anthropology* 28(4): 827–42.
Chudinovskikh, O. and Denisenko, M. 2020. 'Labour Migration on the Post-Soviet Territory'. In *Migration from the Newly Independent States 25 Years After the Collapse of the USSR*, edited by M. Denisenko, M. Light and S. Strozza, 55–80. New York: Springer.
Cieślewska, A. 2021. 'Second Wife, Second Life: Polygyny Among Migrants from Central Asia in Moscow'. *Oriente Moderno* 100(2): 225–47.
Cleuziou, J. 2017. 'Towards Matrifocal Families? Relations in Transnational and Single Parent Families in Tajikistan'. In *The Family in Central Asia: New Perspectives*, edited by S. Roche, 309–36. Berlin: Klaus Schwarz Verlag.
Ibañez-Tirado, D. 2019. '"We Sit and Wait": Migration, Mobility and Temporality in Guliston, Southern Tajikistan'. *Current Sociology* 67(2): 315–33.
International Organization for Migration (IOM). 2019. World Migration Report 2020. M. Mcauliffe and B. Khadria (eds). Geneva.
Kubal, A. 2016. 'Spiral Effect of the Law: Migrants' Experiences of the State Law in Russia – a Comparative Perspective'. *International Journal of Law in Context* 12(4): 453–68.
Reeves, M. 2012. 'Black Work, Green Money: Remittances, Ritual, and Domestic Economies in Southern Kyrgyzstan'. *Slavic Review* 1(1): 108–34.
Reeves, M. 2013. 'Clean Fake: Authenticating Documents and Persons in Migrant Moscow'. *American Ethnologist* 40(3): 508–24.
Schenk, C. 2018. *Why Control Immigration?: Strategic Uses of Migration Management in Russia*. Toronto: University of Toronto Press.
Urinboyev, R. 2020. *Migration and Hybrid Political Regimes: Navigating the Legal Landscape in Russia*. Berkeley: University of California Press.
Voices on Central Asia. 2021. 'Central Asian Migration to Russia: Legalization in 2020', 18 February. https://voicesoncentralasia.org/central-asian-migration-to-russia-legalization-in-2020/?fbclid=IwAR2qsTrLfeE3lTGariM_jnKH0Vc6Lu9GVxQfl0IkEUq6HDQAdJTV6sEJ2v8
Zotova, N. and Cohen, J. H. 2020. 'Left Behind? Russia's Entry Bars and Gender Relations in Tajikistan'. *Nationalities Papers* 48(4): 675–89.

4.6 *Bridezilla* (UK, North America, Australia)
Julia Carter

Akorsu, A. D. 2016. 'Feminization of Labor'. In *The Wiley Blackwell Encyclopedia of Gender and Sexuality Studies*, edited by N. Naples et al. Wiley-Blackwell.

Boden, S. 2003. *Consumerism, Romance and the Wedding Experience*. Basingstoke: Palgrave Macmillan.

Carter, J. and Duncan, S. 2016. 'Wedding Paradoxes: Individualized Conformity and the "Perfect Day"'. *The Sociological Review* 65 (1): 3–20.

Carter, J. and Duncan, S. 2018. *Reinventing Couples: Tradition, Agency and Bricolage*. Basingstoke: Palgrave Macmillan.

Douglas, S. J. 2010. *Enlightened Sexism: The Seductive Message that Feminism's Work Is Done*. New York: Henry Holt & Co.

Engstrom, E. 2012. *The Bride Factory: Mass Media Portrayals of Women and Weddings*. Oxford: Peter Lang.

Illouz, E. 1997. *Consuming the Romantic Utopia: Love and the Cultural Contradictions of Capitalism*. London: University of California Press.

Indeed.co.uk. 2019. 'Wedding Planner Salary in England'. www.indeed.co.uk/salaries/Wedding-Planner-Salaries,-England

Kristeva, J. 1982. *Powers of Horror: An Essay on Abjection*. New York: Columbia University Press.

Lux Life magazine. 2019. 'Global Wedding Awards'. www.lux-review.com/lux_awards/wedding-awards/

McRobbie, A. 2009. *The Aftermath of Feminism: Gender, Culture and Social Change*. London: Sage.

Moorhead, L. 2018. 'Devil in a White Dress: Brides are Too Afraid of Becoming "Bridezilla" to Ask for What They Want'. *Washington Post*, 14 September. www.washingtonpost.com/news/posteverything/wp/2018/09/14/feature/brides-are-too-afraid-of-becoming-bridezilla-to-ask-for-what-they-want/

Samek, A. A. 2012. 'Domesticating Matrimonial Monstrosity: *Bridezillas* and Narratives of Feminine Containment'. In *Media Depictions of Brides, Wives, and Mothers*, edited by A. Ruggerio, 11–25. Plymouth: Lexington Books.

The Wedding Planner (2001) [DVD] Directed by Adam Shankman. United States: Columbia Pictures, Intermedia, Tapestry Films, Dee Gee Entertainment, Prufrock Pictures.

4.7 *Karmir khndzor* (Armenia)
Anna Temkina and Lilit Zakaryan

Carpenter, L. 2005. *Virginity Lost: An Intimate Portrait of First Sexual Experiences*. New York: New York University Press.

de Beauvoir, S. 1949. *Le Deuxième Sexe*. Paris: Gallimard.

Kandiyoti, D. 1988. 'Bargaining with Patriarchy', *Gender and Society* 2(3): 274–90.

Ortner, S. 1978. 'The Virgin and the State', *Feminist Studies* 4(3): 19–35.

Poghosyan, A. 2010. *Some of the Features of the Conversion of the Tradition 'Red Apple': Tradition and Modernity in Armenian Culture*. Yerevan: Gitutyuan.

Poghosyan, A. 2011. *Red Apple Tradition: Contemporary Interpretations and Observance*. Acta Ethnographica Hungarica.

Shagoyan, G. 2011. '"Seven Days, Seven Nights": Panorama of the Armenian Wedding'. *Institute of Archaeology and Ethnography of National Academy of Sciences*: 496–509.

Shahnazaryan, N. 2015. 'O Krasnom Yabloke, Gimenoplastike i Ohote Na Ved'm: Bukva Nashej Tradicii Versus Seksual'naya Revolyuciya?'. The Analitikon. http://theanalyticon.com/?p=7137&lang=ru

Temkina, A. 2008. *Seksual'naya Zhizn' Zhenshchiny: Mezhdu Podchineniem i Svobodoj*. SPb: Izdatel'stvo EUSPb.

Temkina, A. 2010. '"Dobrachnaya Devstvennost": Kul'turnyj Kod Gendernogo Poryadka v Sovremennoj Armenii (na Primere Erevana)'. *Laboratorium* 1: 129–59.

4.8 *Kelin* (Central Asia)
Tommaso Aguzzi

Beyer, J. and Finke, P. 2019. 'Practices of Traditionalization in Central Asia'. *Central Asian Survey* 38(3): 310–28.
Bietsch, K. E., La Nasa, K. H. and Sonneveldt, E. 2021. 'Women Living with Their Mothers-in-Law'. *Gates Open Research* 5: 170.
Brusina, O. I. 2008. 'Sharia and Civil Law in Marital Relations of the Muslim Population in Central Asia'. *Anthropology & Archeology of Eurasia* 47(2): 53–68.
Cleuziou, J. and Direnberger, L. 2016. 'Gender and Nation in Post-Soviet Central Asia: from National Narratives to Women's Practices'. *Nationalities Papers* 44(2): 195–206.
Dildabayeva, Z. 2021. 'Do Movies Like "Kelinka Sabina" Reflect an Attitude of Society Towards Women or Form It?'. Cabar.asia, 6 September. https://cabar.asia/en/do-movies-like-kelinka-sabina-reflect-an-attitude-of-society-towards-women-or-form-it
Golden, P. B. 2011. *Central Asia in World History*. Oxford: Oxford University Press.
Ismailbekova, A. 2016. 'Constructing the Authority of Women through Custom: Bulak Village, Kyrgyzstan'. *Nationalities Papers* 44(2): 266–80.
Kabylova, M. 2021. 'Examining the Causes of Femicide in Kazakhstan', Central Asia Program, https://centralasiaprogram.org/examining-femicide-kazakhstan/
Kudaibergenova, D. 2018. 'Project "Kelin" Marriage, Women, and Re-Traditionalization in Post-Soviet Kazakhstan'. In *Women of Asia: Globalization, Development, and Gender Equity*, edited by M. Najafizadeh and L. L. Lindsey, 379–90. London: Routledge.
Lerman, Z. 2021. 'Gender Gaps in Central Asia: A Reassessment', *Central Asian Journal of Water Research* 7(2): 47–73.
Reynolds, R. 2012. 'Homemaking, Homebuilding, and the Significance of Place and Kin in Rural Kyrgyzstan'. *Home Cultures* 9(3): 285–302.
Turaeva, R. 2020. 'Kelin in Central Asia'. In *The Family in Central Asia: New Perspectives*, edited by S. Roche, 171–83. Berlin, Boston: De Gruyter.
UNFPA Kazakhstan. 2020. 'UN Calls for Peace at Home During COVID-19 Outbreak in Kazakhstan. https://kazakhstan.unfpa.org/en/news/un-calls-peace-home-during-covid-19-outbreak-kazakhstan
UNFPA EECARO. 2014. 'Child Marriage in Kazakhstan'. United Nations Population Fund. https://eeca.unfpa.org/sites/default/files/pub-pdf/unfpa%20kazakhstan%20overview.pdf
Zhussipbek, G. and Nagayeva, Z. 2021. 'Human Rights of Daughters-in-Law (Kelins) in Central Asia: Harmful Traditional Practices and Structural Oppression'. *Central Asian Survey* 40(2): 222–41.

4.9 *Ernai* (China)
Ouxiang Ji

Austen, J. 2003 [1813]. *Pride and Prejudice*. Penguin Classics.
Onnis, B. 2012. 'The Scourge of Prostitution in Contemporary China: The "Bao Ernai" Phenomenon'. *Asian Culture and History* 4(2): 91–8.
Osburg, J. 2016. 'Pleasure, Patronage, and Responsibility: Sexuality and Status among New Rich Men in Contemporary China'. In *Cultural Politics of Gender and Sexuality in Contemporary Asia*, edited by T. Zheng, 108–23. University of Hawai'i Press.
Pardiwalla, A. 2017. 'Sugaring: A New Kind of Irresistible'. *HuffPost*. www.huffpost.com/entry/post_b_9683356
Shih, S.-M. 2007. *Visuality and Identity: Sinophone Articulations Across the Pacific*. Berkeley: University of California Press.
Song, S. 2013. 'Chinese Mistress Culture 101: The Difference Between an Ernai and a Xiaosan'. *International Business Times*. www.ibtimes.com/chinese-mistress-culture-101-difference-between-ernai-xiaosan-1422930
Watts, J. 2007. 'Concubine Culture Brings Trouble for China's Bosses'. *The Guardian*. www.theguardian.com/world/2007/sep/08/china.jonathanwatts

Xiao, S. 2011. 'The "Second-Wife" Phenomenon and the Relational Construction of Class-Coded Masculinities in Contemporary China'. *Men and Masculinities* 14(5): 607–27.

Zurndorfer, H. 2016. 'Polygamy and Masculinity in China: Past and Present'. In *Changing Chinese Masculinities: From Imperial Pillars of State to Global Real Men*, edited by K. Louie, 13–33. Hong Kong: Hong Kong University Press.

4.10 *Toqal/Tokal* (Kazakhstan)
Nursultan Suleimenov

Hussain, S. J. 1965. 'Legal Modernism in Islam: Polygamy and Repudiation'. *Journal of the Indian Law Institute* 7(4): 384–98.

Katsiev, A. 2018. 'Polygamy Officially Banned in Turkmenistan'. *Mir24*. https://mir24.tv/news/16310366/v-turkmenistane-oficialno-zapretili-mnogozhenstvo

Kaziyev, T. 2017. '"Toqalki Life". Prikaspiyskaya Kommuna'. http://pricom.kz/kultura/tokalki-life.html

Khegay, M. 2018. 'Filolog Khakim Omar: Blagodaria Tokal Sostoyalas' Kazakhskaia Natsiia'. Karavan, 9 January. www.caravan.kz/gazeta/filolog-khakim-omar-blagodarya-tokal-sostoyalas-kazakhskaya-naciya-388854/

Najibullah, F. 2011. 'Polygamy a Fact of Life in Kazakhstan'. RFE/RL. 21 June. www.rferl.org/a/polygamy_a_fact_of_life_in_kazakhstan/24242198.html

Nur.kz. 2015. 'Pochemu Kazakhstanskiye Devushki Stanovyatsya Tokal?', Nur.kz. 30 September.

Oka, N. 2018. 'Agashka (Kazakhstan)'. In *Global Encyclopaedia of Informality. Volume 1: Towards Understanding of Social and Cultural Complexity*, edited by A. Ledeneva et al., 464. London: UCL Press.

Shaykov, A. 2008. 'Uzakonit' Mnogozhenstvo ili Net?', Zakon.kz. 20 March.

Sultankyzyl, L. 2013. 'Laila Sultankizy o Fenomene "Tokal" v Kazakhstane'. L'Officiel. 13 January.

The Code of the Republic of Kazakhstan 'On Marriage (Matrimony) and Family'. 2019. Zakon.kz. https://online.zakon.kz/document/?doc_id=31102748

Vallely, P. 2010. 'The Big Question: What's the History of Polygamy, and How Serious a Problem is it in Africa?'. *The Independent*, 6 January. www.independent.co.uk/news/world/africa/the-big-question-what-s-the-history-of-polygamy-and-how-serious-a-problem-is-it-in-africa-1858858.html

Yarmoshchuk, T. and Zhetigenova, A. 2019. '"Kharam i Khalyal". Zachem Muzhchiny v Tsentral'noy Azii Zavodyat Vtoruyu Sem'yu'?. Nastoiashee Vremia. 4 April.

Yensebayeva, M. 2019. 'Gabidulla Abdrakhimov "Ischerpal Kredit Doveriia" za God. Vspominaem Samye Gromkie Sobytiia'. InformBureau.kz. 30 July.

4.11 *Burrnesha* (Albania)
Ellen Robertson

Durham, E. 1910. *High Albania*. London: Edward Arnold.

Gjecovi, S. 2010. *Kanuni i Leke Dukagjinit*. Shkoder: Botime Franceskane.

Horváth, A. 2011. 'Of Female Chastity and Male Arms: The Balkan "Man-Woman" in the Age of the World Picture'. *Journal of the History of Sexuality* 20(2): 358.

Ilia, F. 1993. *Kanuni i Skanderbegut*. Milot: Rosa.

Strochlic, N. 2018. 'Inside the Lives of Girls Dressed as Boys in Afghanistan'. *National Geographic*, 2 March. www.nationalgeographic.com/photography/proof/2018/march/bacha-posh-gender-afghanistan

Young, A. 2001. *Women Who Become Men: Albanian Sworn Virgins*. Oxford: Berg.

Young, A. and Twigg, L. 2009. '"Sworn Virgins" as Enhancers of Albanian Patriarchal Society in Contrast to Emerging Roles for Albanian Women'. *Etnološka Tribina* 32(39): 117–34.

5
Belonging and social exclusion

Introduction: gender, social exclusion and the dark side of informal networks

Sven Horak
St. John's University, New York, USA
and
Fadi Alsarhan
ISC Paris Business School, Paris, France

Informal networking has been regarded as an important accelerator for getting a job and career progression in general (Granovetter 1995, 2017). However, there has been little discussion about whether this holds true for men and women alike, and whether we can generalise across countries. Informal networking can have drawbacks like its vulnerability to cronyism, favouritism and non-transparency that leads to unfair decisions (for example, jobs may be given to incompetent but well-connected individuals). In parallel with a discussion of the dark side of informal networking that currently evolves beyond the traditional themes of corruption and bribery (Horak et al. 2020), policymakers have discovered that social exclusion can become a negative side effect of informal networking. On the contrary, social inclusion is crucial to democratic development.

According to the European Commission (2002), certain factors negatively influence an individual's social inclusion, one of them being gender. In business, gendered social contexts function as barriers to women's careers (O'Neil et al. 2008). This is especially true in male-dominated organisations where female employees are socially isolated and have less access to developmental experiences (Fitzsimmons et al. 2014). While research has been conducted on the dark side of social networks, as well as on the same theme with a focus on social exclusion, so far, both discussions have developed in parallel. In order to connect both, we suggest further development of social exclusion theory by including gender-relevant aspects in an informal network context. How far do informal networks exclude women from access to social resources by obstructing them from accessing informal networks? This is an important question that to date has not been fully explored.

Social exclusion theory has primarily focused on its effects on the individual; little attention has been paid to the exclusion of groups from positions of power in managerial professions. Thus far, poverty has been the major focus of research on social exclusion. However, whereas poverty excludes an individual from certain areas of society on a monetary basis, social exclusion refers to the exclusion from different areas of society, political, economic and civic (Walker and Walker 1997; de Haan 1998). Social exclusion poses questions concerning access to resources and common cultural practices as well as to social networks and support (Saith 2001). Some scholars define it as 'lack of social capital' and regard social participation as a counteragent (Percy-Smith 2000). Furthermore, Nussbaum (2005) and Sen (1999, 2005) focused on the ability to attain self-fulfilment in all aspects of life. Social exclusion itself can be seen as a part of capability poverty (Sen 2000). For instance, this is an approach used by the World Bank to explain poverty in developing countries. However, how far informal networking and cultural practices are intertwined and how this leads to social exclusion as a form of gender discrimination has not been extensively analysed, yet. In the following discussion, we will present two examples of informal networks in order to show how their male dominance and intertwinement with cultural traditions represent sources of social exclusion of women as a facet of gender discrimination. The examples consist of informal networks in Korea, *yongo*, and *wasta* in the Middle East (ME).

Yongo can be described as consisting of effective ties between individual actors that form on an aggregate organisational level; they operate as particularistic and rather exclusive informal networks (Yee 2000; Lew 2013; Horak 2014). The affective nature of *yongo* in the local context is an important aspect of network cohesion. Furthermore, it can be regarded as the central source of identity construction, because in Korea, 'the individual was always viewed in the context of his affection network' (Hahm 1986: 286). The English translation of *yongo* describes the syllable *yon* as an affective tie and *go* as its pre-existence due to shared background. *Yongo* is in principle cause based. It exists based on three pre-existing ties: (1) the same educational institutions that actors attended, isochronous or not (in Korean: *hakyon*), (2) blood ties, through belonging to a family, nuclear and extended (*hyulyon*) and (3) social ties based on the same place of birth or hometown (*jiyon*). These ties are immutable and irreversible.

Since it is common in Korean society to distinguish between in-groups and out-groups, *yongo* can be regarded as exclusive and determines whether people belong to an in- or out-group. Inside a *yongo* circle, there is 'flexibility, tolerance, mutual understanding and trust. While outside the boundary, people are treated as "non-persons" and there can be discrimination and even hostility' (Kim 2000: 179). *Yongo* ties are pervasive in Korea (Kim 2000; Lew 2013; Yee 2015) and important for getting a job and career progression in general. Can *yongo* also be regarded as a source of social exclusion of women? By triangulating studies on gender discrimination in Korea and interview data with managers, we can say that *yongo* is male-dominated and women are usually excluded from these networks.

While extant research suggests that gender discrimination exists in firms independent of their size or industries (Patterson et al. 2013), one of the reasons for social exclusion can be seen in the male dominance within *yongo* networks, which seems to be a result of the sociocultural traditions. As a vice president of a Korean automotive firm explained:

> The huge Korean business conglomerates are male societies. In Confucianism, the father is the head of the family. In Korean business, it just works the same way. Sure, these days you read a lot about promoting more women in business; some bigger firms have a diversity policy in place, but at the end of the day the situation changes very slowly.

Today, the role expectations of females are still pronounced, and societal pressure acts against further progress. As a female manager reports:

> In the past, women were excluded from certain career paths. Expatriate positions abroad, for instance, were often solely filled with male candidates. When pregnant, it was quite common to leave a firm and stay at home. Today there are more opportunities for women, but change is happening very slowly and acceptance by society is still rather low. Women in middle management positions are most affected. They carry a double burden by trying to manage their careers in addition to organising the household and childcare. In most families, expectations towards the genders follow quite traditional conceptions.

Interestingly, although separated by considerable differences in their cultural structures, informal networks in the ME (*wasta*) display a number of commonalities with their Korean counterparts, specifically in regard to gender. Indeed, similarly to *yongo*, *wasta* operates within a tacit yet well-structured system which tends to integrate certain masculinist societal norms. Studies by Alsarhan et al. (2021) and Bailey (2012) found that female professionals in the ME regard themselves as marginalised, even excluded from informal networks. *Wasta* is understood as a means to a certain end (career advancement, access to opportunities, political gains) through connections established with a wide range of individuals. Semantically, the term *wasta* bears two meanings: it can be interpreted as the mediator interceding on behalf of another to secure a gain for the latter, as well as the process of intercession itself. Terminologically, *wasta* can be defined as the intervention on behalf of others with the aim of helping them attain something they could not otherwise achieve (Brandstaetter et al. 2016; Alsarhan 2019; Ali and Weir 2020; Alsarhan and Valax 2020; Al-Twal 2021).

Wasta's origins emanate from social and communal structures, mainly nomadic tribes which stretch across the ME (Cunningham and Sarayrah 1993; Hutchings and Weir 2006; Al-Ramahi 2008). It is also seen as a widespread institution reflecting values such as solidarity, loyalty and reciprocity, which all rely on preferential treatment. Needless to say, these values are indeed normative as they are held in high esteem within Arab societies, where it is even considered unethical to disregard them (Loewe et al. 2008). Through this social setting, and the shaming and shunning tactics, *wasta* becomes a self-sustaining system, capable of enduring changes evolving societies (Alsarhan et al. 2021). However, *wasta* tends to have a rather negative connotation, because it is often used for personal benefits in business settings or in dealing with public authorities. Today, it is often equated with cronyism, favouritism, nepotism and corruption (Abdalla et al. 1998; Aldossari and Robertson 2015; Berger et al. 2015), whereas in the past it was associated with its traditional role of providing mediation to reconcile family/clan conflicts. Since today *wasta* has become a vital component in the coordination of business activities, the rules of reciprocity play an important role in its systems (El-Said and Harrigan 2009; Smith et al. 2012; Sidani and Thornberry 2013). Hence, *wasta* can only flourish between individuals in areas where power circulates.

With these requirements in mind, how far can both genders draw on *wasta* to coordinate activities and get ahead? In Bailey's report (2012), female interviewees who thought of themselves as having *wasta* mentioned they were only able to access it via their fathers or husbands. One woman explained: 'My brother had a teacher who asked him for help. This teacher needed a visa for his daughter so she could come into Dubai. He asked my brother for help because he knew my father could help. These things I could not do. Everyone knows this' (Bailey 2012: 7). Interestingly, the study distinguishes between participants with low and (indirectly) high *wasta* ties. Those with lower *wasta* perceived it as illegal and unfair, while those with better-off *wasta* ties perceived themselves as positively powerful and supporting their families.

The findings of the study indicate that *wasta* intersects with gender and class as a social construction that reinforces patriarchal and class privilege. On the other hand, in a recent study by Alsarhan et al. (2021), the authors state that women in the ME feel largely excluded from *wasta*. They further offered insights into the causes of this exclusion, stating the prevalent masculine nature of Arabic society, which entails social limitations related to the traditional role of women. One female interviewee explained: 'The Jordanian society is a masculine society like other Middle Eastern societies, due to the fact that men are more advanced in social consideration in those societies which is wrong. Therefore, for me, men use *wasta* more than women' (Alsarhan et al. 2021: 138). Moreover, professional determinants such as gendered job segregation and variance in qualifications also affect access to *wasta*. Much more pronounced when compared to *yongo*, *wasta* ties are strongly male-dominated. Social norms do not allow women to use *wasta* ties directly; however, indirectly, that is, through men (fathers, brothers, husbands and uncles) *wasta* can be used by females, but always within the general limitations facing women professionals in the region.

These two network examples imply that from a theoretical perspective there is a need to extend social exclusion theory by including the network dimension, specifically in terms of network access, since informal networks act as gatekeepers for women to launch their careers. Informal networks also act as brokers of social inclusion; hence they are an important factor for societal development. However, there is still a need for more research because informal networks need to be seen as context-specific constructs that are rather heterogeneous, that is, regardless of the respective context in which they are embedded. Some networks may exclude genders, others may be more inclusive. In China, for instance, *guanxi* is employed by all sexes and was even found to narrow the gender earnings gap (Bedford 2015; Shen and Kogan 2017). In Russia, especially during Soviet Union times, women were mainly involved in informal networking (*blat/svyazi*) as it was fundamental to organising daily supplies

(Ledeneva 2003). Whether it is still the case in post-Soviet Russia remains to be researched. Future research should analyse the micro-foundations in order to better understand their causes. Understanding the working mechanisms of informal networks, including their cultural intertwinements, is a precondition for corporations to design effective diversity and inclusion policies and for policymakers to draft legislation adapted to given cultural environments.

5.1 *KhTsB* (Armenia)
Armine Petrosyan
Alumna, School of Slavonic and East European Studies, UCL, UK

KhTsB (pronounced *kh-ts-b*, ԽԾԲ in Armenian) is an abbreviation for an acronym for *khnami* (in-laws), *tsanot* (acquaintance, friend of a friend) and *barekam* (relative) and stands for the use of all social contacts available for solving problems and getting things done, from stronger (relatives) to weaker ties (acquaintances). *Blat* in Russia and *guanxi* in China may be considered as analogous practice to *KhTsB* in Armenia. The impact on different aspects of social and economic life of the practice in Armenia has not yet been thoroughly investigated (although see Harutyunyan 2010; Shakhnazaryan and Shakhnazaryan 2010; Gharagulyan 2011; Jilozian 2017).

Similar to *blat*, the abbreviation emerged in the Soviet context and was particularly used in late socialism, under Brezhnev. It denotes Soviet practices of overcoming shortage and refers to a social contract between the state and its citizens, the so-called 'little deal' (Millar 1987). Since the collapse of the Soviet Union in 1991, however, such practices remained common in Armenia, but its uses and connotations have changed in the context of (neo)liberal markets, shadow economy and present-day corruption.

One of the ways of measuring the use of social contacts is through surveys and in-depth interviews. In 2017, I conducted a short online survey among 100 young Armenians (under the age of 35) to investigate whether they see it as a means of solving problems or a practice that creates problems.

The results of the survey show that *KhTsB* is a widespread practice in Armenia (55.6 per cent reported that the practice is rather widespread and 37.4 per cent of respondents agreed that it is widespread). No one reported an absence of the practice, and only 2 per cent said they had never heard of it.

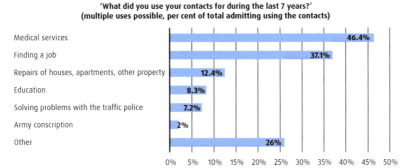

Figure 5.1.1 Survey results on *KhTsB* contacts used to access services.

As suggested by the sample survey, social links in Armenia are most often used in health care (46.4 per cent) and in the labour market (37 per cent). Other areas include repairs on houses, apartments and other property (12.4 per cent) and education (8.3 per cent). While no conclusions can be drawn on the basis of this sample, the information gives us an initial insight into the standard of living and the effectiveness of state policy in Armenia. While providing citizens with the opportunity for a healthy, long life and decent work is stated in governmental policies as the most important goal, such frequent use of social contacts to access health care and employment suggests that citizens are using their own means to tackle the problems the government failed to solve.

The respondents appear to have ambivalent feelings towards *KhTsB*, with 38 per cent finding it difficult to confirm whether the use of practice in society creates problems or solves problems for them – 25 per cent believe that *KhTsB* creates problems for them and for 21 per cent that it solves problems. When given the option to comment on the practice, in the context of jobs being given to unskilled people, one person stated that *KhTsB* indirectly creates problems, another replied that *KhTsB* is terrible and another said that *KhTsB* is a problem. However, these respondents believed it could be effective in a more transparent society.

Employment is one of the areas where social links are used the most in Armenia. Nearly 60 per cent of respondents found a job with the help of their contacts. Moreover, both job seekers' and employers' contacts influenced the securing of the job by providing information and/or influence. In 42.5 per cent of cases, the employee was successfully appointed due to the information passed on by social networks of either the job seeker (26.3 per cent) or the employer (16.2 per cent). Contacts had also 'put in a good word' for the job seeker in 16 per cent of the cases. Jobs found through traditional formal channels accounted for

Figure 5.1.2   *KhTsB*, illustration by the author. © Armine Petrosyan.

only 23.2 per cent of the total responses. Other important aspects to the relationships between contacts and job seekers remain to be examined, for instance the nature of connections, the channels through which information was passed and the factors that facilitated the flow of information through those channels. For example, in the IT sector, which is currently one of the fastest growing and most important sectors in Armenia's economy, current employees are asked to recommend a suitable expert for a new job vacancy and if the referred worker is hired, the referee receives a raise. This hiring practice is used in Google and the IT sector overall, but the main reason behind this practice in Armenia is probably the shortage of qualified experts in IT and the growing demand for them. Here, the use of *KhTsB* can be shown to have an impact on wage rates. Therefore, the use of contacts in the job market may not only have non-monetary but also monetary effects.

There is no evidence of direct monetary effects of using contacts on wages in empirical studies (Granovetter 1995; Mouw 2003), although studies suggest that they can affect wages indirectly via the reservation wage (Montgomery 1992). The reservation wage is the minimum wage rate at which job seekers would be willing to accept a job offer. Individuals with more contacts can expect to receive more job offers, which increases their reservation wage and consequently also their received wage. But even if the monetary effects of the use of social networks in the labour market is less likely, its non-monetary effect can be significant (Franzen and Hangartner 2006). Network members who pass on information about job vacancies are most likely well informed about the education and qualifications of the job seeker and will offer jobs which they believe would be a good match. Hence jobs found through social contacts can have higher educational adequacy than those found independently. However, the broader literature on the impacts of the use of social contacts on the labour market tends to be based on empirical studies carried out in economically developed countries. High unemployment rates, business cycles, economic situations or structure of employment specific to less developed countries, such as Armenia, may shape the labour market in different ways, and the effects of using social networks during times of high unemployment may be significant.

Labour is but one channel through which the use of social contacts affects the economy and citizens' lives. Other areas also deserve the attention of scholars and institutions responsible for policymaking.

5.2 *Pečenje rakije* (Serbia)
Maria Vivod
'Dynamics of Europe' research unit, University of Strasbourg, France and Novi Sad, Serbia

Pečenje rakije refers to distilling beverage alcohol outside of a registered distillery. In the region of the Vojvodina, Serbia, a product of such distillation is called – according to each official language of the province – *rakija* (in Serbian and Croatian), *pálinka* (in Hungarian), *rachiu* (Romanian) or *pálenka* (Slovak). *Rakija* is a type of fruit brandy, similar to the Italian grappa, most often distilled in rural households from local fruit (see also Russian *samogon* and American moonshine). The distillation process, called *pečenje rakije* ('baking' *rakija*) is a small private or communal event in which a mash of ripe fruits that has been fermenting in a barrel for weeks beforehand is treated in an alembic copper distillatory vessel (*kazan za rakiju*). *Pečenje rakije* is often a male gathering and a way for households to procure a yearly quantity of prized spirit alcohol intended for gifts and for guests at special occasions such the family *slava* celebration a feast day celebrating patron saints in the Serbian Orthodox households., birthdays, weddings, *svinjokolj* (pig slaughter) and other social events.

Rakija had an important role in the rural household, as documented ethnographically between 1920 and 1950 (Barjaktarović 1951). It was integrated in the ritual of *slava*. It played a role in Christmas, Easter, wedding and baptism celebrations, and was and still is an indispensable sign of hospitality. It was also a requisite in funerals. A drop from a glass, poured by each mourner, was spilled on the ground for the soul of the deceased. Bottles of *rakija* or wine were also left on graves, as part of the yearly commemoration of the dead.

Rakija has several types and levels of quality. At the end of the nineteenth century, a Serbian author provided chemical and sensory evaluation for over 30 types of Vojvodinian *rakija* (Petrović 1889). Poor households, without access to orchard fruit, were only able to produce low-quality *komadara* made from cereal such as wheat or corn (Barjaktarović 1951; Petrović 1889), or brandy made from foraged fruit such as greengage (*ringlópálinka*) and mulberry (*dudovača*) (Vukmanović 1999). Low-quality brandy was made from pumpkins, although less frequently (Barjaktarović 1951). Fruit brandies with a higher reputation were made from plums (*šljivovica*), apricots (*kajsijevača*) and peaches (*breskovača*). *Rakija* made from grapes was called *komovica* (also *loza* or *törkő*) (Petrović 1889). The sensory properties and alcohol content of *rakija* is often evaluated with a Baumé scale (called *bome*), a hydrometer for measuring liquid density (Dikić and Dikić 2003). Although the method is old-fashioned and less appropriate for measuring alcohol properties accurately (Petrović 1889), using it is perceived as a sign of skill and connoisseurship.

Rakija-making in Vojvodina started to grow from 1718, in the transition period between the Ottoman Empire and the Hungarian crown land. Alcoholic beverages were produced and smuggled into the Ottoman Empire, where Sharia law either taxed them or prohibited their production (Mrgić 2017). According to an imperial Habsburg order from 1772, each Vojvodinian household was ordered to plant on its property and on the street in front of the house 32 mulberry trees (Vukmanović 1999), to encourage and foster the production of silk. In the Bačka area of Vojvodina alone there were 250,000 mulberry trees. The amount of fruit inspired the production of *dudovača*. *Dudovača* used to be considered a poor man's brandy, but nowadays mulberry has become rare and the Vojvodinian *dudovača* has been recently rebranded as a regional specialty (Vukmanović 1999).

Figure 5.2.1 Home *rakija* distillation equipment, August 2019, Novi Sad, Serbia. © Maria Vivod.

The distillation of *rakija* lasts between five and eight hours and is usually conducted by men. The distillation can last from a couple of hours to an entire day depending on the quantity of the fruit mash. Friends and neighbours will often gather for the occasion, although more serious amateur producers will avoid company in order to concentrate on producing quality. Producing good-quality *rakija* is a source of pride and respect in the community. If one does not have the required equipment, a fee can be paid to a communal distiller, who does own the necessary equipment.

Pečenje rakije is a labour- and resource-intensive practice. The chosen fruit is first turned into fruit mash (called *komina*, *džibra*, *kljuk* or *cefre*) in a barrel. The quality of the fruit impacts the quality of the *rakija*, therefore only ripe, never rotten, fruit should be used. Stones are usually removed from the fruit by hand. Sugar is added to the mash to start the process of fermentation in which fruit sugar turns into alcohol. It is desirable to add as little as sugar as possible – too much sugar left after the fermentation gives *rakija* a different taste. *Rakija* with too much sugar is pejoratively called *šećeruša* (from *šećer*, sugar). Fermentation lasts between 7 and 15 days, depending on the sugar content and ambient temperature (ideally between 20 and 25°C). The mash is carefully stirred every few days and monitored for signs that the fermentation process is complete. This is done by checking for the presence of oxygen on the surface with a lit match (the process is carried out if the match stays lit) or by checking if air bubbles are emitted from the mash. Once the fermentation process is complete, the mash is distilled. It is desirable to achieve an alcohol volume of 50 per cent, although to preserve the identifying aroma of the fruit from which the *rakija* was made some *rakije* need to be 'weaker'. A strong yet aromatic *rakija* can be achieved by distilling the mash twice. Such brandy is called *prepečenica* (over-baked *rakija*) and it requires a large amount of fruit: 1 litre of peach brandy requires 20 kg peaches (Vukmanović 2005). The traditional, informal sensory evaluation comprises descriptions of taste, smell and clarity of the liquid. *Rakija* with high alcohol volume is called 'strong' (*jaka*), 'spicy' (*ljuta*), 'lad-like' (*momačka*), 'fierce' (*žestoka*) or 'shoe-stripper' (*izuvača*). *Rakija* with low alcohol content is labelled *slaba* (weak) or *tanka* (thin) and sometimes called *mučenica* (martyr) since the fruits have supposedly 'suffered' during the preparation.

Certain types of *rakija*, such as *travarica* (medicinal herbs macerated in grape brandy) or *komovica* are used for medicinal purposes and are kept on hand in households for home-emergency medical treatments such as toothache, headache, stress-relief and antiseptic. In folk medicine, *rakija* was recommended for treating everything from epilepsy to dandruff, from gout to muscle cramps, from acne to dysentery (Mihajlović 2007). At the turn of the twentieth century, *rakija* was also used as a sleep-inducing substance for infants (Jovanović-Batut 1911).

In March 2019, a 98-year-old woman from Lika in Croatia, a region with a sizeable ethnic Serbian minority, was fined 267 euros for making her own *rakija* in her yard, and 54 litres of *rakija* were seized by the authorities. The news spread rapidly in Serbian online media (Politika 2019) and sparked outrage on social networks The news was interpreted as an impact of the EU-influenced legislation on the older, more tolerant domestic laws. Domestic distilling, despite being a non-authorised practice, is a highly tolerated and rarely fined practice in Serbia. Many rural households own an orchard and distillation equipment, therefore distillation of *rakija* is considered customary. The production of the same 'for own use' is widespread throughout the country and tolerated by the authorities. However, Serbian legislation regarding high-proof distilled spirits recently changed. In the 2009 legislation (*Zakon o rakiji i drugim alkoholnim pićima Sl.glasnik RS br. 41/2009*) the law prohibited the sale and marketing of any alcohol not produced according to the national regulation. It fined all irregular, non-standardised production but it differentiated between *rakija* and other high-proof distilled spirits. In a later edition of the law (*Zakon o rakiji i drugim alkoholnim pićima Sl.glasnik RS br. 92/2015*) this distinction was suspended and *rakija* has lost its special legal status.

5.3 *Hemşehricilik* (Turkey)
Eda Pamuksuzer
Alumna, School of Slavonic and East European Studies, UCL, UK

In Turkey, *hemşehricilik* is the practice of preferential treatment of people of the same origin by doing favours to those 'near and dear'. *Hemşehri* refers to people who come from the same location (composed of *hem*, same or alike, and *şehir*, city). *Hemşehrilik* indicates the state of being *hemşehri* with someone else, while with the derivational affix of *ci*, the expression refers to an occupation or a practice established from this state. *Hemşehricilik* denotes the basic notion of belonging in Turkey.

Hemşehricilik is similar to a number of practices in other parts of the world that rely on collective identity formed through a shared geographical location. For example, the Kazakh practice of *rushyldyq* is defined as a strong feeling of sub-ethnic identity with and loyalty to one's *ru*, a group sharing a territory and united by actual or fictive kinship *ru*. In Russia, people of the same origins are called *zemlyaki*, in South Korea a similar phenomenon is known as *yongo*. In southern Tajikistan, the village identities resemble *hemşehricilik* in forming a collective identity based on prioritising a central geographical origin to form useful social networks (Boboyorov 2013: 126). Concepts referring to shared origins, such as the locality or region, are common worldwide. Practices of giving preferential treatment to a person of the same origin may differ significantly in spread and public perception. In Turkey, the name of the practice is widely used and commonly acceptable, which suggests that the practice is particularly significant.

Hemşehricilik gained importance with the industrialisation in Turkey in the 1950s, which ignited migration from the countryside to the cities (Terzi 2014: 141). In this period of rapid social change, migrants to urban areas held onto their rural roots and thus slowed it down somewhat or adapted to their needs. As rural and urban life continues to transform, the dynamics of social networks have also altered. *Hemşehricilik* practices have spread through migration within or outside Turkey. Although the practice is representative of mobility, it also points to the persistent power of identity and belonging.

The increase in intra- and international migration led to the rise in the number of *hemsehri* associations and the reach of *hemşehri* networks, one of the many channels of *hemşehricilik* (Terzi 2014: 138). *Hemşehri* associations represent a large proportion of civil society organisations in Turkey and countries hosting Turkish immigrants. Establishing a formal *hemşehri* organisation is a straightforward process with a clear legal framework (T.C. Icisleri Bakanligi Dernekler Dairesi Baskanligi 2004) and there are many legally registered *hemşehri* associations with the declared goals of 'bringing together migrants from same town or district' and of solidarity on the basis of co-localism as their declared goal (Erder 1999: 167). Abroad, these associations provide Turks with a space to maintain their distinct cultural values (Terzi 2014: 142), preserve their local cultures, build new ties among compatriots and expand their personal networks. *Hemşehri* institutions help Turkish migrants establish social ties to aid the processes of moving and integration, find jobs and accommodation or overcome similar problems (Erder 1999: 165–6). The associations shape diaspora communities and provide them with exclusive opportunities that are unavailable to outsiders.

Nurturing *hemşehri* relations enables these institutions to accommodate both formal and informal practices within their scope. *Hemşehri* relations may bring voluntary or obligatory contribution requirements such as the expectation of favouritism (*kayırmacılık*), such as *torpil*. *Torpil* (also known as *kıyak*) is an informal practice of exchanging favours to get a job, a promotion, a place in school, to jump a queue and other objectives. This act of 'paving the way' for a person implies favouring them over others and thus undermines the rights of others. The special bonds and relationship of *torpil* can emerge on multiple grounds. *Hemşehricilik* can provide such common ground by producing an 'identity-based belonging and solidarity', characterised by a closed community lock-in effect.

Despite their apolitical appearance, some suggest that the most important function of *hemşehri* associations is their political reach (Erder 1999: 168). Politically active members can use the associations to disseminate political viewpoints and expectations of their parties. *Hemşehri* associations and *hemşehri* networks appear to be a critical resource in urban and diasporic voting and are frequently used as a tool for voter mobilisation. Diaspora communities in *hemşehri* associations are also used to determine the results of critical elections and referendums. Another political ramification of *hemşehrilik* lies in its application in governance, where problems may arise when *hemşehrilik* starts to entail the practice of *hemşehricilik*. Unfair appointments and the creation of locked political circles can have adverse effects. If they become an established practice, *hemşehri* relations in politics may result in political clientelism and favouritism.

5.4 **Ahbap-çavuş ilişkisi** (Turkey)
Semih Ergelen
Sakarya Business School, Sakarya University, Turkey

Ahbap-çavuş ilişkisi is a reliable and intimate relationship among individuals who share a common background, such as friendship established in school, college or the army. The Arabic word *ahbap* means 'beloved ones' (Nişanyan 2009: 9) and is synonymous with pal, crony, buddy or fellow in Turkish. *Çavuş* refers to a military rank equivalent to sergeant but can be applied more generally, for example to refer to work supervisors. *Ilişki* means 'relationship'. An *ahbap-çavuş ilişkisi* is hierarchical as well as peer-based and entails both a vertical and informal exchange of favours. Although the duration of military service has been gradually reducing since 1963, Turkey continues to enlist its army through conscription. Military recruits establish strong bonds due to the considerable amount of time spent together and these bonds persist even after the recruits have left the army. They share memories and maintain relationships for the rest of their lives.

In a nutshell, *ahbap-çavuş ilişkisi* is best represented with the phrase: 'He/she is one of my good friends or acquaintances, so consider it done!' Benefits from these close relationships may include overcoming bureaucratic and legal hindrances or finding alternative solutions to problems for which those in need lack competence. Nevertheless, reciprocity, or mutual obligation, plays a pivotal role in such relationships. If an individual wants to benefit from a close tie, they should feel obliged to return the favour in the future. *Ahbap-çavuş ilişkisi* is similar to 'You scratch my back, I scratch yours'. Once this relationship is established, future favours will be expected, in line with individuals' abilities. There are considerable similarities between *ahbap-çavuş ilişkisi* in Turkey and the use of informal networks elsewhere. Notably, *ahbap-çavuş ilişkisi* is similar to Chinese *guanxi* in that it requires mutual obligation, reciprocity and emotional attachment based on friendship (Provis 2008; Tong 2014). Just as in *guanxi*, a shared biographical path of attending college or army generates friends that are essential for future instrumental use. The Chilean practice *compadrazgo* is similarly based on exchanging favours motivated by a friendship ideology, yet also instrumental. Like the acquaintance support used to avoid formal procedures of the Russian *blat*, *ahbap-çavuş ilişkisi* serves people when formal procedures do not. The differences between the Turkish and analogous informal practices in other societies are likely to be based on the scale and functions in economy, politics and society on the one hand, and the degree of obligation and acceptance on the other. Such comparisons are yet to be made, to establish the ratio of sociability to instrumentality of *ahbap-çavuş ilişkisi* practices and to establish their context-sensitive implications (Ledeneva 2018).

Ahbap-çavuş ilişkisi has negative connotations and is associated with corruption in Turkish politics. Thus, the term *crony capitalism* is translated into Turkish as *ahbap-çavuş kapitalizmi*. Despite being characterised as an illegal and indecent activity, *ahbap-çavuş ilişkisi* is widely spread among Turkish politicians. One politician made the following statement before the 2018 local elections: 'This election, in any manner, is not going to be the kind of "my friend, my acquaintance" election and there will be no *ahbap-çavuş ilişkisi*. We need to nominate candidates who are decent and principled in the eyes of the public' (Yolculuk 2018). Yet these negative perceptions often depend on ideological stances, as well as positions of being an insider or outsider in *ahbap-çavuş ilişkisi*. For example, a member or proponent of the ruling party might regard *ahbap-çavuş ilişkisi* as highly effective and instrumental in getting things done. On the contrary, their opponent will regard *ahbap-çavuş ilişkisi* as corruption or a violation of people's rights. Such double standards are fundamental to partiality and particularism in politics. Reviewing public-private relationships and public procurement agreements reveals how *ahbap-çavuş ilişkisi* permeates the Turkish bureaucratic and political system (Buğra and Savaşkan 2015). For those outside the inner circle, the prospects are grim. Some claimed that the Soma mine disaster which resulted in the death of 301 miners in 2014 was a typical example of *ahbap-çavuş* capitalism in Turkey. Due to close relationships between statesmen and managers, safety conditions were poor and regulations ignored, which resulted in human tragedy (Eğilmez 2014).

Ahbap-çavuş ilişkisi is related to the Turkish informal social network, *torpil*. There are suggestions that ineffective formal institutions are the main reason why Turkish citizens adopt *torpil* (Yay 2018: 216). Yet *torpil* is equally a consequence of *ahbap-çavuş* relationships. Friendships and close ties create *ahbap-çavuş ilişkisi* and may lead to *torpil* relations in a 'knock-on effect'. In contrast, *torpil* relations between parties do not necessarily lead to *ahbap-çavuş ilişkisi*. If pushed to make a distinction, *torpil* may be considered as more instrumental than *ahbap-çavuş ilişkisi*. Social and instrumental aspects are interrelated in both *torpil* and *ahbap-çavuş ilişkisi*, thus making clear-cut categorisations problematic. Turkish people generally perceive *ahbap-çavuş ilişkisi* as a close friendship established for mutual benefit between two parties, while *torpil* is more likely to be seen as a one-sided benefit based on protection. An example of *ahbap-çavuş ilişkisi* would be a chief of police who may overlook a head physician's traffic ticket for the sake of their warm friendship. In return, when the police chief requires hospital treatment, the head physician provides whatever is necessary even if that infringes on other patients' rights. People who benefit from *ahbap-çavuş ilişkisi* in this kind of situation tend to say, 'This is Turkey, and this is how things work here'. An example of *torpil* is an acquaintance with influential people such as members of parliament that gives a job seeker competitive advantage over other candidates.

In both social contexts and private domains, there are no negative connotations of *ahbap-çavuş ilişkisi*. Sezen Aksu, a prominent Turkish lyricist and musical composer, draws on the positive side of the practice in her song 'Ahbap Çavuşlar'. In a part about the intimate relationship of *ahbap* and *çavuşlar*, she sings: 'Let them fill glasses in honour of love, heartbreaks and memories, let *ahbap* and *çavuşlar* sit in the quietest corner, and let them booze.' The strong and affectionate relationship does not need to be negative for those outside the inner circle. *Ahbap-çavuş ilişkisi* is ambivalent just like other practices associated with the use of informal networks. It cannot be conceptualised as good or bad in itself, it is context-bound. To assess both the dark and bright sides of these practices and gain a better understanding thereof, one should explore the economic, political and normative contexts that shape such relationships. The difference between insider/outsider perspectives, and the double standards that emerge from switching from one perspective to another, provide us with the key for understanding how such practices can be criticised, yet are also pervasive. For insiders, *ahbap-çavuş ilişkisi* can be perceived as a problem-solving device or a last resort, while for outsiders, it will be seen as taking advantage of this relationship, gaining access through unethical, if not corrupt, roots. In brief, *ahbap-çavuş ilişkisi* could be useful in problem-solving processes, but it could inevitably lead to corruption when misused.

5.5 *Grypsowanie* (Poland)
Piotr Majda
School of Slavonic and East European Studies, UCL, UK

Grypsowanie as a term originates from the old-German word *grips*, meaning to catch/seize or to understand/grasp. It was originally used to denote all kinds of prison subculture and argot. In Polish prisons, the term identifies a language used by a group of *grypsmen* (*grypsujący*). It is not only a language that is used exclusively within prisons, but also a code of conduct.

The first record of a subculture in Polish prisons associated with *grypsing* goes back to the nineteenth century. In 1867, Karol Estreicher, a journalist for the *Polish Newspaper*, described the prison argot as difficult to decode: 'a philologist would not be able to reach the source of multiple words' (Rodasik et al. 2013). The emergence of modern *grypsing* is associated with Warsaw's 'Gęsiówka' penitentiary system. The term gained popularity within juvenile detention centres and quickly spread across the country to become the most used prison dialect.

In the 1970s, the state launched a campaign against this prison subculture (Szaszkiewicz 1997; Moczydłowski 2002). To identify and isolate subculture members, prison personnel would ask all newcomers whether they were *grypser* as, according to their creed, no *grypser* can deny their membership as this would result in being downgraded in the prison hierarchy (Michalska and Michalski 2020). To conceal their identity as a *grypser* and avoid losing honour, *grypsmen* would change their name to *grypsujący* (Jarosz 2011).

In the case of prison argot, there is a clear attempt to resist the function of penitentiary institutions (Michalska and Michalski 2020). On the one hand, some inmates would say that *grypsing* demonstrates fortitude, steadfastness and honour, while on the other hand, it is a phenomenon conducive to committing crimes, trapping ex-inmates in a downward spiral of violating the law and going back to prison (Szaszkiewicz 1997). Argot is a 'symbolic expression of group loyalty' (Zarzycki 2015: 19), where use and fluency are a measurement of allegiance to and integration into the group. Prison argot functions include consolidating hierarchy, organisation, and imposing rules in the prison, with differences between prisons and countries.

Grypsing regulates every single aspect of prison life, from eating to sleeping regimes, all the dos and don'ts. According to Michalska and

Michalski (2020), the main principles of *grypsing* are usually the same in all prisons across Poland, and they include:

- Opposition to law and justice in all its forms: *grypsmen* cannot cooperate with prison personnel, identify associates in a crime or disclose any information about *grypsing*. They cannot shake hands with prison personnel or inmates of lower status in the hierarchy.
- Group solidarity: *grypsmen* shall protect each other, from both internal and external threats. The former refers to support in prison hardship (sharing resources and so on) and the latter corresponds to planning and committing crimes inside and outside the prison. These rules include joint responsibility for any other *grypsmen* behaviour, support during disciplinary punishments (for example, by sharing food) and not denying membership of the subculture.
- Personal dignity and honour: becoming a *grypsman* improves an inmate's social status, strengthens loyalty and incentivises honesty towards other members. At the same time it endows a mandate to demand respect from outsiders, while treating them with disdain. It is prohibited for *grypsmen* to eat while someone is using the toilet or pick up any items lying next to the toilet, drink water directly from the tap or ask for anyone's help.

The prison hierarchy within the subculture can be divided into three levels (Michalska and Michalski 2020: 9). First, the highest caste of the prison hierarchy includes inmates-*grypsmen*, also known as git-man or humans. They understand and enforce *grypsing* rules, and only recruit by thorough examination and tests. This group consists of elders of the highest authority in the prison, *grypsmen* and fuss-masters, or cell leaders. Second, inmates who do not participate in *grypsing* are referred to as 'inhumans' or 'suckers'. This group is perceived as inferior to *grypsmen*. As outsiders to the code of honour, potential snitches and weaklings, their duties include cleaning and running exploitative errands imposed by *grypsmen*. They are expected to take the blame for the violations of seniors. They cannot eat with *grypsmen* or shake their hands (Kaminski 2004). Third, the lowest caste consists of the so-called 'fags'. Members of this group have no right to speak, and other inmates are highly aggressive and disrespectful towards them. *Grypsmen* perceive them as snitches and prison personnel collaborators. They are given feminine names and often become rape victims as any other interaction with them is forbidden (Kaminski 2004).

Despite a highly hierarchised organisation, the *grypsing* code allows both promotion and demotion. Thus, a *grypsman* can lose his status if he violates the code, for example by using 'fags' utensils, or in the case of major misconduct even becoming a 'fag'. A 'sucker' can be admitted to the *grypsmen* rank if he passes all the tests and demonstrates cunningness, wit and knowledge of the argot. The only group banned from any social mobility are 'fags' as this label cannot be washed away or amended in any way. Attempting to hide it, say, by a transfer to a different prison or cell, can result in serious consequences (Kaminski 2004).

The diagram presents the steps faced by each new inmate upon arrival in the prison. Newbies are inmates who have already served time in prison, while rookies are those entering prison for the first time. At each new arrival, prisoners will be asked whether they participate in *grypsing*, and their answer will determine the next steps. Answering 'yes' automatically indicates a liar who will be beaten and will receive the 'fag' label for pretending to be a *grypsman*. True *grypsmen* know that only

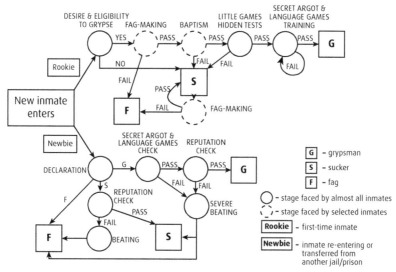

Figure 5.5.1 A diagram showing newcomers' possible paths upon arrival in the cell. At the first stage, rookies are separated from newbies. A rookie is subject both to testing and learning. A newbie is subject only to a verification of his initial declaration. A grypsman may fall into a lower caste after he commits a serious offense against the norms of grypsing. Source: Kaminski, M. M. 2003. 'Games Prisoners Play'. *Rationality and Society* 15(2): 195.

fellow *grypsmen* can vouch for them. However, if a newcomer replies 'no' but shows a desire to learn and join the group, he will be tested for weeks or months to determine his strength, acumen, pain tolerance, alertness and sense of humour (Kaminski 2004). If he passes all the tests, he is allowed to learn argot: experienced *grypsmen* will conduct so-called 'prison university', or *bajera*, at night.

Examples of argot vocabulary include (Małkowski 1971: 138; Kaminski 2004: 192–5; Zarzycki 2015: 20): *piguła* (a pill) for doctor, *fortepian* (a piano) for the prison warden, *zadyma, afera* for affair, *Berło* (sceptre) for a toilet brush. Despite a strict ban on using the language outside prison walls, argot vocabulary has appeared in cinematography [film *Symmetry* 2003], music (especially rap) and eventually into everyday slang, frequently without awareness of the prison-related etymology (Zarzycki 2015).

Between 1945 and 1989, inmates participated in the reproduction of the prison subculture on a much bigger scale than nowadays. *Grypsmen* used to make up to 80 per cent of prisoners, 'suckers' 18–19 per cent and 'fags' no more than 1–2 per cent (Kaminski 2004). Yet, with the fall of communism and 1990s institutional changes in Poland, prisons' rigidity decreased and inmates were granted numerous rights in the process of democratisation and humanisation of the penitentiary system (Moczydłowski 1994). Such measures weakened the need for an internal support network. According to various postcommunist sources, the involvement of prisoners in prison subculture has reduced to 38 per cent or estimated to be as low as 14 per cent (Kaminski 2004).

The number of prisoners using argot decreases rapidly, mainly due to the relaxed selection process (Skręt 2004). *Grypsing* is no longer reserved for the most cunning, physically and mentally strong, but rather used as a support group for inmates unable to cope with reality inside and outside prison walls. *Grypsing* principles were also reduced to just two: do not snitch and do not get involved in sexual relations with other prisoners (Skręt 2004).

5.6 **Meso** (Cyprus and Greece)
George Hajipavli
Oxford School of Global and Area Studies, University of Oxford, UK

Meso(n) is a colloquial term used in Cyprus and Greece. To apply *meso* (in Greek: *vazo [verb] meso [noun]*) means to mobilise personal connections to influence a procedure in order to gain an advantage. While *meso* can benefit the requesting individual, the benefactors may instead be the requestor's immediate or extended family, friends, or friends of friends given that Cypriot and Greek cultures are extensively collective (Georgas et al. 1997; Faustmann 2010: 270). Often used as synonyms to *meso* are the terms *vyzma, donti, akri* (prevalent in Greece), along with *rousfeti*. Although occasionally used as a synonym (for example, Georgiades 2006: 125), *rousfeti* can acquire a more restrictive meaning than usually attributed to *meso*, in that it denotes favours granted by political parties (Trousas 2021).

In contrast to *fakelaki* (see 2.17 Volume 1) (Knight 2018), assistance via *meso* does not necessitate, while it often precludes a financial exchange. It usually relies on a moral obligation to mutual assistance, though it can be used by political and other actors to indirectly obtain support (Faustmann 2010).

The most prevalent means of dispensing *meso* is via political mediation, rendering it particularly widespread in sectors connected to the political sphere. In a 2006 questionnaire, 89 and 54 per cent of Cypriot participants reported that *meso* is diffused in the public and semi-governmental sectors (Georgiades 2006: 127). These two sectors, which constituted the first and third most popular responses in the above survey, are where political mediation is most influential, reflecting the assertion that *meso* is especially prevalent in sectors connected to the political sphere (Faustmann 2010).

However, *meso* extends beyond political mediation. In the same 2006 survey 26 per cent of respondents locate *meso* in the banks, while 57 per cent find it everywhere, which constitute the fourth and second most popular categories, respecively (Georgiades 2006: 127). Therefore, like *veze* (see 1.7 Volume 1) in Serbia, *meso* constitutes an umbrella term for all kinds of mediation. Yet, unlike Greeks and Cypriots, Serbians have coined a dedicated term for political mediation – *političke veze* (Stanojevic and Stokanic 2018). *Meso* can further be held to parallel *torpil* in Turkey (see 6.10 Volume 2) because it similarly calls on powerful individuals to interfere with bureaucratic procedures to skew resource allocation (Yay 2018). Yet *meso* particularly reflects the prevalent role of political parties in Cypriot (Charalambous and Christophorou 2016) and Greek (Papadoulis 2006) societies, especially when it concerns mediation.

Hence, while a variety of actors can be involved in *meso*, political elite usually lead the initiative. This was recently exemplified in 'Cyprus Papers', where leading politicians, including the legislature's president, were accused of exploiting personal connections to circumvent formal requirements in procedures of citizenship acquisition against investment (Al Jazeera 2020). This outlines the existence of hierarchical networks led by the political elite, not too dissimilar to those of political patronage in the post-Soviet region (Hale 2014: 1–18). Apart from parties, other stakeholders act as *meso* power brokers or dispensers, such as military officials, civil servants and ranking members of the clergy. For instance, the Cypriot Archbishop admitted to 'mediating' with the Interior Minister to issue citizenship to a Church donor (Nestoros 2021).

Meso covers a variety of examples. Frequently, *meso* is used to skip the queue or secure preferred reservations at nightclubs. In certain instances, *meso* allows the requestor to circumvent cumbersome administrative procedures, resolving issues of functionality like other informal practices (Baez-Camargo and Ledeneva 2017). An example is mediation for the purpose of securing the timely transportation of a patient in critical condition to a better public medical facility. At other times, *meso* grants an individual undue advantage based on personal connections (favouritism), inclusive of outright exemption from formal regulations, such as the avoidance of prosecution. In the context of the COVID-19 pandemic, reports emerged alleging that individuals deployed *meso* to receive a vaccine ahead of time (Konstantinou 2021). Regularly, *meso* is leveraged to achieve preferential employment, promotion and transfer in the public and private sector and the military.

Certain nuanced differences exist in how *meso* is dispensed in Cyprus compared to Greece. In both instances party linkages are utilised to achieve preferential treatment. In Greece, party favours appear to be based on clientelist linkages, reflecting a particular transactional exchange between the party and the voter (or voter representatives, like trade unions), similar to *Parteibuchwirtschaft* (see 7.6 Volume 2) in Austria (Arbesleitner 2018). In Cyprus, *meso* is usually more reliant on strong interpersonal relations, thus exceeding the conventional boundaries of clientelism (Faustmann 2010: 270–1). For instance, the use of *fakelaki* is rare in Cyprus, while bribery is infrequent both in absolute and relative terms compared to Greece (Pring 2016: 17). While the difference might be exaggerated in literature, a distinction can be recognised. A plausible explanation is the smaller size of society in Cyprus that allows stronger interpersonal relations with political mediators. Interestingly, even though Turkish Cypriots invoke *torpil* and Greek Cypriots *meso*, there are similarities in the two Cypriot communities' social practices, along with common differences in how these terms are deployed in Turkey and Greece. Factors that extend beyond the individual, such as sharing a common domestic origin or enjoying long-standing familial relations are important in incentivising mediation among Cypriots, while transactional aspects appear to be relatively more important in Greece and Turkey.

Akin to multiple informal practices, the public perception of *meso* is ambivalent (Ledeneva 2018). The term is frequently the source of tension due to the inequality it leads to from endowing certain individuals with skewed access to resources and opportunities. Christophoros Fokaides, a former Cypriot defence minister, acknowledged the preferential treatment certain citizens enjoy due to party-based *meso*, resulting in a widespread perceived sense of injustice (Sigmalive 2016). Nonetheless, despite the criticism *meso* often draws, a significant segment of the population feels the practice is justified when it is them or kinship that engages with it.

An understudied aspect of *meso* are the conditions of membership. For example, minority groups with access to *meso* can benefit from added occupational mobility, as with the Roma community in Greece following their acquisition of voting rights (Themelis 2013: 195–8). Yet, individuals who do not belong to the national majority are less likely to possess strong interpersonal relations with local power brokers, leading to reduced access to *meso*, unless they can 'purchase' it.

Recently, the commercialisation of *meso* in Cyprus arising from the country's increasing interaction with global capital is becoming more common. There are frequent reports of wealthy foreigners 'purchasing' bureaucratic access through private service providers, like the expedient or undue acquisition of citizenship and residence permits. Yet, while foreigners can 'purchase' access to domestic networks by financially compensating local service providers, the ultimate application of *meso* rests upon the locals. As such, *meso* ultimately relies on local personal connections, which foreigners are unlikely to possess, generating membership conditions unfavourable to foreigners and leverage for local service providers over wealthy non-natives. As such, certain service firms connected to or comprising of political actors receive preferential access to bureaucracy, as evidenced by the skewed distribution of successful citizenship-for-investment applications among such firms (Zachariou 2020). This highlights that, like other informal practices, *meso* transverses the boundaries of the private and public domains.

5.7 **Palanca** (Mexico)
David Arellano-Gault and Luis Jair Trejo-Alonso
Department of Public Administration, Centre for Research and Teaching in Economics, Mexico City, Mexico

Etymologically, the term *palanca* has a Latin root *palanga*, in turn related to a Greek root φαλαγξ (*phálanx*) or φαλαγγος (*phálangos*). Literally, it means 'wooden roller or trunk, used to move large weights on the ground or to slide boats on the sand until they are thrown into the sea'. In our case, the term lever can be better associated with Archimedes' saying: 'give me a place to stand, and a lever long enough, and I will move the earth'. A lever, with a suitable point of support, can move (almost) anything.

Following this logic, *palanca* is widely recognised in Mexico as the informal social practice of exchanging favours. Due to its informal nature, *palanca* lacks an established definition, yet there are studies aimed at understanding it, either through proverbs and popular sayings (Zalpa et al. 2014) and through semiological analyses of how persons attribute signs and meanings to the practice (Arellano-Gault 2018). *Palanca* is associated with exchanges of favours between people who know each other directly and connect through an intermediary or an 'acquaintance of acquaintances' in order to solve a problem or satisfy a need. It is a problem-solving tool that triggers an intervention of someone in a position to resolve a particular problem faced by an individual, group or family.

The problem-solver generally maintains an expectation of reciprocity for the favour granted, a reciprocity that does not necessarily need to occur immediately and to be pecuniary or material. In this sense, the recipient of the favour becomes indebted to the problem-solver, and

Figure 5.7.1. *Palanca* (lever) in Mexico. CC BY-NC-SA 4.0. © Eduardo Yair Miguel Martínez.

generally in a very ambiguous manner. The recipient's obligation needs to be negotiated and communicated in a subtle way: sometimes explicitly, but more often implicitly, depending on custom, situation and magnitude of the favour delivered.

Expectations of reciprocity create lasting links between people based on mutual obligation or duty to provide support and share their influences and resources with other persons, creating a de facto network of acquaintances sharing different *palancas*. This network is based on the existence of people who, depending on circumstances, are, or are presumed to be, in a position to intervene and help to 'find a way', finding 'the correct route' (by bending the formal rules or allowing an exception) in order to resolve a problem or need of a member of the network. *Palanca* is not exclusive to Mexico. Variations of the practice exist in other countries of Central and South America.

Generally, in Mexico, it is assumed that individuals in positions of high influence achieve such positions, in large part due to their abilities to use *palancas* and build networks through them. Persons are taught to 'invest' in strengthening their networks in order to make them grow in size and influence.

Palancas spread across all strata in Mexican society. However, this does not mean that *palanca* becomes an equaliser in life chances. The bigger and more resourceful the networks of *palancas* are, the more advantages they provide to their members. People in higher strata of society have access to more potent *palancas*.

The practice of *palancas* requires people, regardless of strata, to acquire certain skills, usually involving smart and cunning interpersonal capabilities. A cunning person, cunning in this sense, will invest time and resources to nurture the persons in their network: inviting them for lunch, sending Christmas or birthdays cards, or organising dinners to connect different people. All of these activities are carried out in a systematic manner. Depending on the context of the favour asked, *palanca* involves different rules of etiquette, norms of reciprocity and engagement, and compliance with non-written codes of honour.

Palanca is an old and well-established practice: some propose traces of it can be found in the colonial era in the sixteenth century (Lomnitz 2000). Traditionally, the art of using and maintaining *palancas* is learned informally, within the family, at neighbourhood meetings and through friendships developed at school and college. The means of communication, etiquette, initiation, development and termination are transmitted by word of mouth, through day-to-day social relations, and reproduced through social norms and peer pressure.

Palanca is possible when an individual enjoys a position of formal influence. This position allows a person to intervene in or influence the allocation of resources or entitlements, to modify organisational or legal decisions and thus makes such a person an important asset in a network of people who support each other by exchanging favours. The main reason for using *palancas* is generally to bypass or speed up a high number of regulations or excessive demands imposed by organisations or bureaucracies when attempting to resolve a particular problem. A typical example would involve a person requiring emergency medical care in a public hospital in Mexico. Unless the family finds an acquaintance with a degree of influence to intervene and speed up the process, the person would be forced to wait for a long time. If *palanca* is successful, individuals will be attended to and treated sooner than those without *palanca*, who cannot help but follow the formal procedures and obey the rules. Paradoxically, in Mexico, a family that follows rules and procedures and is unable to bend the rules is considered a failed family and 'justifiably' feels a deep sense of shame.

People justify *palanca*, since it allows a shortcut to circumvent formal procedures and obtain products, services, licences or permits required to solve a specific problem. It is usually not perceived as illegal to search for *palanca*. Social norms in the context of formal inefficiency can make it a legitimate or justifiable action. *Palanca* does not seek revolt against the formal rule itself, but against the fact that the formal rule does not work out in practice.

Just as any social relationship, *palanca* is to be cultivated, maintained and supported by rules of etiquette and norms of reciprocity. The etiquette involves a know-how of managing access to influential persons, mastering skills of asking them for a favour and taking care not to put those persons at risk, for instance. It is essential not to show the instrumentality of the requested favour: issues of 'payment', material or not, and often simply a moral obligation to reciprocate the favour in the future, must be agreed with great *tiento* (tact). If certain codes of conduct are not followed, and the payment offered or insinuated for the favour is taken the wrong way, *palanca* might become suspect and qualify as close to being illegal or corrupt.

The *palanca* is a contradictory mechanism. Similar to the Russian *blat* (see 1.1 Volume 1), the Chinese *guanxi* (see 1.12 Volume 1) or the Brazilian *jeitinho* (1.2 Volume 1), *palanca* in Mexico is considered a balancing mechanism that restores justice when formal institutions malfunction. The justification is that when the authorities fail to offer services or goods efficiently, it is fair to use *palancas* to solve personal or family problems. However, there is less awareness among Mexican people that *palancas* can produce a contradictory social effect. It can perpetuate inequality, since those with more *ties* have informal and opaque advantage over those without or those with only few or low-quality *palancas*. The dark side of *palanca* is that the most influential leverage networks can be highly exclusive, usually permeable only to those with the most money and resources. Nevertheless, for a wider public, *palanca* remains a healthy and functional mechanism, because it is an important source of hope (Nuijten 2003): every person can obtain and use acquaintances in theory and therefore has the potential to obtain and use *palancas*.

There is also little awareness in Mexico regarding the victims of *palanca* (Arellano-Gault 2018). The consequences of 'jumping the queue' in terms of medical treatment are most pronounced for people without levers who have to wait their turn to receive medical treatment according to the formal rules.

Finally, it is necessary to point out that there is a relation between *palancas* and systemic, structural corruption: *palancas* construct parallel, informal ways that legitimate bending the rules to obtain advantages and resources. There might be a blurred (perhaps cynical) borderline between what people in Mexico defines as honest *palancas* and corrupt ones. This is an uncomfortable truth in Mexican society. *Palancas* are an insightful clue for understanding the persistence of corruption in countries like Mexico.

5.8 **Kabel** (Malaysia)
Christian Giordano
Department of Social Sciences, University of Fribourg, Switzerland

Kabel in Bahasa, Malaysia, derives from the English term 'cable', and has literally the same meaning, indicating connection in a technical sense. In Malaysia, however, *kabel* has also developed a parallel meaning, implying connection to people in high places politically or administratively. As Wong Chun Wai aptly observes, *kabel* 'means you need to have the support of an influential figure who is as strong as a cable. It's no longer good enough to "pull strings" but you must be able to "pull a cable" for your plans to get off' (Wong 2017).

In this case, it is not only about sociability, but also the instrumentality of political or administrative networks that can help solve an important problem for those lacking access to resources. The connotations of the phrase 'do you have *kabel*?' include personal relations with those in power, or someone who can solve a problem and can be resorted to in times of need. The term *kabel* is connected to the term *jalan*, which in Bahasa Malaysia means 'road' or 'way'. In fact, the colloquial phrase '*You got jalan ah?*' is very common (Wong 2017: 19) and refers to a way of getting things done. This is a straightforward way of asking an acquaintance or a friend whether they can help solve a complex situation with the public administration through an informal and personalised relationship comparable to those that characterise *kabel*. Therefore, *jalan* is 'the way' to link to *kabel* connections in order to find a quick solution to a specific political or administrative problem.

From an anthropological or sociological point of view, in Malaysia *kabel* primarily implies the existence of specific connections, that is, useful ones or, more precisely, those who can help solve issues. Therefore, *kabel* has to do with informal personal relationships that can guarantee a favourable solution of a given problem which cannot be untangled through formal channels. These lamentable snags are chiefly caused by formal, that is, legal, bureaucratic or political delays or hindrances.

In general, a social relationship linked to the term *kabel* occurs between individuals of different social standings. Since as a rule there is a marked discrepancy between actors A and B in terms of opportunities to wield power and to access economic resources, there will also be a definite socioeconomic difference. *Kabel* is a kind of patron/client relationship entailing reciprocal services, in accordance with the principle of *do ut des* (I give so that you may give), which are indispensable for the client but less so for the patron. The patron/client relationship is characterised by a structural asymmetry because the client is more dependent on the patron than vice versa. The client, therefore, has less access (if any) to power than the patron, who instead is usually a member of the state's political and administrative establishment. In line with research in other societies, Malaysian *kabel* relationships are an integral part of highly complex and informal clientelist coalitions in which the patron often acts as an intermediary between the client and the politician or public official.

As Wong (2017) and Nadeswaran (2016) rightly point out, exchanges of favours in Malaysia are not equally reciprocal because a person with more power will also have important personal connections within the political, bureaucratic and economic machine, more so than someone who lacks connections. Hence, the relationships associated with the term *kabel* are structurally asymmetrical. Though service performances are based on the principle of reciprocity, this does not entail similar or equivalent services. Those with higher political, economic or social positions can exploit and reallocate more important resources than those who lack these connections.

Consequently, *kabel* practices chiefly involve interpersonal and dyadic relationships governed by mutual rights and duties, which are perceived as informal but overall indispensable and practically mandatory. Those with a lower social standing, therefore, will need *kabel* more than those with a higher social standing, rather than vice versa. Thus, a relationship linked to the social logic of *kabel* binds a weaker person to the stronger, and can last for a long period of time. This leads to the establishment of practically indissoluble dependency relationships that are viewed as useful if not indeed mandatory, especially by those who are believed to be in a socially inferior position with limited access to resources.

As observed by scholars, *kabel* does not consist of a single dyadic relationship but rather is grounded in vast interpersonal networks comprising a patron, backed by a considerable number of clients, even if their support is perhaps half-hearted. Thus, *kabel* is best viewed not only as an interpersonal phenomenon, but also as a collective one, especially when *kabel* relationships are mobilised wholesale as at election time. In such cases, they are often patron-driven and oriented top-down to gain electoral support. Where *kabel* practices are initiated by bottom-up requests, and shaped by the need to redistribute resources, *kabel* practices are perceived as clientelist. Both top-down and bottom-up requests enact the co-dependency of *kabel* relationships. Such co-dependency accounts for a lot of behaviours and strategies, servicing the patron-client nature of Malaysian institutions. The mutual – patron-client – use of *kabel* practices characterises the hidden structure of the vast majority of organisations and power structures in Malaysia. Consequently, *kabel* practices and relationships serve both patrons and clients. They are regarded as the underpinnings of a widespread system based on informal networks and practices, but also define the workings of official, and thus formal, public institutions. In the end, what is viewed to be electoral support from the perspective of the patron is considered to be an accelerator to obtain public services for a client.

Ever since achieving independence (31 August 1957), Malaysia has enjoyed remarkable political stability compared to the vast majority of the so-called Third World countries. The exception were the traumatic 'ethnic riots' between Malays and Chinese on 13 May 1969, which have since come to be regarded as the nation's 'negative myth', that is, incidents that must never occur again (Watson and Andaya 2001).

Moreover, there have been no attempted coups and/or challenges to the political and administrative continuity. The parliamentary system in particular has never been challenged, although the reputation of politicians is somewhat tarnished.

Since 2010, this trust deficit worsened in Malaysia, especially after the scandal of the firm 1MDB (1Malaysia Development Berhad) in which Prime Minister Najib Abdur Razak and his family members were involved. Yet, Malaysia has a rather efficient government agency which investigates and prosecutes corruption (Malaysian Anti-Corruption Commission, MACC), and civil society in particular reacted by ousting the entire government at the general election held on 9 May 2018. Thus, it would be a mistake to think that social practices linked to public mistrust in politics and bureaucracy are generalised, even though the personalised relationships that characterise transactions related to *kabel* are still very common throughout the country. In these specific cases there is a noticeable ambivalence between the citizens' participation in current political life and the mistrust in institutions on which typical *kabel* relationships are founded.

Despite the unexpected outcome of the latest election, citizens place very little trust in politicians and bureaucrats and continue to have reservations about trusting impersonal institutions. This results in a fundamental fracture between the State's legality and its corresponding legitimacy. Thus, people are aware of legality but barely respect and acknowledge state authority and do not grant it the necessary legitimacy. According to the penal code, defrauding the state and its institutions is illegal, but from the point of view of the individual subjects, it is an acceptable and often legitimate practice. Thus, although an offence, *kabel* is not perceived by the citizenry as a crime or disloyalty to state institutions. Rather, it is seen to be a form of personalised *justice* and a defence strategy against the arbitrariness of the public sector. Perhaps, a good way to describe the stance of Malaysians towards the state is a confrontation between society and the state, resulting in the neutralisation of the state by infiltrating its institutions through personal connections (Clastres 1974). It is not a case of rebellion or collective open resistance, but rather a set of individual infiltration strategies into the public sector. Such individual strategies constitute highly personalised networks, grounded in clientelist dependence, on the one hand, and ensuring the continuing power of patrons, on the other (Boissevain 1974; Eisenstadt and Roniger 1984; Giordano 2012: 13 ff., 2018: 10 ff.).

5.9 *Fanju* (China)
Lang Liu
Alumna, Department of Political Science and
School of Public Policy, UCL, UK

Fanju is a goal-oriented way to communicate, build social networks, strengthen social ties and transfer interests between individuals or interest groups by throwing a banquet. The Chinese word *fanju* (饭局) has two parts. *Fan* translates as 'meal' and refers to a large group of people eating and drinking together. *Ju* translates as 'gambling' or 'trap' and refers to the banquet's instrumental function. In a *fanju*, people of the same social class, family, interest or professional group gather to strengthen social ties, to redistribute resources or to exchange favours that will benefit them personally.

Fanju is common in all walks of life and regions of China (Li 2017). Chinese people typically participate in some form of *fanju* several times a week. On weekdays, it is customary to share a meal with a colleague or business partner to sustain and improve relationships and to conduct business negotiations. At the weekend, people have *fanju* with family and friends, or they might host or attend a more instrumental *fanju* to solve problems that may not be dealt with through official channels

Figure 5.9.1 A wedding *fanju* in Nantong, Jiangsu, China. © Lang Liu.

(Wu 2011: 11–14). Government officials are often invited to banquets to solicit a promotion or negotiate a reduction or annulment of corporate violation fines (Zhang 2007).

Fanju comprises two categories: ritualised and non-ritualised. Ritualised *fanju* refers to a celebration banquet with an institutionalised form, such as a wedding (*hun yan*) or the full-moon celebration that accompanies the arrival of a baby (*manyue jiu*). *Fanju* hosts rent a restaurant or private room (*baoxiang*) on such an occasion and the guests bring a red envelope (*hongbao*) or a gift. The status and esteem of the host as well as the relationship between guests and hosts are openly displayed. The number of guests at a ritual *fanju* reflects the host family's overall level of social relations and signifies their social capital. Guests usually have an emotional connection to the host. Invitees who do not have a close relationship with the host will send the gift envelope ahead of the celebration banquet without attending it.

Attending a ritualised *fanju* fulfils social or moral obligations. Traditional moral rules require people to participate in institutionalised ritualised *fanju*, to maintain specific social relationships, for example between colleagues and managers, or between unfamiliar distant relatives, even when they dislike each other. It means that a number of Chinese citizens are in the *fanju* system involuntarily (Wu 2011).

Chinese generally divide non-ritualised *fanju* into two types: sociable (such as a family gathering during the holidays) and instrumental. In practice, however, *fanju* with a single characteristic is rare; both sociability and instrumentality are present in different proportions. Instrumental *fanju* refers to a banquet hosted with the purpose of allowing people who lack relationships, or those who have weak ties, to expand their social networks and build new *guanxi* (关系) connections with powerful officials (Wu 2011). The instrumental non-ritualised *fanju* has two common purposes. First, it can serve as an indirect means of conveying and affirming one's loyalty. Accepting an invitation to *fanju* can be an informal way to express approval of the host's goal or exchange expectations. For instance, the host in need of a favour first identifies those in his social network with the ability to help, then invites the guests to attend this type of *fanju* for a formal occasion, such as the Mid-Autumn Festival gathering or National Day of the People's Republic of China, where they can agree on exchanging favours in an informal way. Attending the *fanju* is an indication that the attendees are likely to provide the favour expected by the host. This type of *fanju* can also be used for bargaining, especially where there exists a difference in social status between the two parties, for instance where the invitees have a stronger influence than the host in a specific field. This type of *fanju* maintains the instrumental relationship and does not require the invitees' immediate return of the favour to the hosts (Wu 2011).

Fanju is one of the most important strategies for building, maintaining and expanding an instrumental or sociable guanxi and *quanzi* relationships (Zhang 2007; Osburg 2013). *Guanxi* (关系) is the practice of exchanging favours. *Quanzi* is the Chinese social culture and a product of social interaction. *Quanzi* (圈子) is the cultural preference for working, living and socialising with people with similar social attributes and values and satisfies a sense of belonging, leading people to form small groups, also called *quanzi*. The *quanzi* culture provides an open and common space for finding assistance and cooperation (see also *yong*o in South Korea, 3.5 Volume 1, *joro* in Kyrgyzstan, 6.3 in this volume and *ahbap-çavuş ilişkisi* in Turkey, 5.4 in this volume). Although there are many different types and scales of *quanzi*, including *quanzi* of colleagues, *quanzi* of friends and *quanzi* of students, the common structure of the *quanzi* is – similar to an institution – built around one or more individuals with power or money. The new people who share their value orientation gradually join them for mutual benefits. *Quanzi* culture is extremely exclusive; *quanzi* members will refuse to communicate, socialise and offer favours to those outside of the *quanzi* (Xie 2018; Zhang 2018). These sources suggest that *fanju* is regarded as a crucial socialising method that *quanzi* members use to maintain and expand their social network and emotional connections, specifically the non-ritualised *fanju*, which is initiated by individuals or groups of members. Often, the sole purpose of a *fanju* is just to exchange 'good feelings' (*rengqing*, 人情) or show caring and moral concern. Yet sometimes *fanju* serves the exchange of specific interests, and because *quanzi* relies on a symbiotic relationship between people with varying levels of power it is easy to induce corruption. Corruption in the government usually emerges in a *quanzi* of civil servants who use large amounts of public funds to hold *fanju* in rotation (Xie 2018; Zhang 2018).

Similar practices to *fanju* can be observed in Japan and South Korea. In Japan, *nomikai* is an informal business meeting, often organised at a casual drinking place (*izakaya*) after work. Since Japanese companies have strict boundaries concerning communication between upper and lower corporate levels, *nomikai* is the only opportunity where these limits can be crossed (Li 2005). In South Korea, *hoesik* is a universal company and organisational subculture of eating and drinking together after work (Bader et al. 2018). *Hoesik* helps employees relax, knit stronger ties and resolve workplace conflicts, but can also result in undesirable effects such as excessive or forced drinking, gossip and sexual harassment (Sim 2017).

Fanju originated two thousand years ago, at the Feast at Hong Gate, a banquet held by Xiang Yu, a rebel leader who launched the anti-Qin movement (209–206 BC). The original purpose of the *fanju* was to plot the murder of another rebel leader, Liu Bang (Li 2007). However, Liu Bang escaped this fate by bargaining during the *fanju*. *Fanju* did not become a target of sustained academic and political focus until the end of the twentieth century when it began to be treated as an 'open secret' (Ledeneva 2011) and associated with corruption. The Chinese government has attempted to limit the use of *fanju* as a platform for money laundering deals and political clientelism after President Xi Jinping launched the anti-corruption campaign in 2012 (Shu and Zhang 2018).

Fanju's complex functionality means that its effects on Chinese politics, the economy and society are ambivalent. It can promote integration of social groups, yet it is also susceptible to the abuse of power, particularly when groups use public funds for their private benefit. In 2012, China Net reported that approximately 300 million yuan of public funds were spent on *fanju* annually, an average of more than 820,000 yuan per day. Such high expenses mean that *fanju* costs incurred by officials significantly support the restaurant and entertainment industry as *fanju* is generally held in luxury restaurants with high-end wines and expensive food (Zhang 2007). The launch of the anti-corruption campaign in 2012 – while curtailing corruption – has dramatically reduced the turnover of luxury restaurants and entertainment venues by 35 per cent in Beijing and 20 per cent in Shanghai. Several venues have gone bankrupt as a result (China Net 2014).

5.10 **Enchufismo** (Spain)
Ignacio Fradejas-García
School of Social Sciences, University of Iceland, Iceland

Enchufismo is the practice of granting positions, jobs, assignments, recommendations, resources or benefits through kinship, friendship or political relations, regardless of the merits of the candidate. The term is commonly used in Spain to capture the use of personal networks to overcome constraints in numerous contexts. The term derives from the verb *enchufar* that literally means to plug in, and is synonymous with the verb *conectar*, to connect to someone who has *enchufe*, a socket, in order to access a good position, usually through family or close friendship or their networks.

The term *enchufismo* has the advantage of a powerful metaphor while being semantically close to other pejorative terms such as nepotism, favouritism and *amiguismo* (old-boy network) (Muñoz 2011). There are many metaphorical terms in Latin America with similar meaning. To have *palanca*, or lever, in Cuba, El Salvador or Dominican Republic refers to the ability or influence to obtain something (RAE 2020c). To have *muñeca*, or wrist, implies support from an influential person in Argentina, Bolivia, Peru or Uruguay (RAE 2020b). *Enchufismo* is also similar to cronyism and nepotist practices, such as the Chilean *pituto*, the Italian *recomendazione, pulling the strings* in Anglo-Saxon settings, or *avea o pilă* practices in Romania (Fradejas-García et al. 2022). The term is perhaps more general as it combines both family and friendship, as well as embracing both personal and professional contexts. A recent survey on business perceptions shows that the practices of favouring friends and/or family members in public institutions in Spain is the second highest in the EU (54 per cent) only behind Portugal (59 per cent) and significantly different from the EU average (42 per cent) (Eurobarometer 2019).

The origin of the term *enchufe* is hard to establish but there are references in the media archives in the 1910s (La Vanguardia 1915). It was already in use during the dictatorship of Primo de Rivera in 1923–30, who fostered the practice in order to establish good working positions with people who had kin relationships with the regime elites (García 1980). Then, the term became popular during the Second Spanish Republic in 1931–9, when opponents of the Republic initiated a '*enchufes* campaign' to discredit the government. They used the term *enchufismo* to characterise the case of the deputies who took advantage of their political influence to obtain prestigious positions and resources (García 1980: 52–7). Anthropologists working in Spain have directly linked *enchufismo* practices with politics, where nepotism, patronage systems and other forms of political corruption abound. During Franco's dictatorship in 1939–75, such practices became crucial for circumventing all kinds of bureaucratic obstacles in order to get things done (Kenny 1960; Eisenstadt and Roniger 1984). Local practices of *enchufismo* embrace both clientelist behaviour at the grassroots level (Campbell 2021) and patronal influence in local administrations for granting jobs and resources to friends, families and political allies.

According to the dictionary (RAE 2020a, 2020d), the colloquial and derogatory terms related to *enchufismo* – *enchufar, enchufe, enchufismo, enchufado/a* – tend to emphasise political influence and/or corruption. However, *enchufismo*-based problem-solving is also widespread in spheres beyond politics and state administration, such as the education system or the private job market. Indeed, the term has expanded to mean any social connection to get positions, resources and *sinecura* jobs that are almost effortless.

On the one hand, the idea of using contacts to enter and/or secure a position within an organisation is embedded in the local culture. On the other hand, even when it is clear that someone powerful has 'supposedly' been granted a job, it is not openly recognised. Political influence, kin/friend recommendation or direct help are an open secret, referred to by euphemisms reflecting the power of the connection: 'to be hand-picked' (*dedo* or *dedazo*), and/or 'to have a three-phase electricity' (*trifásico*) that generates, transfers and distributes power.

Enchufismo is a common practice in the Spanish labour market. Although the principle of meritocracy is frequently invoked, it is rarely implemented, so informal networks become the most effective path to getting a job. A 2016 survey shows that 41 per cent of young people in employment (16–34 years old) had obtained their positions through family, friends or acquaintances (INE 2016). Thus, the merit of these appointments is always in doubt. To claim meritocracy for an individual, or an organisation, is to put up a fight against *enchufismo* or *amigocracy* (Kenny 1960). It is not necessary to have a connection with someone in a very powerful position; it is often enough to know someone who can mediate the situation or broker a deal. *Enchufismo* can be related to having powerful parents, a godfather (see also *padrino system* 7.10 Volume 2), or a friend, but it can also be just a recommendation, or a privilege gained on a predilection. Thus, the *enchufe* might be done by an intermediary who is neither close nor directly connected to the beneficiary. Correspondingly, the beneficiary might not need to repay the favour (the fact of belonging to a certain network entitles one to a favour). In most cases, it is just a favour without an obligation to repay, a part and parcel of an extended network of close ties. For example, having a friend who knows someone who is part of the managerial staff of a company or institution is a way of getting your CV to the top of the pile.

Although *enchufe* does not entail a direct reciprocity of the favour or return of the debt, a request for support may occur later. Such requests are rarely symmetrical and may involve the so-called long reciprocity cycle, whereby with time the initial *enchufado* will gain power to *enchufar* someone else in the future. It is accepted that *enchufismo* is negative and pejorative, a practice that everyone has suffered from at some point, and usually reinforces privileged networks and thus structural inequalities. However, it can also be advantageous. Although it might not look good, *enchufismo* is morally accepted when close ties are mobilised to secure a livelihood in precarious situations, which is a common occurrence in Spain nowadays.

5.11 **A molestar a otro lado** (Guatemala)
Jose Godinez and Denise Dunlap
Manning School of Business, University of Massachusetts, Lowell, USA

A molestar a otro lado ('go bother someone elsewhere') is a common expression used by Guatemalan businesses to let potential customers, suppliers and distributors know that they are not welcome. The practice of providing poor service or refusing it to people who look as if they do not have sufficient economic means to afford the items on sale took root when the Spanish began colonising the country nearly five hundred years ago. This attitude is common towards potential customers of modest means, but is more frequently used in dealing with people of indigenous descent, especially if they wear traditional clothes. Irrespective of whether or not such customers can afford goods or services provided by the business, the business often tells them '*a molestar a otro lado*', indicating refusal to deal with them. This discriminatory practice is aided by the fact that businesses are permitted to hang signs outside of their shops saying *nos reservamos el derecho de admision* ('we reserve the right to refuse service to any person').

Guatemala is a country characterised by contrasts and ranked as the tenth most unequal country in the world (CIA 2020). Acute inequality has been in place since colonisation of the country, which allowed people of European descent to accumulate and retain wealth while displacing indigenous people. Due to the unequal allocation of wealth, large businesses are controlled by a small minority. These business groups coined the practice of *a molestar a otro lado*, which occurs commonly in their day-to-day operations. This practice has also permeated smaller businesses and became part of the business culture in the country. Nowadays, this practice is commonly used to provide an impression of exclusivity. However, *a molestar a otro lado* affects a large part of the Guatemalan population since over 60 per cent of the population (or 6.4 million people) live in poverty. In addition, Guatemala has the second highest percentage of indigenous people in Latin America, about 40 per cent of the population (Borgen Project 2017).

A molestar a otro lado is also a common expression used in Latin America to dismiss a person, or group of persons, when their presence is not desired. This expression is used in the Latin American region to discriminate against people on the basis of race. One study found municipal workers in Ecuador telling informal sellers of handicrafts 'to go *a molestar a otro lado*' (Carrillo-Navarrete and Salgado-Andrade 2002). However, its use by Guatemalan businesses to refuse services to possible customers is unique and has not yet been fully analysed and understood. Perhaps, the *a molestar a otro lado* practices in businesses began in the hospitality industry, where customers are often targeted by people begging for spare change or scraps of food. Employees in charge of the businesses turn beggars away with the phrase *a molestar a otro lado*.

While the practice seems illogical from a business point of view – assuming that businesses would like to attract as many customers as possible – in Guatemala companies have a different idea of how to run their business. Specifically, Guatemalan companies think that exclusivity is desirable because it helps to attract wealthier customers. This practice has also been aided by protectionism, allowing larger companies to enjoy subsidies or the enactment of rigid barriers to entry from the central and local governments. As a result, these companies did not need to compete for customers. Nevertheless, social changes, brought about by technical innovations and globalisation, give hope to traditionally excluded Guatemalans since these changes have forced some businesses to reassess their practices.

A molestar a otro lado has been, until the twenty-first century, a deeply embedded practice that seemed unlikely to change. However, the general public has voiced their repudiation of this practice. Indeed, the general public has taken advantage of the globalisation of technology advances to push back against companies that use this practice. While the political and economic elites in the country have embraced the *a molestar a otro lado* practice, the general public have begun to rebel against it. To show their disapproval, people have turned to new technologies, especially social media, to raise their concerns and demand change. This new wave of social conscience has been a unified effort by many different sectors of society irrespective of race or social status. However, not all businesses have been receptive to the demands of the public. One of the few industries that are actually changing is the mobile banking (M-banking) industry.

The M-banking industry can be defined as carrying out financial transactions through a mobile telephone or other mobile device that is linked to a personal bank account (World Bank 2006). Additionally, this industry is characterised by providing banking services to people with little financial resources who nevertheless need to carry out financial transactions but do not have easy access to a traditional bank. Firms within this industry, especially in developing countries, are able to generate attractive returns due to economies of scale, which allow them to provide low-cost services to a great number of clients. Firms within this industry believe that there is no such thing as an unattractive customer.

In Guatemala, the M-banking industry has been generally ignored by the government and thus, unregulated. The lack of regulation has made firms in this industry highly competitive, and as such firms within the M-banking industry realise that ignoring the needs of over 60 per cent of the population is not feasible or desirable if they want to remain in business. Hence, for the first time in Guatemalan history, the practice of *a molestar a otro lado* is being dismantled one small brick at a time. As domestic firms compete against foreign firms that dominate M-banking in Guatemala, they begin to understand that the practice of maintaining the custom of *a molestar a otro lado* will negatively impact their long-term success.

In 2017, we conducted an in-depth research study that examined changes in the mobile banking industry in Guatemala (Godinez et al. 2020). Interviews with 16 members of the Guatemalan government and representatives of six companies from the M-banking industry suggested that domestic firms were beginning to engage with customers and suppliers regardless of their ethnicity and economic status. These changes are the result of the low-profit rates inherent to the industry and thus, the need to increase the number of customers. Our research shows that these firms are creating linkages with traditionally neglected populations and by doing so are better able to compete with their foreign counterparts. These linkages include having direct communication with small suppliers and distributors in order to tailor products and services to customer needs. Also, and more importantly, M-banking firms are, for the first time, opening up and maintaining two-way communication with customers to specifically find ways to accommodate the needs of neglected population groups. Although these groups have limited schooling, they were increasingly using their services. This number is expected to grow since there are on average 1.5 cellular telephones per capita in Guatemala (World Bank 2020). Our research results suggest that firms in the M-banking industry can no longer afford to tell potential clients *a molestar a otro lado* if they want to remain competitive in this global and dynamic sector, and the Guatemalan public are experiencing the benefits of companies competing for their loyalty. With the advent of the adoption of new technologies in Guatemala the practice of *a molestar a otro lado* could be eradicated. Additionally, while the government at many different levels has not yet fully addressed the *a molestar a otro lado* problem, it is possible that social pressures will make them realise the harmful effects of these discriminatory practices, which in turn would bring about change.

Bibliography to Chapter 5

Introduction: gender, social exclusion and the dark side of informal networks
Sven Horak and Fadi Alsarhan

Abdalla, H. F., Maghrabi, A. S. and Raggad, B. G. 1998. 'Assessing the Perceptions of Human Resource Managers Toward Nepotism: A Cross-cultural Study'. *International Journal of Manpower* 19(8): 554–70.

Aldossari, M. and Robertson, M. 2015. 'The Role of Wasta in Repatriates' Perceptions of a Breach to the Psychological Contract: A Saudi Arabian Case Study'. *The International Journal of Human Resource Management* 27(16): 1854–73.

Ali, S. and Weir, D. 2020. 'Wasta: Advancing a Holistic Model to Bridge the Micro–Macro Divide'. *Management and Organization Review* 16(3): 657–85.

Al-Ramahi, A. 2008. 'Wasta in Jordan: A Distinct Feature of (and Benefit For) Middle Eastern Society'. *Arab Law Quarterly* 22(1): 35–62.

Alsarhan, F. 2019. *Factors and Impact of Wasta on HRM Practices in Jordan. Contributions to Theory and Leadership Implications on New Public Management (NPM) Culture of Organization*. PhD thesis, Université Jean Moulin Lyon 3.

Alsarhan, F. and Valax, M. 2020. 'Conceptualization of Wasta and Its Main Consequences on Human Resource Management'. *International Journal of Islamic and Middle Eastern Finance and Management* 14(1): 114–27.

Alsarhan, F., Ali, S. A., Weir, D. and Valax, M. 2021. 'Impact of Gender on Use of Wasta Among Human Resources Management Practitioners'. *Thunderbird International Business Review* 63(2): 131–43.

Al-Twal, A. 2021. 'Narrative Inquiry: A Proposed Methodology for Wasta Research'. *Thunderbird International Business Review* 63(4): 517–21.

Bailey, D. C. 2012. 'Women and Wasta: The Use of Focus Groups for Understanding Social Capital and Middle Eastern Women'. *The Qualitative Report* 17(33): 1–18.

Bedford, O. 2015. 'Crossing Boundaries: An Exploration of Business Socializing (Ying Chou for Guanxi) in a Chinese Society'. *Psychology of Women Quarterly* 40 (2): 290–306.

Berger, R., Silbiger, A., Herstein, R. and Barnes, B. R. 2015. 'Analyzing Business-to-Business Relationships in an Arab Context'. *Journal of World Business* 50(3): 454–64.

Brandstaetter, T., Bamber, D. and Weir, D. 2016. '"Wasta": Triadic Trust in Jordanian Business'. In *The Political Economy of Wasta: Use and Abuse of Social Capital Networking*, edited by M. Ramady, 65–78. New York: Springer.

Cunningham, R. B. and Sarayrah, Y. K. 1993. *Wasta: The Hidden Force in Middle Eastern Society*. Santa Barbara: Praeger Publishers.

de Haan, A. 1998. '"Social Exclusion": An Alternative Concept for the Study of Deprivation?'. *IDS Bulletin* 29(1): 10–19.

El-Said, H. and Harrigan, J. 2009. '"You Reap What You Plant": Social Networks in the Arab World – The Hashemite Kingdom of Jordan'. *World Development* 37(7): 1235–49.

European Union. (2010). *Gender Mainstreaming Active Inclusion Policies*. Luxembourg: European Institute for Gender Equality.

Fitzsimmons, T. W., Callan, V. J. and Paulsen, N. 2014. 'Gender Disparity in the C-suite: Do Male and Female CEOs Differ in How They Reached the Top?'. *Leadership Quarterly* 25(2): 245–66.

Granovetter, M. 1995. *Getting a Job: A Study of Contacts and Careers*. Chicago: Chicago University Press.

Granovetter, M. 2017. *Society and Economy: Framework and Principles*. Cambridge, MA: Belknap Press of Harvard University Press.

Hahm, P. C. (1986). *Korean Jurisprudence, Politics and Culture*. Seoul: Yonsei University Press.
Horak, S. 2014. 'Antecedents and Characteristics of Informal Relation-based Networks in Korea: Yongo, Yonjul and Inmaek'. *Asia Pacific Business Review* 20(1): 78–108.
Horak, S., Afiouni, F., Bian, Y., Ledeneva, A., Muratbekova-Touron, M. and Fey, C. F. 2020. 'Informal Networks: Dark Sides, Bright Sides, and Unexplored Dimensions'. *Management and Organization Review* 16(3): 511–42.
Hutchings, K. and Weir, D. 2006. 'Guanxi and Wasta: A Comparison'. *Thunderbird International Business Review* 48(1): 141–56.
Kim, Y.-H. 2000. 'Emergence of the Network Society: Trends, New Challenges, and an Implication for Network Capitalism'. *Korea Journal* 40(3): 161–84.
Ledeneva, A. 2003. 'Informal Practices in Changing Societies: Comparing Chinese Guanxi and Russian Blat'. Economics Working Papers 45. Centre for the Study of Economic and Social Change in Europe SSEES. London: UCL.
Lew, S.-C. 2013. *The Korean Economic Development Path. Confucian Tradition, Affective Network*. New York: Palgrave Macmillan.
Loewe, M., Blume, J. and Speer, J. 2008. 'How Favoritism Affects the Business Climate: Empirical Evidence from Jordan'. *Middle East Journal* 62(2): 259–76.
Nussbaum, M. C. 2005. 'Capabilities as Fundamental Entitlements: Sen and Social Justice'. In *Capabilities Equality: Basic Issues and Problems*, edited by A. Kaufman, 50–77. London: Routledge.
O'Neil, D. A., Hopkins, M. M. and Bilimoria, D. 2008. 'Women's Careers at the Start of the 21st Century: Patterns and Paradoxes'. *Journal of Business Ethics* 80(4): 727–43.
Patterson, L., Bae, S.-O. and Lim, J.-Y. 2013. 'Gender Equality in Korean Firms: Recent Evidence from HR Practitioners'. *Asia Pacific Journal of Human Resources* 51(3): 364–81.
Percy-Smith, J. 2000. 'Introduction: The Contours of Social Exclusion'. In *Policy Responses to Social Exclusion: Towards Inclusion?*, edited by J. Percy Smith, 1–21. Buckingham: Open University Press.
Saith, R. 2001. 'Social Exclusion: The Concept and Application to Developing Countries'. In *Defining Poverty in the Developing World*, edited by F. Stewart, R. Saith and B. Harriss-White, 75–90. Basingstoke: Palgrave Macmillan.
Sen, A. 1999. *Development as Freedom*. Oxford: Oxford University Press.
Sen, A. 2000. 'Social Exclusion: Concept, Application and Scrutiny'. *Social Development Papers* 1. Office of Environment and Social Development. Manila: Asian Development Bank.
Sen, A. 2005. 'Human Rights and Capabilities'. *Journal of Human Development* 6(2): 151–66.
Shen, J. and Kogan, I. 2017. 'To Whom Is Contact Use Beneficial? The Impacts of Self-Selected Contact Use on Gender Income Differentials in the Transitional Economy of Urban China'. *Studies of Transition States and Societies* 9(2): 1–16.
Sidani, Y. and Thornberry, J. 2013. 'Nepotism in the Arab World: An Institutional Theory Perspective'. *Business Ethics Quarterly* 23(1): 69–96.
Smith, P. B., Torres, C., Leong, C. H., Budhwar, P., Achoui, M. and Lebedeva, N. 2012. 'Are Indigenous Approaches to Achieving Influence in Business Organizations Distinctive? A Comparative Study of Guanxi, Wasta, Jeitinho, Svyazi and Pulling Strings'. *The International Journal of Human Resource Management* 23(2): 333–48.
Walker, A. and Walker, C. 1997. *Britain Divided: The Growth of Social Exclusion in the 1980s and 1990s*. London: Child Poverty Action Group.
Yee, J. 2000. 'The Social Networks of Koreans'. *Korea Journal* 40(1): 325–52.
Yee, J. 2015. 'Social Capital in Korea: Relational Capital, Trust, and Transparency'. *International Journal of Japanese Sociology* 24(1): 30–47.

5.1 *KhTsB* (Armenia)
Armine Petrosyan

Franzen, A. and Hangartner, D. 2006. 'Social Networks and Labour Market Outcomes: The Non-Monetary Benefits of Social Capital'. *European Sociological Review* 22(4): 353–68.
Gharagulyan, A. 2011. 'Voch' dzevakan ts'ants'eri gortsarrut'ayin p'vokhakerpman himnakhndiry hetkhorhrdayin hasarakut'yunnerum'. *Banber Yerevani hamalsarani – P'ilisop'ayut'yun, Hogebanut'yun* 135(4): 16–23.

Granovetter, M. 1995. *Getting a Job: A Study of Contacts and Careers*. Chicago and London: University of Chicago Press.
Harutyunyan, G. 2010. '"Tsanot'i" instituty vorpes sots'ialakan kapitali drsevorman dzev hay hasarakut'yunum'. *Anniversary Scientific Session: Collection of Articles Dedicated to the 90th Anniversary of YSU* 5: 165–71.
Jilozian, A. 2017. 'Gender Politics in Armenia: An Exploration of Legislation, Anti-Gender Rhetoric, and Community Strategies'. *Women Support Center*. www.womensupportcenter. org/wp-content/uploads/2018/01/Gender_politics_final.pdf
Millar, G. R. 1987. 'The Little Deal: Brezhnev's Contribution to Acquisitive Socialism'. *National Council for Soviet and East European Research*. www.ucis.pitt.edu/nceeer/pre1998/1987-801-15-Millar.pdf
Montgomery, J. D. 1992. 'Job Search and Network Composition: Implications of the Strength of Weak Ties Hypothesis'. *American Sociological Review* 57(5): 586–96.
Mouw, T. 2003. 'Social Capital and Finding a Job: Do Contacts Matter?'. *American Journal of Sociology* 68(6): 868–98.
Shakhnazaryan, R. and Shakhnazaryan, N. 2010. 'Sdelai mne uvazhenie: neformal'nye seti podderzhki i neformal'naya ekonomika v Kavkazskix obshchestvakh'. *Laboratorium: Russian Review of Social Research* 2(1): 50–72.
Shirinia, T. 2018. 'The Nation Family: Intimate Encounters and Genealogical Perversion in Armenia'. *American Ethnologist* 45(1): 48–59.

5.2 *Pečenje rakije* (Serbia)
Maria Vivod

Barjaktarović, M. 1951. 'Od čega se i kako peče *rakija* u Banatu'. *Zbornik Matice Srpske. Serija Društvenih nauka* 2: 119–21. Novi Sad: Matica srpske.
Dikić, S. and Dikić, A. 2003. 'Kajsija uzme a bogato vrati: šta se mora poštovati i činiti u privlačnom izazovu: pečenju vrhunske kajsijevače: staro iskustvo: dobra vatra – dobra *rakija*'. *Svet pića* VI (15): 1–5.
Jovanović-Batut, M. 1911. 'Ne uspavljujte plašljivu odojčad otrovima; *Rakija* kao lek'. *Zdravlje-Lekarske pouke o zdravlju i bolesti* VI(1): 1–12.
Mihajlović, B. M. 2007. *Vino, rakija i sirće u narodnoj medicini*. Beograd: Partenon.
Mrgić, J. 2017. 'Aqua Vitae: Notes on Geographies of Alcohol Production and Consumption in the Ottoman Balkans'. *Issues in Ethnology and Anthropology* 12(4): 1309–28.
Petrović, M. 1889. *Proizvodnja Rakije u Našem Narodu. Letopis Matice srpske. Sveska prva. Knjiga 157 & Sveska Druga. Knjiga 158*. Novi Sad: Srpska Štamparija Dra.Svet.Miletića.
Politika. 2019. 'Carinici kaznili 98-godišnju staricu jer je pekla rakiju'. *Politika*. 1 March. www.politika.rs/sr/clanak/423928/Carinici-kaznili-98-godisnju-staricu-jer-je-pekla-rakiju
Vukmanović, Lj. 1999. 'Vaskrs dudare: sirotinjska *rakija* ode u gospodsko piće: sad se flaša dudare menja za flašu viskija'. *Svet pića* II (3–4): 31–4.
Vukmanović, Lj. 2005. 'Mirisi sa gladnoša: retkost iz Sremskih Karlovaca: breskovača od sto sorti bresaka iz podruma Instituta za voćarstvo i vinogradarstvo'. *Svet pića* VIII (20–1): 24–5.

5.3 *Hemşehricilik* (Turkey)
Eda Pamuksuzer

Boboyorov, H. 2013. *Collective Identities and Patronage Networks in Southern Tajikistan*. Munster: LIT.
Erder, S. 1999. 'Where Did You Hail from? Localism and Networks in Istanbul'. In *Istanbul Between the Global and the Local*, edited by C. Keyder, 161–72. Maryland: Rowman and Littlefield Publishers.
T.C. Icisleri Bakanligi Dernekler Dairesi Baskanligi. 2004. '*5253 Sayili Dernekler Kanunu*'.
Terzi, E. 2014. 'Hemsehri Dernekleri, Hemsehrilik Bilinci Ve Kentlilesme Iliskisi Uzerine Bir Arastirma'. *Selcuk Universitesi Journal of Institute of Social Sciences* 32: 37–150.

5.4 *Ahbap-çavuş ilişkisi* (Turkey)
Semih Ergelen

Buğra, A. and Savaşkan, O. 2015. *Türkiye'de Yeni Kapitalizm: Siyaset, Din ve İş Dünyası*. Bülent Doğan (Çev.). İstanbul: İletişim Yayıncılık.
Eğilmez, M. 2014. 'Ahbap Çavuş Kapitalizmi'. 19 May. www.mahfiegilmez.com/2014/05/ahbap-cavus-kapitalizmi.html
Ledeneva, A. 2018. 'Redistribution: The Substantive Ambivalence: Relationships vs Use of Relationships'. In *Global Encyclopaedia of Informality: Understanding Social and Cultural Complexity, Volume 1*, edited by A. Ledeneva, 31–3. London: UCL Press.
Nişanyan, S. 2009. *Sözlerin Soyağacı: Çağdaş Türkçenin Etimolojik Sözlüğü*. İstanbul: Everest Yayınları.
Provis, C. 2008. 'Guanxi and Conflicts of Interest'. *Journal of Business Ethics* 79: 57–66.
Tong, C. K. 2014. 'Rethinking Chinese Business'. In *Chinese Business: Rethinking Guanxi and Trust in Chinese Business Networks*, edited by C. Tong, 1–21. Singapore: Springer.
Türk Dil Kurumu. 2019. '*Ahbap çavuş ilişkisi*'. https://sozluk.gov.tr/
Yay, O. 2018. 'Torpil'. In *Global Encyclopaedia of Informality: Understanding Social and Cultural Complexity, Volume 1*, edited by A. Ledeneva, 213–16. London: UCL Press.
Yolculuk. 2018. 'AKP'li Numan Kurtulmuş: Bu seçim öyle ahbap-çavuş ilişkisi ile olmayacak'. 14 November.

5.5 *Grypsowanie* (Poland)
Piotr Majda

Jarosz, M. 2011. 'Więzienie w krzywym zwierciadle tekstów medialnych' [Prison in the Fun-house Mirror of Media Texts]. *Kultura – Media – Teologia* 5: 34–45.
Kaminski, M. 2003. 'Games Prisoners Play'. *Rationality and Society* 15(2): 188–217.
Kaminski, M. 2004. *Games Prisoners Play*. Princeton: Princeton University Press.
Małkowski, S. 1971. '"Drugie życie" w zakładzie wychowawczym' ['Second Life' in Juvenile Detention Centre]. *Etyka* 8: 135–47.
Michalska, A. and Michalski, D. 2020. *Zachowania niepożądane w zakładach karnych Wybrane zagadnienia* [Undesirable Behaviour in Penitentiary Facilities – Selected Aspects]. Warszawa-Olsztyn: Wydawnictwo AEH.
Moczydłowski, P. 1994. 'Więziennictwo: od systemu totalitarnego do demokratycznego' [Prisons: From a Totalitarian to a Democratic System]. *Przegląd Więziennictwa Polskiego* 8: 3–16.
Moczydłowski, P. 2002. *Drugie życie więzienia* [The Hidden Life of Polish Prisons]. Warszawa: Łośgraf.
Rodasik, R., Ćwiertnia, E. and Zat'ko, J. 2013. '*Język podkultury więziennej – gwara, język migowy, tatuaż*' [The language of prison subculture – argot, sign language, tattoos]. *Kultura Bezpieczeństwa. Nauka-Praktyka-Refleksje* 13: 116–41.
Skręt, R. 2004. 'Obraz podkultury więziennej we współczesnym zakładzie penitencjarnym' [The Image of Prison Subculture in the Contemporary Penitentiary Facility]. *Nauczyciel i Szkoła* 1–2(22–3): 143–52.
Symmetry (Symetria). 2003. Directed by Konrad Niewolski. Poland: SPI International Polska, EM.
Szaszkiewicz, M. 1997. *Tajemnice grypserki* [The Secrets of Grypsing]. Krakow: Wydawnictwo Instytutu Ekspertyz Sądowych.
Zarzycki, Ł. 2015. 'Socio-lingual Phenomenon of the Anti-language of Polish and American Prison Inmates'. *Crossroads. A Journal of English Studies* 8(1/2015): 11–23.

5.6 *Meso* (Cyprus and Greece)
George Hajipavli

Al Jazeera. 2020. 'The Cyprus Papers Undercover', 12 October. www.youtube.com/watch?v=Oj18cya_gvw
Arbesleitner, R. 2018. 'Parteibuchwirtschaft'. In *The Global Encyclopaedia of Informality, Volume 1*, edited by A. Ledeneva, 58–61. London: UCL Press.

Baez-Camargo, C. and Ledeneva, A. 2017. 'Where Does Informality Stop and Corruption Begin? Informal Governance and the Public/Private Crossover in Mexico, Russia and Tanzania'. *Slavonic and East European Review* 95: 367–70.

Charalambous, G. and Christophorou, C. 2016. *Party-Society Relations in the Republic of Cyprus*. London: Routledge.

Faustmann, H. 2010. 'Rusfeti and Political Patronage in the Republic of Cyprus'. *The Cyprus Review* 22: 269–89.

Georgas, J., Christakopoulou, S., Poortinga, Y. H., Angleitner, A., Goodwin, R. and Charalambous, N. 1997. 'The Relationship of Family Bonds to Family Structure and Function Across Cultures'. *Journal of Cross-Culture Psychology* 28: 303–20.

Georgiades, S. D. 2006. 'Favouritism as a Form of Injustice in Cyprus'. *The Cyprus Review* 18: 105–27.

Hale, H. E. 2014. *Patronal Politics: Eurasian Regime Dynamics in Comparative Perspective*. Cambridge: Cambridge University Press.

Knight, D. M. 2018. 'Fakelaki (Greece)'. In *The Global Encyclopaedia of Informality, Volume 1*, edited by A. Ledeneva, 182–4. London: UCL Press.

Konstantinou, G. 2021. 'Limassol: Reports Individuals Vaccinated with Meso', 31 March. Sigmalive. www.sigmalive.com/news/local/761924/lemesoskataggelies-gia-emvoliasmomi-dikaiouxonatoma-emvoliastikan-me-meso

Ledeneva, A. 2018. 'Future Challenges of Corruption Studies'. *Südosteuropa* 66: 418–25.

Nestoros, C. 2021. 'Passport to Jho Low: The Archbishop Admits he Mediated'. *Alpha News*. www.alphanews.live/cyprus/diabatirio-ston-jho-low-paradeheitai-oti-mesolabise-o-arhiepiskopos-binteo

Papadoulis, K. J. 2006. 'Clientelism, Corruption and Patronage in Greece: A Public Administration Approach'. *Teaching Public Administration* 26: 13–24.

Pring, C. 2016. *People and Corruption: Europe and Central Asia*. Berlin: Transparency International.

Sigmalive. 2016. 'Φωκαΐδης: Στα χακί οι 3.000 οπλίτες', 1 August. www.youtube.com/watch?v=jk86IknWg_o

Stanojevic, D. and Stokanic, D. 2018. 'Veza'. In *The Global Encyclopaedia of Informality, Volume 1*, edited by A. Ledeneva, 58–61. London: UCL Press.

Themelis, S. 2013. *Social Change and Education in Greece: A Study in Class Struggle Dynamics*. New York: Palgrave Macmillan.

Trousas, F. 2021. 'Το ρουσφέτι ως ισχυρή ιδιομορφία της ελληνικής κοινωνικοπολιτικής ζωής'. Lifo.gr., 24 January. www.lifo.gr/now/greece/roysfeti-os-ishyri-idiomorfia-tis-ellinikis-koinonikopolitikis-zois

Yay, O. 2018. 'Torpil (Turkey)'. In *The Global Encyclopaedia of Informality, Volume 2*, edited by A. Ledeneva, 213–16. London: UCL Press.

Zachariou, K. 2020. 'This is the Hidden Nouris List – All Those Who "Gave" Golden Passports'. *Diálogos*, 13 December. https://dialogos.com.cy/idoy-i-kryfi-lista-ton-parochon-ypiresion-gia-ta-chrysa-diavatiria/

5.7 *Palanca* (Mexico)
David Arellano-Gault and Luis Jair Trejo-Alonso

Arellano-Gault, D. 2018. 'En México, la vida es una consecución de palancas. Escapando del monstruo burocrático kafkiano: palancas y corrupción'. In *Burocracia en México*, edited by R. Peeters and F. Nieto. Mexico City: CIDE.

Lomnitz, C. 2000. *'Vicios públicos, virtudes privadas: la corrupción en México'*. Mexico City: Ciesas-M.A. Porrúa.

Nuijten, M. 2003. 'Power, Community and the State: The Political Anthropology of Organisation in Mexico'. London: Pluto Press.

Zalpa, G., Tapia, E. and Reyes, J. 2014. 'El que a buen árbol se arrima … Intercambio de favores y corrupción'. *Cultura y Representaciones Sociales* 9 (17): 149–76.

5.8 *Kabel* (Malaysia)
Christian Giordano

Boissevain, J. 1974. *Friends of Friends: Networks, Manipulators and Coalitions*. Oxford: Blackwell.
Clastres, P. 1974. *La société contre l'Etat*. Paris: Editions de Minuit.
Eisenstadt, S. and Roniger, L. 1984. *Patrons, Clients and Friends: Interpersonal Relations and the Structure of Trust in Society*. Cambridge: Cambridge University Press.
Giordano, C. 2012. 'The Anthropology of Mediterranean Societies'. In *A Companion to the Anthropology of Europe*, edited by U. Kockel, M. Craith and J. Frykman, 13–31. Oxford, Chichester: Wiley-Blackwell.
Giordano, C. 2018. 'Klientelismus und Patronage als Sozial- und Kulturphänomen. Theoretische Reflexionen zu informellen Beziehungsstrukturen'. In *Klientelismus in Südosteuropa*, edited by K. Roth and I. Zelepos, 10–28. Berlin: Peter Lang Verlag.
Nadeswaran, R. 2016. *Curi Curi: Stories behind the Stories*. Kuala Lumpur: Self-Publication.
Watson A. and Andaya, L. 2001. *A History of Malaysia*. London: Palgrave Macmillan.
Wong, C. 2017. 'Mind your Words, Please'. *The Star*, 23 April. www.thestar.com.my

5.9 *Fanju* (China)
Lang Liu

Bader, A.K., Froese, F.J. and Kraeh, A. 2018. 'Clash of Cultures? German Expatriates' Work-life Boundary Adjustment in South Korea'. *European Management Review* 15(3): 357–74.
China Net. 2014. 'Meiti jie zhongguo guanchang fanju meitian wan ge yi nian chidiao sanqian yi', 1 January. China Net. http://m.news.cntv.cn/2014/05/14/ARTI1400033868816337.shtml
In, M. 2018. *Jikjanginui Patijungsim Hoesikmunhwaui Baljeon Bangan Yeongu*. Seoul: Sushin Women University Library.
Ledeneva, A. 2011. 'Open Secrets and Knowing Smiles', *East European Politics and Societies* 25(4): 720–36.
Li, G. 2005. 'Shijie geguo fanju'. *Merchant Weekly*, 2 January. http://navi.cnki.net/KNavi/JournalDetail?pcode=CJFD&pykm=ZSTW&Year=&Issue=&Entry=
Li, G. 2007. 'Fanju shi sheme ju'. *Essay Election: The First Half of Month* (12): 31.
Li, C. 2017. *Guizhou Longtancun Gelaozu Yinshi Shejiao Yanjiu*. Chongqing: Xinan University.
Osburg, J. 2013. *Anxious Wealth: Money and Morality Among China's New Rich*. California: Stanford University Press.
Shu, J. and Zhang, L. 2018. 'Xi jinping xinshidai yi tenmin liyi wei zhongxin de siwei fanfu changjianguan tanjiu'. *Journal of Xinyu University* 23(6): 1–5.
Sim, W. 2017. 'Hoesikmunhwaui paereodaim byeonhwawa saeroun silcheonbanganeul wihan modelling surip'. *Cultural Industry Research* (17): 25–32.
Wu, S. 2011. 'Yinshi shejiao zhong di renqing guanxi he quanli jiaohuan'. *Jiling University*, 2 January. https://web.archive.org/web/20190506222406/http://cdmd.cnki.com.cn/Article/CDMD-10183-1011095255.htm
Xie, Y. Y. 2018. 'Dangnei quanzi wenhuade qiyin xingcheng biaoxian weihan yu zhili'. *Journal of Huaibei Vocational and Technical College* 5: 11–13.
Zhang, G. L. 2018. 'Quanzi wenhu jiqizhili'. *Hebei Academic Journal* 6: 212–15.
Zhang, M. 2007. 'Fanju de gongneng yu guocheng yizhong zhongguoren de yinshiwenhua'. *Oriental BBS* 4: 119–23.

5.10 *Enchufismo* (Spain)
Ignacio Fradejas-García

Campbell, B. 2021. 'Pax Regis: Patronage, Charisma, and Ethno-Religious Coexistence in a Spanish Enclave in North Africa'. *Focaal* 1–16.
Eisenstadt, S. N. and Roniger, L. 1984. *Patrons, Clients and Friends: Interpersonal Relations and the Structure of Trust in Society*. New York: Cambridge University Press.

Eurobarometer. 2019. *Business Attitudes towards Corruption in the EU. Flash Eurobarometer 482.* European Commission.
Fradejas-García, I., Molina, J. L. and Lubbers, M. J. 2022. '(Im)Mobilities and Informality as Livelihood Strategies in Transnational Social Fields'. In *Informality, Labour Mobility and Precariousness: Supplementing the State for the Invisible and the Vulnerable,* edited by A. Polese, 33–67. Cham: Palgrave.
García, J. F. 1980. *Léxico y Política de La Segunda República.* Salamanca: Universidad de Salamanca.
INE. 2016. 'Módulo Año 2016 (Base Censos 2011). Los Jóvenes En El Mercado Laboral'.
Kenny, M. 1960. 'Patterns of Patronage in Spain'. *Anthropological Quarterly*: 14–23.
La Vanguardia. 1915. Digitilised Archive. https://hemeroteca.lavanguardia.com/
Muñoz, L. 2011. 'Aspectos de La Recepción Del Léxico En -Ismo e -Ista En La Lexicografía Académica Española y En La Hispanoamericana: Las Actitudes En Los Siglos XVIII, XIX, y XX'. *Cuadernos Del Instituto de Historia de La Lengua*, 45–72.
RAE. 2020a. 'Enchufismo'. *Real Diccionario de La Lengua Española.*
RAE. 2020b. 'Muñeco, Ca'. *Real Diccionario de La Lengua Española.*
RAE. 2020c. 'Palanca'. *Real Diccionario de La Lengua Española.*
RAE. 2020d. 'Sinecura'. *Real Diccionario de La Lengua Española.*

5.11 *A molestar a otro lado* (Guatemala)
Jose Godinez and Denise Dunlap

Borgen Project. 2017. 'Exploring the Poverty Rate in Guatemala', 8 August. https://borgenproject.org/exploring-poverty-rate-in-guatemala/
Carrillo-Navarrete, R. and Salgado-Andrade, S. 2002. *Racismo y vida cotidiana en una ciudad de la sierra ecuatoriana.* Ediciones Abya-Yala: Quito, Ecuador.
CIA. 2020. 'The World Factbook'. https://web.archive.org/web/20181201164345/https://www.cia.gov/library/publications/the-world-factbook/rankorder/2172rank.html
Godinez, J., Dunlap, D., Webb, H. and Bell, V. 2020. 'Navigating Informal Linkages on the Frontier: How Entrepreneurial Firms Uncovered New Sources of Knowledge and Certainty in the Mobile Banking Industry'. Working Paper.
World Bank. 2006. 'Mobile Banking: Knowledge Map & Possible Donor Support Strategies'. http://documents.worldbank.org/curated/en/583091468160508211/pdf/377980infoDev01g1July0200601public1.pdf
World Bank. 2020. 'Mobile Cellular Subscriptions (per 100 people) – Guatemala'. https://data.worldbank.org/indicator/IT.CEL.SETS.P2?locations=GT

6
Alternative currencies of support

Introduction: sharing norms

Elodie Douarin
School of Slavonic and East European Studies, UCL, UK

Sharing norms is the obligation to share and reciprocate favours in a given social group. They translate the moral obligation for reciprocity that cements social groups (Gouldner 1960), but they can go beyond this to encompass social injunctions to share, even when detrimental to the individual. Everywhere, individuals build their identity and social life through belonging to specific groups or networks. And universally, belonging to a specific group means abiding by its rules and customs. Thus, where they exist, these 'traditional sharing norms' are fundamental to maintaining one's place in the relevant social group and they provide informal financial services to members: they can act as social safety nets, insurance, or, if organised as microfinance structures, can facilitate saving aggregation and access to (often micro) credit.

The literature on social sharing norms probably started within the broad field of development studies. There, sharing norms are more frequently studied in the context of kinship networks, that is, social groups formed around the concept of 'extended family', where kinship, as a collective institution, imposes specific constraints on the behaviour of its members. These norms are sometimes described as characteristic of idealised traditional altruistic risk-sharing communities (Scott 1976). However, examples of socially enforced sharing norms can also be found outside traditional societies, because wherever they have appeared in pre-industrial times, they may have persisted to some degree – social norms and culture are 'sticky' after all (Boettke et al. 2008). Importantly, the complex political economy of obligatory sharing norms has long been recognised (Platteau 1991; Hoff and Sen 2006): while they can be protective, they can also be costly to members, imposing a penalty described as the 'dark side of social capital' (Baland et al. 2011). This ambivalence emphasises the need for a careful discussion of the concept of sharing norms, delineating it in conjunction with closely related concepts, and discussing its operationalisation in empirical work. Let us here discuss social capital and cultural values, to clarify what we mean by sharing norms while also discussing some implications of their strength, or weakness, on relevant outcomes.

Social capital, as it is conceptualised in contemporary research, translates the quality of social and economic interactions within a group. It can be defined as 'norms and networks that enable people to act collectively' (Woolcock and Narayan 2000: 225). In other words, social capital has been described as (1) building on a specific structure: as social ties and networks define the relevant social group, and (2) characterised by specific cognitive elements: in the form of the values and norms shared within the group (Andriani and Christoforou 2016).

At first glance, the distinction between social groups with or without strong sharing norms likely overlaps with the distinction between bridging and bonding social capital. Indeed, while bonding social capital essentially refers to connections and shared trust within the family or as embeddedness into a narrow and specific group, bridging social capital is about broader social networks. Bonding social capital implies 'strong ties' and a large number of common ties, while bridging social capital is about 'weaker ties' and a lower number of common ties (Granovetter 1973). With this in mind, the social mechanisms required to impose social sanctions and thus generate a social obligation are more likely to exist in strong ties, bonding capital, types of contexts. To be clear, the moral norm of reciprocity which individuals would subscribe to of their own accord can be found in most social groups, irrespective of whether the reciprocity is applied to individuals linked by weak or strong ties. But contexts where sharing requires a stronger element of social enforcement (whether it is implicit or explicit) might be associated with a structure facilitating this social enforcement, as in contexts with more bonding ties. However, not all bonding capital will be subject to strong sharing norms, and not all bridging capital will be exempt from these either. Maybe an important dimension to this puzzle is the density of the network, rather than its geography or the relative strength of its ties, as density makes it easier for norms to be repeated and thus reinforced within a given group

(Granovetter 2017: 16 and fn 15) – implying density as a condition for sharing norms to exist.

With this in mind, identifying and measuring communities with stronger sharing norms based on structure is difficult, even in contexts where detailed network analysis is possible. That said, in societies *known* for their strong sharing norms, researchers have sometimes used proxies of strong ties – say, number of family members or size of kinship – to measure the extent of social obligation faced by individuals or households (Di Falco and Bulte 2011). Some have instead measured the perceived pressure to share, for example by asking a farmer the number of people in their village they are expected to help (Di Falco et al. 2018). These measures speak directly of the structures that are meant to support these sharing norms, and while they focus on practices of risk-sharing that are meant to be protective to the group, they are shown to encourage individual members to consume, and invest in, goods and services that are less easily shareable with the group (Di Falco and Bulte 2011, 2015), implying costly distortions.

Focusing on social capital as shared norms and values, other studies have theorised on the specific values and norms associated with the obligation to share. For example, Alesina and Giuliano (2014) measure 'family ties' using the World Value Survey. Building on the work of Banfield (1958) or Coleman (1990), Alesina and Giuliano argue that:

> societies based on strong ties among family members, tend to promote codes of good conduct within small circles of related persons (family or kin); in these societies selfish behaviour is considered acceptable outside the small network. On the contrary, societies based on weak ties, promote good conduct outside the small family/kin network, giving the possibility to identify oneself with a society of abstract individuals or abstract institutions. (2014: 180)

Accordingly, they operationalise 'family ties' as holding values reflecting the importance of the family and the importance of respect and love for parents and parental duties. As such they measure cognitive values that translate a specific form of embeddedness: embeddedness in the traditional family structure. A key moral value to consider is thus universalism as opposed to particularism, where altruism can only be targeted towards in-group members. These authors show that the strength of family ties is negatively associated with general trust (arguably a measure of bonding social capital and universalism). Powerful family ties link to lower historical levels of climatic variabilities and are associated today to lower political engagement, a greater focus on home-production, conservative values, favouring relationships over rules, and eventually lower institutional quality and underdevelopment. Importantly and in contrast to this, the strength of family ties also correlates with greater happiness, life satisfaction and better health.

Working on cultural dimensions allows both to define and compare social groups (Inglehart 1997; Hofstede 2001; Schwartz 2004). Summarising her interpretations of different frameworks, Kaasa (2021) points to the association between 'embeddedness' (in a given social group) with sharing and reciprocating favours. She points to the conceptual closeness of embeddedness and collectivism, as both relate to a focus on group interests and members' interdependence. These contrast with individualism, a concept associated with personal interests, economic independence, individual identity and greater universalism (Schulz et al. 2019; Kaasa 2021).

To conclude, strong sharing norms as social obligations are a complex and nuanced concept. They exist in social groups characterised by specific cultural values and structures. There is a distinction between sharing norms as personal moral inclination and sharing norms as social obligation. The inescapability from the latter derives from cultural norms and social structures, and can be costly to members. While these sharing norms are meant to be protective and to support collective risk-sharing, they have become associated with negative outcomes. Even if Western-centred analyses establish that their persistence today is overall inefficient, a broader contextualisation can lead to more nuanced conclusions. Indeed, alternative risk management strategies would require economic actors to focus either on self-reliance or universalistic risk management services. However, if neither self-reliance nor universalistic options are available (or if for some reason the latter are considered unreliable, untrustworthy or lacking in some way), then risk-sharing within smaller groups might be *rationally* preferable, even if considered 'second-best'. Similarly, if people value security, homogeneity and happiness over economic development, sharing norms may actually be seen as 'first-best'.

6.1 *Znaki vnimaniya* (Russia and FSU)
Conor Murray
Alumnus, School of Slavonic and East European Studies, UCL, UK

Translated as 'signs of appreciation', *znaki vnimaniya* are gifts given in post-Soviet countries to facilitate good relations and show sentimentality. There is an expectation to show *vnimanie* (appreciation or attention) through favours and gifts, particularly in the context of a romantic relationship (Kozlov 2006). Ethnographic studies have shown that the practice extends to the use of gifts to 'thank' (*poblagodarit*) schoolteachers, academics (Komu Podarok 2017), medical staff, as well as policemen in order to show that their work is 'valued' (*trud tsenyat*) (Patico 2002; Wanner 2005; Polese 2008). *Znaki vnimaniya* are offered by both children and adults, as it is common practice to give them during one's primary and higher education. *Znaki vnimaniya* are almost always given to someone of superior authority, as the opposite is often interpreted as a sign of harassment (Agapov 2018), or a misuse of office (PhDRu 2014). They are very frequently given on national holidays (such as Teachers' Day), but may also be given whenever feels appropriate.

Znaki vnimaniya, like many types of informality, display high levels of 'predictability and standardisation' (Steenberg 2016: 296). In Russia, formal rules state that a gift to a civil servant must not be worth more than 3000 roubles or be used to further the giver's interests (Bikiyev 2013). Even within these regulations it may still be unclear how noble the intentions of the giver are. The most common *znaki vnimaniya* take the form of chocolate, flowers, cognac, or other expensive alcoholic beverages. Although some studies have found that recipients of these gifts have used them for personal gain by selling them back to the shops they came from (Wanner 2005), to avoid being ascribed to bribery, *znaki vnimaniya* typically take the form of frivolous, perishable things that one 'would not normally buy for oneself' (Patico 2002: 357).

Advice online often focuses on what should be given to a male or female professor (Komu Podarok 2017), and ethnographic studies confirm that flowers are the most acceptable gifts for women, while alcoholic drinks are standard for men (Patico 2002). These sources claim that the gift should have some actual use (whether social or practical) and therefore can take the form of equipment. Money, on the other hand, is seen as unacceptable because it signifies bribery (Patico 2002: 353), and so do very expensive gifts which the recipient may interpret the wrong way. With *znaki vnimaniya*, the only exception to the cash being unacceptable is when it is given to doctors, albeit in very small amounts (Polese 2008: 52). Behavioural standards and types of acceptable gifts also make *znaki vnimaniya* identifiable based on their context and form. Both givers and recipients are aware of these 'standards' to avoid accusations of corruption. In one study, a respondent professor claimed that 'if I receive it, it is a gift. If I demand it, then it is a bribe' (Polese 2008: 53).

The practice can appear suspicious, as it occurs in countries where corruption is rife in academic and medical institutions (Polese 2008;

Shaw et al. 2015; Denisova-Schmidt et al. 2019). However, these sources suggest that *znaki vnimaniya* differ from other forms of corruption as it is based on moral and social values, rather than personal enrichment and preferential treatment. The practice actually serves a much broader range of functions. It can allow those essential to society, such as doctors and teachers, to feel valued and part of a wider network, making up for the shortcomings of the state structure. In post-Soviet states, gift-giving facilitates arrangements that predate the state infrastructure, and therefore is unlikely to ever be considered immoral behaviour (Werner 2000).

Attitudes expressed by those who take part in the practice show that they believe their behaviour is morally justified, often based on the desire to express gratitude and stressing the absence of ulterior motives. The disdain that citizens of the former Soviet Union bear towards bureaucratic state structures (Dimitrova-Grajzl and Simon 2010) is compensated by personalised relationship with teachers, entrusted with children's education, or doctors, entrusted with health and life. Such personalisation results in certain sentimentality rather than intrinsic 'scepticism' towards formal state institutions (Grødeland 2007: 220). Those in the gift cycle feel the benefits of their place in society, as reciprocity is 'not only discussed but experienced in terms of friendship and help' (Pesmen 2000: 131).

The act, however, is ethically questionable. Due to the normalisation of the practice, as distinct from corruption, an individual who does not engage in corruption or even opposes it may accept *znaki vnimaniya* without these two behaviours seeming contradictory. Moreover, although public workers are expected to fulfil their role impersonally, research shows that medical workers appear to consistently expect *znaki vnimaniya* in return (Polese 2008: 54). The moral notions attached to *znaki vnimaniya* mean that classifying them as a simple quid-pro-quo exchange would be too simplistic. It would be more accurate to claim that they enable informal exchanges that could develop into more nefarious ones.

6.2 **Sinnamjai** (Thailand)
Wasin Punthong and Attasit Pankaew
Faculty of Political Science, Thammasat University, Thailand

Sinnamjai (สินน้ำใจ) is a term widely used in Thailand that may be translated into English as a 'token of appreciation'. It refers to an informal relationship of exchange and has its roots in the culture of giving gifts to others as a way of expressing gratitude. The dictionary of the Thai Royal Society defines *sinnamjai* as money or valuables that are presented as a reward (Office of the Thai Royal Society 2011). In this meaning, the term describes an object willingly given by one person to another, thereby reflecting the giver's motivation. However, *sinnamjai* may also take a non-object form, such as a symbolic action. Within a social relationship, *sinnamjai* may be presented by either a giver or a receiver in a reciprocal manner.

Sinnamjai is far from unique to Thailand. Similar practices include *okurimono no shukan* (the practice of giving gifts) in Japan (Rupp 2017) and *songli* (gift-giving) in China (Han 2017), to name but a few. In Southeast Asia, the culture of gift-giving is also related to *saboraschon* (meritorious benefactor) in Cambodia (Hughes 2006) and to *utang na loob* (debt of gratitude) in the Philippines.

Sinnamjai should be distinguished from a patronage network, though it may subtly lubricate relations among actors within such a network. In a formal patronage network, patrons protect and take care of their subjects while the subjects give labour, property and loyalty in return. Patrons who rank highly in the social hierarchy will bestow *sinnamjai* on their subjects when the latter fulfil their assigned tasks. Informally, however, subjects or low-ranking officials may approach other powerful patrons who can guarantee protection (Rabhibhat 1998). In this form of relationship, subjects are expected to repay their patrons by presenting *sinnamjai*. This reflects the emphasis placed by Thai society on the practice of returning favours which, culturally, has a moral implication. Hence, giving *sinnamjai* to other people is, by virtue of the interpretation of returning a favour, morally acceptable in Thai society. The moral roots of *sinnamjai* lie in the values of big-heartedness, generosity and sacrifice, underpinned by Buddhist virtues such as the four *sangaha vatthu* (the four principles of service – generosity, kindly speech, helping others, impartiality), to which Thai people attribute great importance. These values justify the giver's moral motivation in presenting *sinnamjai*.

In traditional times, *sinnamjai* not only was a formal component of the established patronage network but also operated informally in personal relationships between people of different status in the social hierarchy. Even when the feudal system collapsed in the early nineteenth century, the cultural and moral roots of *sinnamjai* remained firm. They were, however, adjusted to fit new social realities. During the transition to the modern state, 'the patrons who used to benefit from their subjects' provision through the self-remuneration system had to adapt themselves by relying upon an extralegal channel to maintain their gains' (Bowie

2008: 476–7). The relationship between patron and subject turned, therefore, into one linking the bureaucrats as a service provider with the people as a service receiver. In other words, the subject turned into a client who expected good service.

One example of this relationship is when a bureaucrat exercises his or her authority to deliver a service swiftly to a certain client. However, the relationship also depends upon the bureaucrat's willingness to accept *sinnamjai*. Hence *sinnamjai*, within this relationship, operates as a lubricant that facilitates the expectations of both parties since the client is expected to present *sinnamjai*, symbolically or materially, to the bureaucrat. In this regard, simultaneous action reflects both an expression of gratitude and the practice of returning a favour.

Presenting *sinnamjai* also highlights the use of practical solutions to deal with bureaucracy. In certain contexts, and especially when state bureaucrats are involved, presenting *sinnamjai* may be regarded as bribery. Therefore – and especially after 1997, the year that marked the beginning of political reforms in contemporary Thai politics – a series of anti-corruption laws was enacted. These include the fundamental anti-corruption law of 1999 that determines the conditions under which politicians and state bureaucrats may receive gifts or other benefits. They may, for example, accept a gift worth up to (but no more than) 3,000 Thai Baht (about 70 euros) as long as the gift meets professional and moral obligations. However, there is no clear definition of such moral obligations. Consequently, presenting *sinnamjai* can be interpreted differently depending on the context, and this demonstrates the ambivalent character of *sinnamjai*. Presenting *sinnamjai* has been practised and, to some extent, accepted not only by Thais but also by foreigners visiting Thailand. For instance, some foreign visitors have presented *sinnamjai* to Thai officers in recognition of special services (ThaiPBS News 2017).

Sinnamjai is often linked with electoral politics. In an opinion survey conducted in the run-up to Thailand's 2011 parliamentary elections, Pankaew (2011) together with King Prajadhipok's Institute examined public attitudes to the behaviour of members of parliament (MPs). Respondents were asked to rank the importance of a range of MPs' activities. The survey found that respondents still considered activities related to *sinnamjai* as important, with more than 50 per cent choosing 'important' or 'most important'.

Table 6.2.1 demonstrates how *sinnamjai* can help to facilitate the relationship between politicians and voters. Such a relationship is multidimensional: it not only reflects the satisfaction of voters' expectations but is also seen as expressing politicians' big-heartedness and goodwill.

Table 6.2.1 Respondents' rankings of the importance of *sinnamjai*

	Most important	Important	Less important	Not important
Attending a ceremony (for example, award-giving, ordination, wedding, funeral (1,312))	16.4	39.6	29.8	14.2
Donating things needed for a ceremony (for example, water, rice, tent (1,316))	8.6	32.6	32.6	26.1
Helping to get somebody's child into school (1,314)	7.9	28.0	33.7	30.5
Seeking funding for one's province (1,312)	23.2	43.3	17.3	16.1
Supporting community activities (for example, donation and volunteer work (1,316))	25.4	50.4	14.7	9.5
Assisting someone to secure a promotion (1,315)	9.4	26.3	35.7	28.6
Regularly attending sessions of parliament (1,314)	33.7	47.6	9.0	9.6
Holding a public forum for local people (1,312)	39.6	48.3	6.6	5.5
Opening an MP's office (1,315)	38.9	47.8	7.6	5.8
Working with provincial bureaucratic bodies to promote specific policies (1,314)	41.1	47.1	6.5	5.3
Working with local bodies to promote specific policies (1,314)	41.6	46.2	6.8	5.3
Cooperating with various bodies in the case of complaints (1,312)	40.9	46.8	6.6	5.6

At the same time, *sinnamjai* is subject to the prevailing vote-buying discourse. It is therefore not possible to determine whether presenting *sinnamjai* in a political context is a form of corrupt practice or just an expression of kind-heartedness. The latter can be justified by moral and cultural underpinnings. This demonstrates the ambivalence in the exchange aspect of reciprocity (Lebra 1975).

Moreover, *sinnamjai* is closely linked to powerful provincial strongmen (*pumeebarameenaichangwat*; ผู้มีบารมีในจังหวัด), more commonly found in rural than in urban areas (Sawasdee 2006: 32). Provincial strongmen who start their careers by building up public support as local politicians satisfy their voters' expectations by securing government funding for local development projects that benefit their constituents, and this in turn enables the politicians to build charismatic popularity (*baramee*; บารมี). Patronage networks channel various resources and favours (Haas 1978: 284–6; Eiawsriwong 2017). Voters return the favour by voting for the politicians. Despite its similarity to pork-barrel politics (Sidman 2017), such a phenomenon can be differently perceived when viewed through the prism of *sinnamjai*. The use of state funding to develop one's own constituency can be portrayed as a provincial strongman showing his big-heartedness. Voters see it as morally acceptable for them to return the favour by casting their votes and expressing their loyalty. In this respect, *sinnamjai* plays a crucial role in sustaining the provincial strongman's popularity.

Nishizaki (2005: 186–8) argues that, while provincial strongmen are often associated with the use of violence in electoral politics, many build their power and popularity without resorting to violence. One way in which they do so is by expressing gratitude to their hometowns by presenting *sinnamjai* in various forms such as donating money to charities or sponsoring construction works. Thinbangtiaw (2010: 196) argues that such practices typify an accumulation of social capital rooted in the combination of big-heartedness, generosity, sacrifice and trust. These values fit well with Thai culture as shown earlier.

Recent research by Satitniramai et al. (2013) affirms that the relationship between patrons and their clients is seen not so much as hierarchical but rather as horizontal, with its focus on caring for each other exemplifying the moral implications of *sinnamjai*. Moreover, there is an old saying in Thai, 'Remember to return a favour'. Accordingly, presenting *sinnamjai* is seen as being more about returning the favour than about vote-buying. Put another way, *sinnamjai* is the act of giving that expresses the giver's goodwill. Hence, the receiver should also act in a reciprocal manner. In this way, *sinnamjai* helps to grease the wheels, containing moral connotations that motivate reciprocity which, in its turn and to a certain degree, sustains the patronage relationship in Thai society.

6.3 *Joro* (Kyrgyzstan)
Arzuu Sheranova
Independent researcher, Kyrgyzstan

Joro is a group of people who get together regularly and socialise over tea or traditional meal (*ash*), usually in a *chaikhana* (traditional public tea- and meal-serving place). *Joro* practice is not specific to Kyrgyzstan; it is common in other Central Asian countries, with some country-specific features, for example, *gaps, gashtaks, ziefats, mushkil-kusho, mavliud* or *bibi-seshanbe* in Uzbekistan and Tajikistan (Madamidzhanova and Mukhtarov 2011; see also *yongo*, 3.5 Volume 1). The word *joro* is of Turkic origin. According to Kyrgyz literary sources, such as the national mythical epic 'Manas', *joro* was organised in winter in order to drink a traditional brew called *bozo* and eventually to share a meal, to relax, to entertain and to have a chat in the village (Beksultanova 2014). Each *joro* member treats other members with *bozo* and hospitality in turn (Kochkunov 2003). Taking part in *joro* is usually referred in Kyrgyz as *joro ichebiz* (literally 'drinking *joro*'). *Joro* has a connotation of belonging and can also be used synonymously with the word 'friend' or 'mate': a member of *joro* gathering.

Joro oturush or gatherings take place on a weekly or bi-weekly basis, with the time and place confirmed in advance by the elected *joro* leader. Along with regular gatherings there are irregular meetings accompanying special occasions such as weddings, funerals, births and so on. When *jorolor* (plural for *joro*) meet to discuss preparations for large occasions, they agree how to distribute responsibilities and duties, how to cover the ceremony expenses and make provisions about other budget matters. Irregular *joro* meetings are called *keneshuu ashy* or *keneshuu dastorkonu* (in Kyrgyz) or *maslyat ashy* (in Uzbek) which means a meal where *jorolor* meet to plan and discuss preparations for upcoming ceremonies.

Joro oturush are popular among people from all walks of life, from high-school students to pensioners. *Joro* usually includes friends, neighbours, classmates or university mates and colleagues. Regular *joro* gatherings vary in size, but on average a *joro* group consists of 10 to 12 people. Depending on a person's social and communication skills as well as financial standing, they can be part of several *joro* groups. Depending on the type of *joro*, it is common to differentiate as *mekteptesh/klasstash*

Figure 6.3.1 A *chaikhana* in Osh, a typical public tea-serving space where *joro* gatherings take place. CC BY-NC-ND 2.0. © Evgeni Zotov.

jorolor (school-based *jorolor*), *universitet/kurstash jorolor* (university-based *jorolor*), *dos-jorolor* (*joro*-friends), *ayildash jorolor* (village-based *jorolor*), *konshu jorolor* (*joro*-neighbours), *ishtegi/kolletiv jorolor* (work-based *jorolor*) and *bala kez jorolor* (childhood friends *jorolor*) and so on. The classifications allow one to organise their life and to not mix up their various gatherings. On average, a middle-aged man is a member of two or three *joro* meetings at the same time: a school- or university-based one, and a work-, neighbourhood- or village-based one. Sometimes *joro* meetings combine a saving fund (see also *chernaya kassa*, 6.8 in this volume).

Joro is best understood as a closed circle of individuals that share a common background, common interests, identity or affiliation. If a region, neighbourhood or organisation are ethnically mixed, *joro* would reflect this diversity. Usually, *jorolor* are of the same age, apart from mixed-age *jorolor* which is common among colleagues or neighbours. *Joro* is a closed network, based on mutual trust and mutual help. Approval for a new membership in *joro* is usually decided collectively by the group. If a *joro* member becomes influential, *joro* has the potential to develop into a client-patron relationship, similar to the dynamics of *gap* or *blat* practices (see 5.12 and 1.1 Volume 1).

In contrast to open networks, a *joro* circle has its own structure and rules. A leader is elected by *joro* members. The *joro* leader is called *joro bashy* (literally 'the head of *joro*') or *emir* (common in Uzbek). The tasks of *joro bashy* are mainly organisational: to mobilise other *joro* members, to collect money, lead meetings and arrange practicalities, to order meals and make other preparations. Major decisions in *joro* are made collectively. These include decisions on fees and donations for special events and contributions for regular *joro* meetings. A *joro* meeting is about more than just eating a meal and drinking tea together. *Joro* is a gathering where each member shares their hardships, discusses plans or ideas, reports successes and offers opportunities to friends. In other words, *joro*, like *blat*, is a networking platform that generates other informal practices, opens up informal connections and satisfies all kinds of needs: regular, periodic, life-cycle or in an emergency (Ledeneva 1998: 118). *Joro* members get a job, learn about career opportunities, get married, find contacts, lend money, solve problems and get support with the help of other group members. During meals, *joro* members discuss topics associated with masculinity, such as women, football, politics, news and cars. The membership helps one raise or lend money in a very short time. *Joro* groups can collect a requested amount of money without bank interest or risk of non-repayment, hence the advantages of a strong group and its lifelong backup go without saying. The disadvantages of *joro* network, following Granovetter's concept of the strength of weak ties in networks, are its closeness and closedness, which may also result in conformity and lock-in effect of social ties (Granovetter 1973). *Joro* gatherings can be held at picnics in the suburbs or in a bathhouse, but most commonly, *jorolor* gather in the tea house, *chaikhana*, where there are no restrictions on how long they can stay for. It offers a public space where *joro* meetings can be held at minimal expense, but also offers a degree of privacy. In case a meal is ordered, the expenses are usually covered collectively, or in turn by each *joro* member. In exceptional cases, the meal may be provided by the meeting organiser. There is an understanding that the *chaikhana* is a masculine space. Usually, *jorolor* gather there without their wives, who would sometimes assemble in a separate room of the *chaikhana*.

The gendered nature of *joro oturush* is changing in Kyrgyzstan as new forms of *joro* gatherings are starting to emerge, such as *kyz jorolor* (female *joro*) and *ui-bulo/semeinyi jorolor* (family *joro*). Women's *joro* is usually a regular (once a month) social gathering for female friends or wives of *jorolor*. Similar to male *joro* gatherings, women meet up to socialise, share interests and discuss personal and family issues. Female *joro* groups include 10 to 12 women or less and run a similar rotational system of covering the cost of meals. *Kyz jorolor* may be combined with running a savings fund. Unlike *joro* meetings, female *joro* meetings are held either in private houses, protected from the public gaze, or cafés, where the meetings are more formal and limited in time. In a mixed-gender format, family or *ui-bulo/semeinyi jorolor* gatherings include families of 10 to 12 friends who meet over a meal, usually once a month. Such *joro* meetings can be held in private houses, cafés or *chaikhanas*. Similar to a single-sex *joro*, families either share the total cost of the meal or take it in turns to pay. Families socialise and tend to run a savings fund. Families agree on the amount of the contribution, the frequency and how they will use the savings (see *chernaya kassa*).

Gendered consumer choices have undergone significant changes in *joro* gatherings. Members only rarely consume *bozo*, the national non-alcoholic brew. Depending on a company's financial standing, social status and religious beliefs, alcoholic drinks are now served, particularly in male companies, especially young or middle-aged. Women's gatherings, however, tend not to include alcohol. Consensus on whether alcohol is consumed at youth *joro* meetings relates to the religious values of members. Gatherings of families, neighbours or colleagues may add alcohol to the menu to celebrate special events. At a *joro oturush* meeting, where both drinking and non-drinking people are present, this is taken into consideration and a mutual adjustment is made. On occasions where alcohol is served, non-drinkers would accept it with understanding. Likewise, members who drink may choose to refrain from consuming alcohol in a predominantly non-drinking *joro*. If alcohol becomes an issue, members may leave their *joro* and enter a non-drinking *joro* where they feel more comfortable. The re-configuration of *joros* reflects the consumer choices of their participants and results in the cohesion of the group.

6.4 *Sadaqa* (Kazakhstan and Kyrgyzstan)
Aisalkyn Botoeva
Institute for European, Russian and Eurasian Studies, The George Washington University, USA

Sadaqa is used in all places with Muslim populations as an umbrella term for charity. It includes obligatory donations (*sadaqa-al-fitr*), made at the time of religious celebration of the end of Ramadan, and voluntary donations (*sadaqa jariyah*). Guidance as to who should give and who should receive charitable funds is provided by the Quran and the hadiths or sayings of the Prophet Muhammad. In Kazakhstan and Kyrgyzstan, *sadaqa* as an Arabic term is used interchangeably with its equivalents in the local Turkic languages, *kairymdylyk* in Kazakh and *kairymduuluk* in Kyrgyz, which similarly refer to charitable actions.

Sadaqa has taken a plurality of forms over time, reflecting how people adapt religious tenets to their traditional customs and practical needs. Historically, Kazakh and Kyrgyz nomadic communities intertwined *sadaqa* with communal food-sharing practices and life-cycle events. When for example someone suffering from a long illness seemed close to death, it was common to sacrifice a sheep in an 'alms for the soul' ceremony (*zhan sadaqa*) that would console the person and beg the deity for a peaceful death (Aljanova et al. 2016). Following someone's death, it was common for families to make seven alms breads (*sadaqa nan*) and distribute them to their neighbours or in the street. Some believed the smell of *sadaqa nan* being cooked would lead the diseased person's soul back home (Aljanova et al. 2016). Even in contemporary urban settings, families are known to make *sadaqa nan* in times of trouble, for example if a family member suffers an accident or other physical injury. In mosque settings, people may also offer sweets as *sadaqa* to be distributed among visitors before prayers (Turaeva 2019).

People may also invoke *sadaqa* if they are robbed or simply lose a valuable item. Although a lost or stolen item may not have been intended as charity, the *sadaqa* wisdom alleviates the misfortune, anxiety and pain of the loss by pointing out that, as long as one's head (here meaning health more broadly) is safe, everything else can be replaced.

The most widely used meaning of *sadaqa* refers to a small monetary donation that one may give to a beggar, or a sack of flour given to a neighbouring family in need. With Islam gaining more salience in public spaces in the post-Soviet period, however, religious authorities have extended discussions of charity to encompass more than just random acts of kindness. In the contemporary period, *sadaqa* has become a popular informal mechanism of local governance and community mobilisation. Religious authorities and community leaders have contributed to this trend, going beyond canonical usage and portraying *sadaqa* as an individual's duty to the community. They now promote the idea that disposable wealth should be directed towards mobilising resources and tackling community needs, ranging from supporting mosques to reconstructing deteriorating school buildings and developing infrastructure such as roads and water canals. Some pious entrepreneurs also extend the meaning of *sadaqa* from monetary donations to good deeds at the workplace and in business.

Religious authorities and community leaders use Quranic idioms and hadiths to prompt community members and well-off sponsors to engage in *sadaqa* and to address broader issues such as public infrastructure, poverty and other areas where they feel the state and its welfare programmes have fallen short. For example, in one of his sermons Abdishukur Narmatov, a notable religious authority in Kyrgyzstan, discusses *sadaqa jariiya* as a deed that will bring God's benevolence even after death (Narmatov 2015). Charitable actions may range from small cash donations to other things such as paving the roads in one's village, building a bridge, planting a tree, making drinking water accessible and generally providing something useful for one's community. Narmatov warns that *shaitan* (Satan) tries to prevent people from enacting *sadaqa* by unleashing doubts about giving: 'Is there no one else who can help people? Maybe it is enough to just give your material possessions to your own family.' In such instances, according to Narmatov, a truly spiritually mature and devoted person should remember the third chapter of the Quran, Al Imran surah, which states that Allah returns everything that is donated or shared as an act of charity (Narmatov 2015).

Inspired by such lessons, pious practising Muslims connect *sadaqa* practices to *sabap* or *so'op* in Kyrgyz and *sau'ab* in Kazakh, which is God's reward returned in forms that range from receiving Allah's mercy and love to subsequent abundance of material possessions and cleansing of one's soul. The head imam of Ali Muhammad Mosque in Kazakhstan, Kanatali Tahirov, adds that a donor also receives healing from disease and that his or her property will be protected and multiplied (Tahirov 2019). Mosque leaders and preachers increasingly connect *sadaqa* to other religious duties, promoting the idea that the pious should engage in charitable acts alongside prayers, fasting and the Hajj pilgrimage. Inspired by such messages, local communities, particularly in rural areas, solve many practical issues such as badly maintained roads or dilapidated school buildings by pooling their resources and efforts, rather than merely relying on the government. In this way, *sadaqa* narratives and practices are related to other forms of collective action in Kazakhstan and Kyrgyzstan such as *ashar* or *yntymak*, where financial resources and labour are pulled together to address a pressing local issue.

Some pious entrepreneurs in both nations are increasingly choosing to identify their businesses as being either explicitly or implicitly 'Islamic' or Shariah-compliant. They merge their capitalist profit-oriented practices with Islamic tenets and argue that both Islamic doctrine and the principles of good modern management dictate certain business ethics. Although interpretations and applications of business ethics vary, some entrepreneurs claim that they treat their workers fairly and respectfully by paying their salaries in a timely fashion and involving them in decision-making. 'It is considered a form of *sadaqa* if you treat your workers respectfully and keep them content', claimed one of the respondents in Botoeva's (2018) study of Muslim entrepreneurs.

However, some religious leaders caution against engaging in *sadaqa* in certain circumstances. Mufti Maksat Aji, leader of the Muftiate in Kyrgyzstan, for example, emphasises that people who already have debts and loans should refrain from practising *sadaqa*. Alluding to the ever-expanding scope of personal loans that individuals take from banks and microfinance institutions, the Mufti has urged people to tackle the issue of credit and debt first. Moreover, other religious authorities state that before making a donation or giving away something of value people should ensure that their own families and friends are well-fed and taken care of. Finally, excessive donations or those that are made to attain public visibility are interpreted not only as being in bad taste, but also as not in keeping with the spirit of Islam. Religious authorities in Tajikistan express similar criticisms (Epkenhans 2011).

6.5 *Ashar* (Kyrgyzstan)
Arzuu Sheranova
Independent researcher, Kyrgyzstan

The term *ashar* (Aşar or Öşür) has a Turkic origin and means 'one out of ten', a basic tax measure which was adapted from the Islamic practice of tax collection during the Ottoman era (see Ihsanoglu 2001: 576). The Ottomans used to collect 1/10 or 5/10 of agricultural crops as tax depending on the type of conquered lands (dry or irrigated), although taxation proportion varied in various regions of the empire (Ihsanoglu 2001: 576). Today *ashar* is not directly related to taxation, referring to the common bearing of the cost of goods or services for those who cannot afford it. This includes material contributions such as cash or in-kind and non-material as physical labour, volunteering and fundraising.

Importantly, the *ashar* tradition goes back to pre-modern times. It was one of the crucial practices within the tribal system of Kyrgyz people. Due to their nomadic way of life Kyrgyz could not imagine their life outside a tribe as only tribes could provide security, food and protection to their weakest members (see Kenčiev 2014: 9). This nomadic legacy justifies the importance of communal help in contemporary Kyrgyzstan. The diffusion of *ashar* has led to the re-employing of the term in other spheres of life. The so-called *ashar* method refers to a collective action undertaken by community members to resolve an issue. *Ashar* is common in rural areas where relatives and neighbours ask for each other's help to collect crops, or to construct a house or building. In these cases, the person who requested *ashar* organises an *ash* meal for relatives and neighbours to show their appreciation.

Ashar often refers to constructing roads, bridges, mosques, schools, or cleaning irrigation canals. *Ashar* serves to solve local social infrastructural problems, frequent in most Kyrgyz peripheries because of the local or state budget constraints. According to the 2017 Bulan Institute for Peace Innovations report, 193 schools out of 2,222 in Kyrgyzstan were considered to be in a state of emergency because most of them were built on *ashar* basis during the post-Soviet transition in the 1990s and did not comply with technical requirements (Azattyk Radiosy 2017). Despite such critique, public infrastructure in Kyrgyz peripheries relies on the *ashar* method. In 2020, in the Alay region of the Osh oblast, local community members erected a playground (KTRK 2020). In a similar way, in 2021, businessmen and residents of Kara-Zhygach village of Batken oblast constructed a road to improve their access to summer pastures (Ala-Too 24 2021).

Ashar is a solution to the limited economic opportunities of local communities in Central Asia. The average family turns to *ashar* to host weddings or funerals due to the increase in cost. As of 2016, an average wedding could cost up to USD 10,220 (Sputnik 2016) compared to 2013 where the figure was between USD 4,500 and 4,750 (Jumasheva 2013). Local communities conduct lavish wedding ceremonies due to social pressure. A family that contributed to the cost of a relative's ceremony expects a contribution from the same relatives when their own ceremony takes place.

In recent years *ashar* has become a popular way of celebrating school or university graduation anniversaries among alumni, whereas previously graduates celebrated their own graduation at cafés. Nowadays, they also collect money to purchase school equipment such as computers or books. Other common forms of social aid among alumni include the construction of houses for families in need or sports fields and kindergartens. Thus, a long-standing cultural tradition of helping each other translates into the practices of volunteering and fundraising at the national level. For example, during the 2010 inter-ethnic conflict in south Kyrgyzstan and the 2021 Kyrgyz-Tajik border clash incident, citizens from various regions of Kyrgyzstan and Kyrgyz labour migrants elsewhere raised funds to send food and clothes to their communities.

In 2020, when the Kyrgyz medical system failed, the community-based response to the COVID-19 pandemic was another shining example of collective action (Ryskulova 2020; Timofeeva 2020). Volunteer groups of young people in Bishkek, Osh and other regions established hotlines and chats on social media platforms (WhatsApp, Facebook and Telegram) to provide first aid to COVID-19 patients. These volunteer groups raised funds to go towards the purchase of protective suits and medical masks for hospital staff and medical workers. These communal efforts were effective in fighting waves of COVID-19 infection in Kyrgyzstan, so that, in 2021 the government officialised the work of these groups by listing them on the online platform administrated by the Ministry of Health of the Kyrgyz Republic (Ministerstvo Zdravoohraneniya i Socialnogo Razvitiya Kyrgyzskoi Respubliki 2021). A final relevant example was the suggestion of members of the Kyrgyz parliament to pay off the state debt to China through the *ashar* method (For.kg 2020).

6.6 *Nisia* (Georgia)
Megi Kartsivadze
Alumna, School of Slavonic and East European Studies, UCL, UK

Nisia refers to a post-purchase payment or an informal interest-free loan, common in urban and rural neighbourhood mini-stores in Georgia. A shopkeeper administering *nisia* keeps a record of every borrower and their debt in a notebook. A similar informal practice called *na zeszyt* or *na kartke* is common in rural areas as well as cities in Poland (Rozanski 2015).

The word *nisia* appears in literary works of the late nineteenth century, which suggests that this practice was present in Georgian society before the formation of the Soviet Union (Vazha-Pshavela 1893). In the literary works of the late nineteenth and early twentieth centuries, *nisia* is mentioned in descriptions of the practices of ordinary citizens (Javakhishvili 1924; Shanshiashvili 1926). *Nisia* was resorted to by Georgian peasants who were excluded from the formal banking and credit system.

Nisia played a significant role in the second economy of Soviet Georgia. During the Soviet Union period, *nisia* became intertwined with *blat*, the exchange of favours to acquire goods or services in shortage (Ledeneva 1998). The second economy of the Soviet Union encompassed illegal and semi-legal retail activities such as *fartsovka* (selling goods brought from abroad) and retail spaces such as *komissionki* (shops officially selling used clothes but offering illegal foreign goods under the counter) and *beriozka* (shops that traded in foreign currency and were therefore not accessible to everyone) (Zakharova 2015). Participating in these transactions required one to have influential connections, *blati*. In Georgia, those with *blati*, allowing them to shop there, also had strong and reliable connections which made them eligible for *nisia*.

After the collapse of the Soviet Union, privately owned enterprises emerged, among them many local mini-stores. The transition to a market economy was accompanied by a severe economic crisis (Papava 2005). Small shopkeepers faced a problem: while the competition among them in the new market economy increased, their customers' incomes significantly decreased. Anticipating the lack of their customers' disposable income to afford the products at their stores, the shopkeepers focused on long-term profit by offering credit to attract and retain local customers. *Nisia* re-emerged in a new shape, disentangled from *blat* and more popular than before. By agreeing to sell something *nisiaze* (on *nisia*), the shopkeepers created a circle of reciprocity (Fehr and Gächter 2000) through which they developed productive interpersonal relationships with their customers who spread positive information about the store through their networks.

Nisia could not have functioned without the cultural elements that created a fertile basis for its emergence. Based on the ethnographic accounts collected from the 5,000 newly arrived immigrants from Soviet Georgia to Israel, Mars and Altman (1983) argued that Georgian society functions through four core values that form the basis of its second economy: (1) the competition for acquiring status in society, (2) a high level of trust as a basis of honour, (3) the development of personal networks and (4) the ability of taking risks. These values were simultaneously revealed and reinforced through informal practices formed as a response to widespread shortage. *Nisia* was one such practice. Without having a legal basis, *nisia* is based on trust. Engaging in *nisia* is a risk-taking activity for both the seller and the customer – the former stakes their funds, the latter their trust and honour. *Nisia* incorporates social excommunication as punishment for those who abuse the trust. Trust and honour have a cumulative impact on the development of personal networks – those who enjoy trust and honour expand their networks of connections, while having large networks grants one further trust and honour.

Georgia's sluggish economy started to recover in 2003 after the Rose Revolution, a peaceful change of government followed by a wave of national anti-corruption reforms. As a result of these reforms, the role of connections, exchanging favours, gifts and other informal practices significantly decreased (Kupatadze 2012). Nevertheless, some informal practices continued to thrive. Over 60 per cent of Georgians reported that they still relied on private social safety nets such as *nisia* (Aliyev 2014).

While microfinance organisations have been proliferating in Georgia since 1999, totalling 69 organisations in 2016 (Dushuashvili 2016), Georgians on low income have had trouble accessing their services. Not certain that they will be able to repay the loan within the stipulated time, they tend to use *nisia* that is free of legal obligations. Although uncertainty about when the amount will be reimbursed, if at all, poses financial problems for local mini-market shopkeepers, they report that they engage in the loss-making informal activity because they feel they cannot refuse to give *nisia* to their acquaintances who might otherwise live in poverty (Giorgelashvili et al. 2016). The primary factor encouraging *nisia* in the decades after the dissolution of the Soviet Union is *natsnoboba*. Replacing *blat*, this Georgian use of networks of acquaintances developed in the 1990s out of the need to survive the economic crisis. The reciprocal relations on which Georgians rely in times of hardship and through which they have established strong connections and networks continue to persist.

The emergence and proliferation of supermarkets affected the business of local neighbourhood shops. Shopkeepers have found it increasingly difficult to retain their loyal customers through *nisia* ever since large retail chains started offering their own credit options. A credit card called More launched by Nikora, a large Georgian retailer, allows customers to make purchases on credit and pay it back at a zero-interest rate within the next 45 days (Nikora 2017). Local mini-markets find these practices almost impossible to compete with. The event of a robbery in Gori, a small Georgian town, where the only thing taken from the local mini-market was a *nisia* notebook (Pisadze 2018), illustrates that customers buying products on *nisia* might be less likely to pay off the loan, as they could alternatively borrow from retail chains. Following Gel'man (2012), *nisia* can be understood as a subversive informal practice, slowly undermining the existence of Georgian mini-markets. Adopted by mini-markets to increase profits and maintain loyal customers in the 1990s, *nisia* has in fact turned against these shops as it began to affect their profits by attracting customers less likely to pay off their debts.

6.7 **Cassa peota** (Italy)
Giulio Benedetti
Alumnus, School of Slavonic and East European Studies, UCL, UK

Cassa peota (pl. *casse peota*) is a trust-based system of micro-credit and mutual insurance used in Venice, Italy. It consists of a common fund from which associates can borrow money at low rates and use it for small investments. The earnings made by the fund are typically spent on collective feasting occasions, redistributed back to associates or donated to charity every year. The latest account of *cassa peota*, published by the Bank of Italy in 2010, recorded 76 associations (Banca d'Italia 2018a).

First regulated by Italian law only in 1999, the practice remained informal for the most part of its history. It dates back to the fifteenth century and appears on written records related to Lorenzo Giustiniani, the bishop and patriarch of Venice between 1433 and 1456 (Tramontin 1985). *Cassa peota* began to operate in the Venice lagoon and the surrounding areas to connect the needs of two key lower-class social groups: small business owners (artisans and merchants) and the oarsmen who rowed the ships of the Venetian Republic (Cacciavillani 2013: 127–9).

For a long time one of the most thriving metropolises of Europe, Venice offered great opportunities to artisans and businessmen. In times of crisis, however, these people ran the risk of being put in prison due to their debts, which led to a vicious circle, as prisoners were unable to earn the money necessary to regain their freedom (Cacciavillani 2013: 127–9). Oarsmen faced an identical problem. Their job was poorly paid, but they were allowed to trade everything they could store under their seat. With some luck, good investments and access to Venetian markets – the best in the world – this personal trade could generate a small fortune (Lane 1978: 62–4, 201). On their return to the capital, having sold their merchandise, the oarsmen needed a way to store their money safely, before heading abroad again for months at a time. *Casse peota* met these two needs: oarsmen deposited their wealth safely, while small business owners were granted loans to avoid prison on the condition that they made weekly payments, called *carato*, which gradually repaid the debt. Failure to do so would result in imprisonment (Cacciavillani 2013: 127–9). The well-known and respected ship pilots were the guarantors of this system. The pilots were often more important to the everyday life of Venetian vessels than the ship captains and they enjoyed great respect among the lower classes of the city. An early interpretation of the name of this practice is associated with their role: *peota* is the Venetian term for 'pilot', while *cassa* can be translated as 'fund' or 'bank', like in *cassa comune*, which stands for the common fund of money (Ragazzini 2007).

In 1913, a survey conducted in Venetian *osterie*, the local traditional taverns and a pillar of the sociability of the working classes of the city, recorded 385 *casse* corresponding to 11,487 associates (Casellato 2002: 1594). Four decades later, a short survey published in the local media estimated the number of *casse* to exceed one thousand (Dell'Oro 1959). In the 1950s, an average *cassa* held around 30 people and served

Figure 6.7.1 *Peota* boats were used for leisure trips funded by the *casse*. CC BY-NC-SA 3.0. © Unknown, La Peàta, 1961. Conoscere Venezia.

the same purpose as in the past: to provide loans at very low rates to their associates, or to make cautious investments (Casellato 2002: 1594–6). *Osterie* were central to the development of the practice (Buonanno 2014: 80).

The *cassa* mechanism was also employed by wealthier retailers, who saw the *casse* as an opportunity to preserve their capital, by factory workers, who interpreted them as collective insurance against injuries and being fired and by piecework labourers, for whom they were a way out of problems and an opportunity for an occasional rich feast. Any earnings made in excess of the insurance coverage were often spent on extravagant meals and trips to the mainland, which in the case of wealthier *casse* lasted for several days. Large fluvial boats, called *peota*, were used to navigate upstream the rivers of the mainland: the latest interpretation of the origin of the name of the practice draws on these trips.

Cassa peota binds participants together in a tight association of economic purpose and is supported by leisure activities such as feasting and travelling, which strengthen trust among participants and represent a guarantee that everybody will keep their economic obligations. It enables individuals without access to the formal banking system to gain credit using interpersonal trust. Because the practice was widespread among the working classes and small traders, *casse peota* were saved by formalisation initiated by Venetian local politicians and regional administration in 1999, when threatened by the EU banking reform (Senato della Repubblica 1998). Today the *casse* are strictly limited operating outside the share of the banking market and are regulated by legislation concerning non-profit private intermediaries (Banca d'Italia 2018b).

Many practices around the world share similarities with *cassa peota*. The closest is the Filipino practice of *sosyudad* (5.15 Volume 1), which combines economic deeds and collective feasting to reinforce mutual trust. Practices such as *lloteria*, *esusu* (5.17 and 5.18 Volume 1) and other credit-oriented associations (ROSCAs) resemble the Venetian practice, but they lack the mechanism of fostering trust through collective leisure (see Ledeneva et al. 2018).

Cassa peota was embedded in the environment of trade relations, which determined its purpose and long-term existence. The formal framework of trade influenced the time frame of the participation, as commercial exhibitions were planned by the public regulator, while the debt laws pushed small business owners to join the *casse*. The practice evolved through the centuries, responding to changes in the formal framework. It reached the factory workers during industrialisation, when it became useful as a means of collective insurance against unemployment and accidents, or as a retirement account. As the state gradually took over the provision of welfare services, with time the factory-based *casse* gradually became less important. Today this practice is closer to the banking system and is used to soften its severity.

6.8 *Chernaya kassa* (Kyrgyzstan)
Arzuu Sheranova
Independent researcher, Kyrgyzstan

Chernaya kassa in Kyrgyzstan is the practice of voluntary and informal credit-giving, similar to the rotating savings and credit associations (ROSCAs) (Neuhauser 1993). The term *chernaya kassa* comes from the Russian language, literally translated as 'black cashbox'. The planned economy of the Soviet Union, defined as an 'economy of shortage', put constraints on the role of money and did not offer any form of consumer credit, which led to the increase of non-cash transactions and the informal credit system of *chernaya kassa* (Kornai 1980; Gaddy and Ickes 1998). Since the collapse of the Soviet Union in Kyrgyzstan, *chernaya kassa* has become an important credit-issuing institution to alleviate the pressure of the transition period. It supported labour-active people, especially women, involved in the informal economy of *bazaars* in order

Figure 6.8.1 A laid *dastorkon* for *chernaya kassa* in Osh, Kyrgyzstan. CC BY-SA 4.0. © Ilhoms.

to supplement family income (Özcan 2006; Cieślewska 2013). Similar to household exchanges of gifts and hospitality, which at the time was aimed at economic survival, *chernaya kassa* can be considered a 'household [survival] strategy' (Werner 1998: 598). During the post-Soviet period, savings supported the travel expenses of family members for labour migration. *Kassa* members stayed behind to provide support for the costs of migration for children or close relatives. *Chernaya kassa* is a common practice in post-Soviet Central Asia beyond Kyrgyzstan (Wolters 2014), as it became a reliable, manageable and widespread informal mechanism of obtaining credit.

The success of ROSCAs relies on the code of honour, reputation and shame: 'Since all members know each other well, the cost of monitoring the use of the funds is low, and the members are in a good position to evaluate a recipient's ability to repay the loan' (Neuhauser 1993: 51). ROSCA-like mechanisms like *chernaya kassa* are common in developing countries of Latin America, African countries and in Asia. An analogous practice in the former Soviet Union was informal credit in the Soviet penal system, called *obshchak*.

The negative connotations of *chernaya kassa* relate to political corruption, illicit party funds and manipulation of the state budget by the elites (Gelman 2002; Barsukova and Zvyagintzev 2006; Zyryanova 2013). However, at a grassroots level in Kyrgyzstan, *chernaya kassa* has a positive image and is associated with mutual help. In contrast with ROSCAs, Kyrgyz *chernaya kassa* is connected to a tradition of setting out food and drink on the floor and is often accompanied by spreading a *dastorkon*, a traditional tablecloth used to serve food. When it is time to rotate the savings, people get together over dinner or lunch, usually organised and paid for by the individual receiving the savings. *Chernaya kassa* usually takes place once a month, and involves families, colleagues, classmates, relatives, neighbours, alumni or friends in a group of 10 to 12, who take turns to collect, interest-free. Similar to *tandas* and *cundinas* (see 5.20 Volume 1) in the northern part of Mexico and the south-west of the United States and *gap* in Uzbekistan (5.12 Volume 1), *chernaya kassa* in Kyrgyzstan is more common among women (Kandiyoti 1998). For female entrepreneurs *chernaya kassa* is a good opportunity to advertise and sell their goods or services among *kassa* members (Turaeva 2018). *Joro* gatherings, popular in Kyrgyzstan (see 6.3 in this volume), often include the *kassa* saving fund system as well. Members of *joro* gatherings agree on the conditions under which *chernaya kassa* would run.

Chernaya kassa as an informal micro credit-issuing scheme permits the taking of a large amount of money at once, interest-free. It enables individuals to get an unofficial extra-fund when in need. Since *chernaya kassa* participants know each other very well and trust each other, conflicts over money are rare. People spend the savings on services and durable goods, such as expensive furniture, household equipment or jewellery, which they would otherwise not be able to afford, or to celebrate life events, such as jubilees, weddings or feasts. Alternatively, they can be spent on travel abroad, tuition fees, or invested in their small family businesses.

Based on drawn lots or collective agreement, *kassa* members determine the rotation order enabling access to funds, the common rules, the number of members in the *kassa* and the amount of saving funds each member will contribute (the contributions vary between USD 30 and 150 and are less in rural areas). As members take their turn to receive the savings, they organise their upcoming *kassa* meeting and notify the others in advance. Depending on their social status and financial standing, an individual can be a member of several *chernaya kassa*. *Chernaya kassa* is normally set to run for at least a year. Because of the pressure of shame and loss of face and reputation (moral and social punishment), there is no need for the rules and payment schedules to be enforced. Even if members do not physically attend the meetings, they ensure their contributions are regular and that the scheme benefits all members (similar shame-based rule-enforcement mechanisms can be found elsewhere, see for example Vietnamese *vay mượn*, 5.16 Volume 1).

Chernaya kassa is a good reason to keep friendship or kinship ties, stay in touch on a regular basis and maintain social networks. This is especially true among kinship-based *kassa* because they often collect a symbolic (very small) amount of money as a reason to chat and meet with each other. This symbolic *chernaya kassa* is popular among housewives with little time and opportunity to escape their routines. As they find it difficult to leave their children and husbands at home to socialise, they can excuse themselves from attending a *chernaya kassa* meeting to see their relatives and friends. In these circumstances, the saving part of *chernaya kassa* is the least important aspect of their gathering; however, this type of *chernaya kassa* is a recent phenomenon. For Kyrgyz with low income, *chernaya kassa* is a way of raising funds when individuals might prefer not to keep their savings in a bank, for example for those with a regular, but unofficial extra income who want to use the funds to launch a small business, contribute to an existing business or purchase a property.

6.9 *Moai* (Japan)
Abel Polese
School of Law and Government, Dublin City University, Ireland

Moai (模合) consists of two kanji: the first (模) is used to relate to imitation and reproduction; the second (合) to meeting or coming together. The two combine to mean the art of sharing a person's company for life and supporting one another financially. The *moai* practices are similar to rotating saving and credit associations such as the *lloteria* Albanian scheme (5.17 Volume 1): a few people pay into a common pool every month (or every agreed period) and the fund is then allocated, in turn, to the person(s) who needs them the most (Imami et al. 2018).

In many respects, *moai* follows the same dynamic: a group of people commit to meet regularly to hand over a small amount of money to a treasurer that collects it and gives the full amount to the person in the group who is in need. For instance, if 12 *moai* participants meet and each of them puts 10,000 yen into the pool, at the end of the evening there are 120,000 yen (1,000 euro) that can be given to someone (or two persons to share, if both are in need). The next time the group meets, everyone will pay the same amount and someone else will get the whole amount for their urgent larger expenses. What makes *moai* unique is not only its conviviality, but also the fact that commitment to the scheme can last more than half a century. Finally, *moai* is regulated and protected by law: a field on bank forms is allocated to the amount of *moai*, and '*moai* bookkeeping notebooks' are for sale at stationery shops (Shimokawa 2006: 144).

People who commit to *moai* do not merely come to contribute money to a common pool but embed this payment in a social occasion. Participants of a *moai* meet for the whole evening, often in an *izakaya* (a place between a pub and a restaurant where dishes and snacks are mostly served to accompany drinks), where only by the end of the evening do they hand money to the treasurer. Meeting with friends for a few drinks is a practice that exists all over the world and it is also accepted that if you are tired or have another commitment you can join next time. Going out for *moai* is different: here not only do you agree to meet your friends, but you also honour your commitment to regularly contribute to a pool of money. Obviously, being seriously ill can be excused, but being absent for a less important reason is to be avoided, because you do not want to give the impression that you are skipping the meeting to avoid paying your contribution. Besides, once you have been meeting these people for 10, 20 or more years, you want to keep the close bonds.

Moai is then a lifelong association: members may join as early as in their school years and continue for several decades, with several *moai* lasting for more than 70 years. That creates not only a bond but also a remedy against loneliness, especially for elderly people. Mental conditions caused by loneliness and isolation have been said to be as fatal as other biological diseases, and *moai* can be a natural cure. As a result, the practice has intrigued people interested in its effects on mental and physical health (Morrow 2019, 2020). Featured in *National Geographic*, *The New York Times* and in the Blue Zones Project, *moai* was presented as one of the possible reasons why people in Okinawa tend to live longer, on average, than any other place on earth.

Still, the practice is not unique to Okinawa, and the diversity of terms used may be indicative of the fact that this practice is used in different contexts and geographical settings. Similar schemes exist in Korea and mainland Japan, where they are known as *mujin* (無尽) and were, after the Second World War, used as alternative financial institutions in other parts of the country (Urban Life Research Project 2009). Morrow (2020) reports that the terms *moyai*, *muyai* and *tanomoshi* (頼母子) are also used, but *moai* remains the most common expression in Okinawa. This expression can occasionally be used to indicate an organisation 'raising funds for new businesses, architecture, land purchases, going on to higher education, travel' (Ryukyu Government Cultural Property Protection Committee 1972: 382).

Mentions of *moai* date as early as the eighteenth century in the Ryukyu Kingdom for the provision and joint production of labour, and foodstuffs such as agricultural products (Watanabe et al. 2008: 502; Urban Life Research Project 2009: 94), but a significant increase occurred during the twentieth century. Although eliminated from public life, *mujin*-inspired practices re-emerged after the Second World War, when the unavailability of initial capital risked jeopardising the development of local financial institutions. In mainland Japan *moai*-like associations were gradually phased out by the 2015 Mujin Industry Law (無尽業法).

In contrast, not only do many Okinawa-based moai remain unaffected, but the institution is also regulated by the 1917 '*Moai* Management Rule' (模合取締規則) adopted for the Okinawa Prefecture. Following a different path from the rest of the country, control and regulation were preferred to repression and liquidation (Okinawa Encyclopedia Publishing Secretariat 1983: 648). This is what has also been referred to as 'purchase of an informal practice' that can be considered an alternative to repression (Polese and Morris 2014). Another example of the practice remaining active is in the Yamanashi Prefecture, although it is mostly used by food establishments (Mynavi News 2013).

Still, *moai* remains mostly practised in the geographical area between Kagoshima and the Okinawa archipelago passing through the Amami islands. Given that access to credit in Japan has become much easier, its raison d'etre is not merely economic. As explained by Gudeman (2015), not all economic transactions are led by economic motives as some uses of money are embedded in societal needs. Similarly, Nelson (2001) sees *moai* as a sort of 'moral economy' that continues to operate in a system of modern globalised capitalism. In many respects, this is crucial for understanding the relationship of Japanese society towards *moai*, and in general, informality. *Moai* is not a practice that survives 'in spite of the state' (Polese et al. 2018). It evolved to replace state functions when people needed support, and to supplement the state in its welfare capacity, while also creating space for social interaction. The social foundation of the practice is possibly the reason why *moai* is still thriving, not so much as an economic phenomenon but as a social cohesion mechanism, whereby money is no longer the end but the means.

6.10 *Koshumcha* (Kyrgyzstan)
Eugenia Pesci
Aleksanteri Institute, University of Helsinki, Finland

The word *koshumcha* can be translated from Kyrgyz as 'additional'. It refers to contributions offered to the organisers of collective celebrations (*toilor*) and memorial events. It can also indicate any kind of assistance given to the groom to pay the *kalym* (bride price), or the gifts part of the *kalym* that are donated by the groom's parents on his first visit to the bride's parents; the latter, in turn, with the help of contributions from relatives, reciprocate the gifts to the groom's parents (Yudachin 1985).

In Kyrgyzstan, *koshumcha* is donated both at joyous celebrations (*zhakshylyk*) and mourning rituals (*zhamandyk*), including weddings (*uilonuu toi*), so-called 'bride farewells' (*kyz uzatuu*), births (*beshek toi*), circumcisions (*sünnöt toi*), first birthdays (*tush¬oo toi*) and meals for relatives and neighbours (*ash*) organised to mark death anniversaries or other meaningful events. All these celebrations and collective social obligations are part of the Kyrgyz customary law (*salt*) (Reeves 2012: 129). Within the ritual economy related to life-cycle events, *koshumcha* is an important informal practice for maintaining social relations. Despite its similarities to other gift-giving practices, *koshumcha* is understood as a form of solidarity and mutual help that mobilises social relationships, similar to *pujogŭm* and *hongbao* (2.3 Volume 1).

The origins of *koshumcha* are unclear but are likely connected to nomadic mourning rituals, where cattle or other goods were donated to the family of the deceased as a form of material support. Kyrgyz used to judge the importance of the deceased based on the degree of organisation of the funeral and the solidarity of the relatives (Abdubaitova 2018). During the Soviet period, *koshumcha* was mainly expressed through gifting consumer goods and commodities that were hard to find in the planned economy, and traditional handmade Kyrgyz clothing, like the *chapan* (winter clothing) (see Turdalieva and Provis 2018: 203). The collapse of the Soviet Union and the transition to a market economy resulted in the emergence of new values shaping more complex social relations, beyond kinship solidarity and support (Turdalieva and Provis 2018: 204). Against a background of dramatic economic hardship, mass migration and low state capacity, neoliberal values were met by the revival of pre-Soviet nomadic traditions, including the celebration of life-cycle events where *koshumcha* is donated.

While gifting clothes, jewellery and furniture is still practised, giving *koshumcha* 'in the envelope' is now very popular in Kyrgyzstan. Unlike other forms of money gifts, *koshumcha* is more a contribution to cover the costs borne by the family organising the celebration, a kind of interest-free loan among one's social network, since those who visit the *toi* constantly owe money, or other people owe them. Guests put *koshumcha* in a sealed envelope with their name on it and hand it to a designated person (usually a male member of the groom's family), who writes down the name of the guest in a notebook and the amount of donated money. Likewise, people who give *koshumcha* keep records of whom, when and how much they had given. In this way, they can estimate how much will be returned to them when they organise a *toi*. In calculating the amount of *koshumcha*, guests usually need to consider inflation and the exchange rate between the Kyrgyz som and the US dollar. The reciprocity principle at the foundation of *koshumcha* is based on mutual trust, but there is always a risk of receiving less or nothing, which means a financial loss for the family organising the celebration, and the shaming of the relatives who could not give a suitable amount of money expected from them. Sometimes, guests who cannot afford to give *koshumcha* write the word *karyz* (debt) on the envelope, meaning that they remain indebted to the family organising the *toi* until they are able to make their contribution. This is made in order not to 'lose one's face' in front of the other guests (Erkebaeva 2018), since refusing an invitation to a *toi* is considered shameful and embarrassing. As pointed out by Reeves (2012: 110), the ritual economy around life-cycle celebrations in Kyrgyzstan is sustained by remittances. Thus, many young people are pushed into labour migration so that the family can afford a *toi* and give the necessary amount of *koshumcha*. Not taking part in these forms of social obligations can even be interpreted as 'leaving kinship' (see Eidson 2017).

Koshumcha is embedded in social relations, norms and traditions and it rests upon mutual obligations and expectations (Granovetter 1985). Since the amount of the contribution towards the family's expenses depends on the degree of kinship, social and material well-being, as well as social and emotional distance (Kochkunov 2018), *koshumcha* can be a way of determining the strength of the ties between givers and receivers. However, new values brought by the market economy and neoliberal ideals are rapidly changing the way *koshumcha* and *toi* are experienced, especially among the better-off urban middle class, also called the 'new Kyrgyz' (see Provis 2015). *Toi* invitations and *koshumcha* then become useful instruments in building strategic relationships with influential acquaintances while excluding poorer, but closer, members of the network. This contributes to the emergence of new patterns of social relationship construction, which further deepens the economic and social gaps between urban and rural populations.

Despite its importance for maintaining social relations, *koshumcha* and the entire ritual economy related to *toi*-making is often criticised because of the financial burden imposed on households. In February 2020, the independent online media outlet *Kloop* conducted a survey on *koshumcha* among 400 respondents across Kyrgyzstan. The answers showed that most of the respondents still give *koshumcha* and are willing to give their last resources for it. According to the estimates of the survey, 62 per cent of the average monthly living wage of a Kyrgyz household is spent on *koshumcha* (Tologonova 2020). Nowadays, the average amount of money for *koshumcha* at weddings is around USD 50, but in big cities like Bishkek and Osh it can be more than USD 100. These are extremely high sums for most Kyrgyz families, especially when considering that the average wage in 2020 was approximately 19,000 som (around USD 224) (National Statistical Committee of the Kyrgyz Republic n.d.). *Koshumcha* can become a real poverty trap as confirmed by the survey respondents: those earning up to 20,000 som per month (USD 240) stated they spent approximately 35,000 som (USD 412) per year on *koshumcha*; those earning more than 60,000 som (USD 700) per month spend approximately 42,000 som (USD 490). This means that low-income households allocate to *koshumcha* a larger portion of their income than those with higher earnings (Tologonova 2020). Another important finding of the survey was that *koshumcha* has a generational dimension: while older generations see participation in every *toi* as necessary in order to maintain social ties, expecting future contributions from relatives, younger ones consider *koshumcha* wasteful and a source of psychological pressure to meet family and community obligations.

Koshumcha, then, is an ambivalent social norm that both enables and constrains by creating a lock-in effect on the basis of kinship, social status or network interests (see Ledeneva et al. 2018). Embedded in norms and traditions of reciprocity and solidarity, *koshumcha* reinforces social ties but also creates a perpetual circle of economic and social obligations. *Koshumcha* is a 'total service' (Mauss 2002), as it pervades all aspects of society, and its logic is dictated at the same time by self-interest and solidarity. *Koshumcha* is characterised by a high degree of ambivalence: it is both a practice of social solidarity and redistribution while also a financial and moral burden for poorer families. The changing nature of *koshumcha* from reciprocity and mutual help to a tool used to create influential networks is the result of a new moral economy where neoliberal principles and traditions related to the celebration of life-cycle events meet.

6.11 *Pujogŭm* (South Korea)

You-Kyung Byun
Institute of Social and Cultural Anthropology, Freie Universität Berlin, Germany

Cash gift-giving is widely practised in South Korea and plays a crucial role in social relationships. The most popular form of cash gift is *pujogŭm*, which is given at weddings and funerals. *Pujogŭm* can be translated into English as 'helping money' (*pujo* means help and *gŭm* means money in Chinese writing; 扶助金). Through *pujogŭm* exchanges, individuals maintain and improve their social relationships. Similar types of gift money have been reported in various countries, especially in the neighbouring East Asian countries, such as in China and Japan. However, unlike *hongbao*, 'red envelope' in Chinese (Tan 2018: 136), and *kōden*, condolence offering for funerals in Japan (Lebra 1976: 99), *pujogŭm* directly indicates the content of such envelopes – money.

The current practice of *pujogŭm* derives from the principles of mutual aid (*sangbusangjo* or *p(b)ujo*) in the primarily agricultural society. Until the intensive industrialisation of the country from the 1960s, mutual aid was an essential principle of village communities in Korea. According to the *pujo* principle, the villagers helped each other in need, such as for farming and ritual ceremonies, and exchanged material and non-material support (Choi 1988: 277–310). The type of exchanges changed to money in the 1960s as ritual ceremonies either disappeared or relocated from private homes to commercial wedding and funeral houses both in city and rural environments (Choi 1988: 161).

Like other gift-giving, *pujogŭm* relies on reciprocity, but unlike other forms it incurs more precision. The given and received amounts are documented in a book or a computer file. Many people rely on their documentation to precisely check the balance in giving and receiving. A continuous imbalance in *pujogŭm* exchanges can disrupt social relationships of the involved individuals. The amount and scale of the cash gifts is standardised. Since the early 2010s, it is customary to give either 30,000, 50,000 or 100,000 KRW (Gallup Korea 2013). Any other given sum is considered odd. A sum is selected on the basis of closeness to the recipient. Thus, the amount of *pujogŭm* is a good indication of the strength of ties between givers and receivers. However, a strong relationship can also result in a smaller amount, due to their strong mutual trust. There are local variations in the reciprocation of the received *pujogŭm*. For instance, in Gyeongsang province, a gift of 10,000 KRW is returned immediately to the visitors at the ceremony as a return gift, to signal

Figure 6.11.1 The front of a *pujogŭm* envelope, with the writing 祝結婚 (*ch'ukkyŏrhon*), meaning 'wedding celebration'. © You Kyung Byun.

consideration and politeness. The making of *pujogŭm* is relatively simple compared to Japanese and Chinese cash-gift envelopes. South Korean *pujogŭm* is a plain white envelope without decoration or knots indicating symbolic meaning, regardless of the type of ceremony. The giver puts banknotes in a white envelope and writes their name lengthwise on the back of the envelope. Next to the name, the donor can also write their affiliation, such as company, church, or school name. In the centre of the front of these envelopes, people write two or three Chinese characters longwise: wedding celebration (*ch'ukkyŏrhon*) or condolence goods (*puŭi*). These characters are the only difference between *pujogŭm* envelopes given at weddings and funerals.

At ceremonies, an appointed person collects *pujogŭm* envelopes at the reception desk. The receptionist, usually a close relative or friend of the host, is responsible for recording the name of the donor and the given sum in a ledger. The host of the ceremony later refers to this record to balance bilateral exchanges. Sometimes guests give their envelopes directly to the host, bypassing the receptionist. The direct delivery to the recipient avoids accounting and possible redistribution to host family members. If one is unable to make it to the ceremony but wants to show support, they will ask another guest to deliver their *pujogŭm* at the ceremony. The proxy payments, called *taenap*, are listed in the documentation book as if the donors were present at the ceremony. Since *taenap* bypasses time spent at the ceremony and the personal attention, hosts also note the actual presence of a guest to determine future exchanges. Due to the development in technology, an increasing number of people send *pujogŭm* via bank transfer.

According to opinion polls, many Koreans find *pujogŭm* exchange burdensome (68 per cent of 1,224 respondents, Gallup Korea 2013). One interviewee reported that he spends nearly 1 million KRW a month on *pujogŭm* exchanges with his business associates (Byun 2020). It is not uncommon for South Koreans to be invited to multiple ceremonies in one weekend during seasons when weddings are more popular, requiring substantial funds for *pujogŭm*. The scale of these informal exchanges has led the government to introduce restrictions. Since 2016, the Kim Yŏng-Ran law prohibits giving *pujogŭm* in excess of 50,000 KRW to employees in public offices and educational and media institutions. The legislation limits the extensive use of *pujogŭm* exchanges for purposes beyond private affairs and indicates the blurred boundaries between *pujogŭm* and bribery in South Korean society. Given that the informal exchange of cash gifts is strongly associated with the stability of social relationship, these measures are unlikely to reduce the circulation of *pujogŭm* exchanges in the near future (Byun 2020).

6.12 **Poclon** (Wallachia, Romania)
Vasile Mihai Olaru
Marie Skłodowska-Curie Individual Fellow, University of Regensburg, Germany

A Slavic term, *poclon* (or *plocon*, pl. *pocloane, plocoane*) entered the Romanian language during the Middle Ages. In Old Church Slavonic the term denoted worship or adoration of the divinity, offering or act of bowing the head or the body, or a kind of penance. Only secondarily, it denoted a voluntary gift (Slovar cerkovno-slavjanskago i russkago jazyka 1847: 306). It was this secondary sense that was used in the Principality of Wallachia from the fourteenth to the nineteenth century. The offerings of *poclon* mostly implied a gift to a socially superior (lord or ruler), a protocol gift in diplomacy, or a gift exchange between in-laws. Later on, its meaning also embraced taxes and fees. Towards the end of the eighteenth century, in the context of administrative reforms and the changing notion of the political power, *poclon* acquired a negative connotation which came to signify a bribe, and was delegalised. Contemporary Romanian dictionaries define the word *poclon* mainly as gift, although variant meanings are also given.

From a gift to tax and fees. The principal meaning of the word adopted in Romanian was that of gift. The term was used interchangeably with *dar* (pl. *daruri*, Slavic origin) and, later on, with *peșcheș* (pl. *peșcheșuri*, Ottoman origin). *Poclon* was not a free gift between equals, but one given to a socially and, sometimes, politically superior person. It was meant to convey the idea of submission of the giver and to secure the goodwill of the receiver. With time, the word and the practice acquired additional nuances due to changing historical circumstances. Initially a spontaneous and occasional gift, *poclon* came to signify an institutionalised obligation, perceived and framed as custom (*obicei*), involving obligation and regularity (Sachelarie and Stoicescu 1988: 364–5). From the fifteenth century onwards, *poclon* practices became associated with tax paid to the prince and fees collected by high official-holders. Thus, the gift offered by subjects at the beginning of a prince's reign turns into the 'gift of the banner' (*poclonul steagului*), paid annually, by all tax-payers, in proportion to their income (Sachelarie and Stoicescu 1988: 364–5). As a privilege, the princedom often exempted monasteries and churches from *poclon* payments along with other taxes (Potra 1961: 271, 326). Similarly, the occasional *pocloane* given to Wallachian officials became regular fees collected from their subordinate officials or from their jurisdiction on a regular basis. The *pocloane* received by the officials contributed to their sustenance and were legitimised, especially in the case of the higher officials, by the latter's superior social status, and not by the services they rendered (see *kula* practices in East Africa and *kormlenie* in Russia, 7.2 and 7.1 respectively, Volume 1). For instance, the high cup-bearer (*vel paharnic*) collected such fees from the sale of wine and brandy (Sachelarie and Stoicescu 1988: 364–5). In the ecclesiastical sphere, the Metropolitan and the two Bishops of Wallachia were collecting *pocloane* regularly from the priests in their dioceses (Urechia

1891: 454). Lesser officials received *pocloane* as payment for their services, usually at an extra 10 per cent on a given tax (Urechia 1891: 402, 406, 411; Giurescu 1962: passim).

From a protocol gift to the tribute. As a practice in the foreign relations of Wallachia, especially with the Ottoman Porte (fourteenth to nineteenth century) and the Crimean Khanate (sixteenth to eighteenth century), *plocon* carried the initial meaning of occasional and ceremonial gift. With the intensification of Ottoman domination, it mutated into regular obligations, akin to the tribute, paid by each prince at the point of accession to the throne (Grecescu 1959: 118) and annually (Giurescu 1962: passim; Greceanu 1970: 144; Potra 1961: 271, 326). In addition, *pocloane* were sent to the Ottoman court each time an Ottoman dignitary, especially the Grand Vizier, was appointed to office, to seek benevolence and favour. At the same time, the initial meaning and practice of *poclon* as an occasional gift persevered. In order to achieve specific objectives, such as border dispute resolution, neutralisation of competitors, prevention of the plunder of the country by the Tatar troops, or simply securing favourable attitude of the Ottoman and Tatar dignitaries, Wallachian princes used to send them *plocoane* (Greceanu 1970: 75, 90, 103, 107, 114, 123). Such 'voluntary' offerings are not easy to distinguish from outright extortion (Greceanu 1970: 231; Eclesiarhul 2004: 80).

From gift to bribe. By the end of the eighteenth century, as part of the administrative reforms introduced by the princes of Wallachia, some variants of *poclon* practices were delegitimised and regarded either as bribe (Urechia VII 1894: 52) or informal payment, which distort the functioning of the administration (Urechia I 1981: 43; Urechia VIII 1897: 476–7). The *poclon*, as an accepted practical norm in administrative and international relations, vanished in the nineteenth century, with the massive administrative overhaul starting from 1830 and the suppression of Ottoman power. It has nevertheless remained in the Romanian language to this day, designating morally and legally problematic practices of gifting in exchange for a favour.

In sum, the practice of *poclon* started as an informal, occasional form of gift-giving. With the development of the state and the stratification of the Wallachian society, *poclon*, while retaining its initial meaning, was institutionalised and came to signify a covert tax system paid to the prince, fees paid to officials and high clergymen and regular gifts offered to prominent figures of the Ottoman empire. By the end of the eighteenth century, it was again 'informalised' and construed as an illegitimate gift leading to corruption.

Bibliography to Chapter 6

Introduction: sharing norms
Elodie Douarin

Alesina, A. and Giuliano, P. 2014. 'Family Ties'. In *Handbook of Economic Growth*. Volume 2, edited by P. Aghion and S. N. Durlauf, 177–215. Amsterdam: Elsevier.

Andriani, L. and Christoforou, A. 2016. 'Social Capital: A Roadmap of Theoretical and Empirical Contributions and Limitations'. *Journal of Economic Issues* 50(1): 4–22.

Baland, J.-M., Guirkinger C. and Mali, C. 2011. 'Pretending to Be Poor: Borrowing to Escape Forced Solidarity in Cameroon'. *Economic Development and Cultural Change* 60(1): 1–16.

Banfield, E. 1958. *The Moral Basis of a Backward Society*. New York: Free Press.

Boettke, P., Coyne, C. and Leeson, P. 2008. 'Institutional Stickiness and the New Development Economics'. *American Journal of Economics and Sociology* 67(2): 331–58.

Coleman, J. S. 1990. *Foundations of Social Theory*. Cambridge, MA: Harvard University Press.

Di Falco, S. and Bulte, E. 2011. 'A Dark Side of Social Capital? Kinship, Consumption, and Savings'. *The Journal of Development Studies* 47(8): 1128–51.

Di Falco, S. and Bulte, E. 2015. 'Does Social Capital Affect Investment In Human Capital? Family Ties and Schooling Decisions'. *Applied Economics* 47(2): 195–205.

Di Falco, S., Feri, F., Pablo, P. and Vollenweider, X. 2018. 'Ties that Bind: Network Redistributive Pressure and Economic Decisions in Village Economies'. *Journal of Development Economics* 131: 123–31.

Gouldner, A. 1960. 'The Norm of Reciprocity: A Preliminary Statement'. *American Sociological Review* 25(2): 161–78.

Granovetter, M. 1973. 'The Strength of Weak Ties'. *American Journal of Sociology* 78(6): 1360–80.

Granovetter, M. 2017. *Society and Economy – Framework and Principles*. Harvard: Belknap.

Hoff, K. and Sen, A. 2006. 'The Kin System as a Poverty Trap'. In *Poverty Traps*, edited by S. Bowles, S. N. Durlauf and K. Hoff, 95–115. New York: Princeton University Press.

Hofstede, G. 2001. *Culture's Consequences: Comparing Values*. 2nd ed. New York: Sage.

Inglehart, R. 1997. *Modernization and Post-Modernization: Cultural, Economic and Political Change in 43 Societies*. Princeton: Princeton University Press.

Kaasa, A. 2021. 'Merging Hofstede, Schwartz, and Inglehart into a Single System'. *Journal of Cross-Cultural Psychology* 52(4): 339–53.

Platteau, J. P. 1991. 'Traditional Systems of Social Security and Hunger Insurance: Past Achievements and Modern Challenges'. In *Social Security in Developing Countries,* edited by E. Ahmad, J. Dreze, J. Hills and A. Sen, 112–70. Oxford: Clarendon Press.

Schulz, J., Bahrami-Rad, D., Beauchamp, J. and Henrich J. 2019. The Church, Intensive Kinship, and Global Psychological Variation. *Science* 366(6466).

Schwartz, S. H. 2004. 'Mapping and Interpreting Cultural Differences'. In *Comparing Cultures: Dimensions of Culture in a Comparative Perspective*, edited by H. Vinken, J. Soeters and P. Ester, 43–73. Leiden: Brill.

Scott, J. 1976. *The Moral Economy of the Peasant: Rebellion and Subsistence in Southeast Asia.* New Haven: Yale University Press.

Woolcock, M. and Narayan, D. 2000. 'Social Capital: Implications for Development Theory, Research and Policy'. *The World Bank Research Observer* 15(2): 225–49.

6.1 *Znaki vnimaniya* (Russia and FSU)
Conor Murray

Agapov, K. 2018. '"Prizhimal k polovomu organu". V Moldaviy professora obvinili v domogatel'stvakh'. *Life.Ru*, 8 August. life.ru/p/1141989

Bikiyev, I. 2013. 'Problemy Otgranicheniya Vzyatki ot Podarka v Rossii i za Rubezhom: Praktika I Tendentsii'. *Aktualniye Problemy Ekonomiki i Prava* 1: 245–9.

Denisova-Schmidt, E., Prytula, Y. and Rumyantseva, N. 2019. 'Beg, Borrow, or Steal: Determinants of Student Academic Misconduct in Ukrainian Higher Education'. *Policy Reviews in Higher Education* 3(1): 4–27.

Dimitrova-Grajzl, V. and Simon, E. 2010. 'Political Trust and Historical Legacy: The Effect of Varieties of Socialism'. *East European Politics and Societies* 24(2): 206–8.

Grødeland, Å. 2007. '"Red Mobs", "Yuppies", "Lamb Heads" and Others: Contacts, Informal Networks and Politics in the Czech Republic, Slovenia, Bulgaria and Romania'. *Europe-Asia Studies* 59: 217–52.

Komu Podarok. 2017. 'Podarki Dlya Professora: Kreativnie Idei'. komu-podarok.ru/podarki-dlya-professora-kreativnye-id/

Kozlov, N. M. 2006. 'Lyubimim Nuzhni Znaki Vnimaniya'. Published 1 January at www.psychologos.ru/articles/view/lyubimym-nuzhny-znaki-vnimaniya

Patico, J. 2002. 'Chocolate and Cognac: Gifts and the Recognition of Social Worlds in Post-Soviet Russia'. *Ethnos* 67(3): 345–68.

Pesmen, D. 2000. *Russia and Soul: An Exploration*. Ithaca: Cornell University Press.

PhDRu. 2014. 'Domogatelstvo k aspirantkam v SSSR'. https://web.archive.org/web/20170707201227/http://phdru.com/domogatelstvo/sexualharassment/

Polese, A. 2008. '"If I Receive It, It Is a Gift; If I Demand It, It Is a Bribe": On the Local Meaning of Economic Transactions in Post-Soviet Ukraine'. *Anthropology in Action* 15: 47–60.

Shaw, P., Katsaiti, M. and Pecorado, B. 2015. 'On the Determinants of Educational Corruption: The Case of Ukraine'. *Contemporary Economic Policy* 33(4): 698–713.

Steenberg, R. 2016. 'The Art of Not Seeing Like a State. On the Ideology of "Informality"'. *Journal of Contemporary Central and Eastern Europe* 24(3): 293–306.

Wanner, C. 2005. 'Money, Morality and New Forms of Exchange in Post-socialist Ukraine'. *Ethnos* 70(4): 515–37.

Werner, C. 2000. 'Gifts, Bribes and Development in Kazakhstan'. *Human Organisation* 59(1): 11–22.

6.2 *Sinnamjai* (Thailand)
Wasin Punthong and Attasit Pankaew

Bowie, K. 2008. 'Vote Buying and Village Outrage in an Election in Northern Thailand: Recent Legal Reforms in Historical Context'. *The Journal of Asian Studies* 67(2): 469–511.

Eiawsriwong, N. 2017. 'Rabob upatham nai kanmuangthai'. Prachatai, 6 July. https://prachatai.com/journal/2017/06/72194

Haas, D. F. 1978. 'Clientelism and Rural Development in Thailand'. *Rural Sociology* 43(4): 280–92.

Han, L. 2017. 'Songli'. Global Informality Project, 17 January. http://in-formality.com/wiki/index.php?title=Songli

Hughes, C. 2006. 'The Politics of Gifts: Tradition and Regimentation in Contemporary Cambodia'. *Journal of Southeast Asian Studies* 37(3): 469–89.

Lebra, T. S. 1975. 'An Alternative Approach to Reciprocity'. *American Anthropologist* 77(3): 550–65.

Nishizaki, Y. 2005. 'The Moral Origin of Thailand's Provincial Strongmen: The Case of BanharnSilpa-Archa'. *Southeast Asia Research* 13(2): 184–234.

Office of the Thai Royal Society. 2011. *Potjananukrom shabab ratchabundittayasatarn*. Bangkok: Office of the Thai Royal Society.

Pankaew, A. 2011. 'Changes, Continuity, and Hope: A Note from the 2011 General Election'. *King Prajadhipok Institute Journal* 9(2): 29–47.

Rabhibhat, A. 1998. *Rabob uppatham lae krongsarngchonchan samai rattanakosintorn ton*. Bangkok: Chulalongkorn University Press.

Rupp, K. 2017. 'Okurinmon no shukan'. Global Informality Project, 3 July. www.in-formality.com/wiki/index.php?title=Okurimono_No_Shukan_(Japan)

Satitniramai, A., Pawakarapand, N. and Mukdawijitra, Y. 2013. 'Final Report: Re-examining the Political Landscape of Thailand'. Bangkok: Thai Health Promotion Foundation (Thai Health).

Sawasdee, S. 2006. *Thai Political Parties in the Age of Reform*. Bangkok: Institute of Public Policy Studies.

Sidman, A. 2017. 'Pork Barrelling'. Global Informality Project, 6 September. http://in-formality.com/wiki/index.php?title=Pork_barreling

ThaiPBS News. 2017. '*Makkutesk Songlka riakrong tormor yokleurk "Nguen sinnamjai" hettamlai-karntongtiaw*'. ThaiPBS, 8 July. https://news.thaipbs.or.th/content/264194

Thinbangtiaw, O. 2010. 'Political Economy on the Local Power Structure in Eastern Part of Thailand'. *Ratchaphruek Journal* 28(3): 184–209.

6.3 *Joro* (Kyrgyzstan)
Arzuu Sheranova

Beksultanova, Ch. 2014. 'Traditsionnye igIy i razvlecheniya kyrgyzov'. *Voprosy istorii Kyrgyzstana* 3(4): 222–30.
Granovetter, M. 1973. 'The Strength of Weak Ties'. *American Journal of Sociology* 78: 1360–80.
Kochkunov, A. 2003. 'Sistema pitaniya kyrgyzov (opyt etnologicheskogo analiza sootnosheniy traditliy i innovatsiy)'. *Manas universiteti.-Sosyal bilimler dergisi* 8: 213–33.
Ledeneva, A. 1998. *Russia's Economies of Favour: Blat, Networking and Informal Exchange*. Cambridge: Cambridge University Press.
Madamidzhanova, Z. and Mukhtarov, I. 2011. 'Cultural Life in the Ferghana Valley Under Khrushchev and Brezhnev'. In *Ferghana Valley: The Heart of Central Asia*, edited by F. Starr, B. Beshimov, I. Bobokulov and P. Shozimov, 164–77. London: Routledge.

6.4 *Sadaqa* (Kazakhstan and Kyrgyzstan)
Aisalkyn Botoeva

Aljanova, N., Borbassova, K. and Rysbekova, Sh. 2016. 'A Semiotic Analysis of the Yurt, Clothing, and Food Eating Habits in Kazakh Traditional Cultures'. *International Journal of Critical Cultural Studies* 14(1): 27–36.
Botoeva, A. 2018. 'Islam and the Spirits of Capitalism: Competing Articulations of the Islamic Economy'. *Politics and Society* 46(2): 235–64.
Epkenhans, T. 2011. 'Defining Normative Islam: Some Remarks on Contemporary Islamic Though in Tajikistan – Hoji Akbar Turajonzoda's Sharia and Society'. *Central Asian Survey* 30(1): 81–96.
Narmatov A. 2015. 'Saadaka beruunun paidasi', 5 April. Nasaatkg. www.youtube.com/watch?v=rVEY8LnECUM
Nasaat Media. 'Sadaka Zhana Zeket Bererden aldyn ushulardy eske alynyz Maksat azhy 2019 Toktomushev nasaat media 2019', 28 September. www.youtube.com/watch?v=4vq6d8Ydqi8
Tahirov, K. 'Chto takoe sadaka?'. *Azan.kz.*, 26 June. https://azan.kz/maqalat/read/chto-takoe-sadaka-11090
Turaeva, R. 2019. 'Imagined Mosque Communities in Russia: Central Asian Migrants in Moscow'. *Asian Ethnicity* 20(2): 131–47.

6.5 *Ashar* (Kyrgyzstan)
Arzuu Sheranova

Abazov, R. 2004. *Historical Dictionary of Kyrgyzstan*. Lanham: The Scarecrow Press.
Ala-Too 24. 2021. 'Doroga, stroyaschayasya metodom ashara' [A Road is Being Constructed by Ashar Method]. www.facebook.com/watch/?v=164284168798499
Azattyk Radiosy. 2017. 'V Kyrgyzstane predlagayut zapretit' stroitel'stvo shkol metodom ashara' [In Kyrgyzstan They Suggest Banning Construction of School by *Ashar* Method]. https://rus.azattyk.org/a/28572933.html
For.kg. 2020. 'Kyrgyzstantsev vnov' prizyvayut pogasit' dolg pered Kitaem metodom ashara' [Kyrgyzstanis Are Again Called to Pay Off Debt to China by Ashar Method], 19 October. www.for.kg/news-672911-ru.html
Ihsanoglu, E. 2001. *History of the Ottoman State, Society and Civilization*. Istanbul: IRCICA.
Jumasheva, A. 2013. 'Srednyaa stoimost svadeb v Kyrgyzstane' [Average Cost of Weddings in Kyrgyzstan]. *Vechernyi Bishkek*. www.vb.kg/doc/237908_sredniaia_stoimost_svadeb_v_kyrgyzstane.html
Kenčiev, J. 2014. 'Sanzhyra Kyrgyzskogo Plemeni "Sarybagysh"'. Berlin: Klaus Schwartz Verlag. https://web.archive.org/web/20200209065321/http://www.klaus-schwarz-verlag.com/manu/14-01-10_Sandsch_kirg.pdf
KTRK. 2020. 'Detskiy park metodom ashara' [A Children's Playground by Ashar Method], 27 July. www.ktrk.kg/ru/news/s/43386
Ministerstvo Zdravoohraneniya i Socialnogo Razvitiya Kyrgyzskoi Respubliki. 2021. 'V Ramkah Pandemii Covid-19 Zapushen Elektronnyi Portal dlya Volonterov' [Within Framework

COVID-19 Electronic Portal for Volunteers was Launched]. https://web.archive.org/web/2021 0803233121/http://med.kg/ru/novosti/4712-v-ramkakh-pandemii-covid-19-zapushchen-elektronnyj-portal-dlya-volonterov.html

Ryskulova, N. 2020. 'Kyrgyzstan: kak volontery zamenili gosudarstvo v bor'be s koronavirusom' [Kyrgyzstan: How Did Volunteers Replace the Government in Fighting against Coronavirus]. BBC. www.bbc.com/russian/features-53791289

Sputnik. 2016. 'Rashody na srednestatisticheskuyu svadbu v Kyrgyzstane – torjestvo na 200 chelovek' [Expenses for an Average Wedding in Kyrgyzstan – A Feast for 200 People]. https://sputnik.kg/ig/wedding/index.html

Timofeeva, D. 2020. 'Brigady poslednei nadezhdy. Kak volontery v Kyrgyzstane spasayut umirauschih, k kotorym ne uspevaet "skoraya"' [How Volunteers in Kyrgyzstan are Saving Dying Patients to Whom Medical Aid is Not Reaching]. *Nastoyaschee Vremja*. www.currenttime.tv/a/volunteers-kyrgyzstan-help-coronavirus/30737441.html

6.6 *Nisia* (Georgia)
Megi Kartsivadze

Aliyev, H. 2014. 'The Effects of the Saakashvili Era Reforms on Informal Practices in the Republic of Georgia'. *Studies of Transition States and Societies* 6(1): 19–33.

Dushuashvili, T. 2016. 'Mikrisafinanso organizatsiebi saqartveloshi'. *Forbes Georgia*. 16 March.

Fehr, E. and Gächter, S. 2000. 'Fairness and Retaliation: The Economics of Reciprocity'. *Journal of Economic Perspectives* 14(3): 159–82.

Gel'man, V. 2012. 'Subversive Institutions, Informal Governance, and Contemporary Russian Politics'. *Communist and Post-Communist Studies* 45(3–4): 295–303.

Giorgelashvili, T., Vachiberadze, I. and Taktakishvili, G. 2016. 'Nisiebis raodenoba gaizarda'. *Maestro TV*. 10 February.

Javakhishvili, I. 1924. 'Jaqos khiznebi'. *Mnatobi*: 7–8.

Kupatadze, A. 2012. 'Explaining Georgia's Anti-Corruption Drive'. *European Security* 21(1): 16–36.

Ledeneva, A. 1998. *Russia's Economy of Favours: Blat, Networking and Informal Exchange*. Cambridge: Cambridge University Press.

Mars, G. and Altman, Y. 1983. 'The Cultural Bases of Soviet Georgia's Second Economy'. *Soviet Studies* 35(4): 546–60.

Nikora. 2017. 'Nikora Supermarket Network Has Launched a New Credit Card More', 18 December. http://nikoraholding.ge/english/news/363

Papava, V. 2005. *Necroeconomics: The Political Economy of Post-Communist Capitalism*. New York: iUniverse.

Pisadze, N. 2018. 'Gorshi, ert-erti maghaziidan e.ts. nisiebis rveuli moipares'. 1TV, 8 June. https://web.archive.org/web/20230401105237/https://1tv.ge/news/gorshi-ert-erti-maghaziidan-e-w-nisiebis-rveuli-moipares/

Rozanski, M. 2015. 'Zakupy na zeszyt? Na wsiach to wciąż norma. W mieście też się zdarza'. *Gazeta Wrocławska*, 3 May. https://gazetawroclawska.pl/zakupy-na-zeszyt-na-wsiach-to-wciaz-norma-w-miescie-tez-sie-zdarza/ar/3843783

Shanshiashvili, S. 1926. 'Ambokari'. *Mnatobi* 4 (24): 5–56.

Vazha-Pshavela. 1893. 'Soflis suratebi'. *Sapolitiko da saliteraturo koveldghiuri gazeti* 123: 1–3.

Zakharova, L. 2015. 'How and What to Consume: Patterns of Soviet Clothing Consumption in the 1950s and 1960'. In *Communism and Consumerism: The Soviet Alternative to the Affluent Society*, edited by T. Vihavainen and E. Bogdanova, 85–112. Leiden: Brill.

6.7 *Cassa peota* (Italy)
Giulio Benedetti

Banca d'Italia. 2018a. 'Attuazione del decreto legislativo 13 agosto 2010, n.141. Pubblicazione degli elenchi ex art. 112, comma 7, TUB'. www.bancaditalia.it/compiti/vigilanza/avvisi-pub/decreto-13082010-141/index.html

Banca d'Italia. 2018b. 'Testo Unico Bancario. Legislative decree n.385/1993, adjourned by the decree n.218/2017'.

Buonanno, I. 2014. 'The History of Wine Shops in Venice'. In *Venice and Viticulture*, edited by C. Favero, 64–83. Cittadella (Pd): Biblos Edizioni.
Cacciavillani, I. 2013. *Il "sociale" a Venezia: Interventi "Sociali" nell'Ordinamento della Serenissima'.* Padova: Panda Edizioni.
Casellato, A. 2002. 'Sestieri Popolari'. In *Storia di Venezia, L'Ottocento e il Novecento*, edited by S. Woolf and M. Isnenghi, 1581–621. Roma: Istituto della Enciclopedia Italiana.
Davydova, I. 2018. 'Pomochi'. In *Global Encylopaedia of Informality, Volume 2*, edited by A. Ledeneva et al., 51–5. London: UCL Press.
Dell'Oro, G. 1959. 'Ancora più di mille in città le "casse peote" e le "mutue"'. *Il Gazzettino*. 27 August.
Imami, D., Polese, A. and Rama, K. 2018. 'Loteria/Lloteria'. In *Global Encyclopaedia of Informality, Volume 2*, edited by A. Ledeneva et al., 63–6. London: UCL Press.
Lane, F. C. 1978. *Storia di Venezia*. Torino: Einaudi Edizioni.
Ledeneva, A. et al., 2018. *Global Encyclopaedia of Informality, Volume 2*. London: UCL Press.
Osabuohien, E. and Oluyomi, O. 2018. 'Esusu'. In *Global Encyclopaedia of Informality, Volume 2*, edited by A. Ledeneva et al., 66–9. London: UCL Press.
Polese, A. 2018. 'Vay mu'o'n'. In *Global Encyclopaedia of Informality, Volume 2*, edited by A. Ledeneva et al., 61–3. London: UCL Press.
Ragazzini, G. 2007. *Dizionario Inglese-Italiano, Italiano-Inglese*. Bologna: Zanichelli.
Sarmiento, R. F. 2018 'Sosyudad'. In *Global Encyclopaedia of Informality, Volume 2*, edited by A. Ledeneva et al., 58–61. London: UCL Press.
Senato della Repubblica. 1998. Written Responses to Parliamentary Interrogations. www.senato.it/service/PDF/PDFServer/DF/17789.pdf
Tramontin, S. 1985. *Venezia e Lorenzo Giustiniani*. Venezia: Comune di Venezia.
Vélez-Ibáñez, C. G. 2018. 'Tandas and cundinas'. In *Global Encyclopaedia of Informality, Volume 2*, edited by A. Ledeneva et al., 72–6. London: UCL Press.

6.8 *Chernaya kassa* (Kyrgyzstan)
Arzuu Sheranova

Barsukova, S. and Zvyagintzev, V. 2006. 'Mehanism politicheskogo ivestirovaniya, ili kak i zachem rossiyskiy biznes uchastvuet v vyborah i oplachivaet partiynuyu jizn'. *Polis. Politicheskie Issledovaniya* (2):110–21.
Cieślewska, A. 2014. 'From Shuttle Trader to Businesswomen: The Informal Bazaar Economy in Kyrgyzstan'. In *The Informal Post-Socialist Economy: Embedded Practices and Livelihoods*, edited by J. Morris and A. Polese, 121–35. London: Routledge.
Gaddy, C. and Ickes, B. W. 1998. 'To Restructure or Not to Restructure: Informal Activities and Enterprise Behavior in Transition'. William Davidson Institute Working Papers Series 134. William Davidson Institute at the University of Michigan.
Gelman, V. 2002. 'The Iceberg of Political Finance'. In *The Contemporary Russian Politics: A Reader*, edited by A. Brown, 179–94. Oxford: Oxford University Press.
Kandiyoti, D. 1998. 'Rural Livelihoods and Social Networks in Uzbekistan: Perspectives from Andijan'. *Central Asian Survey* 17(4): 561–78.
Kornai, J. 1980. *Economics of Shortage*. Amsterdam: North-Holland.
Neuhauser, K. 1993. 'Two Channels of Consumer Credit in the USSR'. Paper No. 38 Berkeley-Duke Occasional Papers on the Second Economy in the USSR. www.ucis.pitt.edu/nceeer/1993-Duke-38-Neuhauser.pdf
Özcan, G. 2006. 'Djamila's Journey from Kolkhoz to Bazaar: Female Entrepreneurs in Kyrgyzstan'. In *Enterprising Women in Transition Economies*, edited by F. Welter, D. Smallbone and N. Isakova, 93–115. Hampshire: Ashgate Publishing.
Turaeva, R. 2018. 'Gender and Changing Women's Roles in Uzbekistan: From Soviet Workers to Post-Soviet Entrepreneurs'. In *Constructing the Uzbek State. Narratives of the Post-Soviet Years*, edited by M. Laruelle, 303–19. Lanham, MD: Lexington.
Werner, C. 1998. 'Household Networks and the Security of Mutual Indebtedness in Rural Kazakstan'. *Central Asian Survey* 17(4): 597–612.
Wolters, A. 2014. 'The State and Islam in Central Asia: Administering the Religious Threat or Engaging Muslim Communities?'. PFH Forschungspapiere/ Research Papers. PFH Private Hochschule Göttingen 2014/03.Göttingen: PFH.
Zyryanova, I. 2013. 'Izbiratelnyi shtab kandidata – subekt korruptsii v izbiratelnom protsesse'. *Aktual'nye problemny ekonomiki i prava* 4(28): 32–7.

6.9 *Moai* (Japan)
Abel Polese

Gudeman, S. 2015. *The Anthropology of Economy: Community, Market, and Culture*. Cambridge: Cambridge University Press.
Imami, D., Rama, K. and Polese, A. 2020. 'Informality and Access to Finance During Socialism and Transition – The Case of the Rotating Lottery Credits Schemes in Albania'. *Journal of Evolutionary Economics* 30: 1367–83.
Morrow, C. 2019. *Moai: The Economy of Trust Medium*. Medium.com, 3 September. https://medium.com/@chicamorrow/moai-the-economy-of-trust-4c26f9e2e8f1
Morrow, C. 2020. 'Does Participation in Moai Affect Individual-level Social Capital or Mental Health in Okinawa?'. MA thesis.
Mynavi News. 2013. 'What is the "Inexhaustible" Custom that Yamanashi Residents are Looking Forward to?', 14 April. https://news.mynavi.jp/article/20130414-a027/
Nelson, C. T. 2001. 'Capitalism, Culture and the Okinawan Moai'. *The Journal of Pacific Asia* (7): 15–26.
Okinawa Encyclopedia Publishing Secretariat. 1983. 'Okinawa Encyclopedia'.
Polese, A. 2021. 'What is Informality? (Mapping) "The Art of Bypassing the State". In *Eurasian Spaces – and Beyond'. Eurasian Geography and Economics* 64(3): 322–64.
Polese, A., Kovacs, B. and Jancsics, D. 2018. 'Informality "In Spite of" or "Beyond" The State: Evidence from Hungary and Romania'. *European Societies* 20(2): 207–35.
Rupp, K. 2003. *Gift-Giving in Japan: Cash, Connections, Cosmologies*. Stanford, CA: Stanford University Press.
Ryukyu Government Cultural Property Protection Committee. 1972. *Okinawa Cultural History Encyclopedia*. Tokyo: Tokyodo Publishing.
Shimokawa, Y. 2006. 'Okinawa That I Fell in Love with More'. *Futabasha*.
Urban Life Research Project Okinawa Team. 2009. *49 Rules for Becoming a Real Okinawan*. Chukei Publishing.
Watanabe, Y. et al. 2008. *Okinawa Folklore Dictionary*. Tokyo: Yoshikawa Kobunkan.

6.10 *Koshumcha* (Kyrgyzstan)
Eugenia Pesci

Abdubaitova, A. 2018. 'Osnovnye traditsii, kotorye dolzhen pomnit' kazhdyi Kyrgyz'. *Kaktus*, 16 September. https://kaktus.media/doc/379489_osnovnye_tradicii_kotorye_doljen_pomnit_kajdyy_kyrgyz.html
Eidson, J. 2017. *Max Planck Institute for Social Anthropology Report 2014–2016. Department 'Integration and Conflict'*. Halle /Saale: Max Planck Institute for Social Anthropology.
Erkebaeva, A. 2018. 'Potratil million na toi i ostalsiya dolzhen gostyam. Kak ustroena kyrgyzskaya traditsiya koshumcha'. *Kloop*, 16 August. https://kloop.kg/blog/2018/08/16/potratil-million-na-toj-i-ostalsya-dolzhen-gostyam-kak-ustroena-kyrgyzskaya-traditsiya-koshumcha/
Granovetter, M. 1985. 'Economic Action and Social Structure: The Problem of Embeddedness'. *American Journal of Sociology* 91: 481–510.
Kochkunov, A. 2018. 'Religious Practices in the Modern Ceremonial Lives of the Kyrgyz People'. *Anthropology of the Middle East* 13: 43–54.
Ledeneva, A. 2018. *The Global Encyclopaedia of Informality, Volume 1: Understanding Social and Cultural Complexity*. London: UCL Press.
Mauss, M. 2002. *The Gift. The Form and Reason for Exchange in Archaic Societies*. London: Routledge.
National Statistical Committee of the Kyrgyz Republic. n.d. 'Srednemesyachnaya zarabotnaya plata'. Stat.kg. www.stat.kg/ru/opendata/category/112/
Provis, R. 2015. 'Shifting Social Dynamics and Economic Inequality in the Post-Soviet Space: Networking and Participation in Toi among the Novyi Kyrgyz'. *Economic Anthropology* 2: 371–84.
Reeves, M. 2012. 'Black Work, Green Money: Remittances, Ritual, and Domestic Economies in Southern Kyrgyzstan'. *Slavic Review* 71: 108–34.
Tologonova, S. 2020. 'Toiekonomika. Koshumcha Privodit k Bednosti?'. Kloop, 1 April. https://kloop.kg/blog/2020/02/01/tojekonomika-koshumcha-privodit-k-bednosti/

Turdalieva, C. and Provis, R. 2018. 'Dynamics of Reciprocity and Networks of the Kyrgyz through Bishkek Toi Making'. *Central Asian Affairs* (4)2: 197–216.

Yudachin, K. 1985. *Kirgizsko-Russkii Slovar*'. Sovetskaya Entsiklopediya. https://eurasica.ru/dict/?l=k&w=4030

6.11 *Pujogŭm* (South Korea)
You-Kyung Byun

Byun, Y.-K. 2020. *The 50,000 Won Friends: Gift Money Exchange In The Alumni Network of South Korea*. PhD dissertation. Freie Universität Berlin.

Choi, J. 1988. *Han'gungnongch'onsahoebyŏnhwayŏn'gu*. Seoul: Iljisa.

Gallup Korea. 2013. 'Gallup Report: Yojŭm kyŏrhonsik ch'ugŭigŭm ŏlmana naesimnikka?', 23 April. www.gallup.co.kr/gallupdb/reportContent.asp?seqNo=414&pagePos=30&selectYear=&search=&searchKeyword=

Lebra, T. S. 1976. *Japanese Patterns of Behavior*. Honolulu: The University Press of Hawai'i.

Tan, L. 2018. 'Hongbao'. In *Global Encyclopaedia of Informality, Volume 1*, edited by A. Ledeneva, 136–9. London: UCL Press.

6.12 *Poclon* (Wallachia, Romania)
Vasile Mihai Olaru

Eclesiarhu, D. 2004. *Scriei alese. Hronograf. Predoslovii*. N. Trandafirescu (ed.). Bucharest: Institutul de istorie literară şi teorie literară 'G. Călinescu'.

Giurescu, D. C. 1962. 'Anatefterul. Condica de Porunci a Vistieriei lui Constantin Brîncoveanu'. *Studii şi materiale de istorie medie* 5: 352–504.

Greceanu, R. L. 1970. *Istoria domniei lui Constantin Basarab Brâncoveanu Voievod (1688–1714)*. Ilieş, A. (ed.) Bucharest: Editura Academiei Republicii Socialiste Românie.

Grecescu. C. 1959. *Istoria Ţării Româneşti de la octombrie 1688 la martie 1717*. Bucharest: Editura Ştiinţifică.

Potra, G. 1961. *Documente privitoare la istoria oraşului Bucarest (1594–1821)*. Bucharest: Editura Academiei Republicii Populare Române.

Sachelarie O. and N. Stoicescu. 1988. *Instituţii feudale româneşti. Dicţionar* . Bucharest: Editura Academiei Republicii Socialiste România.

Slovar cerkovno-slavjanskago i russkago jazyka, Volume 3. 1847. St. Petersburg: Tipographia Imperatorskoi Akademii Nauk.

Urechia, V. A. 1891. *Istoria Românilor: Volume I*. Bucharest: Lito-Tipografia.

7
Gaining an advantage

Introduction: trickster

Mark Lipovetsky
Columbia University, New York, USA

When speaking of tricksters, it is necessary to draw a line between myths, sociocultural roles and tropes. The trickster myth is formed by narratives of tricksters belonging to mythology and folklore. Such is Thoth in Egyptian mythology; Hermes, Prometheus and Odysseus in Greek; Anansi, Eshu and Ogo-Yurugu in West African mythology; Coyote and Rabbit in North American Indian mythology; Loki of the Norse pantheon, and the Raven in Paleo-Asiatic; the Kitsune in Chinese and Japanese folklore; Ivan the fool and Thief in Russian wonder tales; Hershele of Ostropol in Yiddish folklore; Hodja Nasreddin in Turkish; Till Eulenspiegel and Reineke the Fox in German, and so on.

Since the earliest studies of the trickster in the mythology and folklore of various cultures (see the review of literature in Doty and Hynes 1993), this character was associated with motifs of chaos, destruction and the destabilisation of order (see Radin 1956; Kerenyi quoted in Radin 1956: 195–211; Jung quoted in Radin 1956: 173–91). The disorder and destruction that the trickster represents is the *archaic equivalent of freedom*, namely individual freedom, since the mythological trickster is always an egoist, driven only by his appetite – gastronomically and sexually. It is his (typically, it is a he) freedom, joviality and humour that make the trickster's destruction creative and places him next to the culture hero as a parodic double: 'He knows neither good nor evil, yet he is responsible for both. He possesses no values, moral or social, is at the mercy of his passions and appetites, yet through his actions all values come into being' (Radin 1956: xxiii). The trickster myth's implicit philosophy is very close to Mikhail Bakhtin's philosophy of the carnival, and his analysis of the functions of the rogue, jester and fool is highly insightful for the understanding of the trickster's freedom and cultural functions (Bakhtin 1981: 158–67).

Summarising the studies of tricksters in the mythology and folklore of various peoples, William Hynes formulates six partially overlapping characteristics of the mythological trickster: he is (1) ambiguous and anomalous, (2) a deceiver and trick-player who causes disruption and disorder, (3) a shape-shifter, (4) a situation-inverter, (5) the messenger and imitator of the gods, the mediator between the human and divine and (6) changer of the sacred into the profane and lewd, and vice versa (Hynes 1993: 33–46). Other scholars develop the idea of the mythological trickster as an ancient metaphor for the creative possibilities of language (Pelton 1980; Gates 1998; Hyde 1998). The trickster performatively displays the deconstructive work of language, s/he emerges as the living and breathing allegory of language who incessantly destabilises meanings and reveals ambivalence within established beliefs and categories: 'The trickster discovers creative fabulation, feigning, and fibbing, the playful construction of fictive worlds', he is a mediator 'who works "by means of a lie that is really a truth, a deception that is in fact a revelation"'(Hyde 1998: 45, 72).

The folkloric trickster gave rise to a number of later sociocultural roles, such as the carnival clown, the fool, the jester, the impostor, the thief, the holy fool, the adventurer, the con artist, the female trickster, or trick star (Jurich 1998; Mills 2001). There is a vast scholarly literature devoted to each of these types, a review of which would take too much space. In a very rudimentary way, we can divide these derivatives of the mythological trickster into two main categories: those who perform their functions disinterestedly, by virtue of tradition, according to the logic of ritual or for the pleasure of the crowd, and those who use trickery for social climbing or the acquisition of wealth. The first category includes the carnival clown, the fool (liar) and the holy fool, while the roque (picaro), the impostor, the adventurer, the con artist, the hacker and so on belong to the second category. The intermediate position between these categories is occupied by the thief, whose clearly mercenary activity is surrounded in culture with a halo of artistry and even aesthetics (Sinyavsky 2007: 45–58), and the court jester (Otto 2001), whose ceremonial functions are frequently associated with real power, privilege and wealth.

All of these roles differ both from each other and from their common source, the trickster as a mythological hero, but they all share a 'common denominator': the trickster position is specifically designed by culture to manifest what Václav Havel (1985) called 'the power of the powerless'; so that the subaltern can speak freely about the world around him/her and compensate for his/her humiliated and powerless position through deception and tricks. Both functions are visibly combined in the laughter of the trickster. It is this laughter that most clearly embodies their agency.

Mediated by these sociocultural roles, the trickster tradition boils down to what can be defined as the *trickster trope*. The constants of the trickster trope include: (1) ambivalence, understood as a special principle of the deconstruction of binaries, as in Derrida's characteristic of Thoth in *Plato's Pharmacy* (Derrida 1981: 87–94) and the destruction of borders between the sacred and profane, private and public, normative and illicit; (2) transgression – the violation of borders, norms and laws of the social order, the injection of chaos and unpredictability; (3) liminality as the basis for radical freedom connected with non-belonging to social hierarchies (see Turner 1969); and (4) hyper-performativity: the trickster replaces his/her 'self' with numerous performative 'masks' that fuse together the personal and stereotypical, the private and public. The trickster's freedom in this context manifests itself mainly in endless metamorphoses of the subject – liberation from the burden of a given and unchangeable identity serves here as a source of joy and playfulness – as well as the ability to involve others in a kind of participatory theatre. The concretisation of these constants in each specific case generates a specific set of variables, such as, for example, parodying authority and authorship, the aesthetic excess of tricks, the role of mediator, as well as many other characteristics, often directly reproducing the features of the mythological trickster.

The art of the eighteenth to twentieth centuries displays the trickster trope in a rich spectrum of variations. Characters such as Beaumarchais's Figaro; Gogol's Khlestakov, Chichikov and Nozdrev; Mark Twain's Tom Sawyer and Huckleberry Finn; Jaroslav Hašek's Švejk; Tadeusz Dołęga-Mostowicz's political trickster Nicodemus Dyzma; Max Bialystock in Mel Brooks's *Producers*; Eric Cartman from *South Park*; Borat (Sacha Baron Cohen); Bob Odenkirk's 'Saul Goodman' (from the TV series *Breaking Bad* and *Better Call Saul*), as well as cultural personae such as Salvador Dali, Orson Welles, Marcel Duchamp, Andy Warhol, Joseph Beuys, or Banksy, confirm this self-evident thesis.

The modern trickster typically combines features of the picaro, adventurer, impostor and con artist and assumes a new cultural meaning in the modern context as a positive, artistic and incredibly attractive version of a cynic (see Sloterdijk 1987; Žižek 1997). An example of the Soviet trickster is especially illuminating in this respect, although this case reflects general aspects of modernity. Hardly moral beacons by any standard, characters of Soviet literature such as Julio Jurenito (Ilya Erenburg), Benya Krik (Isaac Babel), Ostap Bender (Ilya Ilf and Yevgeny Petrov), or Sandro of Chegem (Fazil Iskander) are nevertheless depicted with sympathy by their authors and adored by their readers, becoming true cult heroes of the entire Soviet culture (unlike no fewer virtuoso tricksters in nineteenth-century Russian literature who are typically represented negatively). Their incredible popularity reflects the dual cultural function of the Soviet trickster – on the one hand, to rebut and mock the cynicism of Soviet state politics and its yawning gap between egalitarian Communist rhetoric and brutal exploitative practice, and, on the other, to aesthetically justify and even elevate normalised survival practices – such as, for example, impostory (Alexopoulos 1998; Fitzpatrick 2005) or *blat* (Ledeneva 1998) – despite their questionable moral value. By embracing the trickster narrative, the cynic, who secretly hates the Soviet system but willy-nilly conforms to its strictures, is transformed from a slave of circumstance into an active and autonomous actor of the social drama, and even an embodiment of artistry and freedom.

In a broader sense, the trickster narratives perform the crucial function of returning social agency to people. Not only actual subalterns but also any marginalised and stigmatised individuals who either avoid (for their own good) the 'official' channels of social mobility and self-expression or are isolated from them, can choose the trickster narrative rather than an outright anti-system position. Entries included in this section demonstrate how trickster narratives are dissipated and, at the same time, fuelled by informal practices of deception and trickery aimed at 'gaming the system' – in socialist and non-socialist conditions alike.

These practices project characteristics of the trickster trope onto the social fabric, blurring the borderlines between the normalised and criminal (as in the Polish concept of *(za)chachmęcenie*, the Indian *chaa pani*, the Malaysian *duit kopi*), the gift and the bribe (as in the South American *aumento* and the Bulgarian *pari pod masata*), the private and public (as in the Central American *chanchullo*), the morally repulsive and playful (as in Spanish *gorroneo*) and so on. Paradoxically, however, many of these practices – much like Soviet tricksters – confront the dehumanising impact of the modern bureaucratic state, as noted by Daniela Peluso in her article on *aumento*, and create channels of power for the powerless – through informal, transgressive, morally and legally ambivalent, yet customary and ubiquitous, practices.

7.1 *Chanchullo* (Central America)
Denise Dunlap and Jose Godinez
Manning School of Business, University of Massachusetts, Lowell, USA

Chanchullo is a term common in Latin America that denotes an illicit act done with the intention of benefiting oneself at the expense of others. *Chanchullo* is defined by the Royal Academy of the Spanish Language as 'fraud'. Its origins can be traced to 1700s Spain where people referred to practical jokes as *chanza* – from the Italian *ciancia* with the same meaning – and the person who performed the practical jokes as *chancero*, which morphed into *chanchullero* (Diccionario Libre 2020). In Central American countries the term *chanchullo* is unique because it specifically denotes practices used by businesses to take advantage of customers, and by governments to take advantage of their constituencies.

Chanchullo can be committed by an individual, a business or a government. An example of this expression in English would be 'John makes ends meet with *chanchullos*'. *Chanchullo* in Spanish-speaking countries has different meanings. In Spain *chanchullo* denotes illicit means to benefit oneself in situations such as gambling or sports, and it generally involves coordination with other people. In Bolivia, *chanchullo* is a piece of paper containing information that can be used to cheat in an exam. In Venezuela and Chile, *chanchullo* is mainly used by the public to describe fraud carried out by public officials or institutions.

In Central America, *chanchullo* encompasses a variety of tricks used to gain an unfair advantage over others. Central American businesses have a bad reputation for swindling the public with impunity. This is the result of the colonial past when groups that controlled most of the wealth lacked competition and could mistreat consumers. Nowadays, the term *chanchullo* is still used to express the view that businesses cheat customers, smaller suppliers or distributors without repercussions. The term *chanchullo* can also be used to refer to the government cheating its constituents to benefit either private companies or government employees.

Chanchullo is different from *chorizo* since the latter is almost exclusively used in relation to the public sector, while *chanchullo* covers both the public and the private. An example of *chanchullo* in the private sector is a recent scandal of collusion to artificially maintain high fuel prices in Guatemala. The reason for the 0.63 USD higher fuel price when compared to neighbouring countries was not due to fuel production, tax structures or physical infrastructure in Guatemala; the reason for the price difference was *chanchullo*: the fuel distributors were found to have colluded in the attempt to maintain artificially high fuel prices, which directly affected the population (Gomez-Estrada 2016).

Another example of *chanchullo* is firms taking advantage of the lax laws regarding classified ads in El Salvador's newspapers. While in El Salvador it is against the law to advertise false claims in the media, some companies have found a loophole that does not restrict advertisements in the classified ads section of newspapers. Companies have been able to post ads for products such as miracle weight loss teas and opportunities with 50 per cent monthly returns on investment (Vanguardia 2017). Such practices have adversely affected the credibility of companies in general, as the public began to distrust businesses due to past abuses of trust and instead favoured informal business transactions with face-to-face interaction and payments made in cash. However, informal trade starves the country of taxes needed to improve the lives of its citizens because cash transactions are rarely reported to central authorities. High reliance on informal business transactions also makes it difficult for the central government to enforce business laws and regulations.

In Central American countries, one of the most common cases of *chanchullo* in the public sector is electoral fraud. The president of Honduras, Orlando Hernandez, was accused of committing *chanchullo* in 2017 when he directed the country's Supreme Court to allow him to run for re-election despite the constitutional ban on presidential re-elections. According to Fang and Mackey (2017), *chanchullo* of the 2017 Honduran elections was systematic; the election was stacked against the opposition candidate who had a slight edge over Hernandez when the polls closed. Following interruptions in the electronic voting systems, the votes necessary for the incumbent to be re-elected began pouring in. While there was national and international outcry, *chanchullo* was accomplished and Hernandez was re-elected president.

Accusations of electoral *chanchullo* were also present during the 2019 elections in Guatemala. In Quetzaltenango, Guatemala's second-largest city, 15 former mayoral candidates filed a suit against the electoral authorities, accusing the winner of *chanchullo*. The former candidates claimed that the electoral process contained irregularities such as inserting extra votes for the winning candidate into ballot boxes and distributing more than one ballot to certain voters. In general, *chanchullo* in electoral processes creates apathy among voters, which further erodes their already weak democracies.

Chanchullo is also found at the intersection of private and public sectors in Central America. For instance, the former Guatemalan president's son and brother's established business issued invoices for services that were never provided in order to recover the expenses for gifts given to allies of their political party. *Chanchullo* in this case was the collusion with an established and reputable business to justify campaign expenses that were used as bribes to people who could benefit the political campaign of the soon-to-be president (Coronado and Monzón 2019).

Another illustration of *chanchullo* at the intersection of the public and private sectors is the case of Trecsa, an energy group controlled by a Colombian firm with operations in several countries. In Guatemala, Trecsa was planning to expand their operations and had bribed the government to get approval for their new project of providing electric energy to rural areas. The project was announced as 'nationally urgent' by the government, despite the fact that Guatemala produces 60 per cent more energy than it consumes and exports the surplus (Escobar 2019). In addition, to expand their operations, Trecsa would have to create infrastructure that would interfere with the ecological balance of the country. The declaration of national urgency was *chanchullo* benefiting the energy company and local politicians. This *chanchullo* not only eroded the government's credibility, but also had wide environmental repercussions.

The wide spread of *chanchullo* has spurred a plethora of studies in Latin America (Varon 2015; Gomez-Estrada 2016; Cabieses Donoso 2019). Because of its wide definition and many uses, most studies analysing this practice have relied on qualitative approaches. This leaves unanswered the question of how detrimental this practice is for economies and the public in the countries where this practice is prevalent. A quantitative analysis of *chanchullo* will allow the public to fully grasp the consequences of this practice and to demand change.

7.2 **Gorroneo** (Spain and Hispanic America)
Ignacio Fradejas-García
Department of Anthropology, Universitat Autònoma de Barcelona, Spain

In Spanish, *gorroneo* refers to the informal practice of eating, drinking and living at the expenses of others. The noun *gorrón* describes a person who 'has the habit of eating, living, giving oneself treats or having fun at someone else's cost', and the related verb *gorronear* refers to eating or living that way (Real Academia Española 2019). While it might be possible to translate *gorronear* as to scrounge, mooch or sponge, this practice of free-riding has specific Spanish cultural connotations and roots.

Asking others for a cigarette and never buying any is one of the most common examples of *gorroneo* in Spain, but similar practices are observable in every culture. Other examples include consuming food and drink that others bring to the workplace or school, eating and drinking without invitation at a party or celebration ceremony, or helping oneself at a bar where a friend works. *Gorroneo* can equally apply to siphoning out resources, such as stealing supplies, one item at a time, usually at work, with the authorities either turning a blind eye or being complicit.

Another common practice of free-riding is associated with *pagar la ronda*, whereby one avoids paying for a round of drinks for an entire group when the norm is for people to take it in turns to pay. Common among family or friends, *pagar la ronda* has no preassigned turns or precise calculations of bills for drinking or eating. Rotation is exercised on the basis of an unarticulated tacit rule that is recognised especially when it is violated. The ritual involves someone paying for the first round and others continuing in sequence, in the spirit of friendship, sometimes pretending to argue over paying. The turn-taking is unproblematic until it is broken, just like a long pause in a conversation or other forms of disruptions of the 'interactive order' (Goffman 1983). The *gorrón* violates the tacit rule by avoiding paying for the round. When people realise that the *gorrón* is taking advantage of them by not paying even though they are capable of doing so, they exclude *gorrón* from the next meeting or ostracise the offender in other ways. The *gorrón*'s free-riding and subsequent sanctions undermine the circle of trust, sharing and reciprocity and may break *pagar la ronda* altogether, resulting in group members paying for their own drinks. In some cases, practices of free-riding are considered to be socially acceptable, particularly in dire economic circumstances, whereby a group of better-off friends allow the *gorrón* to be 'invited'. However, the *gorrón* is at risk of being excluded when circumstances change, for example, if the *gorrón*'s economic situation improves, or if someone in the group stops tolerating the *gorron*'s behaviour.

Gorra means 'hat' or 'cap'. There are two connected interpretations of the origins of *gorroneo* as an expression for free-riding (Sánchez Hidalgo 2018). One emphasises the 'ability to get in' due to wearing a certain hat (*gorra*), whereby greeting the doorman like a gentleman, taking off the hat and blending in allows one to crash a party or sneak into a banquet with guests one does not know. The phrase *entrar de gorra* means 'free entry'. Related expressions are associated with the hat being turned upside down: *vivir de gorra*, in Spanish meaning 'living for free', at the expense of others; *pasar la gorra*, literally asking for money by holding your hat, usually begging, as well as asking for tips after a public spectacle; or *gorrillas*, the self-appointed parking attendants (see *Stoyanshiki*, 5.34 Volume 1).

The second interpretation comes from students' practices documented at the University of Salamanca in the period of the sixteenth to eighteenth centuries. With little money to spare, students became known for their trickery of sneaking into banquets for free meals. They were called *capigorrista* or *capigorrón* because they wore a black cape – *capa* – and a large cap – *gorra* – to give the impression of gallantry and chivalry (Real Academia Española 1729). The character of a trickster and the commonality of the associated practices can be traced back to the Spanish *picaresque* literature in the sixteenth century, starting with the book *The Life of Lazarillo de Tormes and of His Fortunes and Adversities* (Rodriguez Cáceres 1991). The tradition entails diverse *picaresque* novels, poems and plays such as the anonymous 'Entremés de los gorrones'. The term *gorrón* is used in the title of Francisco de Rojas Zorrilla's book *Obligados y ofendidos, y el gorrón de Salamanca* (Rojas Zorrilla 1640).

Jargon around such practices included colloquial words of Germanic origin, with similar meanings (see Rafael Salillas 1896). Salillas mentions *godería*, which means to eat and drink for free, *rozavillón*, a person who lives at the expense of others and *pegote* who is an '(im)pertinent person who does not separate from others, particularly in the hours and occasions in which they usually eat' (Real Academia Española 2019). These words are no longer used, but *gorrón, gorronear* and *gorroneo* remained widely used in colloquial contexts in Spain without an equivalent in formal Spanish (Sanmartín Sáez 2003).

Outside Spain, these terms became common in Latin America from the sixteenth century with the first colonial-indigenous language encounters. They can be found in the Spanish-Quechua vocabulary (González Holguín 1608). The term *garronear* in Argentina and Uruguay, and *gorrear* in Mexico, have similar meanings to *gorroneo*. In Chile and Bolivia, the meaning of *gorrear* has evolved to signify being sexually unfaithful to a spouse. In this sense, the term *gorrona* was also used in Spain as a synonym of 'prostitute' but has since been abandoned. Most of the associated terms carry negative connotations and are morally reprehensible.

Like other informal practices in Spain and worldwide, *gorroneo* can be included in a set of survival and subsistence practices in response to the power constraints of unequal social structures (Scott 1985). However, the character of a *gorrón* can qualify as a case of an archetypal trickster, a rule-bender, border-crosser and free-rider who appears in the mythology of most cultures thus blurring 'the boundary between need and greed' (Ledeneva 2018: 3). In literary contexts, foxy characters tend to be portrayed in an ambivalent fashion: street-smart, good-humoured and entertaining, while also morally reprehensible, unsavoury and parasitic. Beyond the scope of literature and literary critique of the sociological realism of the picaresque genre (Rico 1989; Cabo Aseguinolaza 1992), more research is needed on current *picaresque* practices like *gorroneo* that are embedded in the complex ethos of sharing and friendship specific to the Spanish social, cultural and historical context.

7.3 *(Za)chachmęcenie* (Poland)
Alisa Musanovic
Alumna, School of Slavonic and East European Studies, UCL, UK

(Za)chachmęcenie (verbal form *(za)chachmęcić*) is a Polish colloquial term for behaviours ranging from dishonesty to small-scale theft. Broadly defined as doing something 'vague, indistinct, blurred', the inclusion of the prefix *–za* denotes the more specific act of purposefully 'confusing something ... with the intention of concealing some dishonesty' (Online Dictionary, all translations by the author). The same dictionary defines *zachachmęcenie* as an 'appropriation of someone else's property, using someone's inattention'. The concept therefore assumes a dual meaning. All definitions commonly capture the notion of non-transparency and an element of free-riding. Under Communism, the practice was perceived as a coping mechanism constituting a form of self-help. However, the political system today means that the practice may no longer be interpreted as such.

Many became excluded from the utopian Communist project, which meant that far from the projected ideal of equality, Polish society became highly stratified (Pobłocki 2012: 73). Małgorzata Mazurek's interviews with Polish families demonstrate how people responded to scarcity. They directly refer to their use of *chachmęcenie*, noting how informal taxi drivers' engagement with the practice meant that they were able to obtain extra fuel at petrol stations (Mazurek 2012: 303). While Mazurek translates *chachmęcenie* as 'swindling' (Mazurek 2012: 304) – which captures the deceptive element of the practice – the term is perhaps too strong. According to the Cambridge Dictionary, swindling can also include larger-scale theft or fraud, while *chachmęcenie* relates predominantly to small-scale dishonest interactions for gaining access, or obtaining goods, material benefits or services in short supply.

(Za)chachmęcenie is associated with small-scale theft – routine practices of petty pilfering, workplace or part-time crime, siphoning out and hoarding – and with 'carry-out people' (*nesuny*) – employees who steal things from their workplaces. The 'economics of shortage' experienced

under Communism (Kornai, quoted in Mazurek 2012: 299) normalised the range of behaviours and attitudes of 'honesty, which [also] enabled ... petty stealing from the workplace' (Kochanowicz 2004: 75). Indeed, a Polish newspaper pointed out that 'theft' from factories had become so common that it had almost 'achieved the respectability of custom' (Landy 1961: 20). The gap between the official projection of common ownership and people's actual access to resources means that *(za)chachmęcenie* can be conceptualised as 'repossession' of what people were entitled to have. The casual nature of *(za)chachmęcenie* thus suggests that it was an accepted practice among citizens disillusioned with state failure – a response to shortages and uncertainty. This is reflected in ethnographic observations made by Janine Wedel, who noted that 'the system encourages people to behave dishonestly', demonstrating the flexibility of the (il)legality line (Wedel 1986: 151).

Today, continued preoccupations with resourcefulness in Poland suggest that the erosion of state socialism has not equated to an erosion of the mindset, or practical sense, inherent in practices of *(za)chachmęcenie*. Mazurek's interviews with the same families 30 years later indicate that the logic of *chachmęcenie* was 'passed on from one generation to the next' (2012: 306). Such psychological dimensions of the practice can be linked to Kochanowicz's conception of strategies of calculation as sometimes taking place 'at the subconscious level', suggesting that practices became ingrained during socialism and preserved during its political transformation (Kochanowicz 2004: 76). However, similar practices may be traced back beyond socialism.

The etymological origins of the concept relate to the old Polish noun *chachmęt* or *chachmęć* – dating back to the seventeenth century – which denoted a forest thicket or bush (Online Dictionary). The figurative sense of the word which followed – with *chachmęt* becoming synonymous with chaos or confusion – has likely shaped the meaning of the verb as it is understood today: as becoming 'entangled' in a difficult situation (Karaś 2011: 62). The alternative meaning of *zachachmęcenie* which emerged in the twentieth century can be defined as theft in its least serious form. Indeed, 'theft' in Polish can be described as 'combining (*kombinować*), organising ... in the best case to *zachachmęcić*' (Piętkowa 2014: 158). The more morally neutral idea of obtaining rather than stealing suggests a less calculated thought process and more legitimate practice.

Before becoming a general Polish colloquialism, the word belonged only to the Warsaw dialect. The dual meanings of the concept, as well as its Warsaw origins, are depicted in an apt illustration sourced from the website of the Polish National Centre for Culture (Narodowe Centrum Kultury). Entitled 'To steal something (while) in a bush', it portrays a fox entangled in leaves, while carrying the (presumably 'stolen') Palace of Culture and Science in its arms, an allusion to Warsaw.

(Za)chachmęcenie bears resemblance to the Polish practice of *kombinacja (kombinowanje)*. Loosely translated as 'finagling', *kombinacja*, much like *(za)chachmęcenie*, centres around finding creative ways of coping with difficult situations. The Polish peasants' strategic use of *kombinacja* helped them to negotiate power in their localities following the Second World War (Materka 2017: 1). However, the practice of *(za)chachmęcenie* is more specific because of its association with the distinct act of appropriation or theft. Peasants' employment of *kombinacja* as a 'key method' to 'shift the balance of power into peasant hands' also suggests a more long-term, organised strategy operating on a collective level (Materka 2017: 149), as opposed to the more individual and opportunistic act of *(za)chachmęcenie*. Thus, the smaller-scale nature of *(za)chachmęcenie* means that it has a less political connotation. Finally, *(za)chachmęcenie* does not imply an exchange in 'good *kombinacja* relations' (Materka 2017: 8). The idea of being evasive, confusing or manipulative (or simply a thief) inherent in *(za)chachmęcenie* suggests that the practice is more concerned with self-help than it is with mutual interest and accommodation (see *gorroneo*, 7.2 in this volume).

The articulation of knowledge surrounding the practice today suggests that the existence of *(za)chachmęcenie* is firmly established in the Polish popular imagination. Thus, one online platform includes users' views and comparisons of their understandings of the nuances of *zachachmęcenie*, with the discussion thread being viewed 204,239 times (Maziek 2017)! One user suggests that in their locality, the word can be a 'humorous term' to describe 'moving or hiding something, … it is not being used seriously in the event of real theft' (Forum.lem.pl 2017).

The practice has also been alluded to in the literature of the socialist period. In his 1966 poem 'Lament Wysokiego Dygnitarza' (Lament of a High Dignitary), Janusz Szpotański mockingly explores the grievances of a party official who is outraged at having lost his lavish lifestyle. His hero blames this on 'comrade G', a likely reference to Władysław Gomułka, the leader at the time, who *zachachmęcił* his situation (Szpotański 1966). 'Comrade G' is portrayed as responsible for having meddled with the effortless life previously enjoyed by the speaker, who is no longer allowed to socialise with intellectual elites. Overall, the variety in the usage of the term indicates the wealth of interpretations of the practice and multiple contexts that continue to be relevant in present-day Poland.

7.4 **Nokofio** (Ghana)
Dagna Rams
London School of Economics, UK

Nokofio (also *noko fio* and *noko fioo*) is an expression in Ga, the language of the indigenous population of Accra, the capital of Ghana. The direct translation is 'something small'. The term describes gift transfers within patron–client relations and in political life more generally (see also *Pozornost', d'akovné, všimné*, 2.11 Volume 1). A politician might distribute small bills of money or bags of rice to his constituents at the end of a meeting. The status of *nokofio* is the subject of debate – recipients defend it as a benign sign of reciprocity between representatives and their voters, while critics emphasise its degenerative influence on political accountability. Examples of *nokofio* in the Ghanaian media invoke both laughter and alarm. Inciting to give *nokofio* is a subtle art in its own right and includes referring to seniors as 'Daddy' and 'Mummy', casually reminding potential donors that 'it's Saturday' or that 'Christmas is coming', and making inviting hand gestures.

Gift-giving is prevalent in Ghanaian politics. According to Lindberg (2003), of the 72 MP candidates for the 2000 elections he interviewed, 57 claimed to have spent more than 25 per cent of their campaign budget on personalised gifts. Nugent (2007) reports on a candidate purchasing 'footballs to win over constituency youth, … bottles of schnapps for the chief and pots of wine for the "youth"' (2007: 268). The same person insisted that 'nobody would vote for a candidate who did not demonstrate his/her generosity in this way' (2007: 268). A Ghanaian MP for a Ga district was 'accused of wining over the youth by handing out *nokofio* at campaign rallies and other events' (Paller 2019: 210).

Ghana has returned to multipartyism following the former dictator J. J. Rawlings calling elections and becoming democratically elected president in 1992. Since then, Ghana has shown a growing commitment to democratic process and values. The electoral turnout average is 72 per cent. This commitment to civic values makes research into the consequences of gift-giving difficult, as voters might not want to speak openly about the influence of *nokofio* on their electoral choices. Lindberg's (2010) recent study shows that politicians do not monitor whether gifts translate to votes and similarly, Nugent (2007) says 'money cannot literally buy votes under conditions of a secret ballot: at best it can buy goodwill' (2007: 254–5). A growing number of swing voters demonstrates that Ghanaians are voting on performance and are changing their political preferences. The shifts in power prove that oppositional parties are able to sway elections despite having smaller budgets. The 2016 election that was won by the opposition was decided by the biggest margin in Ghana's history, almost 10 per cent compared to the average of 3.8 per cent for the previous elections in the 2000s.

The importance of *nokofio* in political patron–client relations might mark social inequalities in the democratic process. For less affluent voters, gifts represent more gain than for others, and this could mean that the poorest Ghanaians are more responsive to *nokofio* and thus see their political choice as more circumscribed. Yet the literature urges us not to rush to conclusions about the distribution of power in gift-giving relations. Nugent (2007) cites a political candidate complaining about her constituents: '"You go to them and the approach is a sort of a blackmail. If you can't meet their demands, they tell you the thumb is there. They will definitely not vote for you next time"' (Nugent 2007: 268). *Nokofio* is a practice that implicates both givers and receivers – the former for replacing political agendas with individualised gifts and the latter for demanding or accepting this individuation and obscuration of a political contract. The discussion about who is more to blame – givers or receivers – often reaches a stalemate.

Making fun of *nokofio* is an act of democratic atonement popular with comedians. Comedian Ato Kwamena Dadzie launched a fake 'Noko fio' party as part of the KSM show. Among the proposals of the party were: 'giving every Ghanaian a donkey' (although important people will get camels), the president taking 'at least 40 regular Ghanaians' on all of his international visits so that by the end of the term 'at least half of Ghanaians would have travelled abroad', and creating jobs by employing young people to clean up the dung of the numerous new donkeys. The key criticism underpinning the satire is that *nokofio* does not fundamentally change anything for the better, but rather gives fleeting moments of satisfaction to individual needs or desires.

Documenting cases of *nokofio* in broader politics has been key to Ghana's anti-corruption efforts, perhaps most audaciously spearheaded by the country's foremost journalist Anas Aremeyaw Anas. In his two recent exposés, concerning national football and the judiciary, Anas secretly filmed several officials accepting bribes. Films follow a similar plotline. First, gifts exchange hands at the lowest levels of official hierarchy. Of particular resonance with the public at this stage are two types of bribes – goats and yams – as they result in shenanigans which are especially poignant on camera. Goats do not want to cooperate with the bribe-takers and heavy yams are not the easiest to move around. Accra's streets retorted sarcastically to these exchanges: 'something small to feed on' (*nokofio ni gbomo baaye*). As the films progress, the plots reveal acts of corruption and voluminous bribes in the higher echelons of power, implicating high court judges and the President of Ghana Football Association himself. Rather than circulated on the Internet and viewed in the secrecy of one's private home, Anas' films are screened in the National Conference Centre located opposite the country's Parliament. The spectacle arouses mixed reactions. The attitudes of those accepting bribes invoke laughter – a sly expression of the person accepting the bribe and returning the empty envelope in which it came, or accepting a bribe while pretending to sleep – but it also leads to contempt and frustration. The films successfully present *nokofio* that starts at the peripheries of power as a building block for the overall corruption of the system – and it is at once comical and consequential.

Nokofio is proximate to another Ga term, *kpakpakpa*, popularised by a man randomly interviewed on Accra's streets. When asked about the state of the Ghanaian economy, he explained that he gets by because he moves in a '*kpakpakpa* way', which means 'you pass here, you pass here, and then you elaborate yourself'. The term is accentuated by the man's hand gestures that suggest frantic commotion. For the interviewee, this movement is about buying things in one place and selling them in another and thus getting something small in the process. This less politically overt sense of *nokofio* is the subject of the *Noko Fio* TV series that refers to the term to capture the travails of making ends meet in urban Ghana.

7.5 *Chaa pani* (India)
Ajeet Kaur
Alumna, School of Slavonic and East European Studies, UCL, UK

Chaa pani literally means tea and water. The term originates from the Punjab region in the northern part of India (Positivepurchasing.com 2016). The term has a range of connotations, from bribery in business or government, or paying a little extra to get things done, to obtaining a driving licence or visiting a newborn (Campion 2011). Unlike bribery, *chaa pani* is not always associated with injustice, unfairness or anti-democratic activity. The ambivalent term refers to both paying someone off and to an innocent gesture of hospitality. When it refers to making payments, such payments are made with an expectation of receiving a counter-favour, ordinarily not a monetary one.

In India, although often labelled as the world's largest democracy, informality remains a key part of socio-economic contexts, from informal settlements to the culture of personalised trust. India has strong foundations in unofficial communities and in what is known but not addressed in human interaction. Common informal practices in India include *jaan pehchaan*, using one's social network to further oneself, and *hawala*, an informal money exchange. *Chaa pani* is thought of as legitimate if it takes the form of small-scale informal payments, but not bribery. *Chaa pani* is a gentler version of the more direct term *rishwat*, which translates into the pejorative term for a corrupt bribe. Unlike *rishwat*, the meaning of *chaa pani* is determined by the listener. If used in business or governance, *chaa pani* does not directly point to involvement in corruption, but it does suggest self-interested behaviour or competitive advantage within potentially corrupt institutions. While an informal payment might offer a solution to a person in need, it also creates a problem – a bribe disrupts legitimacy, undermines democracy and subverts the impartial workings of institutions. As both a solution and a problem, *chaa pani* reinforces functional ambivalence (Merton 1977: 92).

Chaa pani draws many semantic similarities to concepts such as the Spanish *mordida* (bite), Arabic *basheesh* (a gift, tip or gratuity), Malaysian *duit kopi* (coffee money), sub-Saharan *l'argent du carburant* and French *pot-de-vin*. These all refer to small sums of money, expressed to include an offer of food or drink. These euphemisms make use of the comfort associated with accepting food, hospitality and tipping, as opposed to the greed and selfishness ordinarily associated with corruption. This distinction is reflected in the difference between 'need corruption' and 'greed corruption' (Bauhr 2016: 561–81). *Rishwat* is an example of the latter as it implies bad traits, injustice, free-riding and the betrayal of trust. In contrast, *chaa pani*, an ambivalent term that helps informal practices remain socially pervasive and acceptable, is an example of the former.

Typical examples of this exchange can be found on the global map of bribe-giving (@IPaidABribe 2019), which shows that the department where bribery was most prevalent in India was the police force. Sixty per cent of all reported bribes involved the police. Integral to the problem of bribery in India is an underlying structural flaw whereby law enforcement agents facilitate and often demand some form of *chaa pani*, suggesting extortion. Data has been collected on 197,740 reports of bribery across India, where 38,130 bribes were paid. The website also reports on circumstances where individuals refuse to pay in a customary way, and documents 3,560 bribes as being resisted (@IPaidABribe 2019).

According to a 2019 report on @IPaidABribe, two police officers stopped a college student on a motorbike and a lorry driver. Neither had documents for the vehicles they were driving. The lorry driver promptly offered the policemen *chaa pani* and the officers let him go. The college student had borrowed his friend's bike and had his driving licence, so when the policemen asked for a payment, he questioned the request. The alleged lack of cooperation from the college student led to him being escorted to the police station for misbehaviour. Non-compliance with a demand to pay a bribe was treated as a punishable offence. Such institutionalised corruption normalises practices of *chaa pani* and makes it difficult to seek an alternative.

Formally, bribery is illegal in the state of India under the Prevention of Corruption Act 2018 and is punishable by up to seven years in prison (Bhaskar 2018: 5). It appears that the Indian government has taken a tough approach towards those engaging in the act of bribery. However, in reality police and investigation authorities are allowed to investigate public servants only when they have received official permission to do so. Inequality in the face of the law, as well as heavy punishment levied on bribe givers in contrast to the bribe-takers, is widely seen as unfair and conducive to 'bribe harassment', whereby a bribe is demanded for services one is entitled to receive for free (Basu 2011: 4). For example, an income tax refund may be withheld until the individual provides adequate payment to the officer. The system criminalises bribe givers even when they report an officer receiving the bribe. The police view such reports as a confession and proceed to punish them (Basu 2011). Although shifting the focus away from the bribe-takers has been debated by anti-corruption scholars, adopting such an approach in practice seems counterproductive as it discourages people from reporting bribery. By interpreting reports of bribery as confessions, officials are accommodating the systemic corruption that frames and facilitates practices of *chaa pani*. The Indian anti-corruption measures seem largely unsuccessful.

Chaa pani in India and similar practices worldwide seem to fall under the radar of global anti-corruption efforts. Websites such as @IPaidABribe, based on grassroots reporting, are key in identifying the degree of systemic corruption which would otherwise be hidden. They also provide an indication of statistics which are less prone to the bias of organisations collecting the data. Yet ultimately, the only way to tackle such informality is to take a top-down approach aimed at fundamentally changing the social norm. Such an approach requires a united front of the government, businesses and social institutions, as well as the political will to condemn the bribe give-and-take practices, while creating non-corrupt channels through which people can satisfy their basic needs. This idea was encapsulated in the proposal that the government of India should strive to work with the bribe giver in order to persecute the bribe receiver (Basu 2011: 4). The fundamental issue in India is that informal payments constitute the social norm, rather than the exception.

7.6 *Duit kopi* (Malaysia)
Christian Giordano
Institute of Social Anthropology, University of Fribourg, Switzerland

Duit kopi, a Malaysian term for 'coffee money', stands for giving money with the expectation of receiving a counter-favour, although generally not a monetary one. In Bahasa Malaysia, *duit* is a very broad term for money, cash in particular, and *kopi* is the local name for coffee. The term *duit kopi* is a metaphorical and metonymical formula for a brief informal transaction between two individuals who do not know each other. It is a euphemism since it reformulates the cruder term *rasuah*, the semantically more exhaustive but pejorative notion of corruption or bribe, into a more specific and more acceptable concept. *Duit kopi* does not point directly to a corruptive action, yet there is a logical contiguity between the two: the implication of an illegal monetary transaction. As a rule, this is a one-off event that will not occur again between the same actors.

An illuminating case is the relationship between drivers and traffic police. Candid video footage shot in Malaysia shows several examples of how drivers, especially those in heavy-duty vehicles, are pulled over by the police for an actual or alleged violation. A veiled invitation to open negotiations in order to avoid a fine may begin with the phrase, '*So, macam mana mau selesai?*' ('How do we settle this?'). After a ritualised transaction, the two actors reach an agreement on the amount of the *duit kopi* to overlook the actual or purported violation, which will be lower than the potential fine. *Duit kopi* does not apply to serious criminal acts.

Foreign drivers, especially white European or American drivers, are exempt from *duit kopi* due to the assumption that they do not speak the language and are unaware of local knowledge. Traffic police officers may either disregard them or pull them over to give them a peremptory lecture without a fine. Behind the ostensibly magnanimous gesture is the risk of losing face or the fear that the foreigner may report them to a higher-ranking officer, thus publicly divulging open secrets to which the authorities turn a blind eye. The police officers' behaviour towards foreigners is also steered by national pride. Giving the impression of requesting *duit kopi*, especially from a white person, could be interpreted as reconfirming old prejudices and stereotypes fostered by the British during the colonial domination of Malaysia. While the illegal practice of *duit kopi* is considered unethical, it is accepted, practised and legitimated by local knowledge.

Based on their research in West Africa, Giorgio Blundo and Jean-Pierre Olivier de Sardan distinguish seven basic forms of corruption: gratuity, commission of illicit service, string-pulling, favours and nepotism, unwarranted fee for a public service, levy or toll, 'white-collar crime' and misappropriation (2006). The Malaysian *duit kopi* may be regarded as a form of tax or toll that these authors have termed a 'racket' – a specific solicitation that is difficult to avoid. Being an implicit imposition, it is expressed by means of everyday semantic codes and the request is perceived by the payer as a parasitic strategy or as an unsophisticated way of cadging money.

The practice of *duit kopi* has clear semantic analogies with the French *pot-de-vin* and the African French *argent pour la bière, argent du thé, argent du café* (Blundo and de Sardan 2006), and functional analogies with the Italian *bustarella* and the Greek *fakelaki* (see also *mordida*, 2.13 Volume 1). *Duit kopi*, however, may also be perceived as a form of micro-extortion and has a pejorative connotation. Its negative repute is reflected in the phrase *nak duit kopi lah tu*, rendered as *hey, listen, don't give away coffee money* – a sincere piece of advice shared among close friends.

Malaysian phraseology regarding corruption is highly diversified. The expressions *makan duit* and *lesen kopi* are semantically related to *duit kopi*. *Makan duit* literally translates as 'eating money' (from *makan*, to eat) and stands for receiving or accepting a bribe, usually a small amount. *Lesen kopi* can be translated as *licence coffee* and refers to a 'voluntary but compulsory' incentive or cash gift to obtain a driving licence (Wai 2017). These terms are typical of petty corruption phenomena, which James Scott (1972) defines as parochial corruption as opposed to market corruption. Yet, differences inherent to this dichotomy should not be overemphasised since market corruption, too, is based on networks of personalised and informal social relationships that can be regarded as parochial.

Malaysia is considered a multi-ethnic and multicultural country. Malaysia's three main ethnic groups are the Muslim Malay majority (the 'children of the soil', the *bumiputra*), the Taoist-Buddhist-Confucian Chinese of Hokkien, Cantonese, Hakka, Teochew and Hainanese origin, and the Indian, mostly Hindu Shivaite Tamil (the *non-bumiputra* or 'immigrants'). Despite its remarkable everyday tolerance, for which Malaysia is often regarded as a plural society, a society characterised by 'two or more elements or social orders which live side by side, yet without mingling, in one political unit' (Furnivall 1944), Malaysia is still an ethnically divided society, with permanent tensions, but no serious interethnic conflict (Giordano 2012). The ethnic groups lead parallel social lives. Although Bahasa Malaysia is the national language and compulsory in the schooling system, the communities use their specific vernacular idioms, which may be highly diversified even within a single group. Ultimately, English remains the spoken lingua franca, though it often takes on local peculiarities so that it is also known as *Manglish*. Despite the remarkable cultural and linguistic diversity, the phraseology of the parochial corruption, such as *duit kopi*, used by every ethnic community is generally expressed in Bahasa Malaysia. Some expressions may be enriched with specific terms, from Chinese in particular, thus generating syncretic and creolised versions.

7.7 **Aumento** (Lowland South America)
Daniela Peluso
School of Anthropology and Conservation, University of Kent, UK

The term *aumento* refers to acceptable forms of corruption in Lowland South America. Related practices operate within the informal economy, an underbelly of the formal economy (Peluso 2018). When individuals are required to make cash payments in excess of what is formally required of them in order to get things done, it is referred to as an *aumento*. Though derived from *aumentar*, 'to increase, augment or expand', in its local usage the term *aumento* is best translated as 'a little more', 'something extra', or a 'top-up'.

Aumento designates an informal cash payment to achieve a goal or desire. Such payments are common in order to establish or maintain social relations and constitute a preferred and amicable way of interacting or 'doing business'. For example, in marketplaces where one can purchase fresh tropical juice, it is common for the vendor to offer 'a little bit more' than a standard serving. Thus, upon finishing one's glass, the vendor will generally smile and say, '*Aumento?*' This simple gesture signals the possibility of building a mutually beneficial relationship of long-term loyalty. A little extra goes a long way, often ensuring the return of the customer. It is thus a means of building both social and financial capital. Inversely, if the vendor does not offer a 'little bit extra', this implies that he or she is not dependent upon the return of the customer. This can happen in cases where the vendor has minimal competition.

Figure 7.7.1 The transportation of illegal wood. © Felipe Werneck/IBAMA.

On a larger scale, *aumento* is used as a euphemism for corrupt practices in timber and logging operations in Lowland South America. Logging companies supply wood from their land as an *aumento*, a top-up to their current provisions, often tied to sustainability regulations. In turn, Amazonians receive their own *aumento* as a cash payment for providing wood that often does not go through formal regulatory channels. The payment they receive for this is less than the open market rate, while the logging companies avoid the extra costs associated with sustainable logging without jeopardising their eco-status.

To comply with inspections by naval officers, the national police or border patrol, individuals must often pay a *coima*, a bribe that is a fraction of the cost of the permit or management plan that is required as part of the formal legal logging protocols (Bridenthal 2013; Stahl 2018). *Coima* is viewed as a necessary payment for bypassing complex forestry regulations, paperwork and fees that would otherwise render most small-scale logging impossible (Peluso 2018).

Indigenous Amazonians have lived in communal territories and cared for different sections of their collective land for generations, therefore they assume that the timber belongs to them. The imposed management plans and logging permits – which, in turn, require the hiring of forestry engineers and involve various bureaucratic procedures – push individuals onto illegal paths. Indigenous people refer to the timber that they deliver to the sawmill of a logging company as an *aumento* to their income. At the sawmill, buyers and sellers alike speak of timber as being 'a little bit extra' as it satisfies the interests of both parties. Indigenous people are aware that these companies claim to follow sustainable practices and receive certification seals for sustainable harvesting.

Despite such credentials, logging companies are eager to acquire additional wood. Indigenous Amazonians say that 'the loggers want their *aumento*' or 'we are providing their *aumento*'. Like those who seek a *coima*, the logging companies are perceived to be helping indigenous people avoid unnecessary bureaucracy. A lower rate of payment is thus accepted for the illegal wood; it is 'extra' money they would otherwise not have. Thus, indigenous people pay 'extra' so as to provide the logging company with their 'extra'. For the sawmill, this illegal timber is 'extra' to the legally sourced timber they deal in and outside of legitimate paths of commerce. This symmetry in language reflects positive social relations and exchange. The 'extra' compensates for what both indigenous individuals and timber workers consider to be unfair and hindering regulation and surveillance by the state. These arrangements continue an ongoing historical legacy of exploitative trade practices towards indigenous lowland South Americans. Yet individuals are confident that by circumventing the rules they can produce a net gain in what is otherwise an uneven playing field.

What might be seen as corrupt from a normative perspective is viewed locally as an exchange of favours (Ledeneva 1998, 2014; Henig and Makovicky 2017). It has parallels in colonial and postcolonial debt systems and related patronage arrangements (Quiroz 2008). Examples of these are *habilitación* in Spanish and *aviamiento* in Portuguese. Whereas the analysis of debt peonage as exploitative is well established, there is also a growing literature that emphasises the mutually beneficial possibilities of the practice (Bauer 1979; Eisenstadt and Roniger 1984; Walker 2012). Extractive economies in Lowland South America have relied upon local knowledge and labour, particularly during and immediately following the first rubber boom of 1879–1912 (Peluso 2014). They have been built on the exchange of housing and credit for work and debt and by facilitating lenders' access to the forest and labourers' access to the cities. Even now, patronage continues to be important in Amazonia, especially in areas far from urban centres (Peluso 2015).

The logging industry is one arena in which patron–client relations continue to thrive. Companies have been seen to present a convincing façade on their international websites, proclaiming their corporate values and social responsibility mission statement. But locally, in places such as Madre de Dios, they thrive on underpaid informal labour involving various forms of contemporary patronage. The role of the patron was, and continues to be, based on advancing loans – in goods and/or cash – in exchange for the guaranteed provision of timber. The debts that local people incur often exceed what they earn.

These patron–client relationships are also intertwined with wider networks of exchange, such as *compadrazgo* (Pinedo 2013: 36; Ledeneva et al. 2018). These networks are seen as a positive part of indigenous moral economies. Social relations are formed through a long-term series of exchanges that underpin economic sustainability in times of hardship. For these reasons, context is key to understanding the relationships between informality, inequality and corruption (Nel 2019). Participation in such social relations is what constitutes moral personhood in Lowland South America (Londoño Sulkin 2005). It can furthermore be viewed as one of the creative forms through which corrupt practices are normalised in Latin America (Goldstein and Drybread 2018). Where bureaucracy, according to Hertzfeld, tends to dehumanise its participants, lowland South Americans use moral-economic practices to recover the humanity that bureaucracy affronts (Herzfeld 1993; Peluso 2018). Part and parcel of moral-economic exchanges, *aumentos* help to restore individually and collectively the moral selfhood that dehumanising bureaucracies otherwise negatively impact.

7.8 *Pari pod masata* (Bulgaria)
Kristina Tsabala
Alumna, School of Slavonic and East European Studies, UCL, UK

Pari pod masata is a colloquial term in Bulgarian that refers to informal payments to public officials. It literally translates as 'money under the table', 'money under the counter' or 'under-the-counter-payments'. These informal payments made by citizens to public servants consist of cash and/or commodities for favours in the public sector (health care, administration, education and customs). The favour provided by the public servant takes the form of preferential treatment such as faster provision, ensured quality, or evasion of state regulations. On the one hand, it is related to the shadow economy because it is an unregulated transaction and represents administrative and civil misbehaviour. On the other hand, 'money under the table' is associated with 'tipping' and 'gift-giving' because it is culturally acceptable in Bulgaria to express gratitude materially to the servant for his/her time and attention (Grodeland et al. 2000: 309). The prominence of this practice was documented in the European Commission's annual report for 2019 where Bulgaria was at the top of the list in the EU for the size of informal payments in the health care sector (European Commission 2019: 56). *Pari-pod-masta* is far from unique. Analogous practices can be found in Greece (*fakelaki*), Latvia (*aploksne*), Hungary (*halapénz*), the Middle East and North Africa (*baksheesh*).

Although studies of informal payments only began to be reported after 1989, films and literature have described *pari pod masata* transactions during the socialist regime. Due to the shortage of commodities, *gifts* were a widespread practice that recognised the official's personality outside of his/her job and aimed at establishing a personal relationship that would later lead to the use of informal networks, known in Bulgaria as *vruzki* (Chavdarova 2018: 64–7). The comedy *Toplo* (Warmth) of 1978 illustrates the hardships of installing a central heating system in a building in Sofia's city centre. In the scene where the residents of the building discuss what they need to do in order to submit the application for the installation to the city council, they state that they had filled out the forms and collected the *pari pod masata* (Yanchev 1978). This scene implies that if they do not provide the informal payment alongside the necessary documents, their application would not be delivered to the appropriate officials.

The transition to market economy after 1989 is commonly seen as the catalyst of informal payments in Bulgaria. Economic reforms during the 1990s intensified the popularity of informal transactions and in-kind payments due to the unstable socio-economic situation caused by market liberalisation. The frequency of informal payments is also associated with the presence of clientelism (*vruzki*) because informal transactions are used in the absence of informal networks.

The economic crisis of 1997 in Bulgaria set a precedent on alternative transactions. Due to rapid inflation the Bulgarian lev fell in value overnight. Consequently, public servants started to refuse cash payments and required alternative commodities, especially food. Thus, goods and cash became mutually substitutable. In 2000, the Bulgarian government introduced a reform that was expected to regulate informal payments in health care (Stepurko et al. 2013: 420). The reform consisted of installing additional formal co-payments for the health services in the benefits package. Nevertheless, a survey of 1,003 people in July 2010 showed that 20 per cent of the respondents had paid informally in cash in the past year and 45 per cent of them had given gifts in-kind (Atanasova et al. 2013: 733). This can be considered an improvement given that in 1997,

86 per cent of the respondents thought that 'it is impossible to obtain adequate health care without giving *bribes*' (Balabanova and McKee 2002: 264, emphasis added).

Pari pod masata identifies extortion when public officials act as gatekeepers. For example, medical officials can also require the payment of an unofficial fee in exchange for general access to free treatment. Similarly, during the 1990s' transition to market economy, the low salaries of public administrative officials led them to demand unwarranted fees for obtaining a document, state provisions, or filing institutional enquiries (Grodeland et al. 1997: 655). Public servants resorting to extortion might abuse their power even further by establishing an informal 'levy' (*red tape*) or 'toll' (Blundo and Olivier de Sardan 2006: 77). This is most frequently reported in relation to custom officials who act as informal tax collectors over travellers' possessions (Kirov 2014). A custom official can earn between 900 and 1,200 euros for a shift at the border with Serbia (24Chasa 2020). They demand informal payments to allow people to access certain administrative and state entities without confiscating anything, regardless of the legality of passengers' belongings.

In the health care sector, *pari-pod-masta* might be offered to the doctor by the patient or his relatives in order to receive quicker access to the service or to ensure the good quality of the treatment. If the payment is given in advance (ex ante), then it bears the resemblance of a bribe. However, the payment can also represent a gift when it is given at the end (ex post) of the treatment, to show gratitude. This conceptual timeframe is important because it differentiates bribes from gifts. Nevertheless, an ex-post payment becomes ex ante for a future exchange, transforming the gift into a bribe (Moldovan and Van de Walle 2013: 386). Expensive gifts might create preferential relationships between the parties. The Bulgarian Physicians' Union officially differentiated between ex-ante and ex-post payments, and the latter was described as ethical (Delcheva et al. 1997: 91).

In the public education sector, *pari pod masata* takes the form of unreported donations for the educational institutions that lack state funding. It is common practice for public schools in Bulgaria to require unofficial donations from parents to improve infrastructures and facilities. These payments are destined for repairs, heating, events, presents, the purchase of extra materials and participation in extracurricular activities. These so-called donations are unregulated but sometimes mandatory.

In 2001, 34 per cent of the population considered informal payments as an unchangeable aspect of the country's culture (Grodeland et al. 2001: 140). Gift-giving, in particular, was seen as legitimate because it is a means to express gratitude and respect to the public servant. Media coverage of informal payments peaked at the turn of the century when major anti-corruption legislation was introduced, and the debates regarding informal payments entered the public discourse following international scandals. For instance, in 2002 Greece declared that it would not accept higher education diplomas issued from Bulgarian universities because of the widespread bribes in the sector. According to media investigations, in the 2000s the cost of passing an exam was between 150 and 300 USD (Coalition 2000 and Center for the Study of Democracy [CSD] 2005: 14). Nowadays, informal payments remain widespread: The Global Corruption Barometer for 2019 reported that 12 per cent of public service users had paid a bribe in the past year (Transparency International 2019). Unregulated donations, showing gratitude to teachers, doctors and officials is still considered a cultural phenomenon rather than immoral behaviour.

7.9 *Otkat vizy* (Russia)
Olga Tkach
Department of Social Sciences, University of Helsinki, Finland

This text was written in 2020, when the practice described had been put on hold since the beginning of the COVID-19 pandemic and the establishment of restrictions for non-EU travellers. It disappeared completely with the full-scale invasion of Russia into Ukraine in February 2022. The phenomenon thus remained in the past.

Otkat vizy is a colloquial Russian phrase that literally means 'taking visa for a ride' and describes the tourist practice of crossing the border for a short visit or one-day shopping trip with the purpose of collecting border stamps and fulfilling the requirements to use a long-term visa properly. This practice is widespread among citizens of the regions of north-west Russia, especially St. Petersburg and the surrounding Leningrad Oblast, in close proximity to eastern Finland. In contrast to other regions of the Russian Federation, St. Petersburg residents enjoy relatively easy access to Finland, developed cross-border transport service and fairly relaxed requirements for acquiring a short-term Schengen visa. Official residents of the region can apply for a short-stay 'C' visa for up to 90 days per half-year, based on a reduced set of documents: (1) international passport with at least six months' remaining validity, (2) completed application form with a photo and (3) travel health insurance. They are not required to submit supporting documents, such as a statement of employment, salary slips, bank statements, proof of real estate property, proof of hotel reservation, or return travel tickets, yet these can be requested from an applicant (Dekalchuk 2014: 11).

In fact, a short-stay multiple-entry Schengen visa, issued by the state of Finland to the residents of its neighbouring region of St. Petersburg, opens up a travel opportunity towards the other 25 EU countries that can be visited via Finland or directly from St. Petersburg. The Schengen Agreement does not stipulate how many days can be spent in each Schengen country. There is a somewhat obscure conditionality to enter the Schengen Area via Finland when using this visa for the first time and this resulted in the practice of 'opening the visa' (*otkrytie vizy*), that is, making a first entry to the Schengen Area via Finland. The related practice of *otkat vizy*, that is, collecting the required stamps by going back and forth from Russia to Finland, therefore, balancing countries of destination with a Finnish priority has become a common way to satisfy the requirements for the Schengen visa. As the 'stamp in a passport' cannot be confirmed as the legitimate and justified purpose of the trip at passport control, the border crossers hide the real purpose of their visits under the pretext of shopping (Studzińska et al. 2018: 122).

Conceptually, *otkat vizy* is the case of 'documentary practices' (Navaro-Yashin 2007) of mobility, or in other words, keeping the letter of the law to exercise the freedom of movement in Europe. Indeed, the travelling practices of the visa-dependent people display a repetitive pattern of cross-border activities that turn highly regulated border controls and visa formalities to their advantage, while also adhering to formal requirements. Other practices include: multiple border crossing to (ab)use a legal duty-free allowance and import goods (see also *mrówki* in small-scale smuggling, 5.25 Volume 1), or the so-called 'marriage of convenience' in order to obtain a visa for regular travel to a more prosperous country (for example. Brennan 2003; Kraler et al. 2011: 221–83). Migrants also use border-crossing strategies to renew a visa/permit of the host country (for example, Green 2015; Schenk 2018: 193). Such patterns can serve long-term and pendulum migration, as well as short-term mobility, which often goes under the radar in migration studies. Much less is known about visa policies and border experiences in contexts, not associated with smuggling, complex borders, ethnicity or entrepreneurship. Yet they have important implications.

For example, the mass *otkat vizy* at the Russia–Finland border has multiple consequences for politics, the economy and everyday life for both countries. Member states at the edge of the EU can individually

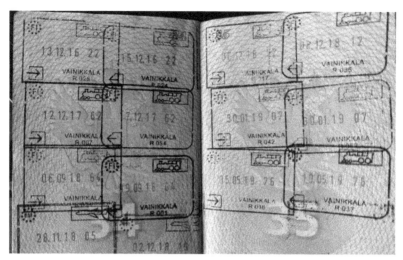

Figure 7.9.1 The practice of *visa running*. © Olga Tkach.

negotiate agreements on local border traffic with neighbouring non-EU countries. By simplifying visa regulations with north-west Russia, the Finnish state balances its commitment to Schengen standards with its national interests. Mass visa issuance and cross-border shopping activities of Russian visitors, interested in *otkat vizy* much more than shopping, boost the local trade and regional development of eastern Finland that had suffered from its geographical and border-induced peripherality, both in Finland and Europe overall (see Eskelinen et al. 2013: 47–113).

The Russia–Finland cross-border tourism industry has flourished since the 2000s, leading to the opening of the Finnish visa application centre in 2011 and the development of a wide net of travel agencies and transport companies. One can easily organise a trip from St. Petersburg to most destinations in Finland, with a choice of a high-speed commuter train, a ferry, luxury or low-cost buses, door-to-door minibuses and cars, car-sharing services, or even a free round-trip bus service in return for spending 100 euro in a shopping mall on the Finnish side of the border.

The number of crossings at the Finnish–Russian land border has grown from 1.3 million in 1991 to 8.4 million in 2010 (Eskelinen et al. 2013: 53). Since the early 2000s, the trend of short trips to this destination continues: 81 per cent of the trips lasted less than eight hours and 94 per cent of the visitors crossed the border at least once a month (Eskelinen et al. 2013: 53). In the late 2000s, about 70 per cent of all

Ночной прокат визы (от Озерков)	20:00	Ср Пт	от 1800 руб.
СПб-Хельсинки (от адреса)	5:55 22:55	ежедневно	от 1390 руб.
Хельсинки-СПб (до адреса)	10:00, 12:00, 14:00, 16:00, 18:00, 20:00	ежедневно	от 1390 руб.
Хельсинки-СПб (до адреса)	21:00, 22:00, 0:00, 2:00	ежедневно	1990 руб.
Шоп-Тур в Лаппеенранту (от адреса)	06:00	Пн. Вт. Ср. Чт. Пт. Сб. Вс.	от 1500 руб. 1600 руб.
Спб-Хамина/Котка (от адреса)	5:55 22:55	ежедневно	от 1190 руб.
Хамина/Котка-Спб (до адреса)	11:00-12:00, 13:00-14:00, 15:00-16:00 17:00-18:00, 19:00-20:00, 21:00-22:00	ежедневно	от 1190 руб.
Котка/Хамина-Спб (до адреса)	23:00 - 00:00	ежедневно	от 1790 руб.
Маршрутка в аэропорт Лаппеенранта	05:00 06:00 07:00 15:00	Ср. Вс. Вс. Ср. Ср. Сб.	1090 руб. 2000 руб.*
Маршрутка из аэропорта Лаппеенранта	10:30 14:00 21:30 12:00	Ср. Вс. Ср. Ср. Сб. Вс.	1090 руб. 2000 руб.*
Трансфер в Лаппеенранту/Иматру (от адреса)	5:30 - 06:00	ежедневно	от 1300 руб.
Трансфер из Лаппеенранты/Иматры (до адреса)	10:00 -12:00, 12:00 -14:00,	ежедневно	от 1300 руб.
Финляндия на 1 час (м.Пл.Восстания, Черная речка)	8:30 - 8:45	Сб. Вс.	1000 руб.
Финляндия на час (без заезда в Лаппеенранту)	5:30 - 06:00	Пн. Вт. Ср. Чт. Пт. Сб. Вс.	от 1500 руб.

Figure 7.9.2 Example of a bus fare list doing daily trips to Finland.
© SPD Lider/spb-tury.ru/raspisanie.

border crossings were same-day tours to Finnish border towns, such as Imatra or Lappeenranta (Studzińska et al. 2018: 122). By 2019, the number of passengers crossing the Finnish eastern border from Russia had exceeded 9.5 million (Findicator 2020).

Qualitative research on selected St. Petersburg residents has shown how the holders of the unified Schengen multiple-entry 'C' visas issued by the state of Finland balance their trips to Finland with other trips to the Schengen Area (Tkach 2021). Interviewed via in-depth semi-structured discussions, the 28 regular travellers reported that *otkat vizy* practices reduced travellers' visa anxiety. By 'imitating' tourism to Finland, even if for short periods, they ensure the right to travel elsewhere in Europe without the additional hustle and costs for visa applications.

These trips can begin at about 4.00 a.m., when the bus driver picks up passengers across St. Petersburg, and end past midnight. The border crossers spend almost the whole day on a bus, moving from one shop to another. It may cost around 15–30 euros for a round bus trip in addition to purchases. Tourism to 'good old Europe' is seen as a reward for the compulsory visits to border towns in Finland that many perceive as shopping trips rather than travel abroad. In fact, *otkat vizy* operates as an aspect of care for the unified Schengen multi-visa that, although partially and fragmentarily, equates St. Petersburg residents as non-EU travellers to Europeans. The purpose of local tourism is dual as it also facilitates tourism deeper into Europe. From September 2019, the visa process requires two additional documents: a preliminary plan of the trip and proof of financial means, but these did not make the procedure more difficult. Finnish authorities mirror the 'imitation of tourism' by imitating tougher constraints on issuing visas, yet without much detriment to their local economy.

The practice of *otkat vizy* illustrates the multi-dimensional nature of border regimes that serve supranational, national and regional policies highlighting the significance of small-scale interactions. Its façade conceals a strategic use of formal institutions of visa and border control, which is beneficial for both sides. It becomes economically and symbolically crucial for the eastern part of Finland, particularly for the towns close to the Russian border. It also maximises mobility chances to the Schengen Area of the Russian citizens, which is of great value for them as 'third-country nationals' with a relatively low passport index.

Bibliography to Chapter 7

Introduction: trickster
Mark Lipovetsky

Alexopoulos, G.1998. 'Portrait of a Con Artist as a Soviet Man'. *Slavic Review* 57: 4: 774–90.

Bakhtin, M. M. 1981. *The Dialogic Imagination: Four Essays*. Edited by M. Holquist. Translated by C. Emerson and M. Holquist. Austin: University of Texas Press.

Derrida, J. 1981. *Dissemination*. Translated and with an introduction by B. Johnson. London: The Athlone Press.

Doty, W. G. and Hynes, W. J. 1993. 'Historical Overview of Theoretical Issues: The Problem of the Trickster'. In *Mythical Trickster Figures: Contours, Contexts, and Criticisms*, edited by W. J. Hynes, 13–32. Tuscaloosa and London: University of Alabama Press.

Fitzpatrick, S. 2005. *Tear Off the Masks! Identity and Imposture in Twentieth-Century Russia*. Princeton and Oxford: Princeton University Press.

Gates, H. L., Jr. 1998. *The Signifying Monkey*. New York: Oxford University Press.

Havel, V. 1985. 'The Power of the Powerless'. *International Journal of Politics*, 15: 3–4: 23–96.

Hyde, L. 1998. *Trickster Makes This World: Mischief, Myth, and Art*. New York: North Point Press.

Hynes, W. J. (ed.) 1993. *Mythical Trickster Figures: Contours, Contexts, and Criticisms*. Edited by W. J. Hynes. Tuscaloosa and London: University of Alabama Press.

Jurich, M. 1998. *Scheherazade's Sisters: Trickster Heroines and Their Stories in World Literature*. Westport, CT: Greenwood Press.

Ledeneva, A. V. 1998. *Russia's Economy of Favours: Blat, Networking and Informal Exchange*. Cambridge and London: Cambridge University Press.

Mills, M. A. 2001. 'The Gender of the Trick: Female Tricksters and Male Narrators'. *Asian Folklore Studies* 60(2): 237–58.

Otto, B. K. 2001. *Fools are Everywhere: The Court Jesters Around the World*. Chicago and London: University of Chicago Press.

Pelton, R. D. 1980. *The Trickster in West Africa: A Study in Mythic Irony and Sacred Delight*. Berkeley, Los Angeles, London: University of California Press.

Radin, P. 1956. *The Trickster: A Study in American Indian Mythology, with Commentaries by Karl Kerényi and C. G. Jung*. New York: Schocken Books.

Sinyavsky, A. 2007. *Ivan the Fool: Russian Folk Belief. A Cultural History*. Translated by J. Turnbull and N. Formozov. Moscow: Glas.

Sloterdijk, P. 1987. *Critique of Cynical Reason*. Translated by M. Eldred. Foreword by A. Huyssen. Minneapolis: University of Minnesota Press.

Turner, V. 1969. *The Ritual Process: Structure and Anti-Structure*. Chicago: Aldine Publishing Company.

Žižek, S. 1997. *The Plague of Fantasies*. London, New York: Verso.

7.1 *Chanchullo* (Central America)
Denise Dunlap and Jose Godinez

Cabiese Donoso. 2019. 'El chanchullo constitucional', 18 December. www.elciudadano.com/especiales/chiledesperto/el-chanchullo-constitucional/12/18/

Coronado, E. and Monzón, K. 2019. 'Absuelven al hijo y al hermano del presidente Jimmy Morales en caso Botín en el Registro de la Propiedad'. *Prensa Libre*, 19 August. www.prensalibre.com/guatemala/justicia/absuelven-a-hijo-y-hermano-de-presidente-jimmy-morales-en-caso-botin-en-el-registro-de-la-propiedad/

Diccionario Libre. 2020. 'Chanchullo'. *Diccionario Libre*, 4 November. http://diccionariolibre.com/definicion/chanchullo

Escobar, L. 2019. 'Trecsa, por mi casa no pasa'. El Periódico, 5 June. https://web.archive.org/web/20210214010817/https://elperiodico.com.gt/opinion/columnistas/2019/06/05/trecsa-por-mi-casa-no-pasa/

Fang, L. and Mackey, D. 2017. 'The President of Honduras is Deploying U.S.-trained Forces Against Election Protesters'. *The Intercept*, 3 December. https://theintercept.com/2017/12/03/the-president-of-honduras-is-deploying-u-s-trained-forces-against-election-protesters/

Gomez-Estrada. 2016. 'Elite de Estado y prácticas políticas: Una aproximación al estudio de la corrupción en México, 1920–1934'. *Estudios de Historia Moderna y Contemporánea de México*, 52: 52–68.

Saenz, E. 2019. 'Chanchullo con los precios del combustible'. *Despacho 505*, 31 March. http://despacho505.com/el-chanchullo-con-los-precios-del-combustible/

Vanguardia. 2017. 'Estafas y empresas piramidales que afectan a los jovenes (parte 2)'. *Vanguardia*, 27 February. https://web.archive.org/web/20180604221514/https://www.vanguardiasv.net/index.php/nacionales/politica-economia/item/821-estafas-y-empresas-piramidales-que-acechan-a-los-jovenes-parte-ii

Varon, A. B. 2015. 'Diccionario de la terminologia politica colombiana'. Master's thesis. *Universita degli studio di Salerno, Italia*. https://repository.ucatolica.edu.co/server/api/core/bitstreams/97bd918d-bc53-4437-b1b2-211b12353a28/content

7.2 *Gorroneo* (Spain and Hispanic America)
Ignacio Fradejas-García

Cabo Aseguinolaza, F. 1992. *El Concepto de Género y La Literatura Picaresca*. Santiago de Compostela: Servicio de Publicaciones e Intercambio Científico de la Universidad de Santiago de Compostela.
Forum.lem.pl. 2017. 'Stanisław Lem – Forum'. https://forum.lem.pl/index.php?topic=1107.1005
Goffman, E. 1983. 'The Interaction Order'. *American Sociological Review* 48: 1–17.
González Holguín, D. 1608. 'Gorrón'. In *Vocabvlario de La Lengva General de Todo El Perv Llamada Lengua Qquichua, o Del Inca*. Lima, imprenta de Francisco del Canto. www.letras.ufmg.br/padrao_cms/documentos/profs/romulo/VocabvlarioQqichuaDeHolguin1607.pdf
Ledeneva, A. 2018. *The Global Encyclopaedia of Informality. Understanding Social and Cultural Complexity, Volume 2*. London: UCL Press.
Narodowe Centrum Kultury, 'Zachachmęcić Coś W Chachmęci' (To Steal Something (while) in a Bush), illustrated by Marcelina Jarnuszkiewicz. https://nck.pl/projekty-kulturalne/projekty/ojczysty-dodaj-do-ulubionych/ciekawostki-jezykowe/ZACHACHMECIC_cos_w_CHACHMECI
Real Academia Española. 2019. 'Gorronear; Gorrón; Pegote; Godería; Rozavillón'. In *Diccionario de La Lengua Española*. Madrid: Real Academia Española. https://dle.rae.es/?id=JMrUqze
Real Academia Española. 1729. 'Capigorrista'. *Diccionario de Autoridades*. http://web.frl.es/DA.html
Rico, F. 1989. *La Novela Picaresca y El Punto de Vista*. Barcelona: Seix Barrl.
Rodriguez Cáceres, M. 1991. [1554, Anonymous.] *Lazarillo de Tormes*. Madrid: Bruño.
Rojas Zorrilla, F. de 1640. *Obligados y Ofendidos, y El Gorrón de Salamanca*. Ciudad de Buenos Aires: Editorial del Cardo. www.biblioteca.org.ar/libro.php?texto=71293
Salillas, R. 1896. *El Delincuente Español. El Lenguaje (Estudio Filológico, Psicológico y Sociológico) Con Dos Vocabularios Jergales*. Madrid: Librería de Victoriano Suárez.
Sánchez Hidalgo, E. 2018. '"Ser Un Gorrón" y Otras Frases Hechas Que Nacieron En La Universidad de Salamanca'. *El País*, 7 October. https://verne.elpais.com/verne/2018/10/03/articulo/1538559769_204176.html
Sanmartín Sáez, J. 2003. 'Lingüística Aplicada y Argot: Los Útiles Lexicográficos Del Traductor'. In *Lexicografía y Lexicogía En Europa y América: Homenaje a Günter Haensch*, edited by G. Haensch, M. T. E Elizondo, and J. P. Sánchez Méndez, 603–14. Madrid: Gredos.
Scott, J. C. 1985. *Weapons of the Weak. Everyday Forms of Peasant Resistance*. New Haven and London: Yale University Press.

7.3 *(Za)chachmęcenie* (Poland)
Alisa Musanovic

Cambridge Dictionary. 'Swindle'. Cambridge Dictionary. https://dictionary.cambridge.org/dictionary/english/swindle
Karaś, H. 2011. *Polska leksykografia gwarowa* [Polish Lexicography of Dialects]. Warsaw: Faculty of Polish Studies at the University of Warsaw.
Kochanowicz, J. 2004. 'Trust, Confidence and Social Capital in Poland: A Historical Perspective'. In *Trust and Democratic Transitions in Post-Communist Europe*, edited by I. Markova, 63–84. New York: Oxford University Press.
Landy, P. 1961. 'What Price Corruption'. *Problems of Communism* 10(2): 18–25.
Materka, E. 2017. *Dystopia's Provocateurs: Peasants, State, and Informality in the Polish-German Borderlands*. Bloomington: Indiana University Press.
Maziek. 2017. 'Pytam:' [Discussion post]. *Stanisław Lem Forum*, 9 June. https://forum.lem.pl/index.php?topic=1107.1005
Mazurek, M. 2012. 'Keeping It Close to Home: Resourcefulness and Scarcity in Late Socialist and Postsocialist Poland'. In *Communism Unwrapped: Consumption in Cold War Eastern Europe*, edited by P. Bren and M. Neuburger, 298–320. New York: Oxford University Press.
Online Dictionary, Malinowski, M. 2019. 'Polszczyzna od Ręki Pana Literki: Chachmęcić' [Polish from the Hands of Mr. Letter: Chachmęcić]. *Obcyjezykpolski.pl*, 10 September. https://obcyjezykpolski.pl/chachmecic/

Piętkowa, R. 2014. 'Pudelek? Polityka? Przybora? Dobór Tekstów do Analizy na Zajęciach Językoznawczych [Pudelek? Polityka? Przybora? Selecting Texts for Analysis on Linguistics Classes]. *Forum Lingwistyczne*, 1: 149–62.

Pobłocki, K. 2012. 'The Struggle over Collective Consumption in Urbanizing Poland'. In *Communism Unwrapped: Consumption in Cold War Eastern Europe*, edited by P. Bren and M. Neuburger, 68–86. New York: Oxford University Press.

Szpotański, J. 1966. 'Lament Wysokiego Dygnitarza' [Lament of a High Dignitary]. *Literatut.ug.edu.pl*. https://literat.ug.edu.pl/szpot/lament.htm

Wedel, J. R. 1986. *The Private Poland. An Anthropologist's Look at Everyday Life*. New York and Oxford: Facts on File Publications.

7.4 *Nokofio* (Ghana)
Dagna Rams

Lindberg, S. 2003. 'It's Our Time to "Chop": Do Elections in Africa Feed Neo-Patrimonialism Rather than Counter-Act It?'. *Democratization* 10(2): 71–140.

Lindberg, S. 2010. 'What Accountability Pressures do MPs in Africa Face and How Do They Respond? Evidence from Ghana'. *The Journal of Modern African Studies* 48(1): 117–42.

Nugent, P. 2007. 'Banknotes and Symbolic Capital: Ghana's Elections under the Fourth Republic'. In *Votes, Money and Violence: Political Parties and Elections in Sub-Saharan Africa*, edited by M. Basedau, G. Erdmann and A. Mehler, 253–76. Uppsala: The Nordic Africa Institute and Natal: University of Kwazulu-Natal Press.

Paller, J. 2019. *Democracy in Ghana: Everyday Politics in Urban Ghana*. Cambridge: Cambridge University Press.

7.5 *Chaa pani* (India)
Ajeet Kaur

Basu, K. 2011. 'Why, for a Class of Bribes, the Act of Giving a Bribe Should Be Treated as Legal'. Ministry of Finance Government of India Working Paper 1: 4.

Bauhr, M. 2016. 'Need or Greed? Conditions for Collective Action against Corruption'. *Governance* 30(4): 561–81.

Bhaskar, R. N. 2018. *The State of Corruption in India*. New Delhi: Observer Research Foundation.

Campion, M. J. 2011. 'Bribery in India: A Website for Whistleblowers'. BBC News, 6 June. www.bbc.com/news/world-south-asia-13616123

@IPaidABribe. 2019. 'I Paid a Bribe' website. www.ipaidabribe.com/#gsc.tab=0

Ledeneva, A. V., Bailey, A. L., Barron, S., Curro, C. and Teague, E. 2018. *The Global Encyclopaedia of Informality: Understanding Social and Cultural Complexity, Volume 1*. London: UCL Press.

Merton, R. K. 1977. *Sociological Ambivalence and Other Essays*. New York: The Free Press.

Positivepurchasing.com. 2016. 'Bribes, Lunches and Chai pani'. Positive Purchasing. https://positivepurchasing.com/bribes-lunches-chai-pani/

7.6 *Duit Kopi* (Malaysia)
Christian Giordano

Blundo, G. and de Sardan, J.-P. O. 2006. 'Everyday Corruption in West Africa'. In *Everyday Corruption and the State: Citizens and Public Officials in Africa*, edited by G. Blundo and J.-P. O. de Sardan, 69–109. London and New York: Zed Books.

Furnivall, J. S. 1944[1939]. *Netherlands India: A Study of Plural Economy*. Cambridge: Cambridge University Press.

Giordano, C. 2012. 'Celebrating Urban Diversity in a Rainbow Nation: Political Management of Ethno-cultural Differences in a Malaysian City'. In *Anthropology in the City: Methodology and Theory*, edited by I. Pardo and G. Prato, 135–54. Farnham: Ashgate.

Scott, J. C. 1972. *Comparative Political Corruption*. Englewood Cliffs, NJ: Prentice Hall.

Wai, C. W. 2017. 'Mind your Words, Please'. *Wongchunwai.com Wordpress*, 23 April. http://wongchunwai.com/2017/04/mind-your-words-please/

7.7 *Aumento* (Lowland South America)
Daniela Peluso

Bauer, A. J. 1979. 'Rural Workers in Spanish America: Problems of Peonage and Oppression'. *Hispanic American Historical Review* 59(1): 34–63.
Bridenthal, R. (ed.) 2013. *The Hidden History of Crime, Corruption, and States*. Oxford: Berghahn Books.
Eisenstadt, S. N. and Roniger, L. 1984. *Patrons, Clients and Friends: Interpersonal Relations and the Structure of Trust in Society*. Cambridge: Cambridge University Press.
Goldstein, D. M. and Drybread, K. 2018. 'The Social Life of Corruption in Latin America'. *Culture, Theory and Critique* 59(4): 299–311.
Henig, D. and Makovicky, N. (eds) 2017. *Economies of Favour after Socialism*. Oxford: Oxford University Press.
Herzfeld, M. 1993. *The Social Production of Indifference*. Chicago: University of Chicago Press.
Ledeneva, A. V. 1998. *Russia's Economy of Favours: Blat, Networking and Informal Exchange*. Cambridge. Cambridge University Press.
Ledeneva, A. V. 2014. 'Economies of Favours or Corrupt Societies: Exploring the Boundaries Between Informality and Corruption'. *The Baltic Worlds* 1: 13–21.
Londoño Sulkin, C. D. 2005. 'Inhuman Beings: Morality and Perspectivism Among Muinane People (Colombian Amazon)'. *Ethnos* 70(1): 7–30.
Nel, P. 2019. 'When Bribery Helps the Poor'. *Review of Social Economy* 78(4): 507–31.
Peluso, D. M. 2014. 'Shajaó – Histories of an Invented Savage'. *History and Anthropology* 25(1): 102–222.
Peluso, D. M. 2015. 'Circulating between Rural and Urban Communities: Multi-sited Dwellings in Amazonian Frontiers'. *The Journal of Latin American and Caribbean Anthropology (special issue), Indigenous Urbanization: The Circulation of Peoples between Rural and Urban Amazonian Spaces*. Guest editor: D. M. Peluso, 20(1): 57–79.
Peluso, D. 2018. 'Traversing the Margins of Corruption Amidst Informal Economies in Amazonia'. *Culture, Theory and Critique* 59(4): 400–18.
Pinedo, D. 2013. 'Bonding or Bridging Ties? Social Relations and Indigenous Activism in Peruvian Amazonia'. *Grassroots Development Journal* 34: 34–9.
Quiroz, A. W. 2008. *Corrupt Circles: A History of Unbound Graft in Peru*. Washington: Woodrow Wilson Center.
Stahl, C. 2018. 'Coima'. In *The Global Encyclopaedia of Informality, Volume 1*, edited by A. Ledeneva, A. Bailey, S. Barron, C. Curro and E. Teague, 174–6. London: UCL Press.
Walker, H. 2012. 'Demonic Trade: Debt, Materiality, and Agency in Amazonia'. *Journal of the Royal Anthropological Institute* 18(1): 140–59.

7.8 *Pari pod masata* (Bulgaria)
Kristina Tsabala

24Chasa. 2020. '2000 evro na smyana ot podkupi na mitnicharite na Kalotina, 50 evro bili za shefa (Obzor)'. *24Chasa.bg*, 7 February. www.24chasa.bg/novini/article/8163285
Atanasova, E., Pavlova, M., Moutafova, E., Rachel, B. and Groot, W. 2013. 'Informal Payments for Health Services: The Experience of Bulgaria after 10 Years of Formal Co-payments'. *European Journal of Public Health* 24: 733–9.
Balabanova, D. and McKee, M. 2002. 'Understanding Informal Payments for Health Care: The Example of Bulgaria'. *Health Policy* 62: 243–73.
Blundo, G. and Olivier de Sardan, J.-P. 2006. 'Everyday Corruption in West Africa'. In *Everyday Corruption in Africa: Citizens and Public Officials*, edited by G. Bludno, J.-P. Olivier de Sardan, N. Arifari and M. Alou, 69–108. New York: Zed Books.
Chavdarova, T. 2018. 'Vruzki'. In *The Global Encyclopaedia of Informality, Volume 1*, edited by A. V. Ledeneva, 64–7. London: UCL Press.
Coalition 2000 and Center for the Study of Democracy (CSD) 2005. *Obrazovanie i antikoruptsiya*. Sofia: CSD.
Delcheva, E., Balabanova, D. and Mckee, M. 1997. 'Under-the-Counter Payments for Health Care: Evidence from Bulgaria'. *Health Policy* 42(2): 89–100.

European Commission. 2019. *State of Health in the EU: Companion Report 2019*. Luxembourg: Publications Office of the European Union.
Grodeland, A., Koshechkina, T. and Miller, W. 1997. '"Foolish to Give and Yet More Foolish Not to Take" – In-Depth Interviews with Post-Communist Citizens on Their Everyday Use of Bribes and Contacts'. *Europe-Asia Studies* 50: 651–77.
Grodeland, A., Koshechkina, T. and Miller, W. L. 2000. 'If you Pay, We'll Operate Immediately'. *Journal of Medical Ethics* 26: 305–11.
Grodeland, A., Koshechkina, T. and Miller, W. 2001. *A Culture of Corruption? Coping with Government in Post-Communist Europe*. Budapest: Central European University.
Kirov, N. 2014. 'Nov podkup izobretiha mitnichari'. *Pariteni.bg*, 24 January. www.pariteni.bg/novini/novini/nov-podkup-izobretiha-mitnichari-181398
Moldovan, A. and Van de Walle, S. 2013. 'Gifts or Bribes? Attitudes on Informal Payments in Romanian Health Care'. *Public Integrity* 15(4): 383–99.
Stepurko, T., Pavlova, M., Gryga, I. and Groot, W. 2013. 'Informal Payments for Health Services – Corruption or Gratitude? A Study on Public Attitudes, Perceptions and Opinions in Six Central and Eastern European Countries'. *Communist and Post-Communist Studies* 46: 419–31.
Transparency International. 2019. 'Our Work in: Bulgaria'. Transparency International. www.transparency.org/en/countries/bulgaria
Yanchev, V. (director). 1978. *Toplo* [film]. YouTube, 17 September. Bulgaria.

7.9 *Otkat vizy* (Russia)
Olga Tkach

Brennan, D. 2003. 'Selling Sex for Visas: Sex Tourism as a Stepping-stone to International Migration'. In *Global Women: Nannies, Maid and Sex Workers in the New Economy*, edited by B. Ehrenreich and A. R. Hochschild, 154–68. New York: Metropolitan Books.
Dekalchuk, A. 2014. 'Schengen Borders in Practice: Facts about Finland (and Russia)'. Working Paper. Series International Relations, No. WP BRP 05/IR/2014. Moscow: National Research University – Higher School of Economics.
Eskelinen, H., Liikanen, I. and Scott J.W. (eds) 2013. *The EU-Russia Borderland: New Contexts for Regional Cooperation*. London: Routledge.
Findicator. 2020. 'Border Crossing'. *Statistics Finland*, 23 March. https://web.archive.org/web/20210506102059/https://findikaattori.fi/en/105
Green, P. 2015. 'Mobility Regimes in Practice: Later-life Westerners and Visa Runs in South-East Asia'. *Mobilities* 10(5): 748–63.
Kraler, A., Kofman, E., Kohli, M. and Schmoll, C. (eds) 2011. *Gender, Generations and the Family in International Migration*. Amsterdam: Amsterdam University Press.
Navaro-Yashin, Y. 2007. 'Make-believe Papers, Legal Forms and the Counterfeit: Affective Interactions between Documents and People in Great Britain and Cyprus'. *Anthropological Theory* 7(1): 79–98.
Schenk, S. 2018. *Why Control Immigration? Strategic Uses of Migration Management in Russia*. Toronto, Buffalo, London: University of Toronto Press.
Studzińska, D., Sivokoz, A. and Domaniewski, S. 2018. 'Russian Cross-border Shopping Tourists in the Finnish and Polish Borderlands'. *Norsk Geografisk Tidsskrift – Norwegian Journal of Geography* 72(2): 115–26.
Tkach, O. 2021. 'Care for the Visa: Maximising Mobility from Northwest Russia to the Schengen Area'. *Nordic Journal of Migration Research* 11(2): 108–23.

8
Informal income

Introduction: informal economy

Colin C. Williams
Management School, University of Sheffield, UK

For over five decades, the International Labour Organization (ILO) have been seeking an overarching definition of the multiple forms of monetary-generating informality that prevail across the world, such as *svart arbete*, *travail au noir*, *caporalato*, *shabashniki*, *paga globale*, *khaltura*, *stacze kolejkowi*, *taksovanie* and *trotro*.

The 15th International Conference of Labour Statisticians (ICLS) in 1993 sought to resolve the multiplicity of forms by adopting an enterprise-centred definition. It did this by defining employment in the informal sector as 'all jobs in informal sector enterprises, or all persons who, during a given reference period, were employed in at least one informal sector enterprise, irrespective of their status of employment and whether it was their main or a secondary job' (Hussmanns 2005: 3). An informal sector enterprise was defined as a small or unregistered, private unincorporated enterprise. In this context, 'small' refers to the numbers employed in the enterprise being below a specific threshold, determined in a national context. 'Unregistered' refers to the enterprise not being registered according to specific types of national-level legislation (for example, tax or social security laws, factory and/or commercial acts, professional group regulatory acts). Meanwhile, a 'private unincorporated' enterprise is a business owned by an individual or household and is not established as a separate legal entity with a complete set of accounts available that would enable the financial separation of the production of the business from its owner's other activities (Hussmanns 2005; ILO 2012, 2013).

When applied to lived practice, problems arose. On the one hand, some wrongly classified all micro-enterprises as informal enterprises. On the other hand, this enterprise-centred definition failed to include informal employment in formal enterprises. Hence, the 17th ICLS in 2003 decided to add to this enterprise-based definition a job-based definition. This sought to include forms of informality not only in informal enterprises but also in formal enterprises. In this job-based definition, 'informal employment' was defined as 'jobs that generally lack basic social or legal protections or employment benefits and may be found in the formal sector, informal sector or households' (ILO 2012: 12).

This job-based definition usefully recognises that forms of monetary-generating informality exist in both informal and formal production units and that formal enterprises sometimes employ informal workers (Hussmanns 2005). It also includes in the definition of informal employment both employers and own-account workers who are self-employed in their own informal sector enterprises, and contributing family workers and members of informal producers' cooperatives, in addition to employees whose employment relationship is, in law or in practice, not subject to national labour legislation, income taxation, social protection or entitlement to certain employment benefits, such as severance pay, notice of dismissal and annual paid leave or sick leave (Hussmanns 2005; ILO 2012, 2013).

The outcome has been that these enterprise- and job-based definitions can be combined to define the informal economy. Taking the enterprise as the unit of analysis, the 'informal sector' covers both formal and informal jobs in informal sector enterprises, while taking jobs as the unit of analysis, 'informal employment' covers informal jobs in both informal and formal enterprises. The 'informal economy' then refers to those workers who in their main job are employed in the informal sector or in informal employment but adding only once those doing both (Hussmanns 2005; ILO 2012). The 19th International Labour Conference in 2002, as well as the ILO's Recommendation No. 204 in 2015, thus defines the informal economy as all economic activities by workers and economic units that are – in law or in practice – not covered or insufficiently covered by formal arrangements (ILO 2002, 2015).

Although these enterprise- and job-based definitions are widely used in the majority world (that is, developing economies), this has been less the case in developed economies and post-socialist transition economies. This is largely because these two definitions depict enterprises and jobs dichotomously as either informal or formal. An enterprise is either formal or informal, and a job either formal or informal. However, in developed and post-socialist transition economies, there has been recognition that enterprises and jobs are often concurrently both formal and informal. On the one hand, a sizeable proportion of formal enterprises conduct a portion of their work in the informal economy such as by not reporting transactions for tax or social contribution purposes (Williams 2006). On the other hand, formal employees can receive from their formal employers a portion of their salary as a declared wage and the rest of their salary as an undeclared ('envelope') wage (Horodnic and Williams 2021; Woolfson 2007). Given that these two prominent types of work in the informal economy work are not included in the enterprise-based definition because these are formal enterprises or in the job-based definition because the worker is in a formal job, the use of an activity-based definition has come to the fore.

One such activity-based definition is that the informal economy involves socially legitimate paid activity that is legal in all respects apart from the fact that it is not declared to, hidden from, or unregistered with, the authorities for tax, social security and/or labour law purposes when it should be declared (Williams 2019). If the economic activity is illegal in other respects and/or perceived as socially illegitimate, then it is not part of the informal economy. Instead, it is part of the wider criminal economy. The goods and/or services exchanged in the informal economy are legal. If the good and/or service traded is illegal (for example, forced labour, selling stolen or counterfeit goods, trafficking illegal drugs), then this is part of the wider 'criminal' economy. Indeed, the term 'shadow economy' often includes both criminal and informal economic activities (Schneider 2013). Activity that is unpaid is also not included in the informal economy. This is the unpaid subsistence economy, not the informal economy.

Nevertheless, and as is always the case, there are sometimes blurred boundaries between the formal, informal, criminal and unpaid subsistence economies. For example, an illegal good or service in one country may be legal in another (for example, cannabis, prostitution), meaning that in one country it might be part of the informal economy if tax, social security or labour laws are not complied with, but part of the criminal economy in another. Meanwhile, the subsistence and informal economies sometimes blur since there is not a dichotomy between a paid and unpaid activity but a continuum. Exemplifying this is that activities can be reimbursed in-kind using reciprocal labour and/or gifts instead of money. Usually, however, only paid activities involving money are included in the definition of the informal economy.

For participants, the informal economy, akin to all the aforementioned other activities, are means of livelihood pursued to secure a living.

In different contexts and among different stakeholders, some of these means of livelihood will be seen more as a problem and something to be deterred and prevented, and in other contexts and among other stakeholders, more as a solution to their problems and beneficial.

8.1 *Svart arbete* (Sweden)
Lotta Björklund Larsen
Tax Administration Research Centre, University of Exeter Business School, UK

Svart arbete, literally 'black work', is the Swedish colloquial term for any informal work performed for remuneration or direct exchange. The actual service (typically construction, home or auto repair) is mostly legal in content, whereas the illegality consists of unreported income and tax evasion. *Svart arbete* is deeply ingrained in Swedish culture, yet as a response to societal changes it continuously takes new forms.

Historically *svart arbete* refers to hard, tiring and dirty work such as in the old proverb *svarta händer gör vita pengar,* literally 'black hands make white money', indicating that a good deed came from hard physical labour (Holm 1964). This moral overtone stands in blatant contrast to the current public connotation of *svart arbete* as a shameful, subversive or abusive practice that cheats the welfare state. The label *svart* signifying economic activities in relation to justice came into Swedish usage after the First World War (SAOB 2006). *Svart* concerned illegal transactions, especially of rationed products, which took place on *svarta börsen*, the black market. *Svart arbete* was probably imported from Germany and Denmark, and the expression *svart arbetsmarknad*, black labour market, was used in Sweden for the first time in 1932 (SAOB 2006 referring to an article reporting on Germans' economic hardship in the *Svenska Dagbladet* newspaper on 5 October1932).

Nowadays *svart arbete* denotes any work in which the required income tax, social fees, pension contributions and even labour laws are evaded. Its spectrum is broad: from the everyday exchange of mundane services between neighbours to organised activities on a large scale, and sometimes even outright criminal transactions. Paying the teenager next door to look after the kids on a Friday evening or offering a plumber 500 *krona* to fix a leaking tap are typical examples of *svart arbete*. Besides cash payments, many exchanges of *svart* services occur as barter between professionals: a carpenter helps build a wall in exchange for an electrician's installation of a sauna oven, a hairdresser needing a car repair offers free haircuts to the mechanic's family. These everyday exchanges, common in all Swedish communities, strengthen social relations while being considerably cheaper than those on the market. For the purchaser of *svart arbete*, the obvious benefit is saving the 25 per cent sales tax on transactions, while the seller, if paid in cash, can avoid declaring income. Practices recalling *svart arbete* can be found in France through *travail au noir* and Italy through *lavoro in nero*.

Svart arbete takes place outside the realm of public institutions. It is hidden, informal and technically illegal. The Swedish Tax Administration plays a large part in distinguishing ordinary, legal exchange of favours between neighbours and acquaintances from more organised *svart arbete* where the intent is to avoid paying VAT or avoid reporting taxable income. Economically, such exchanges of work become *svart* in aggregation, when the economic value of labour provided to others exceeds 20,000 SEK annually. *Svart arbete* is technically illegal but is not always viewed as criminal. The boundary between informal practices of *svart arbete* and unabashed criminal activities is crossed when *svart arbete* is organised and continuous, large scale and affects great numbers of people (Riksrevisionsverket 1997: 59). It then becomes an economic crime (Lindgren 2001).

Svart arbete is common in the construction sector (Polismyndigheten 2017). A developer might appear to be formally compliant, yet the firm will outsource certain tasks to a subcontractor, who in turn finds another subcontractor in an increasingly informal chain of cash payments to foreign workers with insecure contracts. The establishment of the EU single market in the 1990s led to an inflow of skilled craftsmen and other menial workers from neighbouring Eastern countries open to working for considerably lower wages. Although much of this low-skilled work takes place according to laws and regulations, there is also a slippery slope of paying lower wages in cash to people and avoiding safety regulations when deadlines approach. At its extreme, *svart arbete* also includes the mistreatment of immigrants working without permits with no other choice of income – a relationship close to slavery. For instance, Sweden has increasing numbers of seasonal guestworkers picking wild berries, and they have little means to contest inadequate compensation when contracts are breached by unscrupulous employers. *Svart arbete* might also encompass criminal activities such as smuggling, prostitution or the fencing of stolen goods, although in principle such illegal work is not subject to taxation (Skatteverket 2006: 21).

Purchasing *svart arbete* can be seen as a smart move, a way to accomplish cheap and simple transactions (Björklund Larsen 2013).

Exchanging *svart* can be a sign of being well-connected. As a form of citizen protest, it articulates a form of individual opposition to an encompassing state that is seen as meddling in people's everyday life (Leonard 1998: 1; Gudeman 2001: 12). Danes had a saying during the 1980s – 'eat green, vote red, work black' (Sampson 1986: 21). The Danish participants in such an alternative economy can be described as rebels with a cause, since the explicit choice to participate was based on political contempt for all authorities. *Svart arbete* is thus also a form of protest: the individual experiences a discrepancy between society's moral norms and the authorities' laws and regulations (Pardo 1996: 165; Skatteverket 2006: 36; Björklund Larsen 2010: 176).

Yet, not every exchange of *svart arbete* is morally acceptable: people who simultaneously receive public benefits while earning income from working informally are viewed with contempt (Björklund Larsen 2010: 197). By receiving and not providing, theirs is a double abuse of the Swedish state. In contemporary welfare states like Sweden and neighbouring Denmark, *svart arbete* is always viewed as problematic (cf. Viby Mogensen 2003; Organisation for Economic Co-operation and Development [OECD] 2004: 225). In so far as citizens are perceived to be buying *svart* services (thereby avoiding tax, official regulations and union agreements), they are undermining welfare institutions and solidarity (cf. Smith 1989). The impact on society and its institutions is seen to be detrimental, for example as swallowing part of a macroeconomic recovery (Carlberg 2005). *Svart arbete* is often seen as thriving and even growing in devious immoral circles of exchanges. However, this type of work cannot be entirely regarded as a drain on the economy, since much of it would never have taken place if performed formally, with VAT and formal invoices (Skatteverket 2008: 21). With the high-income Swedish taxes, the total payment would have been too expensive. The illegality within *svart arbete* is usually defined in the way it is recompensed, when and to whom, and not within the content of the tasks themselves.

The legal definition of *svart arbete* is in theory quite straightforward, but it is not easily applicable because many labour exchanges do not involve or take place in a neighbourly context. It follows that the extent of *svart arbete*, like any hidden economic activity, is hard to measure (OECD 2002). The Swedish Tax Administration has estimated that its level in 2021 is about the same as it was 15 years ago (Skatteverket 2021) – 6–7 per cent of total income from work. State authorities have applied carrot-and-stick approaches to diminish *svart arbete*. One strategy has been to introduce tax deductions for documented purchase of services such as home repair or household cleaning (known as the

ROT and RUT schemes). Simultaneously, the Swedish tax authorities have attempted to combat *svart arbete* through mobilisation campaigns and third-party reporting, making it increasingly difficult to hide such incomes. Without doubt, the political and moral campaigns, simplified tax reporting, restrictions on cash payments, the increase of legal tax deductions, as well as tax deductions for hiring household services have made *svart arbete* less attractive and less acceptable. It has instead taken more abusive forms, such as exploiting refugees without residence permits or disenfranchised migrant workers.

8.2 *Travail au noir* (France)
Carla Montigny
Alumna, School of Slavonic and East European Studies, UCL, UK

Travail au noir, literally 'black labour' in French, refers to undeclared or unreported employment. The practice is spread worldwide, but similar expressions exist in Italy, where it is called *lavoro sommerso* or *lavoro in nero* (literally 'submerged' or 'black labour'), and in Sweden, under the name *svart arbete*. In French law, in the article of 11 July 1972, *travail au noir* is defined as the money-making act of production, transformation, reparation, or trade, by a person who is not declared and has not fulfilled the social and fiscal obligation linked to their activities, except if they only occur occasionally (Barthélemy 1982).

According to Laé (1990), *travail au noir* can be micro-local or based on group solidarity; it can also be short-term limited work, or a full-time job. It can be divided into two categories: 'self-employment', which includes employers in informal enterprises or own-account workers in informal enterprises, and 'wage employment', which includes employees of informal enterprises or paid domestic workers (Chen, quoted in Stuart et al. 2018). *Travail au noir* is often used as a stepping-stone towards formal employment, as an opportunity to develop a skill before looking for a legal job, specifically in the context of immigration. It is important to note that *travail au noir* often comes with a level of imbalance; indeed, it is usually created by employers rather than sought out by employees (Barthe 1985). It also seems to mostly affect people in a condition of social and economic weakness – for example, someone who is in a desperate economic condition will be more likely to accept undeclared labour. Similarly, immigration or periods of long unemployment often heighten the risk of *travail au noir* for communities. It can also have different implications depending on the demographic; while young people are more likely to engage in *travail au noir* to gain extra income if they still live with their parents or receive money from them, people aged 25–45 are often forced to turn to *travail au noir* due to a situation of extreme scarcity, for example in the context of parenthood or debt (Barthe 1985).

Travail au noir is most prevalent in the contexts of manual labour, such as cleaning, construction or farming jobs, where administrative costs are perceived as excessively burdening. A common form of the practice is a family hiring a cleaner for two or three hours a week. In such a context, informal rules such as morals and social pressure would help regulate the wage received by the cleaner. They might therefore decide, informally, on a salary relatively similar to that received in a formal context. The main difference would therefore be minimised paperwork and tax, rather than the salary itself.

Travail au noir can also take the shape of full-time employment. In France, this is quite common in restaurants, where employees sometimes work 'illegally', as restaurant owners want to keep their costs down, while having access to a large supply of migrant workers who are willing to work despite not being legally allowed to. This could be a transitionary situation, if the employee is waiting to receive their work permit, or it could be permanent. The employee could have no desire or possibility to obtain a work permit. In this situation, there is a clear power imbalance, as the employees are more likely to accept difficult or unsanitary work conditions due to their situations; it is also easier for them to get fired.

Travail au noir can also be '50/50'. Especially in the agricultural context where employers hire workers 'half legally' – in such a situation, there is a contract, and a formal legal framework defining wages and work conditions, but the employer may choose to declare only half of their employee's working hours. By doing so, both employer and employee pay tax on half of the hours effectively worked, but they still benefit from legal protection. This is often seen as a harmless example of *travail au noir*, as the two parties involved pay less tax, and it takes place through a shared understanding that the '50/50' agreement is best for both parties, even if it harms the employee in the long run.

Travail au noir is insidious when one of the parties is unaware of the situation. This happens when an employee (A), for example on a construction site, is momentarily unable to work, and instead sends someone they know and who usually works for them (B). B thus becomes another employee of the construction site. If the employer trusts A, he might not bother to check B's legal situation. If B is working *au noir* for A, the employer will not be aware of this, and he will therefore be unknowingly engaging in *travail au noir*.

Undeclared labour is most prevalent in societies where state institutions are ineffective or absent. The known ineffectiveness of informal institutions (North 1991), or the lack of trust in them, often leads to a desire or need to bypass them (Ledeneva and Efendic 2020). In this context, unreported employment acts as a substitutive institution following the Helmke and Levitsky model (2004). However, unreported labour remains widespread in more developed economies with effective institutions, as evidenced by the prevalence of *travail au noir* in France, where, according to data collected by the European Union in 2013, it involves as much as 11 per cent of the private sector.

This may be due to formal institutions being perceived as intrusive in everyday life; people may struggle to pay tax and their living expenses, they may be disappointed by the perceived unfairness of formal rules, or reject a system they see as invasive. Indeed, in trying to formalise mutual aid through taxation, labour-regulating laws often undermine small-scale cooperation and solidarity. In France, *travail au noir* becomes a competing informal institution in the context of 'over-effective' formal institutions.

The prevalence of *travail au noir* comes with consequences. Beyond the obvious impact on a country's GDP, it also has serious social implications. Since employers and employees do not pay tax on their *travail au noir*, at least a part of their activities evade taxation; while paying less tax seems positive in the short-term, the long-term effects have serious consequences on the community. Indeed, less tax money collected implies that formal institutions, such as welfare, health care (Stuart et al. 2018), education, or the public function will receive less funding, thus lowering their quality. This can lead to a vicious cycle in which, as formal institutions decrease in quality, people are less likely to trust them and more likely to engage in informal activities. The consequences can also be personal and even more dire as *travail au noir* disproportionately affects people in precarious situations. Working *au noir* to have more money at the end of the month often results in a lower pension, among other things; this experience is quite common among members of more precarious groups, such as recent migrants, parents with a large family, or people in unstable economic situations.

Travail au noir is a complex informal practice that falls in a moral grey area with important consequences for communities and for society at large (see also *rad na crno*, 5.24 Volume 2). Being survival-based, people resort to it to fulfil a dire need for money or employment. It is, however, difficult to know where needs end and where greed begins. Is an employer hiring workers *au noir* because he cannot afford to pay tax on their salary, or because it will allow him to have more money at the end of the month? Such grey zones make it hard to establish when *travail au noir* has a more positive or negative impact on those who participate in it.

8.3 **Caporalato** (Italy)
Francesco Bagnardi
Department of Social and Political Sciences, University of Milan, Italy

Caporalato, deriving etymologically from the Latin word for 'head', or 'leader', refers to an illegal form of labour intermediation in which the recruiter, a gangmaster called *caporale*, profits by enrolling and mobilising workers according to the short-term demand of employers. This practice is found mostly in the agricultural sector in specific areas of Italy. The number of workers at risk of being under the control of gangmasters today in Italy are estimated to be between 160,000 and 200,000 (Carchedi 2020).

Within the *caporalato* system, farmers outsource to *caporali* the recruitment, transport and control of workers in the field. *Caporali* enrol the workers for their daily gig, bring them to the field and in some cases provide them with information or access to housing in informal settlements. *Caporali* bargain the tasks and payments with farmers and are paid for the whole team. They are responsible for the output of the team and monitor work intensity and quality. Payment and working hours are negotiated informally, remuneration is often piece-rate and consistently below the minimum wage, and collective provincial contracts and working hour regulations are largely not complied with (Perrotta 2014). *Caporali* take a fee for daily transport and accommodation, and might recruit and retain workers with violence, coercion or simply with the threat of not calling them back to work in the future. In some cases, especially for Eastern European seasonal workers, *caporali* organise transport from the workers' home country to the Italian fields (Perrotta 2015; Corrado et al. 2018).

The *caporalato* system in Italy has existed for more than a century. It persisted despite historical struggles of farmworkers' unions (Mottura and Pugliese 1976; Scotto 2016) and remains crucial to provide cheap and flexible labour to a changing agricultural sector (Piselli 1990; Perrotta 2014) in which asymmetrical agri-food global value chains and the market power of retailers force farmers to stay flexible and minimise labour costs. Today, *caporalato* functions as a 'criminal system without an effective legal alternative' (Poppi and Travaglino 2019: 92): it develops informally and often illegally, but it also ensures labour intermediation and mobility in ways that formal systems fail to (Corrado et al. 2018).

On the one hand, the *caporalato* system might even develop under the control of criminal organisations that directly monitor *caporali*, infiltrate farms, manage informal settlements where migrants live, oversee the relationship between farmers and retailers and even deal with the logistics and transport of produce (Sagnet and Palmisano 2015; Fanizza and Omizzolo 2019). On the other hand, *caporali* can be social brokers (Perrotta 2019) and gatekeepers (Perrotta and Sacchetto 2014) that mediate between agri-businessmen's need for flexible workers and farmworkers' need for income and accommodation.

Since the late 1980s, Italian harvesting activities have been increasingly taken up by migrant workers. *Caporali* and day labourers are today mainly migrants (Avallone 2017). The supply of labour for unskilled farm work exceeds the demand and this favours precarious employment arrangements. The deportability (cf. De Genova 2002) of migrant workers due to European Union and Italian migration regulations contributes to their vulnerability and readiness to accept sub-standard employment conditions. Migrant workers in Italian fields, indeed, are increasingly asylum seekers or refugees with a temporary visa (Dines and Rigo 2015), who often find accommodation in secluded informal settlements. This socio-spatial segregation impairs job mobility and increases dependency on intermediaries (Perrotta and Sacchetto 2014).

Nonetheless, migrant workers maintain agency vis-à-vis their *caporali*, and their relationship is not always based on mere coercion. Farmworkers might frame their *caporali* as entrepreneurial actors and look up to them (Poppi and Travaglino 2019) or they might be linked to them by kinship ties (Perrotta 2019). Workers can escape a coercive relationship with a *caporale* by reaching out to fairer intermediaries or directly to farmers. Forms of misbehaviour and small-scale conflicts to renegotiate the labour process persist too despite the control of *caporali*, giving way to open forms of collective actions like work stoppages and strikes (Perrotta and Sacchetto 2014; Peano 2017).

The spread of the *caporalato* goes beyond specific or marginal Southern Italian areas and sectors. *Caporalato* and other similar exploitative forms of labour contracting are crucial in agriculture in other regions of Italy (Osservatorio Placido Rizzotto 2020), in other Mediterranean countries (Corrado et al. 2016, 2018) and beyond (Barrientos 2013; Palumbo and Corrado 2020). Moreover, exploitative intermediation practices involve not only migrants but also natives (Osservatorio Placido Rizzotto 2020), are common in other traditional industries like construction (Fellini et al. 2007) and are on the rise in technologically advanced sectors such as platform work in the gig economy (Merlo 2020; Inversi 2021).

Policy responses against *caporalato* have abounded in the last few years. In Italy, *caporalato* became a criminal offence in 2011, and since 2016 farmers relying on *caporali* can be imprisoned (de Martino et al. 2016; Santoro and Stoppioni 2019). Policymakers have also introduced measures to provide formalised and regular alternatives to organise agricultural labour markets. These measures, however, achieved only limited results (Santoro and Stoppioni 2019; Bagnardi et al. 2022).

8.4 *Paga globale* (Italy)
Giulio Benedetti
Stockholm School of Economics, Riga, Latvia

Paga globale (literally 'global pay') is an informal wage conveyed through formal channels. Two documents are required for it to function: a sheet recording the hours effectively worked by the employee, who will be paid an agreed fixed sum per hour, and a formal pay cheque calculated on the basis of the national collective contract. The latter is manipulated to match the total amount agreed instead of being based on the hours effectively worked. In this way, taxation is minimised, and the worker exchanges the benefits and guarantees of the formal contract for a net earning that can be higher or lower, depending on the situation.

The practice is often used with migrant workers, as it thrives on price differentials between the region of employment and that of the family's residence. It first appeared in the context of migrations from Southern Italy to the north of the country, alongside the structural changes of the production model that took place during the 1980s, the weakening of trade unions and an increasing individualisation of work through subcontracting (Cillo and Perocco 2016). It is widespread in the metalworking, shipbuilding and construction sectors. It might have first appeared among skilled shipbuilding workers who were posted to work in Northern Italy for short periods of time, but it is also widespread among construction workers commuting to work on short-term contracts (Caputo and D'Onofrio 2011). Initially, a worker paid via *paga globale* could earn substantially more than what he would have earned through the application of the formal collective contract. This practice allows workers to monetise benefits such as paid leave, which would otherwise be unused in the case of short work trips typically lasting a few weeks.

However, the working conditions associated with the practice rapidly deteriorated, and *paga globale* became more common in the following years among foreign workers, who are often paid much less than Italian citizens (Skupnjak-Kapić et al. 2005).

Paga globale appeared at a time of transition towards a production model based increasingly on flexibility and smaller productive units. Useful for employers as a way of reducing taxation and labour costs, *paga globale* allows for the rigidities of formal collective national contracts, more suitable for long-term rather than flexible employment, to be contained. It also allows for the reduction of the cost of labour itself, as workers are paid only for the hours effectively worked, and they are not entitled to paid leave, sick leave, or any other provision guaranteed by formal regulations. From the workers' point of view, *paga globale* somehow represents a coping mechanism, especially viable for migrants. In essence, *paga globale* is the exchange of benefits and guarantees for cash money.

As real salaries in the last decades have progressively decreased, *paga globale* has been on the increase among foreign migrant workers. In this case, *paga globale* can be used in long-term contracts as well as daily, piecework employment. If the latter is a form of further precarisation of labour, long-term contracts paid by *paga globale* usually entail the same pay of a formal contract, but with a higher workload and longer shifts (Panariti 2011). This is made somehow bearable by the even higher differential of prices between Italy and many other workers' country of origin, which allows them to send remittances home that are still relatively conspicuous in light of the favourable currency exchange. In addition, *paga globale* entails the providing of a formal contract that, however violated in practice, provide migrants with the key document to periodically renew their residence permit, without which they would be deported.

The fact that *paga globale* entails a formal transaction makes it more difficult to uncover its informal nature during casual controls by state authorities. *Paga globale* is more easily exposed by the filing of a direct lawsuit by workers. For this reason, the practice is typical of smaller enterprises, where closer relations between workers and employers entail a higher level of reciprocal trust and control. These firms are often subcontractors for larger companies, where maintaining a façade of adherence to formal rules is required.

The spread of *paga globale* among subcontractors for larger companies accompanied a general trend of flexibilisation of labour in the construction and manufacturing sectors in Italy. This process was also underpinned by the easing of controls by state authorities and the gradual decriminalisation of labour offences (Cillo and Perocco 2016). Today, a worker filing a lawsuit against his or her employer on the grounds of *paga globale* is typically only partially refunded. The practice therefore remains economically advantageous for companies. In addition, accessing justice remains a costly endeavour, both in economic terms and for future job perspectives (Panariti 2011: 243).

As *paga globale* gradually expanded from Southern Italian workers posted in companies in Northern Italy to include foreign workers, related practices were translated too. This is the case of the so-called 'hot bed', the use of the same bed by two or three workers working different shifts. Born to contain costs among workers posted for brief periods of time, its use is nowadays organised directly by subcontracting firms. 'Hot bed' is related to *paga globale* much the same as *paga globale* is connected to subcontracting. *Paga globale* is useful to owners of small companies in order to win the race to the bottom of a tender bid because it allows a fixed cost per hour worked to be calculated. Providing shared accommodation is another way of keeping costs down and increasing their predictability (Caputo and D'Onofrio 2011).

When considered in relation to job access, *paga globale* may also relate to patronage and small-scale economies of favours. Finding a job requires a degree of trust, which is often mediated by third parties, or intermediaries. In the case of workers who are in urgent need of a formal contract in order to renew their residence permit, and hence are ready to both accept worse job conditions and to pay to have a contract, the help provided by intermediaries may be paid. Retribution could be either in money or favours, depending on the role of intermediaries. This is often accompanied by ambivalent feelings towards intermediaries, as the latter provide a crucially important and possibly life-saving help, but this doesn't come free of charge.

Paga globale shares similarities with practices related to labour informality such as *alga aploksnē*, *travail au noir* and *svart arbete* (see respectively Sedlenieks 2018; Montigny 2021; Larsen 2021). The difference is that *paga globale* adds an element of façade: the wage is conveyed by formal means, in the way of bank transfers and pay cheques. This difference offers two major practical advantages: being less visible and risky, *paga globale* can be adopted in long-term work relations, and is compatible with the needs of the biggest economic players and contractors. In addition, the façade provided by *paga globale* is also valuable to those migrants who need to renew their residence permit, the main requisite of which is holding a formal job contract, as in the case of *caporalato*.

Today the net starting wage of a metalworking employee is around 1,100 euros per 40-hour week. Workers in subcontracting firms often work up to 10 or 12 hours a day including Saturdays, and in some cases *paga globale* allows them to earn up to 2,000 euros a month (Skupnjak-Kapić et al. 2005: 45). Figures, however, may vary. In the construction sector, where the length of periods of employment can be unstable, earnings through *paga globale* may also reach 2,300–2,500 euros per month (Caputo and D'Onofrio 2011: 124). Judiciary investigations, reported by the media, also uncovered situations in which workers of foreign origin are paid 3 to 4 euros per hour in the shipbuilding sector, with shifts lasting up to 12 hours, six days a week. In this case, the earning is typically between 1,000 and 1,100 euros, the net starting salary of the formal national collective contract (Mion 2021).

Paga globale is not particularly visible and has received only limited media coverage through the years, mainly from local newspapers. Difficult to spot, it emerges through ethnographic accounts and judiciary investigations, often opposed discursively to *paga sindacale* (literally 'union pay'). Despite the denouncements of the trade unions, however, *paga globale* remains a reality mainly known only to those in close proximity to it.

8.5 *Shabashniki* (USSR, Russia)
Nikolay Erofeev
Department of Architecture, State Planning and Landscape Design, University of Kassel, Germany

Shabashniki (literally, 'Sabbath workers', from *shabash*, meaning work done on the side and referring to the Sabbath, the seventh day set aside by God in the Hebrew Bible as a day of rest) is a Russian term used to describe moonlighting brigades who undertook short, illegal or semi-legal contracts in the Soviet Union. Brigades of *shabashniki* were widespread in the spheres of construction, house renovation and decoration. The practice was known as *shabashnichestvo* and the form of work as *shabashka*. Most often the term was used to describe collective brigades, but it was also used to denote individuals working illegally in consumer services such as shoe- or car-repairs. *Shabashniki* were forced to work informally since they were engaged in free-market employment that was illegal under the USSR's command economy. This meant, of course, that their work was not officially reported or taxed. Under Soviet law, individual entrepreneurship was defined as a crime, and workers who accepted money for informal services could be prosecuted for 'private entrepreneurial activity' (Shelly 1990: 17). These official prohibitions notwithstanding, *shabashnichestvo* was extremely widespread in the late USSR. Because the activity, while officially illegal, was both widespread and essential for getting work done, the Soviet authorities had to turn a blind eye to *shabashniki*, whose activities were considered 'morally questionable' yet economically necessary. For some practitioners, *shabashnichestvo* was an informal side job (also known as *levak*) – a way of earning additional money on the side. For others, it was a full-time job. Seasonal short-term contracts triggered seasonal migration of *shabashniki* from the labour-rich republics of Central Asia and the Caucasus to other parts of the USSR. In Armenia, as many as 25,000 *shabashniki* travelled to urban areas and collective farms in Siberia for contracts in the construction sphere every year (Otsu and Ramzes 1992: 367). Migrating brigades of *shabashniki* were also called 'wild' or 'seasonal' brigades or migrant workers in the USSR (Shabanova 1991).

Shabashnichestvo had its origins in the practices of *arteli* – independent, subcontracted gangs that had been working in Russia since the pre-revolutionary period (Valetov 2010: 254) – but the practice was further shaped by the particular circumstances of the Soviet labour market. Following the Marxist doctrine that labour is not a commodity, the Soviet authorities strictly controlled wages in an attempt to suppress competition in the labour market and ruled that workers could not normally have side jobs (Clarke 1999: 13). Out of necessity, however, enterprise and collective-farm directors were allowed to contract work collectives for seasonal short-term contracts. In contrast to these officially approved temporary guest workers (*limitchiki*), *shabashniki* were motivated by higher wages, which were paid informally (see also *alga aploksnē*). The ban on individual entrepreneurship pushed the practice into the grey zone but failed to put an end to it (Shelly 1990: 11–26). Subcontracting teams were also found in other Communist states such as 'autonomous groups' in Poland or 'rogue construction' in Yugoslavia (Łoś 1990: 49; Le Normand 2014: 148).

Shabashnichestvo grew in importance in the late-Soviet period in response to the shortcomings of the centralised system of manufacture and distribution, when state construction companies were unable to retain their workers, encountered difficulties in acquiring materials and rendered services with great delay and at a low-quality level (Valetov 2010: 253). According to some estimates, in the 1970s *shabashniki* accounted for more than half of the construction workers in some regions of the USSR (Shelly 1990: 16; Otsu and Ramzes 1992: 267). *Shabashniki* were also estimated as providing half of all consumer services overall, up to as much as 98 per cent of housing repairs in the Caucasus (O'Hearn 1980: 225; Miller 2017: 89). These extremely high estimates testify to the strong dependence of the Soviet economy on the informal sector. In contrast to other informal practices, *shabashniki* were not just a marginal phenomenon. They played a major macroeconomic role, 'wholeheartedly integrated into Soviet society, while located underground' (Otsu and Ramzes 1992: 367). *Shabashniki* tended also to be more productive and cost-effective for their employers than workers employed on official contracts. Unable to devise a legal framework for this practice, the Soviet authorities largely tolerated it, turning a blind eye to the non-socialist methods employed by their citizens to improve their personal well-being (Millar 1985).

The author's 2017 fieldwork revealed that official and informal practices were intertwined in many state-promoted ideological construction projects. Komsomol-led housing construction (Youth Residential Complexes) brought together the benefits of 'formal' architecture (an expertise in large-slab prefabricated construction) with those of 'informal' practices of *shabashniki*. Officially sanctioned Komsomol construction brigades (*stroiotryadi*) enabled their participants to employ their skills later in the unofficial sector. This amounted, in the words of some practitioners, to a school for learning 'how to get things done' in unofficial or semi-official spheres (Erofeev 2020). *Shabashniki* operated through a network of informal contacts, in acquiring materials, making use of *svyazi* (connections) or 'borrowing' equipment through the practice of kalym (Otsu and Ramzes 1992: 369–70; Valetov 2010: 260). Often they were able to obtain scarce and high-quality building materials and equipment as the result of secret commercial transactions, otherwise unavailable to state enterprises. Serving as mediators for official enterprises, they facilitated their access to the informal sector. The practice testifies to the fact that the official and unofficial spheres strongly complemented each other in the USSR (Ledeneva 2018: 3).

In construction, *shabashnichestvo* was an explicitly male practice (Shelly 1990: 16), a way to earn money to support their families (Morris 2013: 98). Another particular feature of Soviet brigades was that many participants were highly skilled specialists. One such worker, A. Zolotov, who was also a scientist at a research institute at the time, recalled his brigade in 1985:

> There were six of us … all with higher education, two of them candidates of science, aged between 27 and 33. For five years, we

took off to work in the Vologda and Arkhangelsk regions. We were engaged in construction and the overhaul of timber and panelled houses. We over-fulfilled the norms five or six times, working seven days a week for 20–25 days in a row. Daily earnings fluctuated over these years from 48 to 73 roubles. Our brigade was typical in my opinion. (Kruglianskaia 1985)

According to the memoirs of other practitioners, unofficial salaries could exceed the 'normative' wage by as much as 18 times (Valetov 2010: 259). *Shabashniki* were often criticised for receiving high wages and other 'anti-socialist' benefits seen as contradicting Marxist morality. Although performing services required for the official economy, they were frequently fined for violating passport regulations and prosecuted for 'private entrepreneurial activity' (Shelly 1990: 16–17). Directors of the enterprises who hired *shabashki* often took the risk of a 'suspended punishment' (Ledeneva 2006: 13). They could easily be prosecuted due to some law violation, and the punishment could be enforced at any time (Otsu and Ramzes 1992: 364–5). Yet despite this, the Soviet authorities often showed a more benevolent attitude towards *shabashniki* than towards others engaged in the unofficial economy, such as black-market dealers or illegal land 'grabbers' (Arnot 1988: 369, also see *samozakhvat*, 11.3 in this volume). In other cases, Soviet economists suggested that *shabashniki* should even be encouraged as highly skilled and enterprising workers (O'Hearn 1980: 225). Legislation on individual labour activity enacted in 1986 attempted to legalise the practice of *shabashnichestvo*, yet never fully did so (Valetov 2008: 220). *Shabashniki* also appeared in popular culture; they were depicted in several films including *Let's Meet at the Fountain* (Director Oleg Nikolaevskii 1976), *Cat in a Bag* (Director Georgii Shchukin, 1978) and *Love and Doves* (Director Vladimir Men'shov 1984).

Since the collapse of the USSR in 1991, some people with previous experience as *shabashniki* moved into profitable business as the scale of construction projects increased. By 2015, as much as 24 per cent of Russian billionaires made their wealth in the emergent post-Soviet real estate and construction sectors (Treisman 2016: 240). Continuities of Soviet informal practices can also be seen in the contemporary Russian labour market. Employment of moonlighting brigades in an informal sector is widespread in Russia today, similarly involving labour migration from former Soviet republics in the form of *gastarbaiter(y)* and *chelnoki* (Lazareva 2015). These practices testify to the intricacy between the official, semi-official and unofficial spheres, their co-dependency and symbiotic relationship in contemporary Russia, when authorities tend to restrict legal migration (that is, refuse residency and labour rights) and yet are dependent on the presence of informal migrant labour.

8.6 *Khaltura* (USSR)
Taisiia Nahorna
Alumna, School of Slavonic and East European Studies, UCL, UK

Khaltura practices emerged during Soviet times as a response to the rigidity of the system and became deeply rooted in Soviet culture. *Khaltura* has not lost its relevance after the collapse of the Soviet Union and has two present-day meanings. First, it describes an informal side job that provides extra income or refers to such extra income directly. Second, it is used in reference to the low-quality product of accomplished work, produced carelessly or in haste (Kuznetsov 2014).

Khaltura is an unplanned side job that offers the opportunity to earn extra money for a task unrelated to one's main job. The *khalturshchik* (the person exercising *khaltura*) is usually unqualified and paid less than a professional worker. In turn, the 'employer' benefits from getting the job done quickly and at a lower price than if the same were done by a legally hired professional. An example of *khaltura* can be a request for an artist to paint walls for additional income. Another common type of *khaltura* was unloading trains as the task had to be done quickly and people were unofficially hired to perform it.

The meaning of the word *khaltura* has shifted with time. Presumably, *khaltura* originates from the Latin word *chartulatium*. In the fifteenth century, this word described a list containing names of the dead who were to be prayed for. In the seventeenth century, it shifted to describing

Table 8.6.1 *Khaltura* or *shabashka*? A comparison

	Khaltura	*Shabashka*
Period	Year-round	Seasonal
Labour type	Any	Manual
Duration	Short-term	Long-term
Nature	Spontaneous	Planned
Labour migration	Not required	Required
Performance	Individual	Team
Relevance of the term	Still relevant	Losing relevance

wake ceremonies and subsequently free food (Semenov 2003). From the clergy, the word then migrated to the theatre community, where it was associated with side jobs for actors (Karts̆evskiĭ 2000: 213). Its current meaning emerged in the twentieth century. The word *khaltura* was taken from the Russian language and adopted in the spoken languages of the Soviet republics: *haltuura* in Estonian or *xaltura* in Azerbaijani. It was also adopted in the languages stemming from the same language family – Ukrainian, Belarusian, Polish.

Regardless of *khaltura* being a profitable practice, it has its disadvantages. *Khaltura* bears several risks both for the *khalturshchik* and the person who hires him. First, *khaltura* is a form of tax evasion as no official contracts are signed, rendering both the worker and the employer tax fraudsters. Second, it can result in a poorly done task as the worker is usually unqualified or is not granted enough time to accomplish the task properly. Also, the task might not be done on time, if at all, as the parties do not count on any legally binding document. The *khalturshchik*, for his part, receives no health or social protection as no contract is signed or insurance provided. For instance, in the case of an accident no one is held responsible, and the worker cannot take any measures if the 'employer' refuses to pay for the job.

Nevertheless, this practice remains a popular way of getting things done. It is a relatively easy way to earn extra income as no qualifications or special education are required. It also provides an instant profit once the task is complete, as opposed to regular full-time employment, where the salary is paid on fixed dates. The 'employer' usually hires a *khalturshchik* because the service is not offered on the official market or the price is too high. The *khalturshchik* could be willing to do the job for half as much money (Rambler 2018).

The practice of *khaltura* emerged in the Soviet system as a response to economic constraints. It demonstrated that without seeking side jobs, even educated professionals were not able to earn enough money to meet a desired standard of living. On one hand, the practice of *khaltura* was prohibited by the government. All spheres of life were regulated by the government and individual freedoms were restricted. Salaries were established by the state. Opportunities for career development were also limited as people did not have the freedom to choose their place of work. The government allocated a set number of employment opportunities in educational institutions and graduates were then assigned to workplaces all over the Soviet Union (Seichas.ru 1968). Simply applying for a different job to get a higher salary was unimaginable in a Soviet career track. Moreover, behind the Iron Curtain, seeking job opportunities abroad was not an option. The government restricted the development of the business sector by banning all types of private initiatives. Paradoxically, this level of state regulation created an environment where it was impossible to survive without entrepreneurial practices such as *khaltura*, which were considered objectionable by the state itself.

Khaltura and *shabashka* are sometimes used as synonyms, but there are important differences between them. *Shabashka* denotes 'moonlighting brigades undertaking short, illegal or semi-legal contracts in the Soviet Union' (Erofeev 2019) and refers to a seasonal job, related to manual labour, mostly popular in the areas of construction and renovation. *Khaltura* depends more on the opportunity than on the season and includes both manual and intellectual labour: a quick renovation task such as hanging wallpaper, but also writing a text. *Shabashka* is planned, can be of semi-legal nature and requires migration of the labour force. *Khaltura* is spontaneous and does not require migration of the worker. It is not perceived as illegal but as a socially acceptable bending of the rules. *Shabashniki* can work for the state (as in *kolkhozy*, the Soviet collective farms) whereas *khalturshchiki* usually work for a private individual. *Shabashniki* form groups to work for long periods of time whereas *khalturshchiki* work individually on relatively short-term tasks. Today the term *khaltura* is widely used and *shabashka* is losing its relevance.

Khaltura is indirectly related to other informal practices, based on personal recommendations for a *khalturshchik* and ensuring trust of *khalturshchik* through personal or *blat* contacts. *Khaltura* has been described as a 'mysterious, typically Soviet, unseen in the civilised world phenomenon, where low quality is the key precondition of high income' (Dovlatov 1999). The fact that *khaltura* has not lost its relevance within the Russian context today was emphasised in Dmitry Bykov's satirical political poem that comments on Putin's imprisonment of a political critic: 'we have a generous nature, which encompasses both villainy and honour; we have *khaltura* and we have *kultura* [Russian word for culture]' (Bykov 2014).

The practice of moonlighting is global, but the way the side job is defined in different languages reflects the culture of the country and its attitude to labour. Within the English-speaking world, the closest word to *khaltura* is 'gig', 'side gig', 'hustle', defined as 'a job, often a temporary one' (Cambridge Dictionary 2020a) or 'a piece of work or a job that you get paid for doing in addition to doing your main job' (Cambridge Dictionary 2020b). In Vietnam, the practice of taking a second job is called *nghề tay trái*, which means 'left-hand job', implying inferiority to the main job. This negative connotation is also found in the second meaning of *khaltura* in Russian. Brazilian Portuguese also has an informal word for a side gig – *bico*. It does not have a direct translation but designates a quick, informal job for extra money, with no contract and consequently no tax obligations. In some languages, *khaltura* is simply called an extra or second job: *trabajo extra (secundario)* in Mexican Spanish, *ekstra (ikinci) iş* in Turkish. In Romanian, a side job is called *pe langa* – which means 'next to'. In the Tunisian dialect of Arabic, *khaltura* is called *dabbara el'-raas*, which means to organise one's head or behaviour (in a way that would yield extra income).

8.7 *Stacze kolejkowi* (Poland)
Nikolaos Olma
Leibniz-Zentrum Moderner Orient, Germany

Stacze kolejkowi in socialist-era Poland refers to individuals who, amid the severe shortages of consumer goods that plagued the country in the 1980s, stood in the queue for someone else as a means of generating income 'on the side' (*na lewo*). Even though the term literally translates as 'queue-standers', the fact that *stacze kolejkowi* queued for monetary profit largely differentiated them from other 'queuers' (*kolejkowicze* or *ogonkowicze*), who queued to buy a product for either personal use or bartering. The practice is one of many informal structures and arrangements that facilitated the population's provision with consumer goods by filling 'the gray zone between state socialism and the grassroots market economy' (Mazurek 2012: 299). While the collapse of the socialist regime and the transition to market economy resulted in the term falling out of use, the mid-2000s saw its revival, as some individuals began to earn a living by queueing for a fee at box offices, hospitals, state agencies and banks. Outside modern Poland, a similar practice has been recorded in Russia, where those working in this informal line of business are known as *tramitadory*, and in Italy, where the profession of a line-stander – or *codista* – is a legally recognised one.

To a certain extent, shortages of consumer goods and queues as a key allocation mechanism in the shortage economy resulted from structural flaws embedded in socialist-era central planning (Kornai 1980). Accordingly, they were experienced across the entire Eastern bloc. For example, in the late socialist era, Soviet consumers spent between 30 and 40 billion hours a year in aggregate physically queueing for food and other necessities (Larson 1987: 899), which made queueing 'an inescapable quotidian ritual, a waste of time, and a source of irritation'

(Bogdanov 2012: 77). Additionally, consumers throughout the bloc were also habitually registered on one or more waiting lists for larger and more valuable commodities, such as cars, apartments, telephone lines or free vacations. Despite the ideological claims of the advanced nature of socialism, socialist states were unable to produce and allocate resources without queues. Rather, they demonstrated their power by means of a 'dictatorship over needs' (Fehér et al. 1986) and by immobilising citizens and seizing their time (Verdery 1996: 39–57). Hence, to save time and reclaim it from the state, consumers resorted to the informal economy.

This phenomenon laid the ground for the emergence of queue-keepers in Poland as well as in the Soviet Union, where they were referred to as *stoial'shchiki*, literally 'queue-standers', a term that is sometimes used for the present-day *tramitadory* as well.

What made the case of socialist-era Poland somewhat different – and hence rendered *stacze kolejkowi* more popular than their counterparts in other Eastern bloc republics – is that the food shortages were generated less by systemic flaws and more by the decisions made by planners and policymakers (Nørgaard and Sampson 1984). The first signs of a food crisis appeared in 1976, when food prices increased overnight, and sugar was rationed. In the early 1980s, the scale of shortages forced the authorities to extend the rationing system to a wide range of basic consumer goods. As food products became increasingly difficult to obtain, consumers formed long queues in front of otherwise empty shops whenever goods were due – or rumoured – to be delivered. In order to

Figure 8.7.1 People lining up to buy paczki (filled doughnuts) in Warsaw, Poland. © Grażyna Rutkowska/Narodowe Archiwum Cyfrowe.

maximise their chances of obtaining goods, many arrived several hours before the shops' official opening time (Burrell 2003: 190). Rather than queueing only for things they needed, consumers were always on the lookout for any products they could get hold of, knowing that even if they did not need them personally, they could always use them for barter. Such consumer strategies generated further shortages.

Given that demand was much higher than supply, many consumers attempted to obtain consumer goods out of turn by shortening their wait time or by beating the queue. Some deployed creative strategies to enter the shorter separate queues reserved for priority customers – for example, by faking disability and pregnancy or by bringing along little children. Others resorted to the 'familial society' (Wedel 1986), which helped them arrange food provision by means of various kinship- and friendship-centred practices (Mazurek 2012). Still others turned to the 'economy of favours' (Ledeneva 1998), wherein personal ties with shop managers or assistants sped up or facilitated one's access to goods under the counter in return for other goods or services. Individuals who were not well-connected but did not want to or could not queue hired a *stacz kolejkowy*. Even though networks were relatively important to this end as well, *stacze kolejkowi* could also be found outside shops or already standing in a queue. Indeed, many *stacze kolejkowi* queued for particularly attractive products without having been hired to do so, only to later sell their position in the queue – or the products acquired – at an inflated price (Zblewski 2000: 76).

Queueing for goods that were particularly difficult to obtain often ran to several hours, hence the ranks of *stacze kolejkowi* consisted predominantly of people with ample time on their hands, such as pensioners. For many of them, queueing for someone else was a daily practice that, in those times of uncertainty, supplemented their meagre pensions. *Stacze kolejkowi* would stand in a queue from early morning until an interested party bought their position in the queue. If the amount obtained was insufficient, they would move either to the end of the same queue or to another queue altogether, where they would stand again to wait for another client. *Stacze kolejkowi* were also hired ad hoc by individuals who could not skip work on a day that a particularly valuable product became available, or by people unwilling or unable to stand in a queue for appliances, which often stretched over several days. However, not all multi-day queues required constant physical presence, as queueing order was maintained by self-organised 'queue committees' (*komitety kolejkowe*), which kept a 'social queuing list' (*społeczna lista kolejkowa*) onto which all queuers were expected to register. Those registered were allowed to leave the queue but had to be present during roll calls – which took place two to four times a day – as one's failure to be present at a roll call a given number of times resulted in their position in the queue being lost.

Since queuers and queueing committees went to great lengths to keep queues orderly, *stacze kolejkowi* – and the speculation they engaged in – were met with contempt by other queuers. The practice of standing for hours only to sell one's position in the queue for monetary profit was perceived as a disregard for other queuers, as well as a breach of the queue etiquette and of the 'first come, first served' principle. Paradoxically, this reasoning was not usually extended to other forms of 'getting things done' in Poland (*załatwianie*), which offered access to products and services out of turn and hence deprived those who queued of a fair access to products. What made the practice of *stacze kolejkowi* reprehensible was that, in a sphere of life governed by the non-market exchange of goods and services, *stacze kolejkowi* supplanted 'the ethic of the queue (waiting your turn) with the ethic of the market (paying a price for faster service)' (Sandel 2012: 39).

8.8 *Taksovanie* (Uzbekistan)
Nikolaos Olma
Leibniz-Zentrum Moderner Orient, Germany

Taksovanie refers to the widespread practice of private car drivers in Tashkent, the capital of Uzbekistan, providing what across the post-Soviet space is known as 'private carriage' (in Russian: *chastnyi izvoz*), that is, paid rides to their fellow residents as a means of generating income (see also *boda-boda*, 5.33 Volume 2 and *trotro* for similar practices in African cities). The term itself is a colloquial Russian noun stemming from the similarly colloquial verb *taksovat'*, which literally translates as 'to taxi'; accordingly, *taksovanie* can be rendered as 'taxiing'. The majority of the drivers involved in this practice occasionally offer paid rides to passengers whose destination is more or less 'along their way' (Russian: *po puti*), which suggests that much of this mobility paradigm is in fact a form of paid carpooling. However, sustained unemployment and low salaries have forced a considerable part of Tashkent's male population to take up *taksovanie* either full-time, as their primary occupation, or part-time, as a source of secondary income. The majority of part-time drivers are low-wage workers and students who taxi only during after-work hours and at weekends, whereas full-time *taksovanie* is practised by pensioners, the unemployed and, in recent years, scores of young men from the provinces who migrate to Tashkent in search of employment.

While, to the author's knowledge, the noun *taksovanie* is seldom used outside Tashkent, the practice that it refers to is by no means limited to post-Soviet Central Asia's largest city. Offering paid rides in one's private car was already a relatively popular way of generating extra income in large Soviet cities during the socialist era (Siegelbaum 2009). But it was not until the early 1990s that this practice evolved into a fundamental 'survival strategy' (Johnson et al. 1998) employed by people across the former Soviet Union in order to cope with the adverse socio-economic conditions that accompanied the transition to market economy. Thanks to its around-the-clock availability, reliability and relatively low fares, this informal means of transport was immediately embraced by urban populations, for it provided them with an alternative to the mass public transport systems that had collapsed in the aftermath of the Soviet Union's dissolution (Gwilliam 2000). In turn, high demand gave more and more drivers the incentive to take up the practice, and, for most of the 1990s and the early 2000s, such informal taxis constituted a popular means of urban transport and an important element of everyday urban life throughout the region. The widespread occurrence of the practice across countries and socio-cultural contexts resulted in a series of localised colloquial verbs being used instead of or in parallel with *taksovat'* such as *grachevat'* (Kyiv), *kastriuliat'* (Odessa) and *bombit'* (Moscow). The last term is the reason why the individuals engaged in this practice across the post-Soviet space are – often pejoratively – referred to as *bombily*.

Tashkent's informal taxi drivers are essentially moonlighters who transport passengers in their private cars without a licence to do so, and, hence, the cars they drive are devoid of any signs, logos or other markings that distinguish them as taxis. Fares are allocated ad hoc, on the basis of negotiation between driver and passenger, but, nevertheless, they are relatively standard, since most parties involved know, more or less, how much each ride costs by taking into account a series of variables such as distance, car model, weather conditions or time of day. Since the vast majority of this income goes undeclared, *taksovanie* allegedly costs the state budget several billions in lost revenue annually, which has led the authorities, from the mid-2000s onwards, to launch an offensive aimed at curtailing the practice. Similar offensives have taken place in most post-Soviet cities and have, in the majority of cases, led to the practice's marginalisation or even eradication. Nevertheless, in Tashkent, a combination of factors – most notably unemployment and internal migration, low salaries, institutional obstacles hindering formalisation, the personal views and subjectivities of the drivers, as well as the ambivalent stance of the Uzbek state towards *taksovanie* – have all contributed to the endurance of the practice (Olma 2022).

The structural mass unemployment that has beset Uzbekistan's provinces is undoubtedly the most significant socio-economic condition fuelling *taksovanie*, for it steadily forces rural populations to migrate to Tashkent. Most of these rural-urban migrants are young men who come from lower social strata and have little – if any – economic capital, education or professional experience. Accordingly, becoming an informal taxi driver is often their only option (Olma 2021). Yet, the strict civil registration mechanism that is in place in Uzbekistan, known throughout the former Soviet Union as *propiska*, seldom allows poor rural-urban migrants to obtain legal residence status and work permits in Tashkent. Thus, from acquiring a car to finding their way around the city, these rural newcomers constantly navigate a wide array of informal processes, negotiate power relations, adjust to market forces, manoeuvre various regulatory frameworks and deal with the stereotypes that follow them across urban post-Soviet Central Asia. Due to the large volume of informal taxis – some estimates put their number at 30,000 – drivers fiercely compete for clients, which has resulted in relatively low fares that force drivers to work between 10 and 14 hours a day, six or seven days a week. Since most rural-urban migrants do not have another occupation and depend on the income generated from *taksovanie*, they work without any institutional safety net in the form of social security or insurance and notwithstanding the risks stemming from the state-led offensive against them.

Taksovanie is almost exclusively undertaken by men for, even though women often drive cars in Tashkent, they seldom offer rides to their fellow residents. Indeed, throughout his 11 months of ethnographic fieldwork in the city, this male author was never transported in a car driven by a woman, and neither were any of his interlocutors – male or female. Reasons behind the dominance of men over *taksovanie* include concerns by women over their safety and reputation, but also, importantly, the legacy of the Soviet 'gender order' stereotypes (Ashwin 2002) and its influence on post-Soviet labour culture. Throughout the Soviet era, maternalist protective labour regulations blocked the entry of women into professions that were deemed dangerous for their safety and – by extension – that of their family. In this context, *taksovanie* – like most other transport-related professions with the notable exception of trolleybus and tram drivers – is widely seen as 'not a woman's profession' (in Russian: *ne zhenskaia professiia*). This conviction becomes even stronger due to the association of driving and – especially – car ownership with masculinity. In the car-based society that is post-socialist Uzbekistan, cars are seen as an essential part of manhood, a token of coming-of-age among young men and even a prerequisite for marriage. Simultaneously, the extensive time that men in Tashkent spend in garage areas has led to the emergence of a particular 'car culture' (Miller 2001) which reinforces male sociability, male bonding and narratives of masculinity. Finally, the fact that *taksovanie* allows drivers to work for themselves (*rabotat' na sebia*) rather than for someone else (*rabotat' na diadiu*) is seen – especially among rural-urban migrants – as highlighting the manliness of the practice, for it affords them a certain degree of autonomy and freedom (Morris 2016; Sopranzetti 2017).

These associations of *taksovanie* with masculinity often result in rather complex dynamics between male drivers and female passengers, especially when the latter are young and/or unmarried. While physical abuse is uncommon, many female passengers have reported that drivers make them feel uneasy by insistently asking personal questions, making inappropriate comments or staring at them through the rear-view mirror. Among younger drivers, moreover, it is customary to offer young women a free ride in exchange for their phone number. Combined with the fact that many women are concerned about informal taxi drivers knowing where they live, these considerations lead women to book a more expensive licensed taxi to take them home safely, especially when they return from a late night out.

8.9 *Trotro* (Ghana)
Jennifer Hart
Department of History, Virginia Tech, USA

An estimated 85 per cent of the city of Accra, the capital of the West African country of Ghana, moves around in a network of entrepreneurial motor transportation known as the *trotro* (Okoye et al. 2010: 12). The word *trotro* evokes images of a broken-down 15-passenger van, stripped of its once-plush interior, outfitted with locally produced seats of metal frames and plywood bottoms and covered with fake leather. This transformation maximises the number of passengers on any given ride. Mechanics and repairmen in Accra control a process through which vehicles are 'tropicalized' and 'baptised into the system' (Verrips and Meyer 2001).

Along with market trading, *trotro* drivers are quintessential examples of the 'informal sector' or 'informal economy' in Accra, and the history of the *trotro* sector highlights the structural conditions through which

Figure 8.9.1 *Trotro* on the road in Accra, Ghana. © Jennifer Hart.

informal economies grow and thrive. The omnipresence of *trotros* embodies the challenges to contemporary analysis of informality and to development policies that seek to reform the informal economy (Hart 1973).

Trotros emerged in the 1960s out of a broader motor transportation sector through which African owner-operators dominated the transport of goods and passengers (see also *boda-boda* in Uganda, 5.33 Volume 2). Motor vehicles were first introduced in Ghana, then the British colony of the Gold Coast, in the early part of the twentieth century. Cocoa farmers, in particular, saw motor vehicles as a good investment, which allowed them to transport their produce directly to the coast. In purchasing vehicles and transporting their produce, the economic choices of these farmers became a political act. Farmers used their economic power to resist colonial attempts to control the African movement and the flow of profits through the railway.

Throughout much of the twentieth century, Ghanaians used access to vehicles and roads to make powerful arguments about their rights as citizens who deserved investment from the state. In the absence of that investment from both colonial and independent governments, drivers and passengers made motor transportation their own. Drivers valued owning their own vehicle and would work long hours to save up enough money to be able to do so. Vehicles were purchased through importers who shipped new metal engines and chassis from Europe and the United States. New vehicle owners would take their assembled vehicles to carpenters, who added a wooden body, and painters, who decorated the vehicle in their classic blue colour scheme with vibrant decoration and slogans across the rear. These vehicles were popularly known as *mammy trucks* (alternatively *mammy wagons* or *mammy lorries*), emphasising the close connection between motor technology and the passengers who used it most frequently – market women engaged in regional and long-distance trade. Drivers who controlled these valued pieces of technology were respected for their skill in managing risk, for their relative prosperity and for their cosmopolitan ways. Regarded as modern men, they were able to achieve elevated status while bypassing the realms of Western education. The culture and practices of drivers integrated the city and countryside in a sphere of movement of goods, ideas and people.

Before the spread of these wooden trucks, the wealthiest urban passengers drove private cars or hired taxis. The city's most mobile residents, travelling to and from the market to trade, rode the municipal bus system, approved for circulation by the Accra Town Council in 1927. The British-style buses were designed for passenger transport solely, but people travelling to and from the market often also carried goods. These did not fit easily into the tight quarters of the municipal bus. Market women and drivers saw an opportunity: the *mammy lorries* transported passengers around the city and offloaded goods at local markets simultaneously. The city of La was both a gateway for goods entering the city from the agricultural areas to the east and a centre for driver training. Drivers moving between La and Accra with partially empty trucks started picking up market women standing along the roadside with their goods. British colonial officials labelled these vehicles 'pirate passenger lorries', suggesting that these vehicles not only cut into the revenue of the municipal bus system, but also undermined colonial authority and order in the capital city. For market women and other passengers these lorries provided a better way to get around and allowed them to connect neighbourhoods with major markets throughout the city (Hart 2020). The British tried to eliminate the 'pirate passenger lorries' through regulation and restrictions, but they failed to completely stamp out the practice.

The emergence of *trotros* in the late 1950s – first operated by the Ga driver Anane – is an extension of the activities of the colonial-era passenger lorries. Continuing to carry a mixed load of goods and passengers, *trotro* drivers used shorter versions of wooden trucks. Unlike their 'pirate' predecessors, post-independence leaders recognised *trotros* as a lawful form of public transport that could operate alongside municipal buses. *Trotros* operated along the same routes as municipal buses, often charging higher but set fares for travel anywhere within the municipal boundaries of Accra. The term *trotro* itself is drawn from the three-pence fare – the word *tro* in Ga language means 'three'. Beginning in the mid-1960s, the municipal bus system began to steadily decline, hampered by the cost of maintaining the system and the competition from *trotros* (Hart 2013). By the 1970s and 1980s, the public transport system was dominated almost entirely by *trotros* and lorries.

Individual owner-operators often ran the vehicles like a small business. When the cost of maintaining the vehicle or buying petrol increased, so did the fares. When the Ghanaian economy began to struggle in the late 1960s, drivers continued to thrive as men of relative wealth – so much so that women famously aspired to form romantic relationships with drivers because of the stability of their work. The economic crisis worsened throughout the 1970s and 1980s (Hart 2013). Due to the declining value of cocoa, Ghana lost access to enough foreign currency to be able to import goods. Spare parts, tyres and petrol were in increasingly short supply. Yet despite the economic turmoil through the decades – oil shocks in 1979, petrol shortages in 1982–3, famine in the early 1980s – *trotro* drivers continued to flourish. The most successful drivers employed ingenious strategies to keep their vehicles going. When their tyres went flat, they would fill them with rocks in order to continue driving. Improvised spare parts became common. And, when drivers were able to get petrol, they would take passengers at much higher fares. From the perspective of a small business owner, this just seemed like good business practice. From the perspective of passengers, who relied on these vehicles as part of a public transport service, drivers seemed to be profiting from their suffering. The Acheampong (1972–8) and Rawlings regimes (1979, 1981–2001) labelled drivers (and market women) as profiteers, cheats and scoundrels due to their economic prowess in a period of general distress (Hart 2013).

For many, *trotros* are associated with dilapidation, poverty, dirt and criminality. Passengers complain about the smell of the driver's assistant (or 'mate'), the state of the vehicle, the rudeness of their fellow passengers and the danger of the road. Government officials lambast *trotro* drivers over high fares, and newspapers are full of stories of accidents. But the association of *trotros* and their drivers with crime, poverty and danger is relatively new.

The liberalisation of import levies means that vehicles are more available but in worse condition than ever before. Young men, unable to find jobs in the formal sector often come to the *trotro* sector to secure a portion of their income. Even pensioners are using their retirement to drive *trotros* to supplement their small public pensions in an increasingly expensive Accra. The flood of drivers into the system since the 1990s created record-high competition, thus decreasing the profit margins of vehicle owners and limiting the capital available for owners to reinvest in their vehicles (Quayson 2014: 199; Hart 2016: 149–88).

Risky driving is central to the social and cultural identity of a *trotro* driver. On the back of the vehicle are slogans, cut-out of sheets of reflective sticker applied to a rear window or door. These slogans, mostly religious, constitute a sort of folk philosophy – evoking both the values and practices of daily life and the wider existential concerns of drivers and their passengers (Quayson 2014: 129–58, Hart 2016: 20). Phrases like 'My God is Able', 'Nyame Adom' (By the Grace of God), 'Nyame Bekyere' (The Lord Will Provide), 'Only God', 'God's Grace', 'By His Grace', 'Blessings', and many others highlight the importance of a particular vision of religion in contemporary Ghana, which associates faith and piety with material reward. When asked about the meaning of their slogans, individual drivers offer profoundly personal interpretations of the ambivalent sentiment – faith either gave them a vehicle to drive, brought good fortune and took them out of poverty, or protected them from accidents and helped them steer clear of things that didn't happen. Other slogans like 'Jealous', 'Trust No Man', 'Fear Women', 'All Eyes on Me', 'Consider Your Ways', 'Such is Life', 'You Lie Bad', 'Who Is Free' and 'No Mercy for *Trotro* Drivers' are reminders about the uncertainty of life and the difficulty of survival.

8.10 *Pfandsammeln* (Germany)
Annika Kurze
Technische Universität Dortmund, Germany

Pfandsammeln, literally 'collecting refunds', is a common practice in Germany and entails collecting empty and discarded bottles and cans in public or semi-public spaces and returning them to supermarkets for a refund (Duden 2020). People collecting empty drink packaging are called *Pfandsammler*.

The practice of collecting used bottles and cans is not unique to Germany. Recycling of glass bottles, paper and metal were common in the economies of shortage in the former Soviet Union and Yugoslavia (see *budzenje*, 5.36 Volume 2 and *vrtičkarstvo*, 11.8 in this volume). Under socialism, such practices were supported by the infrastructure and promoted through various reward schemes. Practices of waste-recycling, urban foraging or skipping remain operational in the developed markets today but are mainly associated with poverty, squatting and the ethnicity of migrant markets. In Germany, however, *Pfandsammeln* has become an unexpected side effect of the German regulation of packaging (*Verpackungsverordnung*) adopted in 2003. Depending on the kind of bottle, a deposit charge of between 8 and 25 euro cents (depending on the type of packaging) is added to the price of the beverage and can be refunded upon returning them to a supermarket (Voigt 2007: 203). This legal constraint on producers encourages reuse or recycling. The monetary refund system is key for the practice of *Pfandsammler*.

The other important factor is the social custom, whereby people leave behind their bottles in public spaces because they consider returning them an inconvenience, or they leave them in the bin intentionally to benefit those with no income. It is widely held that *Pfandsammler* have no income and that they earn money by returning collected reusable or recyclable packaging. Although the regulation of packaging applies in all 16 German federal states, *Pfandsammeln* is practised much more commonly in urban areas due to the higher number of public spaces and the higher level of poverty in the cities. The income of a bottle collector depends significantly on the number of visitors to a public space. *Pfandsammler* usually collect in city centres, public transport stations and during public events such as concerts or football games (Moser 2014: 1). *Pfandsammler* is associated with urban space and is part of the image that Germans have of city centres.

There are no legal provisions in German law to prohibit collecting refundable bottles discarded by others. However, in public service areas such as shopping centres and train stations, taking anything, including bottles and cans, out of the bins is prohibited (Langhof 2017). Landowners can claim that the contents of the bin belong to them and demand recognition of the emptying of them by the public as theft. The introduction of sub-federal regulations adopting this recognition is often in tune with a general perception of the *Pfandsammler* as a social outcast. Often paired with a rhetoric of order and social security in public spaces, such regulations reinforce social inequality by protecting 'well-behaved' citizens from exposure to those forced to handle public waste. To what extent the regulations are enforced depends on the institution. Some choose to turn a blind eye on the practice as long as the collection is within manageable limits.

The stigma associated with bottle collection, however, disregards the value of bottle collectors' work as ecological duty, voluntary contribution and good civic practice, since the city's streets are cleared of waste for free and glass gets recycled. The less bottles and cans refunded, the bigger the *Pfandschlupf*. Translated as 'deposit slip', the term describes the profit retailers make due to fewer refund payments being redeemed than were charged for (Südwestrundfunk 2020). Without the informal work of *Pfandsammler* and their economical contribution to the German Refund System, this deposit slip would be higher.

Popular initiatives like *Pfand gehört daneben* ('Refundables belong on the side') recognises the role of *Pfandsammler* and calls for people to place their used refundable bottles and cans next to the bin instead of inside it so that collectors can easily take them (Pfand gehört daneben 2020). These campaigns underline the fact that *Pfandsammeln* is not only central to recycling in public spaces, but that communities and municipalities also have to start addressing the issue.

Both public awareness and debates around the issues of *Pfandsammler* are on the rise. There is little scientific research on the topic, with notable exceptions. In a study from 2014, the researcher conducted interviews with *Pfandsammler* and suggested that the motives behind the practice of collecting refundable bottles were complex. Collecting recycling not only generated money but was a way of organising and structuring everyday routine, escaping loneliness and offering engagement in the wider social fabric (Moser 2014: 115). An analysis of the environmental and social aspects of bottle collection based on a case study from Berlin addresses the tension between the ecological and social impact of packaging regulations. While bottle collection contributes to the protection of resources, it also creates an informal economy. The *Pfandsammler* economy is influenced by several external factors. Physical disabilities and mental health issues can make finding a job difficult. Unfair pension systems and migration contribute to the emergence of social and economic outcasts within a society and homelessness. Challenging living conditions may lead people to start to collect bottles and cans.

The practice of collecting refundable bottles and cans emerges on the margins of work or land use. Collectors can spend long hours walking through cities, searching for bottles thrown into bins, scattered in parks or left on pavements in order to secure earnings. They are neither registered workers, nor regulated or supervised (Kainz 2004: 1) and earn money in an informal way, often similarly to the work of street performers and musicians. However, *Pfandsammler* do not rely exclusively on the generosity of passers-by and can stay inconspicuous. They tend to work without disturbing users, although occasionally they wait for people to finish their drink and leave a bottle or can behind. *Pfandsammler* create a self-appointed task that offers them a daily structure, together with the monetary aspect.

Pfandsammeln is a case of a broader set of waste-related informal practices, as well as recycling strategies that the state offloads onto businesses and communities. Making money by returning recyclable bottles and cans without a recycling infrastructure provided by the state is a social contract supported by social norms. The *Pfandsammler* is also an example of claiming a degree of freedom and the right to work informally, without status, assignment or function in a society, and regardless of whether such practices are stigmatised, tolerated or appreciated.

8.11 **Andare in giro** (Italy)
Isabella Clough Marinaro
John Cabot University Rome, Italy

Andare in giro literally means to 'go around' or 'wander' in Italian and is used in multiple contexts. It is, however, also a very specific term employed by some Roma communities in the country to refer to their practice of scouting for and collecting recyclable goods around urban streets and peripheral wasteland. It also includes sourcing items directly from an extensive array of personal contacts. The materials are then cleaned, mended and sold through various formal and informal commercial channels. The practice constitutes a central link in the economies of many camp-dwelling Roma families and is deeply intertwined with urban businesses in Italy more generally.

The artisanal-level collection of discarded recyclable goods occurs around the world, both in the so-called Global South and Global North, providing essential employment for many low-income groups (Fahmi and Sutton 2006; Samson 2015; Cattaneo 2017). In some contexts, it is also becoming recognised as a sustainable, environmentally low-impact means of advancing a circular economy, enabling some communities to demand political and financial recognition for their environmentally protective work (Rutkowski and Rutkowski 2015; Schurman et al. 2017). In Italy, informal waste gleaning is a historically entrenched practice with deep roots in the country's impoverished past. It is not an ethnic-specific activity and, indeed, it has seen a marked rise since the economic crisis of 2008, reflecting the country's ongoing difficulties in addressing the needs of its long-term poor population (ISTAT 2020). Thus, residents of many backgrounds collect what they can for personal use or resale: food, clothing, metals, reusable electronics and household goods (Masia 2016). Notwithstanding this diversity, it is a sector in which many Roma families in particular have developed expertise over various decades, using its elasticity to generate multiple income streams and weave extensive social networks. Although it is largely a consequence of multifaceted discrimination that has forced many Roma groups into poverty – due to frequent exclusion from other employment sectors and the relegation of numerous communities to peripheral slum-like urban camps – it also represents a crucial way of asserting entrepreneurial agency and maintaining economic autonomy from non-Roma (Solimene 2016).

Andare in giro usually involves driving along well-established routes, often various times a week, visiting illegal dumpsites as well as warehouses and bulk stores where Roma collectors have built friendly relations with managers who donate unsold or discarded items. Similarly, foremen at construction sites often allow them to take unwanted materials. However, there are also cases where such actors demand payment for these goods. Salvagers also dedicate time and effort to cultivating contacts in their neighbourhoods, and among NGOs and small business owners around the towns in which they work. Relationships are often so consolidated that clients call requesting the emptying of cellars or the removal of bulky objects. Until the early 2000s, metals were the most lucrative material for collection and resale. However, their falling value on global markets, the intensified legal barriers to transporting and selling them and the physically exhausting and dangerous work of extracting and cleaning metals has forced many reclaimers to diversify into other second-hand commodities. Household goods are often less bulky than metal and do not need to be moved in trucks, thereby attracting less police attention. Moreover, they fall into a regulatory grey zone, making them less easily classifiable as special waste and thus subject to fewer risks of fines and confiscation. Their informal, rather than illegal, status makes the investment of time and petrol to collect them a less risky economic strategy.

In camps where the authorities still allow – or at least informally tolerate – the storage and separation of recovered materials, Roma salvagers then sort and clean the goods in open spaces around homes, with all members of the family participating according to their individual strength and skill. The objects are kept in sheds or under plastic sheeting until they can be resold or reused: old windows and wooden planks are saved for expanding or repairing homes, a battered sofa provides a safe place for small children to play, furniture awaits repair, supermarket trolleys hold items too heavy to carry. Most goods first flow through the domestic sphere; every item is evaluated for its immediate or longer-term utility to the household and for its market value. Some are used temporarily and then sold when a better replacement is found. Long-term stockpiling is impossible, though, as residents fear their goods may be stolen or damaged or that the authorities will evict and demolish the camp and their wares. Consequently, they try to sell them as quickly as possible, at informal street markets or directly to their web of private clients. Indeed, their sales networks are as extensive and diverse as their suppliers. These include collectors and merchants of antiquities and vintage goods, second-hand furniture dealers, metal scrap yards and migrant traders who regularly visit to source specific categories of goods for export primarily to Africa. This last group focuses especially on good-quality second-hand sports shoes, construction tools and machinery, replacement parts for household appliances and electronic components for computers and mobile phones.

The reuse economy within which Roma traders operate is therefore clearly integrated within global consumption and value chains. At the same time, their salvaging work involves the constant weaving of social and cultural capital that reflects their deep embeddedness in Italian local communities and economies. Despite the evidence that these are not marginal or subaltern activities, they are subject to stigmatisation by the authorities and in mainstream media. Gleaning from dumpsters is considered theft in Italian law, and media coverage regularly conflates second-hand wares with generic garbage (Barlozzari and Benignetti 2021). Licences for transportation and sale are expensive and bureaucratically complex, and many city authorities obstruct the creation of street markets for second-hand goods. This resistance to facilitating artisanal recovery and reuse activities is in direct contrast to the EU's policies for sustainable waste management. The recovery of metals and electronic components is of particular importance in the EU's Waste Framework Directive (2008/98/EC), while the more recent European Green Deal has placed even greater emphasis on developing a circular economy that 'work[s] for people, regions and cities' (European Commission 2020). Such goals are echoed in the Italian government's National Strategy for a Circular Economy (MTE [Ministero della Transizione Ecologica] 2022), yet a bill that aims to provide the legal framework for simplifying procedures, tax statuses and licences for reclaimers and traders has been languishing in parliament since 2018 (CdD [Camera dei Deputati] 2018). The bill's proponents estimate that 500,000 tons of materials currently destroyed as waste could be retrieved and reused if a functional system were in place. This would bring Italy more closely in line with countries that support small-scale waste collectors as an environmental asset. For now, though, many Roma waste salvagers continue to operate in legal grey zones that contribute to their financial precarity and their ethnic stigmatisation (Clough Marinaro 2022).

Bibliography to Chapter 8

Introduction: informal economy
Colin C. Williams

Horodnic, I. and Williams, C. C. 2021. 'Cash Wage Payments in Transition Economies: Consequences of Envelope Wages'. Bonn: IZA World of Labor.
Hussmanns, R. 2005. 'Measuring the Informal Economy: From Employment in the Informal Sector to Informal Employment'. Working Paper No. 53. Geneva: ILO. www.ilo.org/wcmsp5/groups/public/---dgreports/---integration/documents/publication/wcms_079142.pdf
ILO. 2002. 'Decent Work and the Informal Economy'. Geneva: ILO. www.ilo.org/public/english/standards/relm/ilc/ilc90/pdf/rep-vi.pdf
ILO. 2012. 'Statistical Update on Employment in the Informal Economy'. Geneva: ILO. www.ilo.org/global/statistics-and-databases/WCMS_182504/lang--en/index.htm
ILO. 2013. 'Women and Men in the Informal Economy: Statistical Picture'. Geneva: ILO. www.ilo.org/wcmsp5/groups/public/---dgreports/---stat/documents/publication/wcms_234413.pdf
ILO. 2015. 'Recommendation no. 204 Concerning the Transition from the Informal to the Formal Economy'. Geneva: ILO. www.ilo.org/wcmsp5/groups/public/---ed_norm/---relconf/documents/meetingdocument/wcms_377774.pdf
Schneider, F. 2013. 'Size and Development of the Shadow Economy of 31 European and 5 Other OECD Countries from 2003 to 2013: A Further Decline'. Linz: Johannes Kepler University, Department of Economics. https://politeia.org.ro/wp-content/uploads/2013/05/ShadEcEurope31_Jan2013.pdf
Williams, C. C. 2006. *The Hidden Enterprise Culture: Entrepreneurship in the Underground Economy*. Gloucester: Edward Elgar.
Williams, C. C. 2019. *The Informal Economy*. Newcastle-upon-Tyne: Agenda Publishing. http://cup.columbia.edu/book/the-informal-economy/9781911116318
Woolfson, C. 2007. 'Pushing the Envelope: The "Informalization" of Labour in post-Communist New EU Member States'. *Work, Employment and Society* 21(5): 551–64.

8.1 *Svart arbete* (Sweden)
Lotta Björklund Larsen

Björklund Larsen, L. 2010. *Illegal yet Licit: Justifying Informal Purchases of Work in Contemporary Sweden*. Stockholm: Stockholm Studies in Social Anthropology N.S. 2.
Björklund Larsen, L. 2013. 'The Making of a "Good Deal". Dealing with Conflicting and Complementary Values When Getting the Car Repaired Informally in Sweden'. *Journal of Cultural Economy* 6: 419–33.
Carlberg, P. 2005. 'Svartjobb ett tillväxthot. Ekobrottsmyndigheten varnar för att uppsving i ekonomin äts upp av ekobrotten'. Interview with Director Gudrun Antemar, *Svenska Dagbladet*, 13 December 2005.
Gudeman, S. 2001. *The Anthropology of Economy: Community, Market, and Culture*. Oxford: Blackwell Publishers.
Holm, P. 1964. *Bevingade ord och andra talesätt*. Stockholm: Bonnier.
Leonard, M. 1998. *Invisible Work, Invisible Workers: The Informal Economy in Europe and the US*. London: Macmillan.
Lindgren, S.-Å. (ed.) 2001. *White-Collar Crime Research: Old Views and Future Potentials*. Stockholm: Brottsförebyggande rådet Report 2001:1.
OECD. 2002. *Measuring the Non-Observed Economy. A Handbook*. Paris: OECD Publications Service.
OECD. 2004. *OECD Employment Outlook*. Paris: OECD Publications Service.
Pardo, I. 1996. *Managing Existence in Naples: Morality, Action, and Structure*. Cambridge: Cambridge University Press.
Polismyndigheten. 2017. *Myndigheter i samverkan mot den organiserade brottsligheten 2016*. Stockholm: Polismyndigheten.

Riksrevisionsverket. 1997. *Svart arbete: 1. Arbetstagare och företagare. Insatser*. Stockholm: Riksrevisionsverket. Report 59.
Sampson, S. 1986. 'Italienske tilstande eller utopi?'. In *Uden Regning*, edited by K. F. Olwig and S. Sampson, 17–43. Copenhagen: Rosinante.
SAOB. 2006. *Svenska akademiens ordbok*. Om Svar Anhålles. http://g3.spraakdata.gu.se/saob/
Skatteverket. 2006. *Purchasing and Performing Undeclared Work in Sweden: Part 1. Results from Various Studies*. Authored by A. Persson and H. Malmer. Stockholm: Skatteverket.
Skatteverket. 2008. *Tax Gap Map for Sweden How Was It Created and How Can It Be Used?, 1B*. Stockholm: Skatteverket.
Skatteverket. 2021. *Skattefelsrapport 2020*. Stockholm: Skatteverket.
Smith, M. E. 1989. 'The Informal Economy'. In *Economic Anthropology*, edited by S. Plattner, 292–317. Stanford: Stanford University Press.
Viby Mogensen, G. 2003. *Danmarks uformelle økonomi. Historiske og internationale aspekter*. København: Spektrum.

8.2 *Travail au noir* (France)
Carla Montigny

Barthe, M.-A. 1985. 'Chômage, travail au noir et entraide familiale'. *Revue Consommation* 3: 19–32.
Barthélemy, P. 1982. 'Travail au noir et économie souterraine: un état de la recherche'. *Travail et Emploi* 12(4).
Helmke, G. and Levitsky, S. 2004. 'Informal Institutions and Comparative Politics: A Research Agenda'. *Perspectives on Politics* 2(4): 725–40.
Laé, J. F. 1990. 'Le travail au noir, vestibule de l'emploi'. *Sociologie du Travail* 32(1): 23–37.
Ledeneva, A. and Efendic, A. 2020. 'The Rules of the Game in Transition: How Informal Institutions Work in South East Europe'. In *Handbook of Comparative Economics*, edited by E. Douarin and O. Havrylyshyn, 811–45. London: Palgrave Macmillan.
North, D. C. 1991. 'Institutions'. *The Journal of Economic Perspectives* 5(1): 97–112.
Stuart, E., Samman, E. and Hunt, A. 2018. 'Informal is the New Normal – Improving the Lives of Workers at Risk of Being Left Behind'. *Shaping Policy for Development*.

8.3 *Caporalato* (Italy)
Francesco Bagnardi

Avallone, G. 2017. *Sfruttamento e resistenze: Migrazioni e agricoltura in Europa, Italia, Piana del Sele*. Verona: Ombre Corte.
Bagnardi, F., D'Onofrio, G. and Greco, L. 2022. 'The State in Chains: Public Policies against Adverse Incorporation in Southern Italian Production Networks'. *Globalizations* 19(1): 34–58.
Barrientos, S. 2013. 'Labour Chains: Analysing the Role of Labour Contractors in Global Production Networks'. *The Journal of Development Studies* 49(8): 1058–71.
Carchedi, F. 2020. 'La componente di lavoro indecente nel settore agricolo. Casi di studio territoriali'. In *Agromafie e caporalato – Quinto Rapporto*, edited by Osservatorio Placido Rizzotto, 183–92. Rome: Ediesse.
Corrado, A., Castro, C. and de Perrotta, D. 2016. *Migration and Agriculture: Mobility and Change in the Mediterranean Area*. London: Routledge.
Corrado, A., Caruso, F. S., Lo Cascio, M., Palumbo, L. and Triandafyllidou, A. 2018. *Is Italian Agriculture 'Pull Factor' for Irregular Migration – And, If So, Why?* Open Society European Policy Institute.
De Genova, N. P. 2002. 'Migrant "Illegality" and Deportability in Everyday Life'. *Annual Review of Anthropology* 31(1): 419–47.
de Martino, C., Lozito, M. and Schiuma, D. 2016. 'Immigrazione, caporalato e lavoro in agricoltura'. *Lavoro e Diritto* 30(2): 313–28.
Dines, N. and Rigo, E. 2015. 'Postcolonial Citizenships and the "Refugeeization" of the Workforce: Migrant Agricultural Labor in the Italian Mezzogiorno'. In *Postcolonial Transitions in Europe: Contexts, Practices and Politics*, edited by S. Ponzanesi and G. Colpani, 151–72). London: Rowman & Littlefield.
Fanizza, F. and Omizzolo, M. 2019. *Caporalato: An Authentic Agromafia*. Milan: Mimesis International.

Fellini, I., Ferro, A. and Fullin, G. 2007. 'Recruitment Processes and Labour Mobility: The Construction Industry in Europe'. *Work, Employment and Society* 21(2): 277–98.

Inversi, C. 2021. 'Digital caporalato: The Uber Italy Srl Case'. *Lavoro e Diritto* 2/202167.

Merlo, A. 2020. *Il contrasto allo sfruttamento del lavoro e al 'caporalato' dai braccianti ai rider: Le fattispecie dell'art.603 bis c.p. E il ruolo del diritto penale*. Turin: Giappichelli Editore.

Mottura, G. and Pugliese, E. 1976. 'Agricoltura, mercato del lavoro e politica del movimento operaio'. In *Problemi del movimento sindacale in Italia 1943–1973: Annali Feltrinelli – Anno Sedicesimo*, edited by A. Accornero, 367–408. Milan: Fondazione Giangiacomo Feltrinelli.

Osservatorio Placido Rizzotto. (ed.) 2020. *Agromafie e caporalato – Quinto Rapporto*. Rome: Ediesse.

Palumbo, L. and Corrado, A. 2020. *Are Agri-food Workers only Exploited in Southern Europe? Case Studies on Migrant Labour in Germany, The Netherlands, and Sweden*. Open Society European Policy Institute.

Peano, I. 2017. 'Migrants' Struggles? Rethinking Citizenship, Anti-racism and Labour Precarity through Migration Politics in Italy'. In *Where are the Unions? Workers and Social Movements in Latin America, the Middle East and Europe*, edited by S. Lazar, 85–102. London: Zed Books.

Perrotta, D. 2014. 'Vecchi e nuovi mediatori. Storia, geografia ed etnografia del caporalato in agricoltura'. *Meridiana* 79: 193–220.

Perrotta, D. 2015. 'Agricultural Day Laborers in Southern Italy: Forms of Mobility and Resistance'. *The South Atlantic Quarterly* 114(1): 195–203.

Perrotta, D. 2019. '"Quando si raccoglie il pomodoro è una guerra". Resistenze e conflitti dei braccianti migranti nei territori del pomodoro'. *Cartografie Sociali. Rivista Semestrale di Sociologia e Scienze Umane* 1(7): Article 7. https://universitypress.unisob.na.it/ojs/index.php/cartografiesociali/article/view/715

Perrotta, D. and Sacchetto, D. 2014. 'Migrant Farmworkers in Southern Italy: Ghettoes, Caporalato and Collective Action'. *Workers of the World: International Journal on Strikes and Social Conflicts* 1(5): 75–98.

Piselli, F. 1990. 'Sensali e caporali dell'Italia Meridionale'. In *Storia dell'Agricoltura in etàcontemporanea: Vol. II-Uomini e Classi*, edited by P. Bevilacqua, 823–55. Venice: Marsilio Editori.

Poppi, F. I. M. and Travaglino, G. A. 2019. 'Parea non Servin: Strategies of Exploitation and Resistance in the Caporalato Discourse'. *Modern Italy* 24(1): 81–97.

Sagnet, Y. and Palmisano, L. 2015. *Ghetto Italia: I braccianti stranieri tra caporalato e sfruttamento*. Rome: Fandango Libri.

Santoro, E. and Stoppioni, C. 2019. 'Il contrasto allo sfruttamento lavorativo: I primi dati dell'applicazione della legge 199/2016'. *Giornale di Diritto del lavoro e di relazioni industriali*.

Scotto, A. 2016. 'Tra sfruttamento e protesta: I migranti e il caporalato agricolo in Italia meridionale'. *REMHU – Revista Interdisciplinar Da Mobilidade Humana* 48: 79–92.

8.4 *Paga globale* (Italy)
Giulio Benedetti

Caputo, G. O. and D'Onofrio, G. 2011. 'Emigrare senza radicarsi: storie di lavoratori pendolari dal Sud al Nord del paese'. *Sociologia del Lavoro* 113–33.

Cillo, R. and Perocco, F. 2016. 'Subappalto e sfruttamento differenziale dei lavoratori immigrati: il caso di tre settori in Italia'. *Economia e Società Regionale* 101–23.

Larsen, L. 2021. 'Svart arbete'. *Global Informality Project*. https://www.in-formality.com/wiki/index.php?title=Svart_Arbete_(Sweden)

Mion, C. 2021. 'I nuovi schiavi, il "caporale" dei subappalti preso a Marghera'. *La Nuova Venezia*, 20 April 2021.

Montigny, C. 2021. 'Travail au noir', *Global Informality Project*. www.in-formality.com/wiki/index.php?title=Travail_au_noir_(France)

Panariti, L. 2011. 'Tute blu e principesse. L'organizzazione del lavoro nel cantiere di Monfalcone (1987–2007)'. *EUT Edizioni Università di Trieste*.

Sedlenieks, K. 2018. 'Alga aploksnē'. In *Global Encyclopaedia of Informality, Volume 2*, edited by A. Ledeneva. London: UCL Press.

Skupnjak-Kapić, S., Milas, G., Mustapi, M. and Karaji, N. 2005. 'Cross-border Labour Migration Flows Croatia-Italy: Focus on Shipbuilding'. *International Organization for Migration*. IOM Publications.

8.5 *Shabashniki* (USSR, Russia)
Nikolay Erofeev

Arnot, B. 1988. *Controlling Soviet Labour: Experimental Change from Brezhnev to Gorbachev*. Basingstoke: Macmillan.
Clarke, S. 1999. *The Formation of a Labour Market in Russia*. Cheltenham: Edward Elgar.
Erofeev, N. 2020. *Experiment in Soviet Architecture and Public Housing, 1955–1990*. Thesis (Dr. phil), Oxford: Oxford University.
Kruglianskaia, I. 1985. 'S diplomom na zarabotki', *Izvestia*, 14 December, 3.
Lazareva, O. 2015. 'Russian Migrants to Russia: Assimilation and Local Labor Market Effects'. *IZA Journal of Migration* 4: 20.
Le Normand, B. 2014. *Designing Tito's Capital: Urban Planning, Modernism, and Socialism in Belgrade*. Pittsburgh: University of Pittsburgh Press.
Ledeneva, A. 2006. *How Russia Really Works: The Informal Practices that Shaped Post-Soviet Politics and Business*. Ithaca and London: Cornell University Press.
Ledeneva, A. 2018. *Global Encyclopaedia of Informality, Volume 2: Understanding Social and Cultural Complexity*. London: UCL Press.
Łoś, M. 1990. *The Second Economy in Marxist States*. Basingstoke: Macmillan.
Millar, J. R. 1985. 'The Little Deal: Brezhnev's Contribution to Acquisitive Socialism', *Slavic Review* 44: 694–706.
Miller, C. 2017. *The Struggle to Save the Soviet Economy: Mikhail Gorbachev and the Collapse of the USSR*. Chapel Hill: The University of North Carolina Press.
Morris, J. 2013. 'Beyond Coping? Alternatives to Consumption within a Social Network of Russian Workers'. *Ethnography* 14: 85–103.
O'Hearn, D. 1980. 'The Consumer Second Economy: Size and Effects'. *Soviet Studies* 32: 218–34.
Otsu, S. and Ramzes, V. B. 1992. *Sovetskii rynok truda: analiz iaponskogo spetsialista*. Moskva: Mysl'.
Shabanova, M. 1991. *Sezonnaia i postoiannaia migratsiia naseleniia v sel'skom raione: Kompleks. sotsiol.-stat. issled.* Novosibirsk: Nauka.
Shelly, L. 1990. 'The Second Economy in the Soviet Union'. In *The Second Economy in Marxist States*, edited by M. Łoś, 11–26. Basingstoke: Macmillan.
Treisman, D. 2016. 'Russia's Billionaires'. *The American Economic Review* 106: 236–41.
Valetov, T. 2008. 'Samoorganizovannye sezonnye brigady (shabashniki) v SSSR v 1960–1980-kh gg.: ekonomicheskie i sotsial'nye aspekty'. In *Ekonomicheskaia istoriia*, edited by L. Borodkin, 203–26. Moscow: Obozrenie.
Valetov, T. 2010. 'Mekhanizmy samoorganizatsii sezonnykh trudovykh migrantov v SSSR i na post-sovetskom prostranstve'. In *Sovetskoe nasledstvo: Otrazhenie proshlogo v sotsial'nykh i ekonomicheskikh praktikakh sovremennoi Rossii*, edited by L. Borodkin, X. Kesslera and A. Sokolova, 253–78. Moscow: ROSSPEN.

8.6 *Khaltura* (USSR)
Taisiia Nahorna

Bykov, D. 2014. 'Dmitrii Bykov: khaltura est' i est' kultura'. *Sobesednik.ru*, 13 March. https://sobesednik.ru/dmitriy-bykov/20140313-hodorkovskiy-na-maydane
Cambridge Dictionary. 2020a. 'Gig'. *Cambridge Dictionary*. https://dictionary.cambridge.org/dictionary/english/gig
Cambridge Dictionary. 2020b. 'Side Hustle'. *Cambridge Dictionary*. https://dictionary.cambridge.org/dictionary/english/side-hustle
Dovlatov, S. 1999. 'Trudnoe slovo'. *Sergeidovlatov.com*. www.sergeidovlatov.com/books/trudnoes.html
Erofeev, N. 2019. 'Shabashniki (USSR, Russia)'. *Global Informality Project*. www.in-formality.com/wiki/index.php?title=Shabashniki_(USSR,_Russia)
Kartsevskiĭ, S. 2000. *Iz lingvisticheskogo nasledii͡a*. Moscow: I͡azyki russkoĭ kul'tury.
Kuznetsov, S. 2014. *Bol'shoĭ tolkovyĭ slovar' russkogo i͡azyka*. St. Petersburg: Norint.
Rambler. 2018. 'U kogo v SSSR byla samaya vysokaya zarplata'. *Finance rambler.ru*, 29 July. https://finance.rambler.ru/money/40440503-u-kogo-v-sssr-byla-samaya-vysokaya-zarplata/

Seichas.ru. 1968. 'Prikaz Minvuza SSSR ot 18.03.1968 n 220'. Seichas.ru. www.lawmix.ru/docs_cccp/6149

Semenov, A. 2003. *Ėtimologicheskiĭ slovar' russkogo iāzyka*. Moscow: IUNVES.

8.7 *Stacze kolejkowi* (Poland)
Nikolaos Olma

Bogdanov, K. 2012. 'The Queue as Narrative: A Soviet Case Study'. In *Russian Cultural Anthropology after the Collapse of Communism*, edited by A. Baiburin, C. Kelly and N. Vakhtin, 77–102. London: Routledge.

Burrell, K. 2003. 'The Political and Social Life of Food in Socialist Poland'. *Anthropology of East Europe Review* 21(1): 189–95.

Fehér, F., Heller, A. and Márkus, G. 1986. *Dictatorship Over Needs: An Analysis of Soviet Societies*. London: Blackwell.

Kornai, J. 1980. *Economics of Shortage*. Amsterdam and New York: North-Holland.

Larson, R. C. 1987. 'Perspectives on Queues: Social Justice and the Psychology of Queueing'. *Operations Research* 35(6): 895–905.

Ledeneva, A. V. 1998. *Russia's Economy of Favours: Blat, Networking and Informal Exchange*. Cambridge and New York: Cambridge University Press.

Mazurek, M. 2012. 'Keeping It Close to Home: Resourcefulness and Scarcity in Late Socialist and Postsocialist Poland'. In *Communism Unwrapped: Consumption in Cold War Eastern Europe*, edited by P. Bren and M. Neuberger, 298–324. Oxford and New York: Oxford University Press.

Nørgaard, O. and Sampson, S. L. 1984. 'Poland's Crisis and East European Socialism'. *Theory and Society* 13: 773–801.

Sandel, M. J. 2012. *What Money Can't Buy: The Moral Limits of Markets*. London: Allen Lane.

Verdery, K. 1996. *What Was Socialism, and What Comes Next?* Princeton: Princeton University Press.

Wedel, J. 1986. *The Private Poland: An Anthropologist's Look at Everyday Life*. New York: Facts on File.

Zblewski, Z. 2000. *Leksykon PRL-u*. Kraków: Znak.

8.8 *Taksovanie* (Uzbekistan)
Nikolaos Olma

Ashwin, S. 2002. 'The Influence of the Soviet Gender Order on Employment Behavior in Contemporary Russia'. *Sociological Research* 41(1): 21–37.

Gwilliam, K. M. 2000. 'Private Participation in Public Transport in the FSU'. Discussion Paper. Washington, DC: World Bank Transport Division.

Johnson, S., Kaufmann, D. and Ustenko, O. 1998. 'Formal Employment and Survival Strategies after Communism'. In *Transforming Post-Communist Political Economies*, edited by National Research Council, 177–202. Washington, DC: The National Academies Press.

Miller, D. (ed.) 2001. *Car Cultures*. Oxford and New York: Berg.

Morris, J. 2016. *Everyday Post-Socialism: Working-Class Communities in the Russian Margins*. London: Palgrave Macmillan.

Olma, N. 2021. 'Driving in the Shadows: Rural-Urban Labour Migrants as Informal Taxi Drivers in Post-Socialist Tashkent'. In *Labour, Mobility and Informal Practices in Russia, Central Asia and Eastern Europe: Power, Institutions and Mobile Actors in Transnational Space*, edited by R. Turaeva and R. Urinboyev, 36–50. London: Routledge.

Olma, N. 2022. 'Under the Auspices of the State: Examining the Endurance of Tashkent's Informal Taxis'. *Geoforum* 136: 302–311.

Siegelbaum, L. H. 2009. 'On the Side: Car Culture in the USSR, 1960s–1980s'. *Technology and Culture* 50(1): 1–22.

Sopranzetti, C. 2017. 'Framed by Freedom: Emancipation and Oppression in Post-Fordist Thailand'. *Cultural Anthropology* 32(1): 68–92.

8.9 *Trotro* (Ghana)
Jennifer Hart

Hart, J. 2013. 'One Man, No Chop: Licit Wealth, Good Citizens, and the Criminalization of Drivers in Postcolonial Ghana'. *International Journal of African Historical Studies* 46(3): 373–96.

Hart, J. 2016. *Ghana on the Go: African Mobility in the Age of Motor Transportation.* Indianapolis and Bloomington: Indiana University Press.

Hart, J. 2020. 'Of Pirate Drivers and Honking Horns: Mobility, Authority, and Urban Planning in Late-Colonial Accra'. *Technology & Culture* 61(2): S49–S76.

Hart, K. 1973. 'Informal Income Opportunities and Urban Employment in Ghana'. *The Journal of Modern African Studies* 11(1): 61–89.

Okoye, V., Sands, J. and Debrah, C. A. 2010. *The Accra Pilot Bus-Rapid Transit Project: Transport-Land Use Research Study.* Columbia University; Accra Metropolitan Assembly: Millenium Cities Initiative.

Quayson, A. 2014. *Oxford Street, Accra: City Life and the Itineraries of Transnationalism.* Durham: Duke University Press.

Verrips, J. and Meyer, B. 2001 'Kwaku's Car: The Struggles and Stories of a Ghanaian Long-Distance Taxi Driver'. In *Car Cultures*, edited by D. Miller, 153–84. Oxford: Berg.

8.10 *Pfandsammeln* (Germany)
Annika Kurze

Duden. 2020. 'Flaschensammler'. *Duden.de*, 27 April. www.duden.de/node/48349/revision/48385

Kainz, K. 2004. *Der urbane informelle Arbeitsmarkt von Entwicklungsländern.* diplom.de.

Langhof, J. 2017. 'Rentnerin (76) sammelt Flaschen – Jetzt ist sie vorbestraft'. *Tz.de*, 19 September. www.tz.de/muenchen/stadt/ludwigsvorstadt-isarvorstadt-ort43328/rentnerin-76-amhauptbahnhof-beim-flaschensammeln-erwischt-jetzt-ist-sie-vorbestraft-8697128.html

Moser, S. J. 2014. *Pfandsammler: Erkundung einer urbanen Sozialfigur.* Hamburg: HIS Verlagsgesellschaft.

Pfand gehört daneben. 2020. www.pfand-gehoert-daneben.de/

Südwestrundfunk. 2020. '1000 Antworten: Wer profitiert davon, wenn ich eine Pfandflasche nicht zum Händler zurückbringe?'. ARD audiothek. www.ardaudiothek.de/episode/1000-antworten/wer-profitiert-davon-wenn-ich-eine-pfandflasche-nicht-zum-haendler-zurueckbringe/swr/68814920/

Voigt, R. 2007. 'Nichts für Flaschen – Verpackungshersteller gegen Einwegpfand'. In *Praxisbuch: Politische Interessenvermittlung*, edited by J. Rieksmeier, 202–14. VS Verlag für Sozialwissenschaften.

8.11 *Andare in giro* (Italy)
Isabella Clough Marinaro

Barlozzari, E. and Benignetti, A. 2021. '"Spegni, ci stiamo inc … zando": Le minacce dei rom a chi mostra il degrado'. *Il Giornale*, 21 January.

Cattaneo, C. 2017. 'Natural Resource Scarcity, Degrowth Scenarios and National Borders: The Role of Migrant Squats'. In *Migration, Squatting and Radical Autonomy*, edited by P. Mudu and S. Chattopadhyay, 257–71. Abingdon: Routledge.

CdD (Camera dei Deputati). 2018. *Proposta di legge. No. 1065. Disposizioni per la disciplina dell'economia dei beni usati e la promozione del settore del riutilizzo, nonché istituzione del Tavolo di lavoro permanente sul riutilizzo.* Atti Parlamentari, Camera dei Deputati. http://documenti.camera.it/leg18/pdl/pdf/leg.18.pdl.camera.1065.18PDL0026380.pdf

Clough Marinaro, I. 2022. *Inhabiting Liminal Spaces: Informalities in Governance, Housing, and Economic Activity in Contemporary Italy.* Abingdon: Routledge.

European Commission. 2020. *Circular Economy Action Plan*. European Commission. https://ec.europa.eu/environment/strategy/circular-economy-action-plan_en

Fahmi, W. S. and Sutton, K. 2006. 'Cairo's Zabaleen Garbage Recyclers: Multi-nationals' Takeover and State Relocation Plans'. *Habitat International* 30(4): 809–37.

ISTAT. 2020. *Le statistiche dell'ISTAT sulla povertà. Anno 2019*. www.istat.it/it/files//2020/06/REPORT_POVERTA_2019.pdf

Masia, V. 2016. 'Dal cassonetto al mercatino, viaggio tra chi di rifiuti ci vive'. *ADN Kronos*, 17 October.

MTE (Ministero della Transizione Ecologica). 2022. *Strategia nazionale per l'economia circolare*. www.cisl.it/wp-content/uploads/2022/07/Strategia-nazionale-economia-circolare.pdf

Rutkowski, J. E. and Rutkowski, E. W. 2015. 'Expanding Worldwide Urban Solid Waste Recycling: The Brazilian Social Technology in Waste Pickers Inclusion'. *Waste Management & Research* 33(12): 1084–93.

Samson, M. 2015. 'Accumulation by Dispossession and the Informal Economy. Struggles Over Knowledge, Being and Waste at a Soweto Garbage Dump'. *Environment and Planning D: Society and Space* 33(5): 813–30.

Schurman, S. J., Eaton, A. E. and Chen, M. A. (eds) 2017. *Informal Workers and Collective Action: A Global Perspective*. New York: ILR Press.

Solimene, M. 2016. '"I go for iron": Xoraxané Romá collecting scrap metal in Rome'. In *Gypsy Economy: Romani Livelihoods and Notions of Worth in the 21st Century*, edited by M. Brazzabeni, M. Cunha and M. Fotta, 107–26. New York and Oxford: Berghahn.

9
Becoming an entrepreneur

Introduction: entrepreneurship
Abel Polese
School of Law and Government, Dublin City University, Ireland

Some years ago, I was looking for a bass player. They were much in demand since everybody at the time seemed to want to start a band, be a guitar player or a singer, and I realised that another ad in a newspaper or on a board would yield little result. So, I found a different way. In a second-hand sale magazine, I looked for people who were selling bass guitars and called them. The first person I called was puzzled by my request: 'I am calling for the bass, but I do not want your bass, I want you in my band.' He appreciated my creativity, and we remained friends ever since that episode. Being entrepreneurial is a state of mind and a skill. How one uses it, and for what purpose, defines the contours and outcomes of entrepreneurship, as well as its borderlines with the formal and the informal.

Two possible meanings can be associated with the word entrepreneur. In a more restrictive sense, the term designates someone who starts a business activity with the goal of generating income. However, a broader, and more inclusive, definition can be deducted from the etymology of the word. 'Entrepreneur' is composed of *entre* (*inter* in Latin) and *prendre* (*prehendere* in Latin) and refers to anyone who undertakes something. It could, therefore, refer to someone who makes ends meet somehow. This would also be in line with my understanding of entrepreneurship that may involve anyone who starts something new, connects actors not connected before and creates new opportunities. One can illustrate the spirit of entrepreneurship with a surprise birthday party: you contact people, create an event and generate value. It may not be monetary but there is a gain of connection, esteem, mood, prestige, respect: currencies people use to build relationships (Pardo 1996; Brennan and Pettit 2005), dependence and reciprocity (White 2004).

Entrepreneurship is about innovation, bringing about novel things with little guesses of where and how they might become useful. It is an attempt to change the status quo that leads in most cases to failure, and in others to impressive results. These nuances are captured in the very essence of the word. In Latin *inter* means 'between' and can be interpreted as someone who finds the link between things not previously connected, the quintessence of entrepreneurship.

What is entrepreneurship?

Is there such a thing as formal entrepreneurship? Innovation is informal in many cases (Phelps 2021). Entrepreneurs move through various channels; they use informal avenues to create opportunities in places where these opportunities did not exist. They liaise through separate aspects of life, parallel worlds, and create synergies to produce results never seen before. This can be done on a micro or macro scale. It could be something small, within your circle of friends, or massive, such as creating a large business. For example, the now world-famous IMDB website started as a post about actresses with beautiful eyes. But a private interest or a sphere of life could become relevant for many and develop into larger structures and organisations. The outcomes of entrepreneurship can be assessed in at least two ways: one that is monetary, measurable and linked to money; the other is still economic, but often embedded in cultural and social dynamics not immediately monetisable (Polese 2021). Grant's idea of givers, whereby entrepreneurs often follow their hearts, do things they really want to do and do not aspire to be the 'taker' in each and every transaction, is what utterly generates the success of entrepreneurship (Grant 2013). As the Turkish proverb goes, 'do a favour and throw it into the sea, if nobody sees it, god will'.

In our surveys with the SHADOW team (Polese et al. 2021, 2022), it emerged quite clearly that a very common tendency of entrepreneurs is to under-declare: income, number of employees, salaries, sometimes more than one of these. This is not a phenomenon of the non-Western world: entrepreneurship is, by default, informal in spite of general perceptions and myths (Jaffe and Koster 2019). Can we differentiate between 'bad' and 'good' entrepreneurship? Between harmful and beneficial? After all, any activity takes place at the expense of some people while benefiting others.

My starting question would then be who (and how many of them) benefits from a new activity and at whose expense, including here not only people and society but also the planet and environmental damage? The practice of selling small water bottles at airports is a necessity for travellers, but it is harmful for the planet as it produces millions of plastic bottles. Free water in restaurants and fountains at airports would be a 'lost opportunity' in the short term, but it would benefit the whole of humanity and the planet in the long term.

A taxonomy of entrepreneurship

Starting with the aforementioned points, I can propose a taxonomy of the practices mentioned in this section and put them on a spectrum from more to less beneficial. What I find the most problematic are those monetary practices that take advantage of loopholes to avoid paying taxes ('double Irish'). The fact that money can be moved to countries where it is taxed at a lower rate, even if such practices are not illegal, clearly undermines state capacity. On the one hand, when a given company has made a certain amount of profit in a country but only pays a fraction of the tax, this is a cause of frustration for people, especially those feeling they are taxed too much. On the other hand, businesses tend to question the efficiency of the state to spend taxes and feel that optimising tax is a legitimate business development strategy.

There is, however, yet another way to look at these practices. People, and organisations, engage with such practices because they have the possibility to do so. This may come from a combination of factors, legality of loopholes, expectation of minimal punishment, existence of safe avenues and cultural attitudes that make this 'bad' but socially acceptable. It is impossible to ensure full compliance in all spheres of the economy. Reducing the percentage of non-conformity and increasing compliance have been the key drivers in economic reforms and development. Russia's success in tax collection since the year 2000 is noteworthy in this respect, and may be related to the effectiveness of informal control and assets takeovers (*otzhim*) undertaken with connivance of the state, as well as a low personal income tax rate. The practice of *otzhim* can be found at different levels of society in a micro (depriving an individual of their assets) or macro form (for example, during the annexation of the Crimean Peninsula).

Next on the spectrum we can place practices such as *combina* in Israel or *tenderpreneur* in South Africa. From a newcomer's standpoint, these practices are barriers to free entry and exit from the market. A new company will have to develop a level of social capital before they can start generating a regular and steady income even if it offers better prices or services. For instance, in the seventies there was a tendency in

Japan to overcharge the government for services offered through a tender. You would not win because you offered the best price or conditions but because you had the best connection while offering a reliable service. From the client's standpoint, it is perhaps more important that the task is completed than it is done with minimal expenditure, dubious quality or unreliable partners. In this respect, one could argue that winning a tender is not only a matter of offering the best conditions in theory but also the assurance that the task will be completed, and that the client will not have to chase the company to get things done, which is somehow associable to effectiveness.

The lack of transparency and flawed procedures in state procurement leads to the possibility that once the tender is assigned, the company disappears, does not deliver or delivers low-quality provision. Money paid against no service or inferior service can also be found in the case of *mertvye dushi* and *bin diwar*, since it entails an expenditure to get someone a salary in exchange for nothing, at least from the state's standpoint. Yet, in a broader context, there is a logic to these practices: not only do they exchange currency for services or support, but they highlight low-quality governance.

This section also includes practices that can be regarded as a weapon of the weak. *Mzungu* price may sound unfair to some and completely fair to others, depending on whether you benefit from the practice or overpay being unaware of local prices. However, it may also be interpreted as payback by oppressed and exploited populations. *Mzungu* price is not unique to Kenya, and entrepreneurial pricing of an item depending on the buyer is something that can be found in all corners of the world. Importantly, it is less a matter of the difference between the Global North and the Global South than it is a conflict between rich and poor. *Palyonka* reflects a similar logic. Normatively, fake goods are bad since they take away revenue from those who thought of the idea and therefore should gain from it. But they also promote the brand and facilitate access to goods with inaccessible prices for most people.

9.1 **Combina** (Israel)
Ina Kubbe
School of Political Science, Government and International Affairs, Tel Aviv University, Israel

Combina (Hebrew: קומבינה, Ladino: *kombina*) – short for combination, or *kombinatzia* – is a colloquial word for a trick (Gilad 2014), or a 'quick unofficial creative solution' to a problem. It refers to the use of personal connections and informal networks to circumvent formal practices and ways for getting ahead or receiving undue benefits. It includes all forms of favouritism such as nepotism, patronage or cronyism. The root *kombina* comes from the old Judeo-Spanish language, commonly referred to as Ladino (there is no 'c' in the alphabet). In Ladino dictionaries one finds (1) *kombina/kombinas* (pl.) as intrigue, (2) *kombinador* as trickster, (3) *kombinasion*, referring to combination, coincidence and opportunity and (4) *profitar la kombinasion*, that is taking advantage of the opportunity. In the Jerusalmic Ladino dialect, *kobima* means trick, ploy, manipulation (Rodrigue-Schwarzwald 2013). *Combinadores* carry connotations of sneaky people, with negative undertones of an underhand service (Hebrew Language Academy 2020). For example, 'if I want to arrange something, I will *combine it* for you' (*lekamben* in Hebrew). Thus, if someone got benefits through connections or even stealing, one is *mekumban* (combined), or has *combina* (see also Rosenthal 2015).

The word *combina* is sometimes translated as a deal 'under the table' or 'off the record' (Big Idea 2020). However, such deals are not necessarily perceived as illegal. They imply a roundabout way of problem-solving through connections and/or creativity. They provide 'an unofficial creative solution' to a problem (Urban Dictionary 2020). As almost every informal practice, *combina* is perceived as useful for reducing red tape in bureaucratic processes to gain documents, to circumvent bureaucracy or bypass the system as a whole by the participants (like *blat* in Russia, see 1.1 Volume 1, *guanxi* in China, see 1.12 Volume 1, *wasta* in the Middle East and North Africa, see 6.8 Volume 1 or *Vitamin B* in Germany, see 1.17 Volume 1).

The trickster's foxy character in the literature is often as morally reprehensible as it is attractive to readers from medieval times to the present day (see *gorroneo*, 7.2 in this volume). One of the most loved Soviet novels in this genre, *The Twelve Chairs* by Ilf and Petrov (2011 [1928]), features a charming *kombinator*, a trickster who outsmarts the Soviet regulations by using *combinatoric* methods (Petrov 2013; Lipovetsky 2010). In such contexts, *combina* can mean an ability to improvise in uncertain situations, overcome obstacles, leverage your skills and contacts, as well as 'cheat the system' in order to achieve the desired outcome. In the great attempt not to be a friar, or a 'sucker', who allows themselves to be cheated or to accept a bad deal, many Israelis succumb to the temptation to take part in *combinot* or underhand deals or ways of cheating the system. They see the 'system' as working against them and believe that their actions are necessary to counterbalance their disadvantaged position.

Combina is deeply rooted in cultural contexts, but also lies at the foundation of the culture of corruption in Israel. It does not include bribery per se, but there is a certain quid pro quo involved. *Combina* is used in all aspects of life and includes both private and professional favours. For example, when taking the car into the garage for its annual check, one can be given special treatment because the mechanic is a lifelong friend of the family, or a friend of a friend. Sometimes, *combina* is a one-off favour, for someone with 'beautiful eyes', or a competitive advantage, such as bypassing a queue saving costs, or bending the rule. It can be a case of *protekzia*, a special arrangement to secure a favour made by someone in the know or on the inside (Halfin 2018). The term embraces a variety of informal practices that penetrate the workings of formal institutions or official settings in Israel. Similar to *blat*, *combinot* are 'people's regular strategies to manipulate or exploit formal rules by enforcing informal norms and personal obligations in formal context' (Ledeneva 2008: 119).

Personal networks allow one to jump the queue in government agencies, speed up administrative processes to obtain government documents or official approvals, gain access to basic social services (for example, in hospital) or secure a place at university or find a job. Contemporary examples of *combina* include getting a parking permit in a specific area because you know someone in the local authority, getting a cushy job through connections, or getting a privileged posting for military service through family connections. Using *combina* is often seen to benefit a family, a circle of insiders, and implies understanding how the system works and knowing how to play the game. It is actually a good thing to be creative, smart and sneaky (Marshadruker 2017).

In Israel, *combina* presents an aspect of a very informal society where 'things always work somehow' and the collective feeling that anything is possible. Organisations tend to be more accessible and work environments more casual, which generates a breeding ground for creativity and new ideas. With a population of 10 million and a size of 22,072 km², Israel is a comparatively small country. There is a saying that anyone is only two phone calls away, and everyone has 30 minutes to help you think through a challenge. Whether you are standing together during the *Yom HaShoah* siren (Holocaust Remembrance Day), on reserve duty, raising kids, or venturing a start-up, Israelis are in it together (Marshadruker 2017). Essential for such 'togetherness' is the national army service, mandatory for all Israeli citizens and inclusive of women (for an elitist model, see *hyvä Veli*, 3.12 Volume 1). During the three years of service, most people acquire networks. There are many cohesion-building rituals, such as weddings, *shivas* (a week-long mourning period for immediate family), or *b'nai mitzvah* and *b'not mitzvah* (Jewish coming-of-age ritual for boys and girls). *Combina* supports the unwritten rule to help others wherever you can.

The argument of inclusivity seems paradoxical, given that Israel is also one of the most diversified countries in the world. Immigrants from all over the world bring over their different traditions, values and norms. In 2014, a quarter of the Jewish-Israeli population were immigrants; a third were children of immigrants and the remainder constituted second-generation immigrants. Founded in 1956, Israel is the only country in the world where the immigrant groups are so substantial that they can sway elections and transform predominant values. It was suggested that such group diversity has a tremendous, positive influence on culture, economy and creativity (Arieli 2017) and that the land itself could be thought of as a start-up where the networking flowed easily and inclusively, regardless of individual accomplishments or titles (Hofstede Insights 2020).

Thus, on the one hand, *combina* generates trust, loyalty and solidarity, or a type of sociability that reduces transaction costs and risks of free-riding. Grounded in family ties, it plays a profound role, especially in structuring access to opportunities. On the other hand, it can also become an endemic problem, reproduce inequality and serve as a vehicle for corruption (Kubbe and Varraich 2019). Therefore, *combina* understood as creativity in its purest forms can turn into anti-social, 'malevolent creativity' (Beaussart et al. 2013) and cause harm. It undercuts transparency, equality, fairness and accountability of institutions. Thus, obtaining building and commercial permits, licences or planning permissions through connections can have serious implications when not issued according to qualification criteria and performance. For ordinary citizens, who lack connections to top officials and power holders and have limited material resources, *combina* in the social, economic and political system is frustrating. *Combina* might have some equalising effect, but does not guarantee equal opportunities, or access to essential services, jobs, administrative paperwork, or other vital aspects of life. This disadvantages people without *combina* and limits career opportunities. Due to this duality, *combina* is difficult to capture empirically and isolate from corrupt acts (Baez-Camargo and Ledeneva 2017).

9.2 *Manteros* (Spain)
Horacio Espinosa
Observatorio de Antropología del Conflicto Urbano, Universidad de Barcelona, Spain

From the Spanish *manta* (blanket), *manteros* are street vendors that offer souvenirs, football T-shirts, footwear, souvenirs, sunglasses and other goods to customers in a public space. In the last decade, this commercial activity has been practised by Senegalese migrants. In *wolof* language they are known as *modou-modou*, which stands for informal traders or migrant workers (Zubrzycki 2016).

Top Manta is another vernacular way to name these street vendors. More in use from the 1990s to the 2010s it is a play on words between *manta* and the pirated CD 'top' hits that *manteros* used to sell. In the video of the song 'Santa Claus' by the Senegalese rapper and ex-*mantero* Lorey Money, the sale of pirated records and DVDs is referred to as 'top manta'. In the same video, the rapper shows another iconic element of the *mantero* sale: a cord device used to secure the merchandise within a blanket. In this way, the blanket becomes a bundle that the *mantero* can carry on his back, allowing him to escape the police. Lorey Money refers to this action as 'doing the Santa Claus'.

In the 1930s, during the government of the second Spanish Republic, *manteros* was practised by Spanish people, which frequently led to clashes with the police in a 'fight for the street' (Ealham 2011: 203). In the 1990s, African immigration to Spain consisted mainly of North Africans, mostly Moroccans, whereas the sub-Saharan community saw Spain as a transit point to traditional destination countries such as France, Germany or the United Kingdom (Robin 1996: 57). Yet, by the early 2000s for Senegalese and sub-Saharan migrants Spain had become 'a migratory destination comparable to Germany, the United Kingdom or France' (Sow 2004: 235). As the new poor, lacking a work permit, Senegalese migrants are drawn to informal activities such as street vending.

In Barcelona, most *manteros* are identified and known to the police, who can go as far as monitoring them from the moment they leave their homes to the point they reach La Rambla, the tourist heart of the Catalonian capital. Still, in the absence of any real integration policies, Spanish authorities are limited to prosecuting street vendors through the work of the police. Moreover, ad hoc regulations are aimed at limiting their mobility. For example, by prohibiting the introduction of 'large

Figure 9.2.1 *Manteros* carrying their packages on their backs, Barcelona, Spain. © Angel García.

packages' into the subway, hence blocking their access to the main means of transport (Lupe 2016).

If they overcome this barrier, *manteros* then need to find a spot where they can sell their products. To this end, street vendors carry out preliminary explorations verifying the presence of the Guardia Urbana, Mossos d'Esquadra (Autonomous Police of Catalonia) or plain-clothes police officers (*secretas*). If they feel insecure, they will wait on different platforms and passages of the Catalonia metro station for the right moment to display the blanket, or what De Certeau calls *kairos*, a term that can be translated 'as the appropriate or opportune moment' (1980: 96).

The Guardia Urbana van, or la *lechera* (milk truck) in street slang, was circulating on the pedestrian walkway of La Rambla with the intention of 'running over' the *manteros*. They would react by pulling the cord to transform the *ambu* (blanket, in *wolof* language) into *sare* (the package). *Manteros* avoided the hit by circling the van and returned to set up their blanket on La Rambla to continue selling in an endless dance that was repeated throughout the night. In Barcelona, due to the eminently touristic character of the city, one of the police's priorities is to safeguard the urban image, so the presence of street vendors is considered incompatible with the image they wish to give to the visitor (Espinosa 2017, 2021).

Figure 9.2.2 Street art depicting a *mantero*, Barrio del Raval, Barcelona, Spain. © Horacio Espinosa.

On 2 October 2015, at the Santa Mónica art centre in Barcelona, a group of about 80 *manteros* organised the Popular Union of Street Vendors of Barcelona (Sindicato Popular de Vendedores Ambulantes de Barcelona). The organisation was founded as a reaction to the death of the Senegalese street vendor Mor Sylla in the tourist area of Salou (Tarragona). Officially, the street vendor 'fell' from a balcony while being chased by the Catalan regional police (Mossos d'Esquadra) in an operation 'against piracy'.

According to the Catalan police force, between 2011 and 2015 the Mossos d'Esquadra had invested 28,000 hours into prosecuting street vendors. When questioned about the death of Mor Sylla, the Minister of the Catalan government justified the fact by declaring that the prosecution of street vendors was unavoidable because their activity 'puts the Welfare State at risk' (El Diario 2015).

On 15 March 2018, the *mantero* Mame Mbayé was killed in a police chase in the Madrid neighbourhood of Lavapiés. His death was followed by a day of riots against the police. The politicisation of street vendors was natural, and a *mantero* has even reached institutional politics, as in the case of the election to the Madrid Parliament of the former *mantero* Serigne Mbayé Diouf in the ranks of the political party *Podemos*.

The 'defence of public space' has been one of the classical arguments used to justify police harassment against African *manteros*, not only in Spain, but also in Argentina (Marcús and Peralta 2021) or Italy

(Molinero and Avallone 2020). On 25 May 2015, Marius Carol, the director of the conservative newspaper *La Vanguardia*, wrote an editorial in which he described the public space as 'the greatest conquest of democracy', quoting Aristotle to justify his discourse in its defence from destructive forces, in this case the street vendors, that he described as 'terrorists of public space' (Carol 2015). These elements testify that in Spain and other countries a large proportion of public opinion is opposed to *manteros* and their survival strategies.

9.3 **Tenderpreneur** (South Africa)
Laurence Piper
Department of Political Studies, University of the Western Cape, South Africa
and
Andrew Charman
Sustainable Livelihoods Foundation, South Africa

Tenderpreneur is a South African colloquialism for a businessperson who uses political contacts to secure government procurement contracts (called 'tenders') often as part of reciprocal exchange of favours or benefits. The term is a portmanteau of 'tender' (to provide business services) and 'entrepreneur'. Today, *tenderpreneurs* are associated with corruption, nepotism and clientelism. This is because the award of many tenders is driven by informal interests and/or political affiliation, rather than the requirements of formal procedure. The informality of *tenderpreneurship* thus resides in these extra-legal social and political relationships.

The term *tenderpreneur* first emerged during the rule of President Thabo Mbeki (1999–2008). Initially, the term had an ambivalent meaning, with both positive and negative undertones (Dlamini 2010). On the one hand, it was associated with the advancement of black entrepreneurs who entered into the private business sector on a legitimate basis under the framework of state policies to enable the advancement of 'black designated groups' in commerce and industry. Thus the South African Constitution, in terms of Section 217, permits organs of the state to implement preferential procurement to advance opportunities for persons previously disadvantaged under Apartheid (Constitution 1996).

These policies successfully enabled commercial opportunities for black businesses as partners and outright suppliers, who would otherwise struggle to compete within a private sector dominated by established white-owned businesses. Key policies to advance this objective include the Preferential Procurement Policy Framework (PPPF 2000) and the Black Economic Empowerment (BEE) Act and subsequent Broad-Based Black Economic Empowerment Act (BBBEE 2017).

On the other hand, *tenderpreneurship* has a negative connotation associated with corrupt practices. The association was particularly noticeable in respect to state procurement processes whereby tenders to supply goods and services were increasingly awarded to individuals with personal linkages to the ruling political party, the African National Congress (ANC) (Dlamini 2010). One of the highest profile early examples was the South African Arms Deal, initiated in 1999, in which bribes were paid to high-ranking politicians, fixers, the ANC and allied community development projects (Southall 2008). Key to this transition is the ANC's ideology of liberation nationalism that defines the party as the champion of the oppressed black, who constitute the primary part of the South African nation; and its intersection with the access to resources enabled by party dominance at election time (Piper 2015).

Tenderpreneurship is distinguishable from other forms of manipulation of the system of black empowerment on the scale of economic theft. Under the objective of advancing opportunities for black business advancement, state organs have instituted regulations to enable favourable procurement through two tracks, one via a system of three competitive quotes, '3Qs' (below a value threshold) and via tenders (above a value threshold) (Corruption Watch 2014). Both tracks have resulted in system manipulation. In the early 2000s, terms such as the '3Qs' emerged to describe black entrepreneurs who had acquired state contracts via the competitive quote pipeline, though these were usually of smaller value (personal communication to Charman, Limpopo entrepreneurs).

These '3Qs' contracts were typically given to those who had a relationship with the government official in charge of minor procurements. These actions constituted a form of nepotism and improper favouritism. Large-value procurements (above R200,000) were subject to more complex tender processes (Corruption Watch 2014). The current PPPF Regulations (2017) detail the criteria for evaluating state tenders, permitting state organs to apply pre-qualifying criteria to advance businesses with high black empowerment (BBBEE) status or smaller businesses. This mechanism is used to exclude less BBBEE-compliant service providers and stack the weighting within the tender evaluation process in favour of business entities with strong BBBEE status and (informal) political connections.

Under the Zuma Presidency, *tenderpreneurship* became synonymous with tender manipulation and corruption in state procurement, notably with respect to large-value contract procurement to supply South African state-owned companies with goods and services (Southall 2011). In South African law, corruption means the private use of public funds, bribery of public officials and improper favouritism by government officials. In 2016 Transparency International (2017) ranked South Africa 64 out of 167 countries in the world. Its score was 45 out of 100, where zero is completely corrupt and 100 is completely clean.

In some of the most celebrated cases, the *tenderpreneur* seeks to cultivate a relationship with politicians (and their families) by supporting and financing their careers. The most famous example of this is the relationship between President Jacob Zuma and the Gupta family, comprising the three brothers Ajay, Atul and Rajesh. Originating in Uttar Pradesh, India, the Gupta brothers immigrated to South Africa in 1993 to establish a foothold for their emerging business, which included Sahara Computers. The Guptas swiftly established political patronage with ANC leaders. In the early 2000s, the Guptas had begun to invest in Jacob Zuma as a future president. The family cultivated their relationship with the future president by employing members of his household, including one of his wives, a daughter, a son and a nephew. Newspaper reports and studies compiled evidence that the Guptas channelled funds to support Zuma and his political career via employment, favours, bribes and kickbacks (Southall 2011; Pauw 2017; Pilling and Cotterill 2017). In return for their financial generosity, the Guptas received substantial government procurement contracts, especially in the energy sector (Conway-Smith 2017). Through preferential procurement, large tenders in particular, the Guptas were able to expand their business interests into the mineral sector, acquiring coal mines and in turn winning a tender with Eskom, the state energy provider, to supply coal, with Eskom paying an inflated price for an inferior product (Pilling and Cotterill 2017).

In governance terms, *tenderpreneurship* has two major implications. First, it is (rightly) associated with poor service delivery and overcharging of the state, with tenders often awarded to companies lacking competency. It is not uncommon for *tenderpreneur* companies to be registered for the sole purpose of accessing state procurement opportunities through preferential bidding (Corruption Watch 2014). The pre-selection process enables corrupt government officials to bias the procurement outcome towards companies deemed to be eligible of high BBBEE status, ignoring matters of competency that are only considered in subsequent phases of the process. In many instances, *tenderpreneur* companies exist as shell organisations that sub-contract other contractors (often established white-owned businesses) to do the actual work. This process is known as 'fronting' (Bolton 2006). Overcharging for goods and services means that both the *tenderpreneur* and their client in the state can extract profits from the fulfilment of the tender. Where *tenderpreneurship* results in poor service delivery, this in turn undermines public accountability and fuels mistrust towards government officials.

Second, *tenderpreneurship* has become associated with maintaining the political status quo through strategies that include undermining civil society. The Guptas, for example, invested in newspapers and TV media to generate positive news around the ANC and President Jacob Zumba in particular, while simultaneously engaging the public relations firm Bell Pottinger to produce 'fake news' and a counter-narrative against *tenderpreneurship* (Plaut 2017). This particular narrative sought to shift the political critique to rally against 'white monopoly capitalism' which was taken as a symbolic name for corporate business and continued dominance of white-owned businesses in the economy. The slogan 'radical economic transformation' (the current anti-business establishment narrative) has linkages (in terms of deriving financial support) to *tenderpreneurs* and 'criminal enterprises' embedded in corrupt relationships with high-ranking officials in the Zuma political fold (Pauw 2017, Pilling and Cotterill 2017).

Political commentators have described *tenderpreneurship* as linked to a 'dominant party syndrome' of the ruling political party, the ANC (Giliomee and Simkins 1999). The ANC has won every national election for the last 25 years with over 60 per cent of the vote. This lack of electoral accountability at the national level (and in most municipalities, apart from the large metropolitan municipalities) means that ANC politicians return to office even when the government has not delivered as promised on development plans, or simply performs poorly. Consequently, many in the ANC take political office for granted and abuse it by enabling non-competitive procurement, *tenderpreneurship* and nepotism in employment. This dominant party syndrome has advanced to a state of kleptocracy, whereby the political elites manipulate the three arms of government (legislature, executive and judiciary) with the intention of capturing resources for self-enrichment, the 'elite capture' (Booysen 2015). The growing perception of Zuma's rule as kleptocracy is beginning to hurt the ANC in the realm of public debates. For the first time, in the local government elections of 2016 four of the largest metropolitan municipalities switched from the ANC to the opposition, the Democratic Allowance party (Chipkin 2016).

9.4 *Mzungu price* (Kenya)
Yunqiao Xu
School of Slavonic and East European Studies, UCL, UK

Mzungu is a popular Swahili term for white people or Europeans (Spitzer 2017). A *mzungu* price is the price charged by Kenyans to usually white foreigners and tourists, which is normally higher than what locals would be asked to pay. Charging foreigners a higher price is common in developing countries in Asia, Africa and the Caribbean. In Kenya, it first appeared in urban street markets and has now become common throughout the country.

Racial inequality contributes to the emergence of *mzungu* price. The word *mzungu* conveys a belief that to be white is to be superior in wealth, which is a lasting consequence of the country's colonial past, as is the phrase 'West is best' (MacOireachtaigh 2015). In a country where racial inequality is substantial, white skin is equated with privilege.

The emergence of *mzungu* price is largely attributed to the growth of informal economic activities in Kenya. In the early 2000s, employment in the informal sector increased by around 5 million, reaching 64 per cent of total employment in 2011 (Escudero et al. 2013). The institutional environment in Kenya disincentivises street traders from acquiring a licence so their activities often remain a part of the informal sector – in 2016, there were over 10,000 street traders in Kisumu, a city with 700,000 inhabitants (Racaud 2017). In major African cities, street trade is an important source of provision for poor urban families (Uwitije 2016).

Figure 9.4.1 Masai Market, Nairobi, Kenya. Source: Unsplash © Bj Pearce.

Passenger taxi services is another typical area where *mzungu* price is charged. The *mzungu* price for a *boda-boda*, a motorbike taxi popular in Kenya, is 3,000–4,000 Kenyan shillings (28–38 USD) more than the local price. Uber drivers are less common, so tourists normally use traditional taxis. Nonetheless, they use the Uber price, or a price suggested by local friends as the benchmark of a fair deal, making the ride-hailing apps a way to uncover and prevent overcharging. Before the expansion of these technologies into Kenya, 'black' taxis, run by drivers without a taxi licence, were prevalent. Nairobi had privately owned minibuses called *matatu*, which provided transportation for locals. However, public transport is difficult for foreigners to use as there are no bus signs or official route maps. The expansion of ride-hailing applications in Nairobi has reduced the window of opportunity for 'black' taxi drivers to charge *mzungu* price and has consequently reduced their earnings. New technologies indirectly act as a means of price regulation for tourists, with direct consequences on the local income.

Persecution of street traders by the authorities is common. Up to 44 per cent of street traders in Nakuru, Kenya have faced mistreatment such as having their goods confiscated without compensation (Roever 2016). Harassment from local officials leads to unstable working conditions and can force traders off the street (Mnyamwezi 2020). This type of repression also leads to social instability and protests (Chepngeno and Lubanga 2020).

Street trade for female street traders is even more difficult, since women often have to care for children while they work. They also earn less compared to male street traders. There are two reasons for this: first, limited access to capital and information, which narrows the range and quantity of commodities they sell and second, working shorter hours because they have to attend to domestic chores (Alila and Mitullah 1999: 11–12).

Charging *mzungu* price often results in tourist dissatisfaction. It can affect tourists' willingness to travel to Kenya, as they prefer destinations where they will not be deceived by the locals (Garg 2015). But *mzungu* price also has a positive impact. First, they contribute to poverty alleviation by providing families with extra income. Second, *mzungu* price indirectly creates a new means of income for Kenyans. Foreigners will sometimes pay local workers to help them buy items in order to access local prices.

In the absence of market regulation, the informal Kenyan traders base the prices of their ware on what they believe *mzungu* are willing to pay rather than on the value of the products. Street traders usually make only minimal profits and do not enjoy social protection. This incentivises them to establish a *mzungu* price. One estimation suggested that street traders made between 1.4 and 14.3 USD daily profit on average in Nairobi Central Business District in 2007 (Kamunyori 2007). The broad range in daily profit depends on the trader's selling skills – the ability to set the highest viable *mzungu* price.

The main barrier to effective regulation is lack of enforcement, despite frequent attempts by the local authorities to limit the growth of the informal sector (Pohl 2002). Police actions are rarely effective as compliance from citizens is low. Regulation becomes even more complicated with formally licensed traders, who nevertheless retain a small margin of freedom when setting prices, thereby enabling prices to be based on unfair subjective decisions. The Micro and Small Enterprises Act issued by the Kenyan government in 2012 was an attempt to register street traders as micro enterprises. However, the trading licences were not issued broadly enough. According to estimates, Nairobi had 500,000 street traders, while only 7,000 licences were issued in 2005 (Lyons and Snoxell 2005). The complex licensing process and the limited number of licences granted discourage people from registering.

Local non-profit policy-making institutions, such as the Kenyan National Association of Street Vendors and Traders and the Kenya Private Sector Alliance, are responsible for adding to the volatility of the street vending environment. These organisations lobby for negotiations between street traders and the government, helping the government to integrate informal trade into urban development and governance. However, inconsistencies in policies from different institutions slow down their implementation (Schlegel and Racaud 2016).

9.5 **Churning** (Canada)
Katie Kilroy-Marac
Department of Anthropology, University of Toronto, Canada

Churning is a term used by professional home organisers (POs) across Canada and the US to describe an unproductive behaviour that they commonly observe among clients. When clients *churn*, they may pick up household items and put them down again, move items from place to place, shuffle piles around, defer decisions about what should be done with this or that object or leave a task unfinished only to start another. Outside of this context, *churning* typically refers to the repetitive motion of mixing, stirring, shaking, blending or otherwise agitating. In North

American English, the word is most commonly associated with the process of making butter (cream is churned into butter), or with a feeling one might have in one's stomach (a churning stomach is an upset or unsettled stomach, related to indigestion or negative emotions).

There are currently more than 4,600 certified POs working across Canada and the US, the majority of whom are white middle-class women between the ages of 40 and 55. The majority of their clients fit a similar demographic. POs are hired by their clients to lend their expertise in organising, decluttering and the optimisation of domestic (or sometimes, digital) space. They work with clients on short-term projects – putting an organisational system in place in a bedroom wardrobe, for example, or sorting and digitising files in a home office – or their visits may stretch over a period of months or even years.

An ethnographic study of POs across southern Ontario in Canada offers unique insights into how, in this historical moment and with such a surplus of stuff everywhere, we are supposed to handle, manage and *be* with our ever-expanding world of material things (Kilroy-Marac 2016, 2018). As part of a larger project designed to track the emergence of *hoarding* in North America – whether as psychiatric disorder, public health hazard or media spectacle – a series of interviews with POs revealed them to be keen observers with a wholly anthropological sensitivity and a great deal of insight into the human condition.

Allie, the first PO to mention *churning* in 2014, had been working in the Toronto area for about four years:

> 'What's really frustrating for me', she admitted, 'is when I start working with a new client and it becomes clear that they don't actually want to get rid of anything. They just want to shuffle things around. They call it *churning*, you know, like you churn butter. They're just moving things from one room to another, or from one spot to another, because they can't make a decision about it.'

Regardless of the client's situation or demands, POs know *churning* when they see it. *Churning*, POs explain, not only keeps clients from achieving their organising goals, but actually makes matter(s) worse because it disperses piles and creates new ones, which themselves attract more stuff. Extending the butter metaphor, we might say that *churning* acts as a 'thickener' of clutter within the home, thereby exacerbating the problem. In clutter, sentimental objects might mix and mingle with important documents, food wrappers, knick-knacks and waste. Take this example: a client starts out with the intention of sorting through a large pile of papers that has accumulated on a kitchen countertop. The client begins sorting, but soon realises that some of the items (receipts, for example) need to be reviewed by another member of the household. There are birthday cards in the pile, too. Should these be thrown away, or digitised or kept in a memento box upstairs? And here is an unsigned school form, and an overdue bill. Each item requires a decision and demands action. 'Decision fatigue' quickly sets in. Overwhelmed, the client decides to move part of the stack into the living room where it can be sorted later, perhaps while watching TV. Now there is a pile of papers on the end table next to the couch, in addition to the pile that remains on the countertop. Both of these piles have become 'landing places' into which more paper, clutter and other items may be set. Clutter, POs say, always attracts more of itself; it grows and thickens. Sophie Woodward describes clutter in relational terms: comprised as it is of multiple, disparate objects that come together to form a '*relational* materiality' (Woodward 2021: 1219, emphasis in original), it is also indexical of social and domestic relations. Clutter, she notes, 'emerges through the relations of the home' and acts as a 'medium through which people negotiate and manage these relations' (Woodward 2021: 1221).

POs have developed many creative methods for addressing clutter and intervening in the relationships clients have with their possessions in order to prevent *churning*. One trick in the POs' toolbox is what is known as 'body doubling'. Body doubling is a technique, first described by Judith Kolberg, a formative figure in the world of professional organising (Kolberg 2007, 2009). When a PO acts as a body double, they work alongside their clients and model behaviour through action. POs keep their clients' attention fixed on the task at hand and gently redirect them when they lose focus. Barbara, a PO working in southern Ontario, explained: 'As a body double, you are an *anchor* and a *mirror* – you are keeping the client rooted in the [sorting] work and you're modelling appropriate behaviour.' In body doubling, POs reorient their clients' habits by example as much as by instruction. In this, physical co-presence is key. Barbara notes that '[a] lot of clients will say to me, "I don't understand why I can only do this when you're here!" … You know, what I'm doing is I'm *lending my focus to my clients* when we are working together. … For some clients … it really is the body doubling that keeps them able to do what they're doing'. In this description, the physical co-presence of PO and client may go beyond simple task-modelling to enable an almost mystical transfer of skill and affect. Indeed, the magical lexicon employed by POs – body doubling, lending focus, becoming an anchor and mirror – suggests that the PO and client join forces to put distance between the client and their material world. It is, in effect, the affective stickiness of things that muddles this distance and leads to *churning* in the first place.

As POs join forces with their clients to bring attention and focus to their material worlds, they encourage their clients to sort and organise what must be kept and let go of the rest. 'Letting go' of an object might mean giving it away or passing it along, donating it or throwing it out. POs generally refrain from using terms like 'purging', 'getting rid of' or 'throwing away' in their practice, for these may be experienced by clients as harsh – even violent intrusions – and result in them holding onto the objects even more tightly. In their work, then, POs recognise that they are not just manipulating objects but also transforming relationships with people and things alike.

In the context of the growing environmental concern, the wide availability of cheap consumer goods has ushered in a growing sense of anxiety about how to manage the ever-expanding world of material possessions. Discourses about excessive accumulation, restricted consumption and the (im)proper handling, organisation and upkeep of objects have come to signal both status and virtue. It is perhaps no wonder, then, that an industry of experts has appeared on the scene to quell these material anxieties and bring order to things.

9.6 **Double Irish** (Ireland)
Julia Schmalz
Alumna, School of Slavonic and East European Studies, UCL, UK

The term *double Irish* referred to a tax strategy employed by multinational companies to reduce their tax liability by shifting profits to a country with a lower-tax legislation. To increase profits, companies, mostly in the technology and pharmaceutical sectors, implemented the *double Irish* to take advantage of the Irish system of territorial taxation and absence of transfer pricing. The *double Irish* strategy required two Irish subsidiaries and drew on an exemption particular to Irish taxation law that allowed companies registered in Ireland to be taxed where their management is located. The territorial taxation regime permitted the Irish subsidiaries to incorporate in Ireland, declare their profits in tax havens and remain in compliance with EU jurisdiction (Darby and Leamaster 2007).

In a *double Irish* arrangement, the first Irish subsidiary declared its tax residency in a tax haven such as the Cayman Islands. The subsidiary held the rights of the parent company's intellectual property and licenced it to a second Irish subsidiary located in Ireland. The profits earned from the licensed rights would normally be taxed at the Irish tax rate of 12.5 per cent. However, the royalties paid to the Irish company in the tax haven were tax-deductible and reduced the profit subjected to taxation in Ireland to a minimum. The lax Irish policy on transfer pricing even exempted multinationals from paying fees on transferring their profits from Ireland to the tax haven. In addition, a shell company located in the Netherlands could be used to transfer profits directly to the Irish company in the tax haven, extending the scheme to a *double Irish with a Dutch sandwich*. As the profits of the Irish company in the Cayman Islands would be taxed according to the corporate taxation rate of this tax haven country, this strategy essentially erased the tax burden of the received royalties (Darby and Leamaster 2007).

Although the *double Irish* strategy was a legal practice within the global system of taxation, several substantial settlement payments have been made on ethical grounds. US companies using *double Irish* to increase their profits have come under special scrutiny from the European Union. In early 2016, Google's parent company Alphabet Inc. settled with the UK on paying an additional £130 million in taxes (Brunsden and Noble 2016; Committee of Public Accounts 2016). In another prominent case, the EU Commissioner for Competition Margrethe Vestager accused the US-based corporation Apple of receiving anti-competitive state aid from the state of Ireland (European Commission 2016), as Apple's main Irish operation had paid a tax rate lower than 0.01 per cent in 2014 (Beesley and Barker 2016). The Commission argued that Ireland had manipulated the market situation by offering Apple the possibility to channel its non-US profits through its Irish subsidiaries. As the corporation avoided taxation to a substantial extent, Vestager declared that this practice amounted to indirect state subsidies. The state of Ireland responded that it would 'appeal before the European Courts to challenge the European Commission's decision on the Apple State aid case'. According to the Irish government, low-taxation environments serve the need to 'remain … competitive as the economy continues to grow' while adhering to the international taxation standards, so treating them as indirect state subsidies was inappropriate (Department of Finance 2016).

Yet, Ireland has recently sought to reform its tax code to better adhere to international taxation standards. The legislative action included an obligation for companies incorporated in Ireland to declare their profits as Irish tax residents and came into effect with the Irish Finance Act

2014 at the beginning of 2015 (Somerville 2015). Corporations currently employing the *double Irish* were granted a transitional period until 2020 to find a new business arrangement. The *double Irish* has attracted much media attention to Ireland (Kahn and Drucker 2016; Scott 2016), but the set-up of the Irish taxation system cannot be considered exceptional in the global context. Several countries are known for offering business-friendly tax environments to attract corporations to their jurisdictions. Tax havens, such as the Cayman Islands, have no corporate tax and represent ideal conditions for businesses to maximise their profits. Within the EU, countries such as Hungary, Liechtenstein and Cyprus have chosen to implement a similar low-tax regime for corporations (Tax Foundation 2022).

The informal economic activity of tax optimisation is often viewed negatively as 'it denies the state revenue and [complicates the planning of] economic ... fiscal and monetary policy' (Danopoulos and Znidaric 2007: 67). In the UK, estimated tax revenues lost from the 700 largest corporations amounted to £12 billion in 2006 (Jones 2015: 110). Tax avoidance is a form of tax non-compliance different from tax evasion in that it systematically uses legal means to reduce tax liability. However, the line distinguishing between 'unacceptable avoidance and legitimate mitigation' is highly debatable (Tax Law Review Committee 1997: 3).

Variations in governmental and judicial attitudes concerning the definition and implementation of anti-tax avoidance measures are partly a result of a country's 'history, experience and cultural perspectives' on taxation (Tax Law Review Committee 1997: 17). At the same time, the *double Irish* scheme was indicative of institutional competition – the conflicts between states competing for economic activity. International pressure has begun to build up for states to limit informal economic activity and reduce the practice and magnitude of tax avoidance in their national territories, as suggested by Ireland's ending the *double Irish* practice by 2020. However, the practice of *double Irish* showcases how national tax rules and tax play a role in shaping corporate strategies. In the *double Irish* case involving Apple, the European Commission has yet to substantiate in court its order for the multinational to pay back €13 billion in Irish taxes (General Court of the European Union 2020). Committing multinationals and states to cooperative, rather than purely legal, taxation standards across borders remains a difficult political endeavour.

9.7 *Palyonka* (Russia)
Zoya Kotelnikova
NRU Higher School of Economics, Moscow, Russia

In Russia, *palyonka* (from the adjective *palyonyi*, meaning singed, burned) is a colloquial term used by consumers to denote counterfeit goods. It originated in late socialism when the term *palyonka* was associated with illegally manufactured vodka. Since the early 2000s, it has been used to refer to a wider range of goods, such as petroleum, documents and clothes, and infringements of intellectual property laws, such as direct copies, imitations or factory overruns. In the 2010s, *pal*, shorthand for *palyonka*, entered youth slang to denote counterfeit branded clothes and footwear (Radaev 2017).

In the late twentieth century, counterfeit products emerged as a global challenge: pirated goods were being produced and consumed in virtually all economies. Russia was no exception and was identified by the European Commission as a country with high infringement of intellectual property rights (Devigne 2008). Russians consume more counterfeit goods than they produce; counterfeit goods in Russia tend to be imported, often from Eastern Europe and the Commonwealth of Independent States, but they primarily arrive from Asia, especially China (Radaev et al. 2008).

Consumers understand *palyonka* as something of poor quality, copied and illegally introduced into commerce. They tend not to draw sophisticated or juridical distinctions between the types of infringements of intellectual property rights and state-quality standards (for example, look-alikes, surrogates or pirated goods). Having no reliable knowledge of brands, consumers tend to lack confidence in determining the originality of goods. They often determine whether a commodity is a counterfeit intuitively, relying on their consumer experience and skills, market signals (price, place of purchase, seller's information) and social ties (Kotelnikova 2017). From the consumer's perspective, *palyonka* goods are loosely associated with deception. Consumers are not always fooled – more than two-thirds of traders openly admit that they sell fakes (BrandMonitor 2018) – and do not always attempt to deceive people regarding the originality of purchased goods (Crăciun 2012). Moreover, deception in counterfeiting is not simply black and white but includes a spectrum of grey: from 'highly-deceptive' where the counterfeit product is virtually identical to its genuine counterpart to 'non-deceptive' where the counterfeit product is easily distinguishable from its genuine counterpart. The degree of deceptiveness varies with consumer experience, their awareness and knowledge (Eisend and Schuchert-Güler 2006).

Since deception and inauthenticity of goods are not necessarily linked, their ambiguous coupling often serves as justification for counterfeit consumption. It was documented that 'about one-third of consumers would knowingly purchase counterfeit goods' (Bian and Moutinho 2009: 368), but they only buy them when they belong to categories where the social, financial and physical risks are low (Chapa et al. 2006: 83). Consumers are more likely to purchase *palyonka* clothing and footwear than medicine and food (Khramova 2012). Although the purchase of counterfeit products varies across income, education, age and gender, empirical evidence on how these demographic factors work in different social contexts is contradictory. The literature highlights that younger people are more likely to purchase counterfeit goods, especially clothing, footwear and digital products. Young consumers adopt more positive attitudes towards unoriginal goods and consciously purchase them (Khramova 2012). At the same time, there is also some evidence that young people are more concerned about safety (Twenge 2017). This could explain why young Russians are less likely to consume counterfeit alcohol than their elders.

Consumer reasons for buying non-deceptive counterfeit goods tend to differ from reasons for choosing deceptive counterfeit goods or authentic goods. Consumers explain their motives for purchasing fakes by strategising between price, quality, brand attractiveness and availability of goods (Wehinger 2013). Counterfeits represent the opportunity to acquire desired branded goods at lower prices, which compensate for their lower quality. However, since expensive goods do not always entail higher quality, people may resent paying high prices for branded goods (Berdysheva and Romanova 2017) and, thus, be more inclined to purchase fakes.

Counterfeiting practices are intrinsically ambivalent: more than 80 per cent of Russians have negative attitudes towards fakes, but about a third of them report buying them consciously (Khramova 2012). This discrepancy between reported attitudes and observed behaviour demonstrates the gap between legality and social legitimacy. It suggests that consumers develop their competencies to serve their own needs and ignore the legal criteria, which better protect brand owners' rights rather than consumer rights.

The line between counterfeit and genuine goods is often very blurred. Experts and brand owners confirm that sometimes it is impossible to distinguish counterfeits from their original counterparts without a special laboratory test. Manufacturers are also known to produce unauthorised overruns (McDonald and Roberts 1994). Moreover, the moral basis for counterfeit consumption lies with the consumer perception of branded goods as unfairly highly priced. This legitimises counterfeits while making original branded goods socially illicit (Crăciun 2012). By purchasing counterfeits, consumers may signal cynicism, dissatisfaction and the desire to challenge the branding paradigm (Holt 2002).

Contradictions in supply policies also reinforce the ambivalence of counterfeit goods. Criminal entrepreneurs involved in providing counterfeits infringe on the intellectual property rights of economic actors and parasitise on popular brands. At the same time, counterfeiters democratise fashion by giving budget-conscious consumers the illusion of success and resolving common market failures such as goods shortages, poor distribution systems and unfair business practices. Evidence exists that the co-existence of brand manufacture and counterfeit production is beneficial for both parties. Brand holders whose intellectual property rights are violated do not always fight against fakes for two reasons: fear that consumers who learn that fakes are circulating on the market will stop buying their goods and, more importantly, the opportunity to gain the advantage of market penetration (Saviano 2008). Counterfeits may introduce a commodity or brand to a new market, form consumer preferences and develop consumer loyalty. In some companies, the local management was found colluding with criminal dealers by making informal agreements and profiting from illegal activity.

After the liberalisation of foreign trade in 1992, fake goods flooded into Russia. The proliferation of counterfeits was also fostered by economic crises, an abundance of cheap labour, the global diffusion of manufacturing technologies, the absence of restrictive legislation and poor law enforcement regarding intellectual property rights. Since the 2000s, the number of counterfeits and enhanced product segmentation has decreased. In 2005, 53 per cent of respondents had purchased counterfeit goods (FOM 2006). In 2011, the number had dropped to 30 per cent (Khramova 2012). Consumer bottom-up attitudes regarding the illegality of counterfeits have changed the counterfeit market much more slowly than the top-down attitudes of brand holders, legal experts and state regulators.

9.8 *Mertvye dushi* (Russian Federation, from 1991)
Ekaterina Vorobeva
Research Centre for East European Studies, University of Bremen, Germany

Mertvye dushi in Russian (dead souls) is an umbrella term describing fictitious employees in Russia. More precisely, *mertvye dushi* are officially employed individuals who have no obligation to attend the workplace or to perform any duties. This hiring practice is used to circumvent official rules and secure personal benefits. It uses creative accounting and window-dressing in order to hide unjust or unpleasant reality behind a deceptive facade (Jameel 2018; Leung 2018).

The practice is found in both the public and the private sectors in present-day Russia. Depending on the sector, however, there are significant differences in how the practice is implemented. In the public sector, top officials and managers hire relatives, friends or members of their inner circle in order to provide them with employment benefits (such as salaries and bonuses) without any corresponding obligations. In some cases, the salaries of *mertvye dushi* are paid to the top officials and managers themselves. This hiring practice is enabled by strong personal networks, the failure of the authorities to exercise efficient monitoring control, the rigid hierarchy of the Russian public sector, and corruption. In the private sector, the practice tends to focus more on benefits and company interests; even so, an owner or top manager also enjoys those benefits, whether directly or indirectly. In private firms, *mertvye dushi* can be represented by anyone – friends, relatives or distant acquaintances – who is registered as officially employed by a company in order for that company to meet certain criteria or to receive benefits. A company might for example need an employee with specific qualifications on its team in order to meet the requirements for a licence or to qualify as a non-commercial organisation. In the private sector, *mertvye dushi* are not usually entitled to a salary or other material rewards, but may receive official work experience (*stazh*) and social contributions paid by the employer.

The practice takes its name from the famous novel *Dead Souls* by Russian writer Nikolai Vasilyevich Gogol. The novel describes the fraudulent actions of Pavel Ivanovich Chichikov, who exploits a flaw in the census procedure in the nineteenth-century Russian Empire (Gornostaev 2021). The fact that at that time censuses were not conducted frequently meant that many dead people remained registered as alive long after they had actually died. In the Russian Empire slavery was practised until 1861, serfs were treated as property and landowners paid taxes based on the number of serfs in their possession. In Gogol's novel, Chichikov travels around Russia, establishing friendships with landowners and purchasing deceased serfs (dead souls) in order, in his words, to free the landowners from unnecessary tax burdens. In reality, however, Chichikov is pursuing his own vested interests since owning a large number of dead souls would qualify him for a huge state loan to purchase land.

Today, the practice involves fraudulent actions undertaken by public officials or owners of private companies. It is most often found in the public sector, as argued by Mingalimova (n.d.), in schools, universities, kindergartens, cultural organisations and hospitals. Top officials and managers exploit not only their personal networks but also the strict hierarchy and non-transparency of the Russian public sector in order to execute their fraud. Enjoying almost full control over a public organisation, managers, accountants and human-resource officials have exclusive access to detailed information concerning the number of employees, the size of their salaries, their attendance and their performance records. Individuals who occupy management positions in a public organisation often collude in order to extract personal benefits in the form of salaries, bonuses, free business trips, retirement benefits and work experience (*stazh*) for themselves or for their relatives and friends.

Mingalimova (n.d.) describes the process of hiring *mertvye dushi* in detail, stressing the essential collusion of managers, accountants and human-resource officials to enable the successful implementation of the practice:

> On the basis of an individual's application, the head of a public organisation issues an order for his or her employment. Knowingly false information about the employee's working hours is then entered on the staff timesheet. On this basis, the accounts department accrues funds in the name of the fictitious employee in accordance with the functional duties and working hours recorded on the timesheet, though these do not correspond to objective reality. The future salary of the fictitious employee is paid in cash or transferred to a bank card, but eventually makes its way into the hands of the head of the public organisation who initiated the action.

An example of such a practice is provided by a hospital manager who hired their young daughter as a salaried receptionist while the daughter was studying abroad. Legally, such actions qualify as a criminal offence, namely, abuse of authority, forgery and theft of budget money.

Public-sector employees who are not part of management are not usually privy to information regarding the number of their fellow workers. When *mertvye dushi* are hired for a certain department of a public organisation, their workload is distributed among actual workers. This often means that the latter have to work extra hours to compensate for the absence of *mertvye dushi*; typically, however, they are not paid overtime. This may negatively affect the quality of work in the public sector because of the lack of necessary manpower.

In the private sector, companies aiming to optimise resources and income-generation are less likely to hire *mertvye dushi*. Even so, the practice may be used as a tool to circumvent official requirements for certain commercial and non-commercial activities. Businesspeople may employ the practice thanks to the relative ease and low cost of hiring an employee in Russia. They may also exploit flaws in the work of monitoring bodies; owners of private firms may report on a certain number of employees and/or a certain qualification in their official reports, meet necessary criteria and thereby reach their corporate goals. Monitoring bodies have few opportunities to check how many employees are working for a private company, or what their qualifications are. As well as meeting criteria for certain (non-)commercial activities, private companies may also use the practice to qualify for loans or governmental support as employment-generating enterprises. While it may look like relatively insignificant fraud, the presence of *mertvye dushi* in private companies distorts information about the real state of a company and the true quality of its services, and thereby represents a tangible threat for investors who have difficulties assessing the actual value of an enterprise. In this case, under law, the practice qualifies as a criminal offence – namely, forgery.

Despite being widespread and well-known in the Russian employment world, the practice has not been studied much in Russia or other former Soviet states. However, it is discussed in various media outlets, on internet platforms and in law firm blogs. Even though the practice seems to be especially popular in Russia, where it has a unique national twist, similar practices have been identified in other countries such as Iran (Jameel 2018), Chile (Sklenar 2018) and Croatia (Šimić Banović 2019). Similar practices are represented by the Kurdish term *bin diwar* and the Arabic *fazaee* (see 9.9 in this volume); both are defined as 'ghost employees' – that is, individuals on public payrolls who are not actually employed in the public service (Jameel 2018). Another example is the Croatian *uhljeb* which is defined as 'a public sector employee whose main "competence" is membership of a political party or a nepotistic relationship' (Šimić Banović 2019: 279). While *uhljebs* resemble *mertvye dushi* in that they use their personal networks to secure employment, *uhljebs* perform their duties at least nominally and show up at their workplace; in this they differ from *mertvye dushi*, whose absence from work is the defining characteristic that gives them their name.

The precise proportion of *mertvye dushi* in the Russian public sector or private companies is unknown. The practice appears to be a burden for a government; it also casts doubt on the quality of the services and products provided by private firms. A reform to eliminate the practice would need to begin with stricter, more independent and less corrupt monitoring institutions. However, during the COVID-19 epidemic, when working remotely became increasingly popular, the practice became even easier to implement and harder to detect. This represents an increasing challenge for the authorities.

9.9 *Bin diwar/fazaee* (Iraq and the Kurdistan Region of Iraq)
Hemn Namiq Jameel
Faculty of Law and International Relations, Soran University, Kurdistan Region of Iraq

The Kurdish term *bin diwar*, used in the Kurdistan region of Iraq (KRI), and the Arabic term *fazaee,* used in the rest of Iraq, describe ghost employees – individuals on the public payroll who are not actual employees in the public service (Al Arab 2015: 7). The Kurdish *bin diwar* translates as 'under the wall'. The Arabic *fazaee* means 'in space' or 'space station'. These concepts are context-specific, but the phenomenon itself encapsulates the universal pattern of putting up facades and benefiting from creative accounting (see also *alga aploksnē*, 6.27 Volume 1, astroturfing, 6.31 Volume 1, *dzhinsa*, 6.32 Volume 1 and *window dressing*, 6.24 Volume 1).

Ghost workers phenomenon affects almost all state institutions in KRI and Iraq. There are around 4 million recorded government employees in Iraq. Together with pensioners and social transfer beneficiaries, there are 8 million public funds recipients in total, in a population of around 39 million population, thus making this the highest proportion in the world (Alhasoon 2017). Official sources estimate that the public institutions require only around half of this number of workers (MEO 2016). There are around 1.5 million people on the payroll of the Kurdistan Regional Government (KRG) (Jameel 2017), and some sources have suggested that most KRG ministries 'could operate as effectively with one-third the staff' (Rubin 2012).

Iraq and KRI have no system of personal income tax or national insurance to contribute to public budgets. Rather, oil provides most of the government's revenue. In both regions, the phenomenon of ghost employees has been on the rise since the 1968 Baath regime led by Saddam Hussein was toppled in 2003 (Hanelt et al. 2004). The reformed governance model offered new positions in public institutions. Political parties and public office holders started allocating public vacancies and funds to their political followers, family and friends in order to insert their influence into the state apparatus.

Fazaee employees have been syphoning public funds in Iraqi public institutions since the rule of the 2003 post-invasion Coalition Provisional Authority (Henneberger 2017; Pringle 2007). *Fazaee* workers have been reported in the army, security and police forces as well as in the Shia militia groups such as Hashd Al Shabi (Al Arab 2015: 7). An official estimate from 2014 puts the number of ghost soldiers and officers in the Iraqi army at 50,000 (Sputnik 2014). Others suggest the number of *fazaee* in different Iraqi institutions is around 900,000, and these estimates are confirmed by the author's research based on interviews with members of the Iraqi and Kurdistan parliaments.

In the KRI, *bin diwar* employees have been observed since 2005, mostly in the KRI army (Peshmerga), and ministries of education, health, finance and religious affairs. In the Iraqi Kurdistan region, politically divided between the 'Yellow zone' of the Kurdistan Democratic Party (KDP) and the 'Green zone' of the Patriotic Union of Kurdistan, both ruling parties have been appointing their own members and followers to public positions, similar to practices of *tazkia* in KRI (see 7.7 Volume 1), or *Parteibuchwirtschaft* in Austria (see 7.6 Volume 1). When the capacities of the public institutions became overloaded, employees took advantage of the situation by not going to work.

Political parties, groups and key leaders can have several motives for encouraging *fazaee* and *bin diwar* practices. First, ghost jobs can be offered as favours in return for political support. Second, as is the case at the Iraqi Ministry of Interior, *fazaee* workers are 'sons, relatives, guards of senior officers' (Alexander and Alexander 2015: 266). Third, the practice can be the result of a deal made between key public officials and individuals to divide the salary (Alexander and Alexander 2015: 266). In the Iraqi army, for instance:

> officers and even the commanders of entire brigades have been suspected of listing more men under their command than really exist. They do so by firing soldiers and not taking them off the payroll, splitting salaries, pocketing half and giving the rest to men who do not show up to work, and even listing soldiers who have defected or been killed. (Sputnik 2014: para 3; Roston and Myers 2007)

Although no official number exists, such informal practices carry a huge economic cost as both governments have to pay salaries to large numbers of people who do not provide any service in return. The ghost employee phenomenon produces a demoralising effect on the performance of actual employees, as they may be discouraged to provide public service upon observing that ghost workers fail to be prosecuted. Governments of KRI and Iraq claim to have taken measures to capture *fazaee* and *bin diwar* workers and cut them from the payroll, yet without much visible results. A comprehensive reform required to remove ghost workers from public institutions will require commitment and true political will.

Bibliography to Chapter 9

Introduction: entrepreneurship
Abel Polese

Brennan, G. and Pettit, P. 2005. *The Hidden Economy of Esteem*. Oxford: Oxford University Press.
Grant, A. 2013. *Give and Take: A Revolutionary Approach to Success*. New York: Penguin.
Jaffe, R. and Koster, M. 2019. 'The Myth of Formality in the Global North: Informality-as-Innovation'. *Dutch Governance International Journal of Urban and Regional Research* 43(3): 563–68.
Pardo, I. 1996. *Managing Existence in Naples: Morality, Action and Structure*. Cambridge: Cambridge University Press.
Phelps, N. A. 2021. 'The Inventiveness of Informality: An Introduction'. *International Development Planning Review* 43(1): 1–12.
Polese, A. 2021. 'What is informality? (Mapping) "the Art of Bypassing the State" in Eurasian Spaces – and Beyond'. *Eurasian Geography and Economics* 64(3): 322–64.
Polese, A., Moisé, G. M., Lysa, O., Kerikmae, T., Sauka, A. and Seliverstova, O. 2021. 'Presenting the Results of the Shadow Economy Survey in Ukraine while Reflecting on the Future(s) of Informality Studies'. *Journal of Contemporary Central and Eastern Europe* 30(1): 101–23.
Polese, A., Moisé, G. M., Tokyzhanova, T., Aguzzi, T., Kerikmae, T., Sagynbaeva, A. Sauka, A. and Seliverstova, O. 2022. 'Informality vs Shadow Economy: Reflecting on the First Results of a Manager's Survey in Kyrgyzstan'. *Central Asian Survey* 42(3): 1–22.
White, J. B. 2004. *Money Makes Us Relatives: Women's Labor in Urban Turkey*. London: Routledge.

9.1 *Combina* (Israel)
Ina Kubbe

Arieli, I. 2017. 'In Israel, Individualism and Collectivism Happily Coexist'. *Israel21c*, 12 July. www.israel21c.org/in-israel-individualism-and-collectivism-happily-coexist/
Baez-Camargo, C. and Ledeneva, A. 2017. 'Where Does Informality Stop and Corruption Begin? Informal Governance and the Public/Private Crossover in Mexico, Russia and Tanzania'. *Slavonic and East European Review* 95(1): 49–75.
Beaussart, M. L., Andrews, C. J. and Kaufman, J. C. 2013. 'Creative Liars: The Relationship Between Creativity and Integrity'. *Thinking Skills and Creativity* 9, 129–34.
Big Idea. 2020. 'Phrases in Israel'. *Big Idea*. https://web.archive.org/web/20201124211909/https://bigidea.co.il/gap-year/10-must-know-hebrew-slang-words-practice-pre-college-gap-year-israel/
Gilad, E. 2014. 'On the Russian Origin of Combina'. *Haaretz*, 19 November. www.haaretz.co.il/magazine/the-edge/.premium-1.2490250
Halfin, J. 2018. 'All the Slang You'll Need for Your Trip to Israel'. *Israel21c*, 9 May. www.israel21c.org/all-the-slang-youll-need-for-your-trip-to-israel/

Hebrew Language Academy. 2020. 'Combina'. *The Hebrew Language Academy*. https://hebrew-academy.org.il/keyword/%D7%A7%D7%95%D6%B9%D7%9E%D6%B0%D7%91%D6%BC%D6%B4%D7%99%D7%A0%D6%B8%D7%94

Hofstede Insights. 2020. 'What about Israel?'. *Hofstede Insights*. www.hofstede-insights.com/country/israel/

Ilf, I. and Petrov, E. 2011 [1928]. *The Twelve Chairs: A Novel*. Evanston, IL: Northwestern University Press.

Kubbe, I. and Varraich, A. (eds) 2019. *Corruption and Informal Practices in the Middle East and North Africa*. Oxon and New York: Routledge.

Ledeneva, A. 2008. 'Blat and Guanxi: Informal Practices in Russia and China'. *Comparative Studies in Society and History* 50(1): 118–44.

Lipovetsky, M. 2010. *Charms of the Cynical Reason*. Brookline: Academic Studies Press.

Marshadruker. 2017. 'Combina, Chutzpah, and a Blooming Desert: Experiencing the Magic of Startup Nation'. *Marshadruker*, 3 May. https://web.archive.org/web/20170507031403/https://marshadruker.com/combina-chutzpah-and-a-blooming-desert/

Petrov, I. 2013. 'Exposure: Y. Petrov Invented the Combine'. *Rotter.net*, 13 October. https://rotter.name/kolot/prime/42621.php

Rodrigue-Schwarzwald, O. 2013. 'Between Hebrew and Juedo-Spanish'. *Hed HaUlpan ha-Hadash* 101: 17–28. http://cms.education.gov.il/NR/rdonlyres/9B57F581-A76B-4CC0-BB11-0BDC12DBFEC9/182452/Ora.pdf%20pp.%206

Rosenthal, R. 2015. 'Literary Culture: The Combination of Declaration: Where Did the Hebrew Slang Words Come From?'. *Maariv*, 23 March. www.maariv.co.il/culture/literature/Article-472587

Urban Dictionary. 2020. 'Combina'. *Urban Dictionary*, 18 January. www.urbandictionary.com/define.php?term=combina

9.2 *Manteros* (Spain)
Horacio Espinosa

De Certeau, M. 1980. *La invención de lo cotidiano, Tomo 1: Artes de Hacer, desarrollo*. México, D.F/Guadalajara: Universidad Iberoamericana/ITESO.

Ealham, C. 2011. 'La lucha por la calle: la venta ambulante, la cultura de protesta y la represión en Barcelona (c. 1930–1936)', *Ayer. Revista de Historia Contemporánea* 81/2011(1): 173–205.

El Diario. 2015. 26 August. www.eldiario.es//

Espinosa, H. 2017. 'El mercadillo rebelde de Barcelona. Prácticas antidisciplinarias en la ciudad mercancía'. *Quaderns-e de l'Institut Català d'Antropologia* 22(1): 67–87.

Espinosa, H. 2021. 'Informal Appropriations in the Face of the State of Exception. Ethnographic Snapshots of the Right to the City'. *AIBR – Revista de Antropología Iberoamericana* 16(2): 266–97.

Lupe, S. 2016. 'Colau expulsa a los "manteros" del metro con un megaoperativo policial'. 20 April, https://www.laizquierdadiario.com/Colau-expulsa-a-los-manteros-del-metro-con-un-megaoperativo-policial

Marcús, J. and Peralta, M. A. 2021. 'La calle en disputa. Narrativas sobre los usos legítimos e ilegítimos del espacio público en la Ciudad de Buenos Aires'. *AIBR, Revista de Antropología Iberoamericana* 16(2).

Molinero, Y. and Avallone, G. 2020. 'El trabajo ambulante: entre derecho a la ciudad y represión. El caso de la resistencia de los trabajadores senegaleses en la ciudad de Salerno'. *MIGRACIONES* 48 (2020).

Robin, N. 1996. 'La multipolarisation de la migration sénégalaise'. In *Mobilités et investissements des émigrés, Maroc, Tunisie, Turquie, Sénégal*, edited by M. Mung, 48–64. París: L'Harmattan.

Sow, P. 2004. 'Prácticas comerciales trasnacionales y espacios de acción de los senegaleses en España'. In *Migración y Estudios sobre remesas y otras prácticas transnacionales*, edited by A. Escrivá and N. Ribas, 235–54. Córdoba: CSIC.

Zubrzycki, B. 2016. 'La migración de los senegaleses "Modou-Modou" en Argentina'. Contra/relatos desde el Sur 13(7): 4–12.

9.3 *Tenderpreneur* (South Africa)
Laurence Piper and Andrew Charman

BBBEE. 2017. 'Broad-Based Black Economic Empowerment Act, 2003'. *Government Gazette* 463(25899), 20 January. www.environment.gov.za/sites/default/files/legislations/bbbee_act.pdf
Bolton, P. 2006. 'Government Procurement as a Policy Tool in South Africa'. *Journal of Public Procurement* 6(3): 193.
Booysen, S. 2015. *Dominance and Decline: The ANC in the Time of Zuma*. Johannesburg: Wits University Press.
Chipkin, I. 2016. 'The Decline of African Nationalism and the State of South Africa'. *Journal of Southern African Studies* 42(2): 215–27.
Constitution. 1996. *Constitution of the Republic of South Africa, Act 108 of 1996*. www.gov.za/sites/default/files/images/a108-96.pdf
Conway-Smith, E. 2017. 'This Is What Happens When a Family of Business Moguls Takes Over a Country'. *Foreign Policy*, 15 May. http://foreignpolicy.com/2017/05/15/the-rise-and-rise-of-south-africas-real-first-family-guptas-zuma/
Corruption Watch. 2014. *Understanding Corruption in Tenders*. www.corruptionwatch.org.za/wp-content/uploads/2015/06/Corruption-Watch-Understanding-tender-corruption.pdf
Dlamini, J. 2010. *Native Nostalgia*. Aukland Park: Jacana Media.
Giliomee, H. and Simkins, C. E. W. (eds) 1999. *The Awkward Embrace: One-Party Domination and Democracy*. London: Taylor & Francis.
Pauw, J. 2017. *The President's Keepers: Those Keeping Zuma in Power and Out of Prison*. Cape Town: NB Publishers.
Pilling, D. and Cotterill, J. 2017. 'Jacob Zuma, the Guptas and the Selling of South Africa'. *Financial Times*, 30 November. www.ft.com/content/707c5560-d49a-11e7-8c9a-d9c0a5c8d5c9
Piper, L. 2015. 'From Party-State to Party-Society in South Africa: SANCO and the Informal Politics of Community Representation in "Imizamo Yethu". Hout Bay, Cape Town'. In *Popular Politics in South African Cities: Unpacking Community Participation*, edited by C. Bénit-Gbaffou, 21–41. Pretoria: HSRC Press.
Plaut, M. 2017. 'A Crushing Defeat for the Dark Side'. *British Journalism Review* 28(4): 37–42.
PPPF. 2000. Preferential Procurement Policy Framework Act, 2000. *Government Gazette* 416(20854), 3 February 2000; 618, No. 40553, 20 January 2017. www.treasury.gov.za/divisions/ocpo/sc/PPPFA/Preferential%20Procurement%20Policy%20Framework%20Act,%202000%20(Act%20No.5%20of%202000).pdf
Southall, R. 2008. 'The ANC for Sale? Money, Morality & Business in South Africa'. *Review of African Political Economy* 35(116): 281–99.
Southall, R. 2011. 'Family and Favour at the Court of Jacob Zuma'. *Review of African Political Economy* 38(130): 617–26.
Transparency International. 2017. 'Corruption Perception Index 2016'. *Transparency International*. www.transparency.org/news/feature/corruption_perceptions_index_2016

9.4 *Mzungu price* (Kenya)
Yunqiao Xu

Alila, P. and Mitullah, W. 1999. 'Women Street Vendors in Kenya: Policies, Regulations and Organisational Capacity'. *International Research Development Centre*. University of Nairobi. https://idl-bnc-idrc.dspacedirect.org/bitstream/handle/10625/35604/127484.pdf?sequence=1
Chepngeno, E. and Lubanga, D. 2020. 'Eldoret Traders Protest over "Rogue" Enforcement Officers'. *Daily Nation*, 5 March. nation.co.ke/counties/uasingishu/Eldoret-traders-close-shops-in-protest/1183334-5479644-o0l0w0/index.html

Escudero, V., Mourelo, E. L. and Rashid, H. 2013. 'Kenya: Making Quality Employment the Driver of Development'. *International Institute for Labour Studies*, 123–9. www.ilo.org/wcmsp5/groups/public/---africa/documents/publication/wcms_231155.pdf

Garg, A. 2015. 'Travel Risks vs Tourist Decision Making: A Tourist Perspective'. *International Journal of Hospitality & Tourism Systems* 8: 1–9.

Kamunyori, W. S. 2007. 'A Growing Space for Dialogue: The Case of Street Vending in Nairobi's Central Business District'. Thesis. *MIT Libraries*. Cambridge: Massachusetts Institute of Technology.

Lyons, M. and Snoxell, S. 2005. 'Creating Urban Social Capital: Some Evidence from Informal Traders in Nairobi'. *Urban Studies* 42(7): 1073–92.

MacOireachtaigh, P. 2015. 'My Skin Colour Represents Privilege and Status. But it Makes Me an Outsider Too'. *Guardian*, 10 September. Https://theguardian.com/commentisfree/2015/sep/10/white-in-africa-outsider

Mitullah, W. 2005. 'Enterprise: Street Trade in Kenya: The Contribution of Research in Policy Dialogue and Response'. In *Urban Futures: Economic Growth and Poverty Reduction*, edited by H. Nabeel. London: ITDG Publications.

Mnyamwezi, R. 2020. 'Kenya Traders on Taveta Border Complain of Harassment by Tanzania Authorities'. *Standard Digital*, 26 November. standardmedia.co.ke/article/2001261321/kenya-traders-on-taveta-border-complain-of-harassment-by-tanzania-authorities

Pohl, O. 2002. 'Kenya Cracking Down on "Beach Boys" Gigolos Serving Tourists'. *The New York Times*, 14 February. nytimes.com/2002/02/14/world/kenya-cracking-down-on-beach-boys-gigolos-serving-tourists.html

Racaud, S. 2017. 'Ambiguous Resource: "Informal" Street Trading in Kisumu, Kenya'. *Articulo – revue de sciences humaines*: 17–18.

Roever, S. 2016. 'Informal Trade Meets Informal Governance: Street Vendors and Legal Reform in India, South Africa, and Peru'. *Cityscape* 18(1): 27–46.

Schlegel, P. and Racaud, S. 2016. 'Urbanization and Street Vending: How Street Vending, an Individual and a Collective Resource Can Be Integrated into the Urban Governance?'. *French Institute for Research in Africa* 38–40.

Spitzer, H. 2017. 'Social Work in East Africa: A Mzungu Perspective'. *International Social Work* 62(2): 567–80.

Uwitije, C. 2016. 'Contribution of Street Vending on Livelihood of Urban Low Income Households in the City of Kigali, Rwanda'. Master's dissertation. *University of Nairobi Research Active* 2–3.

9.5 *Churning* (Canada)
Katie Kilroy-Marac

Kilroy-Marac, K. 2016. 'A Magical Reorientation of the Modern: Professional Organizers and Thingly Care in Contemporary North America'. *Cultural Anthropology* 31(3): 438–57.

Kilroy-Marac, K. 2018. 'An Order of Distinction (or, How to Tell a Collection from a Hoard)'. *Journal of Material Culture* 23(1): 20–38.

Kolberg, J. 2007. *Conquering Chronic Disorganization*. Decatur: Squall Press.

Kolberg, J. 2009. *What Every Professional Organizer Needs to Know about Hoarding*. Decatur: Squall Press.

Woodward, S. 2021. 'Clutter in Domestic Spaces: Material Vibrancy and Competing Moralities'. *The Sociological Review* 69(6): 1214–28.

9.6 *Double Irish* (Ireland)
Julia Schmalz

Beesley, A. and Barker, A. 2016. 'Apple Tax Deal: How It Worked and What the EU Ruling Means'. *Financial Times*, 30 August. www.ft.com/content/cc58c190-6ec3-11e6-a0c9-1365ce54b926

Brunsden, J. and Noble, J. 2016. 'European Commission to Examine Google's UK Tax Deal'. *Financial Times*, 28 January. www.ft.com/content/dc1e3cd4-c592-11e5-808f-8231cd71622e

Committee of Public Accounts. 2016. 'Corporate Tax Settlements Twenty-fifth Report of Session 2015–16', *House of Commons*. http://publications.parliament.uk/pa/cm201516/cmselect/cmpubacc/788/788.pdf

Danopoulos, C. P. and Znidaric, B. 2007. 'Informal Economy, Tax Evasion, and Poverty in a Democratic Setting'. *Mediterranean Quarterly* 18(2): 67–84.

Darby, J. B. and Leamaster, K. 2007. 'Double Irish More than Doubles the Tax Savings – Hybrid Structure Reduces Irish, U.S. and Worldwide Taxation'. *Practical US/International Tax Strategies*: 2–16.

Department of Finance. 2016. *Statement by the Minister for Finance on the Government Decision to Appeal the Apple State Aid Decision*. Irish Department of Finance, 2 September. www.finance.gov.ie/updates/statement-by-the-minister-for-finance-on-the-government-decision-to-appeal-the-apple-state-aid-decision/

European Commission. 2016. *Statement by Commissioner Vestager on State Aid Decision That Ireland's Tax Benefits for Apple Were Illegal*. European Commission, 30 August. http://europa.eu/rapid/press-release_STATEMENT-16-2926_en.htm

General Court of the European Union. 2020. The General Court of the European Union annuls the decision taken by the Commission regarding the Irish tax rulings in favour of Apple. Press Release No 90/20. 15 July.

Jones, B. 2015. *Corporate Power and Responsible Capitalism? Towards Social Accountability*. Cheltenham and Northampton: Edward Elgar.

Kahn, J. and Drucker, J. 2016. 'Google Lowered Taxes by $2.4 Billion Using European Subsidiaries'. *Bloomberg Technology*, 19 February. www.bloomberg.com/news/articles/2016-02-19/google-lowered-taxes-by-2-4-billion-using-european-subsidiaries

Scott, M. 2016. 'Ireland Doesn't Want Apple's Back Taxes, but the Irish Aren't So Sure'. *The New York Times*, 11 September. www.nytimes.com/2016/09/12/business/international/ireland-doesnt-want-apples-back-taxes-but-the-irish-arent-so-sure.html

Somerville, J. 2015. 'Ireland: Irish Finance Act 2014 – Double Irish Finished? How About a KDB?'. *International Tax Journal*, 41(1): 5–8, 45.

Tax Foundation. 2022. Corporate Tax Rates around the World, 2022. https://taxfoundation.org/data/all/global/corporate-tax-rates-by-country-2022/

Tax Law Review Committee. 1997. *Tax Avoidance: A Report by the Tax Law Review Committee*. London: Institute for Fiscal Studies.

9.7 *Palyonka* (Russia)
Zoya Kotelnikova

Berdysheva, E. and Romanova, R. 2017. 'Rethinking Prices During an Economic Crisis: Calculation as a New Mode of Consumer Behaviour in Russia'. *International Journal of Consumer Studies* 41(4): 397–403.

Bian, X. and Moutinho, L. 2009. 'An Investigation of Determinants of Counterfeit Purchase Consideration'. *Journal of Business Research* 62: 368–78.

BrandMonitor. 2018. *Up to 70% Counterfeit Dealers in Russia Admit to Selling Fakes*, 8 November.

Chapa, S., Minor, M. S. and Maldonado, C. 2006. 'Product Category and Original Effects on Consumer Responses to Counterfeits: Comparing Mexico and the US'. *Journal of International Consumer Marketing* 18(4): 79–99.

Crăciun, M. 2012. 'Rethinking Fakes, Authenticating Selves'. *The Journal of the Royal Anthropological Institute* 18(4): 846–63.

Devigne, L. 2008. 'An Urgent Need to Better Respond to the Global Problem of Counterfeiting and Piracy: The EU Answer'. 4th Global Congress: Combating Counterfeiting and Piracy, Dubai, 3 February.

Eisend, M. and Schuchert-Güler, P. 2006. 'Explaining Counterfeit Purchases: A Review and Preview'. *Academy of Marketing Science Review* 6(12): 1–25.

FOM. 2006. *Falsifitsirovannye tovary na segodnyashnem rossiyskom rynke*. FOM, 10 October. http://bd.fom.ru/report/cat/ec_trade/dd064226

Holt, D. 2002. 'Why Do Brands Cause Trouble? A Dialectical Theory of Consumer Culture and Branding'. *Journal of Consumer Research* 29(1): 70–90.

Khramova, Y. 2012. 'Ambivalentnost otnosheniya potrebiteley k kontrafaktnoy produtsii'. *Ekonomicheskaya sotsiologiya* 13(4): 116–54.

Kotelnikova, Z. 2017. 'Explaining Counterfeit Alcohol Purchases in Russia'. *Alcoholism: Clinical and Experimental Research* 41(4): 810–19.

McDonald, G. and Roberts, C. 1994. 'Product Piracy: The Problem that Will not Go Away'. *Journal of Product and Brand Management* 3(4): 55–65.

Radaev, V. V. 2017. 'Crooked Mirror: The Evolution of Illegal Alcohol Markets in Russia since the Late Socialist Period'. In: *The Architecture of Illegal Markets. Towards an Economic Sociology of Illegality in the Economy*, edited by J. Beckert and M. Dewey, 218–41. Oxford: Oxford University Press.

Radaev, V., Barsukova, S. and Kotelnikova Z. 2008. 'Rynki kontrafaktnoy produstsii v Rossii' [Markets for Counterfeit Goods in Russia]. Analytika LESI 2. www.hse.ru/data/2011/02/09/1208661393/ЛЭСИ-2.pdf

Saviano, R. 2008. *Gomorrah: A Personal Journey into the Violent International Empire of Naples' Organized Crime System*. New York: Picador.

Twenge, J. 2017. *iGen: Why Today's Super-Connected Kids are Growing Up Less Rebellious, More Tolerant, Less Happy: and Completely Unprepared for Adulthood (And What that Means for the Rest of Us)*. New York: ATRIA Books.

Wehinger, F. 2013. 'Fake Qualities: Assessing the Value of Counterfeit Goods'. In *Constructing Quality: The Classification of Goods in Markets*, edited by J. Beckert and C. Musselin, 268–87. Oxford: Oxford University Press.

9.8 *Mertvye dushi* (Russian Federation, from 1991)
Ekaterina Vorobeva

Gornostaev, A. V. 2021. 'Mertvye dushi'. *Global Informality Project*. www.in-formality.com/wiki/index.php?title=Mertvye_Dushi_(Russia)

Jameel, H. N. 2018. 'Bin Diwar, Fazaee'. *Global Informality Project*. www.in-formality.com/wiki/index.php?title=Bin_Diwar,_Fazaee_(Iraq_and_the_Kurdistan_Region_of_Iraq)

Leung, D. 2018. 'Window dressing'. *Global Informality Project*. www.in-formality.com/wiki/index.php?title=Window_dressing_(Global)

Mingalimova, M. F. n.d. *Criminal Liability for Employment of 'Ghost' employees*. Wiselawyer.ru. https://wiselawyer.ru/poleznoe/75019-ugolovnaya-otvetstvennost-trudoustrojstvo-mertvykh-dush

Šimić Banović, R. 2019. 'Uhljeb – A Post-Socialist Homo Croaticus: A Personification of the Economy of Favours in Croatia?'. *Post-Communist Economies* 31(3): 279–300.

Sklenar, D. B. 2018. Pituto. *Global Informality Project*. www.in-formality.com/wiki/index.php?title=Pituto_(Chile)

9.9 *Bin diwar, fazaee* (Iraq and the Kurdistan Region of Iraq)
Hemn Namiq Jameel

Al Arab. 2015. 'Report about Ghost Soldiers'. *Al Arab Newspaper*, 2 February.

Alexander, Y. and Alexander, D. 2015. *The Islamic State: Combating the Caliphate without Borders*. Lanham, Boulder, New York and London: Lexington Books.

Alhasoon, N. 2017. '8 Million Iraqis Depend on the State Treasury'. *Alhayat*, 22 November.

Hanelt, C., Luciani, G. and Neugart, F. 2004. *Regime Change in Iraq: The Transatlantic and Regional Dimensions*. Washington DC: Bertelsmann Foundation.

Henneberger, M. 2017. 'Bremer Paid "Ghost Employees" to Avoid Real Trouble', *Slemani News Network*.

Jameel, H. N. 2017. 'A Case Study of Political Corruption in Conflict-Affected Societies (The Kurdistan Region of Iraq 2003–13)', PhD thesis, University of Leicester, Leicester.

MEO. 2016. 'Ghost Employees is Still the Big Corruption File in Iraq'. MEO, 21 February.

Pringle, E. 2007. 'How Iraq was Looted'. *Counter Punch*, 21 April. www.counterpunch.org/2007/04/21/how-iraq-was-looted

Roston, A. and Myers, L. 2007. '"Untouchable" Corruption in Iraqi Agencies'. *NBC News*, 31 July. www.nbcnews.com/id/20043428/ns/nbc_nightly_news_with_brian_williams-nbc_news_investigates/t/untouchable-corruption-iraqi-agencies/#.W11xO7JR3IU

Rubin, M. 2012. 'Why does Barzani Oppose Modern Banking for Kurdistan?' *The Kurdistan Tribune*, 12 October. www.michaelrubin.org/12409/kurdistan-banking

Sputnik. 2014. 'Iraqi PM's Graft Probe Finds 50,000 "Ghost Soldiers"'. *Sputnik*, 30 November. https://sputniknews.com/middleeast/201411301015330267/

10
Living on the edge

Introduction: triangulating ethnicity, networks and migration

Endre Sik
Centre for Social Studies and ELTE University, Hungary

In the context of migration, informality is unavoidably and closely connected to two phenomena which themselves are intertwined: ethnicity and networks. These three dimensions provide us with a model, sensitive and complex enough to offer a proper tool to better understand the operation of the institution of border. It is commonplace that ethnicity has a crucial role in informal activities. Classic sociology texts confirm this association from all over the world and in regard to a wide range of informal activities (Light 1977; Wiegand 1994). The role of networks in the course of various forms of informal processes is also well-known (Sik and Wallace 1999; Sik and Wellman 1999). The value added by this brief introductory treatise is that I first refer to the contributions written for this volume, and second, I present the essence of a case study to demonstrate simultaneous and mutually reinforcing impacts of ethnicity, networks and informality.

Various forms of the combined impact of ethnicity and networks on informality is well illustrated in the first two volumes of this series such as the traditional (*adat*, Chechnya, see 3.1 Volume 1 or *uruuchuluk*, Kyrgyzstan, see 3.3 Volume 1) versus the modern (*joro*, Kyrgyzstan, see 6.3 in this volume, *taksovanie*, Uzbekistan, see 8.8 in this volume, *a molestar a otro lado*, Guatemala, see 5.11 in this volume or *KhTsB*, Armenia, see 5.1 in this volume), the illegal (*blood revenge*, Caucasus, *mzungu price*, East and Sub-Saharan Africa, see 9.4 in this volume or *tenderpreneur*, South Africa, see 9.3 in this volume) versus the a-legal (*ta'arof*, Iran, *partiti*, Corsica, see 13.7 in this volume, *sadaqa* in several regions of Central Asia, see 6.4 in this volume, *ahbap-çavuş*, Turkey, see 5.4 in this volume or *wantoks* and *kastom*, Melanesia, see 3.8 Volume 1).

There are case studies which lucidly illustrate the intertwined and mutually reinforcing role of ethnicity, informality and informality in the context of migration/mobility as well. For example, *hemşehricilik* in Turkey (see 5.3 in this volume) means that rural migrants in cities and/or migrants all over the Turkish diaspora offer favours to those 'near and dear'. This activity contributes to retaining and even strengthening ethnic identity, but it also offers informal advantages for those who belong to these circles such as getting a job and/or higher income, jumping the queue and so on. *Ściągnąć* in Poland (see 10.3 in this volume) is the equivalent of chain migration (literally meaning 'pull down/off from'), for example an apple from a tree or pulling in a fish on a line. The ethnic networks which are embedded into this activity are also the fertile soil of various forms (and not necessarily tensionless) informal activity.

One case study illustrates the complex and strong relations among informality, ethnicity and networks and highlights the importance of context in informal activities: in this case, the border. According to the classic Simmel's concept, the border may act as a bridge, a window and/or a door (van Houtum and Strüver 2002). The strength of control of various commercial activities and the selection criteria for travellers and traders define whether the border acts as a bridge or as a door, and whether there are any ethnicity- and/or network-based informal effects which oil the hinges of this door. The selection processes are often tailored to the needs of the actors involved: just as border control officers need to show their effectiveness to the government, petty traders and cross-border smuggling businesses deliver to their own clients, thus amounting to *practical norms* ranging from bribery to nepotism (De Herdt and de Sardan 2015).

The border-specific intertwined effects of informality, ethnicity and networks can be found practically everywhere when new states with long borders (and more often than not with trans-local ethnic diversity) emerge. This was the case in the 1960s during the decolonisation period in Africa, and this was definitely a core element of the transformation process in the course of the collapse of the Soviet Union (especially if the new states were weak, then all forms of cross-border informal activity had flourished). Between the newly established Croatia and Bosnia-Hercegovina there were about 400 border crossing points which makes border control impossible. The same can be found in the Transnistria region (a quasi-country between Ukraine and Moldova recognised only by Russia) and in several post-colonial countries in Africa (Polese 2006).

Our case study describes cross-border relations in a tri-border zone between Hungary, Slovakia and Ukraine (Sik and Surányi 2014; Sik and Szeitl 2015). This region is characterised by a special form of ethnicity of the so-called quasi-diaspora, that is, a non-migrant population living close to the current border that has been transformed from a majority (in their kinstate) to a minority (in the host-state) (Sik and Tóth 2003; Sik 2012). This ethnic group has a strong ethnic 'We-consciousness' (often encouraged by kinstate politics and policies) and contains strong cross-border networks which are embedded into kin-based and clan-like formation of inter-household cooperation which provide the fertile soil of various forms of informal activities.

The mutually reinforcing characteristics of the four components of this model – ethnicity, networks, informality and border – help the smooth operation of cross-border traffic and explain the high inertia of this complex system. They have well-defined if necessary flexible boundaries in order to: (1) strengthen ethnicity as 'imagined community' (Anderson 2006), (2) maintain the path dependent feature of networks (Sik 2010), (3) reinforce the self-defence mechanisms of informal activities and (4) to define whom to treat as a citizen (Wimmer and Glick-Schiller 2002). Moreover, they have strong capabilities to channel the diverse forms of human, network and financial capitals back and forth as well as to shift these capitals among various informal activities. Thus, identical mother tongue is often a proxy of ethnicity, the basis of selection of belonging to networks, the communication form of informal groups (secrecy) and applying for special treatment at the border (Hungarian ethnicity as the basis to claim compensatory citizenship (Harpaz 2016)).

The role of quasi-diasporic situations in cross-border informal activity becomes especially strong if the border is 'weak', or newly created like in the case of Eastern Europe and in the Balkans following the transformation of the system (Hozic 2004; Egbert 2006). We can envisage that such processes always start small. In the beginning the pettiest forms of informal activities are embedded into ethnically reinforced neighbourhood, friendship, family and kinship ties. Later on, they develop into a larger-scale smuggling business of self-selected, smaller and specialised groups with the same characteristics. The informal trade during the Soviet regime and for a period after it, was also conducted within ethnic inter-household networks (Czakó and Sik 1999; Sik and Wallace 1999). The networks converted their ethnicity-based human and network capital into large informal enterprises specialising in trading goods with a high profit margin (such as gas, alcohol and cigarettes), capital-intensive but profitable forms of trafficking (prostitutes, migrants or refugees) and in smuggling (organs, drugs, weapons or animals).

10.1 *Vorovskie pasporta* (Russia)
Andrey V. Gornostaev
Department of History, University of Toronto, Canada

Several early modern states invented documents to control and regulate the movement of persons both within official borders and outside around the sixteenth and seventeenth centuries. The emergence of identity documents was linked to the states' aspirations to improve their capacity to extract resources from their populations in the form of taxes, military conscripts and labour. At the same time, identity documents facilitated the policies of exclusion, containment and surveillance of various undesirables on the grounds of race, religion, age and other socio-economic factors. Information on places of origin and residence, included in passports, has become a valuable tool to distinguish subjects from foreigners or citizens from non-citizens, and, as such, enabled the emergence of nation-states (Torpey 2000: 1–7).

According to the 1649 Law Code, there were three types of travel documents, called *proezzhie gramoty*: those permitting Russians to travel abroad, those granting foreigners the right to travel to and within Russia and those enabling them to move within Russia for work or business (Franklin 2010: 212–13). While the first two pertain only to a small fraction of official travellers and merchants, the latter affected peasants and townspeople who constituted much of the population and who were also permanently confined to their places of residence by the Law Code of 1649 (see also Gornostaev 2022). According to the household census of 1678, 436,000 peasant households ended up in the hands of nobles, 148,000 belonged to the church establishment, 140,000 were owned by the court and 61,000 were independent tax-paying peasant households residing in the north (Hellie 1990: 308–9). Regardless of the category a person belonged to, carrying such travel documents became the only way to prove the legality of their departures. However, local authorities rarely enforced this requirement, and thousands of people roamed around the country without any papers.

The institutionalisation of the internal passport regime occurred during the reign of Peter the Great (1682–1725) when the imperial state was looking for better ways to collect accurate information about its population and improve the mechanisms of exploitation and mobility control. Between 1719 and 1724, the government carried out a series of measures in this direction: the first population census, the poll tax and, finally, internal passports (Anisimov 1982). Not only did these measures mean that the government had this information at their disposal, but they also forced the tsar's subjects to comply with the new passport regime (Figure 10.1.1).

In 1724, the government drew an official line between those who travelled within their districts – no further than approximately 30 kilometres – and those who searched for jobs outside. For the former, a written permit was sufficient on the condition that it was signed by a landlord, estate manager or a village elder, and specified travel for work as its bearer's objective. The peasants and townsmen intending to work outside of their districts had to obtain formal passports issued on special blanks, signed and sealed by government officials and containing

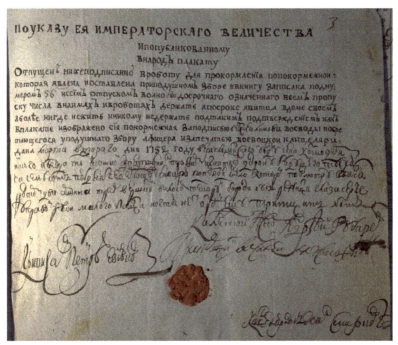

Figure 10.1.1 A counterfeit printed passport, 1752. RGADA, f. 407, op. 1, d. 77, l. 3. © Rossiiskii gosudarstvennyi arkhiv drevnikh aktov (RGADA).

descriptions of the holder's physical features, such as height, hair and beard colour, as well as any distinctive features. Only men could apply for such passports, the term of validity of which ranged from six months to three years (Polnoe sobranie zakonov Rossiiskoi imperii [PSZ] vol. 7, no. 4533). The passport holder had to present the passport to their employers and the local authorities wherever they stayed or sought work.

The introduction of such restrictions led to the problem of passport forgery. Numerous reports about counterfeit passports (*vorovskie pasporta*) prompted the 1726 decree that all passports had to be printed rather than written. Despite this regulation, local authorities struggled with its enforcement because of a shortage of printed blanks. To meet the demand from many itinerant workers who performed seasonal or temporary labour, officials were forced to continue issuing handwritten passports. Such documents were simple to forge as testified by archival records. Counterfeit passports were available virtually everywhere: in taverns, at bazaars and fairs, on barges and along roads. In the town of Viazniki in 1727, for instance, Dmitrii Khabarov produced several false passports for his fellow townsmen in his own house that he signed and sealed himself (Kosheleva 2016: 330). In 1743, the fugitive peasant Semen Akhreianov encountered a barge hauler somewhere near Nizhnii Novgorod who asked whether Akhreianov owned a passport. After receiving a negative response, the barge hauler brought him to a riverboat and wrote out a passport for him, which included the fugitive's real name, physical features and place of residence. The barge hauler then authenticated the passport by sealing and signing it on behalf of Vologda district officials (RGADA [Rossiiskii gosudarstvennyi arkhiv drevnikh aktov] f. 439, op. 1, d. 10, ll. 19–20).

In order to tackle the issue of forgery, Empress Elizabeth restated in 1743 that only passports on official printed blanks were valid (PSZ vol. 11, no. 8,706). The report from the Don region in 1744, however, demonstrated that forgers had already adjusted the process of production, seeking different ways to imitate printed letters. A barge hauler going by the name of Mikhail Ivanov was found to own a printed passport. Although he insisted that the passport was authentic, the investigation deemed it suspicious. The accused's further torture revealed that his passport had been made by a certain Osip, whom Ivanov encountered in a Cossack village. Osip 'put a copy of an official printed passport over a blank piece of paper and used a small tool to engrave the words on the form. Then he took a quill, transcribed the words, wrote his [Ivanov's] name, and signed the passport' (RGADA f. 248, op. 6, kn. 346: 129–30).

Some employers were not that interested in determining whether a person's passport was authentic or not, and could even facilitate his acquisition of a fake one. The serf Averian Sokolov bought a passport from a scribe at a local bazaar in Simbirsk in 1741. In the course of trying to find work on a ship, Sokolov showed his passport to the manager of the ship who immediately identified it as a fake yet also reassured Sokolov that it made no actual difference: 'What is important is not that this passport is counterfeit, but that it is printed' (Gornostaev 2020: 263).

The problem of forgery persisted well into the late eighteenth century. In 1798, the Gatchina authorities uncovered a wide network of people who resided in the town with counterfeit papers. The investigation that began with the discovery of the two main forgers, Aleksei Zmievatskii and Prokhor Popov, led to over a hundred people of dubious status being brought in for questioning. Most men claimed to have left their places of residence with proper documents, but once their passports expired, they had to choose whether to live without official papers, acquire counterfeit ones or travel home to renew their passports (Smith 2020). The latter option was time-consuming and difficult as many workers resided far from Gatchina and would have to have left their current employment, losing time, money and opportunities. For them, falling into illegality with counterfeit papers, or without papers at all, was the only viable choice.

Even during the reign of Alexander I (1801–25), the transition from handwritten to printed passports was far from complete, and cases of forgery were still common. In 1803, the emperor once again decreed that only printed travel documents were legal, after the government learned that several local authorities were continuing to issue handwritten passports due to the lack of official blanks (Franklin 2010: 223). With such passports still in circulation, forgers could continue to practise their craft and help rural and urban dwellers overcome restrictions on geographic mobility in the Russian Empire.

As a tool of social control, the passport could only be of limited use in the early modern period. Without modern technological advances, such as watermarks, photographs, anti-scan patterns and many others, passports lacked essential features that could both facilitate the identification of individuals and prevent forgery. At the same time, the Russian imperial government's continuous efforts to maintain the passport regime underscored the essential role of these documents in the regulation of population movement despite their shortcomings.

10.2 **Saksy** (Poland)
Krzysztof Kruk
Alumnus, Department of Political Science, UCL, UK

Since the late nineteenth century, seasonal economic migration to Germany has been called *saksy* (the terms *obieżysastwo* and *obieżysas* were also used in the past). The etymology of *saksy*, *obieżysastwo* and *obieżysas* is linked to Saxony, a popular destination for Polish peasants seeking temporary employment at the end of the nineteenth century (Morawska 2001: 60; Grabowska and Engbersen 2016: 104). Historical studies suggest that geographical proximity played a role, as many seasonal workers arriving in Saxony and other regions came from areas bordering Germany (Kępińska and Stark 2013: 6). Although the character of Polish economic migration evolved through subsequent decades, *saksy* remains a colloquial name for moving abroad in search of temporary occupation, nowadays regardless of the specific destination country.

The emergence of seasonal work as the dominant form of employment among Polish immigrants developed as a result of the interplay between bottom-up needs and top-down regulations. Demand for cheap agricultural labour and regional economic disparities motivated the movement of people, while the introduction of new crops increased the seasonality of demand for agricultural labour throughout the year (Kępińska and Stark 2013: 4). To demonstrate the size of this practice, the number of migrants from former Polish territories to Germany between 1870 and 1914 is estimated at 3.5 million (Marks-Bielska et al. 2015: 35). Later on, German authorities implemented restrictions on the inflows of immigrants from the Russian and Austrian partitions, preventing Polish migrants from remaining in destination locations for extended periods of time.

With the Polish state recreated after the First World War, temporary migration to Germany was legalised only through a bilateral convention signed in 1927 and restrictions were reinstated only three years later due to the ongoing economic crisis (Marks-Bielska et al. 2015: 35). The outbreak of the Second World War preluded the displacement of hundreds of thousands of Polish forced labourers, used by the Nazis to fill the gaps in the domestic labour market, mainly in agriculture (Kępińska and Stark 2013).

Saksy played a vital role in post-war communist Poland, even as controls imposed by the authoritarian regime raised formal barriers to free movement of labour. With the reforms of the passport law in 1970s, focusing on facilitating mobility within the communist bloc, the number of visits to East Germany reached 9.5 million in 1972 (Stola 2015: 112).

The collapse of communism and Poland's accession to the EU entailed further waves of seasonal migration. In the 1990s, circular economic migration to Western Europe remained the predominant form of emigration from Poland, usually involving temporary employment in construction, agriculture or household services (Grabowska and Engbersen 2016: 103; White et al. 2018). After 2004, the UK overtook Germany as the main receiving country (White 2016: 10). That said, the changing context has transformed the character of *saksy*. Established migration patterns evolved upon the removal of obstacles to legalising permanent stay, which gained importance versus traditional temporary stay (White et al. 2018). The latest critical juncture in the history of Polish migration to Western Europe was the Brexit referendum, which reinstated barriers to the UK labour market.

Saksy are heavily affected by the operation of informal social networks, which organise and transform migration streams (Tilly 2007). Migrants rely on interpersonal trust networks to hedge against risks stemming from lack of information and contacts in an unfamiliar environment. Tilly (2007) observes that the distribution of migration across destinations is not simply a function of associated economic opportunities; channels formed by interpersonal trust networks direct streams of migration into few select destinations. The significance of informal networks for this process is reflected in the informal jargon used to talk about practices surrounding economic migration. The term *ściągnąć* (literally 'to pull down/off from') denotes bringing over friends or family members to a foreign country. Settled immigrants and experienced temporary migrants often have the knowledge, as well as *dojścia* and *znajomości* (personal contacts and acquaintances) in a given location, which predisposes them to assist their fellows. *Dojścia* and *znajomości* are key resources in the *załatwianie* of things (getting things done) for new immigrants, such as jobs and job interviews or accommodation. These practices form a cluster located within the murky borderland between instrumentality and sociability, operating as part of the overarching economy of favours.

Anecdotal evidence highlights the role played by informal networks in shaping Polish short-term economic migration. An illustrative example is provided by the provincial town of Siemiatycze in eastern Poland. Siemiatycze is the origin of an established migrant route to Brussels, with press reports estimating that approximately 3,000 migrants from the town (20 per cent of its population) reside in the Belgian capital at any given time (Widzyk 2017). The town delegated an official available to temporary migrants from Siemiatycze in Brussels, while a regional bus operator runs regular direct services to Brussels. The existence of a migratory route between Siemiatycze and Brussels is attributed to the development of an informal network. In a press interview, the mayor of the town noted that 'nobody knows how it began ... probably someone from Siemiatycze once went to Brussels to work, invited their family and friends – people brought other people over' (Widzyk 2017).

Seasonal economic migration is by no means a distinctive Polish phenomenon, and similar practices are widespread across developing economies with dysfunctional labour markets. Ukrainian *zarobitchanstvo* bears certain similarities to *saksy*, and within the context of the Polish labour market the two remain in a symbiotic relationship as Poland's steady economic growth observed after the democratic transition made it an attractive destination for Ukrainian temporary workers.

Persistent mobility has important implications for family life, such as the division of gender roles. This ties up with the common observation that the informal economy is highly gendered (Marx 2018: 9). Literature suggests that Polish seasonal migration has often been spearheaded by men from small and medium-sized towns and villages (Fiałkowska and Piechowska 2016: 10). When financial pressure begins to mount, it is more likely that men will be exempted from responsibilities of care, with women likely to face a greater ambivalence resulting from competing demands (Connidis and McMullin 2002). Fieldwork studies reported that some female Polish migrants describe migration as an emancipating experience, allowing them to have some 'rest', even when their job in the destination country required substantial physical effort (Fiałkowska and Piechowska 2016: 10).

For many Poles, temporary migration for *saksy* remains an important strategy for making ends meet or finding attractive employment opportunities. The practice has profound implications for Poland's social fabric, to the extent that 'everyone in Poland is touched ... by migration and lives in the transnational social space' (White et al. 2018: 29). The reproduction of a characteristic lifestyle pattern associated with temporary migration affected individual biographies as well as the broader socio-economic structure, by transforming the domestic labour market and provoking the influx of financial but also social remittances, understood as imported norms, values and attitudes (Grabowska and Engbersen 2016). Although similar patterns of behaviour are pervasive across developing countries, *saksy* constitute a historical practice with its own specificities.

10.3 *Ściągnąć* (Poland)

Anne White
School of Slavonic and East European Studies, UCL, UK

Ściągnąć (imperfective form: *ściągać*) means to 'bring over' (literally 'pull down/off from'). The term is used when somebody brings over another person to join them in a foreign country, like pulling down an apple from a tree or pulling in a fish on a line. This is a colloquialism, not mentioned in the 200,000-word Oxford-PWN *Polish-English Dictionary*. Informal migration networking in Poland is part of a wider culture of migration and has its own vocabulary.

As Castles (2010: 1579) points out, 'one of the most widely accepted innovations in migration theory since the 1980s has been the adoption of network theories, which focus on the collective agency of migrants and communities in organising processes of migration and incorporation'. Researchers agree that migration cannot be understood without the lens of informality, even if governments choose to ignore the fact that migrants around the world prefer to go where they have family and friends. Governments aspire to 'immigration control' – making migrants use official channels to go where they are told to go. However, walls do not stop migrants, and attempts at immigration control almost always end up with the triumph of informal practices (Pécoud and de Guchteneire 2007).

This article is based on numerous conversations and 232 interviews regarding Polish migration since 2006, especially 115 interviews with women without higher education (both non-migrants and former migrants) conducted by the author in Poland and the UK (White 2017). The examples are of speakers from locations across Poland, with different population sizes; working-class people across the country use informal networks to migrate. Jaźwińska (2001: 124) contrasted the provinces, where social networks remained strong, with Warsaw, which has weaker migration traditions but where formal institutions could take the place of social networks. However, in my sample even migrants from areas without traditions of international migration used the verb *ściągnąć*. Places of origin are indicated in brackets in the following examples.

The mechanisms of migrant networking have been more extensively studied in the countries of destination than in the countries of origin, where it is often assumed that would-be migrants initiate the use of informal networks as a resource. However, the *ściągnąć* concept suggests that migration might not occur without an invitation from an existing migrant:

'A massive number of people already have friends in the UK, and one person "**brings over**" the next (*jeden drugiego ściąga*).' (Renata, Pabianice)

'The way it works, one person goes first, and then other people "**will bring each other over**" (*się ściągną*) too. So, they went to Manchester and later "**brought**" (*pociągnęli*) some other people from Sosnowiec. They "**brought**" them "**over**" to be with them (*ściągnęli do siebie*).' (Jagoda, Sosnowiec)

'Usually one person "**collects**" (*zabiera*) someone else. Mostly a woman collects her best woman friend, or a man his male friend. That's how the chain is formed as one person "**pulls in**" (*ściąga*) the next ... Sometimes you say, "When you get there, look out for something for me." Then suddenly the link between us breaks, as if they didn't want me to have a better life, just for them to have it better ... I used to request sometimes, and it turned out to be a non-starter; they didn't want to hear what I was saying, so I came to feel that it wasn't worth asking, humiliating myself.' (Celina, Grajewo)

Ściągnąć is sometimes used together with *kusić*, which means to tempt, and which allows the speaker to blame the original migrant for the migration act. In the next quotation, for example, the speaker excuses her husband for leaving their baby daughter to work abroad by blaming the brother-in-law who 'pulled him away'. In the second quotation, low income is offered as an excuse for allowing oneself to be tempted:

'The better earnings "tempted us" (*kusiły*). You know, to earn for the flat, and for a car, well, that was something "you wanted" (*chciało się*). Particularly since his brother was there already, so he "brought him over" (*ściągnął*)'. (Ewa, Grajewo)

'One person will "bring over" another (*jeden drugiego sciągnie*), they'll "pull them" after themselves (*pociąga za sobą*). If someone gets an offer of work, they think it over, and off they go. Not many people refuse. Perhaps only graduates, people with *very* good jobs, such people won't even be "tempted" (*nie kusi się*). But people like us will let themselves be "tempted" (*u nas jest takie środowisko że jednak się kuszą*)'. (Magda, Sanok)

Many other interviewees portrayed invitations as opportunities not to be passed up:

'His brothers simply "brought him" over (*go ściągnęli*). We hadn't really thought about migrating. But it just happened that my brother-in-law phoned, and he said, "You know what, there's a job you could do, come if you like." And my husband said "OK!" and off he went.' (Jolanta, Grudziądz)

However, the use of *ściągnąć* does not always mean that the initiative comes from the person abroad. For example, Bernadeta, originally from Elbląg, reported: 'My brother did want to come [to the UK] recently, but we told him it's too hard to get work, for us to "bring him over" (*żeby go ściągać*)'. Nonetheless, the fact that the process was reported as the migrant potentially pulling the non-migrant establishes a hierarchy, with the migrant in control.

Eagerness to take advantage of invitations is linked to the belief, particularly held in some parts of Poland with a tradition of strong informal networks to the US, that, 'if you go abroad, you must go to someone you know (*do kogoś*)' (Edyta, Grajewo). Conversely, you must never migrate (*w ciemno*) 'into the dark'. It is preferable to wait for an invitation:

'There was always someone in the family … who could "pull you out" of Poland (*ściągnąć z tej Polski*) … It was my cousin who "took me" (*zabrał mnie*) to Sweden. You earn some money, come back to Poland and spend money on all sorts of things, including helping someone out, and you end up without a penny and there's no work here, so you wait for a lucky chance to go abroad. That's how it works … You don't go into the unknown (*w ciemno się nie jeździ*)'. (Leszek, unemployed builder, Grajewo)

Some university graduates interviewed for later projects described themselves as migrating *w ciemno*, but they had more cultural capital and less need to rely on social capital. For instance, Rafał from Lublin reported: 'I went completely into the unknown.' However, he continued by reporting the standard behaviour, using standard vocabulary: 'I "brought over" (*ściągnąłem*) all my friends … Since I was in England, I always helped someone get work. Well, I was on the spot, so it was easier to fix something up for a friend.'

It was curious that interviewees never condemned the use of informal migration networks to find work abroad, while almost universally complaining that it was hard to find a job in Poland because of widespread nepotism. This bears out the truth of Materka's observation about the related concept of *kombinowanie* or *kombinacja*, finding ingenious unofficial ways of accessing resources. '*Kombinacja* used by "us" was cast in a positive light; *kombinacja* used by "them", the perceived competitors, was cast in a negative light' (Materka 2017: 49).

In the 1990s, the use of informal migration networks helped to perpetuate communist-era habits of doing things informally and was thereby harmful for democratisation in Poland (Morawska 2001: 70). Even in the period since EU accession, reliance on networks may be damaging levels of generalised trust since, in sections of society and geographical locations which depend on help from members of informal migration networks, actual instances of being let down readily contribute to widely circulating warnings about Poles behaving 'like wolves to other Poles' or 'Polish conman' (White and Ryan 2008; Garapich 2016: 241–51; White 2018). However, it is also the case that hundreds of thousands of Polish families have bettered themselves thanks to their use of informal migration networks, promoting a degree of prosperity in less economically developed parts of Poland and relieving pressure on the state to provide more generous welfare benefits.

10.4 *Trailing spouses* (India)
Shalini Grover
London School of Economics, UK
and
Sanna Schliewe
Department of Communication and Psychology, University of Aalborg, Denmark

Since the 1990s, when India opened its previously isolated economy to the global market, India has witnessed an influx of foreign nationals settling into its newly cosmopolitan cities. These include many citizens from Australia, East Asia, Europe and the United States. Cultural identities and terminologies such as 'expatriate' and *trailing spouse* are now commonly invoked in the media and in cosmopolitan circles of the new growth economies such as India. 'Expatriate' is now a generic term for the white foreigner in a globalised India (Grover 2018a). Expatriates in India may also be referred to as *gora*, a vernacular term for white people, as well as generic slang for foreign nationals (Grover 2018a). The term *trailing spouse* has for some time been used in the context of global relocations. It is used mainly to describe women who accompany their husbands on transnational postings and expatriate assignments. The gendered phenomenon of wives who 'trail along' as dependent spouses may aptly complement country-specific local terminologies. For expatriate trailing spouses, the Indonesian visa, for instance, is designated *kit swami*, meaning 'following the husband', and does not allow women to accept employment (Fechter 2007: 15). It is often difficult to obtain a work visa as a *trailing spouse* in many countries – including India.

More specifically, *trailing spouse* signifies a married woman's exclusion from the paid labour force in the host country. *Trailing spouses* have long been an invisible part of men's global work performance. In the last decade, however, spouses' well-being and adjustment have received more attention in the academic literature. Likewise, academic interest now sheds light on their everyday experiences in the host country. The practice of 'trailing' may also be considered as reinforcing historical and gendered informal practices. *Trailing spouses* often take primary responsibility for the household, childcare and the emotional well-being of the family (Arieli 2007; Hindman 2013; Boström et al. 2018). To accentuate the gendered outcomes, 'research on couples participating in flows of skilled migration has consistently identified the presence of more traditionally gendered divisions of labour within households, irrespective of nationality' (Walsh 2007: 64). With *trailing spouses* having to renegotiate the marital bond and the household division of labour, low self-esteem, anxiety and depression have been reported among these cohorts (Walsh 2007: 64).

Yet changes that mirror shifting contemporary tendencies in the labour market, such as women's participation in the workforce, are also present. In the past, *trailing spouses* often 'followed' their male partners repeatedly for decades, while they themselves engaged in volunteer and non-paid work for organisations and embassies. Today, by contrast, *trailing spouses* often have their own professional identities, even though these are put on intermittent hold. Such temporary career breaks are voiced by them as challenging due to the loss of work-identity (Cangiá 2017). Moreover, in transnational families with a repeat relocation pattern, the constant underlying uncertainty of the working partner's global mobile career trajectory can act as an obstacle for long-term planning for the *trailing spouse*'s future career options (Cangiá 2018). It is therefore no surprise that such challenges and obstacles are being documented in interdisciplinary research. There has been less emphasis on the fact that moving abroad with the family can be simultaneously experienced as a welcome (short- or long-term) opportunity for trying out alternative life-experiences and reinventing careers. Nonetheless, this manifests a socio-economic upgrade and an alternative cultural identity, particularly when relocating to countries within the Global South.

Studies discuss how many white foreign nationals share a similar vantage point with their colonial counterparts (Fechter and Walsh 2010; Grover 2018a, 2018b). First, the 'expatriate' identity, as opposed to the inferior 'immigrant' or 'migrant' titles, emphasises race-class identities. Second, this superior identity reinforces power relations and international imbalances in the Global South that are long part of erstwhile colonial legacies (Fechter and Walsh 2010). Given that expatriates are perceived as privileged migrants, *trailing spouses* in the Global South may also be negatively characterised by locals (Walsh 2007). For example, in China they are identified as those who go out and have fun (Arieli 2007), while in Dubai they are referred to as *Jumeria Jane*, an idiom directed at their supposedly opulent lifestyles (Walsh 2007).

In India, too, given their class privilege, many *trailing spouses* hire domestic staff who are part of an unregulated labour market (Grover 2018b; Schliewe 2019). The hiring of cheap domestic staff enables expatriate families to lead comfortable lives, liberating them from onerous domestic chores. Living an affluent lifestyle in the Global South, however, without being in paid employment and having full-time domestic workers, can feel like a 'golden cage' for many women (Fechter 2007). In addition, the temporary work contracts that are part of expatriate relocations place the *trailing spouse* in a different relationship to the host country than would likely be the case if the family intended to stay permanently. This may make the case of having domestic staff and endorsing affluent lifestyles seem like an exception, and thus ease its legitimisation (Schliewe 2018). Furthermore, such representations of being placed in an 'exceptional situation' are often shared and reconfirmed within the intimate social networks of expatriates (Schliewe 2019).

For their everyday existence and emotional anchoring in a new country, expatriates often have recourse to what is popularly known as the 'expatriate bubble'. In her Indonesian study, Fechter notes how expatriates construct a spatial and social Western bubble and have little contact with locals other than their domestic staff (Fechter 2007). Furthermore, strong camaraderie often develops informally among accompanying spouses. The latter share not only the experience of being 'foreign' to the local society, but also their particular experiences of 'trailing' in the given setting. In India, *trailing spouses* comfort each other, providing crucial support and reaching out to newcomers, who then quickly become part of these informal networks.

With regard to future research, we believe that a focus on the agency of *trailing spouses* would enrich the literature and counter stereotypes. We also need more data focusing on the dynamics of expatriate bubbles and how these social networks shape and co-create the everyday experiences and ambivalences that legitimise privileges and informal practices. A theoretical lacuna is yet to be addressed on expatriate women who have entered the workforce in the host country, or those who have reinvented their careers, or others determinedly taking career breaks by choice, and what this entails for the outcome of spousal gender equality.

10.5 **Mulas** (Cuba)
Concetta Russo
Department of Sociology and Social Research, University of Milan-Bicocca, Italy

Mula (plural: *mulas*) in Spanish denotes a person who profits from travelling abroad and buying goods to resell informally in Cuba. *Mula* translates into English as 'mule', the offspring of a male donkey and a female horse, all known for their heavy-duty carrying ability, but also used to describe the appearance of someone travelling with heavy bags or smuggling illegal goods across the border (drug mule).

Albeit the term resonates with the concept of smuggling, *mula* in Cuba refers to neither selling drugs nor any other role in illicit cross-border activity, such as money circulation, like *hawala* in Pakistan and Bangladesh (see 5.40 Volume 1). Instead, the term has a distinct meaning associated with a nuanced set of practices that emerged under Cuban socialism characterised by material scarcity and ideological constraints, exacerbated by the US trade embargoes launched against the island from 1958 onwards. Endemic factors that nourish the variety of informal practices encompassed by the *mula* system include: (1) ineffective distribution of goods and shortages of almost every product one needs for a daily life, (2) poor quality and little diversity of circulating commodities on the official market, defined as 'frustrated consumption' (Pertierra 2007), (3) restricted possibility of travelling freely anywhere in the world, which makes it more difficult for common citizens to travel and purchase the goods for themselves and (4) lack of access to e-commerce platforms.

In the 1970s, the term *mula* was colloquially used to allude to a form of kinship-based commodity circulation. It referred to those Cubans who imported goods to the island while living abroad, bringing all kinds of products on request and selling them for profit, thereby covering their travel. This practice, common to most countries with a socialist past, is still active in Cuba. In fact, it constitutes a substantial part of the flow of goods and circulation of items between Cuba and predominantly the US. The scale of the practice is estimated at 50 per cent of remittance transfers, which also points to the strength of the

Cuban diaspora ties for the island's entrepreneurship (Hansing and Orozco 2014).

However, in the last two decades, two factors have stimulated a level of professionalisation of this informal practice. First, the flourishing of small businesses such as private restaurants, beauty salons and stores generated an increased demand for scarce materials. Second, the so-called 'Grandchildren Law' (*Ley de Nietos*) that was operational between 2007 and 2011, gave descendants up to the second generation the right to apply for Spanish citizenship and expanded the possibilities to travel (Israel 2009; Sánchez and Cuesta 2017). According to a 2009 report, during its first two years, nearly 200,000 Cuban applicants claimed this right. Thus, the term *mula* came to acquire another meaning, indicating a *broker*, a dealer and a boss (*negociante*) who moves groups and organises stays in foreign countries where the goods in high demand could be purchased cheaply.

The goods in short supply ordinarily comprise clothes, shoes, household appliances, nail polish and other beauty products. Latin American countries, such as Panama, Ecuador, Colombia, Peru, Venezuela are ideal shopping destinations for both being the neighbouring countries and for granting travel rights for Cubans holding Spanish passports. Mexico and Puerto Rico, which host a considerable number of Cuban migrants, also feature a considerable presence of *mulas*. Other key destinations include Russia and Guyana, where Cubans can travel without visa restrictions, as well as Haiti and Martinique.

A complex coordination network between stores, hotels, hostels and rental houses targeting Cuban *mulas* is operational in the receiving countries. The groups of informal couriers have become the main suppliers for both small businesses and common citizens. *Negociantes* take care of the whole process, from soliciting visas, if needed, to arranging all aspects of *mulas*' stay in a foreign country, such as accommodation and transport to and from the airport. They buy or rent seasonal clothes for their team of *mulas* so that they can travel without personal items and use their luggage allowance for business instead. Being a *negociante* involves not only an investment of substantial financial capital, but also a mastery of equally substantial *confianza* (trust from familiarity), the *negociantes*' social capital.

Opinions on profiling *mulas* differ significantly. In the author's research, *mulas* tend to be women, while Cearns emphasises the role of young men, who start as *mulas* with the intention of becoming *negociantes* (Cearns 2019: 888). Similar to the discussion of gender roles in post-socialist shuttle trading around *chelnoki* (see 5.26 Volume 2), the roles that require mass border crossing involve women, while *negociantes*, the *mula*-bosses who are in charge of organising the trip and protecting the team members, are more likely to be men.

Mulas can import only a limited amount of goods into the country (up to 120 lbs each) and must pay import tax on arrival. Once imported, these goods find customers informally in all classes of society and are sold without income tax or regulation of price, quality or quantity. The connivance of the state with these forms of 'unreported economy', as the Cuban scholar Mayra Espina defines them, is paradigmatic in the way the government exploits the *mula* system (Espina 2010). By collecting heavy tariffs, the government directly profits from this system of importation. Indirectly, the government benefits from the fact that people's needs, which the government is not capable of satisfying formally, are being satisfied informally. By allowing the importation and turning a blind eye on reselling the US-embargoed goods on the shadow market, the state is able to overcome some of the limitations of the restricted access of its citizens to the international market (Russo 2018).

The international circulation of goods put in place by the *mula* system has been compared to the *kula* ring (Malinowski 1922) 'as a lens onto strategies of creating personhood and expanding social worlds through transnational circulation networks of material items' (Cearns 2019: 873). Observing these informal practices offers an opportunity to understand how peripheral economies work (Portes 1983). Indeed, the *mula* ring, as Cearns defines it, not only affects the circulation of commodities in Cuba, but also has a moderate and sometimes considerable impact on the receiving countries too, thus challenging the idea of Cuba being an isolated country. For instance, almost one thousand Cubans travel to Guyana each week, and they purchase goods for the estimated annual amount of GYDD400 million (2 million USD), producing a large impact on the local economy (Semple 2016).

Albeit the crucial role *mulas* play in imports, they are also involved in export activities. The latter include transporting artefacts and other paraphernalia connected with Santeria rituals. Santeria rituals are an Afro-Caribbean religion counting several practitioners in Cuba and in the US, Mexico and Puerto Rico, essential to the embedded nature of the Cuban informal economy (Holbraad 2004). The *mulas* also export tobacco, rum and local *artesania* (craftsmanship), such as a typical Cuban rocking chair made of wood, or wood-carved sculptures, which have come to constitute a distinctive sign in the houses of Cuban diasporas.

The 'transnational networks' (Tilly 2007) put in place by the *mula* system play an important role not only in the constant negotiation between the socialist state and its citizens about the value and distribution of commodities, but also in corroborating the representation of Cuban material identity outside the country.

10.6 **Simsar, samsara** (Middle East and North Africa)
Alberica Camerani
Alumna, School of Slavonic and East European Studies, UCL, UK

In Arabic-speaking countries of the Middle East and North Africa, *simsar* (also *samsar*, female *simsarat*) is an intermediary between the buyer and the seller (Hassan 1986: 255). *Samsar* derives from the Arabic verb *s-m-s-r*, which means 'to act as a broker or middleman' (Lamprakos 2017: 167). A *simsar* is an actor who 'facilitate[s] the transactions between other actors lacking access or trust in one another' (Marsden and Lin 1982: 202). For most, being a *simsar* is a full- or part-time occupation, albeit unregulated. The extensive contacts and abilities of a *simsar* enable transactions that would be otherwise difficult or impossible. Some *simsars* (the correct Arabic plural form is *samasira*) specialise in specific types of goods, such as cars or residential property; others deal with any type of resource. '[T]his kind of man possesses nothing, has nothing, he is always listening to the world around him, and his place of work is simply the outside, the city, the people. [The city] is where the business takes place, and it is definitely his place' (Majdalani 2005: 14).

In the pre-Islamic period, traders in the region were called *al-samasira* (Hassan 1986). In the mediaeval Islamic world, *simsars* were itinerant peddlers, as evident from the documents certifying their existence in the Middle East and in North Africa in the eleventh century (Shatzmiller 1993: 96). The modern profession of *simsar* shares similarities with the commercial brokers who were present in the trading hubs around the Mediterranean and the Indian and Atlantic oceans (Rothman 2012: 36). The Italian noun *sensale* ('a mediator or intermediary in a deal for a fee', Hoepli 2015) and the archaic French noun *censal* ('a broker in the Levant', Dictionnaire Littré 1878), both deriving from the Arabic *simsar*, support this hypothesis (Schacht 1982; Cortellazzo 1989). In the Middle Ages, *samsara* (meaning 'brokerage', also known also as *funduq*, *khan* or *wakala*, depending on the region) was the name of the commercial venue where international and wholesale traders met local buyers and sellers (Gelderblom 2013) and could rent slots from the manager of the property, the *samsari* (Lamprakos 2017).

Although today their meanings are quite distinct, in the Middle Ages, *barrah*, a 'town crier', was one of the synonyms for *simsar* (Colin and Becker 1999). Detailing the negotiations between Arab and European traders mediated by a *simsar*, the Dictionnaire Universel De Commerce refers to them as a 'proper comedy' (Savary des Bruslons 1741: 720–1). If the European buyer did not accept the price requested by the Arab seller and wanted to negotiate, the *simsar* would 'pretend to be angry, cry and shout like a mad man, and would advance as if he wanted to strangle the foreign merchant, but without touching him'. If this would not avert the buyer from further bargaining attempts, he would start to 'tear his clothes, knock his chest with his fists rolling himself on the ground and shout like a deflowered man'. As soon as the negotiation concluded, he 'regained his tranquillity … and finished the piece with *Allah Akbar, Allah Akbir*, "God is great, God is very great", that he pronounced with as much cold blood as if he had not faked all the contortions and the crisis of a possession' (Savary des Bruslons 1741: 601).

Samsara joins the ranks of several other informal brokerage practices that facilitate exchanges, help get things done and create opportunities through social connections and acquaintances. A comparison to other forms of brokerage is instructive in identifying the main characteristics of *samsara*. In contrast to *taps* (see 1.14 Volume 1), a practice in Azerbaijan of obtaining favours for family, friends and contacts through clientelist channels, *samsara* is a market-type exchange, characterised by the presence of cash in the transaction (Jancsics 2015), or a 'quantitative relation between the objects transacted' (Gregory 1982: 41). It involves a commission depending on the value of the transaction; usually, but not necessarily collected from the seller (agent), while *tapsh* is a reciprocal exchange that 'establishes a personal qualitative relationship between the subjects transacting' (Gregory 1982) and thus is not bound by time, quantity or quality of goods (Sahlins 1965: 147). The reciprocal nature of *tapsh* is also maintained in vertical and clientelist transactions (Aliyev 2017).

Tapsh and *simsar* also differ in the relation between the broker and the transacting parties. As an outsider, the *simsar* engages in liaison brokerage, in which the broker 'link[s] distinct groups without having prior allegiance to either' (Gould and Fernandez 1989: 93). This is known as the *tertius gaudens*, 'the third who enjoys' (Simmel 1950:154), gaining advantages such as power, influence and profit from the conflict of others. The *tapsh* broker, on the other hand, has a personal connection with both parties. The *tapsh* broker mediates between the supplier, with whom the broker has a close relationship, and a third party, with whom the broker is acquainted. *Tapsh* is a form of representative brokerage in which a member of a group is delegated to negotiate information or resources with an outsider (Gould and Fernandez 1989).

The difference between *samsara* and *wasta* mediation (see 6.8 Volume 2), which shares the geographical distribution with *samsara*, is less distinct. At first glance, the commission taken by the *simsar* seems to point to the disinterested nature of a *samsara* transaction, in contrast with the more personal *wasta*. Yet *wasta* brokers may also receive compensation in the form of a gift or monetary reward. Reports from Moroccan respondents suggest that a *simsar* 'would be a person they did not know personally and whom they did not trust' (Sommerfelt 2001: 63). The difference between *samsara* and *wasta* is more a matter of degree: choosing to call the middleman a *simsar* or a *wasta* broker indicates the type of social tie that binds him to either party (Sommerfelt 2001). A middleman will be called a *wasta* broker by the party closer to them and *simsar* by the other party. Their relationship is always biased, as scholars note, 'there are no fully neutral forms of brokerage' (Stovel and Shaw 2012; Jancsics 2015: 81). *Samsara* is no exception.

As an informal practice, *samsara* can provide access to goods and services unobtainable through other channels. However, it can also have adverse effects. *Simsars* with a strong presence can become a powerful lobby in the industries based on intermediation, such as real estate property. In Morocco, the lobby of *simsars* 'imposed its law on the real estate market' and left traditional estate agencies bankrupt (Algerie Presse Service 2010).

10.7 **Jak igrač** (North Macedonia)
Borjan Gjuzelov
Alumnus, School of Politics and International Relations, Queen Mary University of London, UK

The Macedonian term *jak igrač* (*јак играч*, 'strong player') refers to someone who is well networked, has the right connections and knows how to manipulate formal and informal rules for their benefit. A strong player is a skilled informality *broker* who understands 'the economy of favours' and is involved in multiple relationships of informal exchange and reciprocity (Ledeneva 1998). The analogy 'player' points to someone who knows how to act according to the informal rules of the game.

The term is used when the speaker wants to emphasise someone's ability to make the most out of complex and uncertain situations. A strong player is someone whose position and authority are not primarily grounded in their professional capabilities or merit, but rather in their ability to make the right decisions at the right time and to take advantage of informal networks and connections. An example of colloquial use would be: 'She's a strong player, she always finds her way ... He's a strong player, watch out!'

In North Macedonia, a strong player is used in limited political or administrative contexts, particularly among insiders knowledgeable about organisational set-ups. Strong players are usually active in politics, business or public administration, or in all of them, and have ties across these sectors which helps them 'get things done'. They are 'masters of informality': they have the social capital and networking resources and use them to maximise their financial or cultural capital. The term 'strong player' is different from the phrase 'strong man' (*jak čovek*); the latter refers to someone above the law due to their political or economic status rather than due to their ability to take advantage of the gaps between the formal and the informal. The term is likely to be used in other Western Balkan countries with a similar connotation.

Strong players thrive in particularistic modes of social organisation. Particularism is a mode of social organisation with a prevalence of non-universally applied rules and a discrepancy between the formal, written rules and the informal ways of 'how things work in practice'. Thus, particularistic regimes are characterised by uncertainty and blurred lines between the public and private interests. The opposite of particularism is universalism; a mode of governance characterised by a prevalence of the universally applied rule of law (Mungiu-Pippidi 2005, 2015). Strong players take advantage of the uncertainty and gaps between formal and informal rules and further expand them to preserve their social position. When good governance reforms seek to install a universal application of the law, strong players may act as veto players to ensure the status quo (Dimitrova 2010).

The Macedonian judiciary, similar to judiciaries in other Western Balkan countries, has numerous characteristics of the particularistic mode of social organisation. It is vulnerable to political interference and informal influence. Judicial professionals are often faced with ambivalent expectations and the need to balance between formal and informal incentives. While obedience and dependency are often rewarded, professionalism and impartiality can be obstacles to a successful career (Gjuzelov 2020; Damjanovski et al. Forthcoming). As a researcher in a multidisciplinary project that analysed the gap between formal rules and informal practices in light of the Europeanisation of the Western Balkan countries, I conducted several interviews with Macedonian judicial personnel (judges, prosecutors and lawyers) in 2018 (Gjuzelov 2020).

Highly ranked judges in the Macedonian judiciary were labelled 'strong players' by their colleagues to illustrate their ability to sustain and expand their position of authority, despite allegations of their corrupt actions and involvement in shadow dealings. Due to their informal connections, strong players were able to manipulate the decision-making of the Judicial Council, the body responsible for the appointment, promotion or dismissal of judges. Moreover, they manifested a 'survival ability': although much of their informal power and authority have been gained through their connection with one political establishment, they remained influential even after the political landscape changed. When asked in an interview about his colleague who was about to be dismissed for malpractice, a judge elaborated with the following:

> Look, he's a strong player, he won't be dismissed so easily, because many of those who decide [members of the judicial council] owe him a favour ... He was involved in so many *quid pro quo* exchanges that he is stronger than the [formal] institutional mechanisms of dismissal. He also knows a lot about others, so everyone will be very careful in their actions.

The pattern of 'survival ability' is supported by other findings from research in the region. In Serbia, neo-patrimonial local leaders maintain their authority despite changes in the regime and remain in power for decades. They are called *lokalni šerifi* ('local sheriffs') and hold a political and economic monopoly in their respective regions based on both formal and informal power. They rely on informal networks of patronage and clientelism on one hand, while staying close to incumbent political powers on the central level on the other. From a bottom-up perspective, they exert political influence on the local population because they provide jobs and solve problems. From a top-down perspective, they are inclined to get (formal and informal) support from the central government in return for predictable and loyal political support from their region. These leaders exhibit the behaviour of strong players because they take advantage of the uncertainties of the particularistic governance to maximise and maintain their local monopoly (Bliznakovski 2020).

The use of the term 'strong player' can also be found in Macedonian public administration, an area usually dominated by incumbent political parties and their informal networks. In this context, the term is used to describe two kinds of people: those with good 'survival ability', despite the changes in the political structure and those who obtain income in addition to their public servant salaries. Extra income may come from both legal activities, such as consulting or doing business, and illegal ones, including direct bribery for abusing their administrative position or revealing sensitive information. Public servants who hold positions of discretionary decision-making power are often able to act as strong players. As one mid-ranked public official in the Macedonian Ministry of Justice elaborated, 'strong players' will more likely be found among those holding a licensing authority for issuing permits or accreditations.

As noted by another interviewed public official, in a small number of cases, the label *jak igrač* is used in the positive sense and refers to public servants with real expertise and institutional memory, whose authority is widely appreciated in their respective institution, regardless of their political affiliation. Reactions to *jak igrač* illustrate the normative ambivalence, as people might assign this label not necessarily out of approval or sympathy with the actions of the strong player, but out of appreciation of their ability to do things informally. Moreover, although *jak igrač*' ability implies 'playing well' primarily to benefit certain personal interests, it may also be directed towards helping others. For instance, the 'institutional veterans' may advise younger colleagues in situations of uncertainty or help them interpret unclear formal procedures. This show of solidarity helps legitimise their actions in the eyes of others. However, despite the normative interpretations, most strong players' actions will primarily serve the private rather than the public interest. Some of their actions may involve illicit activities and shadow dealings in direct conflict with the formal law. At times, *jak igrač* is also a dangerous player (*opasen igrač*), with a similarly ambivalent connotation: to show respect for their abilities but not necessarily acceptance of their activities.

10.8 *Nojukusha* (Japan)
Hideo Aoki
Institute of Social Theory and Dynamics, Nakayama-Nakamachi, Higashi-ku, Hiroshima, Japan

Nojukusha, rough sleepers in Japan, are a demographically interesting, even if statistically insignificant, phenomenon. According to the government's national survey, there were 3,824 homeless people in 2021. Most of the homeless are single, have no children and consist predominantly of elderly men (64 years old, on average). Almost half have never been married. Those who are, are separated from their families. A third are over 70 years old. Only 5 per cent are women.

Nojukusha live off informal jobs, such as day jobs, street jobs or contract jobs in construction sites and factories. During the 'Archipelago Remodeling', the period of high economic growth in the 1960s, day workers took part in the construction of highways, bullet trains and so on. Supported by government-led public investment during the period of economic stability and bubble economy in the 1970s and 1980s, the needs of large-scale construction projects and the expanding manufacturing industry were satisfied by young workers from the agriculture and coal industry and small-scale commerce rather than migrant labour. These workers moved from job to job as day- and contract workers in construction sites and factories. When no jobs were available, the jobless assembled in *yoseba* districts in large cities (*San'ya* in Tokyo, *Kamagasaki* in Osaka and so on), where day- and contract workers co-habited in flophouses (*doya*), obtained jobs from brokers and commuted from *yoseba* to worksites.

The long recession in the 1990s led to a reduction in public investment and construction and civil engineering jobs. The number of unemployed day- and contract workers camping out on the streets, in parks and on riverbanks increased. These workers were at the root of Japan's homelessness problem. In 2003, when the government's national survey began, the average age of the homeless person was 57 and a half years old, so the majority were still in their pre-retirement years. Since then, the prolonged recession, continued unemployment and further ageing has made it difficult for them to escape homelessness. No longer capable of heavy labour, they became homeless, and eked out a living by doing odd jobs collecting empty cans and old newspapers on the streets. In 2021, 40 per cent of the homeless had been living on the streets for more than 10 years.

On the other hand, the economy became focused on services that made employment even more precarious. Many single, middle-aged and young men lost their jobs and were forced to live on the streets, becoming temporarily homeless. Middle-aged men went to job centres and agencies to look for work, while young men registered with online staffing agencies, spent the night in late-night cafes and received calls for work on their phones in the morning. Thus, the homeless population in Japan came to consist of single, middle-aged men, single, young men, as well as elderly people. Before they became homeless, 36 per cent of them had worked in construction and civil engineering, 12 per cent in factories and nearly 50 per cent in the service industry. With the transformation of the economic structure, the origins of the homeless became more diverse.

The homeless are informal itinerant dwellers who move from live-in bunkhouses and company dormitories to the streets and shelters. In 2003, 25,296 people were homeless in Japan: 7,757 in Osaka Prefecture, home to the largest *yoseba*, *Kamagasaki* and 6,361 in Tokyo, home to the second largest *yoseba*, *San'ya*. These are the rough sleepers, but the actual number of practically homeless far exceeded this number. There arose the phenomenon of the blue-sheet tents and camping in public spaces such as streets, parks, riverbeds and train stations in large cities, resulting in the informalisation of formal spaces. Tent villages became a symbol of homelessness and a poignant social issue. The media repeatedly reported on homelessness, raising citizens' awareness and increasing their interest, and the complaints about the homeless camping out in public spaces raised issues, previously unrecognised because of the social invisibility of the homelessness. Moreover, the gentrification of urban spaces increased with the services-oriented economy. The government began to regulate encampments in public space, pseudo-criminalising encampments under the pretext of beautifying the city, thus re-establishing formal control over the space. This resulted in a clash between the police, exercising social exclusion of the homeless, and the homeless/supporters who resisted the exclusion. Media reports helped to articulate homelessness as a serious social issue.

The government launched a full-scale homelessness policy in 2002. They adopted the first homeless law, the Law on Special Measures concerning Assistance in Self-Support of Homeless, and initiated a housing project to accommodate the homeless, allowing them to camp in parks in shelters and helping them find work. However, this law was not able to address the actual situation of some of the homeless, who became unable to find work due to ageing. Hence, the government began a policy of providing welfare to the homeless and providing accommodation in the form of low-rent flophouses and apartments. Many non-profit organisations participated in this project. As a result, the number of homeless on the streets decreased drastically: in 2021, there remained 3,824 homeless in Japan, 6 times fewer than in 2003, 990 in Osaka Prefecture and 889 in Tokyo. The homelessness issue disappeared en masse from the streets of Japan's cities, and thus became invisible again. The government's welfare policy was aimed at alleviating poverty, preventing social exclusion and bringing the homeless back into social life (re-inclusion into formal space). However, in the Japanese welfare system, formality and informality intersect, and people are assigned to and move back and forth between these spaces. Thus, as the number of homeless who became unable to work increased with age, homelessness became a serious welfare issue. Today, the following situation is apparent: a grey spatialisation of formal space, whereby some homeless do not wish to work and refuse the rules of the shelter. They cannot enter shelters, and even if admitted, they are evicted from the shelters when they violate the rules. Some homeless cannot adapt to group living. Others do not want to be taken care of by the government and refuse to receive welfare. Even if they get welfare and get into flophouses or apartments, they do not fit in there. It is a lonely life because there is no one to talk to. Gentrification has caused low-rent apartments to become suburban. In the suburbs, there are no jobs, no living facilities for single people, and no social networks. Hence, tenants are returning to the city centre to live on the street. In the end, they go into shelters, flophouses and apartments again, where they grow old, sick and die alone. Or they die alone in a hospital bed. Or they leave the shelters, flophouses and apartments and die alone on the street. In this way, shelters, flophouses, apartments and the street become human dumping sites for the homeless, who are discarded by society. This is the final stage for the homeless who are excluded from labour and residence, and pseudo-included by welfare. To build human relationships, support each other and die being cared for by friends and peers is only a dream for the homeless in Japan.

10.9 *La débrouille* (Former French and Belgian colonies in sub-Saharan Africa)
Cécile B. Vigouroux
Department of French, Simon Fraser University, Canada

Débrouille, a French term that can be loosely translated in English as 'make do', 'fend for oneself', refers to people's daily ways of navigating their environment and coping with unforeseen circumstances. It is about finding alternative pathways to navigate the harsh socio-economic and institutional realities in which one finds themselves. The notion encompasses a set of socio-economic practices, matrix of perceptions and identity performances, especially in French-speaking sub-Saharan Africa where it is commonly used, although the term is also in usage in Hexagonal France and French-speaking Belgium. *La débrouille* is often associated with a socially valorised *way of being*. Its practitioners characterise themselves as street-smart, quick-minded and entrepreneurial. In the context of Congolese migrants in Cape Town, South Africa, *la débrouille* and the skills and mindset associated with it are essentialised as markers of group identity. On the social ground this identity translates into social stratification along regional and linguistic divides, such as between Lingalaphones from Kinshasa and Swahiliphone from the Eastern provinces.

The term *débrouille* originates in the nineteenth-century European empire-building context (Murphy 2016). It was apparently first coined in the North African French army in the 1850s. In 1872, the noun and its derivatives entered the French lexicon and were extrapolated to new domains. Along with alternative names such as *système D*, short for *système de la débrouillardise*, the term *débrouille* has been 'central to French and Francophone cultural imagination' (Murphy 2015: 351). During the First World War, the French *poilu*, a foot soldier, became the epitome of *la débrouillardise* thanks to his ability to rely on 'brain over brawn' (Murphy 2016: 46). A dictionary of soldier slang defines *système D* in the following terms: 'The "système Dé … brouille" consists in making something out of nothing, in seizing every opportunity or bit of good luck when it arises, in taking advantage of circumstances, the terrain, men and anything you can get your hands on to accomplish' (Déchelette 1918: 206).

In Africa, several categories capture various nuances of *la débrouille*, expressed in indigenous vernaculars. For instance, in Mauritania, an onomatopoeia that imitates the sound of an object falling repeatedly (*tcheb-tchib*) and verbs for 'usurp' or 'seize' (*el-gazra*; < *yag'zar*) are used to index different types of individual or group trajectories. These refer to various strategies for survival and quick social success, as well as the social philosophy of navigating a wide range of contexts, from being jobless to joining the political elite (Salem 2001). In Tunisia, the expression of racing for bread (*al khobza*) encapsulates aspects of the political economy of *la débrouille*, which Meddeb defines as 'a way of life that involves domesticating uncertainties, taming dangers, violence and risks in order to access material resources that are essential to dignity and a decent life' (my translation) (Meddeb 2011: 36).

As a reference to ways of behaving and thinking, *la débrouille* is pervasive in many parts of the African continent. It is less clear how the word spread to the former French and Belgian African exploitation colonies, where it is often constructed as 'African'. *Débrouille* practices have been narrativised in several important cultural performances. For instance, in Senegal, *Goorgoorlou* or *Góor-góorlu* ('Making an Effort, Toughing Up, Doing one's Best') is the name of a popular comic strip turned into a TV series that portrays the daily peregrinations of the main character Goor, who struggles to make ends meet after losing his salaried job. The series created by cartoonist T. T. Fons (stage name for Alfonse Mendy) came out in the late 1980s at the time of the International Monetary Fund's and the World Bank's drastic structural adjustments of terms of loans to Senegal, which led to the rise of the informal economy and the pauperisation of the population. In the Democratic Republic of the Congo (DRC), *la débrouille* has been narrativised by the renowned Congolese musician Pépé Kallé in his 1985 song *Article 15 Beta Libanga* ('Article 15[:] break [a] stone').

Article 15 is commonly used in the DRC as an alternative name to *la débrouille*. It allegedly refers to a fictitious clause in the 1960 constitution of seceded South Kasai. According to Kisangani and Bobb (2010: 31), *Article 15* simply instructed state authorities to do whatever they could (*débrouillez-vous*). Since the Mobutu regime (1965–97), it has become the unofficial motto of the Congolese struggling to make ends meet and, for some, to monopolise local or national state resources (Piermay 1993).

In the literature on sub-Saharan Africa, *la débrouille* has varyingly been associated with survival strategies (Nkuku Khonde and Rémon 2006), creativity (Persyn and Ladrière 2004), coping mechanisms (Waage 2006), pace (de Villers 2002), resilience, everyday resistance to hardship, and/or subversion of a social and political order (Iñiguez de Heredia 2017).

These explanations capture what *la débrouille* means in different situations. It is a social practice that is both shaped by the field in which it is deployed and in turn fashions the latter (Bourdieu 1984). As both a set of practices and a matrix of perceptions, *la débrouille* often involves serendipity. Its practitioners (viz. *débrouilleurs*) are not just reactive to the dire situations in which they are caught; they deploy a range of individual and social resources by tapping into a vast repertoire of cultural practices, norms and beliefs. Anthropologist Janet MacGaffey was the first scholar to coin the expression *débrouille* in reference to informal economic activities in the DRC (MacGaffey 1993; Ayimpam 2014).

La débrouille includes a vast repertoire of practices: small-scale street trading such as selling cigarettes or home-made doughnuts (Vigouroux 2017), hijacking one's neighbour's electrical wires, diamond smuggling or money laundering. However, *la débrouille* need not be reduced to its mercantile dimension because it involves the complex social dynamics within which it is deployed. The accumulation of social capital is essential in *la débrouille*. In some cases, its practitioners can convert the social capital into an economic one. One of the most praised values in *la débrouille* is information, such as knowing the right person, the right time and the right place to buy commodities at a better price. Those who have access to this information may either trade it for money or capitalise on it to create a network of dependents with the expectation of future returns. Failure to honour the social debt may lead to ostracisation.

Researchers doing empirical work on *la débrouille* face methodological challenges. For instance, the wide-ranging nature of the socio-economic practices involved makes it difficult to get an all-inclusive snapshot of the activities it encompasses and the underlying social organisation the latter rest upon. Only a long immersion with the research subject(s) would enable the investigator to access information that leads to a better understanding of the logic of their practices.

10.10 **No. 8 wire** (New Zealand)
Grace Reynolds
Alumna, School of Slavonic and East European Studies, UCL, UK

No. 8 wire practices refer to problem-solving approaches shaped by New Zealand's geographical remoteness. *No. 8 wire* practices and mentality, born from the remote 'pioneer' mindset, are a prized component of New Zealand's national identity and culture. *No. 8 wire* practices occur widely and are impossible to list definitively, yet they are identifiable by two key features: they are normally centred around problem-solving and they are characterised by a lateral-thinking approach, resorting to resources at hand, rather than seeking specialised tools or materials. The solutions are unique, but the practices are generic. Individual *no. 8 wire* practices have analogues elsewhere, themselves the result of scarcity or geographical or political remoteness. *No. 8 wire* as a mindset and part of identity, however, may be unique to New Zealand. The French rural *la débrouille* (see 10.9 in this volume) comes close, although it carries overtones of working-class pride and barter systems which are not present in *no. 8 wire* (Hugues 2022).

No. 8 wire is integral to the New Zealand way of life and national identity. Since these practices emerge from everyday situations, they are inherently informal, even where they occur in ostensibly regulated settings. This creates an ambivalent relationship between *no. 8 wire* and authority: the practices are praised but are also a source of tension between the state and people, because they bypass the rules.

No. 8 wire is a type of wire used for agricultural fencing, and a catalyst for innovation in and of itself. Prior to its introduction in the 1850s, farmers relied on labour-intensive methods of dividing land and corralling sheep. The multiple ways in which the *no. 8 wire* revolutionised farming in remote, sparsely populated areas within its intended application for fencing may have made farmers see it as an innately creativity-sparking product. The modern concept of *no. 8 wire* comes from a situation typical for rural farmers in the nineteenth and early twentieth century. They often had rolls of *no. 8 wire*, so when other, non-fencing, problems arose, due to the remoteness of farms within NZ and the remoteness of NZ itself, and the time other solutions would take, *no. 8 wire* was frequently the only resource available to solve them. From the beginning of formalised government, there was a split: *no. 8 wire* versus the 'official' way. *No. 8 wire* got things done, sometimes in place of government and sometimes despite it.

In New Zealand, the state-led, top-down national identity-formation manifests itself as praise for *no. 8 wire* practices as essential for a remote nation dependent on external engagement – but only when it fits with the values espoused by formal governance. By 1900, New Zealand had the most patents – official evidence of problem-solving – per capita in the world, which the government celebrated, and which nowadays the state cites as 'good' ingenuity (Derby 2010).

The modern concept of *no. 8 wire* – creative resourcefulness, filling in the gaps left by officialdom – remains embedded in the New Zealand national identity. New Zealand is more connected to the rest of the world now, but *no. 8 wire* persists, and remains in tension with formality. Contemporary politicians talk about problem-solving as essential to New Zealand being able to 'punch above its weight'; New Zealanders still disproportionately file patents, and a search for 'Kiwi ingenuity' brings back more than a million results, covering everything from documenting '*No. 8 wire* on screen', 'best of' articles listing innovations, government campaigns about a 'nation of problem-solvers' and articles about particular 'contraptions' – all portrayed positively (Smith 2020). This is partly because these things generate income: inventions regulated via patents are monetised via trade. Creative arts can be profitable or bring in revenue by encouraging tourism.

As well as income, the government also seeks control – states value predictability. *No. 8 wire*'s informality and the ambiguity it represents can threaten control. In New Zealand this creates tension between formal institutions and the governed, on whom the government depends for its existence. National identity is both 'top-down' (shaped by formal entities) and 'bottom-up' (arising from the population). *No. 8 wire* as an element of national identity is paradoxical, constantly negotiated between the government and the governed, and a site for imposing and resisting norms. A classic example of *no. 8 wire* practice in this space are *baches* – holiday homes (Swarbrick 2005). Until the mid-twentieth century, *baches* were frequently home-made from what holidaymakers could acquire and adapt easily and cheaply: old timber, decommissioned trams or agricultural products (literal as well as figurative *no. 8 wire*). Planning legislation introduced decades later would have rendered them illegal but the pre-existing structures were excluded from the regulations.

Even where the state deems *no. 8 wire* positive or non-threatening, there is ambivalence. In a twist which takes *no. 8 wire* simultaneously back to its roots as a prosaic tool but also an inspiration in itself, Waikato Museum's 'No. 8 wire National Art Award' puns on *no. 8 wire*'s history of inspiring creativity by challenging the public to produce artworks made from *no. 8 wire* (Waikato prize 2023). The solutions – a mode of upcycling an agricultural tool into something beautiful – require lateral thinking similar to that employed by early settlers.

The ambivalence exposes a 'zone of discretion' – even in apparently heavily regulated and normative settings, formal rules are not strictly formal. In modern New Zealand, *no. 8 wire* persists and is tolerated even in highly organised official areas: the law, health care and science. In 2006, solicitors adopting a *no. 8 wire* approach to solving problems with unit titles went beyond interpreting and applying law to creating new norms (Thomas 2006). *No. 8 wire* practices filled a regulation gap.

In response to the considerable administrative demands placed on medics and patients by clinical trials, a New Zealand medical ethics committee recommended a '"number-8-wire" ethics alternative' to US-imposed regulations (Tolich and Hapuku 2009). In this case, the regulator was external to (and remote from) New Zealand, so the dynamic was different: *no. 8 wire* as a state-sanctioned marker of New Zealand-ness and identity helped a formal institution (the ethics committee) resist regulation itself. New Zealand's fringe position may have been a factor too: it may have punched above its weight, but it was not likely to threaten the US hegemony.

Scientific *no. 8 wire* practices are another example of informality going against international standards. New Zealand hydrographers applied *no. 8 wire* approaches where traditional instruments and approaches were ineffective (Le Coz 2018). Their research withstood scientific peer review; the techniques were rigorous, but they were also unique and developed for the particular context. Another New Zealand-specific science example is a means of converting car airbags into seismographs (English-Lueck 2003). Standard monitoring equipment can be expensive and hard to access in earthquake-prone New Zealand; airbags are generic, plentiful, cheap – and effective.

The Waikato art prize, *baches*, legal interpretation, clinical trials and scientific measurements give a flavour of the contemporary *no. 8 wire* practices in sometimes surprising sectors. The surprise comes from the ambivalence: despite legislation, ethics, international norms and other types of regulation, *no. 8 wire* 'hacks', inherently informal and norm-disrupting, flourish. If they achieve their ends, *no. 8 wire* means are tolerated – and even celebrated. Tolerance, however, does not always translate into encouragement. Formal institutions would rather regulate, even where this seems misplaced. The New Zealand Productivity Commission's report (2021), which refers to New Zealand's remoteness as a barrier to growth, states that innovation is essential to growth, and that the government's role is to 'facilitat[e] and co-fund innovation'. It recommends that the state should 'discontinue clearly unsuccessful initiatives', encapsulating the state's ambivalence towards innovation and invention. The state should direct ingenuity; but it should also cut off 'unsuccessful' innovation.

Bibliography to Chapter 10

Introduction: triangulating ethnicity, networks and informality
Endre Sik

Anderson, B. (2006). *Imagined Communities: Reflections on the Origin and Spread of Nationalism*. London: Verso Books.

Czakó, Á. and Sik, E. 1999. 'Characteristics and Origins of the Comecon Open-air Market in Hungary'. *International Journal of Urban and Regional Research* 23(4): 715–37.

De Herdt, T. and de Sardan, J. 2015. *Real Governance and Practical Norms in Sub-Saharan Africa*. Oxon and New York: Routledge.

Egbert, H. 2006. 'Cross-border Small-scale Trading in South-eastern Europe: Do Embeddedness and Social Capital Explain Enough?'. *International Journal of Urban and Regional Research* 30(2): 346–61.

Harpaz, Y. 2016. *Compensatory Citizenship*. PhD dissertation, Princeton University.

Hozic, A. 2004. 'Between the Cracks: Balkan Cigarette Smuggling'. *Problems of Post-Communism* 51(3): 35–44.

Light, I. 1977. 'The Ethnic Vice Industry, 1880–1944'. *American Sociological Review* 42(3): 464–79.

Polese, A. 2006. 'Border-crossing as a Strategy of Daily Survival: The Odessa-Chisinau Elektrichka'. *Anthropology of East Europe Review* 24(1): 28–37.

Sik, E. 2010. 'Network Dependent Path Dependency'. *Corvinus Journal of Sociology and Social Policy* 1(1): 77–102.

Sik, E. 2012. 'Trust, Network Capital, and Informality – Cross-Border Entrepreneurship in the First Two Decades of Post-Communism'. *Review of Sociology* 4: 53–72.

Sik, E. and Wallace, C. 1999. 'The Development of Open-air Markets in East-Central Europe'. *International Journal of Urban and Regional Research* 23(4): 697–714.

Sik, E. and Wellman, B. 1999. 'Network Capital in Capitalist, Communist and Post-Communist Countries'. In *Networks in the Global Village*, edited by B. Wellman, 225–54. Boulder: Westview Press.

Sik, E. and Tóth, J. 2003. 'Joining an EU Identity: Integration of Hungary and the Hungarians'. In *Europeanisation, National Identities and Migration*, edited by W. Spohn and A. Triandafyllidou, 223–44. London: Routledge.

Sik, E. and Surányi, R. (eds) 2014. *The Hungarian/Slovak/Ukrainian Tri-border Region*. TÁRKI, Budapest. http://issuu.com/eltetatk/docs/tri-border_hungary/1?e=12707147/11841125

Sik, E. and Szeitl, B. 2015. 'Quasi-diaspora and Cross-border Diaspora in the Hungarian-Slovak-Ukrainian Triborder Region'. *Review of Sociology* 25(4): 107–25.

van Houtum, H. and Strüver, A. 2002. 'Borders, Strangers, Doors and Bridges'. *Space and Polity* 6(2): 141–6. https://web.archive.org/web/20170808062929/http://ncbr.ruhosting.nl/html/files/SpaceandPolity2002.pdf

Wiegand, B. 1994. 'Black Money in Belize: The Ethnicity and Social Structure of Black-market Crime'. *Social Forces* 73(1): 135–54.

Wimmer, A. and Glick-Schiller, N. 2002. 'Methodological Nationalism and Beyond: Nation-state Building, Migration and the Social Sciences'. *Global Networks* 2(4): 301–34.

10.1 *Vorovskie pasporta* (Russia)
Andrey V. Gornostaev

Anisimov, E. V. 1982. *Podatnaia reforma Petra I: vvedenie podushnoi podati v Rossii 1719–1728*. Leningrad: Nauka.

Franklin, S. 2010. 'Printing and Social Control in Russia 1: Passports'. *Russian History* 37(3): 208–37.

Gornostaev, A. V. 2020. *Peasants 'on the Run': State Control, Fugitives, Social and Geographic Mobility in Imperial Russia, 1649–1796*. PhD dissertation, Georgetown University, Washington, DC.

Gornostaev, A. 2022. 'Mertvye Dushi (Russia, 1700s–)'. www.in-formality.com/wiki/index.php?title=Mertvye_Dushi_(Russia,_1700s-)

Hellie, R. 1990. 'Commentary on Chapter 11 (The Judicial Process for Peasants of the "Ulozhenie" of 1649)'. *Russian History* 17(3): 305–39.

Kosheleva, O. E. 2016. '"Bez pashportov i s vorovskimi pashporty", ili mozhno li obmanut' gosudarstvennyi control'. In *Obman kak povsednevnaia praktika. Individual'nye i kollektivnye strategii povedeniia*, edited by O. I. Togoeva and O. E. Kosheleva, 323–48. Moscow: IVI RAN.

Polnoe sobranie zakonov Rossiiskoi imperii (PSZ). 1830. 45 vols.

Smith, A. K. 2020. 'False Passports, Undocumented Workers, and Public (Dis)Order in Late-Eighteenth-Century Russia'. *Journal of Social History* 53(3): 742–62.

St. Petersburg Rossiiskii gosudarstvennyi arkhiv drevnikh aktov (RGADA).

Torpey, J. 2000. *The Invention of the Passport: Surveillance, Citizenship and the State*. Cambridge: Cambridge University Press.

10.2 *Saksy* (Poland)
Krzysztof Kruk

Connidis, I. A. and McMullin, J. A. 2002. 'Sociological Ambivalence and Family Ties: A Critical Perspective'. *Journal of Marriage and Family* 64(3): 558–67.

Fiałkowska, K. and Piechowska, M. 2016. 'New Way, Old Pattern. Seasonal Migration from Poland to Germany'. *Arbor* 192(777): 1–13.

Grabowska, I. and Engbersen, G. 2016. 'Social Remittances and the Impact of Temporary Migration on an EU Sending Country: The Case of Poland'. *Central and Eastern European Migration Review* 5(2): 99–117.

Kępińska, E. and Stark, O. 2013. 'The Evolution and Sustainability of Seasonal Migration from Poland to Germany: From the Dusk of the 19th Century to the Dawn of the 21st Century'. *International Review of Economics and Finance* 28(C): 3–18.

Marks-Bielska, R., Lizińska W., Babuchowska K. and Kaczmarczyk M. 2015. *Conditions Underlying Migrations from Poland to Germany and the United Kingdom*, edited by Z. Chojnowski. Olsztyn: Wydawnictwo UWM.

Marx, C. 2018. 'Introduction: The Puzzles of Informal Economy'. In *The Global Encyclopaedia of Informality: Understanding Social and Cultural Complexity, Volume 2*, edited by A. Ledeneva, 7–10. London: UCL Press.

Morawska, E. 2001. 'Structuring Migration: The Case of Polish Income-Seeking Travelers to the West'. *Theory and Society* 30(1): 47–80.

Stola, D. 2015. 'Opening a Non-Exit State: The Passport Policy of Communist Poland, 1949–1980'. *East European Politics and Societies* 29(1): 96–119.

Tilly, C. 2007. 'Trust Networks in Transnational Migration'. *Sociological Forum* 22(1): 3–24.
White, A. 2016. 'Polish Migration to the UK Compared with Migration Elsewhere in Europe: A Review of the Literature'. *Social Identities* 22(1): 10–25.
White, A., Grabowska I., Kaczmarczyk P. and Slany K. 2018. 'The Impact of Migration from and to Poland since EU Accession'. In *The Impact of Migration on Poland: EU Mobility and Social Change,* edited by A. White et al., 10–41. London: UCL Press.
Widzyk, A. 2017. 'Belgia: Miasto Siemiatycze Chce Pomóc Swej Licznej Emigracji w Brukseli'. *Dziennik Gazeta Prawna.* 11 February. www.gazetaprawna.pl/wiadomosci/artykuly/1019175,belgia-miasto-siemiatycze-chce-pomoc-swej-licznej-emigracji-w-brukseli.html

10.3 *Ściągnąć* (Poland)
Anne White

Castles, S. 2010. 'Understanding Global Migration: A Social Transformation Perspective'. *Journal of Ethnic and Migration Studies* 36(10): 1565–86.
Garapich, M. 2016. *London's Polish Borders: Transnationalizing Class and Identity among Polish Migrants in London.* Stuttgart: Ibidem Press.
Jaźwińska, E. 2001. 'Migracje niepełne ludności Polski: zróżnicowanie międzyregionalne'. In *Ludzie na huśtawce: Migracje między peryferiami Polski i zachodu,* edited by E. Jaźwińska and M. Okólski, 101–24. Warsaw: Scholar.
Materka, E. 2017. *Dystopia's Provocateurs: Peasants, State, and Informality in the Polish-German Borderlands.* Bloomington: Indiana University Press.
Morawska, E. 2001. 'Structuring Migration: The Case of Polish Income-Seeking Travelers to the West'. *Theory and Society* 30(1): 47–80.
Pécoud, A. and de Guchteneire, P. 2007. 'Introduction: The Migration without Borders Scenario'. In *Migration without Borders*, edited by A. Pécoud and P. de Guchteneire, 1–30. Paris: UNESCO; Oxford: Berghahn.
White, A. 2017. *Polish Families and Migration Since EU Accession.* 2nd ed. Bristol: Policy Press.
White, A. 2018. 'Lifestyles, Livelihoods, Networks and Trust'. In *The Impact of Migration on Poland: EU Mobility and Social Change,* edited by A. White, I. Grabowska, P. Kaczmarczyk and K. Slany, 131–59. London: UCL Press.
White, A. and Ryan, L. 2008. 'Polish "Temporary" Migration: The Formation and Significance of Social Networks'. *Europe-Asia Studies* 60(9): 1467–502.

10.4 *Trailing spouses* (India)
Shalini Grover and Sanna Schliewe

Arieli, D. 2007. 'The Task of Being Content: Expatriate Wives in Beijing, Emotional Work and Patriarchal Bargain'. *Journal of International Women's Studies* 8(4): 18–31.
Boström, W. K., Öhlander, M. and Petterson, H. 2018. 'Temporary International Mobility, Family Timing, Dual Career and Family Democracy: A Case of Swedish Medical Professionals'. *Migration Letters* 15(1): 99–111.
Cangiá, F. 2017. '(Im)Mobility and the Emotional Lives of Expat Spouses'. *Emotion, Space and Society* 25: 22–8.
Cangiá, F. 2018. 'Precarity, Imagination and the Mobile Life of the "Trailing Spouse"'. *Ethos* 46(1): 8–26.
Fechter, A.-M. 2007. *Transnational Lives. Expatriates in Indonesia.* Farnham: Ashgate Publishing.
Fechter, A.-M. and Walsh, K. (eds) 2010. Introduction to Special Issue: 'Examining "Expatriate" Continuities: Postcolonial Approaches to Mobile Professionals'. *Journal of Ethnic and Migration Studies* 36(8): 1197–210.
Grover, S. 2018a. 'Who is an Expatriate? Euro-American Identities, Race and Integration in Postcolonial India'. In *Cultural Psychology of Intervention in the Globalized World*, edited by S. Schliewe, N. Chaudhary and G. Marsico, 283–95. Charlotte: North Carolina: Information Age Publishing.
Grover, S. 2018b. 'English-speaking and Educated Female Domestic Workers in Contemporary India: New Managerial Roles, Social Mobility and Persistent Inequality'. *Journal of South Asian Development* 13(2): 186–209.

Hindman, H. 2013. *Mediating the Global. Expatria's Forms and Consequences in Kathmandu*. Stanford: Stanford University Press.
Schliewe, S. 2018. 'The Mobile Life-world Map. A Dialogical Tool for Understanding Expatriates'. In *Cultural Psychology of Intervention in the Globalized World*, edited by S. Schliewe, N. Chaudhary and G. Marsico, 223–44. Charlotte, North Carolina: Information Age Publishing.
Schliewe, S. 2019. 'Inheriting Domestic Workers: A Study of Norm Transmission among Expatriates in India'. *Papers on Social Representations* 28(1): 12.1–12.24.
Walsh, K. 2007. 'Traveling Together? Work, Intimacy, and Home Amongst British Expatriate Couples in Dubai'. In *Gender and Family Amongst Transnational Professionals*, edited by A. Coles and A.-M. Fechter, 63–84. London: Routledge.

10.5 *Mulas* (Cuba)
Concetta Russo

Cearns, J. 2019. 'The "Mula Ring": Material Networks of Circulation Through the Cuban World'. *The Journal of Latin American and Caribbean Anthropology* 24(4): 864–90.
Espina, M. 2010. *Desarrollo, desigualdad y políticas sociales. Acercamientos desde una perspectiva compleja*. La Habana: Publicaciones Acuario, Centro Félix Varela.
Hansing, K. and Orozco, M. 2014. 'The Role and Impact of Remittances on Small Business Development during Cuba's Current Economic Reforms'. Working Paper 69.
Holbraad, M. 2004. 'Religious "Speculation": The Rise of Ifá Cults and Consumption in post-Soviet Cuba'. *Journal of Latin American Studies* 36(4): 643–63.
Israel, E. 2009. 'Spain issues Cuba's first "grandchildren" passport'. Reuters, 6 February. www.reuters.com/article/us-cuba-spain-citizenship/spain-issues-cubas-first-grandchildren-passport-idUSTRE51502U20090206
Malinowski, B. 1922. *Argonauts of the Western Pacific*. Prospect Heights, IL: Waveland.
Pertierra, A. C. 2007. *Battles, Inventions and Acquisitions: The Struggle for Consumption in Urban Cuba*. University of London: London University Press.
Portes, A. 1983. 'The Informal Sector: Definition, Controversy, and Relation to National Development'. *Review (Fernand Braudel Center)* 7(1): 151–74.
Russo, C. 2018. 'Informality in Contemporary Cuban Labor Market. An Anthropological Perspective'. *Interdisciplinary Political Studies* 4(2): 51–78.
Sánchez, C. A. and Cuesta, S. G. 2017. 'Migration and Spanish Citizenship Abroad: Recent Scenarios from the Cuban Context'. *Mediterranean Journal of Social Sciences* 8(3): 91.
Semple, A. 2016. 'Cuban Shoppers Helping to Keep Guyana's Economy Afloat'. *Demerara Waves*, 27 October. https://demerarawaves.com/2016/10/27/cuban-shoppers-helping-to-keep-guyanas-economy-afloat/
Tilly, C. 2007. 'Trust Networks in Transnational Migration'. *Sociological Forum* 22(1): 3–24.

10.6 *Simsar, samsara* (Middle East and North Africa)
Alberica Camerani

Algerie Presse Service. 2010. 'L'Immobilier à Rabat Dominé par le Lobby des Samsars'/*DjaZairess*, 25 September. www.djazairess.com/fr/apsfr/88923
Aliyev, H. 2017. 'Informal Institutions in Azerbaijan: Exploring the Intricacies of Tapsh'. *Europe-Asia Studies* 69: 594–613.
Colin, G. S. and Becker, C. H. 1999. 'Tafilalt'. In *Encyclopaedia of Islam*, edited by P. Bearman, T. Biaquis, C. E. Bosworth, E. van Donzel and W. P. Heinrichs, 102b. Leiden: Brill.
Cortellazzo, M. 1989. *Venezia, il Levante e il Mare*. Pisa: Pacini Editore.
Dictionnaire Littré. 1878. 'Censal'. *Dictionnaire de la langue française, Supplément*. Paris: L. Hachette. www.littre.org/definition/censal
Gelderblom, O. 2013. *Cities of Commerce*. Princeton: Princeton University Press.
Gould, R. V. and Fernandez, R. M. 1989. 'Structures of Mediation: A Formal Approach to Brokerage in Transaction Networks'. *Social Methodology* 19: 89–126.
Gregory, C. A. 1982. *Gifts and Commodities*. London: Academic Press.
Hassan, A. A. H. 1986. *Sales and Contracts in Early Islamic Commercial Law*. University of Edinburgh.

Hoepli. 2015. 'Sensale'. *Hoepli.it*. www.grandidizionari.it/Dizionario_Italiano/parola/S/sensale. aspx?query=sensale

Jancsics, D. 2015. 'A Friend Gave Me a Phone Number: Brokerage in Low-Level Corruption'. *International Journal of Law Crime and Justice* 43: 68–87.

Lamprakos, M. 2017. *Building a World Heritage City: Sanaa, Yemen*. London: Routledge.

Majdalani, C. 2005. *Histoire de la Grande Maison*. Paris: Le Seuil.

Marsden, P. V. and Lin, N. 1982. *Social Structure and Network Analysis*. London, Thousand Oaks, New Delhi: Sage.

Rothman, N. E. 2012. *Brokering Empire: Trans-Imperial Subjects between Venice and Istanbul*. Ithaca: Cornell University Press.

Sahlins, M. D. 1965. 'On the Sociology of Primitive Exchange'. In *The Relevance of Models for Social Anthropology*, edited by M. Banton, F. Eggan and M. Gluckman, 139–237. London: Tavistock.

Savary des Bruslons, J. 1741. *Dictionnaire Universel de Commerce*. Paris: Veuve Estienne. https://gallica.bnf.fr/ark:/12148/bpt6k55968180/f414.item.r=censal.texteImage

Schacht, J. 1982. *An Introduction to Islamic Law*. Oxford: Clarendon Press.

Shatzmiller, M. 1993. *Labour in the Medieval Islamic World*. Leiden: Brill.

Simmel, G. 1950. *The Sociology of Georg Simmel*. New York: The Free Press.

Sommerfelt, T. (ed.) 2001. *Domestic Child Labour in Morocco*. Oslo: Centraltrykkeriet AS.

Stovel, K. and Shaw L. 2012. 'Brokerage'. *Annual Reviews of Sociology* 38: 139–58.

10.7 *Jak igrač* (North Macedonia)
Borjan Gjuzelov

Bliznakovski, J. 2020. 'Political Clientelism in the Western Balkans'. *Conference Report: Political Clientelism in the Western Balkans*: 6.

Damjanovski, I., Lavrič, M., Gjuzelov, B., Obad, O. and Jovanović M. Forthcoming. 'The Gap Between Formal Rules and Informal Practices: Europeanisation Meets Informality'. In *The Gap between Rules and Practices: Informality in South-East Europe*, edited by E. Gordy, P. Cveticanin and A. Ledeneva.

Dimitrova, A. L. 2010. 'The New Member States of the EU in the Aftermath of Enlargement: Do New European Rules Remain Empty Shells?' *Journal of European Public Policy* 17(1): 137–48.

Gjuzelov, B. 2020. *Between Written and Unwritten Rules: On the Ambivalent Context of EU-Sponsored Judicial Reforms in North Macedonia*. PhD thesis, Queen Mary University of London, London.

Ledeneva, A. 1998. *Russia's Economy of Favors: Blat, Networking and Informal Exchange*. Cambridge: Cambridge University Press.

Mungiu-Pippidi, A. 2005. 'Deconstructing Balkan Particularism: The Ambiguous Social Capital Of Southeastern Europe'. *Southeast European and Black Sea Studies*, 49–68.

Mungiu-Pippidi, A. 2015. *The Quest for Good Governance: How Societies Develop Control of Corruption*. Cambridge: Cambridge University Press.

10.8 *Nojukusha* (Japan)
Hideo Aoki

Aoki, H. 2000. *Japan's Underclass: Day Laborers and the Homeless*. Trans Pacific Press.

Aoki, H. 2003. 'Homelessness in Osaka: Globalisation, Yoseba, and Disemployment'. *Urban Studies* 40(2): 361–78.

10.9 *La débrouille* (Former French and Belgian colonies in sub-Saharan Africa)
Cécile B. Vigouroux

Ayimpam, S. 2014. *Économie de la Débrouille à Kinshasa*. Paris: Karthala.

Bourdieu, P. 1984. *Questions de Sociologie*. Paris: Éditions de Minuit.

Déchelette, F. 1918. *L'Argot des Poilus. Dictionnaire Humoristique et Philologique du Langage des Soldats de la Grande Guerre de 1914*. Paris: Jouve & Cie éditeurs.

de Villers, G. 2002. 'Introduction'. In *Manières de Vivre. Économie de la Débrouille dans les Villes du Congo/Zaïre*, edited by G. de Villers, B. Jewsiewicki and L. Monnier, 11–32. Paris: L'Harmattan.

Iñiguez De Heredia, M. 2017. *Everyday Resistance, Peacebuilding And State-Making. Insights From 'Africa's World War'*. Manchester: Manchester University Press.

Kisangani, E. F. and Bobb, S. 2010. *Historical Dictionary of the Democratic Republic of the Congo*. Plymouth: Scarecrow.

MacGaffey, J. 1993. 'On Se Débrouille : Réflexion Sur La Deuxième Économie Et Les Relations Entre Les Classes Au Zaïre'. In *Le Zaïre A L'épreuve De L'histoire Immédiate*, edited by J. Omasombo, 143–59. Paris: Karthala.

Meddeb, H. 2011. 'L'Ambivalence de la Course à "el Khobza". Obéir et se Révolter en Tunisie'. *Politique Africaine* 121(1): 35–51.

Murphy, L. 2015. 'A Brief History of le Système D'. *Contemporary French Civilization* 40(3): 351–71.

Murphy, L. 2016. *The Art of Survival*. New Haven and London: Yale University Press.

Nkuku Khonde, C. and Rémon, M. 2006. *Stratégies de Survie à Lubumbashi* (RD Congo). Paris: L'Harmattan.

Persyn, P. and Ladrière, F. 2004. 'The Miracle of Life in Kinshasa: New Approaches to Public Health'. In *Reinventing Order in the Congo. How People Respond to State Failure in Kinshasa*, edited by T. Trefon, 65–81. London: Zed Books.

Piermay, J.-L. 1993. 'L'article 15, ou le Zaïre à la Recherche d'Articulations de Rechange'. *Travaux de l'Institut Géographique de Reims* 83–84: 99–107.

Salem, Z. O. A. 2001. 'Tcheb-Tchib et compagnie. Lexique de la survie et figures de la réussite en Mauritanie'. *Politique Africaine* 82(2): 78–100.

Vigouroux, C. B. 2017. 'Rethinking (Un)skilled Migrants: Whose skills, What Skills, for What and for Whom?'. In: *Routledge Handbook of Migration and Language*, edited by S. Canagarajah, 312–23. London: Routledge.

Waage, T. 2006. 'Coping with Unpredictability: "Preparing for Life" in Ngaoundéré, Cameroon'. In *Navigating Youth, Generating Adulthood Social Becoming in an African Context*, edited by C. Christiansen, M. Utas and H. E. Vigh, 61–87. Uppsala: Nordiska Afrikainstitutet.

10.10 *No. 8 wire* (New Zealand)
Grace Reynolds

Derby, M. 2010. 'Inventions, Patents, and Trademarks – The "no 8 wire" tradition'. *Te Ara Encyclopaedia of New Zealand*. https://teara.govt.nz/en/inventions-patents-and-trademarks/page-1

English-Lueck, J. A. 2003. 'Number Eight Fencing Wire: New Zealand, Cultural Innovation and the Global Silicon Network'. *Adaptation of Poster presented at the 2003 AAA Annual Meeting*, Chicago, IL. https://svcp.org/pdfs/Number_Eight_Fencing_Wire.pdf

Hugues, F. 2022. 'Getting by in Rural France: La débrouille as a Form of Quiet Popular Resistance?'. *European Journal of Political and Cultural Sociology* 10(1): 2023.

Le Coz, J. 2018. 'L'hydrométrie en Nouvelle-Zélande: l'esprit "Number 8 wire"' (Hydrometry: Efficiency and Resourcefulness). *La Houille Blanche* (*International Water Journal*) 2.

New Zealand Productivity Commission. 2021. 'New Zealand Firms: Reaching for the Frontier. Final Report'. *New Zealand Productivity Commission, April*. www.productivity.govt.nz/inquiries/frontier-firms/

Smith, R. 2020. 'Promoting our Kiwi Ingenuity'. *New Zealand Story*, 2 December. www.nzstory.govt.nz/about-us/news/promoting-our-kiwi-ingenuity/

Swarbrick, N. 2005. 'Creative life – architecture'. *Te Ara Encyclopaedia of New Zealand*, 8 February. https://teara.govt.nz/en/creative-life/page-4

Thomas, R. 2006. 'Fifer, Unit Titles, and No 8 Wire'. *The New Zealand Law Journal* May.

Tolich, M. and Hapuku, J. 2009. 'Number-8-wire Ethics: A New Zealand Ethics Committee's Response to Lengthy International Clinical Trial Information Sheets'. *Journal of the New Zealand Medical Association* 122(1293).

Waikato prize. 2023. National Waikato Museum, Hamilton. https://waikatomuseum.co.nz/artspost/fieldays-no.8-wire-national-art-award/

11
Settling in

Introduction: informal housing and beyond
Anthony Boanada-Fuchs
and
Vanessa Boanada Fuchs
St. Gallen Institute of Management in Latin America, Switzerland

Settling in is one of the most important stages in human life. It often presents problems, which find informal solutions. Hence informality is often connected with the ideas of housing and home. At the same time, the contributions of the authors in this section go beyond that and transgress the mainstream understanding of informal housing.

Informality has been a recurring feature in several distinct discourses and our work focuses on analysing differences and similarities in meanings attributed to the informal. Based on a literature review of different informality discourses, we mapped over one hundred ideas and grouped them into seven overarching dimensions (Boanada-Fuchs and Boanada Fuchs 2021). With such a tool it is possible to dissect a specific discussion, such as on informal housing, and illustrate a range of different ideas. We have reproduced the multi-dimensional visualisation of informality in a graphic (see Table 11.0).

Acknowledging that different discourses on informality do exist and have been developing in parallel to one another with explicit influences (Al Sayyad and Roy 2004), we recognise the role of informal housing as the discourse that has probably produced the largest research output in informality studies after the informal economy. We use the word 'probably' as it is not easy to quantify its actual impact as many different terms

Table 11.0 Informality ideas in various disciplines and discourses

The ideas of economic informality
(1) outside formal economy (2) response to insufficient provision/structural deficiency (3) inefficient/poor quality/low-skill/low-tech/no resource access (4) low productivity/low wage (5) small-scale (6) exploitative (7) harmful to national economies (8) under-employment/part-time/irregular (time-wise)/temporary (9) temporary phenomenon (macro) (10) competitive disadvantage (11) risky (12) cheaper/less expensive/economically efficient/affordable/profitable (13) resource efficient (14) rational choice/not economically irrational (15) a valuable support system, safety net (16) ease of entry/opportunity (17) self-employed (18) other value system/not price-determined (19) non-monetary exchange/barter/unremunerated (20) poverty (21) developing countries (22) dependency (23) vulnerability (24) inequality (25) important (26) no access/excluded (27) solution/successful (28) desperation (29) only option/lack of alternative (30) periphery
The ideas of legal informality
(1) outside the formal legal reach (2) no enforcement of contracts and rights (3) own laws (4) no title/property rights (5) missing legal recognition (6) squatting/land invasion/encroachment (7) unauthorised/prohibited (8) illegal (9) violation of general laws (10) non-compliance with legal rules (11) criminal activities (12) harassment, extortion, repression, discrimination (13) bribery (14) drug trafficking, people smuggling, money laundering, stolen goods (15) produced by laws
The ideas of technical informality
(1) outside regulation (2) uncontrolled/unregulated (3) unauthorised (4) unrecorded/hidden (5) unplanned (6) missing permits/missing registration (7) produced by regulations (8) undermining order/regulation/planning (9) inadequate/sub-standard/dirty/polluting/slum (10) not protected/not insured/insecure/unsafe/instable/poorly maintained (11) lack of services/benefits (12) avoiding taxation, "off the books" (13) avoiding payment of service fees (14) violating work safety regulations and social security (15) non-compliance with technical standards/rules
The ideas of organisational informality
(1) (highly) organised (2) organisationally complex (3) diverse (4) horizontal networks/non-hierarchical (5) brokerage (6) not complying to organisational standards (7) unconventional/unpredictable/ambivalent (8) faster (9) easier/simpler (10) flexible/freer (11) dynamic (12) spontaneous/independent/organic (13) process (14) incremental/gradual (15) adaptive

Table 11.0   (Cont.)

The ideas of political informality
(1) outside official governance (2) unofficial (3) produced/impacted/ stimulated by the state (4) politically tolerated (5) turned a blind-eye upon/ ignored/neglected (6) lack of capacity and means (7) manipulated/patronage (8) excluded from participation/no voice (9) not (politically) recognised (10) destruction/eviction (11) influence politics/political advantage (12) political resistance or political grassroots movement (13) 'anti-state' (14) heroic (15) not visible/omitted
The ideas of social informality
(1) illegitimate (2) corrupted/damaging behaviour (3) immoral/illicit/ indecent (4) socially tolerated/included (5) social struggle (6) resistance (7) trust (8) social/interpersonal relations/friendship (9) reciprocal/ collaborative (10) intimate (11) casual (in social terms) (12) socially excluded (13) marginal (14) not accepted (15) identity
The ideas of cultural informality
(1) self-provision/self-help/self-sufficient (2) self-initiated/intentional (3) survival (4) subsistence/short-term strategy (5) everyday life (6) family or communal-based (7) traditional/rural (8) local/grass-root level (9) indigenous (10) customary (11) anti-modern (12) cultural resistance (13) alternative way of life/own culture (14) creative/improvised (15) cultural similarities

have been used to describe and study situations analogous to informality in housing conditions. This also connects to a major challenge of the discourse which has been partly developed by a related, yet different concept, the one of self-help. The idea of self-help is even older than the term informal economy, coined by Hart in 1972 (Hart 1985), and has become an important policy concern in international development from the 1970s onwards. It informed the first generation of World Bank-supported housing programmes such as sites and services, and slum upgrading schemes. In its Vancouver conference (Habitat 1976), the UN-Habitat also endorsed a housing programme based on the concept of self-help.

This idea can be traced back to the early 1960s and the writings of John Turner, Charles Abrams and William Magnin (Abrams 1966; Magnin 1967; Turner 1977). Turner took interest in the shelter provision logic of the urban poor and carried out extensive field research on squatter settlements in Peru (Harris 2003). His publications describe the efficient and natural way rural-urban migrants met their basic housing needs through auto-construction. The concept of self-help was then used to describe building practices that are irregular, avoid taxes and permits and are organised by the end-user. That discourse perceived the formal and the informal as mutually exclusive. Whereas the informal leans on the use of traditional materials and techniques, related to family networks and imminent subsistence needs, the formal was equated with modernity led by the state. Turner argued that governments should refrain from oppressing and destroying informal construction but acknowledged their valid contribution to solving escalating housing shortages.

Other authors following the categorisation of Drakakis-Smith contextualised building practices of self-help into a larger framework of informal housing options (Drakakis-Smith 1981; Kombe and Kreibich 2000). Such scholars also broadened the analytical gaze to incorporate housing challenges connected to tenure status, regulatory conformity and the politics of land. With this broadened perspective, the definition of informality surpassed the usages related to the concept of self-help (Bredenoord and van Lindert 2010). It is in such later development that the debate on informal housing has much to offer as it highlights the interconnectedness between formal and informal living realities, as well as the selective ways informality is constructed by both laws/policies and social norms/practices.

In line with this brief review and with a view to expanding the debates on housing informality, the entries in this section do not only reflect the history of the discourse with its overlapping discussion of informal housing and self-help, but also transgress the mainstream understandings by focusing on different realities from new geographies indicated on the 'settling in' map.

Colonias in the United States have been a popular object of study and can be seen as a trans-border movement of a housing typology from Mexico to Texas. Early writings can be traced back to Peter Ward and his work (Ward 1976). *Colonias* are substandard housing areas in South Texas inhabited by migrants. They started to emerge when landowners subdivided plots that were vulnerable to natural disasters and/or less suitable for agricultural exploitation. Nowadays they are home to 400,000 residents. Affordability is achieved by low construction and service standards that are often in violation of laws and building regulations. As a consequence of a lack of government responses, the residents often remain marginalised, trapped in poverty and excluded from many important amenities and services.

The case of *samozakhvat* in Kyrgyzstan illustrates the important role that governments play in shaping the living realities of informal residents. The government first attempted evictions, then opposed legalisation and is currently reluctant to provide any basic infrastructure to *samozakhvat*. While such an attitude reflects the early stage of an international learning curve to tackle informal housing (Boanada-Fuchs 2021), it also helps to highlight a very important connection: the relationship between terminology and attitudes. The way informal housing unfolds is not only connected to government positions of action/non-action, but is also influenced by how the informal is perceived by public bodies and society at large. A closer look at the local uses of those terms often grants a glimpse of the latter. If the official or unofficial term stresses the process of squatting, its unlawfulness or substandard quality of housing, such settlements are more likely to be faced with oppression and destruction (see, for example, the early policies in the Philippines [Berner 2000] and the more recent shift in court decisions in India [Ghertner 2008]).

By contrast, several countries define informal housing in more positive terms, most notably the ones based on Islamic law, as legitimate land claims are based on a Hadith (a saying or deed of the Prophet Mohammad) that 'he who turns a dead land into life becomes its owner' (Bukhari 1982: 555). In Turkey, informal settlements are called *gecekondus* (which can be translated into 'put up overnight') that reflect the original meaning of the Hadith, and over the years the government has passed several amnesty laws.

A very peculiar case of informal housing is *zaniato* (Abkhazia and Nagorno-Karabakh, Caucasus). Peculiar, as the informal is connected to a very specific form of occupation in the context of wartime and post-war distribution of goods. In disputed territories, the properties of Georgians who fled Abkhazia were claimed by winners of the Georgian–Abkhaz war. War is by definition the temporary suspension of national laws, also putting informality – hitherto defined by the formal – in a state of flux. What the presented case shares with the more mainstream literature on informal housing is the political dimension of squatting, as governments have also used land invasions in non-war scenarios as a way of benefiting their supporters.

The section on *xiaochanquan* (China) outlines the phenomena of the booming informal housing market in China. The presented findings strongly recall earlier research in a very different context: the *ejido* land in Mexico that was also under the collective ownership of villages and similarly became an important supply of affordable housing options near larger cities (Ward 1990). In the case of China and its fast urbanisation, villages can be surrounded by urban land that is under government control. Villages are islands of legal exceptions and have become a major supplier of affordable housing, often by a common effort of the villagers' committee, developers and investors (Sa and Haila 2021). In such cases, informality is related to the land and the non-conformity of land use, as transforming village land into urban land is a complex and time-consuming process.

Chuồng cop in Vietnam tells a story that could be retold in many countries around the world, but maybe not in such extreme forms. Illegal extensions of existing buildings – because no permits were obtained and they are in violation of building codes – are a common feature of many cities in the Global North. Hanoi, with some of the highest property prices in the world, has seen the development of 'tiger cages', box-like extensions of apartments that may take the form of small additional balconies. This entry allows us to make important connections to the role of governments – the genesis of 'tiger cages' is linked to inappropriate law and non-enforcement of regulations – and how their attitudes can change based on the societal perception of such informality. The author also mentions the potential threats such structures may represent for the structural and fire safety of its residents.

In the entry on *divlja gradnja* in countries of former Yugoslavia, a broader historical development of illegal land occupation and informal constructions is drawn. At the same time, the author addresses the informality of wealth as an important vector of contemporary urban development. Attention to the connections of politics, power, money and informality has originally been developed within the urban informality discourse. The grey city concept developed by Oren Yiftachel within the urban informality discourse underscores the selective attitude of governments, legalising or white-washing the informality of wealth, while the informality of poverty faces oppression and destruction (Yiftachel 2009).

Vrtičkarstvo in Slovenia focuses on allotments in a Slovenian context. This topic is important as it was a primary lens through which to discuss informality in the built environment in the Global North (Hilbrandt 2019). Land dedicated to agricultural activities for urban residents has a long tradition and, in many countries, created legal loopholes or at least grey zones. This regulatory vagueness would enable the construction of more permanent structures that may be used as secondary or sublet homes. In Ljubljana, the *vrtički* are more centrally located which fostered the rise of such informal housing solutions but also government responses to reduce their spread. As a consequence, gardening plots become a more marginal phenomenon, particularly in visual terms – hidden from public scrutiny.

Despite the diversity of contributions in this section, there are also some remarkable commonalities. First of all, informal housing is understood as a substandard housing form that provides affordable space at the expense of construction and service standards. Another major cost reduction is often achieved by building informal housing units on land that is not earmarked for such purpose and/or often disproportionately exposed to risk and hazards. This leads to the second commonality, the prominence of an interlinked discussion between land and housing.

In many instances, informal housing derives not from the structure as such but foremost from land-use violations or the non-conformity of the title transfer. This first source of informality might directly fuel informality in the built form, by not adhering to technical standards and regulations, or failing to obtain permits. But where this is not the case, or at least carried out more subtly, it also means that informality is not easily detectable. This not only creates challenges for formulating appropriate government responses, but is also the underlying reason that one of the most defining features of substandard housing (lack of tenure security is one of five UN-Habitat dimensions to define slums) is not assessed by UN-Habitat (Cities Alliance and GIMLA 2021).

A third common feature is situating informal housing in a broader political force field. The contributions of this section have provided examples of the ways governments influence the nature of informal housing. Within this debate, it is important to devote more attention to the informality of wealth, and the widespread flouting of building regulations by powerful elites, often backed up by politicians. Such insights can further unearth the selectivity of politicians in addressing informal housing as well as advance our understanding of the concept of informality.

In conclusion, the entries in this section insightfully analyse a diverse array of informal problem-solving and housing practices in different geographies (future editions could benefit from broadening the gaze to African and Latin American geographies), while also highlighting the political connections in definitions of informality as well as the necessary relation to land management systems. While each entry has unique qualities, considering them jointly underscores that, more than ever, informal housing cannot be narrowly understood and should be analysed through broader interdisciplinary lenses.

11.1 **Colonias** (USA)
Michael J. Pisani
Department of Management, Central Michigan University, USA

Colonias (singular: *colonia*) are informal, self-built housing units typically clustered together in unregulated and unincorporated subdivisions in the Southwestern United States – California, Arizona, New Mexico and

Texas (Donelson and Esparza 2010, 2016). This low-income housing is often located outside the formal city limits and is characterised by deficient infrastructure (for example, water, roads, electricity, health, police, street lighting, wastewater and trash removal), lack of regulations or enforcement (for example zoning, building codes), poverty and health challenges, and land title ambiguity (Donelson and Esparza 2010). The primary residents of *colonias* are people with contemporary or historical familial ties to Mexico. The majority of *colonias* were built in the post-Second World War era. The name translates to community, neighbourhood or suburb from Spanish (Ward 1999) and originates from low-income urban *colonia* neighbourhoods in Mexico. The legacy of *colonias* in Mexico facilitated the development of *colonias* in the US.

A geographic concentration of Southwestern *colonias* is prominent in South Texas, especially along the US–Mexico border. More than 1,500 *colonias* in South Texas (Texas Department of Housing and Community Affairs 2019) house an estimated 400,000 residents, or nearly 20 per cent of the local population (Richardson and Pisani 2017). *Colonias* in South Texas evolved out of worker camps on larger ranches and farms. Flood- and hurricane-prone areas, less suitable for agriculture, were subdivided into smaller plots by the landowners and sold to Mexican immigrant farm workers. Since the plots fell outside the city borders where building codes were not as stringently enforced, the residents manoeuvred around them to build their housing informally. *Colonias* were also a springboard for engaging in other informal economic activities (Richardson and Pisani 2012).

The poverty that envelops South Texas facilitates the existence of *colonias* (Federal Reserve Bank of Dallas 1996). In 2017, about one third of the population and approximately half of all children lived below the poverty line (Richardson and Pisani 2017). The creation and persistence of *colonia* housing outside of the city borders is a low-income housing strategy that mitigates homelessness and overcrowding, allowing a pathway to home ownership to those on the margins of the economy. Deposits for plots of land, as low as 50–100 USD for a property lot with a price of 10,000 USD, ease entry into *colonia* communities (Durst and Ward 2014). The median price for a *colonia* housing is approximately 40,000 USD for completed homes (Durst and Ward 2014).

Colonias are a conduit for informal economic activities, a social and cultural sanctuary and point towards a failure of formal housing systems. Economic survival in *colonias* is often linked to an engagement in informal work and entrepreneurship (Richardson and Pisani 2012). Since *colonias* housing is cheap, it often attracts the most vulnerable – the undocumented

Figure 11.1.1 *Colonia* home in Hidalgo County, Texas, USA. © Jenny L. Chamberlain.

who cannot legally work (about 30 per cent of *colonia* residents, Barton et al. 2015). But a shared Mexican heritage and identity facilitates social and cultural bonding. *Colonia* residents assist one another in building their homes, provide safety and care to residents and help to access extended social and family networks (Richardson and Pisani 2017). The formal housing market in South Texas is beyond the financial reach of many. There are few public resources devoted to providing public housing, highlighting the inadequate social safety net for housing needs.

The existence of *colonias* also points to deficient regulation. Land development projects often receive insufficient levels of formal scrutiny, leading to deficient infrastructure, missing property sales records, insufficient enforcement of the building code and exploitative financing schemes. The most notorious such scheme was the 'contract-for-deed' property sale, in which the seller retained ownership of the property until the final payment and denied access to the accumulated equity prior to this (which is now illegal).

Since the mid-1990s, the Texas state government has made efforts to understand and ameliorate offences, failures in infrastructure and exploitative financing, but more work is needed (Richardson and Pisani 2012, 2017). *Colonias* are paradoxes for public policymakers. On the one hand, *colonias* can be seen as a free market supply-based response to excess housing demand in border communities. Informal housing has not only offered a solution to a lack of affordable housing stock (Giusti 2008), but has also pushed home ownership rates among *colonia* dwellers to 72 per cent, nearly 10 percentage points above the Texas state average (Richardson and Pisani 2017). Rates such as these may help portray the government as absolved of its financial responsibility to help those in need of housing. On the other hand, *colonias* can be viewed as a blight – a scourge of unregulated housing that encourages crime, disease, inadequate infrastructure, unemployment and settlements of undocumented populations – that needs to be reduced or eliminated. Many public officials denounce *colonias* as eyesores that impede local economic development (Richardson and Pisani 2012).

Colonias face many challenges. The policy emphasis has continued to prioritise the building of infrastructure able to improve the quality of life, such as enabling direct access to potable water, paving roads, provisioning drainage, street lighting and trash collection, and removing wastewater and contaminants. Infrastructure improvements are sporadic and evolving affairs – the gains of which are distributed unequally among *colonias* dependent upon local organising and political will and influence. For example, South Texas-based community organisations La Unión del Pueblo Entero and ARISE have assisted more than 25 *colonia* communities in securing street lighting since 2016 (Taylor 2019). They have done so by organising committed *colonia* residents at the grassroots level and by exerting public pressure, presence and plans at government meetings of county officials.

Ongoing crises in access to health care and health insurance, poverty and public safety are more difficult to address by policy. More than two thirds of *colonia* residents lack health insurance and half of *colonia* households earn below the poverty line (Barton et al. 2015). In contrast to urban neighbourhoods in South Texas with comparable low incomes, *colonias* report lower rates of crime (Richardson and Pisani 2017). This is a remarkable finding, given that *colonias* receive very little public protection and public services. Half of all *colonia* residents engage in seasonal migratory work in agricultural fields or in informal work, which suggests that *colonia* income-earners would benefit from supplemental, complementary or alternative work arrangements (Barton et al. 2015). Half of *colonia* residents also lack a high school education or proficiency in English (Barton et al. 2015). Improving educational access and adult education, including English language training, may reduce pronounced gaps in fuller participation in the larger economy and society.

The stigmas of living in *colonia* communities and the infrastructure challenges are addressed by the residents by relying on a shared culture and strong familial ties. More permanent solutions to problems faced by *colonias* may come in the form of increasing public awareness and investing in meaningful immigration reform (Richardson and Pisani 2017).

11.2 *Chabolismo* (Spain)
Noel A. Manzano Gómez
Departamento de Urbanística y Ordenación del Territorio, Universidad Politécnica de Madrid, Spain

In Spain, *chabola* is a small, poorly constructed dwelling, and *chabolismo* is the condition of abundance of *chabolas* in the urban peripheries. The phenomenon has an extensive historical, sociological and cultural dimension in Spain. In the Catalan-speaking area, this type of dwelling is also known as *barraca* (Tatjer and Larrea 2011).

The word *chabola* is likely to originate from the Basque word *txabola* dating back to the 1800s to denote low-quality peasant housing in central Spain (El Pensamiento Español 1869). In the Spanish capital Madrid, housing for rural migrants was at that time called *choza*, a word with an equivalent meaning but typical from southern Spain (Luque Revuelto and Pulido Jurado 2014). This precarious housing has been documented in the city's northern and southern peripheries since the first half of the nineteenth century (Diez de Baldeon 1983; Pallol Trigueros 2011; Vicente Albarrán 2011). It was outlawed by the authorities within the municipal limits of Madrid in 1898 on the grounds that it was a threat to public health, public order and the city's reputation (Manzano Gómez 2022). However, during the first decades of the twentieth century, more precarious dwellings, often built with waste materials, re-emerged illegally around the city. They became the object of frequent demolition operations by the public authorities, which helped push self-constructed housing further out to the suburbs, outside of the municipal borders (Manzano Gómez 2022). In 1924, national minimum housing standards and urban planning measures were established, which finally banned informal dwellings nationwide. Since then, such housing, built for survival, began to be popularly known as *chabolas* (Rodriguez Chumillas 2010).

After the Spanish Civil War (1936–9), the construction of *chabolas* acquired enormous importance. Rural–urban migration and inadequate

Figure 11.2.1 *Chabolas*, around 1960. © Archivo Regional de la Comunidad de Madrid, Fondo Martín Santos Yubero.

living conditions gave rise to a massive suburbanisation process in larger Spanish cities. In Madrid, in the locations approved in the 1946 prohibited housing land uses, landowners began to sell vacant land plots at lower prices. Yet tenants built housing on them nonetheless, despite having agreed to the terms of the rent-to-buy contracts, which made them liable for any non-compliance with the law (Canosa Zamora and Rodriguez Chumillas 1985). An increasing number of rural immigrants began to build houses during the nights or at weekends to avoid police checks, often without fully owning the land (Montes Mieza et al. 1976; Burbano 2015). At the same time, people were also building homes clandestinely on vacant land, often around areas where illegal housing already existed (Mancha 2018). The illegal dwellings built on legally acquired land were also known as *casas bajas*. This expression had been used since the nineteenth century to denote popular self-built housing legally developed in Madrid's periphery (Vorms 2017) and continued to be used to identify less marginal *chabola* areas.

During the Franco regime (1939–75), the way of life of the *chabola* dwellers was often denoted as a social and cultural pathology (Vorms 2017), reprising the 'scientific racism' representations about pre-Spanish Civil War shantytowns (Manzano Gómez 2021).

In 1945, approximately 150,000 people were living in *chabolas* on the outskirts of Madrid (Comisaría de Urbanismo 1945). In the 1950s, public policies such as the Plan de Urgencia Social ('Social Emergency Plan') and the Plan de Absorción del Chabolismo ('Chabolismo Absorption Plan') aimed to relocate the slum inhabitants and make space for the development of legally approved urban planning (Sambricio 1999; Tamayo Palacios 2011; Vorms 2013, 2017). However, the constant arrival of new populations and the development of new *chabola* neighbourhoods kept the number of *chabola* units stable at about 32,000 well into 1970s (Archivo Regional de Madrid. File 251208/5, 1960, Ministerio de la Vivienda 1977). To protect themselves from slum clearings and private urban planning management (Kreibich 2000; Manzano Gómez and Castrillo Romón 2019), residents formed neighbourhood associations (Castells 1974; Villasante et al. 1989; Schierstaedt 2016; Ofer 2017). The movements to defend the rights of *chabola* dwellers took hold in most of the country's large and medium cities.

In the 'transition' to democracy period after the death of the dictator Francisco Franco in 1975, the fight for housing rights and neighbourhood improvements resulted in the Plan de Barrios en Remodelación ('Neighbourhoods under Remodelling Plan'), carried out in Spanish main cities, but especially relevant in Madrid (Ministerio de la Vivienda 1977). In the late 1970s and the 1980s, the authorities built 38,000 housing units in Madrid alone and rehoused about 150,000 people from deprived neighbourhoods and shantytowns (Aguilera 2021) by constructing subsidised private housing in accordance with the guidelines by the neighbourhood associations (Kreibich 2000). However, the socio-economic

Figure 11.2.2 *Chabolas* in 1981. © Juan Gallego Sanz.

criteria for allocating new housing systematically excluded the Roma population, which generally had lower incomes (Nogués Sáez 2010). The demolition of *chabolas* and the failure to rehouse the Roma population led to the growth of new shantytown areas, constructed more precariously than previously due to the risk of new demolitions (Aguilera 2021).

The public notions linking shantytowns to social marginality were exacerbated by the association of these spaces with a growing drug problem, which led to racist revolts against the *chabola* dwellers (Nogués Sáez 2010). In an effort to control shantytowns, the government developed racialised policies, still in place today, directed not directly at the poor but at the 'culturally different' (Aguilera 2021). Under these policies, the *chabolas* inhabited by the Roma were eradicated and the dwellers relocated to prefabricated houses in areas called Barrios de Tipologia Especial ('Special Typology Neighbourhoods'), far from urban centres. Under the auspices of rehousing dwellers 'without traumatic shocks' and 'avoiding conflicts' with the rest of society, these operations freed up land for legal urban development and strengthened the marginalisation of these areas and their population even further (Lago Ávila 2014). However, new *chabola* neighbourhoods continued to emerge – in 1988 there were still more than a thousand of them around Madrid (Aguilera 2021). The demolitions continued in the 1990s and 2000s when the displaced population was relocated to Cañada Real Galeana, a shantytown existing outside the city since the 1960s and consisting of 11,000 inhabitants in 2012. Despite decades of government effort to eradicate them, *chabola* neighbourhoods continue to exist in Spain. They have been recently studied in the regions of Galicia (Iglesias 2021) and Andalusia (Torres Gutiérrez 2011), but there is no current countrywide analysis. Recent research revealed the existence of new shantytowns built near larger farms, housing agricultural workers (García Padilla 2020).

Demolitions without relocation have recently taken place in the Cañada Real Galeana (Álvarez Agüí 2017) and other shantytowns in the metropolitan periphery of Madrid (Álvarez-De Andrés 2020). A hundred years after the *chabolas* were outlawed, the eradication policies have reduced this type of housing to its minimal expression. However, they have also made its legal status precarious, weakening its inhabitants and exposing them to a constant risk of eviction. Moreover, a new type of informal housing could be replacing *chabolismo*. In the absence of social housing and in the face of the historical, progressive suppression of self-help housing processes, increasingly the only option for populations unable to access the private real estate market is to squat in vacant buildings (Manzano Gómez and Castrillo Romón 2019).

11.3 *Samozakhvat* (Kyrgyzstan)
Eliza Isabaeva
Department of Social Anthropology, University of Zurich, Switzerland

Samozakhvat, literally, 'self-seizure' (*sam* – self and *zakhvat* – seizure), is a Russian term, designating the practice of unauthorised land grabbing in Kyrgyzstan. Although *samozakhvat* can also refer to the seizure of buildings (often government administrative buildings – see also *squatting*, 5.1 Volume 2 and *Schwarzwohnen*, 5.2 Volume 2), in Kyrgyzstan it is predominantly linked to land (*zemlia*) and land squatting (*zakhvat zemel'*). People who practise *samozakhvat* are known as *zakhvatchiki* (literally, 'grabbers') and their settlements are referred to as *zhany konush* in Kyrgyz, or new-builds (*novostroika*). Three waves of squatting can be distinguished.

The first mass land occupation in Bishkek, the capital and largest city in Kyrgyzstan, took place at the end of the 1980s and early 1990s. Following the dissolution of the Soviet Union, unemployed youth from rural areas came to Bishkek in search of employment (Hatcher 2015, Mambetaliev 2016). Lacking housing possibilities, rural youth occupied land plots, formed settlements and demanded formalisation of the

Figure 11.3.1 Ak Zhar squatter settlement to the north of Bishkek. © Eliza Isabaeva.

settlements from the government. The settlements were legalised, and their dwellers registered as Bishkek residents shortly after having claimed the plots. In the early 2000s, the high prices of private property encouraged massive land squatting for the second time. Internal migrants, who after living in Bishkek for several years had not been able to improve their chances of purchasing urban property, began to settle on the outskirts of the capital city. These settlers have likewise managed to formalise their property and register their settlements after several years.

The latest large land seizure in Bishkek took place in the regime change after the Tulip Revolution in March 2005, when President Askar Akayev was forced to resign amid allegations of corruption and authoritarianism. Similar to the previous cases, *samozakhvat* resulted in the emergence of several new shantytown settlements. However, this time achieving the legalisation of the property became more difficult. Opponents of the squatting practice argued that such an expansion of Bishkek would be burdensome for the city's infrastructure and budget and that the unauthorised *samozakhvat* was not a legal act. Considered to be illegal, these settlements were earmarked for demolition. Initial threats notwithstanding, the demolitions have not yet taken place, and the settlers' struggle to obtain property documents, recognition and inclusion into the formal state structures are still acute and relevant issues.

At present, most of the grabbers are urban dwellers who cannot afford urban property or long-term rent and settle on cities' peripheries (see also *favela*, 5.5 Volume 2 and *campamento*, 5.6 Volume 2). The large Kyrgyz cities of Bishkek and Osh have seen geographic expansion as well as demographic growth due to the emergence of squatter settlements on the city fringes. In Bishkek, an estimated 300,000 residents live in approximately 50 peripheral settlements that have emerged in different times since the collapse of the Soviet Union, according to some sources (Shambetov 2015; Ivashenko 2016). According to others, the estimates are down to 168,000 dwellers in 26 settlements (Nasritdinov et al. 2015: 152).

Seen from these developments, *samozakhvat* around Bishkek serves mainly to provide residence and represents an alternative way of obtaining otherwise inaccessible private housing in Bishkek. Due to violating the state law, *zakhvatchiki* have a bad reputation and tend to be viewed as criminals or lawbreakers. This attitude has resulted in the state neglecting the welfare of the Bishkek squatter settlers and their living conditions. The shanty towns that emerged after 2005 lack both material and social infrastructure: the roads are unpaved, there is no sewage system, the electricity and drinking water provision is incomplete, there are no schools, kindergartens or medical services in the area, and waste is not collected. The residents have to provide vital resources such as lighting and water themselves and travel long distances to reach schools or hospitals in the neighbouring formalised settlements or in the city.

Poor living conditions of illegal settlement residents as well as their 'illegal' existence and ensuing invisibility to state authorities have featured heavily in the media covering shanty towns in Bishkek (Abdykalykova 2013; Timofeyenko 2014). Acknowledging the illicit act of squatting, media reports seemed largely sympathetic towards the residents of new-builds (*novostroika*), drawing the public's attention to their hardship and social problems. Rarely have they been depicted as marginalised people and instigators of riots (Mitenko 2011). This has not always been the case. During the mass land squatting following the Tulip Revolution, the popular *Vechernii Bishkek* newspaper described squatters and the urban poor negatively, as *samozakhvatchiki*, and emphasised the authority of the law against illegal acts of squatting.

To politicians, the growing number of *novostroika* residents represent an attractive electoral site. Kyrgyzstan still uses the old Soviet electoral system, by which voters vote in their places of registration. While some residents possess a temporary voter registration or are registered at the address of their relatives, many *novostroika* residents lack such registration in Bishkek and are unable to vote. Amendments of the electoral law for national presidential elections partially resolved this by introducing two special voter application forms for unregistered residents. One allowed a vote to be cast at any polling station, the other enabled voters to add their name to the voting register in case they did not find their name. During election campaigning, the *novostroika* settlements are frequently a target of political promises to resolve the settlers' pressing problems. However, elections for local office (the Bishkek City Council), more important for the particular issues faced by *novostroika* residents, remain subject to mandatory residence registration.

Legalisation of squatter settlements is one of dwellers' major concerns, but the argument of public agencies (regional or city architecture offices, planning agencies and construction departments) poses a serious obstacle. They claim that many new settlements are located on hazardous sites such as close to a landfill, on potentially explosive gas pipelines or under high-voltage power mains. Facing residents' unwillingness to relocate, state agencies drafted a document, requesting the residents to relinquish their right to state protection should such a disaster occur. In a settlement where I conducted my fieldwork, many dwellers have signed this document. They perceived the threats described by the state agencies as a pretext for allowing their eviction and signed the document to prevent it. Squatters have also continued to demand the provision of basic infrastructure to improve their lives and property documents to secure land tenure. Their demands took the form of protests, roadblocks, unannounced visits to influential politicians and so on. Given the absence of public resettlement policies or affordable housing programmes, and strong political pressures by the squatter-settlement dwellers, these settlements will likely be legalised in the near future.

11.4 *Zaniato* (Abkhazia and Nagorno-Karabakh, Caucasus)
Andrea Peinhopf
Department of Social Sciences, Northumbria University, UK

The *zaniato* principle (literally, 'taken' or 'occupied') denotes an informal right of trophy acquisition of real estate in Abkhaz, one of Georgia's breakaway regions. It became widespread during and after the Georgian–Abkhaz war in 1992–3, which was fought between so-called Abkhazian 'separatists' and Georgian government forces and resulted in a mass flight of the Georgian population from Abkhazia and a large-scale redistribution of the abandoned properties among the remaining residents. On a 'first come, first served' basis, people entered empty homes and claimed ownership by writing *zaniato* (often followed by the surname of the occupier) in Russian at the entrance gate or on the walls of a dwelling (Peinhopf 2021). There is evidence that the term and practice was also used in the conflict over Nagorno-Karabakh between ethnic Armenians and Azerbaijani troops in 1988–94 (Day.Az 2021). Beyond the former Soviet Union, the principle has been documented in Cyprus, where it is closely related to the Turkish-Cypriot term *ganimet* (plunder) (Navaro-Yashin 2012; Bryant 2014). Historically, it can be linked to military traditions of looting and trophy taking, now prohibited under international law (ICRC n.d.). Although it occurred primarily in the immediate post-war period, the 'occupied' principle has had long-lasting effects not only on Georgian–Abkhaz relations, but also those among the Abkhaz themselves.

In September 1993, a 13-month war ended with the victory of the pro-Abkhaz forces and the mass flight of the local Georgian population from Abkhazia (HRW 1995). Subsequently, their houses were either destroyed or appropriated by ethnic Abkhazians as a reward for defeating the enemy and became known as trophy houses (*trofeinye doma*) (Peinhopf 2021). Witnesses generally describe the redistribution of property as chaotic and unregulated. A Russian family living in a Soviet apartment bloc

Figure 11.4.1 At the time of the author's fieldwork, there were no more visible signs of *zaniato* in Abkhazia. This photograph was taken in Shusha, Nagorno-Karabakh, where Armenians occupied houses of displaced Azeris after the war in the early 1990s. © Parviz Polukhzada.

remembered the occupation of their neighbouring flat as follows: 'One day, a young man showed up and told me that it was now his and that I should tell this to other people. Later he put a note on the door and then sold it to the current occupants' (Peinhopf 2021). On the surface, these takeovers were seen as justified responses to earlier occupations by Georgian troops in the territories under their control. As an Abkhaz resident, whose flat was occupied by Georgian soldiers during the war, explained:

> One evening a group of thieves broke into our house. The next day, a 'good' Georgian neighbour showed up and said, 'you can't stay here, let me help you escape, I will look after your flat'. After the war, it happened the other way around: Georgians left their keys with neighbours hoping they would be able to return and maintain their property. (Peinhopf 2021)

However, field research conducted by the author in 2017–8 established that not all cases were socially acceptable. While there was an understanding that those whose homes were destroyed during the war had no choice but to 'take' vacant properties, others were seen as using the *zaniato* principle to enrich themselves by occupying, and then selling, multiple dwellings. These sales usually took the form of informal transactions based on private agreements that were not registered with the de facto authorities. Moreover, people targeted not only the so-called 'Georgian' houses, but all kinds of industrial enterprises, raising questions about redistributive justice. According to an Abkhaz man in his late 60s:

> The [occupation of] Georgian houses was one thing, but some people occupied whole guest houses or factories. Take the hotel *Inter-Sukhum* as an example ... I remember, after the war I went inside and saw a couple of guys sitting there. I asked them, 'What were you fighting for? For the hotel or your homeland?' They hadn't built anything themselves or paid a single penny; I don't see how they deserved it. Why do they deserve it and I don't? (Peinhopf 2021)

The redistribution of property according to the *zaniato* principle thus produced a new, privileged segment of society that came to be known as the new Abkhaz (*novye abkhaztsy*). Like the new Russians who are said to have become rich by dubious means and are known for their lavish lifestyle, the new Abkhaz symbolised an unprecedented, overt materialism at the expense of the traditional Abkhaz values of modesty, humility and self-restraint. As a result, they increasingly attracted resentment and mockery from their less well-off co-ethnics. As an older Abkhaz woman once joked, 'The Abkhaz are a nation that likes to adopt bad things from others. For example, the Georgians who lived here had a good life and were working – what we took from them is the "showing off" but not the working [laughs]' (Peinhopf 2021). Similar to what was observed in Northern Cyprus, there was a concern that post-war looting gave rise to a culture of occupation, in which possessions were simply taken rather than earned through one's own work, thus corrupting communal values (Navaro-Yashin 2012; Bryant 2014).

Nearly three decades after the war, the effects of the practice continue to linger on. One example is the ruination of Abkhazia's built environment, which can only partially be explained by wartime destruction. The ubiquity of ruins and abandoned, overgrown spaces has become a defining feature of Abkhazia's landscape. While many abandoned houses appear ownerless because of their decrepit state, most of them are in fact taken rather than simply a 'dead matter' (Stoler 2008: 196). Although the de facto authorities officially nationalised many abandoned buildings after the war, by that time the majority had already been informally claimed. As their ownership remains disputed, numerous buildings – including architectural icons – are left to decay (Zavodskaia 2014). A prominent case is the Soviet-era restaurant *Amra*, which has been neglected despite popular demands for its restoration. Officially owned by a state agency, *Amra* was bought by an investor from an informal owner, who, although willing to restore it, lacks the documents necessary to officially register his ownership. Since neither the investor nor the state have been able to preserve the site, it remains closed off by barricades due to its poor condition (Sharia 2017b).

Another outcome of the *zaniato* principle, whereby some ended up with several properties and others – especially those less involved in the fighting – claimed nothing at all, is a paradoxical housing crisis, with empty dwellings across the city on the one hand, and young families lacking accommodation on the other (JAMnews 2016; Sharia 2017a). One of the areas in question is the so-called 'New District' on the outskirts of the capital Sukhumi, where a number of Soviet-era housing blocks have remained vacant. In recent years, the local media reported several cases of young families – usually from rural backgrounds – who moved into empty properties without legal rights. Having come to the city in search of better employment opportunities but finding themselves without

Figure 11.4.2 Terrace of the abandoned restaurant Amra. © Andrea Peinhopf.

accommodation or state welfare, they took matters into their own hands and occupied houses which others had acquired through occupation during and after the war (JAMnews 2016; Sharia 2017a). As a journalist commented, those who grew up after the war were not always willing to accept the post-war redistribution as legitimate: 'They didn't take part in it for obvious reasons. Now, they suggest making yet another redistribution of property, and they can't understand why they aren't allowed to do what the older generation was allowed to do' (JAMnews 2016).

What this shows is that Abkhazia's poor socio-economic recovery over the 30 years that have passed since the end of the war in 1993 cannot be explained exclusively by such external factors as the lack of international recognition due to its disputed status. It is also a result of internal dynamics, including ongoing property disputes. According to a civil society activist and blogger, 'it is thanks to the "occupied" principle that half of the country is still in ruins. … how many decades must pass for the state to finally put things in order in this area?' (Venediktova 2018).

11.5 *Xiaochanquan* (China)
Cinzia Losavio
Géographie-cités Research Center, University Paris 1
Panthéon-Sorbonne, France

The Chinese term *xiǎochǎnquán* (小产权) literally means 'small property rights' (SPR) or 'limited property rights' but is generally understood as 'small properties'. Contrary to what one might think, *xiǎochǎnquán* is not a legal concept, but a grassroots way to refer to a recent, yet already widespread form of Chinese informal settlement, whose property rights are 'smaller' (weaker) than those of full commercial housing. *Xiǎochǎnquán* designates housing built on collectively owned rural land, mainly developed in peri-urban areas and 'urban villages' (城中村 *chéngzhōngcūn*), namely rural villages that have been encircled by expanding urban settlements. When purchased by outsiders – internal migrants lacking the residence permit (户口, *hùkǒu*) for the place where the SPR housing is located – the transaction can neither be registered by the local government office nor granted legal titling.

The informal status of *xiǎochǎnquán* is an outcome of the controversial development process of the land upon which these buildings are built. Resulting from the Maoist legacy of a rural-urban dual society, a dual ownership system has been legally established in China since the beginning of the 1980s, in order to regulate its real estate market: urban

Figure 11.5.1 Small property rights housing on village residential plot in Zhuhai, Guangdong province. © Cinzia Losavio.

land is owned by the state and rural land is collectively owned by villagers. Subsequent to the 1998 Land Administration Law, only state-owned land-use rights became freely transferable and only state-owned land could be allocated for construction development, while the use of collectively owned rural land remained under tight restrictions for transfers and construction. Hence, only housing built upon urban land can be purchased or sold legally. In rural areas, housing property rights are inalienable and the only legal way to make collectively owned land available for construction is to convert its status to state-owned land through a land requisition process, which requires approval by the Land Resources Department, the Urban Planning Department and the Construction Department. Once legally converted, the land can be transferred to real estate developers for construction and sale, thus systematically excluding its previous owner from the land development process.

In the case of SPR housing, village committees and individual households bypass the formal conversion process and spontaneously proceed to land construction and sale. In this sense, SPR housing transactions generate an informal market, whereby exchanges are not recognised and protected by law (Shen and Tu 2014). This informal market does not only exist on the outskirts of cities, but it has also developed predominantly in urban villages that have mushroomed across most Chinese large cities. In fact, although these rural knots have gradually been sewn into the urban fabric, urban villages retain the collective ownership of rural land as well as their original management model, being administered independently of the city governments.

According to regulations, collectively owned land can only be used by individual villagers for the purpose of residence, agricultural production, township enterprises and public facilities. Such subdivision of rural land use determines the three main types of *xiǎochǎnquán*:

Figure 11.5.2 An urban village in Guangzhou city core being swallowed up by urban encroachment. A group of migrant tenants was still living in what was left of the village before being expelled. Guangdong province, December 2016. © Cinzia Losavio.

- resettlement houses (回迁房, *huíqiān fáng*) – housing built on village residential plots as part of redevelopment projects and sold by villagers' households to outsiders;
- greenhouse-farm houses (大棚房, *dàpéng fáng*)) – housing built on agricultural land; and
- large-scale housing compounds (统建楼, *tǒngjiàn lóu*) – uniformly constructed buildings, built on township enterprises' land or village public facilities' land, where construction and sale involve village shareholding co-operative companies that supply the land and real estate developers that finance the projects.

Depending on the type of SPR housing, the quality and layout of the building vary considerably and can sometimes be more sophisticated than those of formal commercial housing, possibly due to the involvement of architects and designers. These professionals join the heterogeneous network of stakeholders including individual village households, villagers' committees, village co-ops, real estate developers and others. As a recent study has revealed, even the Chinese military actively contributes to the development of the *xiǎochǎnquán* housing market (He et al. 2019). Therefore, if compared to many informal settlements around the world, the informal nature of SPR housing cannot exclusively be associated with inadequate housing standards, poverty or the involvement of disadvantaged groups.

The SPR market primarily targets the Chinese 'sandwich group' (夹心层, *jiāxīn céng*), which encompasses low- and medium-income families as well as internal unregistered migrants squeezed between the soaring prices of the formal real estate market and their ineligibility to highly restrictive social housing programmes. Previous studies on the residential choices of internal migrants in China have focused on the private rental stock in urban villages. Yet, SPR housing has opened a venue for migrants' homeownership in these urban grey spaces. By circumventing the land requisition process, *xiǎochǎnquán* developers do not pay the land conveyance fee or any other taxes linked to it, significantly reducing the costs of development. SPR housing is sold at 40 to 60 per cent of the formal commercial housing price (Cong et al. 2007; Wang and Sun 2014). SPR is perceived to be the only affordable option for homeownership for an estimated 71 million households, or 250 million people in China (Wang et al. 2014).

On 31 December 2007, the Central Committee of the Chinese Communist Party and the State Council used the expression *xiǎochǎnquán* for the first time in an official document (the '2008 No. 1 Document',

China's first, and therefore the most important, policy statement of the year), recognising it as a national issue. Because of its unregulated nature, official data on SPR housing are unavailable. However, scattered empirical research, local surveys and media reports have revealed the huge scale of the phenomenon. It is reported that by 2007, SPR housing could have accounted for at least 20 per cent, or more than 6 billion of the total 33 billion square metres, of Chinese village/township housing construction areas (Guo and Cai 2009; Paik and Lee 2012). The city of Shenzhen (in Guangdong province) is considered to be China's biggest SPR market and covering half of its total constructed area in 2012 (Qiao 2017), compared to 30 per cent of Xi'an, 20 per cent of Beijing and Chengdu, and 15 per cent of Zhengzhou (Tsao 2012). *Xiǎochǎnquán* has spread across China, from Guangdong province, where between the late 1980s and early 1990s, despite the absence of a clear national jurisdiction on rural land, local governments endorsed the informal commodification of rural land to boost urbanisation and economic development in the first special economic zones, such as Shenzhen and Zhuhai (Qiao 2015; Losavio 2022). Such initiatives played a dual role. On the one hand, the informal transfer of rural land served as an incentive to attract foreign and domestic capital and create companies; on the other, its informal development relieved local governments from the onerous role of providing housing to the millions of internal unregistered migrant workers.

The scale and endurance of *xiǎochǎnquán* market invalidates the theory that an efficient market economy cannot form or exist outside a clearly defined property rights system (Barros 2016; De Soto 2000). Informal property rights do affect the property value of *xiǎochǎnquán*, but do not seem to be less secure than formal property rights. Apart from being outlawed by the relevant land and housing regulations, SPR shares analogous development and sale mechanisms, stakeholders and assets with the formal housing market, functioning more as an extension to it rather than its opposite.

11.6 *Chuồng cọp* (Vietnam)
Francisco García Moro
Universitat Politècnica de València, Spain

Chuồng cọp, or 'Tiger cage' is a casual term used in Hanoi to denote illegal extensions added to apartment buildings, thus creating an exuberant streetscape with its own idiosyncrasy and identity. These extensions originate in the Khu thập thể neighbourhoods in Hanoi (KTT), where in the period of 1954–85 'communal dormitories' were built to accommodate the inflow of rural workers relocating to the city. To avoid commuting, these complexes were built close to industrial estates where labour was needed, such as Thượng Đình, Minh Khai or Vĩnh Tuy in the Southwest belt of Hanoi. Both were, until then, peripheral areas dotted by small communal villages (Phuong 2011). These housing blocks were built with the assistance of Soviet architects (Logan 2000). They resembled *Khrushchevka microrayons*, a minimalist architectural style, named after Nikita Khrushchev, the leader of the Soviet Union. He advocated modest but individual living, in opposition to communal flats and Stalinist classicist architecture (Reid 2006). Housing complexes like Kim Liên were built using concrete precast panels on the basis of technology imported from the USSR (Pennec and Ng 2009). In accordance with the Soviet planning guidelines, new neighbourhoods were conceived as autonomous communities, equipped with amenities like schools and markets, and supervised by the *phường* (ward) officers. The design and supervision of KTT housing estates was taken over by Vietnamese architects from 1970s (Schenk 2013).

With the launch of Đổi Mới economic reforms in 1985, the Vietnamese government acknowledged that the Khu thập thể housing model was no longer capable of accommodating the migrants moving to Hanoi (Tran 2016). Economic development was prioritised over strict land law enforcement, implicitly acknowledging that existing regulations were not adaptive enough to respond to the challenges of a fast-changing society. By 2007, the population of Hanoi had reached 3.2 million inhabitants. The threefold increase from one million in 1967 was mainly as a result of the flow of rural migrants into the city (Ledent 2002). Official attitudes became more accommodating of the economic interests and private property (Anh 2017), often resulting in turning a blind eye to the illegal constructions and informal settlements of migrants (Chen 2015). This tolerance gave rise to 'tube houses' (*Nhà ống' Phố Cổ*), narrow but verticalised structures with several floors built on small plots of land.

Since the late 1980s, KTT neighbourhoods have been privatised and subjected to intense re-adaptation process. Apartments were either demolished or sold to tenants through cooperatives (Cerise and Shannon 2010). Privatised properties were then extended individually in a disorderly manner through the addition of apparently shabby structures attached to the façades, sarcastically named 'Tiger cages' (Tran 2016). The common areas on the ground floor were encroached upon by multiple retail stalls, cafés, beauty salons and all sorts of repair shops. The top floors expanded sideways in all directions. The resulting amalgamation

Figure 11.6.1 Khu thập thể Trung Tự. Hanoi, 2019. © Francisco García Moro.

of structures that fill the spaces between existing blocks is known as *xây chen* (Xia 2015).

The Japan International Cooperation Agency (2014) estimated that up to 65 per cent of housing stock built between 1975 and 2009 in

Hanoi lacked legal permits, which implies that approximately 80 per cent of housing transactions remained unregistered and formed part of the informal economy. The emergence of these apparently chaotic constructions was not accidental. It was made possible by a tacit social contract between stakeholders (Geertman 2007). This social agreement consisted of, on the one hand, a precarious but sustained equilibrium among apartment owners who had benefited from the opportunity to develop their property, and on the other, ward officials, who had turned a blind eye to the unauthorised developments (Quinn 2014). Guided by unwritten rules and common understandings that the encroachment should not surpass certain limits, the property owners were careful not to create an open challenge to the city authorities and stay under the radar. The dimensions and configurations of each individual apartment thus reflected a compromise between the government's need to assert its effective authority, the agreement among neighbours and the owner's own status and capacity.

A *Chuồng cọp* comes in a variety of forms and functions. Its actual configuration depends on the structural features of the building, resulting from a tension between formal constraints and informal requirements. A 'tiger cage' may range from a simple balcony equipped with some extra space for flowerpots and laundry, to full liveable compartments, stretching out up to 3 metres from the original façade. These box-like structures are held together by a reinforced steel bar and the floor slabs are supported by steel frames. Windows are made of scraps of standard prefabricated material. Outer surfaces are often made of corrugated sheets, but they can also be made of brickwork or wicker lattice supported by a wire mesh – a technique with a local look. It is not uncommon to see further ventures – 'daughter' extensions of previous extensions – that ultimately endanger the building's stability and push the capacity of the building to its limit due to a lack of formal control over the load that a *Chuồng cọp* may add to an existing structure. Window-based extensions block evacuation in case of fire, while the ground floor encroachments make it difficult for emergency vehicles to access the building. Unregulated drilling and fixtures undermine the joints of the prefabricated concrete walls and cause leaks, contributing to further decay (Anh 2017).

In more prosperous KTTs in good locations, extensions feature lavish interiors and fine furnishings. However, their exterior appearance remains functional, with still rare concessions to aesthetics. This may be due to a combination of an extremely pragmatic approach to habitation standards seen in most Asian cities (for the case of Hong Kong see Wolf et al. 2005) and the tendency to avoid flaunting excessive wealth within small-scale communities. Nowadays, KTTs such as Kim Liên or Giảng Võ have evolved into dynamic neighbourhoods that house multiple social groups and flourishing small businesses. Despite persisting safety concerns, the 'tiger cages' of Hanoi have become a testimony of inventive spirit, entrepreneurship and resilience.

The Vietnamese government has attempted to conceal these informal dwelling practices as embarrassing evidence of the shortcomings of Hanoi's urban policies. Recently however, the state media has reappraised their status by recognising them as monuments of early economic reforms with environmental and cultural value. In 2017, *Nhân Dân*, the official newspaper of the Communist Party of Vietnam, featured an interview with the Uruguayan economist, Martin Rama, who praised the community spirit of these neighbourhoods, their values and called for their preservation and upgrade (*Nhân Dân* 2017). The collective 'Arts build communities', founded by artist Tạ Thu Hương, used the 'tiger cages' as canvases for the display of typical Hanoian imagery in a similar fashion to acclaimed historic districts in the region, such as Penang, Songkla or Melacca. Exhibitions like '8M2' and 'Thay hình đổi mặt' ('Changing faces') by artist Nguyễn Thế Sơn (Nguyễn 2019) were set up to record and celebrate these neighbourhoods of informal architecture before their disappearance leaves room for modern private developments.

11.7 *Divlja gradnja* (Countries of Former Yugoslavia)
Fynn-Morten Heckert
Alumnus, School of Slavonic and East European Studies, UCL, UK and Centre for Southeast European Studies, University of Graz, Austria

'Wild', 'black' or illegal construction (bosn./hr./mtn./srb.: *divlja* or *bespravna gradnja*, slo: *črna gradnja*, al. *ndërtim i paligjshëm*, in the following: *divlja gradnja*) can be defined as the construction of buildings, both residential and commercial, without the prior acquisition of a construction permit, or by modifying a building in a way that it exceeds the originally issued licence. It can also refer to the unlawful change of purpose of a building (Zegarac 1999: 365). *Divlja gradnja* is widespread in the countries which comprised the former Yugoslavia and takes place in relation to nearly all types of buildings, including tourist accommodation, religious buildings (Xharra 2012) and other business-related buildings like shopping malls.

Divlja gradnja can be traced back to the beginning of the twentieth century, as a reaction to the restrictive ownership rules in Belgrade, which put working-class families in a situation in which acquiring property in a legal manner was barely possible (Grubović 2006: 72 f.). *Divlja gradnja*, however, gained momentum as a countrywide phenomenon from the 1960s onwards, with not only individual houses, but entire settlements built informally (Archer 2017: 143 f.). This development can be explained with the urbanisation policy pursued by the Communist regime, as rural populations were incentivised to migrate to urban centres to seek employment at socially owned enterprises, which provided access to certain benefits, such as to health services, and free education. This led to a massive influx of rural migrants to the cities (for Belgrade see: Grubović 2006: 87; for Sarajevo: Kriegl 2011: 163; for Skopje: UNECE and International Federation of Surveyors 2015: 89 f; for Zagreb: Zlatar 2014: 150).

The shortage of housing was exacerbated by natural disasters, such as the earthquake of 1962, which destroyed much of the city of Skopje and left about 80,000 people homeless (UNECE and International Federation of Surveyors 2015: 89 f.). The socialist city authorities were unable to provide enough housing units and thus, many of those who became homeless resorted to 'self-help' by constructing homes without acquiring a construction licence (Grubović 2006: 101 f.; UNECE and International Federation of Surveyors 2015: 89 f.).

Figure 11.7.1 Informal settlement Malo Brdo in the heart of Podgorica, Montenegro. © Fynn-Morten Heckert.

But besides the actual shortage, the authorities were also unable to accommodate the wish of many dwellers for individual housing in suburban areas. As collective housing was favoured by urban authorities, individual housing projects were pushed into illegality (Zegarac 1999: 366; Grubović 2006: 96f). Moreover, following the Skopje earthquake and flooding in the 1960s, the state reconstruction project was focused on the production of collective housing. As many Skopje residents were not willing to leave their local communities and to resettle in the newly built apartment blocks, residents engaged in an informal (re)construction of property on the parcels of land they had lived on before (UNECE and International Federation of Surveyors 2015: 89f).

The wars of the 1990s triggered large migration flows, causing the steep increase of illegal constructions (Grubović 2006: 114). In Belgrade alone, the number of illegal buildings reached 200,000 by 1996 (Grubović 2006: 131). This led to problems both for the environment and the health of dwellers, as settlements often lacked basic infrastructure (Bajić et al. 2016: 3f), or were built on unsuitable land, such as in areas prone to landslides (Grubović 2006: 223 f; Martin-Diaz et al. 2015: 380).

On the other side of the coin there is the informal construction of luxury objects. A notorious example is the Dedinje neighbourhood of Belgrade, where Slobodan Milošević moved to in the late 1980s. Throughout the 1990s, the elite of Serbia, including the political elite and nouveau riche followed his example with the intention of elevating their social status. It was estimated that half of the buildings in the Savski Venac area, to which Dedinje belongs, were built bypassing the official regulations (Grubović 2006: 176–9). Illegal construction of luxurious residential buildings also took place on the Adriatic coast. For example, an informally constructed villa on the coastal line in Dalmatia attracted significant media attention in 2019 (Klaić Saulačić 2019).

In post-socialist Belgrade, politicians and administration massively profited from 'tolerating' the erection of informal settlements. In the area of Zemun, for instance, the ruling party sold state-owned land, which was not residential according to urban plans, without providing adequate infrastructure to residents (many of whom were refugees) (Grubović 2006: 223–5, 253). Business-related informal constructions have become a widespread phenomenon in the last 20 years, ranging from small kiosks to hotels and shopping centres. These commercial developments were realised in defiance of urban plans through informal channels and personal connections (Grubović 2006: 228–33; Pobrić and Robinson 2019: 286f.).

The tourism sector was especially prone to informal construction (for Bosnia see: Pobrić and Robinson 2018: 287; for Dalmatia: Klaić Saulačić

2019; for Montenegro: Müller and Lješković 2008). One of the reasons for this was a ban on land acquisition for foreigners in Montenegro before 2009, which made interested foreign developers enter informal agreements with landowners to build on their land. UNECE estimates that about 15 per cent of all informal buildings in Montenegro, mainly in the coastal area, belong to foreigners (UNECE and FIG 2015: 74). A second category of illegal tourist construction is related to persons having connections to long-standing Montenegrin President Milo Đukanović. These are characterised by grave violations of construction regulations, such as the construction of hotels in especially protected areas (for example, in the Bay of Kotor, a UNESCO World Heritage Site). Nevertheless, in recent years the governments in the region have launched initiatives designed to legalise informal buildings (UNECE and International Federation of Surveyors 2015).

11.8 *Vrtičkarstvo* (Slovenia)
Petra Matijevic
Journalist and independent researcher, Edinburgh, UK

In Slovenian cities, *vrtičkarstvo* is the practice of establishing and maintaining household garden plots, detached from the main place of residence. *Vrtički* (singular: *vrtiček*), meaning small gardens, are tended by residents of housing estates or lodgers in urban family homes. *Vrtičkarji* (singular: *vrtičkar*, female: *vrtičkarica*, *vrtičkarka*) do not have regular access to farmland or a second home and either formally rent or informally take over a plot of land. Surveys suggest that 5 per cent of all Ljubljanans (residents of the Slovenian capital) have an urban plot (Jamnik et al. 2009). Gardeners cultivate land of 50 to 500 square metres, temporarily or long-term, as formal members of an association or through an informal agreement with fellow gardeners. The diminutive term *vrtiček* (compare with *vrt* for garden, and *vrtnar*, *vrtnarica* for gardener) implies an amateur or inconsequential nature of the practice. Such a name, however, disguises its vital social role.

The type of land use analogous to *vrtiček* is called an 'allotment' in the UK, a *Schrebergarten* or *Kleingarten* in Germany, a 'community garden' in the USA, a *działka* in Poland (Sulima 2000), a *hobby kert* in Hungary (Czegledy 2002), a *bašta* in Bosnia and Herzegovina and a *dacha* in Russia and Belarus (Hervouet 2003; Caldwell 2011). The forms of this seemingly universal human activity are locally specific. The practice is contingent upon a number of factors: geographical givens, land-tenure systems and agricultural traditions, rates of rural–urban migration and immigration, formal housing provisions and economic climates. Urban gardening is contextual and highly adaptive.

In contrast to the out-of-town Russian *dachas* used as second homes, hundreds of small and dispersed vegetable *vrtički* sites can be found within walking distance of housing estates in both the inner city and the outskirts of Ljubljana. The geographic and environmental protection regimes have curbed the rate of urbanisation in Ljubljana and kept farmland within reach of residential zones. In contrast to allotments or *Schrebergärten*, *vrtički* are less likely to be organised by a formally recognised institution. *Vrtičkarji* most often cultivate land on the basis of an oral or assumed owner's consent (Jamnik et al. 2009).

Vrtički in Ljubljana can range from a miniature vegetable garden on the side of a railway track to an enclosed plot that houses a second-home cabin. At times, they will serve as a temporary first home for homeless or immigrant urbanites. The majority of garden sites contain dozens of intensively cultivated horticultural plots, accommodating a small shed, a canopy or a polytunnel. The tight proximity of plots encourages an internal system of governance, associated with supervision by an informal gatekeeper, commitment to hard work, the tidy appearance of the plot, a

Figure 11.8.1 View of a housing estate in Ljubljana from *vrtički*.
© Petra Matijevic.

sense of accountability to your immediate neighbours and the use of gossip as a social bond and corrective (Matijevic 2018: 128–59).

Vrtički started to emerge near modernist housing estates in Ljubljana in the late 1960s, following the increase in intra-Yugoslav migration and urbanisation. *Vrtičkarstvo* developed as a private, individual and bottom-up initiative to compensate for the shortcomings in the quality of planned formal housing. Ljubljanans utilised residual and less favourable social land (*družbena zemlja*) around the housing estates, forks of roads, areas under power lines, former landfills or flood-prone fields. Such *vrtičkarstvo* served Ljubljanans in a number of ways:

(a) it supplemented a lack of variety of fruit and vegetable crops available through formal retail channels, improved the quality of the household food supply and contributed to the winter stores;
(b) it provided meaningful work that gave Ljubljanans a sense of control over their lives, and enabled them to express themselves and keep the products of their labour;
(c) it expanded insufficient dwelling-size with a space for hosting and vacationing or a private retreat in the event of domestic fights, and it provided a temporary housing option for migrants, refugees and homeless people;
(d) it facilitated socialising with the neighbourhood community, child-rearing and child-minding, and
(e) it enabled the recycling of food-waste and reuse of clothes, household items and raw materials.

Closer investigation of the dynamics of *vrtičkarstvo* in times of increased unemployment, poverty and uncertainty (in the late 1980s, the 1990s and again after 2009) suggests that the practice not only balanced material shortages, but also made up for the lack of progress and social mobility. Working the soil mended the broken model of the good life by supplying a sense of continuity and certainty (Matijevic 2018: 211–35; 2022).

In the years after Slovenia's secession from Yugoslavia in 1991, *vrtičkarstvo* doubled in size (Simoneti 1997). On the one hand, the expansion followed the 1990s economic crisis and the increased number of migrants from former Yugoslavia. On the other, the land-restitution process threw property rights into temporary limbo, making squatting easier. Media coverage of the spread of the practice acquired a disdainful tone and drew parallels with informal housing settlements (Bogataj 1999). Since Slovenia joined the EU in 2004, local ideas about Europeanness transformed *vrtičkarstvo* into a symbol of dysfunctional governance that characterised

Slovenia's Yugoslav past. Curtailing *vrtičkarstvo* became a key indicator of success of any city administration. Since 2007, the City of Ljubljana has used two techniques to restrain the practice: removal and legalisation.

The area covered by *vrtički* has been reduced to its pre-independence levels (Mestna občina Ljubljana 2018) in three steps. First, the local government acquired the land used for *vrtičkarstvo* from private owners or from the national state. Second, bulldozers removed plot-holders' property from the site. Officials justified the removal by citing environmental, aesthetic or legal concerns. In a questionable legal move employed on one occasion, the city authorities instructed trespassers to remove their belongings themselves in order to avoid legal charges. When one such evacuation provoked an organised protest from the *vrtičkarji*, the news ended up on the front page of the national daily (Petkovšek 2008). Third, the city authorities began to legalise *vrtički* from 2009, when the Eurozone crisis roused the interest in *vrtičkarstvo* and the public agenda of a sustainable economy and green cities started to win EU grants. This last policy recognised *vrtičkarstvo* as a form of household-food self-provisioning only (Mestna občina Ljubljana 2018). Implementing it entailed ordering the measuring and harmonising of individual garden plots, selecting occupiers through an open call and issuing tenancy agreements.

These formal procedures have replaced the informal organisation of gardening sites and impeded the distribution of available plots. They have pushed *vrtičkarstvo* further into the corner: out of the public view, behind tall hedges, between tall buildings, into less populated areas. To hinder municipal attempts to identify, or contact *vrtičkarji*, garden supervisors on the remaining informal sites engage strictly person to person when considering new applicants, collecting rents or settling disputes.

Academic approaches to urban gardening and urban policies rarely see eye to eye. Researchers understand the practice as an indicator of broader trends and social issues yet tend to disregard the multipurpose nature of urban gardening. Narrow comparative analyses of local forms often fail to capture the social role of the practice. To illustrate, Alber and Kohler conclude, based on the reported harvest size alone, that the more productive gardeners in Eastern Europe grow vegetables out of poverty, while their Western European counterparts cultivate gardens as a hobby (2008). While surveys and (historical) aerial photography (Jamnik et al. 2009) are valuable for assessing the spread of the practice, figuring out the particular urban problems to which the practice responds is best achieved with (auto-)ethnography and life histories (Caldwell 2011; Smith and Jehlička 2013; Matijevic 2018, 2022). In contrast, local governments are more likely to treat urban gardening either as a problem in itself, or as a publicly administered panacea that can ameliorate any formal deficiency. What such approaches have in common is that they overlook the ambivalence of urban gardening – it is as much an urban problem as it is a solution. The challenge for policy, then, is to recognise urban gardening as a shadow companion to urbanisation and modernity and thus as a factor to include in formal policy-thinking.

11.9 *Informal housing of the rich* (Global)
Udo Grashoff
Department of History, University of Leipzig, Germany

Research on informal housing has focused primarily on analysing informality of the urban poor in the Global South. There is widespread informality in housing practices of affluent urbanites, but these practices have mostly been ignored by informality studies.

The first reason for this is that informal housing of the rich is less visible; it's not as iconic as *favelas* and shantytowns. As a result, it has been overlooked in the Global North, especially in the United States (Durst and Wegmann 2017).

The second reason for the disregard of informal housing of the affluent is that the focus of scholars of informal housing in the Global South is often accompanied by a neglect of regions where informal housing is not necessarily associated with poverty, such as the Global East and the Mediterranean region. In Italy, Croatia or Greece, normally seen as part of the Global North, informal housing has become a widespread urban development practice. Here, informality has a different function and meaning than in Africa or Latin America. Instead of low-income earners building on land owned by someone else, informal housing outside the Global South predominantly involves middle-class people, who build without public authorisation on plots they rightfully own.

The third reason is that there are fundamental differences in the moral assessment of informal housing, labelling informal housing of the poor as motivated by need, and the other by greed. So far, there exist only a few studies on informal housing beyond the notion of the self-help of the poor. A pioneering study on informal housing for high-income residents in the protected forest area of the eastern hills of Bogotá (Vieda Martínez and Chiodelli 2021) is a rare attempt to fill this research gap. The authors observe three important features of this informal practice – clustering, isolating and concealing. They note that informal housing of the rich is similar to living in gated communities, which makes it look like normal, formal housing of the rich. In a similar vein, widespread informal housing in the Mediterranean, in countries such as Albania, Egypt or

Israel, looks like normal middle-class housing, since the violation of land laws and building codes is hard to see.

Informality is primarily a normative notion, but even from a normative perspective, informal housing of the poor and the rich differ substantially. In order to integrate the unlawful housing practices of the affluent into the field of informality studies, it is necessary to adjust existing notions and make subtle distinctions. There is often no clear-cut boundary between need and greed, and planners must draw a fine line between the two when regulating informality. The preferred reaction to illegal practices aimed at tax evasion might be law enforcement. For informality driven by need, it might be advisable to tolerate it as 'justifiable noncompliance' (Alterman and Calor 2020).

However, the reality of informality of the rich is more complex. Apart from non-compliance, there are forms of 'calculated' informality in the Global North such as non-enforcement and deregulation (Durst and Wegmann 2017), which means passing the buck to public authorities and regulators. With its different manifestations and causes, the 'dark side of informality' (Chiodelli 2019) challenges and complements the somewhat one-sided image of informal housing as self-help of the poor or a weapon of the weak. It can be an expression of selfishness, asocial behaviour and of the abuse of power, too.

Bibliography to Chapter 11

Introduction: informal housing and beyond
Anthony Boanada-Fuchs and Vanessa Boanada Fuchs

Abrams, C. 1966. *Housing in the Modern World*. London: Faber and Faber.

Al Sayyad, N. and Roy, A. 2004. 'Urban Informality: Crossing Borders'. In *Urban Informality: Transnational Perspectives from the Middle East, Latin America and South Asia*, edited by N. Al Sayyad and A. Roy, 7–32. Lanham, MD: Lexington Books.

Berner, E. 2000. 'Poverty Alleviation and the Eviction of the Poorest: Towards Urban Land Reform in the Philippines'. *International Journal of Urban and Regional Research* 24(3): 554–66.

Boanada-Fuchs, A. 2021. *The Challenge of Slums: An Overview of Past Approaches to Tackle It*. Global Review Series on Informality. Brussels: Cities Alliance.

Boanada Fuchs V. and Boanada-Fuchs A. 2021. *Understanding Informality: Towards a Multi-dimensional Analysis of the Concept*. Brussels: Cities Alliance.

Bredenoord, J. and van Lindert, P. 2010. 'Pro-poor Housing Policies: Rethinking the Potential of Assisted Self-help Housing'. *Habitat International* 34(3): 278–87.

Bukhari, M. S. 1982. 'Squatting and the Use of Islamic Law: A Case Study of Land Occupation in Madinah Munawara, Saudi Arabia'. *Habitat International* 6(5): 555–63.

Cities Alliance and GIMLA. 2021. *Data and Slums – A Challenging Relationship*. Global Community of Practice Workshop, 8 October.

Drakakis-Smith, D. W. 1981. *Urbanisation, Housing, and the Development Process*. London: Croom Helm.

Ghertner, D. A. 2008. 'Analysis of New Legal Discourse behind Delhi's Slum Demolitions'. *Economic and Political Weekly* 57–66.
Habitat. 1976. The Vancouver Declaration on Human Settlements, United Nations Conference of Human Settlements, Vancouver, 31 May–11 June. https://sdgs.un.org/sites/default/files/documents/7252The_Vancouver_Declaration_1976.pdf
Harris, R. 2003. 'A Double Irony: The Originality and Influence of John F. C. Turner'. *Habitat International* 27(2): 245–9.
Hart, K. 1985. 'The Informal Economy'. *Cambridge Anthropology* 10(2): 54–8.
Hilbrandt, H. 2019. 'Everyday Urbanism and the Everyday State: Negotiating Habitat in Allotment Gardens in Berlin'. *Urban Studies* 56(2): 352–67.
Kombe, W. J. and Kreibich, V. 2000. 'Reconciling Informal and Formal Land Management: An Agenda for Improving Tenure Security and Urban Governance in Poor Countries'. *Habitat International* 24(2): 231–40.
Magnin, W. 1967. 'Latin American Squatter Settlements: A Problem and a Solution'. *Latin American Research Review* 2: 67–98.
Sa, H. and Haila, A. 2021. 'Urban Villagers as Real Estate Developers: Embracing Property Mind Through "Planting" Housing in North-east China'. *Housing Studies* 1–21.
Turner, J. F. C. 1977. *Housing by People: Towards Autonomy in Building Environments*. New York: Pantheon Books.
Ward, P. M. 1990. 'The Politics and Costs of Illegal Land Development for Self-help Housing in Mexico City'. In *The Transformation of Land Supply Systems in Third World Cities*, edited by P. Baross and J. van Der Linden, 133–68. Brookfield: Avebury.
Ward, P. M. 1976. 'The Squatter Settlement as Slum or Housing Solution: Evidence from Mexico City'. *Land Economics* (3): 330–46.
Yiftachel, O. 2009. 'Theoretical Notes on "Gray Cities": The Coming of Urban Apartheid?'. *Planning Theory* 8(1): 88–100.

11.1 *Colonias* (USA)
Michael J. Pisani

Barton, J., Permeter, E. R., Blum, E. S. and Marquez, R. R. 2015. 'Las Colonias in the 21st Century: Progress Along the Texas-Mexico Border'. www.dallasfed.org/~/media/documents/cd/pubs/lascolonias.pdf
Donelson, A. J. and Esparza, A. X. (eds) 2010. *The Colonias Reader: Economy, Housing, and Public Health in U.S.-Mexico Border Colonias*. Tucson: University of Arizona Press.
Donelson, A. J. and Esparza, A. X. 2016. *Colonias in Arizona and New Mexico: Border Poverty and Community Development Solutions*. Tucson: University of Arizona Press.
Durst, N. J. and Ward, P. M. 2014. 'Measuring Self-help Home Improvements in Texas Colonias: A Ten Year "Snapshot" Study'. *Urban Studies* 51: 2143–59.
Federal Reserve Bank of Dallas. 1996. 'Texas Colonias: A Thumbnail Sketch of the Conditions, Issues, Challenges and Opportunities'. *Federal Reserve Bank of Dallas*. www.dallasfed.org/~/media/documents/cd/pubs/colonias.pdf
Giusti, C. 2008. 'Nuestra Casa [Our House]: A New Model for Self-help & Improvement Along the Texas/Mexico Border'. *Texas Business Review* August: 1–5.
Richardson, C. and Pisani, M. J. 2012. *The Informal and Underground Economy of the South Texas Border*. Austin: University of Texas Press.
Richardson, C. and Pisani, M. J. 2017. *Batos, Bolillos, Pochos, and Pelados: Class and Culture on the South Texas Border*. Revised ed. Austin: University of Texas Press.
Taylor, S. 2019. 'Hidalgo County Asked to Pump Half a Million Dollars into Colonia Street Lights Program'. *Rio Grande Guardian*, 22 May. https://riograndeguardian.com/hidalgo-county-asked-to-pump-half-a-million-dollars-into-colonia-street-lights-program/
Texas Department of Housing and Community Affairs. 2019. '2019 State of Texas Low Income Housing Plan & Annual Report'. *Texas Department of Housing and Community Affairs*. www.tdhca.state.tx.us/housing-center/docs/19-SLIHP.pdf
Ward, P. M. 1999. *Colonias and Public Policy in Texas and Mexico: Urbanization by Stealth*. Austin: University of Texas Press.

11.2 *Chabolismo* (Spain)
Noel A. Manzano Gómez

Aguilera, T. 2021. 'Políticas de erradicación del chabolismo en Madrid (1945–2015): institucionalización, racialización, metropolización'. In *Gitanos rumanos en España. Trayectorias de vida, estrategias y políticas públicas*, edited by C. Bergeon, D. Lagunas Arias and F. Torres Pérez, 153–90. Ed. Le Tirant.

Álvarez-De Andrés, E. 2020. 'Necropolítica de vivienda: 40 años desmantelando la "informalidad" en Madrid (1979–2019)'. *Eure* 46(139): 5–27.

Álvarez Agüí, N. 2017. 'Formulación y tratamiento de un "problema social": En torno a los desalojos forzosos en la Cañada real (Madrid)'. *AIBR Revista de Antropologia Iberoamericana* 12(2): 215–39.

Burbano, A. 2015. *La autoconstrucción de Madrid durante el Franquismo El pozo del Tío Raimundo*. Master's thesis, Universidad Complutense de Madrid.

Canosa Zamora, E. and Rodriguez Chumillas, I. 1985. 'Urbanización marginal en la periferia noreste de Madrid'. *Ciudad y Territorio* (3).

Castells, M. 1974. *Movimientos sociales urbanos*. Madrid: Siglo XXI.

Comisaría de Urbanismo 1945. *Plan de Ordenación de los Suburbios*. File#137043/17. Madrid: Archivo Regional de Madrid.

Diez de Baldeon, C. 1983. *Arquitectura y cuestión social en el Madrid del siglo XIX*. Madrid: Universidad Complutense de Madrid.

El Pensamiento Español. 1869. *La agricultura castellana y su situación angustiosa*, 22 November.

García Padilla, F. M. 2020. *Análisis de la situación de salud de los/as inmigrantes de los asentamientos de Huelva*. Caritas diocesana de Huelva.

Iglesias, B. 2021. *Desde los conjuntos autoconstruidos hasta la infravivienda de producción institucional como expresiones del urbanismo segregativo*. Universidade Da Coruña.

Kreibich, V. 2000. 'Self-help Planning of Migrants in Rome and Madrid'. *Habitat International* 24(2): 201–11.

Lago Ávila, M. J. 2014. 'El otro Madrid: el chabolismo que no cesa. Actuación autonómica en políticas de realojamiento e integración social 1997–2010'. *Estudios Geográficos* 75(276): 219–60.

Luque Revuelto, R. M. and Pulido Jurado, R. 2014. 'Metodología y fuentes para el estudio de una arquitectura rural desaparecida: Las chozas del norte de la provincia de Córdoba'. *Cuadernos Geográficos* 53(1): 68–97.

Mancha, J. J. 2018. *Un cerro de ilusiones: historia del Cerro del Tío Pío*. Madrid: Agita Vallecas (Libros VK).

Manzano Gómez, N. A. 2021. 'The Cleanliness of Otherness: Stigmatization, Epidemics and Informal Urbanization in Early 20th-century Madrid'. *Planning Perspectives* 37(1): 127–47.

Manzano Gómez, N. A. 2022. *The Reverse of Urban Planning. Towards a 20th Century History of Informal Urbanisation in Europe and its Origins in Madrid and Paris (1850–1940)*. Valladolid and Weimar: Universidad de Valladolid/Bauhaus University of Weimar.

Manzano Gómez, N. A. and Castrillo Román, M. 2019. 'From "Chabolas" to Invisible Squats: A Reflection on the Residential Informality Evolution in Madrid'. In *Inequality and Uncertainty: Current Challenges for Cities*, edited by M. Smagacz-Poziemska, M. Gómez, P. Pereira, L. Guarino, S. Kurtenbach and J. Villalón, 253–72. Singapore: Palgrave.

Ministerio de la Vivienda. 1977. *Plan de Barrios*. Anexo I. Grandes Ciudades. File#G25INV(30). Madrid: Archivo Central de la Consejería de Transportes e Infraestructuras CAM.

Montes Mieza, J., Paredes Grosso, M. and Villanueva Paredes, A. 1976. 'Los asentamientos chabolistas en Madrid'. *Ciudad Y Territorio* (2–3/76): 159–72.

Nogués Sáez, L. 2010. *Exclusión residencial y políticas públicas: el caso de la minoría gitana en Madrid (1986–2006)*. Granada: Universidad de Granada.

Ofer, I. 2017. *Claiming the City and Contesting the State: Squatting, Community Formation and Democratization in Spain (1955–1986)*. New York: Routledge.

Pallol Trigueros, R. 2011. *El Madrid moderno: Chamberi (el Ensanche Norte), simbolo del nacimiento de una nueva capital, 1860–1931*. Madrid: Universidad Complutense de Madrid.

Rodriguez Chumillas, I. 2010. 'Chabola'. In *L'aventure des mots de la ville. A travers le temps, les langues, les sociétés*, edited by C. Topalov, L. Coudroy de Lille, J.-C. Depaule and B. Marin. 272–6. Paris: Robert Laffont.

Sambricio, C. 1999. *Arquitectura Vivienda en Madrid en la Decada de los 50. "El Plan de Urgencia Social"*. Madrid: Electa España.

Schierstaedt, N. 2016. 'Los barrios madrileños como áreas de confrontación social durante el tardofranquismo y la transición. Los casos de la meseta de Orcasitas, Palomeras, San Blas y El Pilar'. Historia, *Trabajo y Sociedad* (7): 55–75.

Tamayo Palacios, A. 2011. 'Exclusión Social En El Madrid Del "Desarrollismo": La Influencia Del Modelo Viviendas a Gran Escala Madrid En La Cohesión Social De La Cuidad'. *Revista INVI* 26(73): 73–102.

Tatjer, M. and Larrea, C. 2011. Barraques. *La Barcelona informal del segle XX*. Barcelona: Ayuntamiento de Barcelona.

Torres Gutiérrez, F. J. 2011. 'El territorio de los desheredados. Asentamientos chabolistas y experiencias recientes de erradicación en Sevilla' [The Territory of the Disinherited. Slum settlements and recent eradication experiences in Seville]. *Hábitat y Sociedad* 67–90.

Vicente Albarrán, F. 2011. *Los barrios negros: el Ensanche Sur en la formación del moderno Madrid (1860–1931)*. Madrid: Universidad Complutense de Madrid.

Villasante, T. R. et al. 1989. *Retrato de chabolista con piso. Análisis de redes sociales en la remodelación de barrios de Madrid*. Madrid: IVIMA.

Vorms, C. 2013. 'Madrid années 1950: la question des baraques'. *Le Mouvement Social* 4(245): 43–57.

Vorms, C. 2017. 'Naming Madrid's Working-class Periphery, 1860–1970. The Construction of Urban Illegitimacy'. In *What's in a Name?: Talking about Urban Peripheries*, edited by R. Harris and C. Vorms, 209–31. Toronto, Buffalo, London: University of Toronto Press.

11.3 *Samozakhvat* (Kyrgyzstan)
Eliza Isabaeva

Abdykalykova, M. 2013. 'V Bishkeke u "detei-nevidimok" ogranichennyi dostup k obrazovaniiu'. *Knews*, 30 September. https://knews.kg/2013/09/30/v-bishkeke-u-detey-nevidimok-ogranichennyiy-dostup-k-obrazovaniyu/

Hatcher, C. 2015. 'Illegal Geographies of the State: the Legalization of a "Squatter" Settlement in Bishkek, Kyrgyzstan'. *International Journal of Law in the Built Environment* 7(1): 39–54.

Ivashenko, E. 2016. 'Novostroiki Bishkeka: Zakhvatit' zemliiu, legalizovat'sia i zhit' vozle svalki'. *Ferghana news*, 25 February. www.fergananews.com/articles/8896

Mambetaliev, K. 2016. *Epoha Apasa Dzhumagulova*. Turar: Bishkek.

Mitenko, P. 2011. 'Gde nochuet kirgizskaia revoliutsiia', *Ferghana News*, 11 March. www.fergananews.com/articles/6917

Nasritdinov, E., Zhumakadyr kyzy B. and Asanalieva, D. 2015. 'Myth and Realities of Bishkek's Novostroikasi'. In *Kyrgyzstan beyond 'Democracy Island' and 'Failing State': Social and Political Changes in a Post-Soviet Society*, edited by M. Laruelle and J. Engvall, 143–63. Lanham, MD: Lexington Books.

Shambetov, T. 2015. 'Zhany konushtardyn chechilbegen köigöiü'. *RRL/RL Azattyk*, 18 June. www.azattyk.org/a/kyrgyzstan_suburbs_around_bishkek/27078559.html

Timofeyenko, A. 2014. 'Zhizn' za gran'iu: liudi-nevidimki zhivut na svalke bolee 11 let'. *Vechernii Bishkek*, 25 September. www.vb.kg/doc/287754_jizn_za_granu:_ludi_nevidimki_jivyt_na_svalke_bolee_11_let.html

11.4 *Zaniato* (Abkhazia and Nagorno-Karabakh, Caucasus)
Andrea Peinhopf

Bryant, R. 2014. 'History's Remainders: On Time and Objects after Conflict in Cyprus'. *American Ethnologist* 41(4): 681–97.

Day.Az. 2021. 'Armenians Appropriated the Houses of Expelled Azerbaijanis in Shusha after the Occupation – Archival Photos [*Armiane prisvaivali doma izgnannykh azerbaidzhantsev v Shushe posle okkupatsii - arkhivnye foto*]'. *Day.az*, 13 February. https://news.day.az/politics/1315828.html

HRW. 1995. *Georgia/Abkhazia: Violations of the Laws of War and Russia's Role in the Conflict*. Helsinki: Human Rights Watch Arms Project/Human Rights Watch.

ICRC. n.d. 'Rule 52. Pillage'. *Customary IHL Database*. https://ihl-databases.icrc.org/customary-ihl/eng/docs/v1_rul_rule52

JAMnews. 2016. 'Daite ili zakhvatim' [Give It to Us, Or We'll Grab It]. *JAMnews*, 14 November. https://jam-news.net/ru/дайте-или-захватим

Navaro-Yashin, Y. 2012. *The Make-Believe Space: Affective Geography in a Postwar Polity*. Durham: Duke University Press.

Peinhopf, A. 2020 *Conflict and Co-Existence: War, Displacement and the Changing Dynamics of Inter- and Intra-Ethnic Relations in Abkhazia*. PhD thesis, UCL.

Peinhopf, A. 2021. 'The Curse of Displacement: Local Narratives of Forced Expulsion and the Appropriation of Abandoned Property in Abkhazia'. *Nationalities Papers* 49(4): 710–27.

Sharia, V. 2017a. 'Kvartnirnii vopros: sukhumskie kontrasti' [Housing Questions: Sukhumi Contrasts]. *Ekho Kavkaza*, 25 May. www.ekhokavkaza.com/a/28509113.html

Sharia, V. 2017b. 'Pogruzhenie "galenona" "Amra"' [The Sinking of 'Galleon' 'Amra']. *Ekho Kavkaza*, 17 May. www.ekhokavkaza.com/a/28493949.html

Stoler, A. L. 2008. 'Imperial Debris: Reflection on Ruins and Ruination'. *Cultural Anthropology* 23(2): 191–219.

Venediktova, N. 2018. 'Prezidenty meniaiutsia, a "zaniato" ostaetsia …' [The Presidents Change, but 'Occupied' Stays …]. *Ekho Kavkaza*, 23 January. www.ekhokavkaza.com/a/28998551.html

Zavodskaia, E. 2014. 'Printsip "zaniato" tormozit privatisatsiiu' ['Occupied' Principle Curbs Privatisation]. *Ekho Kavkaza*, 16 December. www.ekhokavkaza.com/a/26747172.html

11.5 *Xiaochanquan* (China)
Cinzia Losavio

Barros, B. (ed.) 2016. *Hernando de Soto and Property in a Market Economy*. London: Routledge.

Cong, J., Chen, J. and Mu, X. 2007. 'Shéi dòng le shéi de nǎilào? wèihé bóyì shínián hòu wènzuì xiǎochǎnquánfáng?'. *Zhōngguó jīngjì wǎng*, 28 September.

De Soto, H. 2000. *The Mystery of Capital: Why Capitalism Triumphs in the West and Fails Everywhere Else*. New York: Basic Books.

Guo, H. and Cai, J. 2009. 'Nóngdì zhìdù ānpái yǔ cūnmín jítǐ xíngdòng – xiǎochǎnquánfáng wèntí tànxī'. *Journal of Finance and Economics* 35(5): 85–93.

He, S., Wang, D., Webster, C. and Chau, K. W. 2019. 'Property Rights with Price Tags? Pricing Uncertainties in the Production, Transaction and Consumption of China's Small Property Right Housing'. *Land Use Policy* 81: 424–33.

Losavio, C. 2022. *La stratification des migrants chinois de l'intérieur au service de la croissance urbaine et économique: les processus différenciés d'ancrage résidentiel à Zhuhai au prisme de l'informalité*. Doctoral dissertation. Paris 1 – Panthéon-Sorbonne University. www.theses.fr/s168719

Paik, W. and Lee, K. 2012. 'I Want to Be Expropriated!: The Politics of *Xiǎochǎnquánfang* Land Development in Suburban China'. *Journal of Contemporary China* 21(74): 261–79.

Qiao, S. 2015. 'Small Property, Big Market: A Focal Point Explanation'. *American Journal of Comparative Law* 63(1): 197–237.

Qiao, S. 2017. *Chinese Small Property: The Co-Evolution of Law and Social Norms*. Cambridge: Cambridge University Press.

Shen, X. and Tu, F. 2014. 'Dealing with "Small Property Rights"'. *China's Land Market Development: What Can China Learn from Its Past Reforms and the World Experience?* Lincoln Institute of Land Policy. Working Paper, 70.

Tsao, H. 2012. 'Zhōngguó dàlù 'xiǎochǎnquánfáng' de zhèngzhì jīngjìxué jīyú chǎnquán lǐlùn de fēnxī'. *Chinese Political Science Review* 53: 1–27.

Wang, L. and Sun, T. 2014. 'Capitalization of Legal Title: Evidence from Small Property Rights Houses in Beijing'. *Habitat International* 44: 306–13.

Wang, L., Sun, T. and Li, S. 2014. 'Legal Title, Tenure Security, and Investment – An Empirical Study in Beijing'. *Housing Studies* 29(8): 1117–38.

11.6 *Chuồng cọp* (Vietnam)
Francisco García Moro

Anh, T. M. 2017. 'Redevelopment of "Khu Tap The" in Hanoi City. How to Make a Livable and Inclusive Living Environment'. *Proceedings of 2017 International Conference of Asian-Pacific Planning Societies*. www.cpij.or.jp/com/iac/upload/file/2017icapps/012.pdf

Cerise, E. and Shannon, K. 2010. 'KTT Transformations in Hanoi'. In *Human Settlements: Formulations and (Re)Calibrations*, edited by K. Shannon, 68–76. Amsterdam: Sun Academia.

Chen, S. I. 2015. 'Hanoi/ KTT CASE STUDY: Architectural Presentation of the Ideal and the Real'. *Asian Cities Research*, 16 December. https://web.archive.org/web/20200516223534/http://fac.arch.hku.hk/asian-cities-research/hanoikkt-case-study-architectural-presentation-of-the-ideal-and-the-real/

Geertman, S. 2007. *The Self-organizing City in Vietnam; Processes of Change and Transformation in Housing in Hanoi*. Eindhoven: Technische Universiteit Eindhoven.

Japan International Cooperation Agency. 2014. *The Study for Basic Information on the Housing Sector in Vietnam*. Japan International Cooperation Agency. http://open_jicareport.jica.go.jp/pdf/1000026720.pdf

Ledent, J. 2002. *La population: évolution passée et développement futur. Hanoi: enjeux modernes d'une ville millénaire*. Montréal: Trames.

Logan, W. S. 2000. *Hanoi, Biography of a City*. Seattle: University of Washington Press.

Nguyễn, T. S. 2019. 'Nguyễn Thế Sơn'. http://nguyentheson.com/

Nhân Dân. 2017. 'Martin Rama, a Uruguayan Economist with Big Love for Hanoi'. *Nhah Dan online*, 29 December. https://web.archive.org/web/20220618045056/https://en.nhandan.vn/culture/item/5743002-martin-rama-a-uruguayan-economist-with-big-love-for-hanoi.html

Pennec, S. and Ng, H. 2009. 'Mass Housing Guide'. *Archis.org*, 1 March. http://volumeproject.org/mass-housing-guide/

Phuong, D. Q. 2011. 'The Impact of "Informal" Building Additions on Interior/Exterior Space in Hanoi's Old Apartment Blocks (KTT)'. *Architecture in the Fourth Dimension* 15–17: 131–8.

Quinn, L. 2014. 'Hanoi: Is It Possible to Grow a City Without Slums?'. *The Guardian*, 11 August. www.theguardian.com/cities/2014/aug/11/hanoi-slums-vietnam-urban-planning-construction

Reid, S. E. 2006. 'Khrushchev Modern. Agency and Modernization in the Soviet Home'. *Cahiers Du Monde Russe* 47(1–2): 227–68.

Schenk, H. 2013. 'Towards a Sustainable View on Social Housing in HaNoi'. *International Conference of Vietnam: Vietnam on the way of integration and sustainable development*. Hanoi 535–54.

Tran, M. T. 2016. *Fabrication du logement planifié sous forme de 'KDTM' (Khu Đô Thị Mới) à Hanoï: la ville de quartiers ou/et la ville de projets?* Doctoral thesis, Toulouse: Université Toulouse, 55–99. https://tel.archives-ouvertes.fr/tel-01260358

Wolf, M., Baker, K. and Young, D. 2005. *Hong Kong: Front Door/back Door*. Hong Kong: Thames & Hudson, pp 115–17.

Xia, C. 2015. 'Hanoi/The Breakdown of the Socialist Housing'. Asian Cities Research, 21 December. https://web.archive.org/web/20200516174342/http://fac.arch.hku.hk/asian-cities-research/the-ward-and-the-breakdown-of-the-socialist-housing-regime/

11.7 *Divlja gradnja* (Countries of Former Yugoslavia)
Fynn-Morten Heckert

Bajić, T., Petrić, J. and Nikolić, T. 2016. 'Fuel Poverty and Perception on Housing and Environmental Quality in Belgrade's Informal Settlement Kaluđerica'. *Spatium* 35: 1–9.

Grubović, L. 2006. *Belgrade in Transition. An Analysis of Illegal Building in a Post-Socialist City*. Ann Arbor: Pro Quest.

Klaić Saulačić, P. 2019. 'A kažu da zakoni vrijede jednako za sve: Investitor gradnjom uništio pomorsko dobro pa nakon kazne – nastavio graditi'. *Dnevnik.hr*, 14 December. https://dnevnik.hr/vijesti/hrvatska/u-dubrovniku-ni-nakon-prijave-nije-rijesen-ozbiljan-slucaj-bespravne-gradnje---586965.html

Kriegl, S. M. 2011. *Stadtgeographie von Sarajevo. Persistente Entwicklung und aktuelle Strukturen*. Graz: Karl-Franzens-Universität.

Martin-Diaz, J., Nofre, J., Oliva, M. and Palma, P. 2015. 'Towards an Unsustainable Urban Development in Post-war Sarajevo'. *Area* 47(4): 376–85.

Müller, Y. and Lješković, S. 2008. 'Illegal Construction in Montenegro'. *Techika Chronika Scientific Journal TCG* 1(1–2): 105–10.

UNECE and International Federation of Surveyors. 2015. *Formalizing the Informal: Challenges and Opportunities of Informal Settlements in South-East Europe*. New York and Geneva: United Nations. https://unece.org/fileadmin/DAM/hlm/documents/Publications/Formalizing_the_Informal_Challenges_and_Opportunities_of_Informal_Settlements_in_South-East_Europe.pdf

Xharra, B. 2012. 'Kosovo Turns Blind Eye to Illegal Mosques'. *Balkan Insight*, 12 January. https://balkaninsight.com/2012/01/12/kosovo-turns-blind-eye-to-illegal-mosques/

Zegarac, Z. 1999. 'Illegal Construction in Belgrade and the Prospects for Urban Development Planning'. *Cities* 16(5): 365–70.

Zlatar, J. 2014. 'Zagreb'. *Cities* 39: 144–55.

11.8 *Vrtičkarstvo* (Slovenia)
Petra Matijevic

Alber, J. and Kohler, U. 2008. 'Informal Food Production in the Enlarged European Union'. *Social Indicators Research* 89(1): 113–27.

Bogataj, M. 1999. 'Zagreti vrtičkarji lope poleti spremenijo v dom'. *Finance*, 9 April.

Caldwell, M. L. 2011. *Dacha Idylls: Living Organically in Russia's Countryside*. Berkeley: University of California Press.

Czegledy, A. 2002. 'Urban Peasants in a Post-Socialist World: Small-Scale Agriculturalists in Hungary'. In *Post-Socialist Peasant? Rural and Urban Constructions of Identity in Eastern Europe, East Asia and the Former Soviet Union*, edited by P. Leonard and D. Kaneff, 200–20. Houndmills, Basingstoke, Hampshire: Palgrave.

Hervouet, R. 2003. 'Dachas and Vegetable Gardens in Belarus. Economic and Subjective Stakes of an "Ordinary Passion"'. *Anthropology of East Europe Review* 1(1): 159–68.

Jamnik, B., Aleš, S. and Borut, V. 2009. *Vrtičkarstvo v Ljubljani*. Ljubljana: Založba ZRC.

Matijevic, P. 2018. *On the Fringes of the European Union: Food Self-sufficiency and the Eurozone Crisis in Slovenia*. PhD thesis. SOAS, University of London.

Matijevic, P. 2022. 'Searching for the Plot: Narrative Self-making and Urban Agriculture during the Economic Crisis in Slovenia'. *Agriculture and Human Values* 39: 301–4.

Mestna občina Ljubljana. 2018. 'Vrtički v Ljubljani'. *Mestna občina Ljubljana*. www.ljubljana.si/sl/moja-ljubljana/podezelje/samooskrba-v-ljubljani/vrticki-v-ljubljani/

Petkovšek, J. 2008. 'Padli prvi nelegalni objekti'. *Delo*, 7 October.

Simoneti, M. 1997. 'Usmeritve in Pogoji Za Nadaljnji Razvoj Vrtičkarstva v Ljubljani: Razvojno Aplikativna Enoletna Raziskava'. *Ljubljana: Ljubljanski urbanistični zavod*.

Smith, J. and Jehlička, P. 2013. 'Quiet Sustainability: Fertile Lessons from Europe's Productive Gardeners'. *Journal of Rural Studies* 32: 148–57.

Sulima, R. 2000. *Antropologia codzienności*. Kraków: Wydawnictwo Uniwersytetu Jagiellońskiego.

11.9 *Informal housing of the rich* (Global)
Udo Grashoff

Alterman, R. and Calor, I. 2020. 'Between Informal and Illegal in the Global North: Planning Law, Enforcement and Justifiable Noncompliance'. In *Comparative Approaches to Informal Housing Around the Globe*, edited by U. Grashoff, 150–85. London: UCL Press.

Chiodelli, F. 2019. 'The Dark Side of Urban Informality in the Global North: Housing Illegality and Organized Crime in Northern Italy'. *International Journal of Urban and Regional Research* 43(3): 497–516.

Durst, N. and Wegmann, J. 2017. 'Informal Housing in the United States'. *International Journal of Urban and Regional Research* 41: 282–97.

Vieda Martínez, S. and Chiodelli, F. 2021. 'Informal Housing of the Rich: Clustering, Isolating, and Concealing in Bogotá, Colombia'. *Habitat International*: 112.

12
Engaging politically

Introduction: political participation

Uta Staiger
European Institute, UCL, UK

The concept of political participation is essential for our definition of politics – democratic politics above all. Indeed, it is arguably what distinguishes democracy from all other forms of government: democracy *depends upon* citizens engaging politically.

As such, the notion has been key to social and political thought over the centuries. For Immanuel Kant, though he favoured restricting the franchise, not only was participation in the civic community indispensable for an individual's moral personhood, but his concept of a social contract implied that citizens – free and equal – were to make the laws they then had to obey (Maliks 2014). Alexis de Tocqueville thought a healthy democracy – characterised by freedom, pluralism and equality as much as by mutable power relations – was sustained not just by frequent elections but by active civil associations that schooled citizens' public vocation (de Tocqueville 2002: 489–92). Political engagement was also at the heart of Hannah Arendt's conception of politics; indeed, what she called action – acting in concert, with others, by speaking in public about public affairs – is authentic politics, she argued (Arendt 2018). Not dissimilar to the Arendtian notion, Jürgen Habermas too accorded citizens' deliberative participation in public affairs a key role in functioning democracies (Habermas 2019).

As these cursory examples show, the significance bestowed on ordinary citizens partaking in political affairs is a historically and typologically distinctive characteristic of democracy. It is also often rather closely tied up with another prevalent concept in the social and political sciences: civic engagement or civil society. Most prominently, perhaps, Robert Putnam observed that levels of trust and cohesion among citizens rise as they participate in civil activities, volunteer in projects or engage with intermediary organisations (Putnam 1993). He argued, consequently, that a direct correlation exists between the vibrance of a state's civil society and the quality or stability of its democracy.

Today, we employ a rather expansive concept of political participation. Conventionally, political participation may have been defined more narrowly as 'those legal acts by private citizens that are more or less directly aimed at influencing the selection of governmental personnel and/or the actions that they take' (Verba et al. 1978: 1). In other words: standing or voting in elections, contacting officials or reaching out to our political representatives about policy matters that may concern us. These days, however, an extended catalogue of types of political participation may encompass areas we may previously have considered as being rather private, social or economic in nature. Such activities would include those we carry out as consumers, as party members, or as citizens making our disagreement with government actions heard through protest and demonstrations (Montero et al. 2006)

These modes of political engagement, then, comprise what Inglehart (2018) called 'elite-challenging issue-oriented' and Tilly and Tarrow (2015) 'contentious' politics. They may even, under certain conditions, cover activities that are not themselves inherently political – but are rather *repurposed* for political ends (van Deth 2016). Political participation can thus describe a whole panoply of formal and informal actions: 'voting, demonstrating, contacting public officials, boycotting, attending party rallies, guerrilla gardening, posting blogs, volunteering, joining flash mobs, signing petitions, buying fair-trade products, and even suicide protests' (van Deth 2016: 1). All of these modes of engagement, different as they may be, seek to shape political decision-making in line with citizens' active preferences or convictions.

Importantly, however, voting and campaign activities, designed and employed as they are to directly influence political processes, continue to be central to the notion of political participation (Kaase 2009). And not randomly so: the role of political representatives and particularly parties remain, after all, the 'most important agents of political representation in modern democracy' (Hagopian 2009: 582). It is arguably in the interest of analytical efficacy that we do not lose sight of this typological fault line of engaging politically. Most (although not all) entries in this section address, after all, the relationship between political parties and voters, or the relationship between political representatives, their own party and the executive.

When it comes to empirical research on this narrower definition of political participation, however, most attention tends to be paid to its *formal* characteristics: turnout and campaigning, party systems and electoral processes, membership and social movements and so on (Kaase 2009). Implicit in most studies is the assumption that the relationship between voters and parties retains an official, distanced character. Electoral choices, in other words, are expected to reside mainly with individual voters responding to a party's class appeal, a shared ideology, or preferences for a party's policy positions. However, there is in fact plenty of evidence that informal modes of politics are also in play, in democracies, too, which transform the party-voter relationship into a much more immediate one – including clientelism or the proffering of pork barrel projects. While often left unconsidered, these informal politics actually represent 'an important part of the dynamics of representation in European democracies' (Hopkin 2012: 199).

It is on these modes of engaging politically that most entries here focus, exploring the limits or indeed the wide-ranging subversion of formal modes of electoral participation and, more broadly, the party-voter relationship. The range of informal political practices discussed include implicit or explicit offers of vote exchange (*voto di scambio*), clientelist or patronage-based strategies (*party soldiers*), outright corruption to obtain votes (*vote buying/selling*; *krumpliosztás*) and the use of violent 'political technologies' to manipulate citizens' political behaviour (*titushky*). These practices may even extend to the diametric other of political engagement itself: when submissive, non-contentious dispositions become socially embedded, citizens do not wish or dare to question any social norms or political status quo (*ne talasaj*). The practices set out in this set of entries thus in fact violate the original principle of political engagement so valorised by political thinkers and scientists. They are no longer forms of 'authentic' political participation, to echo Arendt. Instead, they curb, dull or distort the influence of public opinion, convictions and preference formation on political decision-making. In the case of *ne talasaj*, they even lead to the opposite of action, inactivism.

How can we think more broadly about the conditions that allow such practices – especially in Southern and Eastern Europe or countries of the former Soviet Union, the entries' main focus – to entrench themselves? Informal political participation is encouraged by two interrelated conditions, both of which are particularly prevalent, Hopkin argues, in Southern Europe. On the one hand, this is a tradition of state interventionism, which makes public funds available yet retains only weak judicial oversight of its spending. On the other hand, it is the existence of weak political parties that are only superficially rooted with the electorate (Hopkin 2012: 200–1). The Italian case of vote exchange, or *voto di scambio*, is a key case in point. Italy's electoral system is characterised by low party membership, few associative structures and volatile electoral support; these exacerbate already existing funding shortfalls and rather suboptimal organisational infrastructures. Ergo, there are plenty of incentives to use informal exchanges to ensure citizens support a particular candidate or project.

We can observe similar features in Eastern and Southern Eastern Europe, as the entries from the Balkans, Hungary and Ukraine illuminate. Despite significant developments in recent decades, the region is still characterised by comparatively lower levels of political participation and weaker civil society structures than in Western Europe. Indicators include lower voter turnout and party membership, coupled with high electoral volatility and lack of trust in the authorities, as well as wider political apathy (Ekman et al. 2016). Taken together, this leads to what Cianetti et al. (2018) call a 'relatively stable but low-quality democracy' as the norm. It is not confined to the region, however. Ultimately, we may well see this as indicative of a trend in Northern and Western Europe, too, where the general decline of party membership, apathy and ideological fragmentation may well spell trouble.

Hooghe and Quintelier attribute the reasons for the low and informal political participation in Central and Eastern Europe to three main factors: public perceptions of corruption, bad governance and authoritarian legacies (Hooghe and Quintelier 2014). Particularly the first two, they argue, have a significant negative impact on political participation – it is the *experience* citizens have of ill-functioning governments that determines levels and forms of participation, rather than citizens having been socialised in an authoritarian regime. That said, as particularly the entry on *titushky* in Ukraine shows, the legacy of authoritarian regimes persists in the practices themselves – in this case, the use of post-Soviet 'rent-a-mob' strategies, which in their overt use of violence and state-level organisational requirements far exceed the other party-voter practices discussed here.

Across this set of entries, we see informal practices truly 'infect the system', as Wilson (2011) put it with regard to Ukrainian political technologies. These practices represent a parasitic incursion of party-political systems, which favours obedience over integrity (*party soldiers*) or the material interest of the self or family over the common good (*voto di scambio*). In Mongolia, the practice *mungu idekh* (eating money), a term often employed to critique inefficient leadership, can also carry connotations of practices that are polluted, or pollute, public life. Indeed, by 'eating money', powerful actors self-servingly extracting money from the public purse may literally 'grow fat'.

This notion of ingestion, imbibing, infecting or parasitically feasting upon a host community could not be more prevalent in the Southern American *parillada* – literally, a barbeque (of domesticated pigs) that displaces the (traditionally hunted) tapir, which becomes an exploitative means of engaging with, and ultimately curtailing, the minority rights of indigenous people. While not directly political, this practice is another example of local expertise being extracted without concomitant participation (in decisions or benefits) being offered. Indeed, the only positively connoted example of informal political engagement in this section is the role of non-constitutional but practically recognised representatives (*maliks*) in Afghanistan, who are selected via intra-community consultation processes and function as important intermediaries between their communities and state actors.

Now, political representatives are the link between voters on the one hand, and the government and opposition on the other, which are formed as a result of those voters' choices. Once safely in their seat, they are also active agents in drafting, debating, amending and passing legislation. Usually, parliamentarians are expected to align their positions (and ultimately votes) in line with their party group. Such alignment is thought to arise not only because of a similarity of preferences, institutional conventions and socialisation – but also because of parliamentarians' personal or career considerations and (in)formal party discipline (Bowler et al. 1999; Kam 2011). But dissent and departure from party lines is on the increase (Cowley and Stuart 2012). While the entries at hand do not focus on this particular aspect, an interest in engaging politically must extend also to the coercive practices – legal as well as unconstitutional – that are used to shut down dissent, minimise scrutiny and align members of parliament with party lines or executive actors once in post.

While virtually all entries in this section thus fasten informal practices that are actively harmful to a stable and vibrant democracy, so are of course their direct opposites: inactivism, disinterest and acquiescence. Indeed, we could do worse than recall de Tocqueville, who for all his enthusiasm almost 200 years ago also warned of democracy's potential decline if individual material interests go unchecked, the public's attention to the common good is unnurtured and political apathy reigns. As he argues, such patterns could well develop into a mild yet softly injurious form of democratic 'despotism'. Such despotism:

> does not break wills, but it softens them, bends them and directs them; it rarely forces action, but it constantly opposes your acting; it does not destroy, it prevents birth; it does not tyrannize, it hinders, it represses, it enervates, it extinguishes, it stupefies … it would not be impossible for it to be established in the very shadow of the sovereignty of the people. (de Tocqueville 2002: 663)

12.1 *Voto di scambio* (Italy)
Alberica Camerani
School of Slavonic and East European Studies, UCL, UK

Voto di scambio is an Italian expression (*votu di scanciu* in Sicilian) that can be translated as an 'exchange of vote'. It is used to denote the trade of electoral votes for short-term favours and particularistic benefits. *Compravendita di voti* (literally, 'buying and selling of votes') refers to this practice when the votes are sold for money. According to Parisi and Pasquino (1979), the peculiarity of this kind of vote is the immediate and personalised reward for the electoral act. Historically, *voto di scambio* originated in Southern Italy; however, there is evidence of such practices in Northern Italy as well. For example, in 2012 the councillor for Lombardy Domenico Zambetti was arrested for allegedly buying four thousand votes for 200,000 Euro, 50 Euro for each vote (Ferrarella 2012).

The *voto di scambio* usually occurs within a clientelist relationship, defined by Scott as:

> a special case of dyadic ties involving a largely instrumental friendship in which an individual of higher socioeconomic status (patron) uses his own influence and resources to provide protection or benefits, or both, for a person of lower status (client) who, for his part, reciprocates by offering general support and assistance, including personal services, to the patron. (Scott 1972)

In Italy, two types of clientelism can be observed. In the classic clientelism, the *notabili* (notables) were the patrons in control resources that 'had little to do with the exercise of public power, but flowed from their personal wealth, social standing and prestige' (Caciagli and Belloni 1981: 35).

However, the clientelist relationship that is common nowadays is based on the mass party organisation and it developed in the 1950s, as a result of the expansion of the public sector and the increase in state activities. In this case, the patron is a 'political party which uses its control of public resources to distribute individual benefits (state jobs, pensions, subsidies and even collective benefits such as roads, housing and sport facilities), all in exchange for electoral backing' (Hopkin 2012: 200).

The negotiations surrounding the purchase of votes are not usually conducted directly by the electoral candidate who is seeking votes, but by intermediary agents. In a typical arrangement of the *voto di scambio*, the political candidate agrees with an intermediary on the desired number of electoral votes, then, the agents turn to their networks, formed by smaller intermediaries (*galoppini*), and task them with a number of votes to find. The term *galoppini* may be literally translated as 'galloping minions' and refers to their dynamic and active task of 'going around praising the leader'. Usually, *galoppini* are themselves recipients of 'favours, promises of job, or other tangible benefits for them or members of their family' (Greco 1972: 178). As stated by Allum (1975: 214), 'the politician wanting to expand their network can rely on intermediaries with two types of strategic roles of controlling groups of votes: *grandi elettori* and *capi elettori*'. The difference between them is in the number of groups that they control. The *grandi elettori* (literally, 'great electors') are mayors, parish priests or landowners who can influence several groups, while *capi elettori* ('head electors') control one local group (the mafia is often involved in these).

The benefits received by voters in exchange for their votes can take many forms. Witnesses report electoral votes being exchanged for houses, laundry machines, fridges, jobs, food, streetlights, phone credit, fuel, gas for heating, and insurance and mortgage discounts (Saviano 2013), as well as 'job promotions, construction permits, business licences, artisan certificates and road paving' (Ancisi 1976: 63–4).

The same sources identify mechanisms to ensure that the voters do not break the deal. The investigation '*Il principe e la ballerina*' ('The prince and the dancing ballot'), launched by the District Anti-Mafia Directorate of Napoli, revealed a stratagem based on ballot swapping. Once the terms of the exchange are agreed upon, the voter receives an already completed ballot to take with them to the polling station. In the voting booth, the voter swaps the regular empty ballot with the completed one and inserts it into the ballot box. To claim their reward, the voter must hand the empty ballot to the agent, who will use it for further exchanges (Saviano 2013). Other methods involve the use of a camera or the complicity of 'a member of the polling station or *rappresentante di lista* [literally, 'party-list representative']' (Ancisi 1976: 84).

Scholarship has associated *voto di scambio* with the preference voting system (*voto di preferenza*) (Katz and Bardi 1980; Putnam 1993). The Italian electoral system allows the use of *voto di preferenza* in municipal, regional and European elections. In these types of elections, the citizen votes for the party list and can additionally indicate the name of a preferred party candidate from the list. According to Pasquino, preference voting 'is used as a bargaining chip by the voter and as a commodity that can be bought by the candidate' (1972: 365). For example, *voto di preferenza* allows for one of the most common ways of ensuring that the voters keep their word in a *voto di scambio*. In addition to voting for a party, voters are asked to give their preferential vote to a candidate who is on the party list only as a filler for that particular polling station and is not meant to receive any votes outside it. If the scrutiny later reveals that this candidate did not receive any votes, it means that the voters did not keep their promise.

Scholars have investigated the motivations of the *elettori di scambio*, or 'exchange voters'. Several have relied on Banfield's seminal thesis on 'amoral familiarism' as one of the causes of the 'backwardness' of certain societies (Banfield 1958). While observing everyday life in Montegrano, a South Italian village, Banfield noticed that the self-interested, family-centric society seemed unable 'to act together for their common good or, indeed, for any end transcending the immediate, material interest of the nuclear family'. He claimed this behaviour seemed 'fairly [representative of] the typical south' (Banfield 1958: 10). Among other causes is 'the weakness of the administrative and judicial state structures that favoured the creation and the development of patronage systems which increasingly have undermined the basis of the state authority' (Putnam 1993: 170).

Such weakness is itself, perhaps, grounded in Italy's 'ancient tradition of lack of trust ... [that] produces a general reluctance towards impersonal and extensive forms of cooperation' (Gambetta 1988: 162). An empirical study of political behaviour of the low-income neighbourhood in Palermo highlights 'their extreme social and economic fragmentation and the absence of any associative structures which could serve as poles of aggregation for the population' as a critical factor (Chubb 1981: 81). Moreover, the author observes that 'in the absence of alternative structure to aggregate and mobilise collective interests, every individual seeks to resolve his problems on his own, through whatever channels are open to him' (Chubb 1981: 81).

Research on *vote buying* shows that this practice affects all countries of the Americas (Faughman and Zeichmeister 2011). According to the report, the strongest predictor of the likelihood that an individual is offered a material benefit in exchange for a vote is whether one is politically and civically engaged (the 'participatory citizen'). However, the profile of the Italian *elettore di scambio* presented by Pasquino and Parisi does not include political engagement or 'any motivation to vote when he cannot be guaranteed any remuneration that provides him with immediate and individual benefits' (Cartocci 1990: 107–8).

A 2015–6 report on corruption published by the national Institute of Statistics reveals that the *voto di scambio* was proposed to 1.7 million citizens (3.7 per cent of the citizens between 18 and 80 years old) (ISTAT 2017). According to the data, *voto di scambio* was more likely the subject of municipal elections, and it more likely took place on Italian islands (6.7 per cent) and in the South of Italy (8.4 per cent). The votes were exchanged for 'favours or privileged treatments (34.7 per cent of all vote exchanges), jobs or appointments (32.8 per cent), money (20.6 per cent)' (ISTAT 2017: 12). The indirect experience of the *voto di scambio* is more widespread than the personal direct experience: '3.9 million Italians declared knowing somebody – relatives, friends, colleagues, neighbours – who have been offered something in exchange for electoral backing' (ISTAT 2017: 13). *Voto di scambio* peaked in Puglia (23.7 per cent), while the lowest percentage was reported (1.1 per cent) in Friuli Venezia Giulia.

In Neapolitan popular culture, the ex-major Achille Lauro, who was elected in 1952 with an impressive 300,000 preference votes, has become a legend. He used a 'scheme of handing out shoes to his would-be supporters, the right shoe before the poll, and the left one afterwards, when the vote had been safely recorded' (Dickie 2014: 317). A similar system has been applied to banknotes as well: half of a banknote before the vote and the remaining part on exiting the poll.

In the 2012 movie *Qualunquemente* (it is a made-up word that can be translated as 'in whichever way'), the Italian comedian Antonio Albanese stars in the role of the entrepreneur Cetto La Qualunque ('Mr Whatever') who decides to run for mayor in a small town in Calabria. During the campaign, Cetto La Qualunque is seen engaging in shady activities such as distributing petrol vouchers in the streets or handing out money in cafés to whomever declared to be 'unsure who to vote for'. A more serious depiction of the *voto di scambio* is offered in the movie *Una rete piena di sabbia*, which illustrates the relationship between the mafia and the agents of the *voto di scambio* in the territory of Calabria.

Analogous informal practices include political machineries (from the nineteenth to early twentieth century in the USA) and *caciquismo* (in Spain during the Restoration) for the likeness of their political clientelism. Moreover *veza* (Serbia, the Balkans), with reference to *političke veze* (political connections), is used similarly to obtain privileges and benefits.

12.2 **Vote buying/vote selling** (Western Balkans)
Jovan Bliznakovski
Ss. Cyril and Methodius University in Skopje and Institute for Democracy 'Societas Civilis' Skopje, North Macedonia

Vote buying and *vote selling* are among the most prominent practices of political clientelism worldwide – the exchange of votes for particularistic benefits (see also *voto di scambio*, 12.1 in this volume). In the languages of the Western Balkans, the practices are termed *kupovina glasova/ prodaja glasova* (in Serbian, Bosnian, Croatian and Montenegrin), *blerja e votive/shitja e votave* (in Albanian) and купување гласови / продавање гласови (in Macedonian). The practices of *vote buying/vote selling* have been present across the region since the introduction of the formal multiparty democracy at the beginning of the 1990s. Today, these practices are widely known and recognised in Western Balkans countries as a form of 'corruption' and less frequently as 'clientelism'. Colloquially, the local terms for *vote buying/vote selling* signify an exchange of one's right to vote in the elections for a benefit (typically cash, but also food, clothes, house appliances or minor administrative favours) given, sponsored or assisted by a political party. Both terms, *vote buying* and *vote selling*, point to the same give-and-take practice: the former from the perspective of the patron (a political party), the latter from the perspective of the client (a citizen).

The exchange of electoral votes for material benefits is illegal everywhere in the region, and both cash and non-cash transactions represent a basis for prosecution. The criminal codes of Albania (Art. 328, CCRA 1995) and Kosovo (Art. 215, CCRK 2012) stipulate sanctions of imprisonment of between one and five years for those who participate in *vote buying/vote selling*. The provisions in criminal codes of Bosnia and Herzegovina (Art. 151, CCBH 2003), Montenegro (Art. 186, CCRM 2003) and Serbia (Art. 156, CCRS 2005) go up to three years in prison for *vote buying/vote selling*. In North Macedonia (Art. 162, CCNM 1996), the criminal code stipulates punishment for *vote buying* and *vote selling* of up to one year in prison, or a fine when benefits of minor material value are distributed and a minimum of five years when benefits are substantial.

Despite being an illegal practice, *vote buying/vote selling* is rife in the Western Balkans. A significant number of respondents in the 2017 representative survey in six Western Balkans countries (N= 6040) reported they had been approached with *vote buying* offers in the past (Bliznakovski et al. 2017: 9). Over one-fifth of respondents acknowledged exposure to *vote buying* in Montenegro (22.5 per cent) and Albania (20.6 per cent), followed by 15.4 per cent of respondents in Bosnia and Herzegovina, 12.5 per cent in Kosovo, 8.4 per cent in Serbia and 7.4 per cent in North Macedonia. When compared with surveys from other countries where *vote buying* is considered to be widespread – 5 per cent in Brazil in 2002, 7 per cent in Argentina in 2001–2 and 15 per cent in Mexico in 2000 (Hagopian 2007: 594) – the Western Balkans' average of 14 per cent suggests a significant presence of the practice in the region. *Vote buying* is frequently monitored by external election missions conducted in the region. After monitoring the 2017 parliamentary elections in Albania and the 2018 presidential elections in Montenegro, the Organization for Security and Cooperation in Europe – Office for Democratic Institutions and Human Rights (OSCE/ODIHR) recommended that the prevention of *vote buying* should be a priority for improving the electoral process (OSCE/ODIHR 2017a, 2018a). OSCE/ODIHR noted the presence of the practice in all countries where it conducted monitoring (all but Kosovo) (OSCE/ODIHR 2017b, 2017c, 2018b).

What is the going rate for a vote across the region today? A vote seller's testimony, which helped sentence the mayor of Kavadarci in North Macedonia to two months in prison for buying votes during the 2016 parliamentary elections, cited fees of 16 Euros per vote (Saliu 2017). Wiretap recordings related to the 2017 Albanian parliamentary elections documented a request, made to the Minister of the Interior and the member of the ruling Socialist Party, of 160 Euros for four votes (Tiede 2019). In the city of Cazin in Bosnia and Herzegovina, 150 citizens went on a public protest after they failed to receive the promised 50 Euro compensation for selling their vote in the 2010 general elections (Karabegović 2010). The data we collected through semi-structured interviews conducted as part of the INFORM research project suggest that the price of an electoral vote in the mid-2010s was between 16 and 50 Euros in Albania, 15 and 50 Euros in Bosnia and Herzegovina, from 8 Euros upwards in North Macedonia and from 50 Euros in Montenegro. *Vote buying* and *vote selling* do not always involve cash transactions but can entail the exchange of various goods and services such as food, clothes, house appliances and minor administrative favours.

Political parties in the Western Balkans region employ three main techniques to verify whether the vote sellers keep their end of the bargain. Photographing ballots with mobile phones inside the voting booth is the most common. Parties also instruct vote sellers to mark their ballots with specific symbols or coloured pens, where legal provision does not disqualify such ballots. The third widespread technique of monitoring employed in the region is carousel voting, also referred to as the 'Bulgarian train'. In carousel voting, political party agents hand out already completed ballots to the vote sellers who deposit them in the voting booth, while handing the empty ones received from the polling station to party agents as proof.

The practices of *vote buying* and *vote selling* represent only a fraction of exchanges associated with political clientelism in the Western Balkans. The one-off nature of the vote-for-benefit exchange where a benefit tends to be 'petty' and offered ad hoc during election campaigns distinguishes it from relational clientelism, a type of political clientelism which denotes long-term linking between patrons and clients (Nichter 2018). *Vote buying* and *vote selling* practices are typically reviewed in the literature as examples of electoral clientelism, but political clientelism in the Western Balkans tends to be relational and reaches far beyond activities that support elections directly. Relational clients offer extended services to political parties beyond voting in elections, such as assistance in political mobilisation activities and in the functioning of party organisations, and typically extract greater benefits than the *vote selling* ones such as access to employment, scholarships, subsidies and public procurement contacts. Relational clientelism thus involves a continuous exchange of benefits and services between parties and clients – in the academic literature also referred to as patronage (Stokes et al. 2013: 7).

12.3 *Party soldiers* (Western Balkans)
Jovan Bliznakovski
Ss. Cyril and Methodius University in Skopje and Institute for Democracy 'Societas Civilis' Skopje, North Macedonia

A *party soldier* is a person who offers extended services of political support to political parties in exchange for clientelist benefits. In the Western Balkans languages, *party soldiers* are termed *partijski vojnici* (Serbian, Bosnian, Montenegrin), *militantët e partisë* (Albanian), *партиски војници* (Macedonian) and *stranački vojnici* (Croatian). Unlike *vote buying/vote selling* (Western Balkans), to be a *party soldier* is to not only vote for a given political party in exchange for clientelist benefits, but also to offer services relevant for the building and maintaining of party organisations. *Party soldiers* perform numerous tasks for political parties. They participate in party events such as rallies, conventions and meetings. During election campaigns, *party soldiers* partake in political mobilisation activities such as 'door-to-door' campaigns, put up posters, provide assistance in organising pre-election rallies, mobilise fellow citizens and prepare 'lists of secured voters'. If they are employees of state institutions, *party soldiers* defend the interests of the party while exercising their formal authority. In online social networks, *party soldiers* fiercely promote and defend party interests.

The term has a pejorative meaning and signifies someone uncritically loyal to a political party while enjoying material advantages as a result of party engagement. For example, in one of the interviews conducted by the INFORM project in 2018, a Macedonian respondent explained that: 'the party demands *party soldiers* and acts of obedience … if someone aims to succeed in the party … he only needs to nod his head, he does not need to have any integrity or personal stand on social problems …' A respondent from Kosovo stated that 'employment advantage is given to family members of politicians and to *party militants*'. In the vernacular, it is also often said that political parties 'fill up the ranks of the public institutions with *party soldiers*', that is, with patronage appointments. The title of a news article in Bosnia and Herzegovina reads: '*Party soldiers* are at the head of all public enterprises in Republika Srpska' (Kovačević 2017, emphasis added), while a headline in Serbia reads: 'The heads of public companies should not be *party soldiers*' (FoNet 2019, emphasis added). An alternative term used to describe clientelist engagement is *partijska knižnica* (in Serbian, Bosnian, Montenegrin, Croatian) or *партиска книшка* (in Macedonian), a 'party membership card'. In the common expression, someone obtains a party membership card to get employment or another clientelist benefit.

Since they perform tasks for building and maintaining party organisations, *party soldiers* represent the key base of support for political parties. Political parties carefully record the 'achievements' of their party soldiers. The fiercest activists are first in the queue to extract clientelist benefits, as suggested in the following interview with a former member of party leadership in North Macedonia, conducted by the INFORM project: 'you stimulate activists by making a list [of their attendance in different activities]. And this becomes a party CV, not to be underestimated when the activist will knock on your door looking for employment'. Similarly, in Serbia, an employee in the local administration stated:

> For one to advance, and this depends on the Party, ... he/she has to do something for that party. Maybe he/she will distribute flyers or will partake in a 'door to door' campaign, or will have to collect secured votes – that person has to prove that they are working non-stop. And then, party officials make a list of the most meritorious activist. ... These people are first in the employment cue after the elections, when the party wins power.

Across the region, becoming a *party soldier* is accepted as a viable path towards public sector employment and material benefits. The survey,

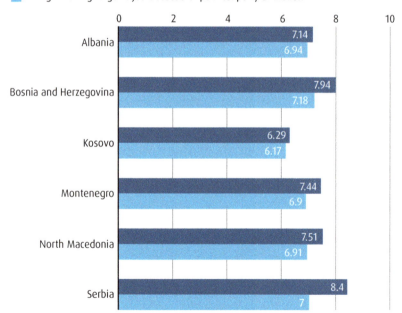

Figure 12.3.1 Influence of political party membership on employment (opinion poll). © Jovan Bliznakovski, based on INFORM survey 2017, created with Datawrapper.

conducted by the INFORM project in 2017, found a strong popular belief that employment and party affiliation were linked in the countries of the Western Balkans. On a scale of 1 to 10, respondents from Serbia agreed with the statement that employment through membership in a political party or party support was widespread in their country with a mean of 8.4, the highest among the surveyed countries (see Figure 12.3.1). The mean of agreement with the statement in other countries was between 7 and 8, apart from Kosovo where respondents agreed with the statement with a mean of 6.3. The survey also suggested that people in the Western Balkans region generally believe that losing or failing to acquire a job because of political party affiliation was widespread (the lowest mean was in Kosovo, at 6.2, and the highest in Bosnia and Herzegovina, at 7.2). Although the depoliticisation of public administration prior to EU integration is high on the agenda in each of the Western Balkans countries (European Commission 2018: 5), these findings indicate an excessive and persistent reliance of political parties on patronage appointments across the region.

Party membership size is another potential indicator of political clientelism. In the Western Balkans, party membership is widespread compared to other European democracies. The 2017 survey by INFORM found that 13 per cent of the respondents in North Macedonia, 10 per cent in Bosnia and Herzegovina, Serbia and Montenegro, 9 per cent in Kosovo and 8 per cent in Albania confirmed they were members of political parties (Bliznakovski et al. 2017: 8), significantly higher than the average in the 27 EU member countries, where it stood at 5 per cent in the period 2004–9 (van Biezen et al. 2012).

Party soldiers are recruited in different ways. Most commonly, they are recruited through social networks (through relatives, friends and acquaintances who hold positions in political parties) and from the rank of public employees (when incumbent political parties coerce employees into joining a party by threatening their employment positions). *Party soldiers* are also recruited from those in dire need of a particularistic benefit (employment). The demand for particularistic benefits is significant in the Western Balkans. Nine per cent of respondents in the 2017 INFORM survey reported that they had reached out to a party official or person of influence for help in the past (14 per cent in North Macedonia, 13 per cent in Montenegro, 10 per cent in Bosnia and Herzegovina, 8 per cent in Kosovo, 7 per cent in Serbia and 5 per cent in Albania) (Bliznakovski et al. 2017: 12).

Citizen engagement in political clientelism, as in the case of *party soldiers*, should be viewed as distinct from citizen engagement present in *vote buying* and *vote selling* (see 12.2 in this volume). While with electoral clientelism clients exchange electoral support for a one-time clientelist benefit, in relational clientelism – a concept proposed by Nichter (2018) – clients support the party for an extended period and extract clientelist benefits on several occasions. In the Western Balkans, relational clientelism with extended party services is associated with higher-value material benefits in comparison to *vote selling*. While vote sellers obtain smaller amounts of cash, food, clothes, household appliances and minor administrative favours, relational clients obtain employment in the public and private sectors, administrative positions on managerial boards of public companies, access to public procurement contracts and other types of preferential access to public services and institutions.

12.4 **Maliks** (Afghanistan)
Jennifer Brick Murtazashvili
Center for Governance and Markets, University of Pittsburgh, USA

In rural Afghanistan, *maliks* are village representatives. They are not leaders but individuals who represent village interests both internally and to the outside world. Often mistaken for village chiefs, they are executives and serve not as headmen or chiefs, but as first among equals, *primus inter pares*. While this entry employs the term *malik*, individuals exercising this role in the Afghan society have a range of regionally specific titles or honorifics. The following terms are to be considered synonymous with the role of *maliks* in Afghan rural life: *qaryadar, khan, qalantar, wakil* (representative), *namayenda* (also representative), *arbab, mir, rais* (leader/head).

'Broadly speaking, the term arbab was used in Western Afghanistan and the term malik is used in eastern Afghanistan' (Kakar 1979: 58). In some cases, the term *malik* is equivalent to a tribe or clan leader, but more often tribal status has little to do with the selection of village representatives. This is because Pashtun tribes have no natural leaders as they are generally acephalous. This does not mean that leaders do not emerge from tribal configurations, but leadership is not a status bequeathed upon individual leaders through hereditary status.

It is also important to note that *maliks* are not the same as large landowning khans that are prevalent in some parts of Afghanistan and in other parts of South Asia, especially Pakistan. In general, *maliks* do not preside over several villages the way that large landowning khans have done in the past. In some villages in Afghanistan, individuals referred to their self-appointed village leaders as khans, but this did not mean that they were powerful. In the past, khans may have been more powerful because they were large landowners, but this power has diminished over the past 50 years. This was noted by anthropologists in the years before the Soviet invasion; it is not a new phenomenon nor a consequence of war (Anderson 1978).

Despite predictions that the customary system would collapse, it actually grew stronger after 2001. Although *maliks* are typically men, there is an increasing number of female *maliks* throughout rural Afghanistan (Murtazashvili 2016).

There are a number of ways for *maliks* to come to power. In some communities the position is hereditary and handed down from one generation to the next. In others, there is some sort of selection process that brings a *malik* to power. This could be through secret ballots or through consensus among community members. Consensus is in fact the most typical way in which these individuals are selected. Typically, male community members, usually through a *shura* process (a process of community consultation and consensus building), select a single person to represent them. By doing so, they give them the authority to make decisions on behalf of the community and represent community interests to the state and outside actors (often to international donors working in villages).

The *malik* is presented by community members to the district governor. In some instances, the district governor will write a letter acknowledging the community decision to local district courts, who may give *maliks* a seal proving the status of village representative (Nojumi et al. 2008: 260). District governments do not always do this: in some cases, *maliks* simply rely upon their signature or their thumbprint on official documents to indicate their authority. The policy of giving stamps and seals to *maliks* is not consistent around the country but has its legacy in histories of cooptation by the state. In the past, the state made seals obligatory. After 2001, *maliks* had no legal status, so when district governors acknowledge their authority to lead communities, this is not a legal act but entirely informal. Of course, this creates enormous confusion, because they are given accoutrements that indicate state support such as seals and appointment letters. Nevertheless, this also indicates the importance of these individuals in mediating community life and underscores the importance of this informal practice. *Maliks* continue to play a vital role in local governance, despite the fact that they are not recognised by any state law or edit.

In many communities, individuals refer to their *malik* as the 'bridge between the people and the government' (Murtazashvili 2016: 79), but the direction of this bridge goes from the village to the state. In other words, the *malik* is not an agent of the state but an agent of the people. *Maliks* most often interact with district governors (*woluswals*), who represent the lowest level of government in post-2001 Afghanistan. Although the constitution calls for elected village councils, these elections have never been held (donor projects, such as community development councils have sought to take their place, but these are not bodies elected through formal processes). The power of *maliks* ranges from community to community and often depends upon how much authority the community is willing to bestow upon them. The further a community is from a seat of power, the more important role the *malik* plays in mediating community life and helping to access the state. In the most populated areas, each community selects its own *malik*, but in more remote areas, it is not unusual for several communities to rely on a single *malik*.

Although communities view *maliks* as leaders who derive their authority to lead based on local consent and custom, their history is deeply interconnected with the state. Throughout Afghan history, state authorities have sought to co-opt *maliks* and use them as agents for their indirect rule. During the 1970s, President Daud tried to establish his own network of *maliks* he could rely upon to collect taxes in rural areas. In the 1980s, the communist People's Democratic Party of Afghanistan tried to appoint its own network of *maliks* to villages to serve as their representatives. Efforts to co-opt *maliks* have generally been unsuccessful.

Maliks can lose power and they are accountable to citizens. In general, when residents become dissatisfied with their *malik*, they can dismiss them from his or her duties. The fact that they are accountable to others is a constraint on their power that generally prevents them from engaging in predatory behaviour. It is for this reason that *maliks* and other customary leaders at the community level enjoy higher levels of trust than any other public organisation in rural Afghanistan (Asia Foundation 2018).

12.5 **Titushky** (Ukraine)
Michal Pszyk
Alumnus, School of Slavonic and East European Studies, UCL, UK

One remarkable feature of post-Soviet regimes is the pervasiveness of 'political technologies' – practices allowing state actors to tip the scales in their favour while simultaneously preserving the façade of democratic procedure (Ledeneva 2006). In Ukraine, *titushky* represents such a practice. *Titushky* describes 'young men of athletic stature wearing sports clothing, serving the role of provocateurs or "protecting" civil actions' (Kukhar 2013).

The term *titushky* was coined in May 2013, and derives from the name of Vadym Titushko, a martial-arts amateur from Bila Tserkva who physically assaulted a female journalist during an opposition protest in Kyiv. The police did not react to the incident despite her cries for help (Ukraiinska Pravda 2013), which raised suspicion of state involvement in the incident. Titushko was subsequently identified as the perpetrator and stated in a video confession that he had been 'offered work on an hourly pay basis', which consisted of 'standing near the oppositionists and maintaining civil order' (Titushko 2013). In that particular case, the task was to create an illusion of emotions expressed by ordinary citizens with no apparent agenda or link to the authorities. The motive for employing *titushky* was to allow authorities to deny any cooperation with hired thugs, who ostensibly acted on their own accord, without being co-opted, and to ensure that reports of *titushky* engaged in overtly violent acts against protesters and journalists did not compromise state actors.

The 'tasks' assigned to *titushky* are not limited to disrupting oppositional protests. Although the name of the phenomenon was coined in 2013, the practice of employing intimidation squads is much older and was used for problem-solving associated with business, in particular during corporate raids. One anonymous source stated that 'a group of men of athletic stature – people older and more experienced than today's

Figure 12.5.1 Vadym Titushko charging at a photographer, Kyiv, 18 May 2013. © Vlad Sobel.

titushky was used for support. They would disperse protesting crowds, take down fences, and provide all sorts of physical support' (Mazanyk 2013). Tasks for *titushky* have included maintaining 'discipline' at rallies (preventing the crowd from dispersing in unwanted directions and upholding 'good morals' through enforcing bans on drinking, smoking and so on), 'monitoring' elections (standing in crowds near polling stations, often sporting 'observer IDs' and, if necessary, resorting to physical coercion) and intimidating opponents planning to disrupt a friendly rally (Chepurko and Ryabokon 2013).

The most notorious instance of *titushky* activity was their involvement in the Euromaidan protests of 2013–14, which ousted pro-Russian President Viktor Yanukovych. These groups of men in civilian clothing acted as an auxiliary force to Berkut, a (now defunct) 6,000-strong anti-riot police unit within the Interior Ministry (Wilson 2014: 78), accused of killing more than 100 people during the revolution's most violent phase in February 2014. The *titushky* assisted Berkut and were held responsible for nearly a dozen documented deaths (Wilson 2014: 79). Among the victims were the protesters assaulted in front of the Supreme Court in Kyiv on 18 February, where the *titushky* reportedly used illegally obtained firearms (Ukraiinska Pravda 2014).

Titushky were initially paid 200 hryvnias per day (17 USD), but as the protests intensified, their pay rose to 500 hryvnias (42 USD), and at times exceeded 1,000 hryvnias (85 USD) for 'active participation'. Active participation involved 'provocation of conflict and disorder' (Mazanyk 2013). One report described a group of *titushky* 'provoking people into brawls and aggression' disguised as members of Svoboda, a nationalist anti-Yanukovych party (Segodnya 2013).

Employing *titushky* as a political technology requires both covert funding for coopting youth and coordination of their activities. During Euromaidan, *titushky* were funded by Serhiy Kurchenko, a Kharkiv-born billionaire with close ties to 'The Family', the inner circle of the former president Yanukovych's allies and his son Oleksandr (Ukrainian Security Service Press Centre 2014). The outcome of the 2014 criminal investigation implicated approximately 20 individuals, including ministers, charged with an 'establishment of a criminal organization', whose illicit profits were 'largely used to finance the suppression of peaceful protests in Kyiv, and particularly to pay for "services" of the so-called "*titushky*"' (Zerkalo Nedeli 2014).

The coordination of these informal activities was handled by the then Interior Minister Vitaliy Zakharchenko, the architect of the anti-Euromaidan media campaign. To ensure deniability, he acted via a proxy, the director of the Kontakt media holding, Viktor Zubrytsky, who was responsible for day-to-day operations. A special investigation charged Zubrytsky with 'coordination of all activities concerning wage payments, distribution of tasks and key instructions regarding who should be given attention and who deserved repression, including activists'. Zubrytsky was also responsible for organising the pro-government rallies in cities where miniature pro-Maidan protests took place (Ukraiinskii Tyzhden 2014).

Titushky groups consisted of unemployed or working-class young men, often with a criminal record, but also 'from a number of backgrounds, like off-duty police officers and state security workers, members of more or less legal combat sports clubs, workers at industrial plants owned by pro-government forces, members of criminal gangs, and common convicts, and most likely also groups of football fans' (Historia Vivens: 2016). They often arrived in Kyiv by bus from 'the east and south of the country', where support for Yanukovych's Party of Regions was the highest (Goncharenko 2014).

Although its idiosyncratic features allow for classifying *titushky* as a Ukrainian phenomenon, such rent-a-mob tactics are hardly unique. Parallels can be drawn with *OBON* (*otdel bab osobogo naznacheniia*), a similar practice observable in Central Asia, particularly in Kyrgyzstan and Uzbekistan. *OBON*, a special-purpose female unit – likely a play on OMON, the Russian government's anti-riot police regiment – is an informal network of groups consisting mostly of rural, middle-aged women who are deployed during protests to fill out crowd numbers, disrupt and delegitimise opposition rallies, and intimidate and assault opponents (Kim et al. 2012).

According to one analyst citing local human rights activists, the first *OBON* groups were formed by Uzbekistan's National Security Service (Szymanek 2012). In order to escape charges of involvement, security officials forcefully recruited socially vulnerable women, such as bazaar traders and former sex workers, to interrupt anti-regime demonstrations, or to target specific individuals, by threatening them with legal problems. In a notorious incident, around 50 women stormed the court trial of human rights activist Abdumannop Khalilov, dragged the defendant out of the building and beat him unconscious. The 30 police officers present at the scene did not react to the incident (Mavloniy 2010). Several days later, an opposition rally in Osh calling for President Bakiyev's dismissal was disrupted by a group of '30 loud women' who 'virtually broke up the demonstration with their yelling' (Evlashkov 2010).

In Kyrgyzstan, the parallels between *OBON* and *titushky* are even more striking. Rather than state coercion, the Kyrgyz authorities have relied on monetary incentives, mostly recruiting women from the ranks of the unemployed. However, oppositionists and private entrepreneurs have also used this practice. *OBON* groups featured prominently in the Kyrgyz Revolution of 2010, when ethnic clashes in the south of the country claimed 2,000 civilian lives and led to the deposition of President Kurmanbek Bakiyev. During one pro-government rally in which Bakiyev himself participated, the speaker's podium was surrounded by 'ranks of strong women' who 'quickly exhibited ready-made posters reading "The opposition seized power with blood!" and "The legitimate president is not guilty!"' (Gabuev 2010).

The use of *OBON* has proven particularly effective due to the image and role ascribed to women in Kyrgyz society. Not only protesters, but even law enforcement officials are hesitant to strike women, seen in Kyrgyzstan as a 'unique embodiment of national character, maternity, and hardship' (Ivashchenko 2015). In the words of one Kyrgyz parliamentarian, 'fighting [them] would be shameful, but so would be running away'. Caught by women, the oppositional leaders had therefore little choice.

12.6 *Krumpliosztás* (Hungary)
Zsofia Stavri
Alumna, School of Slavonic and East European Studies, UCL, UK

The Hungarian practice of *krumpliosztás* can be literally translated as 'potato giving', and it refers to the act of giving food to the electorate in the hope of swaying their votes. The practice dates back to the democratic transition of 1989, when a fall in living standards, growing uncertainty and the deficit of democratic norms were first exploited by political candidates. As the concrete origins of the practice are unknown, it is assumed that the practice could have started as an honest attempt to help the poor.

The recipients are often vulnerable members of society, such as the poor and pensioners (Német 2019). In fact, Hungarian pensioners are in the bottom third in the European Union for the purchasing power of pensions, and with every third person in the country being over 60 years old, they represent a significant voting force. In 2011, an estimated 3.05 million people were living below the poverty line in Hungary, 500,000–600,000 of whom were Roma, almost the entirety of those living in the country (Horváth 2014). In the weeks preceding the 2018 Hungarian parliamentary elections, Dikh TV, a television channel particularly popular among the Roma minority, campaigned against *krumpliosztás*, condemning the fact that sometimes votes are 'sold' for a couple of eggs (Boros 2018).

Politicians usually practise *krumpliosztás* openly, handing food to their constituents. Although the colloquial term refers to potatoes, sometimes it can involve a 'discount market' of sorts for goods at a much cheaper price. Foodstuffs can be decorated with the image of the politician up for election in the given district. Sometimes the politician personally hands out the food to the grateful public, conveying a sense of genuineness and friendliness (Erdélyi et al. 2019; Német 2019).

While *krumpliosztás* relies on ethically ambiguous means, there is a very thin line between *krumpliosztás* and *vote buying*. In 2016, the opposition party Együtt made an official complaint when a candidate of the ruling Fidesz party included a letter urging people to take part in the upcoming referendum on migration in the gifted bags of potatoes (Origo 2016). At the opposite end of the spectrum, the mayor of the thirteenth district in Budapest, József Tóth, changed the date of his municipality's act of charity towards residents to the day after the election to avoid it being seen as a way of buying votes (Haszán 2019).

The origin of funds for the practice is often hard to ascertain, as many politicians cite anonymous donors or declare to have paid themselves (Haszán 2018). These claims are rarely confirmed by trusted sources. The giving can also be initiated by the municipality and seen as a recurring charitable act (Erdélyi et al. 2019). On the other hand, governmental funds are easily funnelled into paying gifts to promote candidates. As such, the practice tends to favour those in power, especially because parties rely on governmental funds for their survival (Transparency International 2017). Hence, this top-down informal practice creates political inequalities, often affecting the reliability of local and general elections (Helmke and Levitsky 2004: 731).

The phenomenon of *krumplosztás* is so iconic in political culture that in 2020 Péter Jakab, leader of the party Jobbik, tried to hand Prime Minister Viktor Orbán a bag of potatoes in an act of protest against what he saw as vote buying in the voting district of Borsod (Herczeg 2020). Jakab had previously dubbed Orbán 'The King of Potatoes' (Sarkadi 2020). *Krumplosztás* is also a trope in popular culture, with many online memes making fun of the practice. One recent example is a picture of US President Joe Biden with the subtitle 'Yes, I did it without giving potatoes'. Another included a list of translations of the word 'potato' in different languages, with the Hungarian version being the word for vote (Krumplis 2019).

Practices similar to *krumpliosztás* exist in other post-socialist countries, such as in Ukraine where politicians give people food packages, sometimes filled with buckwheat (*grechka*) in exchange for votes (Euromaidan Press 2017). In Moldova, pensioners can register to receive cards that enable them to shop in Șor party discount shops, a boon for the constrained financial realities faced by pensioners (Timotina 2018). In Bulgaria, the practice of votes of impoverished ethnic minorities exchanged for foodstuffs is a frequent occurrence (Jordan and Isaev 2009). Finally, beyond the post-Soviet space, similarities can be found with the Italian practice *voto di scambio* (see 12.1 in this volume) (Camerani 2018).

12.7 **Mungu idekh** (Mongolia)
Marissa Smith
Department of Anthropology, De Anza College, USA

Mungu idekh ('eating money') is one of a number of terms used in contemporary Mongolia to criticise ineffective leaders and leadership. In the Mongolian cultural region, leaders' individual qualities of 'moral exemplarship' (Humphrey 1997) are of major importance to political legitimacy. As discussed by High (2017), money and the value of money itself are bound up with the correct management of expansive social relations of production; cash may become polluted and polluting (*buzartai*) if generated through amoral and socially harmful practices or may, alternatively, gain value if generated through exchange with other social groups and networks productive of wealth. High gives the example of a Mongolian gold buyer who travels from a far-flung mining area to the capital to sell gold for Chinese Yuan to Chinese buyers, saying that this 'renews' money and gives the mining area 'good money' as it is invested in local businesses and buys expensive gifts (2017: 121–3). Political leaders must use money to effectively expand social relations and generate fortune from them, for instance through the management of business (Bonilla and Tuya 2018) and construction (Fox 2016). 'Eating' money, on the other hand, means to consume it mundanely and exclusively, in an individual's household, homeland-based, ethnic, corporate or other exclusive networks (from the perspective of which, of course, the money in question may not be seen to be simply 'eaten').

As well as in the context of elections for parliamentary and other public office (Fox 2017), accusations of *mungu idekh* have been repeatedly levelled over the construction of the colossal statue of the Shakyamuni Buddha (*Burkhan Bagsh*) in Erdenet, Mongolia. Between 2010 and 2012, the statue was erected, taken down and rebuilt. It has been 'awakened' (*aravnailakh*) at least twice by the head lama of Mongolia's most powerful monastery (Tuya 2012; Erdenetnews.mn 2014). For members of Erdenet's various networks, particularly those associated with the locally based mining corporation and the provincial government appointed by the Mongolian national government, the statue has been a means to establish political legitimacy through 'donations' (*khandiv*) to kick-start the circulation of wealth and fortune broadly throughout and beyond Erdenet with the mediation of the Buddha. The complicated process of construction has also been a means for these networks to question one another's political legitimacy by branding the money spent on the statue not as broadly beneficial *khandiv* but as *mungu idekh*, 'eaten' within exclusive human networks.

In news outlets owned and operated by networks comprising the community, including the local mining corporation, an exact amount of the money donated by workplaces within the corporation and particular directors as *khandiv* ('donations') appeared on the occasion of the statue's awakening (Tuya 2012) (such detailed listings of donations by specific donors are also commonly posted on Facebook when local, workplace and religious organisations). Other news outlets and stories, funded by networks other than those of the mining corporation and often disappearing from the Internet as quickly as they appear, have levelled accusations of *mungu idekh* at directors of the mining corporation, insinuating that the construction problems visible in the monument itself (for instance, a leaking ceiling that resulted in mould and mildew in the interior of the room at the statue's base) were caused by the movement of money to construction firms that did not utilise the funds for proper materials and building expertise (Byambaa 2013).

While the author was conducting fieldwork inside the corporation, her coworkers were ambivalent about the statue. While they supported the construction of such a monument as an act of collective human 'donation' to a powerful cosmic agent to help repair environmental and social harm related to the industrial pollution that their mining activity had caused locally and that they worked actively as metallurgical and environmental engineers to address, they were loath to associate themselves with the various networks that seemed to be involved in the construction of the statue. A former provincial governor, who also claimed the statue as the product of his donations, was an appointee of the national government as well as an associate of the mining corporation. The mine was established in the early 1970s in the late socialist period; it was well integrated into Soviet and post-Soviet networks and was operated by members of national minority groups. Since the end of the socialist period and the so-called Democratic Revolution of 1988–90, the national government has been controlled by members of the majority Khalkh ethnicity seeking to recentralise control over the mine and its associated logistics infrastructure by the Mongolian state (Bulag 1998). The mining corporation itself is also internally fragmented; in the early 1990s, some sections moved to establish independence, and independent firms with relationships with only some sectors of the mine were successfully established. Thus, there was uncertainty over what sections and directors of the mining corporation were involved in the construction. There was also concern at least on the part of some mine employees who refused to enter the statue and make offerings.

As in the cases of 'eating money' in Greece (see *fakelaki*, 2.17 Volume 1) and Africa (see *kula*, 7.2 Volume 2), the Mongolian case entails the fear that wealthy and powerful actors extract money from the public and 'grow fat' (incidentally, the provincial governor in question was rather overweight). Moreover, however, these cases draw attention to the way in which definitions of the actions involved as either positive or 'corrupt' hinge on the delineation of the networks and publics involved. The construction of the colossal statue succeeds as a politically legitimising act if it solicits the participation of a range of publics, who trust that the actors making the donations are not also engaging in activities that would be systemically harmful – here, for instance, being affiliated with the national government, as the former provincial governor was, that had levied additional taxes on the mining corporation and sought to privatise it, that is, to move control from the locals to the national capital, and to people of another homeland and ethnicity. Also of concern were international relationships (involving, allegedly, China rather than America, Europe and Russia), and a set of professional communities (associated with policy, law and finance rather than with mining and metallurgy). Such actions, as High (2017) has described, make money itself 'polluted' (*buzartai*) and an agent of contamination, and neither the state nor the Buddhist sangha (monastic order) is capable of cleansing (*ugaakh*) the money and its transactors (see also Abrams-Kavunenko 2015 on distrustfulness towards lamas as handlers of *khandiv*).

In contrast to the aforementioned African case, 'feeding' in Mongolia is not overwhelmingly seen as a necessary act of political power. As also shown by the Mongolian concept of *tsartsaani nüüdel* (Fox 2018), exchanging one's vote for 'feeding' is in principle considered unworthy even of livestock, let alone of people, but rather as characteristic of insects. This has not, however, prevented people from 'feeling entitled to' take the money (Fox 2017). It is also significant that, in contrast to the case from Tibetan Rebgong presented by Makley (2018: 127, 140–3), where 'eating money' (*sgor mo za*) characterises the failure of individuals to represent multiple sovereigns at different levels, in the Mongolian context the pre-eminence of a single sovereign or 'aristocratic' network is called for (Sneath 2018). As one commentator on an article about money-eating and the Burkhan Bagsh admonishes, 'Think together, my descendants of Chinggis [Khaan]!' (*sanatsgaa chingisiin ur sad mini*) (Tsolmon 2013).

12.8 **Parillada** (Spanish-speaking Amazonia)
Daniela Peluso
School of Anthropology and Conservation, University of Kent, UK

The term *parillada* refers to a form of bribery and corruption in Lowland South America. It is used among Indigenous Peoples mostly to refer to outsiders, particularly NGO workers, tourism entrepreneurs, oil companies and other local entrepreneurs who specifically aim to enlist indigenous community members to sign an agreement that, in turn, would allow these outside agents to gain access to or rights in the community. Such rights of access could include the building of a lodge, creating a development project, agreeing to an oil concession and so forth. The legal bribe itself operates as part of the informal economy that lays the groundwork, or underbelly for the typically exploitative formal economy that it will serve (Peluso 2018). When indigenous community members are coaxed into making a hasty decision through temptation or when they speak of others being coaxed through enticement or distraction, they say that they have experienced a *parillada*. Although it literally means 'barbecue' – something that smells and looks delicious and is a special much-desired treat, especially for people who live in a hand-to-mouth economy – it is best translated here as a 'distracting bribe'.

Indigenous Peoples' use of *parillada* captures the manner in which other people sometimes try to bribe them. The term is most often used in reference to the NGOs who arrive in the communities and attempt to persuade Indigenous Peoples to approve the NGO's projects, persuaded by the NGO's offer of a range of goods and services. NGOs routinely position themselves as generous potential in the early stages of meeting an indigenous community, endeavouring to create obligations towards themselves while asking the locals to 'cooperate' with their projects. I have witnessed several of these *parilladas*, but the largest was when an adventure ecotourism company hosted such an event and had the community sign an agreement with them while the pigs were roasting on a spit. They presented it as an ultimatum: 'We have been here many times now and if you do not agree we will leave right now and not be returning. If you sign, we can go ahead and celebrate with a *parillada*.' The result is that the NGO currently has a world-renowned tourist lodge inside an indigenous community and is often written about for their exceptional relationship with local peoples. The NGO was adroit in its legal use of bribery, and soon after imposed restrictions and expectations on community members that have curtailed their extractive activities. People often joke: 'we gave up tapir for a mestizo's pig!', referring to the well-prized meat of a tapir that is acquired through indigenous hunting skills and the meat of domesticated pigs which is typically viewed as being unhealthy. In such self-evaluations, individuals are acknowledging their own short-sightedness in the face of inequality while referencing the forfeiture of their own ontologically based economics (Peluso and Alexiades 2005). In this case, a tapir which is a valued 'non-human other' is procured as a source of nourishment on one's own terms for a momentary temptation of inferior meat belonging to people whom they strongly associated with exploitation. The joke serves as a reminder of their improvident exchange.

On a larger scale, *parillada* is used as a euphemism that is inserted into indigenous language to explain the exploitative actions of others towards them. Indigenous Amazonians tend to follow a diverse range of economic practices to ensure their livelihoods as they circulate between rural and urban centres (Alexiades and Peluso 2015, 2016; Peluso 2015, 2021). To varying degrees, Indigenous Peoples have long been integrated into extractive economies in Lowland South America that have rested upon their local knowledge and labour without including their participation in the revenue or benefits share of any overall profits earned. This extractive history precedes the rubber boom becoming particularly punctuated in the seventeenth century via strong colonial trade networks in animal skins, timber, vanilla, cacao and later quinine, rubber and other commodities that propelled personal business pursuits (Alexiades 2009; Peluso 2014, 2016). However, the most acute extractive period was during and immediately following the first rubber boom of 1879–1912 (Cleary 2001). While the prized commodities of extractive economies have changed over time they still rest upon the same formula, the exchange of labour and debt with credit and access to the indigenous forests.

Economically unequal exchanges are reflected in Amazonian colloquial idioms, expressions and euphemisms concerning corruption, such as *parillada* or *aumento* (see 7.7 in this volume), and the respective indigenous moral economies that define what is legitimate and what is not (Peluso 2018, 2020). The language of corruption certainly frames communications and rhetoric (Muir 2016; Tidey 2016; Muir and Gupta 2018), while the local and often intimate vernacular (Ledeneva 1998, 2014; Goldstein and Drybread 2018) normalises it. *Parillada*, as a vernacular idiom, indicates how integrated corruption has become in Amazonian societies and people's everyday lives and how it reflects the larger nation-state (Gupta 1995; Makovicky and Henig 2018a, 2018b) in how people as subjects are often led in particular directions via short-lived benefits and promises.

12.9 *Ne talasaj* (Bosnia and Herzegovina, Croatia, Serbia and Montenegro)
Emina Ribo
Alumna, School of Slavonic and East European Studies, UCL, UK

Ne talasaj literally translates as 'don't make waves', and practices of not making waves are particularly common in Bosnia and Herzegovina, Croatia, Serbia and Montenegro. It is an expression of conformity used in both the private and professional contexts, indicating that it is not desirable to question an unwritten rule, social norm or power structure and disrupt the status quo. While being an expression of conformity, it is considered to be a general attitude of the people associated with powerlessness and inability to change the state of affairs.

Ne talasaj is derived from the Bosnian/Croatian/Serbian verb *talasati* meaning 'to make a wave' (*talas* means 'a wave'). However, *talasati* can also be used figuratively, meaning to 'agitate' or 'disrupt' something. The *ne talasaj* behaviour is a case of ambivalence (Ledeneva 2018: 11). By practising *ne talasaj*, an actor engages in non-action, indicative of conforming with certain rules and power structures, while also tacitly rejecting it. Such dissonance is often associated with an idea of 'doublethink', or a strategy of survival under oppressive regimes. Pursuing *ne talasaj* is a way of willingly or unwillingly supporting the power structures and reproducing norms through conformity. The norms of conforming can affect multiple spheres in citizens' lives and under certain circumstances may become omnipresent.

According to the Croatian online language portal *Hrvatski jezični portal*, a monolingual dictionary, the expression captures the following behaviour: 'Do not ask questions and elicit problems that could disrupt the existing condition and irritate the elite authorities' (*ne postavljaj pitanja i ne pokreći probleme koji bi remetili postojeće stanje i uznemirivali elitu vlasti*). The online Serbian slang dictionary, *Vukajlija*, offers an explanation of the context in which *ne talasaj* practices may occur: the expression is used to warn someone who wants to change an agreement or break a promise in order to let the person know that this action would be disappointing (*izreka kojom nekome ko očigledno želi da promeni dogovor ili prekrži obećanje stavljamo do znanja da bi takav postupak bio razočaravajući*).

The social norms of *ne talasaj* might be more diffuse as there are no particular networks or institutions that support it, as in the case of *kumstvo* (godfather) for example. Instead, it can be described as a practical norm of conformity and inactivism. Just as Janteloven in Scandinavia is a set of norms that takes many forms in different social settings (Jakobsen 2018: 254–5), *ne talasaj* can also occur in different social settings. Both codes of conformity expect people to avoid self-expression and activism while generally supporting the established norms.

The content analysis of the public discourse on *ne talasaj* reveals that most newspaper articles link such behaviour to professional contexts. 'Whenever an employee complained about something or raised his opinion, he was asked to the office for a "conversation in private".' Often they were told, 'Don't make waves, you will get fired, the market is full' (Index.hr 2017). The party patronage system and the limitations of the job market in the Western Balkans are behind the *ne talasaj* compliance that supports the status quo but also creates dissatisfaction with it. Other newspaper articles mention *ne talasaj* in the context of politicians or other whistleblowers who were told to 'not make waves'. In the case of the Mayor of Vir, Kristijan Kapović, who was charged with abusing his political position, allegedly on the grounds of his nonconformity, is quoted as saying: '"Kapović, be silent, don't make waves, be good and you will be good." And when I am not silent, I get reported and sentenced' (Urukalo 2019).

Most entries in the context of the practice in blog or magazine entries deal with *ne talasaj* as a norm that negatively affects society, suppresses freedom of speech and expression while encouraging individual passivity and compliance. The practice is portrayed to prevent people from changing their social circumstances, eventually affecting the private lives of those inactively conforming to power structures as well. *Ne talasaj* is perceived as a vicious circle within which people are trapped. Such social norms account for the so-called implementation gap and eventual failure of reforms, especially in the Europeanisation process and is considered a socio-cultural barrier for the institutional adaptation of the country (see the case of Croatia in Poljanec-Borić and Pilar 2008).

Other sources discuss *ne talasaj* as a behavioural pattern from the Communist era that remains intrinsic to politicians (Veljak 2002) and link it to the existential immobility and the 'ambivalence in the normalizing discourse of waiting out the crisis' (Jansen 2014: 82). Hage (2009) takes the concept of 'waiting out the crisis' or being 'stuck in crisis' further and argues that it represents a form of celebrating the ability to endure a crisis. He argues that 'waiting out' is different to 'just waiting' – it is a specific form of being passive, while disagreeing at the same time. Its ambivalence means that on the one hand, citizens continue to be subjected to certain social conditions by waiting for them to dissipate (inactivism), and on the other hand, they master these conditions as best as they can. This dual character of 'waiting out' is a useful 'governmental tool that encourages a mode of restraint, self-control and self-government' (Hage 2009: 468). This can be linked to the ambivalent nature of *ne talasaj* – a tool that enables the status quo to be maintained.

Academic research confirms the negative implications of *ne talasaj* norms for the implementation of governmental reform or change overall, and links it to the Communist past of the countries in the region. *Ne talasaj* is expected by those in power and used as a mechanism to threaten members of parties with the loss of their position or employees with redundancy if they speak out against any illegal or unregulated acts. Scholars find cultural features to be a major obstacle to economic and business development, labelling them as cultures of keeping the 'status quo' (Šimić Banović 2016: 14). Maintaining the status quo is exactly what happens when pursuing *ne talasaj*: 'when identifying and explaining the cause of certain national-level failures, this saying seems to best reflect the average behaviour of Croatian citizens' (Šimić Banović 2015: 117). The content analysis of media sources confirms that *ne talasaj* is pursued in political, business and other professional spheres.

Ne talasaj either embodies a social norm of conforming to social circumstances or compliance with power structures used as a levelling mechanism to tell others to stay put and refrain from questioning anything. What can be drawn from the context analysis of the perceptions of this practice is that *ne talasaj* is perceived as a societal 'ill', preventing change, activism and individualism, thus reinforcing existing norms and supporting established power structures in both the private and professional sphere. On the other hand, strategies based on the aversion to change do reflect the time-proven effectiveness of dealing with crises, wars and political changes in the region. *Ne talasaj* practices are context-bound and ambivalent, which helps to serve multiple identities and moralities.

Bibliography to Chapter 12

Introduction: political participation
Uta Staiger

Arendt, H. 2018. *The Human Condition*. 2nd ed. Chicago and London: The University of Chicago Press.
Bowler, S. et al. (eds) 1999. *Party Discipline and Parliamentary Government*. Columbus: Ohio State University Press (Parliaments and legislatures series).
Cianetti, L., Dawson, J. and Hanley, S. 2018. 'Rethinking "Democratic Backsliding" in Central and Eastern Europe – Looking Beyond Hungary and Poland'. *East European Politics* 34(3): 243–56.
Cowley, P. and Stuart, M. 2012. 'A Coalition with Two Wobbly Wings: Backbench Dissent in the House of Commons'. *Political Insight* 3(1): 8–11.
de Tocqueville, A. 2002. *Democracy in America*. Paperback ed. Translated and edited by H. C. Mansfield and D. Winthrop. Chicago: The University of Chicago Press.
Ekman, J., Gherghina, S. and Podolian, O. 2016. 'Challenges and Realities of Political Participation and Civic Engagement in Central and Eastern Europe'. *East European Politics* 32(1): 1–11.
Habermas, J. 2019. 'Réflexions sur le concept de participation politique'. *Archives de Philosophie*. Translated by C. Bouchindhomme and J.-M. Durand-Gasselin, 82(1): 11.
Hagopian, F. 2009. 'Parties and Voters in Emerging Democracies'. In *The Oxford Handbook of Comparative Politics*. 1st ed., edited by C. Boix and S. C. Stokes, 582–603. New York: Oxford University Press.
Hooghe, M. and Quintelier, E. 2014. 'Political Participation in European Countries: The Effect of Authoritarian Rule, Corruption, Lack of Good Governance and Economic Downturn'. *Comparative European Politics* 12(2): 209–32.
Hopkin, J. 2012. 'Clientelism, Corruption and Political Cartels: Informal Governance in Southern Europe'. In *International Handbook on Informal Governance*, edited by T. Christiansen and C. Neuhold, 198–218. Cheltenham (UK) and Northampton (US): Edward Elgar Publishing.
Inglehart, R. 2018. *Culture Shift in Advanced Industrial Society*. Princeton: Princeton University Press.
Kam, C. 2011. *Party Discipline and Parliamentary Politics*. Paperback ed. Cambridge: Cambridge University Press.
Kaase, M. 2009. 'Perspectives on Political Participation'. In *The Oxford Handbook of Political Behavior*. 1st ed., edited by R. J. Dalton and H. Klingemann, 783–96. New York: Oxford University Press.
Maliks, R. 2014. *Kant's Politics in Context*. New York: Oxford University Press.
Montero, J., Teorell, J. and Torcal, M. 2006. 'Political Participation: Mapping the Terrain'. In *Citizenship, Involvement in European Democracies. A Comparative Analysis*, edited by J. V. Deth, J. R. Montero and A. Westholm, 334–57. London: Routledge.
Putnam, R. D. 1993. 'What Makes Democracy Work?'. *National Civic Review* 82(2): 101–7.
Tilly, C. and Tarrow, S. G. 2015. *Contentious Politics*. New York: Oxford University Press.
van Deth, J. W. 2016. 'What Is Political Participation?'. In *Oxford Research Encyclopaedia of Politics*, edited by A. P. Djup et al. New York: Oxford University Press.
Verba, S., Nie, N. and Kim, J. 1978. *Participation and Political Equality: A Seven Nation Comparison*. New York: Cambridge University Press.
Wilson, A. 2011. 'Political Technology: Why Is It Alive and Flourishing in the Former USSR?'. *OpenDemocracy*, 17 June. www.opendemocracy.net/en/odr/political-technology-why-is-it-alive-and-flourishing-in-former-ussr/

12.1 *Voto di scambio* (Italy)
Alberica Camerani

Allum, P. A. 1975. *Potere e Società a Napoli nel Dopoguerra*. Translated by A. Serafini. Torino: Einaudi.
Ancisi, A. 1976. *La Cattura del Voto: Sociologia del Voto di Preferenza*. Milano: Franco Angeli.
Banfield, E. C. 1958. *The Moral Basis of a Backward Society*. Glencoe: The Free Press.
Caciagli, M. and Belloni, F. P. 1981. 'The "New" Clientelism in Southern Italy: The Christian Democratic Party in Catania'. In *Political Clientelism, Patronage, and Development*, edited by S. N. Eisenstadt and R. Lemarchand, 35–55. London: Sage Publications.
Cartocci, R. 1990. *Elettori in Italia. Riflessioni sulle Vicende Elettorali degli Anni Ottanta*. Bologna: Il Mulino.
Chubb, J. 1981. 'The Social Bases of an Urban Political Machine: The Christian Democratic Party in Palermo'. In *Political Clientelism, Patronage, and Development*, edited by S. N. Eisenstadt and R. Lemarchand, 35–56. Beverly Hills: Sage Publications.
Dickie, J. 2014. *Blood Brotherhoods: A History of Italy's Three Mafias*. New York City: Public Affairs.
Faughman, B. M. and Zeichmeister, E. J. 2011. 'Vote Buying in the Americas'. *AmericasBarometer Insights* 57. www.vanderbilt.edu/lapop/insights/I0857en.pdf
Ferrarella, L. 2012. 'Regione Lombardia, arrestato assessore di Formigoni per voto di scambio', *Corriere della Sera*, 10 October. http://milano.corriere.it/milano/notizie/cronaca/12_ottobre_10/assessore-lombardia-arrestato-2112186707377.shtml
Gambetta, D. 1988. 'Mafia: The Price of Distrust'. In *Trust: Making and Breaking Cooperative Relations*, edited by D. Gambetta, 158–75. Oxford: Blackwell.
Greco, G. 1972. 'Appunti per una Tipologia della Clientela'. *Quaderni di Sociologia* 2: 178–97.
Hopkin, J. 2012. 'Clientelism, Corruption and Political Cartels: Informal Governance in Southern Europe'. In *International Handbook on Informal Governance*, edited by T. Christiansen and C. Neuhold, 198–215. Cheltenham: Edward Elgar Publishing.
ISTAT. 2017. *La Corruzione in Italia: il Punto di Vista delle Famiglie*. ISTAT. www.istat.it/it/files/2017/10/La-corruzione-in-Italia.pdf?title=La+corruzione+in+Italia+-+12%2Fott%2F2017+-+Testo+integrale+e+nota+metodologica.pdf
Katz, S. and Bardi, L. 1980. 'Preference Voting and Turnover in Italian Parliamentary Elections'. *American Journal of Political Science* 24(1): 97–114.
Parisi, A. and Pasquino, G. 1979. 'Changes in Italian Electoral Behaviour: The Relationship between Parties and Voters'. *West European Politics* 2(3): 6–30.
Pasquino, G. 1972. 'Radici del Frazionismo e Voto di Preferenza'. *Rivista Italiana di Scienza Politica* 2: 353–68.
Putnam, D. P. 1993. *La Tradizione Civica nelle Regioni Italiane*. Translated by N. Messora. Milano: Mondadori.
Saviano, R. 2013. 'Ecco il prezzo dei nostri voti'. L'Espresso, 21 February. www.socialnews.it/blog/2013/02/01/ecco-il-prezzo-dei-nostri-voti/
Scott, J. C. 1972. 'Patron-Client Politics and Political Change in Southeast Asia'. *The American Political Science Review* 66(1): 91–113.

12.2 *Vote buying/vote selling* (Western Balkans)
Jovan Bliznakovski

Bliznakovski, J., Gjuzelov, B. and Popovikj, M. 2017. The Informal Life of Political Parties in the Western Balkan Societies. *Institute for Democracy 'Societas Civilis' Skopje (IDSCS)*, INFORM project. https://idscs.org.mk/wp-content/uploads/2017/11/IDSCS-Informal-Life-of-Political-Parties-Report-27092017.pdf
CCBH. 2003. 'Criminal Code of Bosnia and Herzegovina'. *Official Gazette* no. 3/03.
CCNM. 1996. 'Criminal Code of North Macedonia'. *Official Gazette* no. 37/1996, 29 July 1996.
CCRA. 1995. 'Criminal Code of the Republic of Albania'. *Official Gazette* no. 7895, 27 January.
CCRK. 2012. 'Criminal Code of the Republic of Kosovo'. *Code* no. 04/L-082, 20 April.
CCRM. 2003. 'Criminal Code of the Republic of Montenegro'. *Official Gazette* no. 70/2003.
CCRS. 2005. 'Criminal Code of the Republic of Serbia'. *Official Gazette* no. 58/2005.

Hagopian, F. 2007. 'Parties and Voters in Emerging Democracies'. In *The Oxford Handbook of Comparative Politics*, edited by C. Boix and S. C. Stokes, 582–603. Oxford and New York: Oxford University Press.

Karabegović, D. 2010. 'Stranku Radom za boljitak optužuju za kupovinu glasova'. *Radio Slobodna Evropa*, 28 December. www.slobodnaevropa.org/a/stranka_radom_za_boljitak_optuzuju_za_kupovinu_glasova/2261711.html

Nichter, S. 2018. *Votes for Survival: Relational Clientelism in Latin America*. Cambridge and New York: Cambridge University Press.

OSCE/ODIHR. 2017a. 'Election Observation Mission Final Report. Republic of Albania Parliamentary Elections 25 June 2017'. *OSCE/ODIHR*. www.osce.org/odihr/elections/albania/346661?download=true

OSCE/ODIHR. 2017b. 'Election Observation Mission Final Report. Republic of Macedonia, Municipal Elections 15 October and 29 October 2017'. *OSCE/ODIHR*. www.osce.org/odihr/elections/fyrom/367246?download=true

OSCE/ODIHR. 2017c. 'Election Assessment Mission Final Report. Republic of Serbia, Presidential Elections 2 April 2017'. *OSCE/ODIHR*. www.osce.org/odihr/elections/serbia/322166?download=true

OSCE/ODIHR. 2018a. 'Election Observation Mission Final Report, Montenegro, Presidential Elections 15 April 2018'. *OSCE/ODIHR*. www.osce.org/odihr/elections/montenegro/386127?download=true

OSCE/ODIHR. 2018b. 'Election Observation Mission Statement of Preliminary Findings and Conclusions, Bosnia and Herzegovina, General Elections 7 October 2018'. *OSCE/ODIHR*. www.osce.org/odihr/elections/bih/398957?download=true

Saliu, F. 2017. 'Gradonachalnikot na Kavadarci kupuval glasovi za 1000 denari'. *21TV*, 18 August. https://tv21.tv/mk/gradonachalnikot-na-kavadartsi-kupuva/

Stokes, S. C., Dunning, T., Nazareno, M. and Brusco, V. 2013. *Brokers, Voters, and Clientelism: The Puzzle of Distributive Politics*. Cambridge Studies in Comparative Politics. New York: Cambridge University Press.

Tiede, P. 2019. 'Abhör-Bänder belegen: Regierung manipulierte Wahl'. *Bild*, 17 June. www.bild.de/politik/ausland/politik-ausland/wahl-manipulation-in-albanien-abhoer-baender-belegen-regierung-manipulierte-wahl-62666642.bild.html

12.3 *Party soldiers* (Western Balkans)
Jovan Bliznakovski

Bliznakovski, J., Gjuzelov, B. and Popovikj, M. 2017. The Informal Life of Political Parties in the Western Balkan Societies. *Institute for Democracy 'Societas Civilis' Skopje (IDSCS)*, INFORM project. https://idscs.org.mk/wp-content/uploads/2017/11/IDSCS-Informal-Life-of-Political-Parties-Report-27092017.pdf

European Commission. 2018. 'Communication from the Commission to the European Parliament, the Council, the European Economic and Social Committee and the Committee of the Regions. A credible enlargement perspective for and enhanced EU engagement with the Western Balkans'. *COM(2018) 65 final*, 6 February. https://eur-lex.europa.eu/legal-content/EN/TXT/?uri=CELEX%3A52018DC0065

FoNet. 2019. 'Arsić: Direktori javnih preduzeća da ne budu "partijski vojnici"'. *N1*, 28 March. https://n1info.rs/biznis/a471627-arsic-direktori-javnih-preduzeca-da-ne-budu-partijski-vojnici/

Kovačević, L. 2017. 'DODIKOVA PRIPREMA ZA IZBORNU KAMPANJU: Partijski vojnici na čelu svih javnih preduzeća u RS'. *Žurnal*, 23 August. https://zurnal.info/novost/20642/partijski-vojnici-na-celu-svih-javnih-preduzeca-u-rs

Nichter, S. 2018. *Votes for Survival: Relational Clientelism in Latin America*. New York: Cambridge University Press.

van Biezen, I., Mair, P. and Poguntke, T. 2012. 'Going, going ... gone? The Decline of Party Membership in Contemporary Europe'. *European Journal of Political Research* 51(1): 24–56.

12.4 *Maliks* (Afghanistan)
Jennifer Brick Murtazashvili

Anderson, J. W. 1978. 'There Are No Khāns Anymore: Economic Development and Social Change in Tribal Afghanistan'. *Middle East Journal* 32(2): 167–83.

Asia Foundation. 2018. 'A Survey of the Afghan People: Afghanistan in 2018'. Washington, DC: Asia Foundation. https://web.archive.org/web/20210309203331/https://asiafoundation.org/wp-content/uploads/2019/12/2019_Afghan_Survey_Infographics.pdf

Kakar, M. H. 1979. *Government and Society in Afghanistan: The Reign of Amir Abd Al-Rahman Khan.* Austin, TX: University of Texas Press.

Murtazashvili, J. B. 2016. *Informal Order and the State in Afghanistan.* New York: Cambridge University Press.

Nojumi, N., Dyan, M. and Stites, E. 2008. *After the Taliban: Life and Security in Rural Afghanistan.* New York: Rowman and Littlefield.

12.5 *Titushky* (Ukraine)
Michal Pszyk

Chepurko, V. and Ryabokon, A. 2013. 'Militsiia ne mozhet naiti sportsmena, kotoryi izbil zhurnalistku'. *Komsomolskaya Pravda v Ukraine.* 21 May. http://kp.ua/summary/394666-mylytsyia-ne-mozhet-naity-sportsmena-kotoryi-yzbyl-zhurnalystku

Evlashkov, D. 2010. 'OBON ne proshel'. *Rosiiskaia* Gazeta 81, 16 April: 8.

Gabuev, A. 2010. 'Kurmanbeka Bakieva ukhodiat dekretom'. *Kommersant* 63(12): 8.

Goncharenko, R. 2014. 'Titushki – the Ukrainian President's Hired Strongmen'. *Deutsche Welle*, 19 February. www.dw.com/en/titushki-the-ukrainian-presidents-hired-strongmen/a-17443078

Historia Vivens. 2016. 'Titushki, the Low-cost Beastly Thugs of the Yanukovich Regime …'. *Historia Vivens*, 14 May. https://web.archive.org/web/20160514063748/http://www.historiavivens.eu/2/titushki_the_low_cost_beastly_thugs_of_the_yanukovich_regime_1028900.html

Ivashchenko, E. 2015. 'Pisma iz Bishkeka. Otriad bab osobogo naznachennya'. *Esquire Kazakhstan*, 13 April. https://esquire.kz/pisyma-iz-bishkeka-otryad-bab-osobogo-naznatcheniya/

Kim, A., Osmonalieva, A., Rasulov, B. and Sikorskaya, I. 2012. 'Rent-A-Mob Protests in Central Asia'. *Institute for War and Peace Reporting*, 6 January. https://iwpr.net/global-voices/rent-mob-protests-central-asia

Kukhar, A. 2013. 'Kto takie "titushki", i pochemu ikh tak nazyvaiut v Ukraine?'. *Argumenty i Fakty*, 3 December. www.aif.ru/euromaidan/uadontknows/1036542

Ledeneva, A. 2006. *How Russia Really Works.* Ithaca and London: Cornell University Press.

Mavloniy, D. 2010. 'Znakomtes: OBON – otriad bab spetsialnogo naznacheniia'. *Radio Azattyk*, 13 September. http://rus.azattyq.org/a/obon_woman_kyrgyzstan_uzbekistan/2154268.html

Mazanyk, L. 2013. 'Pokolenie titushek'. *Gordon.ua.* http://gordonua.com/specprojects/titushki.html

Segodnya. 2013. 'Po Kievu khodiat "titushki", zamaskirovannye pod "svobodovtsev" – aktivist Maidana'. Segodnya, 11 December. www.segodnya.ua/ukraine/po-kievu-hodyat-titushki-zamaskirovannye-pod-svobodovcev-aktivist-maydana-481850.html

Szymanek, M. 2012. 'OBON: Rent-A-Mob Groups in the Volatile Kyrgyzstani Reality'. *New Eastern Europe*, 6 December. https://neweasterneurope.eu/2012/12/06/obon-rent-a-mob-groups-in-the-volatile-kyrgyzstani-reality/

Titushko, V. 2013. 'Interviu Titushko Vadima'. *YouTube.* www.youtube.com/watch?v=IbeJqWers9o

Ukraiinska Pravda. 2013. 'Molodyky do krovi pobyly zhurnalistiv, militsiia ne vtruchalasia'. *Ukraiinska Pravda*, 18 May. www.pravda.com.ua/news/2013/05/18/6990166/

Ukraiinskii Tyzhden. 2014. 'Antymaidan i titushok koordynuvalo kerivnytstvo MVS'. *Ukraiinskii Tyzhden*, 3 April. http://tyzhden.ua/News/106646

Ukrainian Security Service Press Centre. 2014. 'SBU ta Henprokuratura rozsliduiut protypravnu diialnist holovnoho finansysta "sim'ii" Yanukovycha'. *Portal.lviv.ua*, 8 October. https://portal.lviv.ua/news/2014/10/08/125000

Wilson, A. 2014. *Ukraine Crisis: What It Means for the West*. New Haven and London: Yale University Press.
Zerkalo Nedeli. 2014. 'Genprokuratura obvinila Kurchenko v finansirovanii "titushek"'. *Zerkalo Nedeli*, 24 March. http://zn.ua/POLITICS/genprokuratura-obvinila-kurchenko-v-finansirovanii-titushek-141829_.html

12.6 *Krumpliosztás* (Hungary)
Zsofia Stavri

Boros, J. 2018. 'Ne az legyen, hogy egy doboz tojással megveszik a cigányok szavazatát' [Don't Let Them Buy the Votes of the Roma with a Box of Eggs]. *444.hu*, 26 February. https://444.hu/2018/02/26/ne-az-legyen-hogy-egy-doboz-tojassal-megveszik-a-ciganyok-szavazatat

Camerani, A. 2018. 'Voto di scambio (Italy)'. *Global Informality Project*. www.in-formality.com/wiki/index.php?title=Voto_di_scambio_(Italy)

Erdélyi, P., Sarkadi, Z., Halász, J. and Kiss, B. 2019. 'Újkori feudalizmus: országszerte étellel és adományokkal tömik a választókat a politikusok' [New Age Feudalism: Around the Country Politicians are Stuffing the Electorate with Food and Gifts]. *444.hu*, 12 October. https://444.hu/2019/10/12/ujkori-feudalizmus-orszagszerte-etellel-es-adomanyokkal-tomik-a-valasztoikat-a-politikusok

Euromaidan Press. 2017. 'Why Ukrainian Parliament Voted to Change the Election System Against its Own Will'. *Euromaidan Press*, 11 November. http://euromaidanpress.com/2017/11/11/why-the-ukrainian-parliament-voted-to-change-the-election-system-against-its-own-will/

Haszán, Z. 2018. 'A Fidesz úgy talpra állította a gazdaságot, hogy a kampányoló kormánypárti politikusok nem győznek közkívánatra ingyen ételt osztani a rászorulóknak' [Fidesz has Strengthened the Economy So Much That Campaigning Politicians of the Party are Overwhelmed with Giving Free Food to the Needy]. *444.hu*, 25 January. https://444.hu/2018/01/25/a-fidesz-ugy-talpra-allitotta-a-gazdasagot-hogy-a-kampanyolo-kormanyparti-politikusok-nem-gyoznek-kozkivanatra-ingyen-etelt-osztogatni-a-raszoruloknak

Haszán, Z. 2019. 'Máris kettőre ugrott az olcsókrumpli számláló' [The Cheap Potato Counter has Already Jumped to Two]. *444.hu*, 16 October. https://444.hu/2019/10/16/maris-kettore-ugrott-az-olcsokrumpli-szamlalo

Helmke, G. and Levitsky, S. 2004. 'Informal Institutions and Comparative Politics: A Research Agenda'. *Perspectives on Politics* 2(4): 725–40.

Herczeg, M. 2020. 'A Fidesz-KDNP megszavazta Jakab Péter 4,4 millió forintos rekordbírságát, majd elvették tőle a szót, amikor Tiborczról kezdett el beszélni' [Fidesz-KDNP Voted for Péter Jakab's 4.4 million Forint Record Fine and Then Took the Right to Speak from Him When He Started to Talk about Tiborcz]. *444.hu*, 30 November. https://444.hu/2020/11/30/a-fidesz-kdnp-megszavazta-jakab-peter-44-millio-forintos-rekordbirsagat

Horváth, B. 2014. 'Az ombudsmani jelentés szerint hárommillió szegény él Magyarországon' [The Ombudsman's Report Says There Are Three Million Poor People in Hungary]. *444.hu*, 30 March. https://444.hu/2014/03/30/az-ombudsmani-jelentes-szerint-harommillio-szegeny-ember-el-magyarorszagon

Jordan, M. J. and Isaev, O. 2009. 'The Business of Politics'. *Jordanink Wordpress*, 13 October. https://jordanink.wordpress.com/2009/10/13/the-business-of-politics/

Krumplis, B. 2019. 'Krumpli=szavazat' [Potato=Vote]. *Facebook.com*, 2 October. www.facebook.com/krumplisbence/photos/501833667048109.

Német, T. 2019. 'Mit kínál a magyar kampány?' [What Do Hungarian Campaigns Offer?]. *Index.hu*, 12 October. https://index.hu/belfold/2019/10/12/mit_kinal_a_magyar_kampany/

Origo. 2016. 'Szavazásra buzdít Wintermantel Zsolt' [Zsolt Wintermantel Encourages Voting]. *Origo.hu*, 27 September. www.origo.hu/itthon/20160927-krumpliosztas-miatt-a-valasztasi-bizottsaghoz-fordul-az-egyutt.html

Sarkadi, Z. 2020. 'Jakab Péter: Krumplikirály van Magyarországon, ma koronáztuk meg' [Péter Jakab: There Is a Potato King in Hungary, We Crowned Him Today]. *444.hu*, 11 October. https://444.hu/2020/10/11/jakab-peter-krumplikiraly-van-magyarorszagon-ma-koronaztuk-meg

Timotina, M. 2018. 'Sor's Web. How a Practical Businessman Gave Shops the Function of Territorial Party Organisations'. *Vedomosti.md*, 22 January. www.vedomosti.md/news/pautina-shora-kak-praktichnyj-biznesmen-pridal-torgovym-toch

Transparency International. 2017. 'Választások, politikafinanszírozás' [Elections, Financing Politics]. *Transparency International Hungary*. https://transparency.hu/kozszektor/valasztasok-part-es-kampanyfinanszirozas/

12.7 *Mungu idekh* (Mongolia)
Marissa Smith

Abrams-Kavunenko, S. 2015. 'Paying for Prayers: Perspectives on Giving in Postsocialist Ulaanbaatar'. *Religion, State and Society* 43: 327–41.
Bonilla, L. and Tuya, Sh. 2018. 'Electoral Gifting and Personal Politics in Mongolia's Parliamentary Election Season'. *Central Asian Survey* 37: 457–74.
Bulag, U. E. 1998. *Nationalism and Hybridity in Mongolia*. Oxford: Clarendon Press.
Byambaa, B. 2013. 'Burkhan Bagshiin Sereg Dur Nurj Unakhad Belen Boljee'. *ErdenetInfo*, 5 September. http://erdenetinfo.mn/node/1226 (inactive)
Erdenetnews.mn. 2014. 'Burkhan bagshiin sereg duriin dakhin aravnailna'. *Erdentenews*, 11 April.
Fox, L. 2016. 'The Road to Power'. *Emerging Subjects Blog*, 24 August. https://blogs.ucl.ac.uk/mongolian-economy/2016/08/24/the-road-to-power/
Fox, L. 2017. 'The Price of an Election: Split Hopes and Political Ambivalence in the Ger Districts of Ulaanbaatar'. *Emerging Subjects Blog*, 13 March. http://blogs.ucl.ac.uk/mongolian-economy/2017/07/13/the-price-an-election-split-hopes-and-political-ambivalence-in-the-ger-districts-of-ulaanbaatar/
Fox, L. 2018. 'Tsartsaani nüüdel'. In *The Global Encyclopaedia of Informality, Volume 2*, edited by A. Ledeneva, 460–3. London: UCL Press.
High, M. 2017. *Fear and Fortune: Spirit Worlds and Emerging Economies in the Mongolian Gold Rush*. Ithaca and London: Cornell University Press.
Humphrey, C. 1997. 'Exemplars and Rules: Aspects of the Discourse of Moralities in Mongolia'. In *The Ethnography of Moralities*, edited by S. Howell, 25–46. London: Routledge.
Makley, C. 2018. *Battle for Fortune: State-Led Development, Personhood, and Power Among Tibetans in China*. Ithaca: Cornell University Press.
Sneath, D. 2018. 'Commonwealth, Inalienable Possessions, and the Res Publica: The Anthropology of Aristocratic Order and the Landed Estate'. *History and Anthropology* 29: 324–41.
Tsolmon, G. 2013. 'Burkhan bagshiin sereg dur buteekh mungunuus zavshigchdig ATG-t shalgaj ekheljee'. *Mongolnews.mn*, 9 October. http://mongolnews.mn/i/46481 (inactive)
Tuya, B. 2012. 'Burkhan Bagshiin Sereg Dur Ene Sariin 16-nd "amilna" '. *Shine Medee* 81(843), 10 September: 2.

12.8 *Parillada* (Spanish-speaking Amazonia)
Daniela Peluso

Alexiades, M. N. (ed.) 2009. *Mobility and Migration in Indigenous Amazonia: Contemporary Ethnoecological Perspectives*. London: Berghahn Books.
Alexiades, M. N. and Peluso, D. M. 2015. 'Introduction: Indigenous Urbanization in Lowland South America'. *The Journal of Latin American and Caribbean Anthropology* 20(1):1–12 (special issue), *Indigenous Urbanization: The Circulation of Peoples between Rural and Urban Amazonian Spaces*. Guest editor: D. M. Peluso.
Alexiades, M. N. and Peluso, D. M. 2016. 'La urbanización indígena en la Amazonia. Un nuevo contexto de articulación social y territorial' [Indigenous Urbanization in Amazonia: A New Context for Social and Territorial Articulation]. *Gazeta de Antropología* 32(1): 1–22 (special issue), *Minorías Étnicas, Procesos De Globalización Y Contextos Urbanos*. Guest editors: J. M. Valcuende and E. I. S Idrovo Landy.
Cleary, D. 2001. 'Towards an Environmental History of the Amazon: From Prehistory to the Nineteenth Century'. *Latin American Research Review* 65–96.
Goldstein, D. M. and Drybread, K. 2018. 'The Social Life of Corruption in Latin America'. *Culture, Theory and Critique* 59(4): 299–311.
Gupta, A. 1995. 'Blurred Boundaries: The Discourse of Corruption, the Culture of Politics, and the Imagined State'. *American Ethnologist* 22(2): 375–402.
Ledeneva, A. V. 1998. *Russia's Economy of Favours*. Cambridge: Cambridge University Press.
Ledeneva, A. V. 2014. 'Economies of Favours or Corrupt Societies: Exploring the Boundaries between Informality and Corruption'. *The Baltic Worlds* 1: 13–21.
Makovicky, N. and Henig, D. 2018a. 'Neither Gift nor Payment: The Sociability of Instrumentality'. In *The Global Encyclopaedia of Informality, Volume 1*, edited by A. Ledeneva, 125–28. London: UCL Press.

Makovicky, N. and Henig, D. 2018b. 'Neither Gift nor Commodity: The Instrumentality of Sociability'. In *The Global Encyclopaedia of Informality, Volume 1*, edited by A. Ledeneva, 36–40. London: UCL Press.
Muir, S. 2016. 'On Historical Exhaustion: Argentine Critique in an Era of "Total Corruption"'. *Comparative Studies in Society and History* 58:(1): 129–58.
Muir, S. and Gupta, A. 2018. 'Rethinking the Anthropology of Corruption: An Introduction to Supplement 18'. *Current Anthropology* 59(18): 4–15.
Peluso, D. M. 2014. 'Shajaó – Histories of an Invented Savage'. *History and Anthropology* 25(1): 102–22.
Peluso, D. M. 2015. 'Circulating between Rural and Urban Communities: Multi-sited Dwellings in Amazonian Frontiers'. *The Journal of Latin American and Caribbean Anthropology* (special issue), *Indigenous Urbanization: The Circulation of Peoples between Rural and Urban Amazonian Spaces*. Guest editor: D. M. Peluso, 20(1): 57–79.
Peluso, D. M. 2016. 'Global Ayahuasca: An Entrepreneurial Ecosystem'. In *The World Ayahuasca Diaspora: Reinventions and Controversies*, edited by B. C. Labate, C. Cavnar and A. K. Gearin, 203–21. London: Routledge.
Peluso, D. M. 2018. 'Traversing the Margins of Corruption amidst Informal Economies in Amazonia'. *Culture, Theory and Critique* 59(4): 400–18.
Peluso, D. M. 2020. 'Aumento'. In *The Global Encyclopaedia of Informality, Volume 3*, edited by A. Ledeneva. London: UCL Press.
Peluso, D. M. 2021. *Ese Eja Epona: el poder social de la mujer en mundos múltiples e híbrido*. Lima: The Centro Amazónico de Antropología y Aplicación Práctica.
Peluso, D. M. and Alexiades M. N. 2005. 'Indigenous Urbanization and Amazonia's Post-Traditional Environmental Economy'. *Traditional Settlements and Dwelling Review* 16(11): 7–16.
Tidey, S. 2016. 'Between the Ethical and the Right Thing: How (Not) to be Corrupt in Indonesian Bureaucracy in an Age of Good Governance'. *American Ethnologist* 43(4): 663–76.

12.9 *Ne talasaj* (Bosnia and Herzegovina, Croatia, Serbia and Montenegro)
Emina Ribo

Hage, G. 2009. 'Waiting Out the Crisis: On Stuckedness and Governmentality'. *Anthropological Theory* 5(1): 463–75.
Index.hr. 2017. 'U Mjesec Dana 119 Prijava za Mobing u Vrtićima; Ne talasaj, puna je burza nezaposlenih' [In the Course of a Month There have Been 119 Reports of Mobing in Kindergartens; Don't Make Waves, the Market is Full of Unemployed People]. *Index.hr*, 24 April. www.index.hr/vijesti/clanak/u-mjesec-dana-119-prijava-za-mobing-u-vrticima-donosimo-popis/965532.aspx
Jakobsen, M. 2018. 'Janteloven/Jantelagen (Scandinavia)'. In *The Global Encyclopaedia of Informality, Volume 1: Towards Understanding of Social and Cultural Complexity*, edited by A. Ledeneva, 254–8. London: UCL Press.
Jansen, S. 2014. 'On Not Moving Well Enough: Temporal Reasoning in Sarajevo Yearnings for "Normal Lives"'. *Current Anthropology* 55(9): 74–84.
Ledeneva, A. 2018. 'Introduction: The Informal View of the World – Key Challenges and Main Findings of the Global Informality Project'. In *Global Encyclopaedia of Informality, Volume 1: Towards Understanding of Social and Cultural Complexity*, edited by A. Ledeneva, 1–27. London: UCL Press.
Poljanec-Borić, S. and Pilar, I. 2008. 'Transfer of Governance Culture: A Case Study of Socio Cultural Barriers for Institutional Adaptation in Croatia'. *Revija za sociologiju* 39(3): 123–44.
Šimić Banović, R. 2015. 'Cutting the Red Ribbon but Not the Red Tape: The Failure of Business Environment Reform in Croatia'. *Post-Communist Economies* 27(1): 106–28.
Šimić Banović, R. 2016. 'Is Culture an Underpinning or Undermining Factor in the Business Environment of the Transitional Countries?'. In *Economic Development and Entrepreneurship in Transition Economies*, edited by J. Ateljević and J. Trivić, 11–38. Cham: Springer.

Urukalo, V. 2019. 'Podignuta optužnica protiv načelnika Vira, a opis djela za koje ga terete je, u najmanju ruku, vrlo neobičan: Ako sam kleptoman, onda nisam za USKOK, nego za psihijatriju!' [An Indictment Has Been Filed against the Mayor of Vir, and the Description of the Offences for which He Is Charged Is, to Say the Least, Very Unusual: If I Am a Kleptomaniac, then I Am not for USKOK, but for Psychiatry]. *Slobodna Dalmacija*, 26 September. www.slobodnadalmacija.hr/vijesti/crna-kronika/podignuta-optuznica-protiv-nacelnika-vira-a-opis-djela-za-koje-ga-terete-je-u-najmanju-ruku-vrlo-neobican-ako-sam-kleptoman-onda-nisam-za-uskok-nego-za-psihijatriju-625070

Veljak, L. 2002. 'Zašto je problem globalizacije akademske naravi?'. *Habitus* 8(6): 23–32.

13
Ageing power

Introduction: demystifying ageing and power

Gemma Carney
Queen's University Belfast, Northern Ireland
and
Mia Gray
Cambridge University, UK

The relationship between human ageing and power is complex and fascinating. The significance of how power is distributed across age groups deserves our immediate attention given the significant increase in life expectancy over the course of the last century. The relationship between power and age is full of contradictions. Even democracies tend to prefer older politicians, leading to the claim that democracies are gerontocracies (that is, ruled by the aged). This is intriguing given that it is well established that old age is not an advantage in other contest situations (Magni-Berton and Panel 2020: 5). However, one only has to glance at a photograph of world leaders meeting at international summits like the G7 to conclude that power lies largely in the hands of older men. The entries in this section outline a range of practices which demonstrate differing cultural values when it comes to age and power.

Old age, once an important and accepted stage of life, has, over the last century, been reclassified as a period of declining physical and mental productivity (Cole 1992). In Western industrial societies, our obsession with productivity and individualism has led to the devaluing of any groups of people who do not engage in paid work. The institution of retirement, where one must give up paid work after a certain age (normally around 66–7 years), places older people in this category of 'other'.

In Western societies, the positioning of old age as a period of 'senescence' and decline has deep historical significance (Carney and Hannan 2021). Once we remove the idea that living a long life is intrinsically valuable, old age becomes little more than a costly period of health care use and unmet needs (Macnicol 2015).

When policymakers extrapolate the individual needs of older people onto the population level we end up with narratives of decline and metaphors like the 'demographic time-bomb', the term used to describe the economic cost of an ageing population (Carney and Gray 2015). This 'narrative of decline' (Gullette 2017) is based on a combination of economic reasoning and a medical model of ageing. Economists use influential but ultimately simplistic models to predict 'dependency ratios' where there are fewer workers to the growing number of retirees (Carney and Nash 2020). Meanwhile, well-funded medical researchers present ageing as little more than a series of ailments and disease. Few will dispute the fact that pensions are expensive or that most of our health care needs are in the first and last years of life. However, by failing to acknowledge that all older people were young once, and that all young people (if they are lucky) will be old one day, we ignore the universality of ageing as part of the human condition.

Some theorists and thinkers have sought to question the idea that age equals decline (Gullette 2017). For instance, Cohen (1988: 124) coined the phrase 'the elderly mystique' to describe the process of internalisation where, as we age, we learn to accept lower social status: 'the participant in the elderly mystique knows society finds it hard to accept, let alone forgive, his existence … The old person expects derogation in explicit terms'.

Taking up the baton from Cohen (1988), we argue that while the focus is largely on *ageing*, it is *ageism* that presents the biggest challenge for society and policy in responding to the increasing longevity of the human race (Carney and Gray 2015). It is not age, per se, which presents a problem for ageing societies. Rather, it is the way we use age to shape every aspect of human life. The process of devaluing older people is based on a form of biological determinism which places a high value on physical health and mental capacity, while lived experience is given a much lower value. For instance, we see physical health in binary terms – youthful vigour versus old age and decline. Chronological age is institutionalised in our systems of work, education and employment, as well as the criminal justice system (Kohli 2007). In some instances, age barriers are explicitly ageist. For instance, there are age limits on civic and political roles such as jury service (76 years in the UK), or on holding certain political offices (for example, you must be over 35 to run for President of Ireland). The young can also suffer institutional ageism – as seen in the application of the UK's minimum wage law, which allows employers to pay less than the minimum wage to those under 23 years of age – although there are many more examples of ageism which apply to older people.

Some older people, such as those living in residential care, or who lack 'mental capacity', are utterly powerless. They are rarely helped to vote or take part in other aspects of civic society, which, arguably, reinforces the low levels of political attention devoted to sub-standard eldercare in many countries (Glasby et al 2020). Finally, perhaps the most obvious example of the elderly mystique is ageist humour in popular culture. The continued use of age as the last identity that it is socially acceptable to laugh at is evident in everything from birthday cards to TV panel shows and the use of terms like 'bed blocker' or 'pensioner' in mainstream media. More extreme versions of this kind of ageism were evident during the pandemic when the #BoomerRemover went viral on Twitter (Carney et al. 2022).

Despite millions of pounds of investment in research and development in longitudinal studies of ageing, cures for dementia and anti-ageing serums, humanity has not really progressed much since the publication of Cohen's elderly mystique in 1988 or indeed from Butler's (1975) question – *Why Survive? Being Old in America*. Indeed, in a review of the work of G. Stanley Hall, seen as the father of modern gerontology, Carney and Hannan (2021: 19) conclude that, despite Hall's attempts to systematise old age, 'Hall (1922) shows us that ... as much can be learned from the *experience* of living through old age as can be learned from the *study* of it as a set of conditions, maladies, or statistics that apply to someone else'.

Experience is central to informality and ageing. The entries in this section offer examples of how, despite institutionalised ageism, older people continue to influence and lead through informal practices. For example, *Duang muang*, the Thai practice of using astrological guidance to make political decisions, leads to important long-term relationships between leaders and professional astrologers. Other entries in this section offer real world examples of one of the emerging theories of ageing, which is that older women have a particular contribution to make (Friedan 1992; Hawkes et al. 2000; Carney 2018; Fegitz 2022). While some of these practices may be controversial, such as the case of *OBON*, they reflect the achievements of women as grassroots activists over the life course. As women are often excluded from official or patriarchal institutions of the state, they build a lifetime of social networks and capacity at local level. In the case of the *OBON*, older women using informal practices can shift the narrative from shame and humiliation around poverty to entitlement and rights.

The use of the term 'elders' to describe the *Jirga* in Afghanistan denotes respect and authority that is now seldom seen in youth-obsessed Western cultures. There is much to be learned from how these practices of elder statehood can translate traditional practices into human rights. *Amakudari* is practised in Japan, where retired civil servants are re-employed by public institutions. While the practice is not popular with the public, who view it as collusion, others argue that it can be useful for smoothing relations between the private and public sectors.

Age-old practices, informal rules and norms are the main mechanisms for distributing political power. Informal practices are important means of understanding the complex relationship between age and power, particularly in the context of ageing societies.

13.1 **OBON** (Kyrgyzstan)
Elmira Satybaldieva
Conflict Analysis and Research Centre, School of Politics and International Relations, University of Kent, UK

The term *OBON* stands for *Otryad Bab Osobogo Naznacheniya* and translates as 'Women's Unit for Special Purposes'. It refers to older female leaders in post-Soviet Kyrgyzstan, aged 55–65, who have emerged as informal intermediaries between marginalised citizens and state institutions in the period of increasing social inequalities and distrust in formal political institutions.

OBON has become part of the everyday lexicon and is widely used by the media and lay people. The term has a negative connotation and instantly evokes images of older women as paid protesters, who act in aggressive and confrontational ways, such as shouting at officials and storming and occupying government buildings (Alymkulova et al. 2012; Szymanek 2012; cf. *titushki*, see 12.5 in this volume). The media and political elites cultivate this negative image to condemn and to delegitimise older women's participation in political processes. The origin of the term is attributed to a former politician and filmmaker, Dooronbek Sadyrbaev, who suggested that politicians would mobilise older women similar to special police units (*OMON – otdel militsii osobogo naznacheniya*) to intimidate their rivals.

Despite the negative media portrayal, *OBON* women are important informal leaders, whose mediating role is crucial for understanding community micropolitics, women's political agency and broader state–society relations in the post-Soviet context.

In developing countries, the possibility of accessing formal political channels or effecting change is limited. Instead, people use informal representational mediators to achieve their goals. This form of mediation is distinct from arbitration and dispute resolution, where the mediator is a neutral actor. It refers to third-party representation of a marginalised social group to a political authority and primarily consists of bargaining and negotiation, as well as group mobilisation and protests (Piper and Von Lieres 2015). Notably, this form of representational practice is not based on legal frameworks but rests on 'an enduring assertion of the right to speak for certain social groups due to shared identity, interests, proximity, efficacy and the like' (Piper and Von Lieres 2015: 697).

In Kyrgyzstan's political field, communal leadership is regularly contested by a variety of actors, such as criminal groups, religious leaders or professional brokers, all claiming to represent the voices of the poor. The *OBON* women set themselves apart, because they developed their informal political legitimacy through grassroots activism, cultural and gendered resources (motherhood status and age) and concerns for social justice.

A particular form of neopatriarchy in Central Asia grants women authority and status recognition in old age, if they have produced male progeny and have ensured a reproduction of patriarchal structures – a phenomenon Kandiyoti (1988) refers to as a 'bargain with patriarchy'. Using motherhood as a symbolic capital is not unique to Central Asia. Others have documented how Mothers of the Plaza de Mayo in Argentine and the mothers of soldiers in Russia, for example, use age and status to legitimate their struggles and to achieve their objectives (Sutton 2007; Zdravomyslova 2007).

An important aspect of *OBON* women's political legitimacy is their informal leadership on the ground. They reflect the identity and experiences of their followers and serve as effective problem-solvers to help channel resources to their communities. Their political legitimacy is not achieved immediately but develops through several years of collective action and sustained efforts.

In an empirical study on informal politics in Kyrgyzstan, this author conducted 12 semi-structured interviews with *OBON* women in the city of Osh in south Kyrgyzstan (Satybaldieva 2018). The study sheds light on how *OBON* women mediate on behalf of poor groups on a number of issues reflecting their communities' beliefs about tackling social inequalities.

Housing became an important subject after the evictions of former textile employees from their communal dormitories, whose rights to accommodation were denied as a result of fraudulent privatisation of the dormitories. In response to these evictions, the *OBON* women mobilised 83 families to occupy a disused public building. In the subsequent years, they organised numerous protests, sit-ins and land-grabs to try and force state officials to recognise the evicted families' demand for accommodation. Their efforts expanded to include a campaign for the rights of rural migrants to social housing. After a decade-long process of negotiations with the state authorities, the *OBON* women succeeded in obtaining enough land to accommodate approximately forty-five thousand people.

Financial malpractices by banks and microfinance agencies constituted another focus. Most lenders targeted women as loan recipients and charged them exorbitant interest rates. Many borrowers became heavily indebted and defaulted on their loans, causing the lenders to seize their homes. The *OBON* women acted to prevent the extrajudicial seizure of property. They held protests outside and inside the banks and microfinance agencies, picketed in front of the White House and petitioned the Ombudsman. They asserted the borrowers' rights by negotiating for concessions with the lenders and demanding that the National Bank enforce stronger regulation of the financial sector.

The *OBON* women's mediation also emerged as a spontaneous response to inter-communal clashes between ethnic Kyrgyz and Uzbeks that erupted in south Kyrgyzstan in the aftermath of the overthrow of President Kurmanbek Bakiev in June 2010. They became involved in the distribution of humanitarian aid to families affected by the violence. They also took action to search for missing persons, and to campaign for compensation for the affected families.

OBON's mediatory strategies are entwined with contentious activism to pressure state elites to hear them out. Confrontation was used as either a tactic or was undertaken out of frustration. While the state and financial elites were not emotionally moved by their accounts of injustice and suffering, the women's perseverance and effective tactics pushed them into negotiations. Their informal mediatory strategies were particularly successful during elections or political uprisings when several elite factions vied for public support and were seeking *OBON* women to mobilise local communities.

The study shows that *OBON*'s informal mediatory practices achieved several meaningful changes in southern Kyrgyzstan. First, they advanced the needs of rural migrants and urban poor people. They were instrumental in negotiating and forcing the central and local authorities to distribute land for housing. This was a significant outcome given that habitable land is scarce in the region. Second, the mediation process empowered certain marginalised groups to participate in politics. For example, several older women initiated a protest movement against banks and their policy of high interest rates. Their movement developed into a national cause, gaining the attention of the government, which passed an anti-usury law in consequence. Third, the *OBON* women helped to politicise practical needs and pragmatic issues such as housing and credit. Their collaboration with political leaders resulted in protests and popular mobilisation. The *OBON* women were active in the events leading up to the 2005 Tulip Revolution, the first popular uprising that ousted President Askar Akaev from power. Fourth, the *OBON* women's contentious strategies challenged gendered norms, ideas of shame and masculine power. Although political elites and the media demonised their subversive tactics, they refused to stay passive and docile. Fifth, the women's informal mediation was crucial for raising awareness about injustices and violations. In particular, they shifted feelings of shame and humiliation about debt and homelessness into ideas of entitlements and rights.

13.2 *Jirga/shura* (Afghanistan)
Madeleine O. Nosworthy
School of Slavonic and East European Studies, UCL, UK

Jirga is a gathering of elders for the purpose of local or national conflict resolution. *Jirga* is a word in Pashto, Dari and Turkish language that means a gathering and consultation among a group of people. Originally from the Pashtun tribe, the practice has spread to the entire Afghan country. In areas of Afghanistan that are dominated by non-Pashtun ethnicities, including Tajiks and Uzbeks, this type of gathering is named *shura*.

In the Pashtun tribe, *jirgas* are usually formal events following the rules of reciprocity of the tribal code of conduct, the Pashtunwali. *Jirgas* are also organised to resolve conflict at the local level, among villagers. In a *jirga*, the local representatives (usually the community's elders) sit in a circle, a formation that dissolves the perception of inequality. The negotiators reach a settlement for the dispute through consensus or a majority vote, and the settlement is binding for all parties involved.

An example of a conflict settled through a local *jirga* is the story of Kobra (Gang 2011: 62–3), who lost her husband in the civil war when she was pregnant. Years later, having remarried, she faced financial difficulties and decided to claim her late husband's land for her son. Her late husband's brother refused to recognise his nephew's inheritance rights, saying that Kobra's remarriage invalidated her claim. Kobra sought mediation from a *jirga* of elders to resolve the dispute and secured a piece of land for her son.

Jirgas are highly ritualised. A *jirga* usually starts with the recital of verses of the Qur'an and ends with a prayer. It is held in a specific location and in the shape of a circle. The reconciliation also occurs according to rituals, which vary according to the type of conflict being resolved.

A *jirga* that takes place at the national level is called *Loya Jirga*. The Constitution of the Islamic Republic of Afghanistan states that:

> *Loya Jirga* is the highest manifestation of the will of the people of Afghanistan and gives it an all-important role in national governance. *Loya Jirgas* are held to lend representative weight to decisions such as formulating a new constitution, making agreements

Figure 13.2.1 A Grand *Jirga* in Moqur, Afghanistan. CC BY 2.0 © ResoluteSupportMedia.

with foreign forces on their presence in Afghan territory, or debating the extent of the authority of a new leader. Rather than convening different members of the public for each national assembly, the members of *Loya Jirga* are fixed and consist of members of the National Assembly and residents of provincial and district assemblies.

A notable *Loya Jirga* took place in June 2002. The Bonn agreement of 2001 intended to re-install the Afghan government after the US military intervened in Afghanistan in response to the 9/11 attacks. Signed by twenty-three Afghan officials and a UN representative, the Bonn agreement nominated Hamid Karzai, later long-term president of Afghanistan (2004 to 2014), as chair of the interim administration. His role was to be, amongst other things, to set up an emergency *Loya jirga* 'to decide on a Transitional Authority, including a broad-based transitional administration, to lead Afghanistan until such time as a fully representative government can be elected through free and fair elections'. (United Nations Peacemaker 2001: I.4)

In the 2002 *jirga*, 1,600 delegates representing various Afghan ethnic groups confirmed Karzai's interim nominations for cabinet posts and his own nomination as Head of the Transitional Government.

The oldest record of a *jirga* dates to 977, when one of the first Afghan heads of state in the Ghazni province was chosen. The tradition of the *jirga* practice is an important foundation of its surviving popularity. When asked about the justice delivered through *jirga* and *shura*, Afghans consistently give higher ratings to *jirga*s and *shura*s than the state courts and consider them fair and trustworthy, effective, timely and prompt (Rennie et al. 2009: 91, 152; Ayoubi et al. 2011; Shawe 2013: 86). The Afghanistan Human Development Report (Wardak et al. 2007: 91) estimates that *jirga*s and *shura*s settle more than 80 per cent of judicial cases in Afghanistan. In a context where the rule of law is impeded by the lack of institutional checks and balances, *jirga* and *shura* are 'meeting an urgent need' as an alternative conflict resolution mechanism (Wardak et al. 2007: 91).

Jirgas have been critiqued for their violation of human rights. Women lack inclusion and representation in *jirga*s and settlement practices. Disputes are often settled with *baad*: a woman of the offender's family is given to the victim's family for marriage. Another criticism of *jirga*s and *shura*s is that their members can be influenced or bribed.

Research into the 2002 *Loya jirga* which resulted in Hamid Karzai being nominated head of state suggested that there were irregularities in the methods of selection of the delegates, procedural difficulties and concealed dealings that might have influenced the outcome of the *Loya jirga* (Saikal 2002: 48). He adds that Zalmay Khalilzad, who was envoy to Afghanistan under US President George W. Bush, allegedly cajoled the former Afghan King Mohammed Zahir Shaw to withdraw his candidacy, securing an easier win for Karzai. Despite the potential foreign influence, Saikal considers this *Loya jirga* to have been a first step towards a democratic process nonetheless, as it was the first time a *Loya jirga* provided indirect popular legitimacy to a leader.

Warlords or armed local leaders can also influence a *jirga/shura* through positioning loyalists within them. A report by Rashid found Afghan warlords 'enlisting more and more men in order to increase their power base before the convening of the *Loya jirga*', with some military leaders commanding 'more than 15,000 troops' (2002). 'Armed political groups, commanders, and warlords have strategically targeted traditional customary justice systems (*jirga* and *shura*) throughout rural Afghanistan in their attempt to control local populations' (Wardak 2006: 97).

Programmes of hybrid conflict resolution explore the possibility of joining traditional norms with the development of human rights. A research project on conflict resolution in a part of Kabul named Afshar examined 'the value and possible mechanisms for linking state and non-state justice systems' (Gang 2011: 1) and set up a hybrid conflict resolution programme using principles of Sharia law, rights from state law and local traditions as well as creating space for women's participation (Gang 2011). A hybrid model for the justice system in Afghanistan was proposed in 2007 (Wardak et al. 2007: 129). It allowed for a thorough system of checks and balances between traditional conflict resolution methods and state justice, and was later expanded to account for women's participation with a female-dominated human rights unit (Braithwaite and Wardak 2013: 203). Researchers noted a positive policy shift that saw *jirgas* and shuras as 'sometimes abusing rights, but also ... as reformable'. They reported that '*baad* as *jirga* outcome [has] become increasingly rare' (Braithwaite and Wardak 2013). They gave examples of *shuras* which have ended traditions of forced marriages and ruled that beating of wives was no longer allowed (Braithwaite and Wardak 2013). These examples suggest that a dual or hybrid approach to lawmaking in Afghanistan might be a way forward to bring about durable change.

13.3 *Aqsaqal* (Kazakhstan)
Talshyn Tokyzhanova
Department of Business Administration, Tallinn University of Technology, Estonia

Aqsaqal (Kazakh), *aksakal* (Kyrgyz) or *oqsoqol* (Uzbek) – literally, 'white-bearded', denotes someone who is old, elderly, wise and who has gained wisdom through life experience. These well-respected male community members sit on the *aqsaqal* council of elders in Kazakhstan, Kyrgyzstan (*Aksakaldar keneshi*), and Uzbekistan (*Oqsoqollar kengashi*). This informal institution nowadays has the task of mediating and resolving local disputes. The younger generation is expected to follow the elders' guidance, and *aqsaqals* have the authority to summon citizens if they misbehave. After the collapse of the Soviet Union, the majority of Central Asian countries used *aqsaqal* councils as consultative, administrative or even judicial organisations in their efforts to construct their nations.

The model for these councils was influential in pre-Soviet Central Asian societies. In Uzbekistan, wards comprised roughly 30–60 dwellings, and it was a close-knit community administered by an elder council. Without the community's permission, an outsider could not purchase a home in the ward (Bacon 1966: 72). When in the nineteenth century, Bukhara was split into different quarters based on common descent and the professions of the residents, the senior citizens in each quarter generally competed for the position of *aqsaqal*. The elders and religious leaders of the quarter played a significant role in the decision-making process. Also, *aqsaqals* had to be approved by urban powers as their official representatives. In quarters with two or more ethnic groups, each ethnic group chose their *aqsaqal* (Sengupta 2000).

A conflict between two members of the same village in Kazakhstan was generally settled by one of the village's respected elders (Martin 2001: 28). *Aqsaqals* listened to all parties and rendered a decision based on the merits of the specific case, as well as the family's overall interests. When cases were more complicated, or there was a need for arbitration between villages or kin groups, the disputing parties often turned to clan leaders known as *biys*.

During the Russian Empire, while clan leaders' (*biys*) judicial power gradually decreased, the more traditional function of the *aqsaqal* was still alive. As a result, there was a parallel system of civic authority within Kazakh communities: a visible state-sanctioned structure and an 'invisible' customary one. *Aqsaqals* were instrumental in creating *assar*, community cooperation, and mutual assistance. Activities such as the construction of private houses were often organised under the guidance of an *aqsaqal* (Bankoff and Oven 2019: 385). This dualism remains a characteristic of contemporary village society today, with political, judicial and moral authority shared between formal and informal institutions (Martin 2001: 112; Bankoff and Oven 2019: 381).

Due to the ethnic and geographic variety of Kazakhstan, nowadays, these councils are not universally apparent in the country; however, they are noticeable in some instances (Earle et al. 2004: 17). In February 2020, after the interethnic clashes in the village of Masanchi, in the Kordai district, Kazakh authorities held a meeting with the village elders. They agreed to establish a joint *aqsaqal* council which would include the elders of nearby settlements. The joint council members discuss the village problems. They are mandated to educate young people and organise cooperative cultural and sporting activities to foster a sense of solidarity among all nationalities residing in the district (Prime Minister of the Republic of Kazakhstan 2020).

Aqsaqal councils were put to work in labour conflicts among Kazakhstani steelworkers in 2013 when the management of the ArcelorMittal Temirtau invited the mill's elder, highly positioned former labour to join a newly formed veterans' council. The new council was inspired by traditional *aqsaqal* councils, and it was intended to be used to re-establish amicable connections with workers and to discuss the company's challenging circumstances (Trevisani 2019: 382).

The *aqsaqal* council was established under the Religious Administration of Muslims of Kazakhstan in 2022. The council is responsible for organising a national Forum of Elders, as well as the National *Äjeler forumy* (Forum of Grandmothers). The administration hopes that the elders will give a new impetus to the work of the Religious Administration in the field of public relations (Qazaqstan musılmandarı dinï basqarması 2022 [Religious Administration of Muslims of Kazakhstan 2022]). Local administrations have also been using the *aqsaqal* council as advisors for the prevention of domestic crimes in the Karaganda region, by conducting individual preventive interviews with over 200 people in rural areas and small towns (Polisia.kz 2022).

Aqsaqal councils are diffused in universities as well. They usually consist of well-known, older teachers and professors who have worked at the university for many years. The councils are established as a public advisory board to develop proposals and discuss issues related to the development of the educational, scientific and social life of the university (Kazakh National Medical University 2013). On occasion universities form *aqsaqal* councils as associations of honorary professors to connect with well-established, older professors to teach special new programmes (Satbayev University 2017).

The court of elders is nowadays a regular feature of Kyrgyz village life. The former Kyrgyz president Askar Akaev and his government launched the court of elders in 1995. These courts, according to the law, judge based on: 'moral criteria that reflect the Kyrgyz customs and traditions'. Offences, family disputes, land, property and water conflicts can all be handled by these courts (Beyer 2006: 142). The courts responded to increased demand from international organisations to democratise and decentralise the state bureaucracy. Also, a weak state, without the capacity to administer justice, was able to decentralise judicial power (Beyer 2015: 55).

External donors in Central Asia have also recognised the value of engaging with *aqsaqals* before launching a project. Their presence legitimises the project from a local standpoint and motivates people to participate in the initiative. The *aqsaqals*' authority is frequently required to encourage community members to commit their time and money to a specific project (Earle et al. 2004: 43). However, research undertaken in a village in the Osh Oblast showed that by doing this, donor initiatives reinforce power dynamics and social inequality in rural areas. As a result, women and poorer community members are excluded from the decision-making process. In particular, women in the village did not have the opportunity to express their disagreements during the hearings led by the *aqsaqal*. They believed that he would not have listened, and at the same time, they did not feel comfortable challenging a well-respected man in the village (Earle et al. 2004: 29).

13.4 **Mullahs** (Afghanistan)
Jennifer Brick Murtazashvili
Center for Governance and Markets, University of Pittsburgh, USA

In Afghanistan, *mullahs* are village-level religious leaders. Sunni Islam, which is this entry's focus of discussion, does not have a hierarchal leadership. In terms of status, however, *mullahs* have the lowest among religious leaders because they typically have the lowest level of education. This means they are distinct from other categories of religious leaders with more formal education and training such as imams, judges (*qazi*) and scholars (*mawlawi*). According to anthropologist Louis Dupree, in Afghanistan *mullahs* are 'at the bottom of the hierarchy [who] function as part time religious leader. Technically, Islam has no organized clergy, and every man can be a mullah. Anyone can lead in prayer' (Dupree 1973: 107–8). Imams are the most formal religious leader and represent doctrinal interests rather than community interests. In some communities, there are also *mawlawis*, who possess more formal religious training.

In the context of Sunni communities in Afghanistan, those with official training lead prayers. A *mullah* is someone who does not have formal religious training, but who practises religious functions 'regularly and professionally' (Dorronsoro 2005: 48). Unlike their more educated counterparts, the *ulama*, who are typically involved in developing and interpreting Islamic Law, *mullahs* are the individuals who are responsible for the implementation of religious law and practice. Despite their lack of formal training, they are able to apply fundamental religious principles to everyday practice (Shahrani 2002).

Mullahs are ubiquitous throughout Afghanistan. In rural areas, residents will often describe the size of their village in terms of the number of mosques and *mullahs* that they have (for example, 'We have a large village: we have six mosques'). Many communities have Shia and Sunni mosques that exist side by side in one community. These mosques have distinct spiritual leaders. In Afghanistan, mosques are the centre of the community and religious life. Mosques often function as important community centres where residents meet to try to settle disputes or discuss issues of common concern.

In addition to their religious and spiritual functions, in Afghanistan *mullahs* play an important role in governance – especially in rural areas. They are usually not appointed by outsiders, rather they enjoy this role within the community because of their own personal reputation for piety and wisdom (Roy 1990: 32). Through honest works they can craft their own legitimacy.

Mullahs have a range of responsibilities that go beyond simply performing religious rites and leading services. They play a pivotal role in solving disputes, especially those that involve family or personal issues. They are particularly active in issues involving inheritance matters, divorce, and resolving controversies within and among families.

Mullahs have also played a key role in local politics, resolving disputes that arise within and between communities. The political significance of *mullahs* in community life has also made them the target of government policy over the centuries. Religious leaders were heavily persecuted under the rule of the People's Democratic Party of Afghanistan (PDPA), which ran the government in Kabul from the Saur Revolution in 1978 until its collapse in 1992. Just as *mullahs* were persecuted by the communists, they were celebrated by the Taliban, which sought to elevate their role as the epicentre of village governance, replacing *maliks*, who previously held this position.

During the Taliban rule in Kabul (1992–6), the government tasked *mullahs* with a wide range of goals, from implementing Taliban legal codes to collecting local taxes. This presented a challenge because *mullahs* often had very low levels of formal training or they relied on almost syncretic forms of religious interpretation, which wove customary law with formal religious law. For example, customary law among *Pashtuns*, *Pashunwali*, often contradicts some aspects of Islamic jurisprudence. *Mullahs* gained very little from their rule at the community level because they were not prepared to take on such roles. Similarly, individuals in communities had little expectation that *mullahs* could handle these additional responsibilities.

After 2001, *mullahs* played an important, although less prominent, role in society. They worked alongside other informal community organisations, such as *maliks* (informal village representatives) and community councils (*jirgas/shuras*) providing advice to both. *Mullahs* are not usually the most powerful actors in the community. Community governance consists of three organisations that co-exist and divide power at the community level: *maliks*, *mullahs* and *jirgas/shuras*. These organisations not only co-exist, but the authority of the three bodies ensures not only a separation of power at the community level, but also checks and balances on such authority, preventing one actor from becoming too powerful over the others (Murtazashvili 2016). This separation of power promotes the ability of *mullahs* to resolve disputes more successfully in communities, because these officials know they will be held accountable for their actions.

Another constraint on the authority of *mullahs* are social norms that make it acceptable to 'venue shop', or to choose to approach a *mullah* who they believe might be most inclined to rule in their favour. This means that *mullahs* are often brought into conflict with one another by citizens whose interests they are supposed to represent. *Mullahs* play an important role in communities, but residents often make light of *mullahs*, their lack of education and often their lack of formal education (Barfield 2004). Citizens frequently joke about the fact that *mullahs* can be bought off with a good meal, which is often seen as the key to getting an amenable result from their ruling (Murtazashvili 2016: 77).

13.5 **Amakudari** (Japan)
Hayato Moriyama
Alumna, School of Slavonic and East European Studies, UCL, UK

The Japanese term *amakudari* (天下り) can be translated as 'revolving door' in English, although the literal translation is 'descent from heaven' (Mizoguchi and Van Quyen 2012: 813). The term describes the practice of employing senior civil servants, who have retired from their position in ministries, in managerial positions in corporations, non-governmental organisations or local governments overseen by these ministries. The senior bureaucrats are figuratively referred to as Gods and the places of their new employment are described as the Earth (Mizoguchi and Van Quyen 2012: 813–14). Arranging jobs for civil servants and accepting *amakudari* officials in the private sector rests on a long-term relationship between the ministries and the industries (Mizoguchi and Van Quyen 2012: 816).

Amakudari is widespread in Japan. A search on the Newspaper Trend search engine reveals that Japanese newspapers have referred to the word more than 6,000 times from 2013 to 2018. Both public agencies and re-employment organisations are motivated to participate in *amakudari*. One possible reason is the tradition of recommending early retirement in central ministries (Kobayashi 2012: 28–9). In Japanese central ministries, officials progress in their career through an annual promotion review. The role of vice-minister at the top of the ladder can normally be reached between the ages of 55 and 60. Since the organisational structure is pyramidal, officials not offered the highest position, but in line for promotion, will be recommended for early retirement and redeployed in the private sector or special governmental corporations (National Personal Authority of Japan 2002). Another motivational factor is the promise of a high salary in the private sector at the end of one's career, which motivates junior civil servants to work harder for low wages (Mizoguchi and Van Quyen 2012: 815–16). The incentive for pushing out senior employees from private organisations with the promise of lifetime employment and promotion of seniority – that promotions become increasingly costly to the organisation (Johnson 1974: 959) – seems less applicable to the Japanese civil service since the number of employees and the labour cost budget in this sector are both fixed.

Although the National Civil Service Law has banned securing private posts for civil service officers by the ministries in 2007, the number of *amakudari* placements between 2006 and 2008 totalled 1,872 according to a press release of the Ministry of Internal Affairs and Communications (MIAC 2009). *Amakudari* in the Ministry of Land, Infrastructure and Transport (MLIT), with coveted positions in the construction and real estate industries (Quah 2011: 452), increased from 180 to 218 between 2007 and 2008 (MIAC 2009). As evident from Table 13.5.1, ministries that hold authority over private companies (such as the MLIT and Ministries of the Economy, Trade and Industry, and Finance) have significantly more positions than those without such supervising roles (like the Ministry of Foreign Affairs).

Amakudari has analogous practices in other countries. In the US, the revolving-door phenomenon has three forms: industry-to-government, government-to-industry and government-to-lobbyist movement. In industry-to-government, 'the appointment of corporate executives and business lobbyists to key posts in federal agencies establishes a pro-business bias in policy formulation and regulatory enforcement' (Revolving Door Working Group 2005: 7). In the movement of public officials to the private sector, ex-officials help the new employers navigate governmental procurement and regulations (Revolving Door Working Group 2005: 8). Finally, in movement from the civil servants to lobbyists, former government connections are employed to advance the interests of corporate clients (Revolving Door Working Group 2005: 8). In *amakudari*, government-to-industry is the only direction of employment exchange. The practice of revolving doors in the US is more elaborate. The French analogue is *pantouflage*: leaving the civil service for employment in the private sector, usually on secondment that allows a return to the position in the public sector (Alexandre-Bailly and Muratbekova-Touron 2018: 239). Upon entrance to certain French universities, students are guaranteed they will become civil servants and retire early in their careers in order to pursue senior positions in the private sector (Colignon and Usui 2003: 5).

Table 13.5.1 First *amakudari* posts in selected ministries and government agencies

	2006	2007	2008	Total
Ministry of Land, Infrastructure and Transport	199	180	218	597
Ministry of Economy, Trade and Industry	77	83	69	229
Ministry of Agriculture, Forestry and Fisheries	62	66	67	195
Ministry of Finance	67	59	66	192
Coast Guard	49	56	54	159
Ministry of Internal Affairs and Communications	45	44	28	117
Ministry of Education, Culture, Sports, Science and Technology	25	24	28	77
National Police Agency	19	22	31	72
Ministry of Foreign Affairs	5	8	7	20
Other ministries and government agencies	78	79	57	214
Total	**626**	**621**	**625**	**1872**

Amakudari can trigger a number of other informal practices in the public sector. Civil servants lobby for their own future positions in private companies and organisations, and retired officials lobby for the promotions of senior bureaucrats. Strong ministry-to-business ties result in bureaucratic corruption in the construction industry in the form of the illegal *dangou*, or secret bid-rigging system (Quah 2011). In *watari*, an elaborate derivative form of *amakudari*, retired bureaucrats move between different positions in private firms supervised by their former ministries (Cheung 2013: 140–1).

The implications of *amakudari* are manifold. The practice has been criticised as one of the root causes of collusion in Japan's 'iron triangle', a mutually supportive relationship among politicians (especially in the Liberal Democratic Party), public servants and private companies operating in Japan (Colignon and Usui 2003: 191). When ex-bureaucrats lobby for favours, younger officials oblige their esteemed former colleagues by providing information or steering towards company-friendly legislation because these junior officials will seek an *amakudari* position in the future (Colignon and Usui 2003). This reciprocity makes *amakudari* an instance of *jinmyaku*, the informal network of business contacts (Horak 2018: 94–6).

Amakudari can serve as the vehicle for the maintenance and acquisition of public subsidies. In 2015, Daisuke Yoshida, the former director-general of the Higher Education bureau in the Ministry of Education, Culture, Sports, Science and Technology of Japan (MEXT), the body allocating higher education subsidies, was appointed professor at Waseda University within two months of his retirement. While the public investigation found evidence of the director-general having arranged for his future placement while in his post as the bureau head (Secretariat of Reemployment Surveillance Commission of Japan [SRSC] 2017), the bureau claimed no such subsidy favours were possible (Ministry of Education, Culture, Sports, Science and Technology of Japan [MEXT] 2017).

Although mostly a form of collusion, *amakudari* can have positive effects. Employing experienced public officials, well versed in regulation, can improve the effectiveness of administrative guidance of private companies (Johnson 1974: 963–4). *Amakudari* can help break tensions between the government and private sector. Employing *amakudari* officials can also be more cost-efficient for private firms than lobbying for favours (Mizoguchi and Van Quyen 2012: 815–16).

The Japanese public is not sympathetic towards *amakudari*. A public opinion survey conducted by the Cabinet Office showed that more than 75 per cent of respondents, who held that civil servants did not meet public needs, believed that this was due to extensive *amakudari* (The Cabinet Office of Japan [CAS] 2007). While legislative revisions have been attempting to curb the practice since the 1990s, public officials persist in finding detours.

13.6 *Jajmani* (South Asia)

Soumya Mishra
Department of International Development, University of Oxford, UK

The terminology of *jajmani-kameen* signifies a reciprocal relationship between landed upper castes (*jajman*) and occupational lower castes (*kameen*). It is a form of patron-client relationship, or a moral economy based on an exchange of goods and services. In contrast to capitalism, it operates without money. The practice is prevalent in the Indian subcontinent across India, Pakistan (Barth 1960; Ahmad 1970), Nepal, Sri Lanka and Bangladesh (Arens and van Beurden 1978). It has similarities to feudalism in mediaeval Europe and to practices that exist in Peru (*compadrazgo*) and Uzbekistan (*xokimiyat*). Introduction of market economy has transformed the *jajmani* system and operations of the caste-based networks.

The practice has various names across India: *jajmani, yajmani, jajman-kameen, jajman-kaam karney waale* and *jajman-kaamgaar*. The term was first coined and conceptualised as an interaction between castes in Uttar Pradesh (William and Charlotte Wiser 1930). The term *yajman* or *jajman* originates in the Sanskrit word *yajna* meaning 'a sacrificial offering'. The derivative *yajmaan* or *jajmaan* refers to priests performing the sacrifice. Later, the term was for land-owning upper castes (Brahmins, Kshatriyas). The *yajman* became synonymous with a village landlord, who could get services or goods in exchange for patronage of particular lower-caste families. Those supplying the services are called *kameen, kamgaar* or *kaam karne waaley*, or those who work (Lewis and Barnouw 1956).

Opler and Singh 1948) examined *jajmani* relations in Eastern Uttar Pradesh. Reddy (1955) did a systematic study of *jajmani* system in North India. It is also known as *batuldari* (Maharashtra), *vetha/vethi-chakiri* (Deccan India), aya or *bitti-chakiri* (Karnataka), *gaikh* (Himachal Pradesh) or *sepidari* (Punjab, see Darling 1934). Gould (1986) found a replication of the *jajmani* system among the lower castes with lower-status groups acting as *kameens* for upper-status groups. Lewis and Barnouw (1956) took the case of the village of Rampur in Uttar Pradesh and observed its evolution from a relationship framework of personal bonds to an exploitative regime of control of *kameens* by *jajmans*. In South India, studies focused on Mysore (Srinivas 1952), among others, an exclusive and hereditary tie between families, belonging to difference castes, which cannot be broken easily by either party (see Chapter 3 Volume 1 on lock-in effect).

Not every caste is necessarily a part of the *jajmani* system, and the ties may vary depending on what service one offers (Orenstein 1962). A barber can be a *kameen* or service-provider for several families, as a barber is needed once every few weeks, while a cleaner may be needed more frequently. Some families have a *jajmani* relationship with the whole village rather than with particular families, but the generations are still linked together by affective ties. This creates opportunities for exploitative demands on the part of a *jajman*, who provides a *kameen* with social security, access to credit and patronage. In contrast to precarious daily waged work, a social obligation exists between the parties that underpins the informal safety net.

The *kameens* have a caste court (*panchayat*), which functions as a trade union based on kinship. A *kameen* cannot leave the *jajmani* system without finding a replacement from his own extended family (not even from another family of the same caste), the caste courts ensure that. Similarly, a *jajmaan* cannot dismiss a *kameen*, as it is a hereditary relationship which is passed down from one generation to the next, hence becoming a right, a kind of the family's property similar to land (Lewis and Barnouw 1956).

The role of the *jajmani* system in patronage of regional music and art was critical in the past and continues in some form today (Rudner 2003; McNeil 2007). It is common in a classical Indian music or dance performance in India to term audience members as *jajman* or patron. The practice also continues in rituals of marriage ceremonies or thread ceremonies, in which the washerman (*dhobi*) plays a significant role. The *dhobi*'s wife becomes a bridesmaid, applying a beauty mask (*ubatan*) before the wedding.

This lock-in arrangement derives from the caste system based on the concepts of purity and pollution. As it was impure for upper castes to do certain manual jobs, the lower castes provided these services. Yet when they refused to do so, the *jajmans* had to do it themselves. A *kameen* could not be replaced easily, so this system emerged to guarantee job security for generations of *kameens* and security of the provision of services for generations of *jajmans*. As *jajmans* acted as a moneylender for the *kameens* in times of need, they often charged an interest rate that made the debt impossible to return. Such help also created a trap for the 'bonded labourer', who could not buy their freedom, as depicted in film, oral history and literature (see for example the film *Mother India*, 1957; Munshi Premchand's short stories and many others). Urmila Pawar's autobiography *Aaidan* (2006) recounts growing up in Phansawala, Maharashtra in a *kameen* community and the hypocrisy of the concepts of purity and pollution. Similarly, Dangle's *Poisoned Bread* (1992) speaks of the Mahar community and the clashes between a traditional older generation and a rebellious younger generation willing to fight against caste exploitation.

The *jajmani* system has political and economic implications. Politically it legitimises oppression and prevents individuals from seeking to exercise their constitutional rights. Traditional forms of organising society are deeply entrenched. Economically, it saves labour costs as peasants or lower castes are duty-bound, according to their caste status in Hindu cosmology, to do what is asked of them by their *jajman*. The *kameen* enjoys security of livelihood but also experiences insecurity, as breaking away from the *jajmani* system is not easy and it is hard to find work afterwards.

Presently, the *jajmani* system continues to exist, with modifications, in villages. Sociologists disagree on the degree of its dominance, with some arguing that education, employment opportunities and commercialisation have eroded the caste-based patronage (Parry and Bloch 1989; Gurjar 2019). Yet, the caste networks become important in contractual labour and kinship networks that help individuals to find work. The system has evolved into a form of social network or *jaan-pehchaan* or *guanxi*. The exploitative institution of *jajmani* is seen as a driver for *kameens* to migrate to cities seeking work outside of the local social inequality in villages. The kinship-based networks of *kameens* help them to migrate to cities and look for jobs. Factories also utilise caste and kinship networks to control migrants, as the labour contractor is often from the same village as the workers. On the one hand, it creates some job security in a precarious economy, as contractors prioritise saving jobs for workers from their own village or region over those from other regions. On the other hand, the caste system is still prevalent in attitudes and expands into the city.

13.7 *Partiti* (Corsica)
Paul Thomé
Alumnus, School of Slavonic and Eastern European Studies, UCL, UK

Partiti (singular: *partitu*) comes from the Italian *partito*, which means 'party' in the political sense. In Corsican, it is more associated with the idea of a faction or a clan. While *partiti* is a name used to designate a clan, the practice covers the system of favours and clientelism used between members of the same clan. The favours can be wide-ranging, from a simple gesture in everyday life to weaving cunning criminal or political schemes. The stability of the system is ensured by the Corsican culture of honour. Therefore, a member of a *partiti* is duty-bound to help other members of the same *partiti*.

A *partiti* comprises three components: *parenti*, *amici* and *clienti*, Corsican words meaning 'parents', 'friends' and 'clients', equally used to refer to the different clans (see also *KhTsB*, 5.1 in this volume). *Parenti* (singular: *parente*) in Corsican refers to all the blood relations of an individual. *Parenti* are the foundation of a Corsican clan, replacing the traditional family structure.

Figure 13.7.1 The isolated location of Corsican villages contributes greatly to a Corsican sense of identity and to the formation of *partiti*. © Pierre Bona.

Amici (singular: *amicu*), meaning 'friends', must be understood in its wider sense, as referring to everyone with whom an individual is on friendly terms. Because of the isolated location of Corsican villages, families and clans tend to live in the same location their entire lives, thus reinforcing the sense of Corsican identity, as well as the ties between villagers. This sense of community is therefore extended to anyone from the blood-related *parenti* (Gaudry 2007) to a neighbour, a family friend or the mayor of the village.

Clienti (singular: *cliente*), on the other hand, represent the part of the clan outside of the village. These are clients of the clan who gain its protection in exchange for services. This type of patron-client relationship seems to be in existence since the late nineteenth century (Briquet 1990: 79–80), when clan leaders would gather scarce resources and distribute them to the *clienti* in exchange for their loyalty. With the modernisation of the economic structure in Corsica, *clienti* are now understood to be individuals in a position of power, working for the clan's best interests, such as doctors and lawyers. The clan structure represents the foundation of all forms of interaction in Corsica. Because of this, last names are not as important in denoting lineage or ancestral village and are often omitted (Candea 2010). The names symbolise a code shared among Corsicans, unknown to outsiders.

Its location in the Mediterranean Sea sets Corsica apart from other insular cultures. Mediterranean cultures place an emphasis on solidarity, kinship, as well as honour and justice (Adrey 2009: 145). Corsica's isolation, its harsh environment and its history have also influenced its culture. Unique circumstances have shaped unique social relations, which led to unique informal practices (Adrey 2009: 143–7). Among them, *partiti* represents a form of clan-based clientelism, endogenous to the island.

Being part of a clan ensures long-standing solidarity and strong mutual help in achieving success. The importance of lineage in this insular context generates a 'lock-in effect', whereby local and closed communities reward members with a safety net and support, expecting reciprocation (see Chapter 3 Volume 1 on lock-in effect). The effect creates and reinforces the idea of a shared identity, which in turn solidifies bonds of solidarity between clan members and ensures their protection and 'help with difficulties'. Clan members are loyal to one another and help each other in times of need. To serve his *partiti*, a clan member working as a civil servant will find a way to help other members in need by using state resources, for example granting construction permits without requiring paperwork. The practice of *partiti* exists to solve problems, it represents the Corsican 'way of getting things done'.

Like *partiti*, relationships such as *yongo* from South Korea, *hemşehricilik* and *ahbap-çavuş* from Turkey and *rushyldyq* from Kazakhstan refer to helping people of shared origins. The *yongo* personal ties are based on kinship, shared locality or education. The Turkish *ahbap-çavuş* relationships are made on the basis of shared educational or military experience, while *hemşehricilik* is the basis of mutual help among Turkish emigrants. The Kazakhstani *rushyldyq* is the feeling of loyalty to one's *ru*, a sub-ethnic identity.

The Mediterranean concept of *amici, amigos* is close to the idea of *amici* in Corsica, especially to the instrumentalisation of friendship and the impossibility of refusing a request. However, *amici* in Corsica need not be of the same social standing, and reciprocity is not expected. The continuity of the *partiti* practice is ensured by honour, an important concept in the Mediterranean. Refusing a request brings shame to both the individual and his or her clan. By offering protection, the protector's honour is at stake, and honour is valued more highly than reciprocity or material interest (Lenclud 1993).

The political dimension of *partiti* in Corsica comprises four elements: two-party system, mandatory affiliation, clientelist organisation and partisan exercise of power (Lenclud 1986: 138). Their combination is what makes the political climate of Corsica unique. Bipartisanism means that in every locus of power there can only be one party in power (the *partitu*) and one party in the opposition (the *contrapartitu*). This antagonism between clans contributes to the formation of their identities: one clan exists because it opposes another (Briquet 1990). Clientelism refers to 'protection' from the *partiti*. The dyadic relationship between protector and client, although instrumentalised, relies on the basis of emotional friendship. This ambivalence between 'affective and effective friendship' (Briquet 1990: 37) represents another fundamental characteristic of *partiti*, in which substantial favours are neither gifts, nor commodities, nor payment – as is often the case in informal practices (Ledeneva et al. 2018: 10). In Corsica such favours are symbols of friendship, an important component of this relationship (Lenclud 1986: 142). They showcase the values of honour and trust that are pre-eminent in the Corsican culture. Even a small favour to a member of a *partiti* entails a deeper meaning: the sense of belonging to a clan (Pomponi 1978). The nature and quality of the act matter less than the act in itself, as a favour is remembered by the clan. This means that favours will be returned by other members of the *partiti*. Finally, *partiti* is part and parcel of a personalised system of power in Corsica, creating the conditions for a subjective exercise of power, where the members of one's own clan take precedence.

13.8 *Caciquismo* (Mexico)
Fausto Carbajal Glass
Department of Security and Crime Science, UCL, UK

Caciquismo refers to the exercise of political, economic and social influence in a geographic area, based on informal control and co-optation mechanisms. It is a widespread phenomenon in Latin American countries, probably as the result of pre-Columbian power hierarchies and a shared colonial past. The Spanish crown kept the indigenous social structures so that *caciques* remained political chiefs (Hobsbawm 1971: 90). Since the nineteenth century, the term has evolved to denote those individuals – predominantly men – who exercised power to the point of consolidating subnational regimes (O'Donnell 2004: 183). In Mexico, *caciquismo* still refers to a person who exerts influence in public affairs in a geographic area, starting at the local level of municipality, the lowest politico-administrative unit in Mexico preceding state and federal authorities (Ugalde 1973: 124). Until present-day, *caciquismo* has been a distinctive trait in the Mexican state-making process as it has been a source of para-institutional power of social and political control (Pansters 2012: 25). The *caciques* have influenced, if not shaped, most major transformations of twentieth-century Mexico, such as the 1910 revolution, as well as the early twenty-first-century democratisation process and the contemporary security crisis.

In the late 1890s and early 1900s, President Porfirio Díaz managed to align his presidency with both the formal and informal power brokers (Krauze 1998: 10). During the *Porfiriato*, as this period is commonly known, *caciques* became an oligarchic network that produced a new breed of magnates, for it gathered landowners, industrials, merchants and lenders into a single network that appeased the Mexican society and maintained power (Meyer 2000). Although the revolution ousted Díaz in 1911 after a 35-year dictatorship, *caciquismo* survived the civil war. Once the revolution's political and social turmoil ended in the 1930s, and the Institutional Revolutionary Party (PRI) 'routinized' the post-revolutionary regime in the 1940s, *caciquismo* was once again a fundamental way to bring about peace and effective governance to the country. The *cacique* were again the informal intermediary that connected local politics to the national political project (Meyer 2000).

In essence, the post-revolutionary regime was characterised by a single-party government, a centralised authority of the president, a corporatist pact among the party, interest groups, and bureaucratic leaders and a clientelist pyramid composed of political officials and local powerbrokers – *caciques* – to enhance state capacity in remote areas (McAdam et al. 2001: 294). Through this period, *caciques* were selected, controlled and funded by the central government. They were responsible, on the one hand, for providing solid electoral results and, on the other, for maintaining peace and order in their stronghold (McAdam et al. 2001).

Caciques would ensure electoral support of the population in exchange for access to public benefits and state resources. Such practices became known as *clientelismo*, whereby the *cacique* became the patron and the population its client (O'Donnell 2004: 182). In this sense, *caciquismo* is a paternalistic relationship whereby a local magnate holds power on the basis of influence over those who put themselves under his protection (Hobsbawm 1971: 57). This informal institution is similar to the *padrino* system in the Philippines (Pak-Nung and Joyce 2018: 380–2). Both systems presume co-optation practices based on distribution of goods, services, employment or political positions. *Caciquismo* reinforces itself by a collective attitude of social consent and cooperation. Although *caciquismo* is an undemocratic way to concentrate power, paradoxically, it has also been a mechanism for serving democratic needs and power redistribution, albeit discretional and arbitrary. The way *caciques* mediate relations between citizens and the state also resembles the *dalali* brokers in India who alleviate complexity for the federal authorities (Martin 2018: 211–13).

To maintain peace in remote areas, the federal government endowed *caciques* with control over public order with the help of the military (Benítez-Manaut 2017). In other cases, *caciques* would exert control primarily through the engagement of private militias or paramilitaries in order to rapidly suppress any uprising (Maldonado-Aranda 2013: 48). Even nowadays, local landowners-cum-patrons-cum-politicians treat the municipal police forces as private armies (Felbab-Brown 2013: 14).

Caciques were empowered to compensate for the defects and insufficiencies of the national government, but their influence spread to the detriment of municipal-level institutions. Their informal power undermined the effectiveness of law enforcement that exacerbated Mexico's ongoing security and violence crisis, even more so in association with the criminal underworld becoming increasingly fragmented, diverse and localised (Carbajal Glass 2019). The coercive nature of *caciquismo* is inevitably coupled with repression and impunity (Pansters 2012: 25). In its darkest aspects, *caciquismo* shares similarities with the Indian *Goonda Raj* (Michelutti 2018: 383–5) and the Russian *krysha* (Zabyelina and Buzhor 2018: 256–9).

In 2000, the centre-right National Action Party (PAN), the main opposition party at the time, ousted the PRI, thus ending its federal hegemony of over 70 years. The political changes associated with the democratisation 'undermined the pyramidal composition of power structures (single-party government and centralised authority of the president) meaning the loss of social control' (Villarreal 2007: 484). In this new context, *caciques* adopted a more competitive approach. The democratisation made it even clearer that *caciquismo* was in reality a subsystem operating within the context of a national polity and economy (Anderson and Cockroft 1972: 12). The dissolution of the centralised top-down, one-party structures gave more autonomy to local state and municipal authorities often controlled by the *caciques* themselves (Maldonado-Aranda 2013: 52). The democratisation and the redistribution of power gave way to a *federalización caciquista* (*cacique*-like federalisation), as was predicted years earlier (Castillo-Peraza 1995).

Caciquismo operates on the basis of multiple elements of coercion, co-optation, patronage and consensual interaction between patrons and clients. Its core is best grasped by related concepts of corporatism, patrimonialism, clientelism and personalism (Powell 2012). With deep historical and political roots, *caciquismo* is ubiquitous in Mexico. It will be interesting to study how this informal institution evolves under increasing democratisation, deep security challenges and a lack of institutional design at the local level.

13.9 **Maan tapa** (Finland)
Simo Mannila
Department of Social Sciences, University of Helsinki and University of Turku, Finland

The Finnish term *maan tapa* refers to a parallel legal system that applies when no primary, or written, legislation is available. The term can be translated as a 'custom law'. To become a *maan tapa*, an established practice needs to be considered binding, accepted by all parties and not be prohibited explicitly by legislation. The Finnish Parliament (2017) also refers to *maan tapa* as custom law, but states that situations where *maan tapa* would constitute a source of law are very rare. In juridical literature the term dates back to the eighteenth century. It is included in the Swedish 1734 legal code, historically an important source of Finnish law (Finnish Parliament 2009; Finnish Wikipedia 2017).

Legally reprehensible links of *maan tapa* in Finland often exist within *hyvä veli* networks. These follow the principle 'I scratch your back, you scratch mine'. The *hyvä veli* term originates in the correspondence between old Swedish-speaking civil service, whose letters typically started with 'Dear brother'. The connotations of the term changed in the course of history from neutral to critical and ironic ones when used in press and everyday language.

In the Finnish vernacular, *maan tapa* describes a widely accepted but legally or morally questionable practice (Finnish Wikipedia 2017). Thus, a strictly legal term has developed into a popular expression used by the media and the public. It came to denote the interactions within *hyvä veli* networks – elite connections and forms of informal influence bordering on corruption. There have been important lawsuits, where defendants had pleaded *maan tapa* but their plea was found to be in conflict with the legislation and turned down. Examples of such cases have included reprehensible links between politicians, civil servants and business, such as failures to observe a conflict of interest in decision-making, financial scheming and lack of transparency in policymaking. In public discourse the term is now used ironically to refer to any malpractice, its original sense becoming rather obsolete (Mahlamäki 2017).

The change in the use of the term reflects a changing reality. Finnish law enforcement today seems alert to identifying problematic cases of *maan tapa* and bringing them to court. Academic research into *maan tapa* is still lacking, but since its meaning is linked to informal influence and corruption, research into corruption or administrative malpractice in Finland is relevant for its understanding (Salminen 2010; Salminen and Mäntysalo 2013; Peurala and Muttilainen 2015; *hyvä Veli* at Shala 2018; 3.12 Volume 1). According to the Transparency International corruption perception index (Transparency International 2016) Finland is a country with the lowest levels of corruption in the world, but there are concerns that corruption in Finland has a structural character (Salminen and Viinamäki 2017). Therefore, to address its nature, future research on *maan tapa* should include studies of relevant historical lawsuits and their normative and public argumentation, studies on the use of the term in the media and the development of indicators such as legal lawsuits statistics or relevance of *maan tapa* in various contexts.

Maan tapa is the subject of Jarmo Korhonen's book on the funding of Finnish political parties (2015; cf. Joutsen and Keränen 2009). In Finland, as well as other European countries, there is a wealth of organisations attached to political parties. Some organisations attempt to influence them, also via financial scheming. Political funding often comes also from the business sector, sometimes via intermediaries, and is aimed at specific politicians, rather than political parties. Between 2000 and 2010, electoral funding was the subject of litigation cases in which businesspeople, typically men, were accused of bribing political parties and were condemned by district courts, yet subsequently acquitted in higher courts, either partly or completely. Korhonen, the secretary of the Centre Party between 2006 and 2010, was himself involved in lawsuits related to irregularities in financing the elections. In the book spanning 776 pages, Korhonen argues that all Finnish political parties have to some extent used financial scheming. Korhonen states that '*maan tapa* describe[d] Finnish society in the 2000s' and adds that 'it is important for the reader to understand that the media was a part of *maan tapa*' (Korhonen 2015: 7). The media was implicated by selectively covering political lawsuits. While the back cover prominently linked *maan tapa* to corruption in Finland, Korhonen's book did not receive any major attention and did not spur any legal action despite its detailed contents.

An interesting reference to *maan tapa* is a 2012 album *Maan tapa* by Finnish rapper Paleface and Julkinen Sana. In the album, the term has lost both its original sense and its more common ironic meaning. It offers a broad, aggressively critical analysis of contemporary Finnish society. The title of the album suggests that the term is widely used and its meaning is constantly changing, depending on the time period, the users and the context.

13.10 **Duang muang** (Thailand)
Akkharaphong Khamkhun,
Pridi Banomyong International College, Thammasat University, Thailand
and
Wasin Punthong
Faculty of Political Science, Thammasat University, Thailand

In Thailand, *duang muang* literally means 'the fate of the city'. In a Thai Lao language, *muang* simply means city, town, or network of administrative units, and it is also colloquially used to refer to the whole country, *Muang Thai*. The term *duang* means a pre-determined fate, or destiny, controlled by supernatural powers. Everyone's life is preordained from the exact moment of birth. The destiny cannot be changed but reading its astrological movements and forces at work can help achieve some control. Thus, *duang* is professionally calculated by astrologers, who are highly visible in Thailand. Most magazines and newspapers around the globe feature horoscope sections, but in Thailand it is common for people to use it and for astrologers to give advice through mainstream media and in almost every national daily. When people are about to get married or open a new business, they usually seek consultation from astrologers or monks who have astrological knowledge. Interpreting *duang* based on its astrological revelations is therefore a no-nonsense social practice, and trade, in Thailand.

Figure 13.10.1 A *duang* tablet forecasts and enhances one's *duang*. Numbers engraved in the circle on the tablet are calculated by a professional astrologer. © Wasin Punthong.

Historically, the practice of *duang* reading plays an important part in several royal ceremonies. During a coronation ceremony, the monarch's birth *duang* (ดวงพระราชสมภพ: *duang phrarajchasompob*) is engraved on the surface of a golden plaque. According to the chronicle of Ayutthaya Kingdom, since the fourteenth century, the court astrologers played a prominent role in providing advice to the king. The title of the court astrologer, *Phraya Horathipbodi* (พระยาโหราธิบดี), was given to those overseeing the *Hora* department responsible for guidance to the kingdom's destiny. Although this title was abolished, together with the formal advisory role of court astrologers, their ceremonial role endures. Nowadays, the king appoints a *Phra Maha Raja-Kru* (พระมหาราชครู), an informal advisor. In this respect, for centuries, interpreting *duang muang* had been a method of political analysis and influence that shaped political decisions of the ruling class.

Prior to the 1932 revolution initiated by the People's Party, which changed the country's regime from absolute monarchy to a democratic regime, *duang muang* was considered a common practice especially in the royal court. With modernisation, *duang muang* gradually lost its formal prescriptive role in politics. Destiny reading became an obsolete spiritual practice associated with the bygone age that contradicted modern political practices, presumed to be based on scientific grounds and empirically tested decision-making. Beyond the formal political realm, interpreting *duang muang* by well-known astrologers remains politically relevant for Thai leaders and socially significant for many Thai people. The practice of seeking spiritual guidance is widespread in the private sphere, in Thailand and elsewhere (see, for example, Green et al. 2005 for a serious study of mundane astrology in the US). However, the scale and the public domain of its application make the divination practices in Thailand specific. The specific feature of *duang muang* can be associated with its potential to influence a course of political action in highly uncertain contexts, such as a *coup d'état* (Songsamphan 1991). *Duang muang* has political implications, whereby cultural elements embedded in Thailand's social fabric can be used pragmatically. Recent research findings on the role of astrological heuristics have confirmed the psychological influence of *duang muang* (Hamilton 2015).

Political leaders use *duang muang* as an enabling, or problem-solving, tool that helps them assess, or improve, a highly volatile political situation. *Duang muang* helps build political consensus because of beliefs that the country has inherited its own destiny and that the movement of the stars influences the political life of the country, thus legitimising political decisions, if they had been made in accordance with *duang muang*. For instance, it is widely known among Thais that the date of installing

Bangkok's city pillar, 21 April 2325 BE (Buddhist Era), was selected with reference to its most auspicious *duang muang* (Likitkijsomboon 1994: 78). This particular conception of *duang* is collective in the sense that all members of a political community are united under the same *duang muang*. This belief purports that political changes are to some extent conditioned by *duang muang* at every moment in time. The right to an interpretation of *duang muang* can also be contested. Only a handful of elite astrologers are widely acknowledged in the society as being able to accomplish a political reading or divination, and their number is kept under control. The Thai Astrologer Association, an active professional organisation under the Patronage of Her Majesty the Queen, was founded in 1947. Its founders include several prominent members of establishment, including an Oxford graduate, ex-privy council member, Phraya Srivisarnvaja (Tienliang Hoontrakul) [(พระยาศรีวิสารวาจา (เทียนเลียง ฮุนตระกูล)].

Most of the political elites and governmental leaders today use the expertise of political consultants who provide analyses of the political context, forecasts, and advice on policy responses to particular situations. These experts tend to be qualified in economics, political science or similar disciplines. Parallel to this practice, political leaders often develop close relationships with astrologers. Politicians, including the prime minister and cabinet members, approach astrologers for advice and divination in order to boost their popularity. In reverse, such close interactions with politicians enable professional political astrologers to gain access to the elite networks, exercise political influence, and even get a political appointment. For example, Prime Minister Prayuth Chan-o-cha, who staged a coup in 2014, appointed his once spiritual advisor and an acclaimed astrologer Panuwat Punwichatkul (ภาณุวัฒน์ พันธุ์วิชาติกุล) to the political affairs unit of his Secretariat (101World 2020).

In times of political uncertainty, when they are expected to be the pillars of stability and leadership, governmental agencies and political analysts tend to be overruled by leading political astrologers who publicly reveal the *duang muang* through mass media and de facto substitute for, if not clash with, the functions of these agencies. This practice can be understood as a form of informal political analysis that attempts to explain politics with reference to astrological patterns. As those astrologers are socialised and integrated into the society, their interpretation of *duang muang* reproduces an existing metanarrative, accepted by Thai society. *Duang muang* provides a political frame through which political activities are enacted, perceived and assessed, as if supernatural forces kept the country in a mould. From this perspective, *duang muang* creates a space free of secular political control. It is an objective movement of the stars that enables or disables events from occurring.

Duang muang plays a crucial role in Thai society since it shapes the way political activities are enacted. Political elites tend to cling to an astrological prophecy when making a decision on critical matters, such as forming a new government or staging a coup. Before the bloodless coup that changed Siam from an absolute monarchy to a constitutional monarchy, the People's Party, the group that planned and staged the coup, consulted the astrological constellation (Museum Siam Knowledge Center 2019). *Duang muang* is also used instrumentally to legitimise political incumbency by mounting evidence that the current leaders' personal astrological registers could enrich the *duang muang* (see Tipyamasgomen 1996; Panpeerapit and Pongsawat 2019). In parallel with the formal hiring of political consultants to provide political insights, politicians and leaders benefit from the informal advice of astrologers able to interpret *duang muang* in both political and personal domains. The coexistence of the two practices highlights the political and social significance of interpreting *duang muang*.

13.11 **Okkul't** (Russia)
Valeriy Solovey
Independent researcher, Moscow State Institute of International Relations, Russia

In Russian society, a significant proportion of people take magic, astrology and extrasensory perception seriously. Thirty-one per cent say they believe in magic, 31 per cent believe in the possibility of predicting the future and 18 per cent believe in psychic phenomena (transmission of thoughts and telekinesis), while 15 per cent say they trust astrology (WCIOM 2019). According to anecdotal evidence, the proportion of such people is even higher among the Russian establishment, including the top elite, and has been rapidly increasing since 2012. In the context of the growing turbulence of the political situation in Russia since the annexation of Crimea and the 2022 warfare in Ukraine, the establishment seeks, with the help of the *okkul't*, to look into the future, to gain and/or retain power, to ensure guarantees of personal security and to preserve their wealth. The *okkul't* (mystical or magical) practices and shamanism (shamans are believed to have access to, and influence in, the world of good and evil spirits) play an instrumental role for the Russian establishment.

Recourse to the *okkul't* is typical of the Russian elite in a time of uncertainty. In the early twentieth century, the family of Russia's last emperor, Nicholas II, came to rely on the services of the famous French medium Philip and the well-known Orthodox mystic Grigory Rasputin.

Okkul't and Orthodox mysticism were intricately intertwined and most popular among the Russian aristocracy at that time. When the Soviets came to power in Russia in 1917, atheism became officially propagated and enforced, yet occult followers continued to be found among communists (Znamenski 2011). Within several decades, interest in esotericism revived in the Soviet Union (USSR) in the 1960s. This research into paranormal human capabilities was headed by the General Staff of the Soviet Armed Forces together with the Committee for State Security (KGB) (Vilkov 2019a).

The period from the second half of the 1980s to the first half of the 1990s saw intense interest in extrasensory phenomena in the USSR. Indeed, this interest acquired the character of an epidemic: the most famous psychics (Allan Chumak and, in particular, Anatoly Kashpirovsky) attracted whole stadiums to their sessions and even conducted them on state television. In the first half of the 1990s, parapsychology (the study of paranormal or psychic phenomena such as telepathy and telekinesis) was intensely developed within the framework of the Federal Security Service (FSB) and the Presidential Security Service (SBP), organisations that guarded Russia's first president Boris Yeltsin and other senior officials in the newly established Russian Federation (Vilkov 2019b). *Okkul't* activities and esoteric experiences by the Russian establishment and society are described in grotesque and phantasmagorical yet somewhat accurate ways in several novels by the Russian writer Viktor Pelevin (Pelevin 2003, 2006, 2017, 2018).

In the 2000s, interest in extrasensory perception and occult practices prevailed among the Russian establishment, especially following the outbreak of war in Southern and Eastern Ukraine in 2014 (Baltic Worlds 2021). There is an obvious historical analogy with Russia in the early twentieth century when, as noted earlier, interest in the *okkul't* increased as political turbulence spread in the Romanov empire. A second analogy is the interweaving of occultism with Orthodox mysticism. A qualitatively new feature of the modern situation is the use of shamanism (that is, attempting to communicate with and harness the power of the spiritual world) and syncretic (that is, bringing together and combining different philosophical, religious or cultural principles and practices) religious cults such as Santa Muerte, Voodoo and other African cults that are not normally found in Russia.

Today's Russian establishment readily turns for advice to so-called Orthodox elders (monks and priests believed to have mystical abilities). Father Iliy (Elijah) Nozdrin is considered especially influential and is someone with whom Russian President Vladimir Putin and members of the top Russian elite reportedly meet from time to time (Rubin et al. 2019). Bishop Tikhonov (Shevkunov), considered to be the confessor of the Russian president, is one of the most influential Orthodox advisers too. The main requests addressed to the elders include predicting the future of a specific official, healing and providing protection against the intrigues of competitors. Mystical rites have been employed to fight against COVID-19 (RIA Novosti 2020). The elders, including Iliy, also play an important psychotherapeutic role, legitimating the decisions taken by the authorities from the point of view of Orthodox mysticism.

The Russian establishment use astrology and fortune-telling, including tarot cards, in order to predict the future and to seek advice on how to behave in a specific situation; they resort to magic in order to influence a specific situation, ensure security, gain protection against competitors, and eliminate competitors. As a rule, wives, daughters and mistresses of members of the Russian establishment turn to fortune-tellers for advice. Men, on the other hand, prefer to take part in magic rituals. Rituals often involve sacrifices: a black bird or animal will be brought to the ceremony. Magicians try to satisfy the demands of their high-ranking clients and to build confidence in the effectiveness of the rituals. All levels of the Russian establishment, including the topmost elite, engage in occult practices.

Attempts to influence political decision-making are conducted by means of shamans. The Russian establishment uses representatives of mainly two shamanic traditions: Siberian and Amazonian. President Putin flew several times to Siberia, Tuva and Khakassia (most recently in March 2021), where he allegedly took part in shamanic rituals. In the mid-2010s, the establishment sought the services of shaman Kolya, an ethnic Nenets (the Nenets being one of the aboriginal peoples of the Russian North), who made predictions of the events in eastern Ukraine.

In 2019, a Yakut shaman, Alexander Gabyshev, began a march of approximately 5,000 miles (8,000 km) from his native Yakutsk to Moscow with the aim of performing a ritual that would remove President Putin from power (Sugueva 2021). In September 2019, the Russian authorities arrested Gabyshev and sent him against his will to a psychiatric hospital in Yakutsk (*The Moscow Times*, 2019). The police stopped Gabyshev when he made a second attempt to walk in December 2019. After he announced his third attempt in May 2020, he was again detained and committed by court order to a mental hospital (AFP 2020).

To sum up, an influential syncretic system of religious, *okkul't* and shamanic practices has developed in Russia and is used by at least part of the Russian establishment. There was a noticeable increase of interest in such rituals in 2014 that has intensified further since 2020. According to some estimates, the total annual turnover of the magic-services market in Russia before the onset of the COVID-19 pandemic was about 30 billion roubles (450–500 million USD) (Efimkina et al. 2019). The rituals and their practitioners (fortune-tellers, astrologers, magicians, sorcerers and shamans) do not directly determine key government decisions, but they do play an important psychotherapeutic role, helping to build their clients' confidence in their decisions and activities, as well as solve personal problems. These include predicting the future, achieving personal success, securing protection against competitors and outer forces alike.

Bibliography to Chapter 13

Introduction: demystifying ageing and power
Gemma Carney and Mia Gray

Butler, R. N. (1975). *Why survive? Being old in America*. New York: Harper & Row.
Carney, G. and Gray, M. 2015. 'Unmasking the "Elderly Mystique": Why It Is Time to Make the Personal Political in Ageing Research'. *Journal of Aging Studies* 35: 123–34.
Carney, G. and Hannan, L. 2021. '"To Write My Autobiography and Get Myself in Focus Genetically": G. Stanley Hall's *Senescence*'. *Age, Culture, Humanities: An Interdisciplinary Journal. Special Issue: Narratives of Ageing in the Long Nineteenth Century.*
Carney, G. and Nash, P. (2020) *Critical Questions for Ageing Societies*. Bristol: Policy Press.
Carney, G. M., Maguire, S. and Byrne, B. 2022. 'Oldies Come Bottom of Grim Reaper Hierarchy: A Framing Analysis of UK Newspaper Coverage of Old Age and Risk of Dying during the First Wave of the COVID-19 Pandemic'. *Journal of Social Policy*: 1–22.
Carney, G. 2018. 'Toward a Gender Politics of Aging'. *Journal of Women & Aging* 30(3): 242–58.
Cohen, E. S. 1988. 'The Elderly Mystique: Constraints on the Autonomy of the Elderly with Disabilities'. *Gerontologist* 28 Suppl: 24–31.
Cole, T. 1992. *The Journey of Life: A Cultural History of Aging in America*. Cambridge: Cambridge University Press.
Fegitz, E. 2022. 'Neoliberal Feminism in Old Age: Femininity, Work, and Retirement in the Aftermath of the Great Recession'. *Gender, Work & Organization*: 1–16.
Friedan, B. 1992. *The Fountain of Age*. New York: Atlantic Books.
Glasby, J., Zhang, Y., Bennett, M. and Hall, P. 2020. 'A Lost Decade? A Renewed Case for Adult Social Care Reform in England'. *Journal of Social Policy* 1–32.
Gullette, M. M. 2017. *Ending Ageism, or How Not to Shoot Old People*. New Brunswick: Rutgers University Press.
Hall, G. S. 1922. *Senescence: The Last Half of Life*. New York: D. Appleton and Company.
Hawkes, K., O'Connell, J., Blurton Jones, N., Alvarez, H. and Charnov, E. 2000. 'The Grandmother Hypothesis and Human Evolution'. In *Adaptation and Human Behaviour: An Anthropological Perspective*, edited by L. Cronk, N. Changnong and W. Irons, 1st ed. London: Routledge.
Kohli, M. 2007. 'The Institutionalization of the Life Course: Looking Back to Look Ahead'. *Research in Human Development* 4(3–4): 253–71.
Macnicol, J. 2015. *Neoliberalising Old Age*. Cambridge: Cambridge University Press.
Magni-Berton, R. and Panel, S. 2020. 'Gerontocracy in a Comparative Perspective: Explaining Why Political Leaders Are (Almost Always) Older Than Their Constituents'. *Sociology Compass* 15(1): e12841.

13.1 *OBON* (Kyrgyzstan)
Elmira Satybaldieva

Alymkulova, A., Aitmatova, J. and Mamaraimov, A. 2012. 'OBON kak zerkalo: razvitie politicheskogo aktivizma ili ispol'zovanie zhenskogo resursa dlya tselei grup interesov v Kyrgyzstane'. *Tsentr Pomoshi Zhenshinam*.

Kandiyoti, D. 1988. 'Bargaining With Patriarchy'. *Gender & Society* 2(3): 274–90.

Piper, L. and Von Lieres, B. 2015. 'Mediating Between State and Citizens: The Significance of the Informal Politics of Third-Party Representation in the Global South'. *Citizenship Studies* 19(6–7): 696–713.

Satybaldieva, E. 2018. 'A Mob for Hire? Unpacking Older Women's Political Activism in Kyrgyzstan'. *Central Asian Survey* 37(2): 247–64.

Sutton, B. 2007. 'Poner el Cuerpo: Women's Embodiment and Political Resistance in Argentina'. *Latin American Politics & Society* 49(3): 129–62.

Szymanek, M. 2012. 'OBON: Rent-A-Mob Groups in the Volatile Kyrgyzstani Reality'. *New Eastern Europe*, 6 December. https://neweasterneurope.eu/2012/12/06/obon-rent-a-mob-groups-in-the-volatile-kyrgyzstani-reality-2/

Zdravomyslova, E. 2007. 'Soldiers' Mothers Fighting the Military Patriarchy'. In *Gender Orders Unbound? Globalisation, Restructuring and Reciprocity*, edited by I. Lenz, C. Ullrich and B. Fersch, 207–28. Opladen & Farmington Hills: Barbara Budrich Publishers.

13.2 *Jirga/shura* (Afghanistan)
Madeleine O. Nosworthy

Ayoubi, N., Haqbeen, F. R. and Tariq, M. O. 2011. *Afghanistan in 2011: A Survey of the Afghan People*. Kabul: The Asia Foundation.

Braithwaite, J. and Wardak, A. 2013. 'Crime and War in Afghanistan Part II: A Jeffersonian Alternative?'. *British Journal of Criminology* 53(2): 197–214.

Gang, R. 2011. *Community-Based Dispute Resolution Services in Kabul City*. Kabul: Afghanistan Research and Evaluation Unit. https://areu.org.af/wp-content/uploads/2016/02/1107E-CBDR-Processes-in-Kabul-City-CS-2011-web.pdf

Rashid, A. 2002. 'Signs of Internal Chaos Dog Afghanistan's Government – Fighting Among Warlords Escalates as Preparations Begin for Loya *jirga*'. *Wall Street Journal*, 22 February.

Rennie, R., Sen P. and Sharma, S. 2009. *Afghanistan in 2009: A Survey of the Afghan People*. Kabul: The Asia Foundation.

Saikal, A. 2002. 'Afghanistan after the Loya *jirga*'. *Survival* 44(3): 47–56.

Shawe, K. 2013. *Afghanistan in 2013: A Survey of the Afghan People*. Kabul: The Asia Foundation.

United Nations Peacemaker. 2001. *Agreement on Provisional Arrangements in Afghanistan Pending the re-Establishment of Permanent Government Institutions*. https://peacemaker.un.org/sites/peacemaker.un.org/files/AF_011205_AgreementProvisionalArrangementsinAfghanistan%28en%29.pdf

Wardak, A. 2006. 'Structures of Authority and Local Dispute Settlement in Afghanistan'. In *Conflicts and Conflict Resolution in Middle Eastern Societies: Between Tradition and Modernity*, edited by H. Albrecht, E. Kiza, H. Rezaei, H.-C. Rohne and J.-M. Simon. Berlin: Duncker & Humblot.

Wardak, A., Saba, D., Kazem, H. and United Nations Development Programme. 2007. *Afghanistan Human Development Report 2007, Bridging Modernity and Tradition: Rule of Law and the Search for Justice*. Kabul: Kabul University.

13.3 *Aqsaqal* (Kazakhstan)
Talshyn Tokyzhanova

Bacon, E. E. 1966. *Central Asians under Russian Rule: A Study in Culture Change*. Ithaca: Cornell University Press.

Bankoff, G. and Oven, K. 2019. 'From Nomadic Communitarianism to Civil Socialism: Searching for the Roots of Civil Society in Rural Kazakhstan'. *Journal of Civil Society* 15(4): 373–91.

Beyer, J. 2006. 'Revitalisation, Invention and Continued Existence of the Kyrgyz Aksakal Courts: Listening to Pluralistic Accounts of History'. *The Journal of Legal Pluralism and Unofficial Law* 38: 53–4.

Beyer, J. 2015. 'Customizations of Law: Courts of Elders (Aksakal Courts) in Rural and Urban Kyrgyzstan'. *PoLAR: Political and Legal Anthropology Review* 38(1): 53–71.

Earle, L., Fozilhujaev, B., Tashbaeva, C. and Djamankulova, K. 2004. 'Community Development in Kazakhstan, Kyrgyzstan and Uzbekistan'. Occasional Paper No. 40.

Kazakh National Medical University. 2013. 'Aqsaqal keñesi'. https://kaznmu.kz/a-sa-al-ke-esi/

Martin, V. 2001. *Law and Custom in the Steppe: The Kazakhs of the Middle Horde and Russian Colonialism in the Nineteenth Century*. 1st ed. Richmond: Routledge.

Polisia.kz. 2022. 'Sovet aksakalov sodeystvuyet v profilaktike bytovoy prestupnosti'. *Polisia. kz*, 1 February. https://polisia.kz/ru/sovet-aksakalov-sodejstvuet-v-profilaktike-bytovoj-prestupnosti/

Prime Minister of the Republic of Kazakhstan. 2020. 'Council of Aksakals to be created in Korday region'. *Official Information Source of the Prime Minister of the Republic of Kazakhstan*, 10 February. https://primeminister.kz/en/news/sovet-aksakalov-sozdadut-v-kordayskom-rayone

Religious Administration of Muslims of Kazakhstan. 2022. Council of Elders Has Been Established under the Religious Administration. *Religious Administration of Muslims of Kazakhstan*, 22 February. www.muftyat.kz/kk/news/qmdb/2022-02-09/38638-kmdb-zhanynan-aksakaldar-kenesi-quryldy-foto/

Satbayev University. 2017. 'V Kazakhstane sozdan Mezhdunarodnyy nauchno-obrazovatel'nyy tsentr atomnoy promyshlennosti'. *Satbayev University*, 21 April. https://satbayev.university/ru/news/v-kazakhstane-sozdan-mezhdunarodnyy-nauchno-obrazovatelnyy-tsentr-atomnoy-promyshlennosti

Sengupta, A. 2010. 'Imperatives of National Territorial Delimitation and the Fate of Bukhara 1917–1924'. *Central Asian Survey* 19(3–4): 394–415.

Trevisani, T. 2019. 'The Veterans' Gala: The Use of Tradition in an Industrial Labour Conflict in Contemporary Kazakhstan'. *Central Asian Survey* 38(3).

13.4 *Mullahs* (Afghanistan)
Jennifer Brick Murtazashvili

Barfield, T. J. 2004. 'An Islamic State Is a State Run by Good Muslims: Religion as a Way of Life and Not an Ideology in Afghanistan'. In *Remaking Muslim Politics: Pluralism, Contestation, Democratization*, edited by R. W. Hefner, 213–39. Princeton: Princeton University Press.

Dorronsoro, G. 2005. *Revolution Unending: Afghanistan, 1979 to the Present*. New York: Columbia University Press.

Dupree, L. 1973. *Afghanistan*. Princeton: Princeton University Press.

Murtazashvili, J. B. 2016. *Informal Order and the State in Afghanistan*. New York: Cambridge University Press.

Roy, O. 1990. *Islam and Resistance in Afghanistan*. Cambridge: Cambridge University Press.

Shahrani, M. N. 2002. 'Local Knowledge of Islam and Social Discourse in Afghanistan and Turkistan in the Modern Period'. In *Turko-Persia in Historical Perspective*, edited by R. L. Canfield, 161–88. New York: Cambridge University Press.

13.5 *Amakudari* (Japan)
Hayato Moriyama

Alexandre-Bailly, F. and Muratbekova-Touron, M. 2018. 'Pantouflage (France)'. In *The Global Encyclopaedia of Informality, Volume 2*, edited by A. Ledeneva, 240–3. London: UCL Press.

Cheung, A. B. L. 2013. 'NPM in Asian Countries'. In *The Ashgate Research Companion to New Public Management*, edited by T. Christensen and P. Lægreid, 131–44. Farnham: Ashgate Publishing.

Colignon, R. A. and Usui, C. 2003. *Amakudari: The Hidden Fabric of Japan's Economy*. Ithaca: Cornell University Press.

Horak, S. 2018. 'Jinmyaku (Japan)'. In *The Global Encyclopaedia of Informality, Volume 1*, edited by A. Ledeneva, 94–6. London: UCL Press.

Johnson, C. 1974. 'Reemployment of Retired Government Bureaucrats in Japanese Big Business'. *Asian Survey* 14(11): 953–65.

Kobayashi, K. 2012. 'Kokkakoumuin no amakudari konzetsu ni muketa kinnen no torikumi', *Reference* 739: 27–63. http://dl.ndl.go.jp/view/download/digidepo_3525594_po_073902.pdf?contentNo=1&alternativeNo=

Ministry of Education, Culture, Sports, Science and Technology of Japan (MEXT). 2017. 'Monbukagakushou ni okeru saishuushokutoumondai ni kakaru chousahoukoku – saishuu matome'. *Ministry of Education, Culture, Sports, Science and Technology of Japan*. www.mext.go.jp/component/a_menu/other/detail/__icsFiles/afieldfile/2017/04/19/1382987_04.pdf

Ministry of Internal Affairs and Communications of Japan (MIAC). 2009. 'Press Release: Heisei 18 nen kara heisei 20 nenmatsu madeno saishuushoku no assenkensuu no chousa ni tsuite'. Ministry of Internal Affairs and Communications of Japan. www.soumu.go.jp/menu_news/s-news/02jinji02_000003.html and www.soumu.go.jp/main_content/000019232.pdf

Mizoguchi, T. and Van Quyen, N. 2012. 'Amakudari: The Post-Retirement Employment of Elite Bureaucrats in Japan'. *Journal of Public Economic Theory* 14(5): 813–47.

National Personnel Authority of Japan. 2002. 'Heisei 13 nendo nenjihoukokusho'. *National Personnel Authority of Japan*. www.jinji.go.jp/hakusho/h13/jine200202_2_062.html

Quah, J. S. T. 2011. *Curbing Corruption in Asian Countries an Impossible Dream?* Bingley: Emerald.

Revolving Door Working Group. 2005. 'A Matter of Trust: How the Revolving Door Undermines Public Confidence in Government – and What to Do about It'. https://core.ac.uk/download/pdf/71339481.pdf

Secretariat of Reemployment Surveillance Commission of Japan (SRSC). 2017. 'Press Release: Monbukagakushou shokuin oyobi motoshokuin ni yoru saishuushokutou kiseiihankoui ga okonawareta jian ni kansuru chousakekka ni tsuite'. Secretariat of *Reemployment Surveillance Commission of Japan*. www5.cao.go.jp/kanshi/pdf/houdou/290120/tyosakekka.pdf

The Cabinet Office of Japan (CAS). 2007. 'Koumuinseido tokubetsuchousa ni kansuru gaiyou'. *The Cabinet Office of Japan*. www.gyoukaku.go.jp/senmon/dai8/siryou14.pdf

13.6 *Jajmani* (South Asia)
Soumya Mishra

Ahmad, S. 1970. 'Social Stratification in a Punjabi Village'. *Contribution to Indian Sociology* 4(1): 105–25.

Arens, J. and van Beurden, J. 1978. *Jhagrapur: Poor Peasants and Women in a Village in Bangladesh*. Amsterdam, Birmingham: Third World Publications.

Barth, F. 1960. 'The System of Social Stratification in Swat, North Pakistan'. In *Aspects of Castes in South India, Ceylon and North-west Pakistan*, edited by E. R. Leach, 113–48. Cambridge: Cambridge University Press.

Dangle, A. 1992. *Poisoned Bread: Translations from Modern Marathi Dalit Literature*. Bombay: Orient Longman.

Darling, M. 1934. *Wisdom and Waste in the Punjab Village*. London: Oxford University Press.

Gould, H. 1986. 'The Hindu Jajmani System', *Journal of Anthropological Research* 42(3): 269.

Gurjar, V. P. P. 2019. 'Why Caste Matters Reading Electoral Outcomes through the Optic of Caste'. *Economic and Political Weekly* 54(32): 76–8.

Lewis, O. and Barnouw, V. 1956. 'Caste and the Jajmani System in a North Indian Village'. *The Scientific Monthly* 83(2): 66–81.

McNeil, A. 2007. 'Mirasis: Some Thoughts on Hereditary Musicians in Hindustani Music'. In *Context: Journal of Music Research* 32.

Opler, M. and Singh, R. D. 1948. 'The Division of Labor in an Indian Village'. In *A Reader in General Anthropology*, edited by C. S. Coon, 464–93. London: Jonathan Cape.

Orenstein, H. 1962. 'Exploitation or Function in the Interpretation of Jajmani'. *Southwestern Journal of Anthropology* 18(4): 302–16.

Parry, J. P. and Bloch, M. 1989. *Money and the Morality of Exchange*. Cambridge and New York: Cambridge University Press, Cambridge Core.

Reddy, N. S. 1955. 'Functional Relations of Lohars in a North Indian Village'. *Eastern Anthropologist* 8: 155.

Rudner, D. 2003. 'Jajmani'. In *South Asian Folklore: An Encyclopedia*, edited by M. Mills, P. Claus and S. Diamond. New York and London: Routledge.
Srinivas, M. N. 1952. *Religion and Society Among the Coorgs*. Oxford: Oxford University Press.
Wiser, C. V. and Wiser, W. H. 1930. *Behind Mud Walls*. New York: R. R. Smith.

13.7 *Partiti* (Corsica)
Paul Thomé

Adrey, J.-B. 2009. 'Unity and Diversity in Corsica: Patterns of Identity and Political Separatism'. In *Discourse and Struggle in Minority Language Policy Formation: Corsican Language Policy in the EU Context of Governance*, edited by J.-B. Adrey, 142–59. London: Palgrave Macmillan.
Briquet, J.-L. 1990. 'Les amis de mes amis … Registres de la mobilisation politique dans la Corse rurale'. *Mots. Les Langages du Politique* 25: 23–41.
Candea, M. 2010. 'Anonymous Introductions: Identity and Belonging in Corsica'. *Journal of the Royal Anthropological Institute* 16: 119–37.
Gaudry, F.-R. 2007. *Les grandes familles de Corse: l'île aux clans*. LExpress.fr.
Ledeneva, A. et al. (ed.) 2018. *The Global Encyclopaedia of Informality: Understanding Social and Cultural Complexity, Volume 1*. London: UCL Press.
Lenclud, G. 1986. 'De bas en haut, de haut en bas: Le système des clans en Corse'. *Études Rurales* 137–73.
Lenclud, G. 1993. 'S'attacher. Le régime traditionnel de la protection en Corse'. *Terrain, revue d'anthropologie et de sciences humaines*: 81–96.
Pomponi, F. 1978. 'Structure de clan et structure de classe en Corse'. *Cahiers de la Méditerranée* 3: 143–57.

13.8 *Caciquismo* (Mexico)
Fausto Carbajal Glass

Anderson, B. and Cockroft, J. D. 1972. 'Control and Co-optation in Mexican Politics'. In *Dependence and Underdevelopment: Latin America's Political Economy*, edited by J. D. Cockroft, A. G. Frank and D. L. Johnson, 219–44. New York: Doubleday.
Benítez-Manaut, R. 2017. Seguridad interior: otro dilema del 2017, 'Revista Nexos', 30 January. https://seguridad.nexos.com.mx/?p=31
Carbajal Glass, F. 2019. 'The Mexican National Guard: Challenges, Opportunities and Fundamental Questions'. *RUSI*, 13 March. https://shoc.rusi.org/blog/the-mexican-national-guard-challenges-opportunities-and-fundamental-questions/
Castillo-Peraza, C. 1995. 'La yugoslavización del PRI'. *Diario Reforma*, 2 February.
Felbab-Brown, V. 2013. 'Peña Nieto's Piñata: The Promise and Pitfalls of Mexico's New Security Policy against Organized Crime'. *The Brookings Institution* 1–30.
Hobsbawm, E. 1971. *Primitive Rebels*. London: Brown Book Group.
Krauze, E. 1998. *Mexico: Biography of Power; A History of Modern Mexico, 1810–1996*. New York: Harper.
Maldonado-Aranda, S. 2013. 'Stories of Drug Trafficking in Rural Mexico: Territories, Drugs and Cartels in Michoacán'. *European Review of Latin American and Caribbean Studies* 94: 43–66.
Martin, N. 2018. 'Dalali'. In *The Global Encyclopaedia of Informality, Volume 2*, edited by A. Ledeneva, 211–13. London: UCL Press.
McAdam, D., Tarrow, S. and Tilly, C. 2001. *Dynamics of Contention*. New York: Cambridge University Press.
Meyer, L. 2000. 'Los caciques de ayer, hoy y mañana'. *Letras Libres*, 31 December. www.letraslibres.com/mexico/los-caciques-ayer-hoy-y-manana
Michelutti, L. 2018. 'Mafia Raj/Goonda Raj'. In *The Global Encyclopaedia of Informality, Volume 2*, edited by A. Ledeneva, 383–85. London: UCL Press.
O'Donnell, G. 2004. 'Cuatro temas para una agenda de debate'. In PNUD *La democracia en América Latina: el debate conceptual*. New York: PNUD.
Pak-Nung, W. and Joyce, K. 2018. 'Padrino System/balimbing'. In *The Global Encyclopaedia of Informality, Volume 2*, edited by A. Ledeneva, 380–82. London: UCL Press.

Pansters, W (ed.) 2012. *Violence, Coercion, and State-Making in Twentieth-Century Mexico: The Other Half of the Centaur*. California: Stanford University Press.
Powell, K. 2012. 'Political Practice, Everyday Violence, and Electoral Processes During the Neoliberal Period in Mexico'. In *Violence, Coercion, and State-Making in Twentieth-Century Mexico: The Other Half of the Centaur*, edited by W. Panters, 212–32. California: Stanford University Press.
Ugalde, A. 1973. 'Contemporary Mexico: From Hacienda to PRI, Political Leadership in a Zapotec Village'. In *The Caciques: Oligarchical Politics and the System of Caciquismo in the Luso-Hispanic World*, edited by R. Kern. Albuquerque: University of New Mexico Press.
Villarreal, A. 2007. 'Political Competition and Violence in Mexico: Hierarchical Social Control in Local Patronage Structures'. *American Sociological Review* 67(4): 477–98.
Zabyelina, Y. and Buzhor, A. 2018. 'Krysha'. In *Global Encyclopaedia of Informality, Volume 2*, edited by A. Ledeneva, 256–9. London: UCL Press.

13.9 *Maan tapa* (Finland)
Simo Mannila

Finnish Parliament. 2009. *Lakikirjanäyttely*. Finnish Parliament. 1734 laki. www.eduskunta.fi/FI/naineduskuntatoimii/kirjasto/aineistot/kotimainen_oikeus/Documents/Lakikirja250-1734.pdf
Finnish Parliament. 2017. *Yleisistä oikeuslähteistä ja oikeudellisesta informaatiosta*. Finnish Parliament. www.eduskunta.fi/FI/naineduskuntatoimii/kirjasto/aineistot/kotimainen_oikeus/kotimaiset-oikeuslahteet/Sivut/Yleista-oikeuslahteista-ja-oikeudellisesta-informaatiosta.aspx
Finnish Wikipedia. 2017. 'Maan tapa'. Finnish Wikipedia. https://fi.wikipedia.org/wiki/Maan_tapa
Joutsen, M. and Keränen, J. 2009. *Corruption and Prevention of Corruption in Finland*. Helsinki: Ministry of Justice.
Korhonen, J. 2015. *Maan Tapa*. Helsinki: Tammi.
Mahlamäki, M. 2017. 'Selvitysmies Olli Mäenpää: Yleissä on ongelmia vain Atte Jääskeläisen toimituksessa – On päässyt muodostumaan maan tavaksi että Yleen voi vaikuttaa'. *Etelä-Saimaa*, 15 May. www.esaimaa.fi/paikalliset/3828399
Paleface and Julkinen Sana. 2012. 'Maan tapa', www.youtube.com/watch?v=xkdw4wqJp38
Peurala, J. and Muttilainen, V. 2015. 'Korruption riskikohteet 2010-luvun Suomessa'. *Poliisiammattikorkeakoulun raportteja 115, Tampere: Poliisiammattikorkeakoulu*.
Salminen, A. (ed.) 2010. *Ethical Governance: A Citizen Perspective*. Vaasa: Vaasan yliopiston. www.uwasa.fi/materiaali/pdf/isbn_978-952-476-328-8.pdf
Salminen, A. and Mäntysalo, V. 2013. *Epäeettisestä tuomittavaan: korruptio ja hyvä veli –verkostot Suomessa*. Vaasa: Vaasan yliopiston. www.univaasa.fi/materiaali/pdf/isbn_978-952-476-429-2.pdf
Salminen, A. and Viinamäki, O.-P. 2017. *Piilokorruptio Suomessa: Mitä kansalaiset kertovat?* Vaasa: Vaasan yliopiston. https://osuva.uwasa.fi/bitstream/handle/10024/7972/isbn_978-952-476-740-8.pdf?sequence=1&isAllowed=y
Transparency International. 2016. Corruption Perception Index. *Transparency International*, 25 January. www.transparency.org/news/feature/corruption_perceptions_index_2016

13.10 *Duang muang* (Thailand)
Akkharaphong Khamkhun and Wasin Punthong

Green, H. S., Carter, C. E. O. and Raphael. 2005. *Mundane Astrology: The Astrology of Nations and States*. Lanham, MD: Astrology Classics.
Hamilton, M. A. 2015. 'Astrology as a Culturally Transmitted Heuristic Scheme for Understanding Seasonality Effects: A Response to Genovese (2014)'. *Comprehensive Psychology* 4: 1–11.
Likitkijsomboon, P. 1994. *Horasatwipak [Critique of Astrology]*. Bangkok: Namthai Publishing.
Museum Siam Knowledge Center. 2019. 'Horasat: Kruengmue Kanmuang Bab Thai [Astrology: A Thai-Style Political Tool]. Museum Siam Knowledge Center, 5 April.

Panpeerapit, K. and Pongsawat, P. 2019. 'The Relationship Between Astrology and Military Coup in Thailand'. *Journal of MCU Buddhapanya Review* 4: 115–32.

Songsamphan, C. 1991. *Supernatural Prophecy in Thai Politics: The Role of a Spiritual Cultural Element in Coup Decisions*. PhD thesis, The Claremont Graduate University, California.

Tipyamasgomen, S. 1996. *An Analysis of Politically Astrological Content in Printed Media During 1991–1993*. Master's thesis, Chulalongkorn University, Bangkok.

101World. 2020. 'Jorluek Hora Thai: Muea Duang Muang Shu Thahan Rerng Amnaj' [Understanding Thai Astrologers: When *Duang Muang* Complements the Military]. *101World*, 20 January. www.the101.world/thai-astrology/

13.11 *Okkul't* (Russia)
Valeriy Solovey

AFP. 2020. 'Anti-Putin Shaman Forced into Mental Asylum in Siberia'. *The Moscow Times*, 20 June. www.themoscowtimes.com/2020/06/02/anti-putin-shaman-forced-into-mental-asylum-in-siberia-a70460

Baltic Worlds. 2021. *Occultism Survived Communism. Special Issue*, XIV(4). CBEES: Södertörn University.

Efimkina, N., Zhurenkova, O. and Bulygina, Y. 2019. 'Godovyye oboroty rossiyskikh magov otsenili v 30 mlrd rubley' [The Annual Turnover of Russian Magicians Has Been Estimated at 30 billion Rubles]. *RIA Novosti*, 28 March. https://360tv.ru/news/obschestvo/godovye-oboroty-rossijskih-magov-otsenili-v-30-mlrd-rublej/

Pelevin, V. 2003. *Chisla*. Moscow: Eksmo.

Pelevin, V. 2006. *Empire V*. Moscow: Eksmo.

Pelevin, V. 2017. *Lampa Mafusaila, ili Kraynyaya bitva chekistov s masonami*. Moscow: Eksmo.

Pelevin, V. 2018. *Taynyye vidy na goru Fudzi*. Moscow: Eksmo.

RIA Novosti. 2020. 'Izvestnyy starets obletel Moskvu i Peterburg s molitvoj ot koronavirusa' [A Well-known Elder Flew over Moscow and St. Petersburg with a Prayer against the Coronavirus]. *RIA Novosti*, 3 April. https://ria.ru/20200403/1569528602.html

Rubin, M., Badanin, R., Lukyanova, Y. and Zholobova, M. 2019. 'The Kremlin's Elder. How the Russian Government Fell in Love with Mysticism'. *Project Media*, 29 May. www.proekt.media/en/article-en/kremlins-elder-elijah/

Sugueva, Y. 2021. 'Ya luchshe syadu v koloniyu, no ne nado menya lechit. Dvukhletniy put' shamana iz Yakutska v psikhiatricheskuyu kliniku' [I'd Rather Go to the Colony, You Don't Need to Treat Me. Shaman's Two-year Journey from Yakutsk to Psychiatric Clinic]. *Zona Media*, 21 May. https://zona.media/article/2021/05/21/shaman

The Moscow Times. 2019. 'Russia Sends Shaman en Route to Exorcise Putin to Psychiatric'. *The Moscow Times*, 20 September. www.themoscowtimes.com/2019/09/20/russia-sends-shaman-en-route-to-exorcise-putin-to-psychiatric-hospital-a67364

Vilkov, S. 2019a. 'Upravleniye Genshtaba po delam nechistoy sily' [Department of the General Stuff for evil spirits]. News.ru, 5 April. https://news.ru/society/upravlenie-genshtaba-po-delam-nechistoj-sily/

Vilkov, S. 2019b. 'Pogony russkikh magov: kak "ekstrasensy" stali generalami FSO' [Shoulder Straps of Russian Magicians: How 'Psychics' Became Federal Protective Service Generals]. News.ru, 17 April. https://news.ru/society/pogony-russkih-magov-kak-ekstrasensy-stali-generalami-fso/

WCIOM (All-Russian Public Opinion Research Centre). 2019. 'Vera v neob'yasnimoye: Analiticheskiy monitoring' [Belief in the Unexplained: Analytical Monitoring]. WCIOM, 2 July. https://wciom.ru/analytical-reviews/analiticheskii-obzor/vera-v-neobyasnimoe-monitoring

Znamenski, N. 2011. *Red Shambhala: Magic, Prophecy, and Geopolitics in the Heart of Asia*. Wheaton, IL: Quest Books.

14
Informal care and the end

Introduction: elderly care and ambivalence

Elena Zdravomyslova
European University at St. Petersburg, Russia

When we study and conceptualise care – a big, if not central, topic of the twenty-first century – we have to take into account its *spirit of informality*. Regardless of their forms and contexts, caring practices are informal in nature. They can be neither fully formalised (institutionalised, bureaucratised), nor commercialised. Despite the attempts to list the responsibilities of professional caregivers in job contracts (carer, nurse, social worker), certain personalised features of a carer's performance cannot be captured in a contract. Good carers are in high demand, but what makes a good carer eludes formalisation. Bureaucratisation (though inevitable and partly efficient) is constantly under attack in critical studies, often branded as a trend that can subvert the very ethics of care. The spirit of care reveals itself in the ability to express sympathy, compassion and the capability to understand and respond to personal needs. Trust and rapport are the core of care logic; it is impossible to formalise such intrinsic human qualities. The expectation of a good carer is to exercise primarily physical care but also to have a human touch, to engage in emotional work.

Care resembles a 'fictitious commodity' that loses its value when commodified, that is reduced to its exchange value (Polanyi 1944; Burawoy 2021: 155). Care work is sold and paid for; it seems to follow the logic of exchange when carers are employed to help family members partially delegate caring chores. However, there is a limit in the course of commercialisation, and carers may become open to exploitation due to their emotional ties to the patient. The global trend of the commodification of care is also criticised as an expression of 'global cooling' (Hochschild 2003). The logic of care is different from the logic of market and public choice (Mol 2008).

The modern regimes of care are complex. They include contributions from the state, market, family, community and civil society, as opposed to more controversial, spiritual sources, presented in this chapter. The very idea of care is about wholehearted personalised engagement in the improvement of well-being on both an individual and a collective level. An academic definition of care attempts to grasp the modus of true commitment and intrinsic tensions of caring (Tronto 2013). Robert Merton has captured the ambivalent logic of some professions (Merton 1976: 6). On the one hand, doctors, he wrote, should be both impartial and distanced from the patient in order to do a good job (thus, surgeons are prohibited from operating on their family members). On the other hand, they have to be personable, interested in a patient and have a personal touch. The clash of contradictory demands on a doctor causes what Merton named 'oscillating behaviour', whereby performance is context-bound and changes accordingly.

Along these lines, there are contradictory demands on the holder of the status of carer. Merton's idea of ambivalence is central to the understanding of caring, its informal spirit and the core of caring practice. Caring is a sustainable circular chain of interactions of a vulnerable dependent person, primary caregiver and other supportive actors. The work involves multiple never totally calculable, ever-changing tasks; drawing on physical, cognitive and emotional resources. Feminist researchers identify this specific type of work as love-work (Graham 1991). Love-work is not an oxymoron. Zygmunt Bauman defines ambivalence as the possibility of assigning an object or an event to more than one category and views it as a language-specific disorder (quoted in Ledeneva et al. 2018: 9). Simultaneously love-work belongs to two worlds of meanings – the one where instrumentality and exchange rules clash/or co-exist with that of sociability and selfless devotion. When conservative ideologies claim that care is a duty and a normative role, feminist discourses reveal that this role is love-work that could be both the realm of exploitation of caregivers and abuse of care-receivers.

Emotional ambivalence of the love-work operates in a similar way as a psychological ambivalence of love-hate. Medical professionals (doctors, nurses, helpers, paramedics) as well as family caregivers are expected to provide compassion and warmth, tuned to the changing demands of a suffering patient while at the same time exercising emotional self-control, which enables them to implement caring procedures. Professional carers become experienced in implementing such emotional ambivalence on a daily basis. However, formal training in medical colleges and universities (nursing departments) is detached from actual professional practices. When emotional warmth is not provided, ambitious patients claim *khamstvo*, or unacceptable rudeness of personnel (see 1.2 in this volume). Research on the practices of nursing confirms that playing ambivalence in professional life is in high demand, but it is also psychologically costly and could be costly for the institutions. This skill of oscillation mobilises the emotional and cognitive resources of professional carers that are exhaustive in principle, and this intensive long-term mobilisation results in care workers burning out (Becker et al. 1961; Borozdina 2015; Temkina 2019).

The emotional turn in contemporary research of private and public spheres helps to see the importance of emotional work and mobilisation of informal rules of emotional conduct in an uncertain world (Hochschild 1979; Illouz 2007; Lerner and Rivkin-Fish 2021). Emotional intelligence as a skill to resolve ambivalence in context becomes an increasingly explicit demand in both public and private institutions (Khalili 2012).

Ambivalence in care work reveals itself in dramatic emotional duality typical for narratives of caregivers. On the one hand, they feel and say that they made the right choice when deciding to keep their elderly at home and to provide care following the cultural model of familial domestic care; they are good people, good daughters, in-laws, true friends; some would say that they follow Christian rules of benevolent behaviour. On the other hand, they feel guilty for not being good enough, nor being able to provide the best help, in cases of emotional breakdowns when they could not exercise self-control. Narratives of caregivers confirm emotional oscillation between self-respect for proper behaviour and resentment that they lack autonomy, lack time and lack the energy to do anything other than care. Research shows that informants constantly face moral dilemmas because of the lack of institutional help and the strict code of familyist elderly care. This emotional ambivalence in the narratives is especially self-critical when institutional care for the elderly is poor and inadequate.

The emotional ambivalence described earlier is essential for analysing practices of care, in addition to the four dimensions – substantive, functional, normative and motivational – already identified and illustrated in the first two volumes of the encyclopaedia. Just like many entries in this chapter, the empirical research on caregiving for the elderly led by the Gender Studies Centre at the European University at St. Petersburg highlights the centrality of informal caregiving in the domestic realm. Informal care provides solutions where formal care or resources are in short supply, or where the wider context of uncertainty needs an urgent shortcut.

The elderly care crisis in the twenty-first century is part and parcel of the global ageing trend. Demographic ageing not only signifies the social and cultural achievements of humanity, but also presents multiple challenges. The need for care and the corresponding demand to transform elderly care regimes are pressing. Informal domestic care, a gendered realm of practices in many societies, becomes less available and less efficient for a number of reasons. First, family members have other needs and things to do. Second, intergenerational family ties grow weaker, especially as the elderly live apart from their adult children at great distances or abroad. Third, women en masse tend to be employed and are not able to provide full-time domestic care. Fourth, the so-called 'sandwich generation' has to provide care for both the frail elderly and still dependent children, so the pivot family member is literally torn between the obligations of these family roles. Fifth, the balance of work and elderly care is still not sufficiently addressed at the institutional level. Caring responsibilities for the elderly do not entitle one to annual leave or reduced hours according to the majority of work policies, while the responsibilities and required competencies continue to grow.

A study of long-term caring practices of family members supporting elderly relatives with dementia in Russia provides some insights into the issues of informal care. First, families are perceived to be the key actors providing elderly care. Care institutions exist and there have been some improvements in ageing policies, but the overall format of date is best conceptualised as modernised familial (Kremer 2007; Rostgaard and Pfau-Effinger 2011; Bogdanova 2019; Zdravomyslova and Savchenko 2020). Second, it is a gendered model: everyday primary care tends to be women's responsibility. Female family members and female medical professionals exercise multiple caring tasks and learn many skills in their caring career. Third, informality in caring practices goes together with formal engagements. Carers gain legal status of a guardian and heir; they act as sick/elderly life-managers; and represent their interests on various institutional occasions. Fourth, they develop expert knowledge regarding their client's health conditions, pharmaceutics, perks and benefit entitlements, as well as regarding ways to deal with bureaucrats and benefit from the system. Fifth, formal institutions need help from informal caregivers especially with the elderly suffering from cognitive impairments. Caregivers monitor treatment and observe the compliance of a patient, which is not an easy task.

The mode of functional ambivalence, whereby the carer is a family member but also a quasi-professional carer with expertise, is intrinsic to the role. It is an acquired skill, and not without consequences for the carers themselves. Dealing with cognitive disability in the family aggravates the caregiver's burden, changes their status and identity, their whole life. Sometimes their care work schedule seems impossible – during periods of health aggravation of the patient. The breakdowns are often reported in the narratives of caregivers. They feel that their other duties are neglected and their health worsens. They tend to disengage themselves socially. It becomes more difficult to carry on when a caregiver is employed and/or finds themselves in the sandwich generation syndrome. Their functionality breeds dysfunctionality.

The substantive form of ambivalence reveals itself in the coexistence of loving commitment and instrumentality. Observers may claim that caregiving is just the price to pay for being the first in line for inheritance, and emphasise instrumentality in the attitude of the caregiver. But this is only one side of the story. Our research based on carers' lifestories suggest that caregivers with instrumental interest also expresses true familial attachment. Inequality is an additional factor of care of the elderly. Extended families with low income often depend on their elderly relatives, who are often the only reliable economic providers of benefits and pensions. If adult children are unemployed or have an unstable or low income, they are keen for the elderly pensioners to contribute to the family income for as long as possible. So they care out of love but also out of self-interest. Such motivational ambivalence goes hand in hand with the substantive ambivalence where the love-work aspects of caring co-exist.

The gendered pattern of caregiving involves double-standards, or normative ambivalence. Women are expected to be more skillful and socialised in such a way that make them good caregivers. Well-off families employ migrant domestics and claim that they are 'more traditional' and they know how to provide care better than urbanised middle-class women. 'Chains of care' that are activated by migrant labour globally and in the Russian context (Hochschild 2003; Rotkirch et al. 2012) shift the gender inequality picture by giving professional women the opportunity to climb the occupational ladder. It is perhaps not surprising that most entries on informal spiritual care in this chapter refer to women – *baksy, bajanie, vilarka, ThetaHealing*, whereas power-related religious and ritual practices are less so.

The cultivation of this cultural model and the nostalgic moralising about the lack of piety towards elderly parents by egoistic adult children prevents the actual modernisation of elderly care regimes and the easing of the burden of family caregivers. The feelings of personalised family responsibility and the reliance of the elderly on the family prevent society from building new institutions, including long-term care systems. Many societies comply with this cultural model and do not articulate demands for social policy innovations.

The final point on ambivalence of caring as an expression of the dialectic of power in the system of interactions of caregiver and care-receiver. To describe the power imbalance as a source of conflict and specific tension in care work some use the term 'dependency work' (Kittay 1995). A sick person seems to be the one who is totally dependent on the powerful caregiver. However, caregivers are also dependent. Their whole life is adjusted to meet the needs of the care-receiver. The dependency work and love-work are themselves ambivalent constructs, aimed at capturing the challenges of informal problem-solving that only institutional changes in elderly care can help alleviate. Informality in care has to be supported by caring institutions.

One of the main concerns of the elderly is that they are advancing towards death not only existentially, but also, in a daily routine that involves catching up with people of their age, checking on their ills and conditions, counting friends who depart and who are still around, seeking confirmation that people older than them still live well, even if elsewhere. The routine of approaching the end prolongs life but also prepares for the departure. Bronnie Ware, an Australian nurse in palliative care, looked after patients in the last 12 weeks of their lives. She writes of the phenomenal clarity of vision that people gain at the end of their lives and shares the wisdom behind their top five regrets: not living true to oneself, working too hard, not showing emotions, not staying in touch with friends and not allowing oneself to be happier (Ware 2019).

14.1 *Baksy* (Kazakhstan)
Lyazzat Utesheva
Alumna, School of Slavonic and East European Studies, UCL, UK

The Kazakh term *baksy* stands for a shaman, defined by Cambridge Dictionary as a person with special powers to influence spirits and as a form of religious belief. Although the word shaman also exists in Kazakh, the word *baksy* is more commonly used. Etymologically, the word *baksy* originates from a common Turkic root, *bag/bak*, which means 'to look, peer or see'. Scholars write about *baksylyk*, referring to a shaman's path (Wood 2016) and explain the meaning of the word *baksy* as 'looking out for the soul of the patient' (Kuspanova 2019). The main difference between *baksy* and a healer (*yemshi*) is that *baksy* is engaged not only in healing but also in prophecy and communication with the spirits (Stasevich 2009). The word *baksy* may also include other meanings associating man with the cosmos or eternity, expressing their predetermined connection (Kokumbayeva 2012). *Baksy* act as mediators connecting the world of people and the world of spirits.

Baksylyk is an integral part of the ancient Turkic shamanic tradition and the ancient Kazakh culture that go back to the pre-Islamic era (Kulsariyeva et al. 2016). Kazakhs believe in the extraordinary gift endowed to *baksy* by spirits. Some *baksy* learn their destiny in early childhood, while others seek training or discover their gift late in life.

According to Kazakh folklore, only someone able to tame evil spirits (*zhyn*) and defeat them in oneself can become a real *baksy*. A *baksy* should both succumb and control the spirits, one being the reverse of the other (Naumova 2016). According to such beliefs, there are good spirits – the spirit of the ancestor (*aruak*), angel (*perish*) and fairy (*perizat*), and there are evil ones (*zhyn*), Devil (*shaitan*), and other demonic creatures (*albasty*) (Somfai-Kara et al. 2006). While the former may protect people, they should seek protection from the latter. Embodying the spirits, and mastering them, is what makes a *baksy*. If the spirits left the *baksy*, they would become an ordinary person. In order to acquire and maintain the reputation of a 'strong' shaman, *baksy* must continuously demonstrate the power of making the spirits help. Otherwise, they cannot count on the respect of others (Kandyba 1988).

The patron of Kazakh *baksy* is Korkyt (or Korkut), both a real character and a mythical one. Their canonic text is *The Book of My Grandfather Korkyt*, written around the fifteenth or sixteenth century. Korkyt was a legendary epic narrator of the Oguz tribe, conveying the worldview of shamanism (Konyratbay 2016). He led a pious way of life, was a sage and blessed the Khans on military campaigns.

The *baksy* had significant influence on society and were respected by the rulers of Asian states. According to some sources, the supreme rulers of the nomadic empires resorted to *baksy* for help. Since people, feeling their helplessness before nature, did not know another way of salvation from diseases and misfortunes, they relied on *baksy* for guidance (Abdimomynova 2015). All this strengthened the perception of power of *baksy* among people. *Baksy* were recognised as having the ability to communicate with the forces of the other world, predict the future, heal, besiege and prophesy.

During the rule of Islam in the fifteenth century, the *baksy* in the territory Kazakh Khanate (*Qazaq handyǵy*) lost their role of regulating the life of society and were limited mainly to healing. Traditional Islam considers shamanism to be a sin (Bersnev 2014). Although the existence of demons, devils and spirits is recognised in Islam, establishing communication with them was taboo. As a result, Islam reduced the social and ritual functions of the *baksy*, and the main function for Kazakh *baksy* until the present day was the healer. As such, the practices of healing did not contradict the norms of Islam, since *mullahs* and *imams* themselves were engaged in healing during the Soviet Union (Larina 2016), in contrast to the practice of divination and prophecy which is forbidden by Islam and condemned by representatives of the Muslim clergy.

The policy of the Soviet government in Kazakhstan (1936–91) also presented an obstacle to the development of the institution of *baksylyk*. Since the Soviet Union persistently fought any religious manifestations and conducted active anti-religious propaganda, it undermined and weakened traditional shamanic practices. Shamans were repressed, forced to renounce their faith and cease shamanic activities, as well as donate to museums or destroy their shamanic attributes (Kharitonova 2003).

Since the collapse of the Soviet Union, the Kazakhs turned to their traditions and values, and the *baksy* became perceived as martyrs of the Soviet regime and symbols of the rebirth of the nation's ethnic identity. Healers and *baksy* re-launched their healing practices on a massive scale, organising sessions in large stadiums and in concert halls attended by thousands of participants (Essy 2006). At the same time, in the 1990s, the overall economic and social situation in Kazakhstan deteriorated sharply, and unemployment and poverty increased, especially in rural areas. The Soviet-era health care system was in crisis, hospitals and polyclinics in villages were closed and doctors resigned from their jobs because they were not being paid. Neither the government nor the official Muslim clergy could alleviate the people's suffering, left to bear the cost of the post-Soviet transition. The *baksy* picked up the burden of people's despair. They spoke the language understood by ordinary people and relied on shamanic traditions to offer the help of the spirits in solving people's social, economic, medical and psychological problems (Penkala-Gawęcka 2013).

In the twenty-first century, the *baksy* in Kazakhstan are as popular as they were hundreds of years ago. They are mainly engaged in healing but also practise divination. Some Kazakhs still believe in their ability to foresee the future, control human destiny, recognise thoughts, openly talk about the past, cause changes, summon spirits. Modern Kazakhs do not see any conflicts of interest when turning to *baksy* for help when they need some good luck, help in decision-making or assistance in business and family problems. Most commonly, *baksy* are asked to cure diseases such as alcoholism, tuberculosis, paralysis, childhood diseases, female infertility. They can also protect or remove damage from 'an evil eye'. The methods of treatment of contemporary *baksy* are varied: they use spells, prayers and touch healing. For example, many *baksy* bring their patients to the graves of saints in order to treat female infertility. Others practise from their homes. During 'treatment', they can also fumigate a patient with smoke, use candles, sprinkle various essences or give them mixtures to drink.

From the traditional range of shamanic attributes, present-day *baksy* use a whip (*kamshy*), a protective measure against evil forces and for expelling diseases from the patient's body. *Kobyz* and *dombyra*, in the past the main attributes of Kazakh *baksy* to communicate with the spirits in the past, are no longer in use. At present, the main attribute is the Koran. Perhaps, paradoxically, the legacy of Islam on the taboo traditional Kazakh institution of *baksylyk* includes, first, the use in ritual practices of reading the Kuran, prayer formulas and appeals to various saints (Stasevich 2009) and, second, the obligatory ritual washing of the healer and the patient before the beginning of the session (as before *namaz*). The tension of Islamic beliefs and the Kazakh pre-Islamic tradition of *baksy* is somewhat resolved by gender. The religiosity of men is closer to the 'classical norms' of Islam, condemning the practice of folk healing (Rakhimov 2009), while the majority of *baksy* are female. According to research, Kazakh women are more oriented to the preservation and use of pre-Islamic ideas and cults than men, which may be interpreted as a specificity of the modern religiosity of Central Asian or within a wider set of Eastern religious dualism. It is noteworthy that appeals to *baksy* tend to be secularised and normalised. The Kazakhs do not consider the *baksy* 'abnormal', cynics may view them as shrewd businessmen and observers did not see them as people with an upset psyche. Eyewitnesses emphasised sincere faith *baksy* in the reality of the world of spirits (Zenin n.d.).

14.2 *Bajanje and vilarkas* (Serbia and the Western Balkans)
Maria Vivod
'Dynamics of Europe' research unit, University of Strasbourg, France and Novi Sad, Serbia

Bajanje is the pronouncement of a verbal text or charm (*basma*) to achieve a desired effect. The charmer is called *bajalica* (also *basmara*, *bajarica*, *bajaluša*) (Radenković 1996) and is usually a woman, who has been initiated during an illness suffered in childhood, was born with a mark or impairment, or through a matrilineal knowledge-transmission. During the pronouncement of the *basma*, *bajalice* refer to themselves with special names or attributes (Radenković 1996), such as *lakodušnica* ('one with an easy soul'), *lakobajka* ('one who easily casts spells'), or *petoprsnjača* ('the five-fingered one'). Pronouncing a spell, known only to the initiated, is done in a particular manner, for instance whispering in the ear of the individual or standing above a person's head or chest with a water bowl and murmuring the verses (Radenković 1996). According to material collected by Serbian ethnographers in the late nineteenth century and during the first half of the twentieth century, *bajanje* was conducted on specific days – especially Tuesdays and Thursdays. These days were believed to be chthonic, favoured by the south Slavic (pre-Christian) gods ruling the world of spirits and therefore favourable for activities invoking this world (Radenković 1996). Nowadays, *bajalica* in Serbia and Montenegro avoid charming on 'red days' (*crvena slova*), days dedicated to Christian orthodox saints, presumably named for being marked with red letters in the calendar (Vivod 2008).

Like most verbal magic rituals, pronouncing *basma* is goal-oriented: some *basme* are healing charms, others are meant to protect against demons, for instance against *babice* who attack newborns and their mothers (Conrad 1983; Vivod 2008; Kropej 2009). The disorders treated with *bajanje* are most often 'culture-bound syndromes', that is, symptoms of illness found only within a specific society or culture. In the Western Balkans, one such condition is called *strava*. *Bajanje* is often accompanied by an act of melting lead, also called 'melting fear' (*salivanje olova* or *salivanje strave*) (Đorđević 2011). The researcher describes a process of pouring hot, molten lead into a bowl of water and then interpreting the cause of illness from the shape of metal. This act is both a divination and a protection against an evil charm (*urok*). By 'seeing' and naming the cause of the fear in the molten piece of lead, the individual is cured, and the *strava* (fright) – a personified emotion, imagined as an evil spirit – is 'chased away' (Đorđević 2011). *Strava* can be compared with the Latin-American *susto*, or the Chinese-Polynesian *hak-tao*. A similar practice is 'extinguishing coals' (*gašenje ugljevlja*), where instead of molten lead, hot coal is thrown into the water. That water is later given to the patient to drink (see Figure 14.2.1).

Bajanje can be accompanied by a ritual bodily practice performed by *bajalica*, such as *provlačenje* (pulling through), *merenje* (measuring) and *kupanje* (washing). *Provlačenje* is an act of pulling the patient through a barrier, such as the chains of the cauldron (*verige*), a garland of flowers, or a specially shaped tree branch. In *merenje*, *bajalica* measures the patient's limbs with a cord before and after *bajanje* and compares the two results. If they differ, *bajalica* determines an evil spell as the cause of illness. The cord is destroyed (burned or thrown into a stream) after the treatment. *Kupanje* takes place in the stream or well where *bajanje* is conducted, or in the water in which the coal or molten lead was thrown. It is believed that these techniques help the patient 'pass through' between worlds and leave the illness in the other, chthonic world (Đorđević 2011). The charms take the shape of a formula or a statement. Some involve counting backwards (Lecouteux 1996), some are folk versions of canonical Christian prayers or apocryphal prayers, often invoking God, Jesus, or a saint to ask for help or protection.

Folk medicine practices such as *bajanje* tend to resurface in periods of crisis or uncertainty. The detailed ethnographies of folk medicine from the Yugoslav socialist period following the Second World War mostly openly

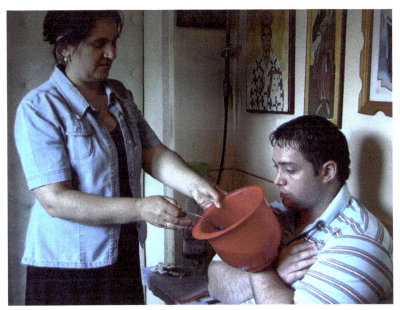

Figure 14.2.1 *Salivanje strave* ('melting the fear'). © Maria Vivod.

condemn *bajanje*, designating it as originating in the backward beliefs of the poor, oppressed and primitive people. Folk medicine in that period was deemed incompatible with communist ideals. Yet, in a post-communist context, defined by war and in the absence of resources, modern medicine was not able to provide relief to the sick or to a family in crisis, especially in the countryside. Charmers were the last resort for those seeking relief for psychological disorders or those who had been failed by biomedical treatments. The traditional healing of 'souls' made it into the twenty-first century as informal care to individuals and families in need.

Thus, community members visit *vilarke*, the seers, for treatment of illnesses believed to be fairy-induced and evil spells, to consult on personal matters and divination, and to communicate with the deceased loved ones. Visiting *vilarka* often serves to alleviate grief, reach out to the deceased or reduce uncertainty. *Vilarka*'s clients reward her with gifts and, more commonly recently, money. There are two broad theoretical perspectives on the belief in communication with fairies (*vile*) and practices of communicating with them. First, they are rooted in pre-Christian systems of beliefs and witch-hunt trials (see Ginzburg 1966 for Italy, Klaniczay 1983 for Hungary, Henningsen 1993 and Čiča 2002 for Croatia). Second, they are remnants of folk customs and beliefs about beings with malevolent or benevolent powers exceeding human ones (Pòcs 1989 for Central Europe, Bošković-Stulli 1960 for Croatia).

Figure 14.2.2 The fairy-seer Ivanka, in Kulma Topolnica, Eastern Serbia, April 2015. © Maria Vivod.

Healing and divination are in high demand in contemporary societies in the Balkans. *Vilarka*'s services are sought by people unable to solve their problems in other ways. The Vlach seers are particularly known in Serbia for their psychic powers and ability of lifting evil charms and enjoy special status. People from outside the Vlach region travel to seek out their help. *Vilarke* also serve as informal advisors and mediators in conflicts in communities. Their social roles as self-taught psychologists, social workers, counsellors are essential tools for the well-being of the communities and individuals, even if performed informally. In a practical sense, *vilarke* bring economic advantages to the remote and poor regions where they live. In a symbolic sense, as these women develop national and even international reputations (see documentary by VICE), they become cultural icons of their region and ethnicity. Their practices generate media attention, which bring further benefits to the region.

14.3 *Tchop* (Caucasus)
Maria Vyatchina
Department of Ethnology, Tartu University, Estonia

Tchop (or *tchup*) is a local term that is used in the traditional medical practice found in different regions of the Northern and Southern Caucasus (Anuchin 1884: 387; Gasanov 1928: 208–23; Konjus 1946: 21; Lalajan 1988: 187–8; Lisician 1992: 159). Etymologically, the word originates from the Turkish root *çöp* that literally means 'splinter that got stuck'. The practice is based on the belief that a person could suffer a range of long-term symptoms as a result of pieces of food or other kinds of small objects getting stuck in the nose or throat. The condition is thought to affect mostly children; however, adults may suffer too. Usually, the case is treated with a throat massage or a special blowing technique. Currently, the term is used for both the condition and the treatment.

Traditionally, in the North Caucasus region, *tchop* is distinguished from the 'evil eye'. Although the symptoms appear similar, their causes are believed to be of a different nature. Thus, if someone has been affected either by *tchop* or by the evil eye, they become physically ill, suffering from fever, weakness, diarrhoea, nausea and/or inability to eat. It is believed that only a ritual specialist is able to identify the underlying cause. Spiritual healing is needed for evil-eye ailments while *tchop* is assisted manually. However, some advanced *tchop* specialists can treat the evil eye too. In some cases, *tchop* substitutes for tonsillitis, acute upper respiratory infections and other medical diagnoses. Professional doctors tend to express scepticism and disdain towards *tchop*. Besides, the *tchop* treatment, due to its growing commercialisation, is regarded as a fraudulent practice.

A specialist in *tchop* treatment is called *tchopchy*. There are several ways of becoming a *tchopchy*. Some *tchopchy* claim that their skill runs in the family, for example, from grandmother to granddaughter. Another option is *tchop* as a calling. In some cases, the special ability of the *tchopchy* is supplemented with formal medical qualifications.

Usually, *tchop* assistance is sought out by people unable or unwilling to solve their own or their children's health problems in other ways,

Figure 14.3.1 The advertisement for *tchop* treatment on public transportation. Makhachkala, 2019. © Maria Vyatchina.

for instance, by visiting a professional doctor. Traditionally, *tchop* practicians were women. However, in Dagestan, due to the diffusion of Islam orthodoxy that curtails physical contact between non-related men and women (even if it is a physician-patient contact), nowadays services by male *tchopchy* tend to be in great demand. A female *tchopchy* may refuse to treat boys or men if she considers it contrary to her religious beliefs. Thus, the principles of this historically gendered practice have shifted from the domestic female space to being strongly influenced by the religious norms common in the area.

The Dagestani inhabitants explain the endemicity of *tchop* in several ways. First, they consider the specific climate conditions in Dagestan such as high humidity, which supposedly can affect the throat anatomy. Second, they blame the regional diet. Finally, the high incidence of *tchop* is linked to children's unsupervised behaviour. All these explanations are based on the underlying idea of small holes in the throat anatomy where items can get stuck. Moreover, recently, local people started using the term *oesophageal diverticula*, which sounds scientific but appears to be a non-existent medical theory. It is worth mentioning that visits to *tchopchy* tend to be viewed as medical appointments.

In Dagestan, information on *tchop* experience is widely spread by word of mouth and social media, such as Instagram. Also, *tchop* advertisements can be found everywhere, including on public transport, street posters and inscriptions on the gates of *tchopchy* houses. Despite high numbers of *tchopchy*, the practice continues to be practically invisible to non-locals.

Nowadays, *tchopchy* services are in high demand also in other regions of the Russian Federation where migrants from the Northern Caucasus settle. For example, there are large Dagestani communities in Moscow, St. Petersburg, Surgut, Tyumen due to increasing migration (Kapustina 2019: 103–18). Migration gave a new meaning to the *tchopchy* practice. The migrant families visit *tchopchy* during vacations at the place of their origin following older relatives' advice and recommendations. Thus, a *tchopchy* visit could be described as a sign of belonging because locals strongly believe that '*tchop* happens to the Dagestanis only'.

Studying *tchop* helps to reveal certain aspects in the relationship between older and younger generations within the extended family, between science-based medicine and traditional medical knowledge, urban and rural ways of life, and the relationships within migration networks.

14.4 *Kako mati* (Greece)
Eugenia Roussou
Centre for Research in Anthropology, Portugal

Kako mati (κακό μάτι) is the Greek sociocultural version of the belief widely known around the world as the 'evil eye', which is popular in Mediterranean countries as well as in the Middle East (Maloney 1976; Galt 1982; Dundes 1992 [1981]; Veikou 1998: 71–80). Its practice is directly connected to Orthodox Christianity, the 'prevailing religion' of Greece (Alivizatos 1999: 25; Molokotos-Liederman 2004: 404–5). *Kako mati* occupies a central cultural space in the context of Greek 'vernacular religion' (Primiano 1995; Bowman and Valk 2012), since it is practised informally, in the context of everyday social and religious life. At the same time, it may be considered as a tool for negotiating informal social interactions, social status, gender and power.

Kako mati is based on the belief that when an individual is jealous of another person, s/he can cast a negative gaze on, or gossip about, that person, and can subsequently transmit negative emotions that may cause the latter to fall ill. These exchanges are believed to occur through direct visual communication, when people informally interact in the street, or via indirect verbal communication, that is, gossip or, according to the Greek term, *glossofagia*, which literally means 'being eaten by the tongue'. For example, those who are beautiful, enjoy high social status, own many material goods, or generally stand out from the crowd in one way or another, are most likely to attract evil gazes and evil tongues. Babies are considered to be especially susceptible to *kako mati*, as are small children, animals and plants.

According to one of the most popular socio-scientific explanations, giving someone the evil eye functions as a form of social control: whoever has higher social status or exhibits elements of difference compared to the rest of their social surroundings is likely to be symbolically punished by the community (Veikou 1998). Such an explanation is usually based on the stereotype according to which *kako mati* is principally encountered in Greek villages, where the sense of 'community' is tight, as is the need to maintain informal social equality within it. In addition to its popularity in rural communities, *kako mati* also plays an active role in Greek discourse and everyday practice in urban social settings, being considered an everyday means of informal sensory interaction and energy-exchange that leads to symptoms of bodily illness.

Figure 14.4.1 A lay healer performing *ksematiasma* in northern Greece. © Eugenia Roussou.

When someone is affected by *kako mati*, s/he becomes physically ill, experiencing symptoms such as headache, upset stomach, dizziness and physical weakness. These symptoms need to be treated through specific healing rituals, which draw on religious symbolism and are performed predominantly by female lay healers. According to the most popular Greek ritual performance against *kako mati* (*ksematiasma*), the lay healer uses a small coffee cup filled with water, dips her fingertip into oil (usually taken from the oil lamp in the household's icon stand) and, while reciting an Orthodox Christian prayer, drops oil into the water. If the person is evil-eyed, the oil drops directly to the bottom of the cup and dissolves; if not, it stays on the surface. She repeats the process until the oil begins to stay on the surface of the water, which is seen as a signal that *kako mati* has been removed. She then crosses the evil-eyed person's forehead with the water-oil mix and makes him/her drink from the water-oil solution three times, in the name of Holy Trinity. The rest is thrown into a flowerpot or onto the ground since the water, having been sacralised, may not be treated as normal waste.

Kako mati and its ritual healing create a symbolic and actual conflict between informal religious belief and the official discourse of the Orthodox Christian Church and its priests. According to the Greek Orthodox Church, the only legitimate term to describe belief in the evil eye is *vaskania*, a word derived from the ancient Greek verb *vaskaino*, which means 'to look at someone with envy'. The Church, its priests and its religious devotees perceive the process of being evil-eyed as an act of the Devil that possesses individuals who in turn cast envious evil gazes on others and make them evil-eyed. It follows that the only way to get rid of *vaskania* is for a priest to perform an exorcism on the evil-eyed person, usually in the form of reading certain prayers against the evil power of the Devil. Through the negation of the existence of *kako mati* and the refusal of the efficacy of *ksematiasma*, the Greek Orthodox Church and its priests formally (re)claim their sociocultural and religious authority, which is challenged significantly by the informal religious and healing power of the lay healers. It is also a matter of gender power-struggle: the male authority of the Orthodox priest is defied by the female lay healer who, through her evil-eye ritual empowerment, renegotiates the ownership of religious power in the Greek sociocultural context; she thereby acquires a far more active role of spiritual empowerment in the male-oriented Greek Orthodoxy, where a woman's spiritual role continues to be regarded as inferior to that of the male priest (Roussou 2013a).

In practice, *kako mati* and *vaskania* share ritualism, sacredness and performative engagement (Stewart 1991) and, above all, a common goal: the expulsion of the evil-eye effects. At the informal level of everyday performance, the distinction between an evil-eye healer (*ksematiastra*) and a priest, and between lay and doctrinal interpretations of religious practice, collapses. Most lay evil-eye healers are Orthodox believers and almost always recite Orthodox Christian prayers and use Orthodox symbolism in *ksematiasma*, interpreting the Orthodox doctrine in their own creative ways. Furthermore, there are many priests who informally recognise the power of female evil-eye healers and even ask to have a *ksematiasma* performed by them, thereby accepting, even if unofficially, their spiritual authority.

Along with the process of giving, receiving and healing, another important aspect of *kako mati* is the various material objects used as protective amulets against it. These are usually blue beads that represent an eye. They are believed to act as a prophylactic mirror that reflects back the negative energy of the evil-eye giver. (According to popular belief, it is blue-eyed individuals who are most likely to transmit the evil eye through their powerful gaze.) In recent years, and due to globalised spiritual trends such as the so-called 'New Age' spiritual movement (Heelas 1996), the usual evil-eye amulets are worn and/or placed together with

Orthodox (crosses and religious icons) and 'New Age' ones (mainly Chinese *feng shui* good-luck charms, crystals, Eastern spiritual figures and so on), so as to offer protection against *kako mati*, the Devil and all other types of evil energy. This creative and novel use of evil-eye material objects represents a more general and crucial change that has happened recently in the field of Greek religiosity, where religious pluralism and an amalgamation of Orthodox and 'New Age' discourses, practices and concepts can be observed in the informal everyday exchange and practice of *kako mati* (Roussou 2013b).

14.5 **Marmotagem** (Brazil)
Giovanna Capponi
Department of Human Sciences, State University of Rio de Janiero, Brazil

The term *marmotagem* derives from the Portuguese *marmota* (literally, 'marmot') and is commonly used as a slang term to describe someone or something that is dishonest, strange or suspicious. In the context of Afro-Brazilian religions like Candomblé and Umbanda, *marmotagem* is a derogatory term that describes the improper or fraudulent practising of magical or religious rituals, often aimed at extorting money from followers or clients (Goldman 1985). The *marmoteiro* (female, *marmoteira*) is a priest(ess) who is considered to either perform the rituals incorrectly because of incompetence or lack of knowledge, or pretend to have credentials to act as a religious authority in order to gain prestige or profit. Accusations of *marmotagem* among Afro-Brazilian practitioners highlight notions of authenticity, grounds for recognition and realms of competition in religious communities.

Afro-Brazilian religions consist of various religious beliefs, with Candomblé and Umbanda being the most widespread. They draw upon elements of traditional African ritual practices resulting from the deportation of enslaved African people from West and Central Africa to Brazil. In Brazil, and also in Europe and the US since the 1990s, regional variations of these religions include ritual practices under numerous names: *Candomblé ketu, Candomblé Angola, Xangô in Recife, Tambor de Minas, Batuque* and many others. Afro-Brazilian deities (*orixás*) are closely associated with natural elements of the landscape (ocean, forests, rivers, crossroads and so on), linked to human temperaments, and associated with different stages of life and matter. Rituals involve a complex manipulation and assemblage of multiple objects, artefacts and ingredients in order to 'feed' the *orixás* with animal sacrifice properly and/or to make food offerings to ensure the return of sacred energy and favours.

Afro-Brazilian religious communities are held together by an initiation ritual and a rigid hierarchical structure, based on the combination of age, competence and status. Each role in the hierarchy presumes different abilities, obligations and taboos, and it helps to secure the legitimation of one's performance of rituals as being 'traditional'. In general, accusations of *marmotagem* are based on a perceived deviation from tradition (Araújo 2018 45–7). In specific contexts, such accusations are often a way to claim that one's own ritual tradition is the most authentic and the most efficacious (Capone 2010: 12). Accusations of *marmotagem* often imply the fact that the *marmoteiro/a* did not undergo the initiation ritual, and/or that they pretend to have an initiated knowledge to gain prestige or profit. Similarly, someone who initiates others without being ordained as priest or priestess (which should ordinarily happen at least seven years since initiation) or acts as if they already have a higher position in the hierarchy can be accused of being a *marmoteiro/a* by both external and internal members of religious communities.

The priest(ess) who initiates a novice should have expertise, through divination or specific rituals, to be able to define if the person is either *rodante* (someone who can go into trance) or *não-rodante* (someone who cannot and should take a different role in the hierarchy). When a novice, determined to be *não-rodante* suddenly goes into trance, the priest(ess) can be accused of wrongdoing (*fazer errado*), of incompetence and lacking credentials for the role. Trance possession is the key ritual event in which the *orixás* manifest themselves on earth, so the claims of authenticity or charlatanry tend to centre upon it. Faking trance and/or not complying with the physical performance, right timing, or other parameters of trance possession are commonly regarded as signs of charlatanry. Most practitioners admit having a 'trained eye' for recognising if the trance is faked or real. Such expertise includes an ability to estimate the trance physical performance, and its various features such as movement of the eyes, eyelids, physical shaking, emitting sounds and talking.

Doing it wrongly (*fazer errado*) may relate to the performance of the ritual itself and mixing elements that are considered incompatible. For example, a priestess can be accused of being *marmotagem* based on leading ceremonies using a recording of sacred chants rather than live drums (Opipari 2009: 102). Similarly, there can be accusations of offering palm oil (which is bright red) to Oxalá, the *orixá* of whiteness and purity, while red and black colours are not allowed, or not complying with the rigid rules and prescriptions of body purity for the required period after initiation rituals (like abstaining from wearing coloured clothes, drinking and having sex). In all such cases the rituals are performed without the 'right' knowledge to administer and manipulate the sacred energy.

As noticed by Brazeal (2014), *marmotagem* practices are often motivated by economic interests, as religious priests or priestesses respond to the demand from clients asking for rituals to solve problems related to health, family, romance or business. In order to attend the most diverse requests, self-proclaimed religious authorities would mix different elements belonging to different traditions in order to impress their clients. *Marmoteiros* may also subvert the tradition of the verbal transmission of knowledge, and learn rituals from books, or even websites, instead of submitting themselves to the hierarchy and learning from the elders as prescribed. However, the ultimate test for authenticity in such contexts is the ritual efficacy. While it is impossible to determine the ritual efficacy in advance, the money charged for the ritual is one indicator that determines whether the ritual practice might be fraudulent (when too expensive) or simply non-efficient (when too cheap) (Brazeal 2014: 136).

In cases of deviation from orthodox practices, the efficacy of rituals gives priests and priestesses the power to renegotiate the notions of authenticity and to promote innovation and change within the religious practice. At the same time, indicators of ritual efficacy are often related to client satisfaction, which is subjective, or to the correctness of inducing trance that depends on the respect that priests and priestesses have in their religious milieu.

14.6 *ThetaHealing* (USA, Russia)
Tatiana Loboda
Department of Sociology and Philosophy, European University at St. Petersburg, Russia

ThetaHealing® (registered trademark) is the official name of the practice ('healing technique') developed in the USA by Vianna Stibal. According to Stibal, the *ThetaHealing* technique can 'heal' on the physical, emotional and spiritual level. A person trained in this method is called a *Theta* practitioner. Stibal has been teaching this technique and issuing qualification certificates since 2000. *Theta* practitioners can 'heal' themselves, relatives, friends and clients. The name of the technique contains the letter of the Greek alphabet *theta* (θ), which in neurophysiology denotes one of the rhythms of the brain during deep relaxation. *Theta* practices allegedly work their 'healing' in this rhythm. Stibal claims this technique can cure many diseases and solve psychological problems through the reliance on the 'unconditional love' of the 'Creator Of All That Is' with the help of special meditation (Stibal 2010: 6, 46).

ThetaHealing is an informal New Age social practice. New Age in a broad sense is a theosophical and anthroposophical expectation of an early coming of the 'Age of Aquarius' and 'spiritual' world transformation. In a narrow sense, it is a variety of alternative ideas and activities, including a mix of spiritualism, science fiction and popular psychology (Hanegraaff 1998: 97). Many of these trends represent an alternative to the value system of social institutions such as medicine and established religions. It is conceptually difficult to draw a line between some of them; however, not all supporters of alternative ways (for instance, homoeopaths) share New Age ideas. Holistic spirituality is a group within alternative spirituality and includes characteristics such as (1) an alternative approach to the treatment of physical diseases, (2) a neoliberal discourse regarding personal (emotional, financial) well-being as the main value in life and (3) a gendered practice. The majority of holistic spirituality supporters are female (Heelas and Woodhead 2005; Sointu and Woodhead 2008). *ThetaHealing* belongs to the field of holistic spirituality. Fields similar to *ThetaHealing* include the Reiki, CosmoEnergy, Challenging, Regressology and Dr Joe Dispenza's teaching. Practices they have in common are 'viewing past soul lives' and 'manipulating energy' to treat physical, emotional and psychological problems. In general, the boundaries between these fields are a matter of personal opinion, and practitioners in their own practice often combine different approaches and teachings.

Methods such as semi-structured interviews, participant observations and text analysis were used in my research on *ThetaHealing* conducted in 2017–19 in St. Petersburg (Loboda 2020). The research consisted of 22 interviews with *Theta* practitioners from St. Petersburg; of these, 19 were women, three were men, all aged between 22 and 66, with a median age of 43.5 years. Twenty-one people had higher education, 11 of whom held two or more university degrees. In addition, I attended seven meetings of *Theta* practitioners in the club where the method was taught and where insight retreats as well as '*ThetaHealing* sessions' were held. I analysed 35 textual sources about *ThetaHealing*: books by Stibal, blogs of *ThetaHealing* instructors, video footage about meditation and personal examples of *ThetaHealers*.

The *Theta* practitioner works with a client, either in person or by phone, as follows: they sit opposite the client and hold their hands (but not necessarily so). The client usually closes their eyes and the

ThetaHealer tunes in to the 'theta wave'. The client articulates the problem, for example, infertility, and the *ThetaHealer* meditates and walks into the '7th plane of Existence' to appeal to the 'Creator' about the cause of the 'disease'. Usually, the *ThetaHealer* explains to the client the psychosomatic cause of the 'disease', which is called a 'negative subconscious belief systems', for example, the fear of being a mother. The *ThetaHealer* offers to change the 'negative belief' to a 'positive' one, for instance, that being a mother is safe. Beliefs are formulated in such a way that they are related to the client's personal experience and feelings. For example, the fear of being a mother may derive from the violence that the client experienced from her mother during childhood. That is, deliverance from the fear of motherhood is followed by the necessity to forgive one's mother and other negative beliefs that may be associated with this. In *ThetaHealing* it is claimed that the success of the healing is largely achieved due to the 'energy of unconditional love' with which the *ThetaHealer* accompanies all belief changes. As a result, during several consultations ('*ThetaHealing* sessions') with the help of the *ThetaHealer* the client should be able to articulate the problem with its root causes and reinterpret it, and thereby, recover, resolve the problem or suffering and find their new 'Self'. *ThetaHealing* resembles an accelerated practice of a longer and more expensive psychotherapy (Illouz 2008). *ThetaHealing* is considered to be one of the therapeutic techniques which belong to the cultural landscape of coaching, training and 'self-help' books (Perheentupa and Salmenniemi 2019).

All the informants in my research had experience of attending the Orthodox Church (and some, in addition, the Catholic Church or Buddhist teaching), but in general they were not regular churchgoers. The *ThetaHealers* explained their favouring of alternative spirituality over established religions by their unwillingness to follow a strict code of behaviour and, as they said, to have an intermediary in the form of the clergy between themselves and God. The *ThetaHealers* were convinced that they, themselves, were responsible for their lives and their decisions, and that God provided them only with 'energy support' but did not direct their lives. During *ThetaHealing* courses, they learnt to analyse their lives (and the stories of their future clients) in the following format: 'Why did I do this to myself?' Because practitioners do not blame social structures for their failures and lack of resources and do not expect support from the state, *ThetaHealing* echoes a neoliberal social policy.

Of my informants, three women earned their living entirely by offering *Theta* sessions, and 16 women combined their *Theta* earnings with other employment. Usually, they conducted between one and five

Theta sessions a week. To attract clients, they used social networks, personal websites and open clubs. A single session can cost from 500 to 5000 roubles, the price mostly depends on the number of qualification certificates (awarded by ThetaHealing Institute of Knowledge, THInK) that are held by the healer. Between three to seven sessions are held with each client, aimed at resolving short-term emotional problems, problems of personal growth and health issues. Almost all clients are middle-income working women. Their problems often concern finding a partner, infertility, emotional burnout in marriage, the struggle to combine their professional and domestic roles, and a general feeling of losing the meaning of life (tiredness from the monotony of daily routine).

According to the official website, in July 2020 there were 5,864 *Theta* practitioners in Russia, 89.5 per cent of them were women. My research suggests that women use spiritual techniques to release the emotional stress caused by traditional gender roles (Loboda 2020) that researchers have described as the 'working mother contract' (Temkina and Rotkirch 2002). Women can gain emancipating potential as they strengthen their agency and try to become psychologically more independent and well-adjusted personalities. However, at the same time they do not try to go against the existing gender order and do not refuse the 'contract' but prefer to 'normalise' and adjust their femininity to better emotional family management and continue working in their professions.

ThetaHealing is spread throughout the world. According to the official *ThetaHealing* website, over 32,000 people globally have completed at least one certified course. The number of followers is growing rapidly: since 2018 the number has increased by 30 per cent – from 24,560 to 32,756; Stibal herself claims that there are now about 300,000 *Theta* practitioners in 30 countries. There are official 'country event coordinators' in Switzerland, Australia, Brazil, Canada, Croatia, Germany, Greece, India, the Netherlands, Hungary, Israel, Italy, Japan, Latin America, Philippines, Lebanon, New Zealand, Russia, Romania, Slovenia, Serbia, Spain, Sweden, Turkey and the United Kingdom. There may also be *ThetaHealers* in other countries who have completed courses abroad and then returned to their homeland.

To be officially considered a *ThetaHealer*, one has to attend certified courses conducted by people at 'instructor' level. Stibal founded the THInK to affiliate all certified *Theta* practitioners. She also developed core curriculum programmes that must be taught in a unified system and at an equivalent cost in all countries (depending on the course, the price varies from 20,000 to 60,000 rubles). Students are allowed to develop their own courses but must certify their content with Stibal. The practice of *ThetaHealing* (which includes meditation, terminology and the world-view) can be learnt from books, videos and in clubs free of charge – the number of people interested in *ThetaHealing* in such a way is impossible to calculate. However, without taking courses people cannot register on the official website and are not allowed to consult clients through the official system. A *ThetaHealing* instructor can independently conduct training and issue certificates on behalf of Stibal. A 'Master certificate' confirms advanced training, being awarded on completion of 11 courses on various topics related to *ThetaHealing* (for example, 'Disease and Disorder', 'Dig Deeper', 'Manifesting and Abundance' and so on).

14.7 **Indulgence** (Global)
Elena Denisova-Schmidt and Sibylle Krause
University of St.Gallen, Switzerland and Protestant Church, Jestetten, Germany

According to *Encyclopadia Britannica*, *indulgence* is a 'feature of the penitential system of the Western mediaeval and the Roman Catholic Church that grants full or partial remission of the punishment of sin' (Duggan 2020). It is a buy-out-of-sin option that secures preferential treatment from God and eventually a place in Paradise.

Catholics believe that only a few people are sinful enough to descend to hell or virtuous enough to ascend to heaven immediately. The majority find themselves in a grey zone, an 'intermediate place', Purgatory. The Church developed the idea for *indulgence* in the twelfth century, during a period of the emergence of cities and a solvent bourgeois class (Duggan 2020). It is based on the power and 'righteousness of God' not to leave a sin unpunished. Man must atone or face the punishment – in this world or thereafter but the punishment for sins in the afterlife is decided in Purgatory, upon the balance of sins and good deeds. With a letter of *indulgence*, the time spent in Purgatory can be shortened. This letter may be acquired for (a) sins already committed, (b) sins only planned in the future or (c) the deceased.

In the Middle Ages, the initial idea of *indulgence* as spiritual support for the faithful was appropriated to 'camouflage' a stable source of income for several stakeholders:

> The donation of money with good intentions, which was only ancillary, often turned out to be the primary concern. … [T]he *indulgence* was pulled down from its ideal height and degraded to

a financial operation. It was no longer the attainment of spiritual grace but the need for money that ... became the real reason why *indulgences* were requested and conferred.

(Pastor IV 1: 231, quoted in Paulus 1923: 450)

The price for a typical *indulgence* letter issued by the Apostolic Chancery was calculated as follows, based on four different taxes: a tax for the original copy (*taxa scriptorum*), for the concept (*taxa abbreviatorum*), for the registration (*taxa registro*) and for the affixing of the bull or lead seal (*taxa plumbai*) (Paulus 1923). While the revenue from the first two taxes went to the Colleges of Scribes and Abbreviators, the bull tax and, in part, the registration tax was channelled towards the Papal Treasury, which used this income to pay civil servants, and benefitting the Roman Curia directly. Initially, the total price for a letter was low, but the price rose over time. In the mid-fifteenth century, a letter that granted *indulgences* to the addressee for seven years cost about 200 Groschen or 20 ducats. In the early sixteenth century, an *indulgence* letter that cost 20 ducats would only be valid for two years. Moreover, the price for *indulgence* depended on the status and wealth of the individual. According to the 1517 set of *indulgence* instructions from the city of Mainz, the prices ranged from around 1 gulden for ordinary citizens to more than 6 guldens for those with annual income of 200 guldens, and as much as 25 Rhenish gulden for kings, queens, princes and archbishops. People without income were able to acquire *indulgence* by praying or fasting. Over time, the non-monetary commutations came to include various services, obligations or goods equivalent to a monetary value (Paulus 1923).

Although abuses of *indulgence* such as letters granting *indulgence* for an unusual duration (for example, a period of a hundred or a thousand years) and fake *indulgences* were strongly criticised, the money collected with the letters became a common way of raising revenue. According to Paulus, 'the Papal Treasury receive[d] a considerable amount of money from the bestowal of *indulgences*, [hence] it is easy to understand why ... those very Popes who struggled with great financial difficulties ... evinced a special generosity in the bestowal of *indulgences*' (Paulus 1923: 457). Yet the Church representatives allowed – and the Popes even encouraged – commutations at different levels, including donations to build a hospital or a cathedral. But whether *indulgences* could be 'sold' was always a point of contention. The Church began to shift its views on the sale from the fourteenth to the fifteenth century when local secular governments began to demand a substantial share of the revenue from any bestowed *indulgence*, sometimes even up to two-thirds of the total yield and weakening the papacy as a result. In 1567,

Pope Pius V formally abolished the sale of *indulgences*. However, its theological underpinnings remained largely intact until 1967 – four hundred years later – when Pope Paul VI moved the emphasis away from the fulfilment of punishment to the promotion of good works. This significantly reduced the number of plenary *indulgences* and eliminated the ancient system of partial *indulgences*. The *indulgence* could be interpreted as a scheme or an example of window dressing, were the church not so central to the ethical upbringing and judgement. Five hundred years ago, Martin Luther (1483–1546) established Protestantism after starting to doubt the practice of *indulgences*. Luther argued that forgiveness could not be purchased; God granted it for free. The only 'preconditions' were the act of salvation of Jesus Christ, the faith of the sinner, and the awareness of sin. The practice of *indulgence* letters corrupted this awareness as they granted forgiveness of sins and the remission of guilt in exchange for money, making a sincere repentance and intention for improvement no longer necessary. The latter were essential in order to share God's forgiveness. In his argumentation against *indulgences*, Martin Luther issues a call to start questioning and reflecting on one's own unethical behaviour:

> Why does the Pope not liberate everyone from Purgatory for the sake of love (a most holy thing) and because of the supreme necessity of their souls? This would morally be the best reason. Meanwhile he redeems innumerable souls for money, a most perishable thing, with which to build St. Peter's church, a very minor purpose. (Duggan 2020)

From a contemporary perspective, *indulgences* are a fraud against believers, even from the viewpoint of the modern Catholic Church (Jansen 2014). Yet *indulgences* are still sold in the Catholic world in both monetary and non-monetary forms, including praying at home, the church, the cemetery, or on pilgrimages. 'Every believer may gain partial *indulgences* or plenary *indulgences* for himself or on behalf of the deceased' (quoted in Direktorium 2019: 259).

14.8 **Ehsan** (Azerbaijan)
Turkhan Sadigov
Department of Political Science, University of
Wisconsin–Madison, USA

In Azerbaijan, a funeral feast is called *ehsan*, which implies a broader connotation in Islam: *ihsan* means to 'do beautiful things' in a bid to reach 'perfection', 'excellence'. Consequently, *ihsan* in Islam denotes demonstration both in deeds and actions of social responsibility drawn from a religious conviction (Ayoub 2013). Examples of these may include (among other deeds) showing compassion, kindness, mercy to others in everyday life (Azerbaijan National Encyclopaedia 2016: 434–5).

However, in Azerbaijan *ihsan* (or *ehsan* as pronounced in local language) has another, narrower meaning. In a historical context, *ehsan* denotes a charity food and water provision during *Ashura* (Shia religious mourning ceremony commemorating the martyrdom of prophet Muhammad's (*pbuh*) grandchildren Huseyn and Hasan) by well-off citizens and establishments. In a narrower sense, *ehsan* denotes a food banquet during funerals. Historically in Azerbaijan, Ashura charity served as a vivid example of Islamic *ihsan* – a selfless devotion to Shiism and service to its religious pillar – deeds that were seen as 'exemplary', marking 'excellence', 'perfection'. There is a small difference between a religious Ashura ceremony and a family funeral for the deceased relative – both being mourning ceremonies. Consequently, food provision as a religiously meritorious action (that is, *ihsan*) emerged in Ashura charity, and later started to be applied to the provision of food during ordinary funeral ceremonies with the same connotation of a religious merit.

Hadiths and generally Muslim tradition insist that the family of a deceased is not obliged to provide food during a funeral. On the contrary, other people should help the family of a deceased person with food:

> It is better for neighbours and relatives to make food in their own houses then bring it to the household (of the deceased), because it was narrated that when the Prophet (peace and blessings of Allah be upon him) heard that his cousin Ja'far ibn Abi Taalib (may Allaah be pleased with him) had died in the Battle of Mu'tah, he told his family to make food for the family of Ja'far, and said, 'Because there has come to them that which will preoccupy them.' But it is not permitted for the family to make food for people because for the sake of the deceased. (Al-Shaykh al-'Allaamah 'Abd al-'Azeez ibn 'Abd-Allah ibn Baaz 2022)

Thus, it may be hypothesised that food provision in Azerbaijani funerals has its roots not in religious precepts. Rather food provision started as the reflection of a religiously meritorious charity of Ashura. It is from this historical narrative that a funeral food provision as *ehsan* gradually started to take root as applied to ordinary funeral services. Food provision by the relatives of a deceased person served as a religiously meritorious act of charity showing their affection and devotion to the person who passed. Today, *ehsan* is also provided by the Azerbaijani government and foundations in the country to commemorate servicemen fallen during military operations (Anews 2016). Ultimately, the usage of the term in both Ashura and ordinary funeral ceremonies shows specific actions, which, in the eyes of the local population, serve as notable examples of the Islamic concept of *ihsan*.

In contemporary Azerbaijan, food provision (*ehsan*) attains a central part of a funeral ceremony and accounts for the bulk of ceremony spending. As with other rituals (Sadigov 2020a), *ehsan* also experiences the pressure of overspending. It is no coincidence that the government regulation conceived to keep in check population overspending on funerals focuses mostly on *ehsan* (BBC 2016), whereas other aspects of funerals do not get comparable attention (Jamnews 2018).

This tradition of providing an exemplary tribute requiring a considerable financial investment seemingly serves several broader functions. First, through providing an opulent *ehsan*, a person/family earns moral capital: as noted earlier, the very provenance of the term *ehsan* links it to religious merit. Consequently, it is assumed that a person/family who spends generously on a funeral feast is a meritorious Muslim, with all the ensuing religious implications of this status for religious reward in the afterlife.

The second function of *ehsan* is linked to social capital. Through demonstrative consumption, aggressive hospitality, co-optation of useful contacts and network maintenance funeral feasts serve to boost horizontal links within one's social circle. An opulent funeral feast (or at least the one which does not fall short of social expectations) contributes to family prestige in broader social networks.

Finally, *ehsan* has a third psychological implication: people spend a large amount of money on funerals to emphasise their love and emotional affection for a deceased family member through the aforementioned opulent funeral paraphernalia and lavish funeral feasts. Funeral feasts, hence, symbolically represent the affection felt towards the deceased. While death may deal a big blow to traditional family and clan solidarity, elaborate funerals with generous food provision serve to re-integrate and strengthen social bonds (Sadigov 2020b). Consequently, *ehsan* may also serve as a psychological function of quenching a sense of loss.

The cited reasons may create social pressure to spend a significant amount on funeral feasts. Once the incentives to spend are introduced, then a societal competition for religious, social and psychological capital may force individuals to overspend (that is, to spend beyond what they may reasonably afford) on funerals. Many poor families, faced with social pressure to provide funeral feasts risk financial ruin, which, in turn, increase social tensions and discontent. Consequently, many governments interfere in order to regulate funeral spending in a bid to keep in check social pressure to overspend (Sadigov 2021).

14.9 *Pomeni* (Moldova)
Gian Marco Moisé
School of Law and Government, Dublin City University, Ireland

Pomeni, literally, 'handouts', are parcels containing a painted hard-boiled egg, *colaci* (round braids of bread), candy, a small cotton towel, a candle and matches wrapped in a plastic bag. In Moldova and Romania, the bundle is gifted to visitors at the cemetery during *paștele blajinilor*, the day of remembering the dead, literally, the 'Easter of the Blessed Ones'. When gifting *pomeni*, people will say: 'For the soul of' (*pentru sufletul*) followed by the name of the relative they wish to remember. To this the recipient responds '*bogdaproste*', an abbreviation of the Bulgarian '*bog da prosti*', 'may God forgive'.

Arrangements for *paștele blajinilor* are similar to those of the Orthodox Easter celebration. Ghosts of the ancestors are believed to roam the cemeteries and consume the meals prepared by their relatives, and leftovers are never brought back home. Wine is sometimes poured on the tombstones. According to one interpretation, the wine will get the Devil drunk and spare the souls of relatives; according to another, the wine allows the deceased to celebrate (Sofronia 2021). Moldovan tombs often contain a built-in small table and chairs so that the living and the dead can share a meal. A candle is then lit near the tomb, weeds are cleared out and fresh flowers are laid. Older women are expected to clean the tombs no longer tended by the relatives of the deceased.

While younger generations tend to not partake in the practice, older generations continue to prepare *pomeni* with care, days in advance. In some Moldovan areas such as Soroca, in northern Moldova, *pomeni* have become an extravagant display of wealth, involving plasma TVs and laptops instead of eggs and bread. Attendants dress up for *paștele blajinilor* as they would for a night out. Women in high heels and revealing dresses often infuriate priests, who accuse visitors of violating the sacred ground of the cemetery (Transilvania Report 2019). Visitors snap selfies in front of the tombs or document their celebration on social media. The town, already well-known for its kitsch architecture, has a cemetery with tombstones that reach impressive dimensions and carry life-sized carved pictures of the deceased, often dressed in tracksuits or sitting on thrones. In a game of blame, in local newspapers Romanians attribute the degeneration of the practice to Moldovans. On the other hand, Moldovans put the blame on Roma, whose presence is particularly high in the district of Soroca.

Gifting *pomeni* to visitors to the cemetery is the core practice of *paștele blajinilor*. In Romanian, *paștele* means 'Easter'. The term *blajinilor* has Slavic origins meaning a 'gentle, kind, or pious soul' (Stimpovschii

Figure 14.9.1 Built-in table and chairs in tombs. © Gian Marco Moisé.

2015). By celebrating *paștele blajinilor*, people from Banat, Transylvania, Bukovina, Bessarabia and Maramureș regions between Moldova, Romania and Ukraine, celebrate their mythical forefathers. The ancestors, believed to guard the villages, are called to celebrate Easter by releasing red-coloured eggshells to float down the river. Another way to call the ancestors is to put an ear on the ground, but according to a popular belief, the voices of *blajini* can cause deafness. According to another popular belief, if people do not celebrate the Easter of the Blessed Ones with care, the fields will no longer bear fruit, the sheep will get sick and their hands and feet will ache (Radio Chișinău 2018).

While in Romanian references to the ancestors are vague, in Ukrainian the celebration has a protohistoric etymology. *Paștele blajinilor* is called *rahmanskii velikdien'*, the great day of the Rahmans (Boris Grinchenko Dictionary, n.d.b). It is believed that the forefathers of people from these regions, the *blajini*, were the Rahmans, a mythical nation of righteous Christians in Ukrainian folklore (Sofronia 2021). Other interpretations present *blajini* as the descendants of Seth, the third son of Adam and Eve, incapable of doing harm and living at the border between the 'seen' and the 'unseen'. According to researchers, the name Rahmans (Boris Grinchenko Dictionary n.d.a) comes from the Thracian language, and is the nickname of Zeind-Roymenos (holy light), a deity present in Dobrogean, Oltenian and Transylvanian folklore. In a section of the mediaeval epic *Alexandria* (Vrăjitoriu Enache 2015), Alexander the Great met the Blajini at the edge of heaven, where their king Evant gifted him with the water of eternal life (Radu n.d.). This shows that *paștele blajinilor* is a pagan celebration reinterpreted by the Christians from these regions. Similar to *paștele blajinilor*, Russians from the Smolensk region celebrate *radonitsa* (Mostowicz 2018), and in Belarus the same festivity is called *radaunitsa*.

Celebrated on the Monday following Saint Thomas Sunday, eight days after Orthodox Easter, *paștele blajinilor* takes place after 'light week' (*săptămâna luminată*), during which believers are supposed to abstain from household or farm work or they risk going blind (Sofronia 2021). Only during the 'dark week' (*săptămâna neagră*) can they commemorate the dead. Most of these beliefs have been lost in modern-day practice. During Soviet times, *paștele blajinilor* was celebrated on Sunday instead of Monday, a working day since Soviet authorities did not acknowledge the holiday. After the dissolution of the Soviet Union and Moldova independence, the celebration became a national holiday. In Chișinău, the capital of Moldova, during *paștele blajinilor*, buses form long queues on the side of Albișoara street to bring passengers to Saint Lazarus cemetery located on the outskirts. It is prohibited to travel to the cemetery by car during the *paștele blajinilor* holiday, because the cemetery's car park is too small to accommodate large numbers of visitors.

14.10 **Mingbi** (China)
Yizhou Xu
Department of Communication and Theatre Arts, Old Dominion University, USA

The Chinese term *mingbi* (冥币) refers to paper offerings burned as part of mourning as part of ancestor worship. The practice occupies a significant role in directing the everyday social and spiritual life in China. Each year, during Tomb Sweeping Day (*Qingming Festival*), millions of people travel to cemeteries across the country to venerate their ancestors through the ritual of paper burning. The paper offerings, more colloquially known as 'spirit money' or 'joss paper', are paper replicas of items such as money, houses or furniture, as well as modern everyday possessions like cars, laptops, cameras and iPhones. The offerings are burned and ritually destroyed as a form of symbolic offering to the dead. Paper burning is often performed at cemeteries and other venues of remembrance as a way of communicating with the deceased. With the adoption of the Internet and digital technologies in China, the use of joss paper and other forms of ritual tribute have migrated online (Xu 2022). It has become a popular means of fulfilling one's filial obligations with the convenience of digital platforms and without the need to physically travel to cemeteries.

Confucian practices of ancestor worship require the material transfer of food, money and other items to the deceased, often in the form of joss paper items, ritually burned as a means of communicating with the spirit world. The perennial practices of ancestor worship are the bonds that unite families and clans as the basis for sociality in Chinese society and an inseparable part of Chinese identity. 'Death does not terminate the relationship of reciprocity among the Chinese, it simply transforms these ties and often makes them stronger' (Watson and Rawski 1988: 9). In this regard, Chinese eschatological practices represent a radical break from the Western notions of the afterlife. In contrast to the linear or teleological view in Abrahamic religions, the Chinese traditions have a unitary and cyclical view of the world. Rather than having a clear distinction between the material and the immaterial world, life and death in China exist in parallel. This is reflected by the binary worldview of the *yin-yang*.

Mingbi can also be considered a type of spiritual gift exchange linked to the traditional practices of ancestor worship that are a crucial part of the Chinese conception of the afterlife. Accordingly, death does not sever the social obligation between family and clans but extends into a cult of lineage worship (Jankowiak 1993) that is reciprocated through mortuary rituals. Central to the perpetuation of Chinese sociality into the afterlife is the exchange of spiritual gifts in the forms of joss paper items and money. These items signify the ritualistic bridging of two worlds by which spiritual gifts are rendered immaterial through their ritual destruction. In exchange, people receive good blessings from their ancestors, creating a reciprocal relationship of material/immaterial gift exchange, maintained by every generation.

The continuity between afterlife and social life is also closely tied to the roles of the traditional Chinese state and its governing bodies. Both worlds share similar functions to that of the state bureaucracy, in that the afterworld contains parallel bureaucratic organs that mirror society. Paper offerings of imitation money were some of the earliest manifestations of joss paper, despite having no standard design. Imitation money exists in a huge range of styles and denominations, always depicting authorities and institutions governing the afterlife. Joss paper notes, often called 'hell notes' are issued by the 'Bank of Hell', which references the Chinese term for the netherworld, *difu*, ruled by King Yan and other deities of the Chinese religious pantheon.

The parallel existence of state apparatuses denotes the inseparability of the afterlife with that of the living governance. In drawing from the Foucauldian notions of biopolitics, Mayfair Yang points to the complexity by which power is distributed across different mediums of economic exchange in China, specifically '(1) the state distributive economy, (2) the gift economy, and (3) resurgent commodity economy' (Yang 1994: 178). The ritual gift economy in this case constitutes what Yang calls *minjian*, the people's realm that operates in tandem with, but is distinct from, the logic of the state and market economy. Gift exchange in the form of *guanxi*, the cultivation of personal relationships, makes up a significant portion of the contemporary cultural and political economy of China. China's biopolitical governance provides a useful way of thinking about how the state-distributed economy works in controlling social life. It also inversely implies that *minjian* can be applied to the Chinese concept of *yinjian*, the nether-realm, in looking at gift exchange beyond the mere circuits of exchange in the living context and demonstrating its necropolitical implications.

In recent years the Chinese government has heavily promoted the digitisation of paper burning rituals via online cemeteries to adopt more sustainable mourning practices. These so-called 'green funeral practices' discourage traditional rituals of paper burning, firecrackers and food offerings in order to curb air pollution and waste from burning. Instead, there have been renewed calls to adopt online practices that substitute traditional joss paper with digital gifts that can be purchased and shared on online virtual cemeteries. This effectively reframes the practices of mourning into productive acts by which users must work to turn material objects into digital imitations to be accumulated and shared online. As a result, the practices of ancestor worship and private mourning are gradually being replaced by the notions of preservation, memorialisation and public ceremony. The traditional ritual gift economy is increasingly subsumed by the formal digital commodity economy. Digital platforms work to rematerialise the ephemerality of the gift into new spheres of socioeconomic exchange, deemed productive to the interest of the state.

The state's intervention in traditional rituals is not surprising, as paper burning had long been categorised as a form of *mixin*, or superstition, and was seen as a backward, counterrevolutionary activity (Chu 2010: 182). But since the market reform of the 1980s, there has been a resurgence of folk religions and traditional practices. These are often tolerated but remain illicit and unsanctioned by the state and local authorities. The state's promotion of modern mortuary practices via online commemoration signifies the removal of traditional filial ties and the waste associated with paper gifts, while promoting a collective public memorialisation. The platformisation of mourning and its promotion by the state can be viewed as a means of regulating and standardising an aesthetic practice that is commensurate with what the Chinese government views as a modern, clean and civilised society. Such discourses in official policy can be considered as a form of 'aesthetic governmentality' (Ghertner 2015). In the case of China, individuals are conditioned to practise proper funereal conduct that is sanitised as opposed to unsightly, and productive as opposed to destructive.

Yet the remediation of material practices into the online realm also necessitates new ways of reifying corporeal practices vis-à-vis the digitisation process. The transformation of paper imitation into digital imitations requires a different way of thinking about what constitutes materiality within this new online space of ritualised mourning. Online cemeteries therefore serve as the site of exchange by which joss paper and other votive offerings are digitised in ways that alter Chinese traditional practices. The digitisation of joss paper demonstrates the biopolitical means by which the state and market forces work to subsume traditional ancestor worship into controllable and commodifiable forms of mourning. The subversive acts of waste and destruction of the gift is replaced by its accumulation and preservation online. Digitisation highlights the process by which otherwise dead objects take on a different materiality, and different values, aesthetics and productive labour practices.

Bibliography to Chapter 14

Introduction: elderly care and ambivalence
Elena Zdravomyslova

Becker, H., Geer, B., Hughes, E. and Straus, A. 1961. *Boys in White: Student Culture in Medical School*. Chicago: University of Chicago Press.
Bogdanova, E. 2019. 'Rezhim zaboty o pozhilykh malomobil'nykh ljudjakh' [Elderly Care Regime of Low-mobile People]. In *Kriticheskaya sotsiologiya zaboty* (in Russian), edited by E. Borozdina, E. Zdravomyslova and A. Temkina, 277–311. St. Petersburg: European University at St. Petersburg.
Borozdina, E. 2015. Zabota i sotsialnoe grazhdanstvo [Care and Social Citizenship]. *Sotsiologicheskie issledovaniya* 10: 84–93.
Burawoy, M. 2021. *Public Sociology*. Cambridge and Oxford: Polity Press.
Graham, H. 1991. 'The Concept of Caring in Feminist Research: The Case of Domestic Service'. *Sociology* 25(1): 61–78.
Hochschild, A. 1979. 'Emotion Work, Feeling Rules, and Social Structure'. *American Journal of Sociology* 85(3): 551–75.
Hochschild, A. 2003. *The Commercialization of Intimate Life: Notes from Home and Work*. Los Angeles and London: University of California Press.
Illouz, E. 2007. *Cold Intimacies: The Making of Emotional Capitalism*. London: Polity Press.
Khalili, A. 2012. 'The Role of Emotional Intelligence in the Workplace: A Literature Review'. *International Journal of Management* 29(3): 355.
Kittay, E. F. 1995. 'Taking Dependency Seriously: The Family and Medical Leave Act Considered in Light of the Social Organization of Dependency Work and Gender Equality'. *Hypatia* 10(1): 8–29.
Kremer, M. 2007. *How Welfare States Care: Culture, Gender and Parenting in Europe*. Amsterdam: Amsterdam University Press.
Ledeneva, A. (ed.) 2018. *The Global Encyclopaedia of Informality: Understanding Social and Cultural Complexity, Volume 1*. London: UCL Press.
Lerner, J. and Rivkin-Fish, M. 2021. 'On Emotionalisation of Public Domains'. *Emotions and Society* 3(1): 3–14.
Merton, R. K. 1976. *Sociological Ambivalence and Other Essays*. New York: Simon and Schuster.
Mol, A. 2008. *The Logic of Care: Health and the Problem of Patient's Choice*. London: Routledge.
Polanyi, K. 1944. *The Great Transformation*. Boston: Beacon Books.
Rotkirch, A., Tkach, O. and Zdravomyslova, E. 2012. 'Making and Managing Class: Employment of Paid Domestic Workers in Russia'. In *Rethinking Class in Russia*, edited by Suvi Salmenniemi, 129–48. London: Ashgate.
Rostgaard, T. and Pfau-Effinger, B. 2011. 'Welfare State Change, the Strengthening of Economic Principles, and New Tensions in Relation to Care'. *Nordic Journal of Social Research* 2: 1–6.
Temkina, A. 2019. 'Devushki v Belom: gender I obuchenie praktikam professionalnoi zaboty v sestrinskom dele' [Girls in White: Gender and Learning Professional Caring in Nursing]. In *Kriticheskaya sotsiologiya zaboty* (in Russian), edited by E. Borozdina, E. Zdravomyslova and A. Temkina, 25–58. St. Petersburg: European University at St. Petersburg.
Tronto, J. C. (2013). *Caring Democracy: Markets, Equality, and Justice*. New York: New York University Press.
Ware, B. 2019. *The Top Five Regrets of the Dying*. UK: Hay House.
Zdravomyslova, E. and Savchenko, A. 2020. 'A Moral Career of Caring for Elderly Relatives Living with Dementia'. *Laboratorium: Russian Review of Social Research* 12(2): 90–123 (in Russian).

14.1 *Baksy* (Kazakhstan)
Lyazzat Utesheva

Abdimomynova, G. 2015. 'Traditional Life in the Steppe: Kazakh People and Shamanism'. *E-history. kz*, 21 July. https://e-history.kz/en/news/show/8337

Bersnev, P. 2014. *Sacred Cosmos of Shamans. The Archaic Consciousness, the Worldview of Shamanism, Traditional Healing and Plant-teachers*. 3rd ed. St. Petersburg: Academy of Culture Research Publishing House.

Essy, P. 2006. 'Sufi Ideology, Shamanistic Rituals: How Religious Groups Have Reached Popularity in Kazakhstan'. *Central Asian Survey* 25(3): 359–71.

Kandyba, V. 1988. *Magic*. St. Petersburg: s.n.

Kharitonova, V. 2003. 'Shamans Without Tambourines'. *Oriental Collection* 130–40.

Kokumbayeva, B. 2012. 'Culturology of Tengrian Art'. Pavlodar: Pavlodar State Pedagogical Institute.

Konyratbay, T. 2016. 'Korkyt in the Folklore of the Turkic Languages'. *Internauka* 11(50): 8–16.

Kulsariyeva, A., Sultanova, M. and Shaygozova, J. 2016. 'The Satified Nature of Metals in Turkic and Kazakh Ministry and Healing Traditions'. *KazNU Bulletin, Philosophy, Political and Cultural Sciences Series* 2(56): 169–78.

Kuspanova, D. 2019 'About Kazakh shamans baksy'. Astrakhan: s.n. https://web.archive.org/web/20210509205431/http://astrakhan-musei.ru/article/article/view/15728

Larina, E. 2016. 'Materials for the Study of the Cult of Saints among the Kazakhs (Evidence from West Kazakhstan Region)'. *Bulletin of the Kalmyk Institute of Humanities of the Russian Academy of Science* 27(5).

Naumova, J., 2016. 'Modern Demonological Ideas of the Kazakhs about Jinn and Peri'. *Bulletin of the RSUH, Series History. Philology. Culturology. Oriental Studies* 3(12): 48–60.

Penkala-Gawęcka, D. 2013. 'Mentally Ill or Chosen by Spirits? *Shamanic Illness* and the Revival of Kazakh Traditional Medicine in Post-Soviet Kazakhstan'. *Central Asian Survey* 32(1): 41.

Rakhimov, R. 2009. 'Central Asia: Islam at the hearth'. In *Central Asia: A Tradition in the Face of Change*. St. Petersburg: Museum of Anthropology and Ethnography named after Peter the Great of the Russian Academy of Sciences.

Somfai-Kara, D., Kunkovács, L. and Sipos, J. 2006. 'Batïrkan, a Kazakh Shaman from the Altay Mountains (Mongolia)'. *Field Reports* 14(1–2): 117–38.

Stasevich, I. 2009. 'Baksylyk and the Practice of Traditional Healing in Modern Kazakhstan'. In *Central Asia: A Tradition in the Face of Change*. St. Petersburg: Museum of Anthropology and Ethnography named after Peter the Great of the Russian Academy of Sciences.

Wood, N. B. 2016. 'Shamans at the Centre of the World'. *Sacred Hoop* 91: 36–43.

Zenin, Y. V. n.d. 'Metaphysics of Being'. https://proza.ru/2013/03/11/1440

14.2 *Bajanje and vilarkas* (Serbia and the Western Balkans)
Maria Vivod

Bošković-Stulli, M. 1960. 'Kresnik–Krsnik, ein Wesen aus der kroatischen und slovenischen Volksüberlieferung'. *Fabula* 3: 275–99.

Čiča, Z. 2002. *Vilenica i vilenjak, Sudbina jednog pretkršćanskog kulta u doba progona vještica*. Zagreb: Etnografija.

Conrad, J. L. 1983. 'Magic Charms and Healing Rituals in Contemporary Yugoslavia'. *Southeastern Europe* 10(1): 99–120.

Đorđević, S. 2011. 'Priče o (uspešnim) izlečenjima: okviri govornog žanra'. *Izlaganje na konferenciji* 165–89.

Ginzburg, C. 1966. *The Night Battles, Witchcraft and Agrarian Cults in the Sixteenth and Seventeenth Centuries*. Baltimore: John Hopkins University Press.

Henningsen, G. 1993. 'The Ladies from Outside in Early Modern European Witchcraft'. In *Centres and Peripheries*, edited by B. Bengt Ankarloo and G. Henningsen, 191–215. New York: Oxford University Press:.

Klaniczay, G. 1983. 'Benandante-kresnik-zduhač-táltos. Samanizmus és boszorkányhit érintkezési pontjai Közép-Európában'. *Ethnographia* 94 (1983): 116–34.

Kropej, M. 2009. 'Slovenian Charms Between South Slavic and Central European Tradition'. In *Charms, Charmers and Charming. International Research on Verbal Magic*, edited by J. Roper, 145–62. London: Palgrave Macmillan.

Lecouteux, C. 1996. *Charmes, conjurations et bénédictions, Lexique et formules*. Paris: Honoré Champion.

Pòcs, É. 1989. *Tündérek, démonok, boszorkànyok*. Budapest: Akadémiai Kiadò.

Radenković, L. 1996. *Narodna bajanja kod Južnih Slovena*. Beograd: Prosveta/ Balkanološki institut SANU.

VICE International. www.youtube.com/watch?v=XKN8WxSoGns

Vivod, M. 2008. 'Die Beschwörerin (Bajalica) Biljana aus Budisava, Wojwodina. Rekonstruktionsversuche einer ethnischen Identität im postsozialistischen Nachkriegsserbien'. *Curare* 30(2007)2&3: 153–62.

14.3 *Tchop* (Caucasus)
Maria Vyatchina

Anuchin, D. 1884. *Otchet o poezdke v Dagestan letom 1882 goda*. St. Petersburg: Tipografija A. S. Suvorina: 387.

Gasanov, S. 1928. 'medicina v Azerbajdzhane'. *Izvestija obshhestva obsledovanija i izuchenija Azerbajdzhana* 6: 208–23.

Kapustina, E. 2019. 'The Boundaries of the Djamaat: The Particular Features of Dagestan's Translocal Communities in the Context of Migration Flows within the Russian Federation'. *The Journal of Social Policy Studies* 17(1): 103–18.

Konjus, E. 1946. *Istoki russkoj pediatrii*. Moscow: Medgiz.

Lalajan, E. A. 1988. *Trudy v pjati tomah*. Yerevan. T.2.

Lisician, S. D. 1992. *Armjane Nagornogo Karabaha. Etnograficheskij ocherk*. Yerevan.

14.4 *Kako mati* (Greece)
Eugenia Roussou

Alivizatos, N. 1999. 'A New Role for the Greek Church?'. *Journal of Modern Greek Studies* 17: 23–40.

Bowman, M. and Valk, Ü. (eds) 2012. *Vernacular Religion in Everyday Life: Expressions of Belief*. London: Routledge.

Dundes, A. (ed.) 1992 [1981]. *The Evil Eye: A Casebook*. Wisconsin: University of Wisconsin Press.

Galt, A. 1982. 'The Evil Eye as a Synthetic Image and Its Meanings on the Island of Pantelleria, Italy'. *American Ethnologist* 9: 664–81.

Heelas, P. 1996. *The New Age Movement: The Celebration of the Self and the Sacralization of Modernity*. Oxford: Blackwell.

Maloney, C. (ed.). 1976. *The Evil Eye*. New York: Columbia University Press.

Molokotos-Liederman, L. 2004. 'Sacred Words, Profane Music? The Free Monks as a Musical Phenomenon in Contemporary Greek Orthodoxy'. *Sociology of Religion* 65(4): 403–16.

Primiano, L. 1995. 'Vernacular Religion and the Search for Method in Religious Folklife'. *Western Folklore* 54(1): 37–56.

Roussou, E. 2013a. 'Spirituality within Religion: Gendered Responses to a Greek "Spiritual Revolution"'. In *Gender and Power in Contemporary Spirituality: Ethnographic Approaches*, edited by A. Fedele and K. Knibbe, 46–61. London: Routledge.

Roussou, E. 2013b. 'The New Age of Greek Orthodoxy: Pluralizing Religiosity in Everyday Practice'. In *The Best of All Gods: Sites and Politics of Religious Diversity in Southern Europe*, edited by J. Mapril and R. Blanes, 73–92. Leiden: Brill.

Stewart, C. 1991. *Demons and the Devil: Moral Imagination in Modern Greek Culture*. Princeton: Princeton University Press.

Veikou, C. 1998. *To Kako Mati: I kinoniki kataskevi tis Optikis Epikoinonias*. Athens: Ellinika Grammata.

14.5 *Marmotagem* (Brazil)
Giovanna Capponi

Araújo Carneiro, P. 2018. *Segredos do Poder: hierarquía e autoridade no Candomblé (Secrets of Power: Hierarchy and Authority in Candomblé)*. São Paulo: Arché.
Brazeal, B. 2014. 'The Fetish and the Stone: A Moral Economy of Charlatans and Thieves'. In *Spirited Things: The Work of 'Possession' in Afro-Atlantic Religions*, edited by P. C. Johnson, 131–54. Chicago and London: University of Chicago Press.
Capone, S. 2010. *Searching for Africa in Brazil. Power and Tradition in Candomblé*. Durham and London: Duke University Press.
Goldman, M. 1985. 'A construção ritual da pessoa: a possessão no Candomblé' [The Ritual Construction of Personhood: Possession in Candomblé]. *Religião e Sociedade* 12(1): 22–54.
Opipari, C. 2009. *O Candomblé: Imagens em Movimento [Candomblé: Moving Images]*. São Paulo: Editora da Universidade de São Paulo.

14.6 *ThetaHealing* (USA, Russia)
Tatiana Loboda

Hanegraaff, W. J. 1998. *New Age Religion and Western Culture: Esotericism in the Mirror of Secular Thought*. New York: Suny Press.
Heelas, P. and Woodhead, L. 2005. *The Spiritual Revolution: Why Religion is Giving Way to Spirituality*. Oxford: Blackwell.
Illouz, E. 2008. *Saving the Modern Soul: Therapy, Emotions and the Culture of Self-help*. Berkeley: University of California Press.
Loboda, T. 2020. *Spiritual Strategies of Women for Achieving Agency on the Example of Theta-healing in Russia*. Dissertation. St. Petersburg: European University.
Perheentupa, I. and Salmenniemi, S. 2019. 'Treading the Tightrope of Femininity: Transforming Gendered Subjectivity in a Therapeutic Community'. *European Journal of Women's Studies* 26(1): 1–15.
Sointu, E. and Woodhead, L. 2008. 'Spirituality, Gender and Expressive Selfhood'. *Journal for the Scientific Study of Religion* 47: 259–76.
Stibal, V. 2010. *Theta Healing: Introducing an Extraordinary Energy Healing Modality*. UK: Hay House UK.
Temkina, A. and Rotkirch, A. 2002. 'Sovetskiye gendernyye kontrakty i ikh transformatsiya v sovremennoy Rossii'. *Sotsis* 11: 4–15.

14.7 *Indulgence* (Global)
Elena Denisova-Schmidt and Sibylle Krause

Direktorium. 2019. Direktorium Erzbischöfe Freiburg. Erzbischof.
Duggan, G. L. 2020. Indulgence. In *Encyclopædia Britannica*. www.britannica.com/topic/indulgence
Jansen, T. 2014. 'Ein Mann des klaren Wortes'. *Katholisch*, 5 January. www.katholisch.de/artikel/2897-ein-mann-des-klaren-wortes
Paulus, N. 1923. *Geschichte des Ablasses im Mittelalter vom Ursprunge bis zur Mitte des 14. Jahrhunderts*, 3rd edition. Paderborn: Ferdinand Schöningh Verlag.

14.8 *Ehsan* (Azerbaijan)
Turkhan Sadigov

Anews. 2016. 'Ehsan Given to Commemorate Azerbaijani Martyrs'. *Anews*. https://anews.az/en/201604081044-ehsan-given-to-commemorate-azerbaijani-martyrs
Ayoub, M. M. 2013. *Islam: Faith and History*. New York: Simon and Schuster.

Azerbaijan National Encyclopaedia. 2016. 'Ehsan entry'. In *Azerbaijan National Encyclopaedia, Volume 7*. Baku: Scientific Centre of Azerbaijani National Encyclopaedia.

BBC. 2016. 'Yas mərasimləri ve biznes' [Funeral Ceremonies and Business]. BBC. www.bbc.com/azeri/azerbaijan/2016/06/160625_luxurious_memorial_ceremonies

Jamnews. 2018. 'Azerbaijani Government to Strictly Regulate Graveyards'. *Jam News*, 10 December. https://jam-news.net/az/az%c9%99rbaycanda-dovl%c9%99t-q%c9%99biristanliqlari-ciddin%c9%99zar%c9%99t-altina-goturur/

Sadigov, T. 2020a. 'Household Overspending on Marriage: The Scale of the Problem and Government Reactions around the World'. *International Journal of Sociology and Social Policy* 40(11/12): 1509–32.

Sadigov, T. 2020b. 'Burying Instability: Post-Soviet Governments' Regulation of Funerals'. *Problems of Post-Communism* 68(1): 74–87.

Sadigov, T. 2021. 'Death beyond the Means: Funeral Overspending and its Government Regulation around the World'. *Rationality and Society* 33(3): 363–98.

Salih Al-Munajjid, S. M. 2022. 'Making Food during the Mourning Period'. *Kitaab Majmoo' Fataawa wa Maqaalaat Mutanawwi'ah li Samaahat al-Shaykh al-'Allaamah 'Abd al-'Azeez ibn 'Abd-Allaah ibn Baaz*, 9: 325. https://islamqa.info/en/answers/13307/making-food-during-the-mourning-period

14.9 *Pomeni* (Moldova)
Gian Marco Moisé

Boris Grinchenko Dictionary. n.d.a. 'Rahman'. Словарь української мови (Словарь украинскаго языка). Борис Грінченко. http://hrinchenko.com/slovar/znachenie-slova/50547-rakhman.html#show_point

Boris Grinchenko Dictionary. n.d.b. 'Rahmanskii Velikdien'. Словарь української мови (Словарь украинскаго языка). Борис Грінченко. http://hrinchenko.com/slovar/znachenie-slova/4405-velykden.html

Mostowicz, I. 2018. 'A Ritual of Death or Life? The Case of Radonitsa in the Smolensk Region, Russia'. *Sibirskie Istoriceskie Issledovania [Siberian Historical Research]* 2: 224–43.

Radio Chișinău. 2018. 'DOCUMENTAR | Paștele Blajinilor'. *Radio Chișinău*, 15 April. https://radiochisinau.md/documentar-pastele-blajinilor---66176.html

Radu, M. n.d. 'Paștele Blajinilor – legendă, tradiție și mister' [Paștele Blajinilor – Legend, Tradition and Mystery]. www.academia.edu/43212859/Melania_Radu_Pa%C5%9Ftele_Blajinilor_legend%C4%83_tradi%C5%A3ie_%C5%9Fi_mister

Sofronia, D. 2021. 'Tradiții în Săptâmâna Neagră. Când e Paștele Blajinilor sau al Rohmanilor, o sărbătoare cu origini păgâne' [Traditions in the Black Week. When it is the Easter of the Blessed Ones or the Rohmans, a Feast of Pagan Origins]. *Adevarul.md*, 5 May. https://adevarul.ro/locale/piatra-neamt/traditii-saptamana-neagra-e-pastele-blajinilor-rohmanilor-sarbatoare-origini-pagane-1_6091275e5163ec4271aee3d6/index.html

Stimpovschii, D. 2015. 'Moldovenii sărbătoresc păgânește. Paștele Blajinilor înseamnă fericire. În cimitir nu se intră cu mâncare și băutură' [Moldovans Celebrate Pagan. The Easter of the Blessed Means Happiness. Food and Drink Are Not Allowed into the Cemetery]. *Adevarul.md*. https://adevarul.ro/stiri-externe/republica-moldova/moldovenii-sarbatoresc-paganeste-pastele-1616249.html

Transilvania Report. 2019. 'Paștele Blajinilor în Republica Moldova, între tradiție creștin – ortodoxă și practică păgână' [Easter of the Blessed in the Republic of Moldova, between Christian-Orthodox Tradition and Pagan Practice]. *Transilvania Report*, 18 April. https://transilvaniareporter.ro/actualitate/pastele-blajinilor-in-republica-moldova-intre-traditie-crestin-ortodoxa-si-practica-pagana

Vrăjitoriu Enache, A. 2015. 'The Food of the Happy Ones'. *DICE* 12(1): 183–94.

14.10 *Mingbi* (China)
Yizhou Xu

Chu, J. Y 2010. *Cosmologies of Credit: Transnational Mobility and the Politics of Destination in China*. Durham: Duke University Press.

Ghertner, A. 2015. *Rule by Aesthetics. World-class City Making in Delhi*. New York: Oxford University Press.

Jankowiak, W. R. 1993. *Sex, Death, and Hierarchy in a Chinese City: An Anthropological Account*. New York: Columbia University Press.

Watson, J. L. and Rawski, E. S. 1988. *Death Ritual in Late Imperial and Modern China*. Berkeley: University of California Press.

Xu, Y. 2022. 'Digitizing Death: Commodification of Joss Paper on Chinese Online Cemetery'. *Journal of Cultural Economy* 15(2): 151–67.

Yang, M. M. 1994. *Gifts, Favors, and Banquets: The Art of Social Relationships in China*. Ithaca: Cornell University Press.

Concluding remarks: the Big Three and informality

Jan Nederveen Pieterse
Distinguished Professor and Mellichamp Chair in Globalization, University of California, Santa Barbara, USA

The Big Three – state, market, society – are pillars of social science. Society is the foundation. Social life takes shape (clan, tribe), markets evolve (surplus produce, artisanal goods, caravanserai, souk, fair) and organisation follows (village councils, chief, bey, sheikh, lord) to settle disputes, provide services and secure trade routes.

Without a society, there is no state, but there can be a society without a state. States are extensions of society. The origins of state institutions are the administrative bureaucracies of feudal lords, kingdoms and empires, with security, census taking and tax collection among the key functions (Strayer 1970; Anderson 1986; Scott 2017). Society, the deepest layer, sprawls in many directions. Markets and states arise from the growing division of labour and differentiation of society; over time they become functionally autonomous and specialise. Economies and states spread out in many spheres. Talcott Parsons and structural functionalism – an influential approach in American sociology in the 1960s and 1970s – added culture as a fourth domain.

In Thessalonica, visit the National History Museum and its emphasis is on national, Greek histories, costumes, narratives. Now go on to the Folk and Ethnological Museum and it tells much older stories, in which Ottoman and Greek worlds intertwine and rural mountain routes, dress and cuisine overlap. Visit the Archaeological Museum and the angle pivots to Macedonia and Thrace.

'Society', often equated with the nation-state, is older than nation and state, is layered and unfolds in myriad ways. Social cooperation long preceded state formation. Why then is the conventional sequence that of 'state, market, society'? Does it imply a rank order in the power to shape society? It goes back to the nineteenth century when social science disciplines took shape. Approaches were state-centric from the Westphalen Treaty of 1648 until the late nineteenth century when civilisational history and other genres of history evolved, economic, social and so on.

The state came in first place because it was held to possess the largest database and the widest range of agency. Hegel (2001[1840]) viewed the state as the leading embodiment of consciousness and agency: what it takes to awaken to the 'spirit of history', to become a subject rather than an object of history, is awareness of what is happening and the ability to act upon this knowledge. This lineage includes, among others, Jacobinism, the French revolution that set the stage for the French educator state, Prussia's robust state, Lenin's New Economic Policy, Nkrumah's postcolonial state, and the developmental state of Japan, East Asian economies and China.

Adam Smith and Manchester liberalism criticised the royal chartered companies and deemed market forces to be more competitive and capable than government. This view moved up with neoclassical economics, Mises and Hayek and the Chicago school, became dominant from the 1980s onwards and established another network of power. The limitations of market forces as societal guidance emerged in financial and economic crises during the 1990s, culminating in the crisis of 2008, which showed that neoliberalism was 'oversold'.

The informal underlies and enables the formal; the formal is an organisation and regulation of the informal. The informal, like a diamond, has many facets, and which sides show up depends on where the light shines from. From the point of view of the formal, the informal lacks standing and status and is merely ordinary, everyday casual as in dress and manner. From the viewpoint of states, the informal lacks features such as records, legibility, regulation, taxation (black market). From a business viewpoint, the informal means risk (no written contract, no recourse, unpredictable) yet also entails opportunities for cheap deals and backdoor scams. In many developing countries, the informal sector is the largest and those who work in this sector such as street hawkers and rickshaw drivers have tacit rules of their own. In the words of the bard, 'To live outside the law you must be honest'. In advanced economies, informal and low regulation work have been on the increase in migrant work and the gig economy, and with it the precariat grows, while the informal circulation economy of sharing and reuse also grows. In organisation studies, the informal is part of the infrastructure of the formal; the front door, side door and backdoor are interdependent. Informal organisation is a resource of morale, trust, resilience (water cooler, Thank God it's Friday) as well as a source of intrigue, sabotage, backbiting.

Viewed from an existential angle, the informal is wide and profound, layer upon layer of old strata, from folk wisdom down to ancestral knowledge. It is irreverent, ribald, a wellspring of the sage, the bard, the jester, of humour and bawdry jokes. It is concealed (as in an Ethiopian saying, 'when the great lord passes, the peasant bows and silently farts') and hidden from view alongside the power of the weak and their hidden texts (Scott 1985), their subterfuge, sources of comfort, healing and resistance. All social movements, peasant uprisings, mutinies, trade union organising, women's emancipation arise from and are grounded in informal resources.

Erasmus mocked the posturing and hypocrisy of Roman Catholic dignitaries ('In Praise of Folly', 1511), and Qawwali music from rural Pakistan offers ribald mockery of the urban mullahs and their rules.

Formality, too, comes in many guises. Rules and procedures are markers of organisation. Formality is a gatekeeper to the nodal points of institutional change and decision-making. Courtrooms require gravity, parliaments require procedure. Also part of the equation are bureaucracy and red tape (disorganisation is a byproduct of organisation), ritualism, pomposity, deception (Potemkin façade) and guile (promise, don't deliver), guises that are not always neatly distinguishable.

The informal and formal are a continuum, not a binary. The distinction between formality and informality is also an administrative fiction, a tool of governmentality. The actual boundary between formal and informal lies in the twilight zone, a moving target that looks different by day than by night. A pirate may be an envoy of the king. Relations between formality and informality are not easy to map due to lack of transparency. The spectrum of the informal is wider than that of the formal. After all, the secrets of the formal are informal (networks, backroom, 'personnel is policy').

American corporations and Hollywood studios tuck the informal away in Non-Disclosure Agreements, which are formal. Media discreetly follow codes of no-go under the code word 'classified information'. The informal works through and in the crevices of the formal – like the police moonlighting for gangs, secret services shielding crime syndicates in East Europe and Russia (Glenny 2009), intermediary judges for hire, billionaires' dark money funding right-wing movements and think tanks that design policy papers for Congress. The secrets of the US' 'longest war' in Afghanistan include 'imaginary institutions' and 80 per cent of US funds going to large contractors (van Bijlert 2009; Ackerman 2022).

In developing countries, the informal sphere is often more knowledgeable on the ground, better organised, more effective than government agencies. The government hoards the limelight but has limited grasp. In developing countries, the government and civil society often compete for legitimacy and foreign aid. In Bangladesh (BRAC, Grameen), Pakistan (Jamaat-e-Islami), Egypt, religious organisations and charities often function better than government agencies. This follows the 'retreat of the state' in the wake of markets opening up and government spending cutbacks. In several countries NGOs are stronger in some domains than government agencies, with uneven ramifications (Hanlon 1991; Duffield 2019).

According to Serif Mardin, in Ottoman Turkey the tax collectors were the centre, tax payers were the periphery (1973). The periphery survived by informal means. Thus, one view is that the problem is not informality, that is simply how people get by, as people ever did; the actual problem is formality, the quality of governance that is superimposed on much older informality in various ways. Susan George's advice (1977) is don't study the poor, they get by (with the kind of community help discussed in this volume). Study the rich, that is where the problem lies.

Several entries in this volume refer to patron-client relations, which often go back deep in time and cross strata of caste, class, slave, an underestimated dimension of social cohesion. What goes under the bulky heading of 'corruption', then, forks in at least two directions – social cooperation and cohesion, and abuse and fraud. Abuse and fraud fork in two further paths – small fry and big fish. The big fish are a big problem.

Folklore is much older than the state and the nation. Many entries in this volume refer to folk legacies, custom and tradition. The revocation of the old also refers to the creation of new hiding places and forms of camouflage. Are the informal practices discussed in this volume, with their wide range and geographical scope, transformative?

According to an entry in this volume, in Mexico, *palanca* is the 'informal social practice of exchanging favours …' (see 5.7 in this volume). Similar to the Russian *blat* (see 1.1 Volume 1), the Chinese *guanxi* (see 1.12 Volume 1) or the Brazilian *jeitinho* (see 1.2 Volume 1), *palanca* in Mexico is considered a balancing mechanism that restores justice when formal institutions malfunction. The justification is that when the authorities do not offer services or goods efficiently, it is fair to use *palancas* for solving personal or family problems … *Palanca* does not seek revolt against the formal rule itself, but against the fact that the formal rule does not work in practice' (Arellano-Gault and Trejo-Alonso 2023: 107, 108). 'Restoring justice' is an interesting perspective. Does it work? The entry also points out limitations: 'The dark side of *palanca* is that the most influential leverage networks can be highly exclusive, usually permeable [accessible] only to those with the most money and resources' (Arellano-Gault and Trejo-Alonso 2023). Thus, the rich not only bask in wealth and power, but they also get favours.

The informal, of course, shapes formal decision-making. The 'quiet encroachment' of the poor (for example, street hawkers move to a slightly better position when the police aren't watching; Bayat 1998) is no match for the quiet encroachment of the rich. In the words of Warren Buffett, one of the world's wealthiest persons: 'There's class warfare, all right', Mr. Buffett said, 'but it's my class, the rich class, that's making war, and we're winning' (Stein 2006). How come mega corporations and billionaires pay little or no taxes? The rich leverage their wealth and power to secure a favourable tax code. Lawyers turn tax evasion (illegal) into tax avoidance (legal). Big Tech, Big Pharma, Big Oil, Big Banks, Big Agrobusiness and so on spend millions on lawyers and lobbyists. Their lawyers and lobbyists tweak Congress legislation so that regulation stifles competition from smaller firms (Derber 2007). The gap between Big Cap, Wall Street and Main Street keeps growing. Financialisation has been trendsetting since the 1980s, and swindle is profuse in the finance sector (Nesvetailova and Palan 2021). Tax havens and what the Panama Papers and Paradise Papers convey are informal too (Bernstein 2017) while the US Senate policies that uphold them are formal.

Inequality has risen to staggering heights. In the US, the top 0.01 per cent of Americans, about 200,000 families, own as much wealth as the bottom 90 per cent, about 110 million households (Piketty et al. 2018). Most Americans live from paycheck to paycheck. Worldwide, 'The richest 10 per cent today snap up 52 per cent of all income. The poorest half get just 8.5 per cent' (IMF 2022). The use of informal means by the wealthy and powerful turns the world into a world of scams. The balance is not in favour of the majority.

Bibliography

Ackerman, E. 2022. *The Fifth Act: America's End in Afghanistan*. New York: Penguin.
Anderson, J. (ed.) 1986. *The Rise of the Modern State*. Brighton: Wheatsheaf.
Arellano-Gault, D. and Trejo-Alonso, L. J. 2023. Palanca (Mexico). In *Global Encyclopaedia of Informality, Volume 3*, edited by A. Ledeneva. London: UCL Press.
Bayat, A. 1998. *Street Politics: Poor People's Movements in Iran*. Cairo: American University in Cairo Press.

Bernstein, J. 2017. *Secrecy World: Inside the Panama Papers Investigation*. New York: Henry Holt.
Derber, C. 2007. *The Wilding of America*. 4th ed. New York: Worth.
Duffield, M. 2019. *Post-humanitarianism: Governing Precarity in the Digital World*. Cambridge: Polity.
Erasmus, D. 1511. *Stultitiae Laus*. Basel.
George, S. 1977. *How the Other Half Dies: The Real Reasons for World Hunger*. 2nd ed. Harmondsworth: Penguin.
Glenny, M. 2009. *McMafia: A Journey through the Global Criminal Underworld*. New York: Vintage.
Hanlon, J. 1991. *Mozambique, Who Calls the Shots?* London: James Currey.
Hegel, G. W. F. 2001 [1840]. *The Philosophy of History*. Kitchener: Batoche Books.
IMF. 2022. *Finance & Development*, March.
Mardin, Ş. 1973. 'Center-periphery Relations: A Key to Turkish Politics?'. *Daedalus* 102(1): 169–90.
Nesvetailova, A. and Palan R. 2021. *Sabotage: The Hidden Nature of Finance*. London: Penguin.
Piketty, T., Saez, E. and Zucman, G. 2018. 'Distributional National Accounts: Methods and Estimates for the United States'. *Quarterly Journal of Economics* 133(2): 553–609.
Scott, J. C. 1985. *Weapons of the Weak: Everyday Forms of Peasant Resistance*. New Haven: Yale University Press.
Scott, J. C. 2017. *Against the Grain: A Deep History of the Earliest States*. New Haven: Yale University Press.
Stein, B. 2006. 'In Class Warfare, Guess Which Class Is Winning'. *New York Times*, 26 November. www.nytimes.com/2006/11/26/business/yourmoney/26every.html
Strayer, J. R. 1970. *On the Medieval Origins of the Modern State*. Princeton: Princeton University Press.
van Bijlert, M. 2009. 'Imaginary Institutions: State Building in Afghanistan'. In *Doing Good or Doing Better: Development Policies in a Globalising World*, edited by P. van Lieshout, M. Kremer and R. Went, 157–75. Amsterdam: Amsterdam University Press.

Glossary

A molestar a otro lado (Guatemala): refusing to serve poor or indigenous customers, lit. 'go bother someone elsewhere'.

Ahbap-çavuş ilişkisi (Turkey): a close fraternity entailing mutual support and exchange of favours, associated with friendship established in school, college or army.

Ala kachuu (Kyrgyzstan): lit. 'take the girl and run', kidnapping a woman, with or without her consent, with the purpose of marrying her.

Amakudari (Japan): appointing retired senior civil servants to executive positions in private companies.

Andare in giro (Italy): scouting for and collecting recyclable goods for mending, repurposing and reselling.

Aqsaqal (Kazakhstan): old male members sitting on the elderly council, tasked with mediating and resolving local disputes.

Ashar (Kyrgyzstan): community effort to solve a common or individual issue.

Aumento (Lowland South America): lit. 'to augment, something extra', used when someone is giving or receiving something above what is considered standard practice.

Babushki (Russia): lit. grandmothers, a family-based support system associated with childcare and household help by those excluded from formal labour markets.

Bajanje and Vilarkas (Serbia and the Western Balkans): the pronouncement of a verbal text or charm to achieve a desired effect.

Baksy (Kazakhstan): a healer, prophet and communicator with the spirit world, originating in the ancient Kazakh culture.

Bin diwar, fazaee (Iraq and the Kurdistan Region of Iraq): ghost employees; those who receive salaries from the public budget but do not perform a public service.

Bridezilla (UK, North America, Australia): labelling for a bride, striving for perfection and power in an aggressive but also victimised fashion, moulded and targeted by the wedding industry and media.

Burrnesha (Albania): women who adopt masculine appearance and behaviour to preserve the honour of their birth families.

Caciquismo (Mexico): the exercise of political, economic and social influence with measures of control and co-optation.

Caili (China): lit. 'bride price', betrothal gifts for the bride and her family by the family of the groom.

Caporalato (Italy): labour intermediation in which the recruiter profits by enrolling workers on short-term jobs.

Cassa peota (Italy): a trust-based system of micro-credit and mutual insurance, used in Venice, Italy.

Catfishing (Global): faking one's online profile on a social networking site, typically using another person's name and/or images, to form an intimate relationship.

Chaa pani (India): euphemism for petty bribery; informal payments for a service.

Chabolismo (Spain): abundance of shacks in the suburbs of large cities.

Chanchullo (Central America): fraud; illicit act of benefiting oneself at the expense of others, committed by business owners and public officials.

Chéngzhōngcūn (China): rural villages encircled by rapidly expanding urban settlements.

Chernaya kassa (Kyrgyzstan): informal trust-based credit and savings system accompanied by gathering over a meal.

Chuồng cọp (Vietnam): illegal extensions of apartment buildings that infringe on public space.

Churning (Canada): lit. 'mixing', the act of hoarding material things.

Colonias (USA): informal settlements housing migrant populations in unincorporated and unregulated areas.

Combina (Israel): a trick used for solving a problem or manipulating an outcome in one's favour.

Cumătrism (Moldova): quasi-family ties, established through rituals of godparenthood to turn weaker ties into lifelong support networks; instrumental in economies of favours.

Divlja gradnja (Countries of Former Yugoslavia): buildings constructed or modified without legal permits.

Double Irish (Ireland): a corporate tax optimisation strategy of shifting profits to the country with lower taxes by exploiting Ireland's tax legislation allowing multinationals to register profits at the location of their headquarters.

Doxing (Global): releasing targets' private and personal information online.

Duang muang (Thailand): fortune-telling and spiritual guidance; a method of political analysis and influence shaping political decisions.

Duit kopi (Malaysia): lit. 'coffee money', a small sum of money given to a public servant as an inducement payment.

Ehsan (Azerbaijan): an opulent funeral feast with religious implications.

Enchufismo (Spain): nepotism, granting opportunities and favours to the nearest and dearest; use of personal connections.

Ernai (China): lit. 'second wives', nowadays refers to mistresses in relationship with married men in exchange for material support.

Fanju (China): socialising in banquets to celebrate, build social networks and exchange interests between the host and the guests.

Follower buying (Global): increasing the number of one's online followers by paying an intermediary supplier.

Gaser (Serbia and the Western Balkans): young adults with a luxurious and void lifestyle.

Gorroneo (Spain and Hispanic America): free-riding; eating, drinking and living at the expense of others; siphoning off resources.

Grypsowanie (Poland): prison jargon used by inmates.

Hemşehricilik (Turkey): doing favours for people of one's own origin, especially within diasporic and political communities.

Hikikomori (Japan): social withdrawal of people driven away by societal shame.

Indulgence (Global): a monetary or in-kind payment in exchange for a full or partial remission of the punishment for sin in the Roman Catholic Church.

Informal housing of the rich (Global): a widespread urban development practice, resulting from non-enforcement and deregulation. Gated communities predominantly involve the middle- and upper-class people, building without public authorisation on plots they rightfully own, making it less visible than informal housing of the poor.

Jajmani (South Asia): patron-client relationship originating in ritual and hierarchical organisation of the village economy between landholders and service providers.

Jak igrač (North Macedonia): label for a skilled informality broker who knows how to manipulate formal and informal rules in a particularistic mode of social organisation.

Jirga/Shura (Afghanistan): a gathering of elders in order to resolve local or national conflicts.

Joro (Kyrgyzstan): closed informal trust and mutual help-based network; a company of people that share either a common background, interests, identity or affiliation and socialise over a meal or tea.

Kabel (Malaysia): political or administrative connection to people in positions of influence.

Kako mati (Greece): a popular belief that everyday visual and verbal communication can cause people to suffer symptoms of illness that can then be removed by the performance of ritual healing.

Karmir khndzor (Armenia): the ritual of inspecting bedsheets to verify the bride's virginity on the wedding night and rewarding her parents with a gift.

Kelin (Central Asia): lit. 'daughter-in-law', a newlywed woman who moves in with her husband's family.

Khaltura (USSR): informal side job offering extra income or a low-quality product of the side job.

Khamstvo (USSR, Russia): rude, impudent and abusive way of communicating, used especially in the Soviet public sector service provision.

KhTsB (Armenia): the use of social contacts, in-laws, friends or relatives, for solving problems and getting things done.

Koshumcha (Kyrgyzstan): contribution given on important social celebrations.

Krumpliosztás (Hungary): electoral candidates distributing food and discounts to voters in exchange for votes.

La débrouille (Former French and Belgian colonies in sub-Saharan Africa): lit. 'make do', 'fend for oneself'; refers to people's daily ways of navigating their environment and coping with unforeseen circumstances.

Lesboseksprosvet (Russia): lesbian sex education; grassroots initiatives disseminating information about safer sex among queer women in Russia.

Les rallyes mondains (France): gathering of young aristocrats for cultural and networking events.

Maan tapa (Finland): lit. 'custom law', a parallel system of justice for members of the elite, based on personal connections and political influence.

Maliks (Afghanistan): spokesperson representing the interests of the villagers.

Manteros (Spain): informal street vendors displaying their merchandise on a blanket.

Marmotagem (Brazil): improper or deceitful practising of Afro-Brazilian religious rituals.
Mei bao ma (China): 'birthright tourism'; travelling to give birth in the USA in order to acquire American citizenship for the child.
Mendanghudui (China): lit. 'marriage of the matching doors', is the practice of pairing couples based on similar social and educational backgrounds.
Mertvye dushi (Russian Federation, from 1991): lit. 'dead souls', an umbrella term describing fictitious employees in Russia. More precisely, *mertvye dushi* are officially employed individuals who have no obligation to attend the workplace or to perform any duties.
Meso (Cyprus and Greece): mobilisation of personal connections to influence formal procedures.
Mianzi (China): lit. 'face', a person's reputation and its social implications and consequences.
Moai (Japan): collecting saving scheme characterised by lifelong social bonds.
Mulas (Cuba): shuttle traders who resell goods purchased abroad.
Mullahs (Afghanistan): religious leaders without formal religious training, responsible for applying principles of Sunni Islam to everyday practice.
Mungu idekh (Mongolia): lit. 'eating money', the use of public funds in a way that does not enrich the people socially or economically.
Mzungu price (Kenya): a higher price charged to foreigners and tourists, usually white people.
Ne talasaj (Bosnia and Herzegovina, Croatia, Serbia and Montenegro): avoiding problems by complying with unfair unwritten rules.
Neijuan (China): growth without development caused by intense competition.
Nikoh (Tajikistan): informal Islamic marriage ceremony.
Nisia (Georgia): interest-free loan for food and other necessities, administered by local shopkeepers.
No. 8 wire (New Zealand): refers to problem-solving approaches and creative resourcefulness mentality. Born from the 'pioneer' mindset and geographical remoteness, it is a prized component of New Zealand's national identity.
Nojukusha (Japan): lit. 'rough sleepers', people living on the street.
Nokofio (Ghana): lit. 'something small', gifts given by politicians to their constituents, also a euphemism for bribe.

Obnalichivanie (Russia): the use of fraudulent property transactions to extract money illegally from the Russian maternity benefit system.

OBON (Kyrgyzstan): older female intermediaries negotiating with state institutions on behalf of marginalised citizens.

Okkul't (Russia): mystical or magical practices and shamanism.

Otkat vizy (Russia): crossing the border under the pretext of shopping tourism to collect passport stamps required for a multi-entry Schengen visa; 'running a visa'.

Paga globale (Italy): informal wage paid through manipulated formal channels to match the originally agreed 'global pay' for the month.

Palanca (Mexico): the exchange of favours to solve problems and satisfy needs.

Palyonka (Russia): the production, trade and consumption of counterfeit goods.

Pari pod masata (Bulgaria): lit. 'money under the table', gifting or tipping as gratuity for health and education services.

Parillada (Spanish-speaking Amazonia): lit. 'a mixed grill of meats, barbecue', often used as a euphemism for corruption when someone bribes through the enticement of food.

Parovoziki (Russia): slang for foster or adopted siblings; the practice of rule-following in child placement or adoption of siblings that prevent foster families from separating the group.

Partiti (Corsica): a system of favours and clientelism between members of a clan.

Party soldiers (Western Balkans): person offering support to political parties in exchange for clientelist benefits.

Pečenje rakije (Serbia): distilling brandy from local fruit in rural households, used as a gift or to show hospitality.

Pfandsammeln (Germany): collecting bottles and cans from bins and public places to obtain a refund.

Poclon (Wallachia, Romania): the practice of giving money or other goods to a superior in order to obtain a favourable attitude or various advantages.

Pokhorony okurka (Russia and USSR): type of physical and psychological punishment for violating non-smoking prohibitions in the Russian and Soviet army.

Pomeni (Moldova): lit. 'handouts', parcels of food gifted at the cemetery during 'Easter of the Blessed Ones' in memory of dead relatives.

Pujogŭm (South Korea): cash gift exchange common at weddings and funerals that mobilises social relationships.

Rabenmutter (Germany, Austria, German-speaking Switzerland): a mother combining family and career, regarded as underperforming in both; a bad, egoistic mother.

Revenge porn (Global): non-consensual disclosure of private, sexually graphic, images of an individual.

Runs (Nigeria): cheating and malpractice by students and staff in higher education.

Sadaqa (Kazakhstan and Kyrgyzstan): Muslim charitable giving, usually a donation of a small amount of money or food; also functioning as a mechanism of local governance and community mobilisation.

Saksy (Poland): seasonal economic migration.

Samozakhvat (Kyrgyzstan): unauthorised settling on vacant suburban land.

Ściągnąć (Poland): term denoting a migrant bringing over another person to join them in a foreign country.

Sdelat' ZAGS (Tajik diaspora in Russia): lit. 'to do the marriage registration' to facilitate the obtaining of Russian citizenship.

Selektivni abortus/tuđa večera (Montenegro): son preference, expressed in the deliberate termination of pregnancy with a female fetus; and in the pejorative referring to female inferior social position within a patrilocal residence system.

Shabashniki (USSR, Russia): moonlighting brigades undertaking short, illegal or semi-legal contracts in the Soviet Union.

Shuahaoping (China): publishing false online user reviews to improve the reputation of one's enterprise.

Simsar, samsara (Middle East and North Africa): an intermediary between the buyer and the seller.

Sinnamjai (Thailand): an informal exchange of gifts and favours, widely used and morally acceptable.

Słoiki (Poland): lit. 'jars', used to describe people migrating from the countryside to cities.

Stacze kolejkowi (Poland): individuals who queue for someone else as a means of generating income.

Svart arbete (Sweden): unregistered and untaxed labour and services.

Taksovanie (Uzbekistan): providing paid rides in privately owned cars as a means of generating income.

Tchop (Caucasus): traditional medical practice based on the belief that small items when stuck in the throat or nose cause illness.

Telefon gap zadan (Tajikistan): lit. 'to talk on the phone', clandestine courtship practice of young people before marriage.

Tenderpreneur (South Africa): entrepreneurs offering favours, benefits and help with securing government procurement contracts to clients lacking political contacts and willing to pay for the service.

ThetaHealing (USA, Russia): a practice of holistic spirituality, treating physical, emotional and psychological problems through meditation and therapy.

Ticket touting (Global): re-sale of tickets at inflated prices.

Titushky (Ukraine): members of intimidation squads, unofficially recruited and paid for disruption of oppositional rallies; notable for their involvement in the Euromaidan protests.

Toqal/Tokal (Kazakhstan): second or 'unofficial' wife.

Trailing spouses (India): women accompanying their husbands on transnational postings and expatriate assignments, excluded from the paid labour force in the host country.

Travail au noir (France): lit. 'black labour', unregistered or partially registered employment.

Travel influencers (Global): social media opinion leaders focused on travel and tourism.

Trotro (Ghana): converted vehicles used as public transport.

Uklonenie ot alimentov (Russia): evasion or reduction of child support payments by a parent, normally the father.

Vorovskie passporta (Russia): counterfeit passports.

Vote buying/Vote selling (Western Balkans): practice of induced vote-mobilisation.

Voto di scambio (Italy): trading electoral votes for short-term benefits, pay or favours.

Vrtičkarstvo (Slovenia): establishing and maintaining garden-plots by landless urban households in order to improve welfare.

Xiaochanquan (China): informal settlements with limited property rights, built on collectively owned rural land in 'villages within the city' and peri-urban areas.

Xiaoerni (China): a family's second-born girl; the girl has an elder sister which is given to another family in order to have a son, meaning that she grows up in an adoptive family.

(Za)chachmęcenie (Poland): practice of self-help involving non-transparency and elements of rule-bending or free-riding.

Zaniato (Abkhazia and Nagorno-Karabakh, Caucasus): lit. 'taken', occupying empty property and marking the building as 'taken'.

Znaki vnimaniya (Russia and FSU): gifts to teachers and physicians, intended to show respect and appreciation.

Index

3Qs, 366
9/11 attacks, 93
996 system, 79
8050 problem, 87

a molestar a otra lado, 220–3, 607
abduction, *see* kidnapping
Abkhazia, 437, 450–4, 614
abortion, 28, 30, 36–8, 144
absurdity, 85
abuse, 152
accountability, 56, 106, 287, 361, 368, 467, 494, 531
accounting, creative, 380, 383
activism, 91, 122, 166, 454, 489–90, 497, 506, 507, 519, 521, 522
administration, 205, 210–11, 213, 266, 267, 297, 318, 360–1, 425, 464, 484, 486–7, 492, 525, 534, 541, 544, 545, 601, 603
   federal, 95, 219
   local, 218, 468, 490, 527, 528
   public, 299, 415–17, 491
   regional, 254
   religious 528
adoption, 38–41, 42, 43
adult education, 442
advantage, gaining an 275–304
advertising, 113, 114, 280, 572, 573
Afghanistan, 175, 481, 492–4, 520, 523–6, 529–31, 603, 609–11
Africa, 255, 369, 394, 395, 502
   North, 298, 412–14, 421, 613
   sub-Saharan, 290, 362, 420–3, 610
   West, 293
Afro-Brazilian religions, 577–9
age, 87, 517–35, 550–2
ageism, 518–19
agriculture, 79, 318, 320–2, 400, 423–4, 446, 263
ahbap-çavuş ilişkisi, 197–9, 540, 607
aid
   first, 249
   humanitarian, 522
AIDS/HIV, 90, 91
ala kachuu, 144–7, 165, 607
Albania, 37, 172–5, 257, 470, 486–8, 490–1, 608
alcohol, 235, 244
   counterfeit, 377, 378
   homemade, 191–5
   see also pečenje rakije; *rakija*
alga aploksnē, 324
alimony evasion, 29, 30, 53–6
allotments, 438, 465, 466
altruism, 233
amakudari, 87, 520, 531–5, 607
ambiguities, 21, 94, 118, 123–4, 156, 208, 276, 378, 424, 440, 499
ambivalence, 20
   elderly care, 559–64
   emotional, 20, 22, 27–30
   functional, 21, 22, 561, 563
   mastering, 21–3
   motivational, 21, 22, 561, 563
   normative, 21, 22, 561
   sociological, 20–1
   substantive, 21, 561, 563
   types of, 1, 21–3
amici, 538–40
ancestors, 591–4
andare in giro, 345–7, 607
anonymity, 21, 110, 121–3, 125, 499
anthropologists, 17, 30, 38, 106, 218, 372, 422, 493, 529
anthropology, 17, 106, 107, 175, 211
anti-corruption campaigns, 28, 217, 238, 250, 288, 291, 300
apartheid, 365
apartments, 48, 75, 189, 333, 419–20, 438, 450, 458–9, 461, 464
appointments, 171, 196, 267, 384, 416, 485, 489, 491, 493, 502, 533, 534, 547–8
appreciation, tokens of, 234–41, 248
aqsaqal, 527–9, 607
area studies, 3, 12, 18–19
Argentina, 218, 283, 364, 487, 521
argot, 200, 203
aristocracy, 287
Armenia, 38, 141, 160–3, 188–91, 610
Armenians, 326, 450
arrangements, informal, 28, 54, 321, 332
arrests, 482, 551
art, 117–21, 536
ashar, 246, 247–9, 607
Asia, 369, 377, 461
   see also Central Asia; East Asia; South Asia; Southeast Asia

615

assistance, mutual, 204, 208, 216, 242, 251–4, 256, 260, 262, 263
astrology, 519, 545–9, 551
asylum seekers, 95, 321
atheism, 550
aumento, 278, 294–7, 505, 607
Australia, 89, 91, 93, 95, 156–60, 607
Austria, 50–3, 205, 384, 613
authenticity, 73, 109–14, 117, 165, 169, 378, 398–9, 477, 479, 577–9
authoritarian regimes, 448, 480
autonomy, 160, 338
Azerbaijan, 38, 330, 413, 585–8, 609

babushki, 29, 56–9, 607
bajalica, 568–9
bajanje, 568–71, 607
baksheesh, 290, 298
baksy, 564–7, 607
Balkan trep music, 88–9
Balkans, 142, 174, 175, 395, 480, 486–92, 568–71, 607, 609, 612, 614
Bangladesh, 535, 604
Bangkok, 548
bank(s), banking, 204, 247, 249, 254, 522, 523
    mobile, 221–2
banqueting, 214–17
baptism, 192
bargaining, 215
    see also negotiations
barter, 314–15, 332, 334
    see also exchange; reciprocity
bazaars, 254, 398, 399, 497
begging, 221, 245, 282
Belarus, 121–2, 330, 465, 590
Belgium, 401–2, 420
Belgrade, 463, 464
belonging, 183, 187–220, 241–4
beriozka, 249
    see also komissionki
betrothal gifts, 141, 142–4, 145
bid rigging, 534
bin diwar, 358, 382, 383–5, 607
birth, 27, 29–36
birthright tourism 28, 31–3
bitcoin, 121, 126
blackmail, 77
blaga rakija, 161
blanket party, 85
blat, 20, 187, 188, 198, 209, 242, 243, 249–50, 251, 278, 331, 604
blockchain, 107
blogs, 113
body doubling, 373
Bogotá, 469
Bolivia, 218, 279, 283
border(s), 393–6, 442
    border control officers, 394
    border crossings, 300–4
    border patrol, 295
    see also boundaries
Bosnia and Herzegovina, 175, 394–5, 465, 486–91, 505–8, 611
bots, 116, 117, 118–19
bottles and cans recycling, 342–5

bottom-up approaches, 4–5, 12
boundaries, 395
    see also borders
boys, 36–9, 51, 75, 77, 123, 128, 175, 573
Brazil, 9, 28, 209, 332, 487, 577–9, 604, 611
bribes, 76, 77–8, 183, 205, 235, 238, 265, 266, 267, 278, 281, 288–92, 293, 295, 299, 300, 366–7, 394, 417, 503–4, 525, 545
bride brokers, 37–8
bride price, 141, 142–4, 145, 151, 164
bride price, 260
bridezilla, 141, 156–60, 607
brokerage, 77, 118, 120
brokers, 3–87, 47–9, 78, 118, 410, 412–17
Budapest, 499
Buddhism, 237, 581
Bulgaria, 89, 278, 297–300, 500, 612
Bulgarian train, 488
bureaucracy, 75, 198, 206, 209, 218, 296, 297, 359, 592
bureaucratisation, 559
bureaucrats, gifts to, 238
burrnesha, 172–5, 608
buses, 302–3, 340–1, 402
business ethics, 246–7
business sector 216–17, 220–3, 252, 254, 279, 290, 331, 365–8, 380–3, 534, 544–5

caciquismo, 485, 541–3, 608
caili, 75, 142–4, 608
camaraderie, 408
Cambodia, 237
campaigns, 38, 52, 165, 200, 218, 281, 287, 317, 344, 424, 449, 478–9, 485, 488–90, 496, 499, 522
    anti-corruption, 28, 217, 238, 250, 288, 291, 300
camps, 345–7, 419, 440
cans recycling, *see* bottles and cans recycling
Canada, 31–3, 95, 371–4, 608
candidates, 41–2, 44, 53, 80, 185, 198–9, 217, 280, 287–8, 327, 480, 483–4, 498–9
Candomblé, 577
cannabis, 313
capital
    cultural, 71, 347, 405, 441
    maternity, 46–50
    moral, 587
    symbolic, 521
    see also social capital
capitalism, 125, 246, 259, 368, 535
    crony, 198
    petty, 120
    surveillance, 107
caporalato, 320–2, 324, 608
care/caring
    commodification, 560
    elderly 559–64
    family members, 559, 561–4
    gender, 562–3
    institutional, 561, 562, 564
    lay healers, 573–7, 579–83
    medical, *see* folk medicine; health care

professionals, 560–1
residential, 519
spells, 568–71
spiritual healing, 571–3
Caribbean, 369
carnival, 276
carousel voting, 488
cash, 297–300
charitable donation, 245, 246
corruption, 294–7
gifts, 235, 260–1, 263–5, 292–4
for good reviews, 110
transactions, 280
vote buying/selling, 486–8
cassa comune, 252
cassa peota, 251–4, 608
caste, 535–7
catfishing, 123–6, 608
Catholicism, 581, 583–5, 603
Caucasus, 164, 326, 437, 450–4, 571–3, 613, 614
North, 49, 571, 573
South, 571
Cayman Islands, 374–6
celebrations, 260–1, 262
Central America, 208, 278, 279–81, 608
Central Asia, 129, 142, 151, 163–6, 241, 248, 255, 326, 497, 521, 527, 567, 610
Central Europe, 14, 480
ceremonies, 267, 547
see also rituals
chaa pani, 278, 289–92, 608
chabolismo, 443–6, 608
chachmęcenie, 278, 284–6, 614
chaikhana, 241, 242, 243, 244
chanchullo, 278, 279–81, 608
charities, 244–7, 252, 499, 586, 604
charlatanry, 578
charms, 568–71
chav, 89
cheating, 76–9, 279, 359
chelnoki, 328
chéngzhōngcūn, see *xiaochanquan*
chernaya kassa, 254–7, 608
child support, 29, 30, 53–6, 172
childbirth, 27, 29–36
childcare, 164, 370
children, 28–9, 38–46, 50–3, 56–9, 69–72, 80, 96, 168, 171–2, 235, 334, 571–3
see also youth
Chile, 9, 197, 218, 279, 283, 382
China, 19, 20, 31–3, 38–41, 73–6, 79–81, 95, 108–12, 116, 118, 120, 122, 127, 141, 142–4, 148–50, 166–9, 187, 188, 197, 209, 214–17, 237, 263, 264, 377, 408, 437–8, 454–8, 568–9, 591–4, 604, 608, 609, 611, 613, 614
chorizo, 279
christening, 44–5 see also family relations; godparents
Christianity, 561, 569, 570, 588–91
Orthodox, 192, 549–51, 568, 574–7, 581, 588, 590
chuồng cọp, 438, 458–62, 608
churning, 371–4, 608

circular economy, 345, 347
citizenship, 28, 31–3, 153–5, 204, 205, 206, 395, 410
civil servants, 235, 520, 531–5, 539, 544
civil service, 205, 216
civil society, 213, 478, 480, 519, 604
civil wars, 58, 152, 154, 443, 444, 524, 541
clans, 538–40
class(es), 149, 150, 187, 407
lower, 252, 337
middle, 32, 58, 80, 82, 116, 167, 261, 372, 469–70
upper, 116, 169, 313
see also aristocracy
working, 497
click-farming, 109, 116
clientelism, 218, 298, 365, 416, 479, 482–3, 538, 540, 541–2
political, 197, 205, 217, 486–9, 491–2
clients, 29, 32, 44, 48, 212, 222, 240, 337, 346–7, 371–4, 394, 488, 492, 533, 538–9, 543, 551–2, 570, 577 579, 581–3
clienti, 538–9
climate change, 2, 93
clothes, 220, 260
club(s)
Bilderberg, 5
Club, The (London), 4
History of Ideas Club (Baltimore), 4
nightclubs, 205
Ration Club (London), 4
Vienna Circle, 4
clutter, 371–4
coercion, 543
coercive control, 141
cognitive impairment, 562–3
cohabitation, 170–1
cohesion, 12, 70, 72, 184, 244, 361, 478
social, 106, 259, 604
coima, 295, 296
collective action, 14, 247–9
collective identities, 195
see also belonging; identities
collectivism, 234
collusion, 279–80, 281, 381, 520, 534
Colombia, 281, 410, 469
colonialism, 15, 220, 279, 293, 339, 340, 369, 407–8, 504, 541
colonias, 9, 436, 439–43, 608
combina, 357, 358–61, 608
command economies, 325
commissions, 413, 414
Commonwealth of Independent States, 377
communism, 15, 75, 82, 166, 203, 278, 284, 285, 401, 406, 463, 507, 530, 570
Communist Party, 166, 462
communities
closed, 196, 539
ethnic, 294
imagined, 395
local, 4, 22, 39, 246, 248, 347, 464, 522
rural, 574
village, 263
compadrazgo, 197, 297, 535
compensation, 57, 142, 168, 206, 315, 414, 487, 522

INDEX   617

competition, 79–81, 111, 115, 142, 144, 250, 290, 294, 326, 342, 360, 375–6
competitiveness, 28, 74, 79–80, 222, 375, 543, 602
concubines, 166, 168
confidence, 296, 377, 551, 552
conformity, 505–8
Confucianism, 75, 81, 185, 591
connections, 29, 31, 70, 72, 110, 148, 186, 190, 215, 232, 250, 327, 355, 358, 361, 465, 528, 565
  emotional, 215, 216
  informal, 243, 416
  network, 30, 216, 250–1, 414–15, 544
  personal, 10, 203–6, 210–13, 359–60, 413, 464
  political, 366, 416, 439, 486, 533
  social, 216, 219, 413
consensus, 16, 105, 163, 244, 493, 523, 547
consent, 126–7, 129, 140, 144–7, 170, 466, 494, 542
  sexual, 90, 92
constituencies, 240, 279, 287
constitutions, 280, 365, 422, 494, 524–5, 537, 549
constraints, xxi, xxiii, 22, 117, 461
construction sector, 315, 318, 322, 323, 325, 326, 328, 331, 346, 418, 534
consumerism, 157–8, 166
contacts, 34, 219, 243, 346, 359, 412, 413, 488, 587
  informal, 11, 83, 327, 534
  personal, 331, 345, 401
  political, 365
  social, 188–91
contempt, 127, 289, 316, 335
context sensitivity, 20–1, 23
contraception, 91, 92
contract-for-deed system, 441
contractors, 324, 368, 537, 603
contracts, 105, 169, 315, 318, 320–7, 331–2, 408, 418, 537, 602
  civil, 150
  government, 358, 365–8, 492
  job, 324, 559
  political, 288
  rent-to-buy, 444
  social, 188, 345, 461, 477
  working mother, 582
control, 29, 34–6, 54, 56, 95, 130, 141, 147, 156, 158, 160–1, 163, 165, 220, 259, 279, 320–1, 323, 326, 338–40, 380–1, 394, 396–7, 399, 400, 419, 424, 437, 446, 451, 461, 502, 526, 536, 537, 594
  informal, 22, 357, 541
  mechanisms, 163
  political, 482–3, 541, 548
  social, 541–3, 574, 592
co-optation, 22, 494, 541–3, 587
coronation ceremony, 547
corruption, 45, 169, 183, 186, 199, 209, 213, 216, 217, 235–6, 238, 267, 288–97, 300, 360, 361, 365–8, 380, 448, 480, 485, 502, 503, 505, 534, 544, 604
  elite, 76
  official, 167
  petty, 76, 293
  political, 198, 218, 240, 255, 367–8, 479, 486
  systemic, 77, 210, 291
Corruption Perception Index (CPI) 544
Corsica, 538–40, 612
councils of elders, 527–9
counterfeit goods, 358, 362, 364, 377–9
counterfeit passports, 397, 398–9
court jesters, 276
courtesy, 81
COVID-19 pandemic, 93, 94–6, 166, 205, 248–9, 383, 519, 551
CPI (Corruption Perception Index), 544
creative accounting, 380, 383
credit, 249–59, 296
crime, 200–1, 341, 442
criminal economy, 313, 315
criminal networks, 49
criminal organisations, 321
criminality, 84, 278, 379, 381–2
Croatia, 175, 194, 382, 394–5, 469, 486, 488–9, 505–8, 611
crony capitalism, 198
cronyism, 186, 218, 359
cross-disciplinarity, 17–18, 23
  see also interdisciplinarity
Cuba, 218, 409–12, 611
cultural capital, 71, 347, 405, 441
cultural informality, 435
cumătrism, 28–9, 44–6, 608
custom law, 543–5
customers, 220–3, 249–51
customs, 38, 44, 46, 151, 168, 231, 245, 529, 570
customs officers/officials, 299
cyber
  crime, 118, 120
    security, 116
  space, 105–31, 591, 593–4
  stalking, 128
Cyprus, 203–6, 376, 450, 452, 611

dachas, 465, 466
Dagestan, 573
dalali, 120, 542
dastorkon, 255, 256
dating, 123–6, 129–31, 149
dead
  commemoration of the, 192, 588–91
  communication with the, 570
  rituals of, 192, 591–4
  worship of, 591–4
  see also funerals; rituals
death, 245
  approaching, 564
  digitalising, 591–4
  see also funerals
débrouille, 420–3, 610
debts, 247, 296–7, 523
deception, 377–8
decision makers, 605
deep fakes, 106, 128–9
dementia, 562
democracy, 477–9, 481–2, 486, 494, 498, 517, 526, 541–3

Democratic Republic of the Congo (DRC), 422
demolitions, 443, 446, 448
Denmark, 314, 316
dependency work, 564
deportation, 155, 321, 323
despotism, 482
developed economies, xix, 17, 31, 191, 312, 319
development studies, 4, 231
dichotomies, 19, 23
digital age, 105–31, 591, 593–4
diligence, 80, 81
disability, 42–3, 47, 344
   fake, 334
disapproval, 52, 221
discipline, 83–6, 201
discretion, 36, 56, 83, 154, 425, 542
discretionary power, 54, 417
discrimination, 220–3, 346
   gender, 184–5
dishonesty, 284–6
dismissal, 220–3
dissent, 166, 481
distributed ledger technologies (DLTs), 107
distrust, 280, 319, 368, 480, 484, 502, 520
diversity, 36, 185, 188, 307, 345, 361, 394
divination, 547–8, 566–8, 570–1, 578
divlja gradnja, 438, 462–5, 608
divorce, 29, 30, 53–6, 58, 140–1, 147, 152–3, 155, 168
doctors, 30, 34, 235, 236, 300, 560, 566, 572
domestic labour, 164–5, 167, 370, 407, 408
domestic violence, 75, 128, 147, 152, 165–6
dominance, 15, 58, 93, 168, 337, 366, 368, 537, 602
domination, 21, 160, 293, 339, 341, 365, 368, 416
Dominican Republic, 218
donors, 260–2, 501–2, 584
double deed, 21
double incentives, 21
double Irish, 357, 374–6, 608
   with a Dutch sandwich, 375
double motivation, 21
double standards, 20, 21–2, 159, 161, 198, 199, 563
doublethink, 505
   see also double deed; double incentives; double motivation; double standards; double utility; paradoxes
dowries, 142, 147, 164
doxing, 121–3, 608
driving licences, 293
drugs, 313, 446
duang muang, 519, 545–9, 609
Dubai, 408
duit kopi, 278, 290, 292–4, 609

earnings, *see* salaries; wages
East Asia, 263
East Germany, 401
Eastern Europe, 14, 332–3, 377, 395, 468, 480, 603
Eastern Europeans, 320
economic migration, 400–2
   see also migration

economic status, 148–50, 165, 166–9, 171, 256
economies
   command, 325
   formal, 32, 294, 503
   informal, 6–9, 311–47, 369, 402, 422, 434, 461, 503
   market, 250, 260, 261, 298–9, 332, 336, 458, 535
   planned, 33, 254, 260
   second, 249–50
   shadow, 6, 188, 297, 313
Ecuador, 221, 410
education, 32, 47, 51–3, 71, 148, 149, 171, 189, 191, 219, 248, 299, 300, 442
   adult, 442
   higher, 76–80, 235, 360, 528, 533–4
   lesbian sex, 89–93
   online, 96
   pre-school, 80
   primary, 235
   sex, 89–93
Egypt, 470, 604
ehsan, 585–8, 609
El Salvador, 218, 280
elders, 59, 258, 418, 517–35, 550–2, 559–64, 588
elections, 287–8, 449, 478–80, 482–8, 496, 522, 542, 549, 551
   parliamentary, 238, 487, 499, 501
   presidential, 53, 280, 449, 487
electoral campaigns, 281, 489
electoral fraud, 280
electoral funding, 545
electoral support, 212
elites, 76, 168, 218, 439, 478, 506, 522, 544, 548
   economic, 221
   intellectual, 286
   political, 14, 204, 221, 255, 368, 421, 464, 520, 523, 548–9
elopement, 144, 146
embeddedness, 234
employment, 183, 185–6, 189–91, 196, 219, 360, 369, 379–85, 400–2, 406–9, 418
   formal, 317
   informal, 17, 55, 311–42
   opportunities, 9, 87, 330, 402, 454, 490, 537
enchufismo, 217–20, 609
enforcement, 32, 39, 54, 56, 72, 161, 201, 231, 256, 371, 398, 440, 522, 533, 550
   law, 49, 146, 147, 155, 280, 290, 328, 379, 459, 470, 498, 542, 544
   selective, 146, 151, 343, 396, 441
   social, 232
entertainment, 117–21
entrepreneurship, 115, 118, 120, 167, 245–7, 256, 301, 325–6, 327, 331, 346, 355–85, 410, 420, 440
envelopes, 289
   gift, 215, 260–1, 264–5
   red, 215, 263
   see also rituals
ernai, 166–9, 609
Estonia, 330

esusu, 254
ethics, 106, 110, 118, 246, 425, 426, 559
ethnic networks, 393–6
ethnicities, 139, 147, 195, 242, 293–4, 301, 343, 347, 365–6, 369–71, 393–6, 500, 502, 522, 525, 527–8, 566
ethnography, 27–9, 107, 108, 130, 153, 161, 163, 166, 192, 235, 250, 285, 325, 337, 372, 468, 568–9
etiquette, 208, 309, 335
etymology, 203, 206, 285, 320, 355, 400, 564, 571, 590
euphemisms, xxiii, 74, 76, 78, 219, 290, 292, 295, 504, 505
European Commission, 183, 298, 375, 376, 377
European Union, 82, 96, 119, 194, 218, 254, 298, 301, 315, 321, 347, 374–6, 401, 406, 467–8, 491
Eurozone crisis, 468
evasion, tax, 54, 314, 330, 376, 470, 605
everyday life, 33, 47, 57, 67, 252, 301, 316, 319, 484, 538, 586
evictions, 446, 450, 522
evil eye, 571–2, 574–7
exams, 76, 78, 279
exchange, xxiv, 18, 20, 45, 47, 73, 76–8, 106, 107, 118, 166, 204, 205, 215, 216, 236, 266, 288, 296–7, 322, 338, 358, 416, 487–9, 492, 500, 504–5, 533, 535, 539, 542, 559–60, 574, 577, 592–3
  economic, 255, 592–3
  of favours, 197, 207, 211, 214, 249, 267, 296, 315, 365, 413, 485
  informal, 6, 21, 236, 263–5, 313–16, 414, 456
  market(-type), 413
  monetary, 34, 263–5, 290, 299, 323, 585
  networks, 297
  non-market, 335
  reciprocal, 240
  sexual-economic, 152
  social, 21, 69, 297
  vote, 479–81, 482–6, 503
exclusivity, 221
exorcism, 576
expatriates, 406–9
expenses, 81, 146–7, 169, 217, 241, 243, 255, 257, 261, 281, 219
expertise, 1, 2, 5, 12–13, 30, 68, 91, 106, 327, 345, 372, 417, 481, 501, 548, 563, 578
experts, 34, 43, 52, 58, 95, 112, 113, 165, 175, 190, 374, 378, 379, 548, 562
exploitation, 12, 27, 31, 38, 41, 128, 131, 155, 201, 204, 212, 278, 296, 317, 321, 358, 360, 380–2, 397, 411, 421, 436, 441, 481, 498, 503–4, 536–7, 559–60
export(s), 411 171, 281, 347
exposure, 79, 106, 114, 117, 121, 127, 153, 323, 343, 487
expressions of gratitude, 234–41, 248, 297, 299–300
extended families, xxv, 40, 58, 141, 204, 231, 536, 563, 573
extensions to buildings, 438, 458–62
extortion, 267, 290, 293, 299, 577
extrasensory perception, 549–50

façades, 14, 27, 55, 115, 296, 304, 323, 324, 380, 383, 459, 461, 494
face, 73–6, 80, 256, 261, 292
see also reputation
fake
  documents, 76, 78–9
  employees, 379–85
  followers, 114–17
  goods, 358, 362, 364, 377–9
  identity, 123–6, 128–9
  news, 125, 368 136
  Reviews, 108–12
fakelaki, 204, 205, 293, 298, 502
families/family relations, 27, 29, 38–44, 50–9, 81–2, 140–52, 160, 162–5, 233–4, 243, 244, 361, 402, 404–9, 559–64
  close, 162, 255, 265
  daughters, 29, 37–41, 57, 59, 75, 146, 152, 160, 171, 187, 367, 381, 404, 551, 561
  extended, xxiv, 40, 58, 141, 204, 231, 536, 563, 573
  fathers, 29, 30, 37, 55–9, 148, 185, 187, 219
  grandparents, 29, 56–7, 59, 141, 164
  host, 215, 265
  husbands, 29, 36–7, 46, 51. 72, 75, 148, 152, 156, 163–5, 167–8, 171, 174, 187, 257, 404–6, 524
  in-laws, 46, 163–4
  mothers, xxiv, 27–32, 34–5, 42, 46–7, 50–3, 55, 56–8, 70, 75, 93, 146, 160, 162, 164, 185, 521, 568, 581–2
  nuclear, 27, 57, 93, 164, 484
  parents, 27, 31–2, 36, 37, 39–44, 47, 49, 53–5, 57, 59, 71, 75–6, 80, 86–7, 130, 140–6, 149, 160, 162–4, 219, 233, 260, 299, 318, 319, 538, 564
  poor, 587
  sons, 37–9, 164
  spouses, 71, 140, 142, 144, 149, 153–4, 155, 170, 172, 283, 406–9
  see also husbands; wives
  wives, 46, 70, 75, 142, 146, 148, 151, 152, 155, 156, 166–72, 243, 406–9, 526, 536, 551
see also marriage; relationships
fanju, 214–17, 609
farmers, 233, 320–2, 339, 423–4
farms, 263, 318, 321, 423–4, 440, 446, 590
  collective, 326, 331
favouritism, 186, 196, 197, 205, 218, 359, 366–7
see also favours: exchange of
favours, 46, 216, 219, 231–4, 235, 240, 289, 292–4, 297, 360, 394, 413, 483, 485, 534, 538, 540, 578, 605
  administrative, 486, 487, 492
  ambivalence of, 21
  economies of, 324, 334, 401, 414
  exchange of, 197, 206–12, 214, 249, 267, 296, 315, 365, 413, 485
  personal, 195
  short-term, 482
  social exchange of, 204–5, 604
fazaee, 382, 383–5, 607
feasts, 252, 253, 585–8
see also festivities, 215

femininity, 158–60, 163, 174, 582
feminism, 159, 161, 166, 560
fencing of stolen goods, 315
fertility, 39–40, 49
fictitious employees, 379–85
films, 85, 124, 156, 159, 203, 288–9, 298, 328, 537
finagling, 286
fines, 41, 48, 194, 215, 328, 346
Finland, 300–4, 543–5, 610
folk medicine, 568–71
folklore, 275–6, 565, 590, 604
follower buying, 114–17, 126, 609
food, 81–3, 214–17, 241, 243, 244, 248, 252, 253, 256, 258, 282, 290, 498–500, 585–91
forced marriage, 140, 165
forgery, 381–2, 398–9
formal
  channels, 189, 211, 322
  constraints, xxi, xxiii, 22, 117, 461
  economies, 32, 294, 503
  employment, 17, 317, 528
  institutions, 4, 8, 13, 15, 16, 19–20, 87, 198, 209, 304, 319, 360, 403, 416, 424–6, 562, 604
  procedures, 198, 209, 365, 417, 468
  rules, 16, 17, 208–10, 235, 319, 323, 360, 415–16, 425, 603–5
  sector, 15, 312, 341
  systems, 321
formalisation, 12, 56, 254, 319, 322, 337, 448, 559
formality, 19, 118, 419, 424, 603, 604
fortune-telling, 551–2
foster care, 41–4
France, 11, 69–72, 112, 118, 126–7, 290, 293, 315, 317–20, 420, 533, 610, 614
fraud, 48–50, 78, 111, 117, 279–81, 330, 381, 572, 577, 585, 604
freedom, 275–7, 338
  of expression, 506
  of movement, 301
  of speech, 506
free-riding, 281–4, 290, 361
friendship, 197–9, 257, 284, 334, 538–40
  see also relationships
fronting, 368
FSU, *see* Soviet Union: former
Fundamentalist Mormonism, 140, 168
funerals, 142, 192, 248, 260, 263, 265, 585–8
  see also rituals

Gabor Roma, 140–1
galoppini, 483
gangmasters, 320–2
gaps, 242, 256
gardens
  community, 465
  plots, 438, 465–9
  see also dachas
gaser, 88–9, 609
gastarbeiter(y), 328
gatecrashing, 282
gatekeepers, 467, 603
  brokerage, 118

gender
  caregiving, 562–3
  change of, 142
  discrimination, 184–5
  earnings gap 51–2, 187
  employment, 51–3, 187
  gatherings, 243–4
  identity, 159, 172–5
  imbalance, 141, 142–4
  inequality, 8, 51, 55–6, 75, 91, 96, 159, 563
  norms, 162, 523
  power-struggle, 576
  religion, 567, 573
  roles, 53, 402
  selective abortion, 36–41
  social exclusion 183–8
  violence, 96
  see also domestic violence
gendered 28, 55, 56, 128, 154, 159, 183, 187, 243, 244, 402, 406, 407, 521, 523, 562, 563, 573, 580
generosity, 237, 240, 287, 331, 344, 367, 504, 584, 587
Georgia, 38, 249–51, 450–4, 611
German Democratic Republic, *see* East Germany
Germany, 50–3, 314, 342–5, 400–1, 465, 612, 613
  see also East Germany
gerontocracy, 517
gestalt, 20
Ghana, 77, 125, 287–9, 338–42, 611, 614
ghost employees, 379–85
gift-giving, 160, 162, 236–7, 263, 267, 287–8, 297, 299
gifts, 30, 41, 44, 88, 130, 145, 191, 215, 234–41, 260–2, 265–7, 278, 287–90, 292–4, 297–300, 313, 588–91, 592
  to academics, 235, 236
  alcohol, 235
  betrothal, 142–3
  dead, remembering the, 588–90
  exchange of, 21, 45, 73, 82, 266
  flowers, 235
  funeral, 263
  return, 263
  wedding, 160, 162, 263
gig economy, 322, 331, 602
girls, 36–40, 51, 70, 75, 77, 123, 128, 152, 175
global financial crisis, 93
globalisation, 221, 259
gorroneo, 278, 281–4, 609
governance, 196–7, 358, 383, 415, 424, 480, 592
  informal, 6, 15, 17, 245, 367–8, 466, 493, 524, 530, 531, 541
government(s), 216, 217, 279, 281, 290, 360, 371, 411, 424, 426, 403, 436–9, 441–2, 446, 462, 468–9, 481, 501–2, 507, 533, 604
  contracts, 358, 365–8
  officials, 215, 365–8, 397
governor(s)
  district, 493–4
  lokalni šerifi, 416
  provincial, 501–2

INDEX 621

gratitude, tokens of, 297, 299–300
gratuities, 290, 297
Greece, 203–6, 293, 298, 469, 502, 574–7, 601, 610, 611
greed, 20, 28, 283, 290, 319, 469, 470
  see also need
Greek Orthodox Church, 574–7
grey
  areas, 115, 118, 319
  city concept, 438
  salaries, 54–6
  shades of 17
  wages 54, 55, 56
  zones, xviii, 12, 14, 19, 20, 22, 320, 326, 346, 347, 377, 438, 583
  see also gray zone, 332
growing up, 67–96
grypsowanie, 200–3, 609
guanxi, 20, 41, 73–4, 111, 148, 187, 188, 197, 209, 215, 216, 537, 592, 604
Guatemala, 220–3, 279–81, 607
guest workers, 326
Guyana, 410, 411

habilitación, 296
hackers, 121, 126
hacktivism, 126
Haiti, 410
halapénz, 298
haltuura, 330
Hanoi, 438, 458–62
haopingfanxian, 110
hashtags, 117
hawala, 290
health care, 29–30, 32–6, 90–2, 95–6, 118, 189, 194, 205, 209, 235, 236, 248–9, 298–9, 300, 360, 425, 518, 560–1, 566–71
hemşehricilik, 195–7, 394, 540, 609
hierarchy, xxvi, 35, 51, 57, 82, 94–5, 142, 148, 158, 162, 164, 197, 200–2, 204, 237, 240, 277, 288, 380–1, 405, 529, 541, 578–9
higher education, 76–80, 235, 360, 528, 533–4
hikikomori, 86–7, 609
Hispanic America, 281–4
HIV/AIDS, 90, 91
hoarding, 284, 372
holistic spirituality, 580–3
homelessness, 344, 417–20, 463, 466, 467, 523
homophobia, 91, 93
homosexuality, 89–93
Honduras, 280
Hong Kong, 122, 167
hongbao, 260, 263
honour, 130, 160, 163, 164, 173, 174, 200, 201, 208, 250, 255, 538, 539, 540
  code of, 201, 208, 255
hospitality, 70, 164, 192, 221, 241, 255, 289, 290, 587
  hostesses, 71
hospitals, 28, 32, 34, 118, 199, 209, 249, 332, 360, 381, 420, 449, 566, 584
  psychiatric, 551

house renovation and decoration, 325, 327, 328, 331
housework, 164–5, 167, 370, 407, 408
housing, 48–9, 58, 80, 189, 433–70, 522, 523
hukou, 40–1, 80
humour, 85, 203, 286, 288–9, 519
Hungary, 298, 376, 395, 465, 480, 498–500, 610
hymenoplasty, 163

identities, 82
  bridal, 158–9
  collective, 183, 187–220, 241–4
  consumer, 157–8
  ethnic, 195
  fake, 123–6, 128–9
  gender, 159, 172–5
  group, 82, 231, 421
  national, 163, 423–4
  networks, 184
  nonconsensual revealing of, 121–3, 126–9
  youth culture, 89
identity documents, 396
  see also passports
ihsan, see *ehsan*
ill health, 246
  see also health care
illegality, 15, 28, 41, 76, 116, 118, 121, 146, 147, 154–5, 209, 249, 285, 291, 292–3, 314, 315, 316, 322, 325–6, 462–5, 486–7
imams, 529, 566
immigration, 32, 94–5, 196, 250, 293, 315, 317, 361–2, 367, 400–1, 403, 408, 440, 443–4, 466
impartiality, 21, 237, 290, 415, 560
impersonation, 123–6
imports, 301, 409–12
impunity, 279, 542
inclusions, 12, 21, 82, 183, 187–8, 419, 448
independence, 147, 156, 171, 212, 234, 339, 340, 502, 582, 590
independent media, 92, 262
India, 9, 38, 96, 116, 120, 127, 278, 289–92, 406–9, 437, 535–7, 542, 608, 614
indigenous peoples, 220, 287, 295–7, 481, 503–5
individualism, 234
Indonesia, 152, 406–7, 408
indulgence, 583–5, 609
inequality, 75, 82, 88, 95–6, 142, 143–4, 166, 187, 206, 210, 219–20, 288, 291, 297, 343, 361, 442, 499, 504–5, 520, 522, 529, 605
  gender, 51, 55–6, 75, 91, 96, 159, 563
  income, 96, 166, 220
  political, 499
  racial, 369
  rural–urban, 82
  social, 88, 288, 343, 520, 522, 529
influencers, 112–17
informal
  channels, 34, 464
  connections, 243, 416
  contacts, 11, 327
  control, 22, 357, 541

622 INDEX

economy, 6–9, 311–47, 369, 402, 422, 434, 461, 503
employment, 17, 55, 154, 312
exchange, 6, 21, 197, 236, 265, 414, 480
governance, 6, 15, 17, 245, 367–8, 466, 493, 524, 530, 531, 541
  see also 3Cs model of informal governance, 22
groups 4, 69, 395
housing of the rich, 469–70, 609
influence, 17, 415, 544
institutions, xxiv, 13, 17, 20, 319, 527, 528, 542, 543
markets, 456
networks, 10–12, 19, 29–30, 34, 44–6, 49, 71, 83, 183–8, 195–9, 208–20, 241–4, 250–1, 298, 327, 331, 401–6, 408
norms, 360, 520
payments, 34, 267, 289–300, 315, 320
politics, 15, 479, 521
power, 17, 22, 416, 541, 542, 563–5, 571, 574, 576
practices, xxi–xxv, 1, 2, 5–6, 8, 14, 16–21, 23, 27–30, 34, 46, 124, 140, 149, 196, 198, 205–6, 243, 249–51, 259, 260, 278, 281, 283, 290, 315, 319, 327–3, 331, 345, 359–60, 384, 403, 407–11, 414, 416, 469, 480–1, 485, 493, 499, 519–20, 534, 539, 540, 604
relationships, 28–9, 236
rules, 318, 414–15, 520, 561, 602–3
sector, 15, 311–12, 327–8, 369, 371, 602
services, 326
settlements, 6, 9, 433–70
structures, 332
trading, 280, 362, 371, 395
welfare, 57
informalisation, 267, 419
informality, technical, 434
informality studies, 1–23
information technology, 190
injustice, 206
inner circle, 81
innovation(s), 356, 423–6
institutions
  formal, 4, 8, 13, 15, 16, 19–20, 87, 198, 209, 304, 319, 360, 403, 416, 424–6, 562, 604
  informal, xxiv, 13, 17, 20, 319, 527, 528, 542, 543
  political, 520
  public, 29, 212–13, 218, 279, 315, 383–5, 489, 492, 520
  religious, 151
  state, 213, 236, 319, 383, 489, 520, 601
  total 34, 42, 85–6
instrumentality, xxiv, 20, 21, 173, 197–9, 209, 210, 214–16, 401, 482, 560, 563
insurance, 31, 231, 251–4, 300, 330, 337, 442, 483
intellectual property rights, 377, 379
intermediaries, 73, 78, 110, 114, 117, 155, 203–7, 211, 219, 254, 320–2, 324, 327, 412–14, 478, 481, 483, 520–4, 541, 544, 581, 603
intermediation, 276, 320–1, 414

internal depletion, 79–81
internalisation, 67–8, 72
Internet, xxvi, 2, 13, 30, 48, 80, 106, 112, 113, 115–16, 121–30, 382, 501, 591
intimacy, 123, 126–9, 163, 197, 199
intimidation, 495–6, 520
investments, 37, 57, 72, 76, 114, 204, 206, 208, 233, 252–3, 256, 280, 339, 342, 346, 368, 410, 418, 443, 519, 587
investors, 382, 437, 453
@IPaidABribe, 291
Iran, 151, 152, 382
Iraq, 383–5, 607
Ireland, 357, 374–6, 608
ishk gap zadan, 129–31
Islam, 129–31, 147, 150–3, 156, 163, 168, 170, 244–7, 384, 524, 529–31, 566–7, 573, 585–8
  see also Sharia
isolation, 35, 84, 95–6, 258
  see also social exclusion
Israel, 357, 358–61, 470, 608
Italy, 86, 120, 174, 218, 251–4, 279, 293, 315, 317, 320–5, 332, 345–7, 364, 469, 480–1, 482–6, 500, 607, 608, 612, 614

jaan pehchaan, 290, 537
jajmani, 535–7, 609
jak igrač, 414–17, 609
janteloven, 124, 506
Japan, 53, 81, 86–7, 118, 127, 216, 237, 257–9, 263, 264, 358, 417–20, 520, 531–5, 607, 609, 611
Java, 79
jeitinho, 209, 604
jinmyaku, 534
jirga, 520, 523–6, 531, 609
job
  contracts, 324, 559
  second, 325–35
Jordan, 187
joro, 241–4, 256, 610
judiciary, 415–16
jury service, 518
jus soli, 31, 33
justice, 209, 324, 526, 539, 604–5
  extra-judicial, 123
  personalised, 213

kabel, 18, 210–13, 610
kako mati, 574–7, 610
kameen, 535–7
karmir khndzor, 160–3, 610
kastom, 142
Kazakhstan, 142, 152, 168, 169–72, 195, 244–7, 527–9, 540, 564–7, 607, 613, 614
kelin, 163–6, 610
Kenya, 358, 369–71, 611
Kenya Private Sector Alliance, 371
Kenyan National Association of Street vendors and Traders, 371
kept women, 168, 171
khaltura, 329–32, 610
khamstvo, 29, 33–6, 561, 610
khans, 492–3

khrushchevka, 459
KhTsB, 188–91, 610
kidnapping, 141, 144–7, 165
kinship, 27, 29, 30, 38–41, 44–6, 163, 164, 231, 233, 257, 261–2, 334, 537, 538
　see also families/family relations
kleptocracy, 368
knowledge, 2–3, 18–19, 23
kōden, 263
kombinacja/kombinowani, 286, 405
komissionki, 249
Komsomol construction brigades, 327
Korea, 184–6, 258
　see also South Korea
koshumcha, 260–2, 610
Kosovo, 175, 486–7, 489–91
KRI (Kurdistan region of Iraq), 382, 383–5, 607
krumpliosztás, 479, 498–500, 610
krysha, 542
ksematiasma, 575, 576
kula, 411, 502
　see also feeding
kumstvo, 44
　see also family relations
Kyrgyzstan, 44, 141, 144–7, 151, 241–9, 254–7, 260–2, 436, 447–50, 497, 498, 520–3, 527, 607, 608, 610, 612, 613
kyz jorolor, 243–4

la débrouille, 420–3, 610
labour law, 313, 314
language, 200, 203, 276
Latin America, 218, 220–1, 255, 279, 281, 283, 410, 541, 568, 609, 612
　see also South America
Latvia, 298
law enforcement, 49, 147, 290, 379, 459, 470, 498, 542, 544
legal
　constraints, 38, 56
　frameworks, 94, 116, 119, 128, 146, 152, 153–4, 170, 171, 194–5, 196, 252, 254, 259, 265, 316, 327
　immunity, 44
　informality, 434
　maturity, 140
　principles, 31
legality, 36, 40, 121, 154, 213, 285, 314, 378
les rallyes mondains, 11, 69–72, 610
lesboseksprosvet, 89–93, 610
LGBTQ, 89–93, 94
licences, 154, 209, 336, 338, 347, 361, 369–71, 375, 380, 417, 462, 464, 483
Liechtenstein, 376
line standers, 332–5
Ljubljana, 438, 465–8
lloteria, 254, 257
loans, 247, 522
　interest-free, 249–51, 261
lock-in, 11, 83, 196, 243, 262, 536, 539
logging operations, 295–7
loneliness, 258, 344
longevity, 258
looting, 450, 452
love-work, 560, 563, 564

lower class, 252, 337
Loya Jirga, 524–5, 526
loyalty, 200, 215, 294, 361, 379, 489, 539
lynching, 123

maan tapa, 543–5, 610
Macedonia, 161, 486, 489
machine learning, 128–9
Madrid, 364, 443–6
mafia, 483, 485, 524
magic, 549, 551–2, 568–71, 577–9
Malaysia, 18, 210–13, 278, 290, 292–4, 609, 610
maliks, 481, 492–4, 531, 610
manteros, 362–5, 610
manufacturing sector, 323
Mariana Islands, 33
market, relationship with state and society, 601–2
market economy, 250, 260, 261, 298–9, 332, 336, 458, 535
marketing, 115, 116–17
　see also advertising
marmotagem, 577–9, 611
marriage, 70–2, 75–6, 130, 139–75, 406–9
　arranged, 140, 163–4
　of convenience, 301
　fictive, 153–6
　forced, 525, 526
　remarriage, 140–1, 152, 166–72
　second, 140–1, 152, 166–72
　see also weddings
Martinique, 410
Marxism, 326, 328
masculinity, 29, 55, 167, 174, 186, 187, 243, 338
mass media, 44, 548
material interests, 480–1, 540
material goods, 574
material motives, 259, 344, 384, 469, 484–5
materialism, 149
maternity, 165
　capital, 46–50
maternity care, 29–30, 32–3, 34–6
mating, assortative, 149–50
Mauritania, 420
media, 419, 462, 464, 467, 468, 496, 499, 501, 506, 507, 519, 520–1, 532, 544, 545, 603
　independent, 92
　mass, 44, 548
　national,
　social, 109, 112–17, 131, 139, 158, 221, 249, 573, 588
mediators, 565
　see also brokerage; brokers; intermediaries
medical care/treatment, see health care
medicines, 378, 573, 580
　folk, 194, 569–70
mei bao ma, 31–3, 611
Melanesia, 142
men, 29, 30, 36–8, 51, 55–9, 75, 91, 128, 130–1, 142–57, 160–1, 163–72, 187, 191, 193, 235, 243, 327, 335–8, 340–1, 370, 398, 406–9, 410–11, 418, 493, 494–8, 523–9, 541, 550–1, 567, 573
　women living as, 172–5

mendanghudui, 148–50, 611
mental capacity, 519
mental illness, 167, 344
meritocracy, 219
mertvye dushi, 358, 379–83, 611
meso, 203–6, 611
metalworking sector, 322, 325
metaphors, xvii, 74, 83, 218, 276, 292, 372, 518
Mexico, 206–10, 256, 283, 332, 410, 411, 436, 437, 440, 487, 541–3, 604–5, 608, 612
mianzi, 73–6, 80, 611
microfinance agencies, 522
microfinance, 247, 251
middle class, 32, 58, 80, 82, 116, 167, 261, 372, 469–70
Middle East, 186–7, 298, 412–14, 574, 613
migrant networks, 401–6
migration, 8, 37, 81–3, 95, 152, 153–6, 162, 165, 166–8, 195–6, 255, 261, 301, 315, 317–26, 328–9, 331, 336, 337, 338, 343, 344, 347, 361–2, 393–6, 400–6, 436, 440, 457, 466, 467, 563, 573, 602
  see also rural–urban migration
military, 83–6, 197, 205, 360–1, 384, 542
mingbi, 591–4
minimum wages, 191, 320, 519
mining/miners, 198, 501–2
ministers, 205, 206, 364, 487, 496
minorities, 94–6, 128, 150, 153, 194, 206, 395, 481, 499, 500, 502
misappropriation, 293
mistrust, *see* distrust
moai, 257–9, 611
mobile banking (M-banking), 221–2
mobile phones, 129–31, 147
mobility, social, 202
Moldova, 28–9, 44–6, 500, 588–91, 608, 612
money, 155, 243
  coffee, 293
  for grades, 76, 77–8
  imitation, 592
  laundering, 217
  political waste of, 500–3
Mongolia, 95, 481, 500–3, 611
Montenegro, 36–8, 44, 144, 175, 465, 486–91, 505–8, 568, 611, 613
moonlighting, 325–9, 331, 336
moonshine, 191
moral capital, 587
  see also material interests, materialism
morality, 129
Mormonism, 140, 168
Morocco, 414
mosques, 151, 172, 245, 246, 248, 530
motivational ambivalence, 21, 22, 561, 563
mourning rituals, 260
mulas, 409–12, 611
mullahs, 529–31, 566, 611
multinational companies, 374–6
mungu idekh, 481, 500–3, 611
murder, 147, 166
music, 88–9, 203, 536, 545
mutual help/assistance/aid, 204, 208, 216, 242, 251–4, 256, 260, 262, 263
mysticism, 549–51

mythology, 241, 275–7, 565, 590
mzungu price, 358, 369–71, 611

Nagorno-Karabakh, 437, 450–4, 614
nationalism, 147, 165
natsnoboba, 251
navigating, 21–2, 72, 112, 130, 235, 337, 420, 421
ne talasaj, 479, 505–8, 611
need, 283, 470
  see also greed
negociantes, 410–11
negotiations
  business, 214–15
  commodity distribution, 412
  dispute resolution, 523
  family, 164
  intermediaries, 414, 521–3
  labour, 320, 321
  land, 522–3
  loans, 522
  marital bond, 407
  monetary transactions, 292, 336, 413
  power, 286, 337, 576
  reciprocity, 208
  religious context, 576, 579
  social contexts, 67, 69, 574
  state, 302, 412
  street traders, 371
  vote purchase, 483
  weddings, 157
  see also navigating
neighbourhood associations, 445
neighbourhoods, 71, 82, 208, 242, 249, 251, 340, 346, 395, 440, 442, 445–6, 459, 462, 464, 467, 484
neighbours, 73, 162, 164, 193, 241–2, 244–5, 247–8, 256, 260, 314–15, 422, 451, 461, 467, 485, 539, 586
neijuan, 79–81, 611
neo-institutional theory, 4
neoliberalism, 260, 261, 602
Nepal, 535
nephews, 524
nepotism, 186, 218, 359, 365, 366, 368, 382, 394, 405
Netherlands, 375
networks,
  blat, 20, 187, 188, 198, 209, 242, 243, 249–50, 251, 278, 331, 604
  guanxi, 20, 41, 73–4, 111, 148, 187, 188, 197, 209, 215, 216, 537, 592, 604
  informal, 10–12, 19, 29–30, 34, 44–6, 49, 71, 83, 183–8, 195–9, 208–20, 241–4, 250–1, 298, 327, 331, 401–6, 408
  kinship, 75, 231, 537
  old-boy, 218
  patronage, 237, 240
  personal, 30, 196, 212, 217, 250, 360, 380–2
  social, 22, 34, 72, 167, 184, 189, 191, 194, 195, 214–16, 232, 257, 261, 290, 346, 401, 403, 408, 420, 489, 491, 519, 537, 582, 587
  trust, 401
torpil, 196, 198–9, 204

INDEX   625

New Age, 576–7, 580
new normal, 93–6
New Zealand, 95, 423–6, 611
Newsweek, 121
nghề tay trái, 331
NGOs, 147, 162, 346, 503–4, 604
Nigeria, 76–9, 125, 613
nikoh, 150–3, 156, 611
nisia, 249–251, 611
no. 8 wire, 423–6, 611
nojukusha, 417–20, 611
nokofio, 287–9, 611
nomadism, 163, 183, 245, 247, 260, 565
nomikai, 216
nonconsensual pornography, 126–9, 131
normative ambivalence, 21, 22, 561
norms, xxiv, 16–17, 28, 37, 45, 67, 72, 129,
    160, 186, 262, 277, 328, 361, 402,
    424–5, 505, 526
  ambivalence, 21, 22, 561
  cultural, 234, 422
  democratic, 498
  gender, 162, 523
  informal, 360, 520
  international, 426
  moral, 316
  practical, 394
  religious, 131, 566, 567, 573
  sharing, 231–4
  social, 14, 127, 131, 187, 208–9, 231, 261,
    345, 436, 479, 506–7, 531
  see also etiquette
North Africans, 362
North America, 156–60, 607
North Caucasus, 49, 571
North Macedonia, 89, 414–17, 486–7,
    489–91, 609
Norway, 8

obedience, 165, 415, 480, 480
obligations, 5, 28–30, 45, 53, 72, 85, 107,
    196–8, 204, 208–9, 215, 231–4, 238,
    244, 251, 253, 260–2, 266–7, 317, 332,
    360, 375, 493, 504, 536, 562, 578,
    584, 591–2
obnalichivanie, 46–50, 612
OBON, 497–8, 519–23, 612
occupation of properties, 450–4
officials, 171, 217, 237, 266–7, 279, 288, 291,
    297–300, 361, 367, 370, 380–1, 384,
    398, 442, 461, 478, 520, 525, 531–5,
    541, 550
  colonial, 340
  corrupt, 167
  government, 215, 341, 367–8, 397, 468
  law enforcement, 498
  military, 205
  party, 490
  police, 147
  public, 211, 279, 297–300, 367, 381, 384,
    416–17, 441–2, 478, 533–5
  school, 77
  security, 497
  state, 46, 380, 522
okkul't, 549–52, 612
okurimono no shukan, 237

older people, *see* elders
online shopping, 108–12
open secrets, 34, 45, 55, 217, 219, 292
operationalising informality, 16–17, 23
opposites, coexistence of, 19
opposition, 146, 201, 316
  political, 280, 287–8, 368, 481, 495, 497–8,
    455, 540, 543
organisational informality, 434
organisational theory, 14
Orthodox elders, 550–1
otkat vizy, 300–4, 612
outsiders, 12, 16, 22, 83, 185, 196, 198, 199,
    201, 413–14, 454, 457, 503, 527,
    530, 539
overcharging, 358, 367–71
owners, 79, 252, 254, 318, 324, 339, 342, 346,
    378, 381–2, 461, 468
ownership, 285, 338, 437, 440–2, 450, 453–4,
    456–7, 463, 576

packaging recycling, 342–5
padrino, 44, 542
paga globale, 322–5, 612
Pakistan, 127, 535, 603, 604
palanca, 206–10, 218, 604–5, 612
palyonka, 358, 377–9, 612
pantouflage, 533
paradoxes, 20–1, 22, 111, 160, 209, 278, 331,
    335, 361, 424, 441, 453, 542, 567
parapsychology, 550
parenti, 538–9
pari pod masata, 278, 297–300, 612
parillada, 481, 503–5, 612
parliamentary elections, 487, 499, 501
parovoziki, 41–4, 612
Parteibuchwirtschaft, 205, 384
particularism, 233, 415
parties, 204, 205, 206, 281, 255, 287–8, 366,
    384, 478–80, 482–3, 491, 506, 544
partiti, 538–40, 612
partners, selection, 139–40, 148–50
party membership, 478, 480, 489–91
party soldiers, 479, 480, 488–92, 612
passengers, 299, 303–4, 335–42, 370, 590
passivity, 505–8
passports, 300–1, 304, 328, 396–9, 400
paștele blajinilor, 588–91
patriarchy, 147, 156, 159, 161, 163, 165, 521
patronage, 204, 218, 237–8, 240–1, 296–7,
    324, 359, 367, 416, 479, 484, 489, 491,
    542, 543
  patron–client relations, 211–12, 213, 240,
    242, 287–9, 296–7, 482–3, 535–7, 539,
    542, 604
patrons, 212, 213, 237, 482, 488, 542
payments, 47, 80, 155, 209, 249, 252, 256,
    258, 265, 266, 280, 294, 314, 316–17,
    344, 346, 375, 441, 497
  informal, 34, 267, 289–300, 315, 320
peasants, 161, 169, 249, 286, 396, 443, 537
pečenje rakije, 191–5, 612
peer pressure, 13, 14, 45, 165, 208
peers, 70, 80, 88, 90, 96, 420
pensioners, 334, 335, 341–2, 498, 500
pensions, 57, 58, 314, 319, 334, 341, 344, 518

626 INDEX

peota, 252, 253
perceptions
 business, 218
 consumer, 379
 customary, 37
 external, 72, 73
 gender, 51, 75
 general, 343, 356, 565
 generational, 162
 inequality, 523
 influencers, 113
 marriage, 148
 matrix of, 420, 422
 normality, 93
 political, 198, 368
 public, 195, 205, 480
 self-, 85
 societal, 438, 507
persistence, 28, 51, 153, 195, 197, 210, 231, 234, 251, 320, 321, 399, 424, 425, 440, 462, 480, 491
personal
 connections, 10, 203–6, 211, 213, 359, 413, 464
 contacts, 345, 401
 networks, 30, 196, 212, 217, 250, 360, 380–2
 relationships, 105, 127, 211, 213, 236, 237, 250, 293, 298, 592
personalisation, 21, 36, 84
personal connectedness, 213
persuasion, 113, 145, 503
Peru, 218, 410, 435, 535
petty capitalism, 120
petty corruption, 76, 293
 see also bribery; bribes
petty theft, 284–6
Pfandsammeln, 342–5, 612
Philippines, 44, 237, 254, 437, 542
physicians, *see* doctors
pilferage, 284
pirated goods, *see* fake goods
pituto, 218
planned economies, 33, 254, 260
 see also command economies; communism
poclon, 265–7, 612
pokhorony okurka, 83–6, 612
Poland, 81–3, 120, 121, 200–3, 249, 278, 284–6, 326, 330, 332–5, 394, 400–6, 465, 609, 613, 614
police, 235, 290–2, 295, 346, 362–4, 371, 384, 419, 496, 497
 harassment, 155
 officers, 121, 147, 290, 292, 363, 497
 traffic, 189, 292
political
 apathy, 480
 campaigns, 287, 478–9
  see also electoral campaigns
 clientelism, 197, 205, 217, 486–9, 491–2
 coalitions, 211
 connections, 366, 416, 439, 486, 533
 consultants, 548–9
 corruption, 198, 218, 240, 255, 367–8, 479, 486
 decision-making, 551

elites, 14, 204, 221, 255, 368, 421, 464, 520, 523, 548–9
funding, 544–5
influence, 196–7, 416
legitimacy, 501, 502, 521
mediation, 204, 205, 206
networks, 210–11
opponents, 280, 287–8, 368, 481, 495, 497–8, 455, 540, 543
participation, 477–508, 520–3
parties, *see* parties
patronage, 204
rallies, 478, 489, 496, 497
politicians, 198, 213, 238–40, 281, 287–9, 367, 439, 479, 481, 499, 506, 507, 517, 519, 534, 545
politics, 218, 255, 364, 530, 547–9
polygamy, 140, 142, 150–3, 155–6, 166–72, 170–1
polygyny, 142, 150–3, 155–6
Polynesia, 568–9
pomeni, 588–91, 612
pork barreling, 240, 479
pornography, 126–9, 131
Portugal, 218, 296
post-communist transformation, 12, 15
postfeminist societies, 159
post-purchase payments, 249–51
post-Soviet states, 56, 57, 90, 188, 204, 234, 236, 245, 248, 255, 328, 335–7, 480, 494, 502, 520–1, 566
poverty, 78, 88, 154, 184, 220, 192, 245, 251, 262, 288, 341, 343, 345–6, 362, 369, 436, 438, 440, 442, 467, 468, 498, 520, 521, 523, 529, 566, 587
 see also need
power, 15, 18, 33–5, 37, 42, 56, 73–4, 106, 142, 148, 156, 159, 184, 186–7, 267, 276–8, 286, 318, 337, 339, 408, 413–14, 477, 481, 592, 602–3, 605
 abuse of, 204–5, 216–17, 299, 439, 470
 ageing, 517–35, 550–1
 discretionary, 54, 417
 informal, 17, 22, 416, 541, 542, 563–5, 571, 574, 576
 networks, 602
 political, 52, 159, 266, 287–8, 416, 490, 499, 502, 520, 540, 549
 positions of, 211, 213, 215, 219, 237, 240, 289, 416, 493–4, 507, 539, 579
 state, 29, 333
 structures, 72, 212, 283, 505–7, 543
practical norms, 394
 see also norms
preferential treatment, 87, 186, 195, 205–6, 236, 297, 365–7, 583
 see also discretionary power; favouritism
pregnancy, 31–3, 34, 185
 fake, 334
pre-school education, 80
presidential elections, 238, 487, 499, 501
pressure, 13, 22, 40, 52, 57, 80–1, 87, 185, 223, 233, 248, 256, 262, 318, 376, 402, 406, 442, 450, 522, 587–8
 peer, 13, 14, 45, 165, 208
prestige, 30, 71, 73, 75, 84, 88, 144, 154, 161, 218, 355, 48, 577, 578, 587

prices, 48, 79–80, 303, 322, 323, 329, 330,
    333, 335, 343, 357–8, 367, 378–9, 440,
    444, 448, 457, 499, 582, 584
  higher, 33, 117, 120, 279–80, 334,
    358, 369–71
  votes, 487
pride, 29, 30, 115, 193, 292, 423
primary education, 235
principal–agent models, 14
prison, 200–3
prisoners, 252
  former, 84
privacy, 123, 243
private sector, 205, 279, 281, 319, 365, 380,
    382, 492, 532–3, 534
privileges, 20, 22, 29, 166, 187, 219, 266, 276,
    360, 369, 408, 452, 485, 486
  see also preferential treatment
problem-oriented approach, 2–5
problem-solving, 19, 423–6, 521, 547, 564
professional home organisers (POs), 371–4
promotion, job, 44, 80, 185, 196, 202, 205,
    215, 416, 483, 532, 534
property, 37, 42, 47–50, 55, 142, 173 189,
    246, 257, 284, 380, 414, 437–8,
    440–1, 450–1, 453–4, 461, 463–4, 468,
    522, 536
  private, 448, 459
  rights, 172, 454–8, 467
  see also public: goods; public: resources
prosecution, 49–50, 205, 213, 326, 328, 362,
    364, 385, 486
prosecutors, 154, 416
prostitution, 77, 78, 168, 283, 313, 315
protection, 221
  protekzia, 360
protests, 122, 147, 316, 487, 495–8,
    499, 520–3
Protestantism, 585
provocateurs, 494–8
public
  administration, 299, 415–17, 491
  funds, 48, 216, 217, 367, 383–4, 480
  goods, 6
  institutions, 29, 212–13, 218, 279, 315,
    383–5, 489, 492, 520
  interest, 115, 123, 417
  officials, 211, 279, 297–300, 367, 381, 384,
    416–17, 441–2, 478, 533–5
  opinion, 95, 365, 479, 534
  procurement, 198, 488, 492
  resources, 441, 483
  schools, 299
  sector, 14, 33, 213, 279, 280, 297, 380–5,
    483, 490, 520, 533–4
  services, 33–4, 212, 442
  space, 29, 48, 130, 243, 245, 342–4, 362,
    364–5, 419
  sphere, 46, 561
  transport, 336, 340–1, 343, 370, 573
Puerto Rico, 410, 411
pujogŭm, 260, 263–5, 612
pulling strings, 210, 218
  see also brokerage; connections;
    intermediaries
punishment, 83–6, 146, 201

puns, 425
puzzle(s), 232

Qualunquemente, 485
quanxi, 216
quarantines, 95
queue committees, 334–5
queue jumping/skipping, 205, 209, 210, 360
queue standers, 121, 332–5

Rabenmutter, 50–3, 613
race, 96, 407
racial
  discrimination, 221
  inequality, 369
racism, 444
rakija, 191–5
rallyes mondains, les, 11, 69–72, 610
rape, 145, 201
rationing, 333
real estate, 8, 167, 301, 328, 414, 446, 450,
    455–7, 532
  see also protests
rebellion, 69
recipients, 21, 207, 235, 263, 265, 588
  see also donors
reciprocity, 186, 197, 207–8, 209, 211, 219,
    231–4, 237, 240–1, 250–1, 261, 262,
    263, 282, 287, 313, 323, 365, 534, 535
recluses, 86–7
recomendazione, 218
recruitment, 70, 201, 320
recycling, 342–7
refugees, 317, 321, 464, 467
  see also migration
regimes, authoritarian, 448, 480
registration
  civil society organisations, 196
  companies, 116, 367
  consumers, 333–5
  children, 40–1, 172
    non-existent, 49
  employees, 380
  household, 40, 80
  job agencies, 418
  marriage, 150–6, 172
  migrants, 337
  pensioners, 500
  property, 55, 448, 453, 454
  residents, 448, 449
  school, 49
  street traders, 371
  tax, 8, 584
  voters, 449
regulations, *see* rules and regulations
relations/relationships
  affective, 184, 536, 540
  extramarital, 166–9, 171
  friendships, 197–9, 257, 284, 334, 538–40
  godchildren, 29, 30
  godfathers, 44
  godmothers, 162
  godparents, 29, 30
  informal, 28–9, 236
  instrumental, 216
  long-term, 166, 519, 532

patron–client, 211–12, 213, 240, 242, 287–9, 296–7, 482–3, 535–7, 539, 542, 604
 personal, 45, 73, 105, 127, 205–6, 211, 213, 236, 237, 250, 293, 298, 592
 personalised, 211, 213, 236
 romantic, 123–6, 129–31, 171, 235
 sexual, 126–9
 social, 164, 209, 211, 215, 237, 260, 261, 263, 265, 293
 symbiotic, 216, 329, 402
 see also families/family relations
reliance, 280, 406, 491, 564, 580
 see also confidence; trust
religion, 15, 70–1, 94, 139, 151, 168, 192, 205, 244, 265–7, 342, 411, 527, 550, 577–9, 592, 604
 see also Catholicism; Christianity; Islam; Mormonism; Protestantism; shamanism
remittances, 18, 154, 165, 261, 323, 402, 409
rent-to-buy contracts, 444
rents, 448, 465, 468
repairs, 189, 299, 314, 216, 325, 327, 346, 460
repayment, 219, 237, 251–2, 255
 see also reciprocity
reproduction, 27–8
reputation, 30, 39, 52, 74, 80, 108–9, 111, 116, 117, 127, 130, 144, 192, 213, 255, 256, 337
 see also face
residence permits, 206, 323, 324
resilience, 13, 442, 462, 603
resistance, 16, 22, 30, 34, 39, 40, 93, 140, 153, 200, 213, 347, 419, 424, 425, 603
 everyday, 422
resourcefulness, 285, 420–6
resources, 4, 8, 15, 22, 37, 51, 79, 111, 149–50, 158, 196, 204, 209–10, 214, 217–19, 240, 245, 282, 344, 368, 382, 396, 403, 412, 414, 415, 423–4, 449, 482, 521, 560–2, 603, 605
 access to, 12, 73, 108, 184, 206, 210, 212, 285, 366, 405
 educational, 32
 financial, 41, 58, 164, 211, 221
 human, 58, 381
 key, 401
 limited, 5, 35
 material, 22, 361, 421
 natural, 171
 pooling, 5, 201, 208, 246
 public, 441, 483
 scarce, 8, 33, 95, 333, 539
 social, 148, 184, 422
 societal, 105
 sociocultural, 68–9
 state, 422, 539, 542
 symbolic, 22
restaurants, 215, 217, 318
retirement, 58–9, 517, 531
 early, 532, 533
revenge porn, 126–9, 131, 613
reviews, fake, 108–12
revolving door, 531–5
rhetoric, 28, 52, 89, 165, 278, 343, 505

rights
 human, 147, 525, 526
 property, *see* property rights
risks, 231, 233, 234, 250
rituals, 260, 262, 263, 361, 411, 524, 551–2, 567, 568–71, 575, 576, 577–9, 586, 591–4
 red apple, 160–3
 red envelopes, 215, 263
 see also gifts
Santeria, 411
 see also ceremonies; seers
Roma, 206, 345–7, 446, 498–9, 589
Roman Catholicism, *see* Catholicism
Romania, 8, 89, 140–1, 218, 265–7, 332, 588–90, 612
ROSCAs (rotating savings and credit associations), 254, 255, 256, 257
rudeness, 33–6
rule of law, 415, 525
rulers, 266, 565
rules and regulations, 1, 14, 22, 33–4, 36, 67, 73, 76, 94, 110, 122, 200–1, 231, 234, 242, 256, 296, 331, 376, 420, 423, 463, 505, 560, 579
 of behaviour, 51
 duty-free allowance, 301
 formal, 16, 17, 208–10, 235, 319, 323, 360, 415–16, 425, 603–5
 of good conduct, 70, 72
 informal, 318, 414–15, 520, 561, 602–3
 moral, 215
 official, 380
 of reciprocity, 186, 523
 safety regulations, 315
 social, 173
 state regulation, 295, 315, 316, 321, 323, 343, 346, 371, 439, 441, 456
 unwritten, 18–19, 461
ruling parties, 198, 384, 464
runs, 76–9, 613
rural areas, 37–8, 39, 81–2, 142, 143, 144, 148, 151, 152, 162, 191–2, 194, 195, 240, 246, 247–8, 423–4, 454–8, 492–4, 530, 566, 603
 see also agriculture; peasants
rural–urban migration, 337, 338, 394, 435, 443–4, 453, 459, 463–4, 466, 522, 523, 537
rushyldyq, 195, 540
Russia, 20, 29–30, 33–6, 41–4, 46–50, 51, 53–9, 83–6, 89–93, 94, 95, 116, 123, 141, 152–6, 168, 187–8, 191, 195, 198, 209, 234–6, 278, 300–4, 325–9, 332, 336, 357, 377–9, 396–9, 410, 465, 466, 521, 542, 549–52, 562, 579–83, 590, 603, 604, 607, 610, 612, 613, 614
 Imperial, 380, 396–9, 527
 Federation, 379–83, 550, 573, 611

sacrifices, 245, 551
sadaqa, 244–7, 613
saksy, 400–2, 613
salaries, 54, 55, 56, 80, 313, 318, 323, 325, 328, 330, 335, 337, 380, 384–5, 532
 see also wages

INDEX 629

salivanje olova/strave, 568, 569
samogon, 191
samosud, 123
samozakhvat, 436, 447–50, 613
samsara, 412–14, 613
sandwich generation, 562, 563
satire, 288–9
savings, 254–7, 242–4, 257–9
Scandinavia, 506
scarce resources, 8, 33, 95, 333, 539
 see also state: resources
Schengen visa, 300–4
schools, 90, 248, 381, 449, 459
 private, 32, 71
 public, 299
Schrebergarten, 465, 466
ściągnąć, 394, 403–6, 613
sdelat' ZAGS, 153–6, 613
search engine optimisation, 113
second economy, 249–50
 see also informal: economy; shadow economy; underground economy; unofficial economy
secrecy, 139–40
secrets, open, 34, 45, 55, 217, 219, 292
seers, 570–1
 see also vilarkas
self-censorship, 85
self-help, 435–6
semeinyi jorolor, 243, 244
Senegal, 421–2
Senegalese, 362
SEO (search engine optimisation), 113
Serbia, 88–9, 175, 191–5, 204, 416, 486–91, 505–8, 568–71, 607, 609, 611, 612
services, 8, 32, 35, 44–5, 47–8, 108, 158, 189, 206, 209, 220–2, 231, 233, 247, 249, 256, 266–7, 284, 291, 313–17, 325–8, 334–5, 357–8, 361, 366–8, 382–3, 414, 418, 487–8, 503, 535, 604
 illicit, 293
 informal, 326
 public, 33–4, 212, 442
settlements, 528
 informal, 4, 6, 9, 290, 320–1, 437, 442, 454, 457, 459, 463–4, 467
  see also favelas; shantytowns; slums; squatting
sex
 education, 89–93
 for grades, 76, 77–8
 ratio, 36–7, 143, 152
 videos, 128–9
sex-selective abortion, 36–8
 see also selektivni abortus, 36–8, 144, 613
sexism, 159
sexual
 abstinence before marriage, 90
 harassment, 127
 minorities, 128
 orientation, 128
 unfaithfulness, 283
sexuality, 89–93
sexually transmitted infections (STIs), 90, 91, 92
shabashka, 329, 331

shabashniki, 325–9, 613
shadow economy, 8, 188, 297, 313
 see also informal: economy; second economy; underground economy; unofficial economy
shamanism, 549–52, 564–7
shame, 35, 81, 86–7, 91, 127, 160, 209, 255, 256–7, 261, 523
shantytowns, 445–6, 448–9
Sharia, 15, 146, 170, 192, 246, 437, 526, 530–1
sharing, 231–4, 282, 284, 324
shipbuilding, 322, 325
shops, 220–3, 249–51, 300–2, 304
shortages, 9, 13, 22, 35, 58, 82, 118, 188, 249–50, 254, 284–5, 298, 332–4, 341, 342, 379, 409, 436, 463–4, 467
shuahaoping, 108–12, 114, 613
shura, 523–6, 531, 609
side jobs, 325–35
simsar, 412–14, 613
Singapore, 95
single parents, 29, 58
sinnamjai, 236–41, 613
siphoning, 284
skills, 5, 16–23, 38, 46, 108, 192, 208, 209, 315, 317, 322, 327–8, 346, 355, 359, 317, 373, 377, 407, 414, 421, 561–3, 572
 social and communication, 70, 72, 241
slang, xxiii, xxvi, 43, 77, 203, 363, 377, 406, 421, 506, 577
slava, 191–2
slavery, 315, 380
słoiki, 81–3, 613
Slovakia, 395
Slovenia, 89, 438, 465–9, 614
slums, 9, 439, 445
small traders, 79–80
small property rights (SPR), 454–8
smuggling, 192, 315, 394, 395
 small-scale, 301
sociability, xix, 12, 20, 21, 198, 210, 215, 216, 252, 338, 361, 401, 560
 see also instrumentality
social
 agency, 68, 278
 capital, 31, 70–1, 72, 82, 184, 188–91, 215, 231–3, 240, 257, 260–2, 263, 265, 266, 290, 294, 297, 315, 316, 334, 346, 347, 357, 359–61, 401–6, 408, 410, 414–17, 422–3, 441, 491, 519, 587
 bonding, 232–3
 bridging, 232
 informal, 9–10, 198, 293, 401, 574
 class(es), see class(es)
 connections, 216, 219, 413
 contacts, 188–91
  see also connections; networks; relationships; ties
 context, 67, 68–9
 contract, 188, 345, 461, 477
  see also negotiation
 exchange, 21, 69, 297
  see also arrangements, informal; contracts; understanding

630   INDEX

exclusion, 183–8, 201–3, 220–3, 419
    see also belonging; inclusion
groups, 33, 45, 59, 72, 217, 231–2, 234, 252, 462, 500, 521
housing, 446, 457, 522
inclusion, *see* belonging; exclusion
inequality, 88, 288, 343, 520, 522, 529
informality, 435
isolation, 84, 86–7
justice, 521
life, 241–4, 257, 258–9
media, 109, 112–17, 131, 139, 158, 221, 249, 573, 588
mobility, *see* mobility, social
networks, 22, 34, 72, 167, 184, 189, 191, 194, 195, 198, 214–17, 232, 257, 261, 290, 346, 401, 403, 408, 420, 489, 491, 519, 537, 582, 587
    online, 123, 125–6
norms, 14, 127, 131, 187, 208–9, 231, 261, 345, 436, 479, 506–7, 531
    see also customs; etiquette; informal: institutions; traditions
relationships, 164, 209, 211, 215, 237, 260, 261, 263, 265, 293
    see also connections; networks; ties
sciences, 2–3, 105, 108, 113, 601–2
status, 71, 73–6, 80, 143, 144, 148–50, 152, 160–1, 164–5, 167, 174, 201, 215, 221, 237, 244, 250, 256, 262, 266, 464, 482, 518, 574
structures, 88, 161, 234, 283, 541, 581
ties, 44, 185, 196, 214, 232, 243, 262, 377, 414
    see also connections
withdrawal, 86–7
socialisation, 67–8, 69, 85
socialism, 285, 286, 298, 332–3, 336, 342, 377, 409, 412, 463, 569
social network analysis (SNA), 6
society, relationship with state and market, 601–2
soirées dansantes, 70, 71
solidarity, 10, 81, 93, 163, 186, 196, 201, 260, 262, 316, 317, 319, 361, 417, 528, 539, 587
Solomon Islands, 142
songli, 237
sosyudad, 254
South Africa, 357, 365–8, 614
South America, 208, 278, 294–7, 481, 503–5, 607
    see also Latin America
South Asia, 535–7, 609
South Korea, 38, 44, 81, 195, 216–17, 263–5, 540, 612
Southeast Asia, 237
Soviet Union, 33–6, 42, 58, 83–6, 144, 146, 151, 162, 170, 187–8, 249–50, 254, 260, 278, 325–33, 359, 394, 395, 459, 550, 566, 590, 610, 612, 613
    former, 234–6, 255, 328–9, 342, 382, 614
space, public, 29, 48, 130, 243, 245, 342–4, 362, 364–5, 419
Spain, 94, 112, 127, 217–20, 278, 281–4, 279, 290, 296, 362–5, 443–6, 486, 608, 609, 610

special economic zones, 458
spells, 568–71
    see also seers
sponsorship, 112, 115
squatting, 435, 437, 446, 447–50, 467
    see also settlements: informal
Sri Lanka, 535
stacze kolejkowi, 121, 332–5, 613
standards, double, 20–2, 159, 161, 198, 199, 563
state
    actors, 481, 494, 495
    agencies, 332, 449–50, 453
    authorities, 213, 316, 323, 422, 449, 484, 494, 522
    bureaucracy, 238, 529, 592
    companies, *see* state-owned companies
    institutions, 213, 236, 319, 383, 489, 520, 601
    officials, 46, 380, 522
    power, 29, 333
    procurement, 358, 366, 367
    regulation, 295, 315, 316, 321, 323, 343, 346, 371, 439, 441, 456
    relationship with market and society, 601–2
    resources, 422, 539, 542
state-owned companies, 367
status, 22, 27, 34, 44, 46, 56, 95–6, 148, 150, 164, 166, 169, 174, 202, 222, 340, 374, 415, 461, 492, 493, 521, 529, 535–6, 537, 563, 571, 578, 584, 602
    social, 71, 73–6, 80, 143, 144, 148–50, 152, 160–1, 164–5, 167, 174, 201, 215, 221, 237, 244, 250, 256, 262, 266, 464, 482, 518, 574
stereotypes, 81, 90, 94, 171, 174, 277, 292, 337, 408, 574
stigma, 15, 22, 30, 53, 56, 96, 160, 278, 343, 356, 347, 443
stockpiling, 346
stoial'shchiki, 333
strategies, xxiii, xxiv, 6, 14, 31, 36, 77, 82, 131, 154, 155, 212, 213, 285–6, 301, 304, 316, 341, 345, 346, 357, 374–6, 440, 479, 508
    coping, xix, 22
    informal, 28–9, 39–41, 54–6, 74, 111, 114–17, 119–20, 139–40, 216, 293, 334, 360, 368, 378, 402, 411, 480, 522–3
    survival, xxiv, 81, 255, 336, 365, 421, 422, 505
street traders, 362–5, 369–71
strength, 4, 5, 10, 159, 174, 203, 232–4, 346
    of family ties, 233–4
    of individuals, 346
    of informal networks, 4, 5, 10, 232
    of prisoners, 203
    of social capital, 232
    of women, 159, 174
strong players, 414–17
structures
    power, 72, 212, 283, 505–7, 543
    social, 88, 161, 234, 283, 541, 581
students, 2, 8, 32, 43, 53, 76–80, 88, 96, 108, 130, 216, 241, 283, 290–1, 335, 533, 582

subcontractors, 315, 322–6, 368
subcultures
    marriage, 139–40
    organisational, 216
    prison, 84, 200–3
    youth, 88–9
subordinates, 75, 85, 266
    see also superiors
sub-Saharan Africa, 290, 362, 420–3, 610
subsistence, 313
substantive ambivalence, 21, 561, 563
suburbanisation, 444
subversion, 15, 22, 76, 110, 251, 290, 314, 422, 479, 523, 559, 579, 594
suicide, 147
superbride, 157–8
superiors, 74–5, 79, 84, 235, 266
    see also subordinates
superstitions, 593
    see also rituals
support, 231–67
    groups, 127, 203
    mutual, 204, 208, 216, 242, 251–4, 256, 260, 262, 263
    political, 384, 416, 488–92
    public, 240, 522
surrogacy, 27–8, 30
surveillance, 129
surveillance capitalism, 107
survival, 75, 82, 111, 278, 283, 319, 331, 342, 416–17, 440, 499, 604
    strategies, xxiii, xxiv, 81, 255, 336, 365, 421, 422, 505
suspicion, school of, 12
svart arbete, 314–17, 324, 613
Sweden, 314–17, 543–4, 613
swindling, 284
Switzerland, 50–3, 613
sworn virgins, 172–5
symbiotic relationships, 216, 329, 402
symbolic capital, 521
symbols, 19, 22, 94, 123, 142, 145, 148, 162, 163, 174, 200, 237, 238, 257, 264, 304, 368, 419, 452, 468, 488, 539, 540, 566, 571, 574–6, 587, 591
synonyms, 122, 197, 204, 217, 241, 283, 285, 331, 367, 413, 492, 535
synthetic media, 128–9
système D, 421
systemic corruption, 77, 210, 291

Tajik diaspora, 153–6, 613
Tajikistan, 129–31, 141, 150–5, 195, 241, 611, 613
taksovanie, 335–8, 613
Taliban, 530–1
tandas, 256
tangping, 81
tapsh, 413–14
taxes, 53, 247, 266–7, 280, 291, 293, 313–19, 322–3, 325, 330, 332, 357, 374–6, 380, 470, 584, 604, 605
    tax authorities, 317
    tax avoidance, 376, 605
    tax evasion, 54, 314, 330, 376, 470, 605
    tax havens, 374–5, 605
taxis, 284, 335–8, 370

tazkia, 384
tchop, 571–3, 613
tea money, 293
teachers, 20, 80, 187, 235–6, 300, 528
technology companies, 79
telefon gap zadan, 129–31, 613
television, 123–5, 159, 165, 172, 277, 289, 368, 373, 421, 499, 550
    see also media
tenderpreneur, 357, 365–8, 614
tenders, 358, 365–8
Thailand, 236–41, 519, 545–9, 609, 613
theft, 284–6, 314, 343, 347, 381
ThetaHealing®, 579–83, 614
thieves, 276, 286, 451
ticket touting, 117–21, 614
timber, 295–7
tipping, 290, 297
titushky, 479, 480, 494–8, 614
tobelija, 174
toi, 260–2
tokens
    of appreciation, 234–41, 248
    of gratitude, 297, 299–300
tolerance, 168, 185, 194, 282, 293, 327, 345, 346, 425–6, 459, 464, 470, 593
top-down approaches, 3–5, 15
toqal, 168, 169–72, 614
torpil, 196, 198–9, 204
total institutions 34, 42, 85–6
tourism, 28, 31–3, 112–14, 300–4, 424, 465, 504
tourists, 369–71
townships, 457, 458
trabajo extra 332
trade, 110, 252, 254, 296, 302, 313, 317, 340, 409, 412–13, 424, 504, 601
trade relations, 254
trade unions, 316, 322, 325
traders, 347, 362, 377, 394, 412–13
    bazaar, 497
    petty, 394
    shuttle, 410
    small, 253
    street, 369–71, 422–3
trading,
    informal, 280, 369–71, 395–6
    licences, 371
traditions, 15, 39, 44, 83, 143–7, 151–2, 156, 160, 163, 165–6, 168–72, 175, 184, 185, 241, 245, 247–8, 256, 260–2, 276–7, 283, 450, 466, 525–9, 565–7, 577–9, 586–7, 591–4, 604
    see also rituals
trailing spouses, 406–9, 614
tramitadory, 332, 333
transition, 14–15
Transnistria, 395
transparency, 106, 107, 189, 361
transportation, 284, 300–4, 335–42, 370, 402
travail au noir, 315, 317–20, 324, 614
travel influencers, 112–14, 614
treatment, preferential, 87, 186, 195, 205–6, 236, 297, 365–7, 583
    see also discretionary power; favouritism
trep folk music, 88–9
tribalism, 247, 492, 523

tribes, 186, 247, 492, 523, 565
tribute, 267
    see also feeding
tricksters, 275–8, 283, 358–61
trolls, 116
trotro, 338–42, 614
trust, 105–8, 111, 117, 127–8, 130, 167, 213, 232, 233, 242, 250, 253, 254, 256, 261, 263, 282, 290, 323, 324, 331, 361, 406, 410, 478, 494, 525, 540, 559
tsartsaani nüüdel, 503
tuđa večera, 36–8, 144, 613
Tunisia, 152, 332, 421
Turkey, 164, 195–9, 204, 205, 332, 394, 437, 540, 604, 607, 609
Turkmenistan, 170–1

uhljeb, 382
ui-bulo jorolor, 243, 244
UK, *see* United Kingdom
uklonenie ot alimentov, 29, 53–6, 614
Ukraine, 330, 336, 395, 402, 480, 494–8, 500, 550, 590, 614
Umbanda, 577
Una rete piena di sabbia, 485
unanimous internal competition, 81
uncertainty, 13–14, 21, 23, 122, 251, 285, 334, 342, 359, 407, 415–17, 421, 467, 498, 502, 547, 548, 549, 561, 562, 569–70
underground, 327
    economy, 82
        see also informal: economy; second economy; shadow economy; unofficial economy
    groups, 116
        see also informal: groups
    market, 109
understanding
    gatherings, 243, 244
    informal networks, 188
    mainstream, 436
    mutual, 185, 318
    property extensions, 461
    theft, 286
    unspoken, 169
    vacant properties, 452
unemployment, 86–7, 191, 317, 335–7, 418, 467, 497, 498, 566
United Kingdom, 89, 91, 96, 118, 119, 127, 156–60, 375, 376, 401, 403–5, 465, 518, 607
United Nations-Habitat, 435, 439
United States, 9, 27–8, 31–3, 53, 57, 85, 91, 94, 95, 116, 121, 123, 127, 128, 191, 256, 371–2, 375, 405, 409, 411, 436, 439–43, 465, 469, 485, 526, 533, 579–83, 603, 605, 608, 614
universalism, 233, 234, 415
unofficial economy, 328
unpaid subsistence economy, 313
unwritten rules, 18–19, 461
upper class, 116, 169, 313
    see also aristocracy
urban areas, 8–10, 37–8, 39, 81–3, 143, 162, 167, 195, 337, 343, 369, 419, 435, 438, 443, 447–8, 454–6, 463–4, 522, 523

urban centres, 296, 446, 463, 504
urban gardens, 438, 465–9
urban planning, 443, 445
urban spaces, 343, 419
urban studies, 4
urbanisation, 437–8, 458, 463, 466, 467, 469
urbanites, 466, 469
Uruguay, 218, 283
US, *see* United States
used bottles and cans, recycling, 342–5
    see also recycling
user reviews, fake, 108–12
USSR, *see* Soviet Union
Uzbekistan, 151, 241, 256, 335–8, 497, 527, 535, 613
Uzbeks, 522

values, 13, 14, 39, 67, 89, 90, 139, 186, 216, 232–4, 237, 240, 250, 287, 342, 361, 402, 422, 424, 452, 462, 540, 566, 594
    corporate, 296
    cultural, 196, 232, 234, 517
    moral, 72, 76, 236, 275
    neoliberal, 260, 261
    religious, 244
    social, 169, 236, 275
    socialist, 122
vendors, 49, 294, 362–5, 371
Venezuela, 279, 410
vengeance pornographique, 127
veza, veze, 204, 486
Vietnam, 38, 331, 438, 458–62, 608
vilarkas, 568–71, 607
    see also seers
villages, 43, 167, 174, 195, 233, 241–2, 263, 437–8, 454–9, 492–4, 523, 527–31, 535–9, 566, 574, 590
    Potemkin, 115, 603
violence, 4, 88, 123, 320, 421, 522, 581
    domestic, 75, 128, 147, 152, 165–6
    fear of, 165
    gender-based, 96
    kidnapping, 144
    physical, 480, 495–6, 542
    political, 240
virginity, 145, 160–3, 172–5
visas, 300–4, 321, 406–7, 410
vorovskie passporta, 396–9, 614
voters, 478–81, 498–500, 519
votes
    buying/selling, 240, 287–8, 479, 482, 484–8, 492, 499, 614
    exchange, 479–81, 482–6, 503
voting rights, 51, 206, 449
voto di scambio, 479, 480–1, 482–6, 500, 614
vrtičjartstvo, 438, 465–9, 614
vruzki, 298

wages, 190–1, 313, 315, 318, 322–5, 326, 328, 532
    envelope, 54, 313
    grey, 54, 55, 56
    house-buying process, 80
    minimum, 191, 320, 519
waiting lists, 333
Wallachia, 265–7, 612
wang hong, 112

INDEX   **633**

wantoks, 142
warlords, 526
wasta, 186–7, 414
waste recycling, 342–5
wealth, 438, 439
  disposable wealth, 245
  see also inequality
weddings, 139, 142, 150–3, 156–60, 192
  banquets, 214, 215
  costs, 146, 147, 152, 248
  gifts, 260, 261, 262, 263, 264, 264
  rituals, 536
welfare
  informal, 57
  state, 314, 316, 364
Western Balkans, 88–9
Western Europe, 468
whistle-blowing, 123, 506
widows, 170
women, 28, 29–38, 46, 50–3, 56–9, 70, 75, 89–93, 128, 130–1, 141–75, 183–8, 235, 243, 254, 256, 257, 337–8, 340, 341, 370, 372, 406–9, 410–11, 418, 493, 497–8, 519–23, 525, 526, 529, 562–3, 567–71, 573, 576, 580–2, 588
work
  permits, 318, 337
  stoppages, 321
  visas, 407
working conditions, 79, 323, 325, 370
working mothers, 50–3

xiaochanquan (*chéngzhōngcūn*), 437–8, 454–8, 608, 614
xiaoerni, 38–41, 614

yongo, 44, 184–6, 195, 540
youth, 96, 317–18, 341, 447–8, 495–7
  ageism, 519
  consumption, 378
  culture, 88–9
  dating, 129–31
  gifts to, 287
  identities, 125
  marriage, 139–40, 151, 166
  see also children
Yugoslavia, 326, 342, 569–70
  former, 88–9, 438, 462–5, 608

zachachmęcenie, 278, 284–6, 614
zakhvatchiki, 447–8
załatwianie, 335
zaniato, 437, 450–4, 614
znaki vnimaniya, 234–6, 614

Printed in the USA
CPSIA information can be obtained
at www.ICGtesting.com
LVHW050228270824
789126LV00019B/207